KU-524-096

Cardiff Libraries
www.cardiff.gov.uk/libraries

Llyfrgelloedd Caerdy
www.caerdydd.gov.uk/llyfrgell

CARDIFF
CAERDYDD

THE ROUGH GUIDE TO

Myanmar (Burma)

written and researched by

Joanna James, Gavin Thomas and Martin Zatko

ACC. No: 03232133

ROUGH
GUIDES

roughguides.com

Contents

Introduction to
Myanmar (Burma)

The largest but least-known nation in Southeast Asia, Myanmar is – to borrow Churchill's phrase – a riddle wrapped in a mystery. For half a century, the country languished in self-imposed obscurity under the rule of its despotic and enigmatic military rulers, little visited and even less understood. All that is now changing, and with spectacular speed. Following tentative recent economic and political reforms, the national landscape is being transformed in ways unimaginable even a few years ago, and visitors have begun flocking to Myanmar in unprecedented numbers. All of a sudden, the country is now hot property.

Ironically, it's precisely these decades of suffocating political isolation, combined with economic stagnation, that have helped preserve (albeit at a terrible human cost) much of Myanmar's magically **time-warped character** into the twenty-first century. The old Burma immortalized by Kipling and Orwell is still very much in evidence today: this remains a land of a thousand gilded pagodas, of ramshackle towns and rustic villages populated with innumerable red-robed monks and locals dressed in flowing, sarong-like longyi, their faces smeared in colourful swirls of traditional *thanaka*. It's a place in which life still revolves around the temple and the teahouse, and where the corporate chains and global brands that have gobbled up many other parts of Asia remain notably conspicuous by their absence.

It's also a uniquely diverse nation. Physically, Myanmar encompasses **landscapes** ranging from the fertile plains of the majestic Ayeyarwady River to the jungle-covered highlands of Shan State, and from the jagged, snowy Himalayan peaks bounding the northern edge of the country down to the emerald confetti of tropical islands that dot the Andaman Sea in the far south. **Culturally**, too, it's a bewilderingly eclectic place, sandwiched between Bangladesh, India, China and Thailand – all of which have exerted their own distinctive influence on Burmese architecture, culture, cuisine and much more. Myanmar's position at one of Asia's great cultural watersheds also accounts for its extraordinary **ethnic diversity**, with well over a hundred minority peoples who

ABOVE A FISHERMAN ON INLE LAKE; NUNS' SANDALS OUTSIDE A TEMPLE

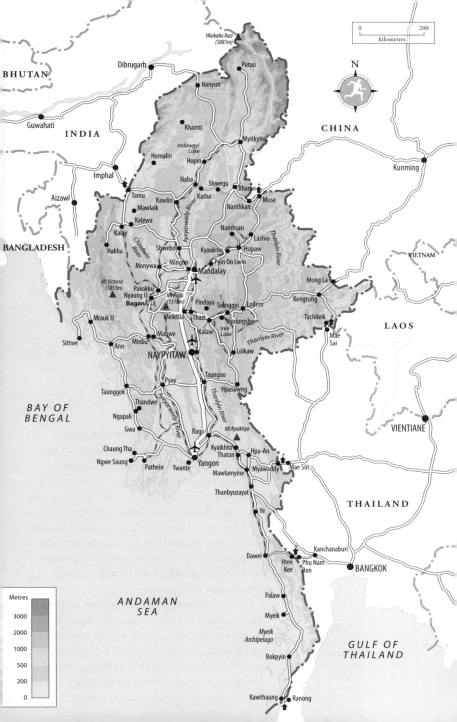

FACT FILE

• According to the results of a (controversial) census taken in 2014, Myanmar has a **population** of 51.4 million. Yangon is the largest city (5.2 million), followed by the national capital Naypyitaw (1.6 million) and Mandalay (1 million).

• At 676,000 square kilometres, Myanmar is slightly smaller than Turkey, and slightly larger than France.

• Buddhism is the main **religion** (around 90 percent of the population), though there are also sizeable populations of Christians, Muslims and Hindus.

• The country was formerly named Burma after its majority **ethnic group** – the Bamar, who are thought to represent around 68 percent of the population. Other major groups include the Shan (9 percent), Kayin (7 percent), Rakhine (4 percent) and Mon (2 percent).

• Three major **linguistic families** are represented in Myanmar: Sino-Tibetan (which includes Burmese), Tai-Kadai (which includes the Shan languages) and Austro-Asiatic tongues such as those of the Mon, Palaung and Wa tribes.

• **George Orwell** lived in Burma from 1922 until returning to England after catching dengue fever in 1927; his *Burmese Days* (see p.363) remains one of the most-read books about the country. **Rudyard Kipling** had also popped by in 1889; though this gave rise to his vaunted poem "Mandalay", he never actually visited the city.

(despite systematic government oppression) continue to follow their traditional culture and beliefs, from the long-necked ladies of the Padaung tribe to the warlike Wa, whose fierce reputation remains to this day.

For the visitor, it's the images of old Burma – the spectacular temples of Bagan; the great golden stupa of Yangon's Shwedagon Pagoda at sunset; traditional leg-rowed boats bobbing across Inle Lake – that provide the touchstone of the Burmese experience. The **political challenges** faced by modern Myanmar, however, continue to cloud the country's future, despite recent reforms, while the fight for democracy and justice goes on, symbolized by the unceasing defiance of Nobel laureate **Aung San Suu Kyi** and embodied by the many thousands of nameless Burmese who have sacrificed their liberty, and often their lives, in the battle for freedom over the past five decades. Given their tragic recent past, what is perhaps likely to linger most in the memory is the sheer warmth of the Burmese people, starved of contact with the outside world for so many years, and who remain among the friendliest and most welcoming in Asia. Visit now, before it all changes.

Where to go

Though no longer the capital, **Yangon** remains Myanmar's commercial heart and the core of its spiritual life. Its glorious Shwedagon Pagoda is a Myanmar must-see, while the downtown area is a magnificent showpiece of colonial architecture, with streets full of memorably decaying Raj-era buildings. Whether you get lost in the city's animated markets, seek out beer and barbecue in Chinatown, visit Hindu temples or take an eye-opening ride on a commuter train, Yangon provides a vibrant and engaging introduction to the country.

The fertile **Delta region** south and west of Yangon was devastated in 2008 by Cyclone Nargis, after which the military regime closed the area off to foreign travellers; it's now open again, with most hurrying straight to the beaches at **Chaung Tha** and **Ngwe Saung**. Heading north along the west coast, you reach the long and thin stretch of Rakhine State; the most

BURMESE CHIC

Want to dip your toes into Burmese culture? Don a longyi, and slap on some *thanaka*. The **longyi** is a sarong-like lower-body garment worn by men and women across the land; though both wear essentially the same thing, patterns vary by gender, as does the style of folding. You may notice certain colour-related traits – green, for example, is strongly associated with education and thus de rigueur with students, while those working in the service industry often opt for sky blue. Many travellers end up buying one and wearing it around – usually made of cotton, longyis are extremely comfortable in hot weather, and very affordable at K2000–6000 each.

Then there's **thanaka**, a bright yellow face paint sported – often in rather spectacular styles – by more or less every woman and child in the country, as well as a few gents. Made from ground tree bark, it's usually applied in the morning, the purpose manifold – it's a sunblock, a perfume, decoration and a skincare product, all in one. Again, it's easy to partake yourself: just hunt it down from a shop selling it in powder form, then mix with a little water to form a paste – locals love to show you the ropes.

touted destination here is **Ngapali Beach**, though rising hotel prices have squeezed out anyone on a strict budget, and many travellers prefer to make for **Mrauk U**, capital of Rakhine when it was a separate kingdom.

Easily overlooked by tourists in the rush to head north from Yangon, **southeastern Myanmar** more than justifies a diversion, and is far more accessible now that border crossings with Thailand have opened to foreigners. A wealth of golden stupas and some giant Buddha statues make **Bago** an appealing destination, while pressing on further south you'll find the boulder-and-pagoda balancing act of Kyaiktiyo, best known as the **Golden Rock** – a feat of apparent gravity defiance which will live long in the memory. South of here, don't miss the boat trip along the Thanlyin River from the former British capital of **Mawlamyine** to **Hpa-An**, a town that makes a great base for day-trips into the surrounding karst-littered countryside. In the far south of the country is the **Tanintharyi Region**, which is gradually being opened up to international tourism – many make a beeline for the gorgeous white-sand beaches of the undeveloped Myeik Archipelago.

The highlight of **central Myanmar**, and perhaps of the whole country, is **Bagan**, nestled beside the Ayeyarwady River and surrounded by sweeping plains covered in an astonishing profusion of ancient temples – one of Asia's greatest spectacles. Most other towns in the central plains still remain off the mainstream tourist circuit, although if you have time its worth visiting the skyscraper-sized Buddha statue at Maha Bodhi Tataung, near the town of **Monywa**, while the sprawling remains of the great Pyu city of Sri Ksetra can be seen just outside the enjoyable Ayeyarwady town of **Pyay**. Most travellers give the national capital, **Naypyitaw**, a wide berth, though this is one of Asia's fastest-growing cities and visually arresting in a manner unique to Myanmar.

With Kayah and Kayin states mostly off-limits to tourists, it's large Shan State (a good deal of which is itself closed) that epitomizes the appeal of the hilly **east** of the country. Most travellers choose to base themselves in **Nyaungshwe**, which sits close to the north end of spectacular **Inle Lake** – a day-trip on its waters, visiting stilt villages and colourful markets, is the prime attraction hereabouts. Adventurous sorts can opt to hike to the lake from **Kalaw**, a lofty town with its own appealing ambience – two or three days of gentle walking will give you the opportunity to see how some of the area's many ethnic minority groups go about their lives.

Mandalay, Myanmar's second city, doesn't quite live up to the magic of the eponymous Kipling poem, but linger and you'll find the place will grow on you. There's Mandalay Hill to climb for one thing, memorable both for its views and for the experience of joining throngs of locals doing the same. Then there are the day-trips to former Burmese capitals such as the once-mighty **Inwa**, now a sleepy backwater scattered with stupas that you can visit by horse and cart.

Most of **northern Myanmar** is closed to foreigners, largely due to the history of conflict between the army and ethnic militias in Kachin State. The parts that *can* be visited are safe, however, and provide some of the country's best opportunities to spend time with local people. One of the most memorable ways to do this is on a boat trip on the Ayeyarwady north of Mandalay up to **Katha** and **Bhamo**, where long journey times

---

BURMA OR MYANMAR?

This is a land with two names – three, in fact, for the country's official appellation has been the **Republic of the Union of Myanmar** since 1989. That was the year in which the ruling military junta decided to officially change the name from **Burma**, in line with a policy that also saw Rangoon renamed Yangon. The official line put forth was that Burma's name derived from the majority Burmese population, and that unlike neighbouring Thailand, Laos and Vietnam, they wanted a title more inclusive of minorities. **Myanmar** was thus born – or reborn, in fact, since the first known usage of the name (actually "Myanma" in the local vernacular) dates back to the thirteenth century, thus predating Burma as a national title.

While those sympathetic to (or at least tolerant of) the military regime, and some minority groups, are happy to call the country Myanmar, those in opposition – including the **National League for Democracy** and many international governments – tend to prefer the name Burma. Most travellers end up picking one, whether intentionally or otherwise, and using that for the rest of their trip – you'll be placing yourself in no danger by using one or the other. In this book, the term "Myanmar" has usually been used when describing the country, though the difficulty in forming a demonym from this (some locals use "Myanmar people") means that "Burmese" has been used as the generic adjective for local people or traditions.

Author picks

Our authors made their way across every (accessible) corner of Myanmar for this first ever Rough Guide to the country. Aside from the major sights, here are some of their personal favourites.

Big Buddhas Big is definitely best when it comes to Buddhist merit-making, as exemplified by the super-sized Buddhas of Yangon (p.76) and Bago (p.137) or the stupendous, sky-high statue at Maha Bodhi Tataung, near Monywa (p.221).

Cycling The country abounds with cycling possibilities (p.30) – it's one of the best ways to see Mandalay and its surrounding sights (p.274), and there are a variety of enticing routes around Nyaungshwe and Inle Lake (see box, p.240).

Teahouses Teahouses (see box, p.37) are an integral part of daily Burmese life, and many travellers find themselves making a daily pilgrimage of sorts. The tea is typically sweet, and served with tasty snacks – the local doughnuts, sometimes flavoured with coconut, are highly recommended.

Markets Every town, however small, has a market, and this will invariably be one of the most entertaining places in which to spend your time (p.33). Those in Shan State are particularly fascinating (see box, p.230), though wherever you are, head to the local market to grab some cheap noodles, shop for a longyi, or ruin your teeth the local way by chewing a betel parcel.

Remnants of the Raj Examples of crumbling colonial architecture dotted around the land provide evidence of Myanmar's time under British control – step back to another era by taking afternoon tea in Yangon's *Strand Café* (p.88), or a horse-drawn-carriage ride around Pyin Oo Lwin (p.299).

Nat ceremonies Don't leave Myanmar without experiencing a raucous *nat* (spirit) ceremony (p.40). Khayone Cave (Mawlamyine) has daily *nat*-driven séances (p.157), and Taungbyone's *nat pwè* (see box, p.266) is a magnet for energetic transvestite *nat kadaw* (see box, p.49).

> Our author recommendations don't end here. We've flagged up our favourite places – a perfectly sited hotel, an atmospheric café, a special restaurant – throughout the guide, highlighted with the ★ symbol.

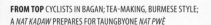

FROM TOP CYCLISTS IN BAGAN; TEA-MAKING, BURMESE STYLE; A *NAT KADAW* PREPARES FOR TAUNGBYONE *NAT PWÈ*

BETEL JUICE

Anyone who spends more than a day in Myanmar will notice two particularly curious features of the country – the wretched state of many locals' teeth, and the odd red blotches peppering each and every road across the land. These are both related to the chewing of **betel** (*ku-nya*), a popular pastime with male and female, young and old. To make betel, areca nuts are placed, together with tobacco and other optional ingredients, into a leaf pasted with **slaked lime**. Users experience a slight rush, similar to that of coffee or a cigarette. Addiction can develop quickly and repeated use can lead to **oral cancer**, though more of a guarantee is wretchedly **damaged teeth**.

One or two parcels are unlikely to hurt, however, and some travellers are keen to see what all the fuss is about; the tastiest is said to come from the Kalaw area (see box, p.234). Parcels are sold in packs from roadside stalls all over Myanmar, with prices as low as K100 for a pack of three. If you're chewing, remember to spit out the first few times your mouth fills with saliva, since the slaked lime can (ultimately) destroy your liver.

and a scarcity of foreigners make it easy to get a sense of provincial life. Heading northeast from Mandalay instead, through quaintly colonial **Pyin Oo Lwin** towards the Chinese border, the areas around **Kyaukme** and **Hsipaw** offer the chance to stay in ethnic minority homes in traditional mountain villages, while the truly intrepid will want to travel further north still, to **Indawgyi Lake**, for a taste of Kachin State's wilderness.

When to go

Myanmar boasts a **tropical climate**, and as such the flux of hot versus cold and wet versus dry is far more applicable than notions of spring, summer, autumn and winter. The main tourist season runs from November to February, when the country is blessed with a winning combination of azure-blue skies and relatively low temperatures, though things also get very busy around Burmese New Year, which usually falls in April and can wreak havoc with travel plans. **November** is a grand month to visit – both temperatures and visitor numbers are still quite low, and much of the country remains a lush green from the rains. **December** and **January** see Western tour groups arriving en masse, with accommodation at its most scarce; if Chinese New Year falls in January, things can get particularly busy with domestic travellers and those from neighbouring countries added to the mix. Chinese New Year can also fall in **February**, which is when temperatures start to pick up. In Yangon, the huge Shwedagon Festival often takes place in February, though it can fall in March too.

As long as you don't mind getting hot or wet, it's perfectly feasible to visit Myanmar outside the main season; New Year aside, you'll also see the country at its most refreshingly tourist-free. The country starts to sizzle in **March**, and by **April** temperatures are at their year-round high – all the more excuse for Thingyan, a huge water festival which occurs

RIGHT RICE TERRACES NEAR KENGTUNG

AVERAGE MONTHLY TEMPERATURES AND MONTHLY RAINFALL

	Jan	Feb	March	April	May	June	July	Aug	Sept	Oct	Nov	Dec
YANGON												
Max/min (°C)	32/18	35/19	36/22	37/24	33/25	30/24	30/24	30/24	31/24	32/24	32/22	31/19
Rainfall (mm)	5	3	7	15	301	545	557	603	368	204	61	8
MANDALAY												
Max/min (°C)	29/13	32/15	35/20	38/24	37/26	34/26	34/26	32/25	32/25	32/24	30/19	28/15
Rainfall (mm)	5	2	1	39	134	153	87	113	153	129	35	7
MYITKYINA												
Max/min (°C)	24/10	27/12	30/16	33/20	33/22	31/24	30/24	30/24	31/23	30/21	27/16	25/12
Rainfall (mm)	8	18	27	48	156	536	512	412	283	158	27	9

around this time … be prepared to get very, very wet, whether you want to or not. Those arriving after Thingyan may get the same kind of feeling, since **May** sees the sudden onset of the rainy season – be aware that during the monsoon some places are inaccessible and transport services may not run. Things only get wetter in **June**, and conditions stay that way through the month of **July** before the rains subside slightly in August. **September** is already usually dry enough to make for pleasant travel, and **October** even more so.

Large as Myanmar is, this month-by-month advice generally applies across the board. Temperatures do tend to be slightly lower the further north you head, and the sheltered position of Mandalay and Bagan helps them escape the worst of the rainy season, though this also makes them bake more in hotter months. If the heat's getting too much for you, head up to loftier, cooler climes on the Shan plateau, such as Kalaw, Pyin Oo Lwin or Lashio.

19

things not to miss

It's impossible to see everything that Myanmar has to offer in one trip – and we don't suggest you try. What follows, in no particular order, is a selective and subjective taste of the country's highlights, from impressive Buddhist monuments to spectacular journeys. All entries have a page reference to take you straight into the Guide, where you can find out more. Coloured numbers refer to chapters in the Guide section.

1

1 BAGAN
Page 188

One of the great wonders of Asia – and the world – with (literally) thousands of majestic temples rising from the Ayeyarwady plains.

2 TAUNG KALAT (MOUNT POPA)
Page 216

Dramatic volcanic plug covered in shrines dedicated to Myanmar's bizarre *nat* spirits.

3 COLONIAL ARCHITECTURE, YANGON
Box, page 62

They may have seen better days, but Yangon's colonial-era buildings and streetscapes remain among Asia's most impressive Raj-era relics.

4 U BEIN BRIDGE
Page 282

The small town of Amarapura makes a great half-day trip from Mandalay, not least because of its lengthy – and highly picturesque – teak bridge.

 5 ETHNIC MINORITY GROUPS

Box, page 230

Myanmar is a real jigsaw of colourful ethnic groups. An easy way to delve into minority culture is to explore the wonderful markets that spiral around Shan State on a rotating five-day cycle.

 6 SHOPPING

Page 46

Myanmar's markets and shops serve up plenty of unusual souvenirs, including beautiful parasols, jade jewellery, lacquerware, wood ornaments and all sorts of traditional textiles.

 7 SHWE OO MIN CAVE

Page 236

Peering down over the country village of Pindaya, this spectacular cave is filled with more Buddha statues than anyone can count.

 8 HPA-AN

Page 143

Watch the sunrise from a mountaintop monastery and disturb squeaking clouds of bats in holy caves outside laidback Hpa-An.

9 BOAT TRIPS ON THE AYEYARWADY

Box, page 273 & box, page 311

Float downstream from Mandalay to Bagan or foray into the far north along Myanmar's most important river, jumping ship at remote villages as you go.

8

9

10 HIKING TO INLE LAKE
Box, page 232

Trekking from Kalaw to must-see Inle Lake you'll see minority folk aplenty, and experience the pleasure of staying a night or two in farmhouse accommodation.

11 MOHINGA
Page 34

This hearty fish broth – flavoured with lemongrass, lime, chilli and coriander – is Myanmar's essential power-breakfast.

12 GOKTEIK VIADUCT
Box, page 300

Steel your nerves for the slow trip across Myanmar's highest bridge on this creaking railway viaduct.

13 KYAIKTIYO
Page 140

Join thousands of pilgrims gazing in awe at the precarious Golden Rock, held steady by a few strands of the Buddha's hair.

14 YANGON STREET LIFE
Box, page 89

Traditional and modern Myanmar meet in downtown Yangon, with some great street eats to hunt down amid the bustle.

15 NGAPALI BEACH
Page 108

Legendary beach in deepest Rakhine, with smooth white sands, stylish resorts and super-fresh seafood.

16

16 NYAUNGSHWE AND INLE LAKE

Pages 238 & 246

Dreamily pretty Inle Lake is, deservedly, one of Myanmar's most popular sights, though there's also a lot to be said for Nyaungshwe, a small town sitting just off its northern edge – its relaxed, traveller-friendly vibe may well tempt you to stay far longer than you'd anticipated.

17 SHWEDAGON PAGODA, YANGON

Page 70

One of the world's greatest Buddhist temples, its soaring golden stupa dominating the skyline of Yangon.

18 MANDALAY SHOWS

Page 279

Myanmar's second city boasts an assortment of intriguing entertainment options, from the slapstick actions of the Moustache Brothers to dance and puppet performances.

19 MRAUK U

Page 119

The historic capital of the kingdom of Arakan, with monumental fortified temples (such as the magnificent Shittaung Paya, pictured) and hundreds of stupas scattered across a beautiful landscape of wooded hills and twisting rivers and lakes.

17

18

19

Itineraries

Myanmar is a large country, and you could spend months here and still not see everything. At a bare minimum, seven days would provide just about enough time for a whirlwind tour of the "big four" sights of Yangon, Inle Lake, Mandalay and Bagan. With more time on your hands you'll be able to work some farther-flung possibilities into the mix.

THE GRAND TOUR

Myanmar's default itinerary follows a vaguely kite-shaped route around the country, taking in the "big four" with a visit to the Golden Rock – the kite's string – as an optional side-trip from Yangon. Many travellers are happy to spend the duration of their entire 28-day visa in these places alone.

❶ Yangon The country's largest city, home to the stupendous Shwedagon Pagoda, with its huge clusters of gleaming golden spires, as well as one of Asia's most perfectly preserved colonial centres. **See p.56**

❷ Kyaiktiyo (Golden Rock) Join local pilgrims on a night-time walk up Mount Kyaiktiyo, at the summit of which sits a golden, apparently gravity-defying boulder. **See p.140**

❸ Kalaw The most enjoyable way to reach Inle Lake is on a two- or three-day hike from this relaxed – and occasionally chilly – mountain town. **See p.228**

❹ Inle Lake Take a boat trip around spectacular Inle Lake, which features "floating" villages and farms, and a truly photogenic cast of locals. **See p.246**

❺ Mandalay Markedly more relaxed than Yangon, Myanmar's second city also has its fair share of sights and restaurants, and is the best place in the land for local-style entertainment. **See p.260**

❻ Bagan Quite simply, one of Southeast Asia's must-sees – catch sunrise or sunset from one of its thousands of temples. **See p.188**

ETHNIC MINORITIES

The chance to see colourfully attired minority folk is one of Southeast Asia's major tourist draws, and Myanmar is no exception to this regional rule. The national government does, of course, have something of an axe to grind with certain groups, but the danger zones are all off-limits to travellers.

❶ Hpa-An The startling limestone karst scenery around Hpa-An is home to the Kayin, resplendent in their distinctive striped longyi. **See p.143**

❷ Mrauk U Much of Chin State remains off-limits to travellers, though you can get an easy sampler of Chin culture on a boat trip from Mrauk U – the tattoo-faced old ladies hereabouts are particularly photogenic. **See box, p.119**

❸ Myitkyina Catch the colourful Kachin National Day celebrations way up north in multicultural Myitkyina. **See box, p.320**

❹ Kyaukme and Hsipaw Head for the tea-swathed hills north of these two towns, where Shan-dominated valleys give way to tea-growing hills tended by the Palaung, crisscrossed with great trekking routes and peppered with homestay opportunities.

ABOVE ARTWORK ON DISPLAY, BOGYOKE MARKET, YANGON; BOAT, NEAR NYAUNGSHWE

Hsipaw itself is a laidback town offering a taste of Shan culture. **See p.300 & p.301**

❺ **Inle Lake** Myanmar's most easily accessible minority folk live around Inle Lake – most notable are the long-necked "giraffe" women of the Padaung group, though those trekking here from Kalaw, or visiting the umpteen local markets, will also see pockets of Pa-O and Danu. **See p.246**

❻ **Kengtung** A small Shan State city surrounded by Akha, Lahu and other colourful ethnic groups, yet almost entirely tourist-free – and even more tempting now that restrictions have been lifted on the nearby Thai border. **See p.252**

ROADS LESS TRAVELLED

With Myanmar becoming ever more popular as a tourist destination, would-be travel renegades are having to try a little harder to get their off-the-beaten-track fix. With a little advance planning, and by avoiding the corners of "The Kite" (see opposite), you could max out your visa without seeing a single tour bus.

❶ **Tanintharyi Region** Head down to Myanmar's deep south, whose abundance of beaches and islands are becoming easier to explore. **See p.159**

❷ **Pyay** An enjoyable stopover on the slow road from Yangon to Mandalay, with ancient Pyu ruins, the towering Shwesandaw Pagoda and one of central Myanmar's best night markets. **See p.82**

❸ **Meiktila** This little-visited crossroads town has a beautiful lakeside setting, a clutch of quirky temples and stand-out street food. **See p.179**

❹ **Pindaya** Those staying in Kalaw or Nyaungshwe often make a day-trip to see Pindaya's wonderful Buddha-filled cave – trump this by staying the night in this wonderfully chilled-out town. **See p.235**

❺ **Katha** Inspiration for the town of Kyauktada in Orwell's novel *Burmese Days*, Katha's

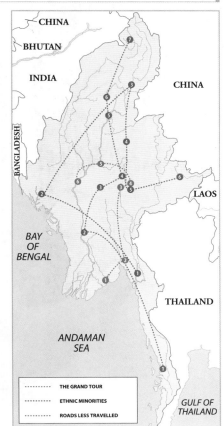

backstreets are dotted with atmospheric colonial buildings; the 1924 tennis club still hosts matches today. **See p.314**

❻ **Indawgyi Lake** Kayak across or bike around Myanmar's biggest lake to seldom-visited villages and Shwe Myitzu, a golden pagoda that floats above the water's lapping waves. **See p.325**

❼ **Putao** Discover Kachin State's wild side in the thickly forested Himalayan foothills outside this remote far northern town. **See p.327**

BUDDHIST MONK WITH CHEROOT

Basics

Getting there

Travelling to Myanmar used to be a question of flying into Yangon or catching one of the few international flights to Mandalay. Then, in 2013, four of the five border crossings between Myanmar and Thailand opened fully to independent foreign travellers, creating some interesting possibilities to enter Myanmar overland, especially in the south of the country.

For the time being, however, most visitors arrive at the ageing **Yangon International Airport** on regional flights from around Asia. The least expensive way to get here is to travel through a regional hub. Bangkok and Singapore are the best options, with regular low-cost flights to both Yangon and **Mandalay International Airport**. Flight prices are slightly higher during the winter peak season (December to February) and over the Thingyan Water Festival, or Burmese New Year (see p.41), which falls in April each year.

There are plans afoot to build a new international airport 80km east of Yangon, near the town of Bago, but at the time of writing these were firmly stuck on the drawing board, and it seems that the airports in Yangon and Mandalay will need to handle the rapidly increasing volume of visitors on their own for the time being.

Whichever way you arrive in Myanmar, it helps to have a valid **visa** before boarding your flight or arriving at the border, as the country's visa-on-arrival system is in its infancy (see p.48). At the time of research the **overland border crossings** from Thailand had been reliably open for a year, but there's always a chance that this will change. Make sure to check the latest information before relying on a particular crossing.

Flights from the UK and Ireland

At the time of writing there were no direct flights from the UK and Ireland to Myanmar. The most convenient (and frequently the cheapest) indirect flights transit through **Bangkok** (11hr 30min), **Kuala Lumpur** (12hr 30min) or **Singapore** (12hr 50min), with daily flights from each of the three cities directly to Yangon, as well as from Bangkok direct to Mandalay (see p.24). Air China and Qatar Airways also operate daily flights from London to their airport hubs, with several direct flights on to Yangon each week.

Other airlines that fly to Bangkok or Singapore with a stop en route include Air France, Cathay Pacific, Emirates, Jet Airways, KLM and Lufthansa. If you're travelling to Myanmar from another UK airport or from the Republic of Ireland you will need to fly to London Heathrow or another hub city first.

From the UK, the lowest available return fares to Yangon, changing planes in Bangkok, KL or Singapore, start around £500.

Flights from the US and Canada

When flying to Myanmar from US and Canadian cities on the **east coast**, your route might see you transiting through Europe or via Asia, with the latter often being more direct, as well as slightly cheaper. There are regular flights from New York, Chicago and Toronto to Beijing on Air China, to Hong Kong on Cathay Pacific, Seoul on Asiana and Korean Air and Tokyo on ANA and JAL, with direct flights from all of these cities to Yangon. Chicago and New York are also served by daily flights to Doha on Qatar Airways, from where you could take one of the three weekly flights to Yangon. Return fares start from $1300 (Can$1420), and flight times are all upwards of 20hr.

Major Asian airports are also the most convenient transit points between the **west coast** and Myanmar. There are direct flights from Los Angeles, San Francisco, Seattle and Vancouver to Beijing, Hong Kong, Seoul, Tokyo and Taipei (the latter on China Airlines), with direct flights from all of these Asian hubs to Yangon. Return tickets start at around $1100 (Can$1200), and the shortest flights take around 18hr, including time spent in transit.

Flights from Australia, New Zealand and South Africa

When travelling to Myanmar from the southern hemisphere, **Bangkok**, **Singapore** and **Kuala Lumpur** are the most convenient places to transfer onto a flight to Yangon. From Australia, Kuala Lumpur is typically the cheapest destination of the three, with direct flights from Adelaide, Brisbane, Sydney, Melbourne and Perth starting from just Aus$400 return, thanks to the presence of **budget carriers** (including Jetstar, Scoot and Tigerair) on various routes, along with full-price airlines. There are also daily direct flights from Brisbane, Melbourne, Perth and Sydney to Singapore (from Aus$470) and Bangkok (from Aus$700).

A BETTER KIND OF TRAVEL

At Rough Guides we are passionately committed to travel. We believe it helps us understand the world we live in and the people we share it with – and of course tourism is vital to many developing economies. But the scale of modern tourism has also damaged some places irreparably, and climate change is accelerated by most forms of transport, especially flying. All Rough Guides' flights are carbon-offset, and every year we donate money to a variety of environmental charities.

Thai Airways operates several flights from Auckland (from NZ$1700) and Johannesburg (from ZAR8500) to Bangkok each week. Singapore Airlines flies direct to Singapore from Auckland and Christchurch (from NZ$1650) and Johannesburg (ZAR9250). And Malaysia Airlines operates daily flights from Auckland (from NZ$1385) to Kuala Lumpur. All prices are for return airfares.

Flights from Southeast Asia

Flights between **Bangkok** and **Yangon** (50min) start at $120 return, with the cheaper airlines often flying out of Don Mueang International Airport (DMK), rather than the larger Suvarnabhumi Airport (BKK), which is preferred by standard-price carriers. Ensure that you leave enough time between connections if you're flying into one airport and out of the other – it can take over an hour to drive between the two. Airlines flying between Bangkok and Yangon include Bangkok Airways, Thai Airways, Golden Myanmar Airlines and Myanmar Airlines International (out of Suvarnabhumi) and Nok Air and AirAsia (out of Don Mueang).

The longer flight from **Singapore** to Yangon (3hr) is well served by budget airlines, with Jetstar Asia and Tigerair operating daily services between the two cities. Return airfares start from $150. Full-price carriers, including Golden Myanmar Airlines, SilkAir and Singapore Airlines, also operate daily flights, with airfares from $360 return.

Airlines that fly directly to Yangon from cities around Southeast Asia include AirAsia and Malaysia Airlines from **Kuala Lumpur**, Myanmar Airways International from **Phnom Penh** and **Siem Reap** and Vietnam Airlines from **Hanoi** and **Ho Chi Minh City**. Air Bagan and Golden Myanmar Airlines also fly between Yangon and **Chiang Mai** several times each week.

Regional airports

Mandalay International Airport is served by an increasing number of direct international flights. At the time of writing there were non-stop flights from Mandalay from Bangkok Suvarnabhumi (daily, 2hr, around $200), Bangkok Don Mueang (daily, 2hr, around $150) and Singapore (2 weekly, 3hr 25min, $360), as well as Kunming in Yunnan, China, and Gaya in Bihar, India.

In addition, Bangkok Airlines operates five flights each week between Bangkok Suvarnabhumi and **Naypyitaw**'s recently expanded airport (2hr 30min, $245). China Eastern flies to the capital from Kunming (1hr 50min; from $220) twice each week, and there are also occasional charter flights from further afield.

Finally, Nok Air runs a daily flight between Mae Sot in Thailand and Mawlamyine in Mon State (1hr), although this was suspended at the time of research.

Overland from Thailand

Of the five border crossings between Myanmar and **Thailand**, four were fully opened to independent travellers in August 2013. **Ranong–Kawthaung** (see box, p.166) and **Phu Nam Ron–Htee Kee** (see box, p.162) in Tanintharyi Region, **Mae Sot–Myawaddy** (see box, p.150) in Kayin State and **Mae Sai–Tachileik** (see box, p.256) in southern Shan State are all now open to travellers with valid Myanmar visas. The fifth checkpoint, **Three Pagodas Pass** between Sangkhlaburi in Thailand and Payathonzu, is also open but only allows day-trips into Myanmar – useful for visa runs, but little else. Thai visas are available at the border but Myanmar visas are not, other than a one-day permit ($10 or 500 baht) used for visa runs.

If you plan to cross at Mae Sai–Tachileik, note that it is not possible to travel overland further into Myanmar beyond Kengtung. Travellers planning to use the Phu Nam Ron–Htee Kee crossing should also note that the road on the Myanmar side of the border is largely impassable during the rainy season, when it's best to enter the country elsewhere.

Overland from China

The **Myanmar–China** border crossing between Muse in northern Shan State and Ruili in China's Yunnan province (see box, p.308) is nominally open to foreigners, but it's necessary to hold a permit and to be part of an officially sanctioned tour in order to either enter or leave Myanmar.

Overland from India, Laos and Bangladesh

The crossing between Moreh in **India** and Tamu in Sagaing Division is theoretically open to foreigners, but onerous **permit requirements** – which (if you're lucky) take several months to negotiate – mean that it is not a feasible route.

There are no official border crossings along Myanmar's short borders with **Laos** and **Bangladesh**.

AIRLINES

Air Canada ⓦ aircanada.com
Air China ⓦ airchina.com
Air France ⓦ airfrance.com
AirAsia ⓦ airasia.com
American Airlines ⓦ aa.com
All Nippon Airlines (ANA) ⓦ ana.co.jp
Asiana ⓦ flyasiana.com
Bangkok Airways ⓦ bangkokair.com
British Airways ⓦ ba.com
Cathay Pacific ⓦ cathaypacific.com
Delta ⓦ delta.com
Emirates ⓦ emirates.com
EVA Air ⓦ evaair.com
Japan Airlines (JAL) ⓦ jal.com
Jet Airways ⓦ jetairways.com
Jetstar and Jetstar Asia ⓦ jetstar.com
KLM (Royal Dutch Airlines) ⓦ klm.com
Korean Air ⓦ koreanair.com
Lufthansa ⓦ lufthansa.com
Malaysia Airlines ⓦ malaysiaairlines.com
Myanmar Airways International ⓦ maiair.com
Nok Air ⓦ nokair.com
Qantas ⓦ qantas.com.au
Qatar Airways ⓦ qatarairways.com
Scoot ⓦ flyscoot.com
SilkAir ⓦ silkair.com
Singapore Airlines ⓦ singaporeair.com
Thai Airways ⓦ thaiairways.com
Tigerair ⓦ tigerair.com
United ⓦ united.com
Vietnam Airlines ⓦ vietnamairlines.com

AGENTS AND OPERATORS

Operators specializing in cycling tours are covered under "Getting around" (see p.30).

Absolute Travel US ☎ 1 212 627 1950, ⓦ absolutetravel.com. High-end private tours, customized to your budget and interests, with most tours between ten and fifteen days.

Adventure Center US ☎ 1 800 228 8747, ⓦ adventurecenter .com. Dozens of Myanmar tours, from a nine-day whizz around the "big four" to two-week treks in northern Kachin State. Small-group and private journeys.

Adventures Abroad US ☎ 1 800 665 3998, ⓦ adventures -abroad.com. Small-group specialists with a range of itineraries that feature Myanmar alongside its Southeast Asian neighbours.

Asian Pacific Adventures US ☎ 1 800 825 1680, ⓦ asianpacific adventures.com. Offers several group and private tours of Myanmar, the most interesting of which focus on ethnic minority regions in Chin and Shan states.

Backroads US ☎ 1 800 462 2848, ⓦ backroads.com. Short cycling and hiking tours around Myanmar's main tourist sights.

Belmond UK ☎ 0845 217 0799, US ☎ 1 800 524 2420; ⓦ voyagesinmyanmar.com. Formerly known as Orient Express Travel, Belmond operates high-end cruises on its two boats, *Road to Mandalay* and *Orcaella*, along several Ayeyarwady itineraries.

Exodus UK ☎ 0845 287 3647, ⓦ exodus.co.uk. Offers a small selection of two-week trips around the usual suspects of Yangon, Mandalay, Inle Lake and Bagan, along with a more interesting (and challenging) trekking trip that will see you ascend Mount Victoria in Chin State.

Exotissimo Thailand ☎ 02 633 9060, ⓦ exotissimo.com. Bangkok-based company with offices in Yangon (see p.83) and Mandalay (see p.274) offering a good selection of tours countrywide from one to fourteen nights plus overland journeys from Mandalay to Yunnan, Chiang Mai to Kengtung and Yangon to Phuket. Also runs good local tours of Bagan (but avoid the useless branch office in Bagan itself and book via Yangon or Mandalay).

Explore UK ☎ 08436 368009, US ☎ 1 800 715 1746, Canada ☎ 1 888 216 3401, Australia ☎ 1300 439 756, New Zealand ☎ 0800 269 263; ⓦ explore.co.uk. Big range of small-group and tailor-made trips around Myanmar, ranging from nine to 24 days, with a flexible approach and reasonable mid-range prices.

InsideBurma Tours UK ☎ 0117 244 3381, ⓦ insideburmatours .com. Reliable outfit offering tailored tours and a selection of off-the-peg group itineraries; the latter include an interesting "Kipling's Burma" option, which weaves together aspects of colonial heritage and local culture.

Intrepid UK ☎ 08082 745111, US ☎ 1 800 970 7299, Australia ☎ 1300 797 010; ⓦ intrepidtravel.com. Small-group tours with an emphasis on cross-cultural contact and low-impact tourism, organizing a range of standard trips, plus a few to more out-of-the-way destinations including Bago, Kyaiktiyo and Tanintharyi.

North South Travel UK ☎ 01245 608291, ⓦ northsouthtravel .co.uk. Friendly competitive travel agency, offering discounted fares worldwide. Profits are used to support projects in the developing world, especially the promotion of sustainable tourism.

Panoramic Journeys UK ☎ 01608 676821, Ⓦ panoramic journeys.com. With a focus on ethical travel, this operator has recently added Myanmar to its short list of destinations. Tours are often arranged to coincide with festivals, with a focus on the main sights, and there are also several trekking trips and occasional forays off the beaten track. Private tours also possible.

Regent Holidays UK ☎ 020 7666 1244, Ⓦ regent-holidays.co.uk. Specializing in offbeat tours, this operator has a range of itineraries that include trips on Myanmar's railways plus cruises along the Ayeyarwady and through the Myeik Archipelago.

STA Travel UK ☎ 03333 210099, US ☎ 1 800 781 4040, Australia ☎ 134 782, New Zealand ☎ 0800 474 400, South Africa ☎ 086 1781781; Ⓦ statravel.co.uk. Worldwide specialists in independent travel; also providing student IDs, travel insurance and a range of other services. Good discounts for under-26s.

Steppes Travel UK ☎ 08436 368323, US ☎ 1 855 203 7885; Ⓦ steppestravel.co.uk. UK-based tour operator with an Asian focus offering a range of tailored private tours around Myanmar.

Trailfinders UK ☎ 0207 368 1200, Ireland ☎ 021 464 8800; Ⓦ trailfinders.com. One of the best-informed and most efficient agents for independent travellers.

Travel CUTs Canada ☎ 1 800 667 2887, Ⓦ travelcuts.com. Canadian youth and student travel firm.

USIT Ireland ☎ 01 602 1906, Ⓦ usit.ie. Ireland's main student and youth travel specialists.

Travel Indochina US ☎ 1 800 342 1957, Ⓦ travelindochina .com. Covers the obvious Myanmar sights, but goes a bit beyond them, as well as taking bookings for Belmond's luxury Ayeyarwady cruise boat, *Orcaella*.

Wild Frontiers UK ☎ 020 7736 3968, Ⓦ wildfrontierstravel.com. A small range of standard Myanmar journeys with an emphasis on sustainable travel, and one or two more adventurous options.

Getting around

Getting around Myanmar can take as much or – at least travelling between major cities – as little time as you like. At one end of the scale, it's possible to zip around the major destinations by plane, while at the other you can join the locals on bumpy trains and unhurried river-boats. Somewhere in the middle lies Myanmar's surprisingly modern bus network, its speedy air-conditioned coaches providing a winning combination of quick(ish) journeys and reasonable ticket prices.

By plane

In addition to state-owned **Myanma Airways** (Ⓦ myanmaairways.aero), which has a poor reputation for the condition of its aircraft, an array of **private airlines** – among them Air KBZ (Ⓦ airkbz .com), Air Mandalay (Ⓦ airmandalay.com), Air Bagan (Ⓦ airbagan.com), Asian Wings (Ⓦ asianwingsair .com), Golden Myanmar Airlines (Ⓦ gmairlines.com) and Yangon Airways (Ⓦ yangonair.com) – run services on domestic routes and have offices in major towns and cities.

Given the long journey times overland, travelling by plane can be an attractive choice if you're not on a tight budget (one-way airfares from Yangon to Mandalay start from $120), and in a

---

PERMITS: GO OR NO-GO?

While independent travel is straightforward in much of central Myanmar, you will quickly run into **travel restrictions** if you want to explore the country's mountainous fringes. In some areas – such as large parts of Shan and Kachin states – foreigners' access is limited as a result of government conflict with ethnic minority groups, while other areas are cut off to protect dubious business interests – among them jade and gem mines, as well as drug-dealing hotspots. Many of these regions are either completely closed to foreign visitors or require permits that may take several weeks to obtain.

Myanmar's no-go zones are in constant flux – parts of Rakhine State, for example, have closed and reopened repeatedly in the last few years – and these closures and requirements can change without warning. Our map (see p.28) shows regions where travel was restricted at the time of writing, but for the latest information contact Myanmar Tours and Travels (MTT; Ⓦ myanmartourism.org) or get in touch with an authorized tour operator.

Make sure to plan well in advance if you would like to visit a restricted area. **Permits** take at least a month to arrange, with a private tour operator approved by MTT (these are listed under "Services" on the MTT website) making the application on your behalf. You will be required to book onto an **official tour** or – at the bare minimum – hire a guide to make sure you don't misbehave. Permit **costs** themselves are nominal, but the strings attached to the permit (often requiring you to be accompanied by a guide and driver, or to join a group) drive up the price of visiting off-limits regions.

few cases, such as visiting Kengtung, air travel is the only option as overland routes are closed to foreigners. Many services fly on **circular routes**, stopping at several airports on the way, and it may therefore be easier to make a journey one way than the other.

Besides Yangon and Mandalay, the most useful regional airports for visitors are **Bagan** (Nyaung U) and **Heho** (for Inle Lake, Kalaw and Pindaya). Note that flights are always heavily booked over the Thingyan Water Festival, when you will need to book well in advance. The luggage weight limit on domestic flights is 20kg per person.

There are a number of **downsides** to domestic air travel. For one thing, it may not save you much time as schedules are subject to change at short notice and delays are common. For another, most domestic airlines still do not sell tickets online – although they may allow you to make an online reservation and then pay once in the country. In addition, travellers should avoid flying if they are trying to limit the amount of their money that ends up with the government or its cronies (see box, p.42).

By bus

Buses are usually much faster than trains, and are generally the best way to get around on a budget. There are many different bus companies and most are privately owned. Taking buses can be quite tiring, however, since most long-distance services run through the night, stop roughly every three hours for toilet or food breaks (not all the buses have toilets on board), and arrive before dawn.

Most **long-distance buses** are reasonably comfortable, and an increasing number offer luxuries such as small television screens in each seat and complimentary toothbrushes and snacks. Do make sure you bring warm clothes, as they tend to crank up the air-conditioning, and earplugs if Burmese pop music isn't your thing. On major routes, it's often possible to take a slightly faster and more comfortable "VIP" or "**express**" bus service for a small additional fee. **Ordinary buses** also run segments of longer routes, such as Taungoo–Mandalay (rather than the full Yangon–Mandalay trip); these are usually in worse condition but are cheaper for shorter trips, as on long-distance buses you will pay the fare for the full journey even if you get on or off part-way through. You'll also find smaller, 32-seat buses – these should be avoided if possible for long trips, as they tend to be jam-packed with luggage. As for **prices**, the 9hr trip between Yangon and Mandalay costs around K20,000 on express bus, compared to K15,000 by ordinary bus. Note that on express buses, large items of luggage are stowed in compartments underneath the coach, while on ordinary buses bags are stored anywhere the owner can find space.

Some bus routes are **off limits** to foreigners (such as Bhamo–Mandalay), while elsewhere bus passengers escape permit requirements demanded of train travellers (such as Mawlamyine–Dawei). If in doubt about your route, check with local guesthouse staff at either end of the journey, as they are often the most clued in on the local situation.

It's a good idea to **book** a day or two ahead for busy routes (such as Bagan–Nyaungshwe), ones where only a few buses run (e.g. Ngwe Saung–Yangon) or where you're joining a bus part-way through its route (in Kalaw, for example). Guesthouses can often help book tickets for a small fee (usually K2000–3000), or you can buy them either from bus stations (which in some cases are outside of town), from in-town bus company offices or from local travel agents. Tickets booked privately often include **transfers** to and from the bus station, particularly convenient when the station is out of town.

Note that all of Myanmar's bus services **close down** for a week or more over the Thingyan Water Festival; make sure that you have alternative arrangements – typically by plane or train – if you need to travel over that period. Finally, prepare for **delays**, particularly if travelling during Myanmar's rainy season (June–Oct) each year.

By train

The **railway system** in Myanmar is antiquated, slow and generally uncomfortable. The entire network, which dates from the days of British Burma, is narrow gauge, and although frequent repairs have been made (thankfully), train journeys in Myanmar are often comically bouncy and timing unpredictable in the extreme. On most routes buses are faster and more reliable – it is not uncommon for express trains to be delayed by several hours, and local trains are even worse.

All that said, there are reasons why you might want to take a train at least once during your trip. One is that on a few routes, such as from Mandalay up to Naba, Katha and Myitkyina, road transport is closed to foreigners. Another is for the experience

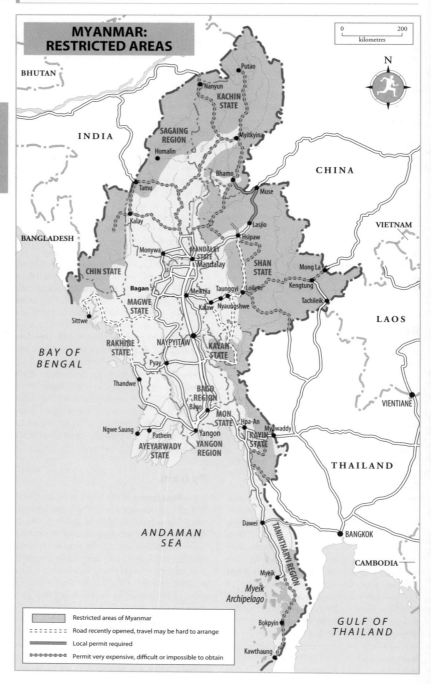

MYANMAR: RESTRICTED AREAS

0   200
kilometres

N

BHUTAN

INDIA

CHINA

VIETNAM

BANGLADESH

Putao
Nanyun
KACHIN STATE
SAGAING REGION
Homalin
Myitkyina
Bhamo
Tamu
Muse
Kalay
Lasjio
Monywa
Hsipaw
MANDALAY STATE
Mandalay
SHAN STATE
Mong La
CHIN STATE
Bagan
Meiktila
Taunggyi
Loilem
Kengtung
MAGWE STATE
Kalaw
Nyaungshwe
Tachileik
Sittwe
RAKHINE STATE
NAYPYITAW
KAYAH STATE
LAOS
BAY OF BENGAL
Pyay
Thandwe
BAGO REGION
Bago
MON STATE
Hpa-An
Myawaddy
Ngwe Saung
Pathein
Yangon
KAYIN STATE
VIENTIANE
AYEYARWADY STATE
YANGON REGION
THAILAND
ANDAMAN SEA
Dawei
TANINTHARYI REGION
BANGKOK
CAMBODIA
Myeik
Myeik Archipelago
Bokpyin
GULF OF THAILAND
Kawthaung

	Restricted areas of Myanmar
- - - - - - -	Road recently opened, travel may be hard to arrange
━━━━━	Local permit required
◆◆◆◆◆◆	Permit very expensive, difficult or impossible to obtain

itself: many routes run through areas of great beauty, for example the rickety Gokteik Viaduct between Pyin Oo Lwin and Kyaukme (see box, p.300). Trains also offer more opportunities than buses to interact with local people.

Routes and train types

The country's most important line (and one of the few stretches of double track) runs between Yangon and Mandalay via Naypyitaw, and this line has the most modern rolling stock. Additional **major lines** run from Myitkyina in the far north to Mandalay, and south of Yangon as far as Mawlamyine. **Branch lines** connect towns to the east and west of the main railroad to the network. Myanmar's railways are currently being extended in several directions, with **new track** being laid to Bhamo in the northeast, Kengtung in the east, Myeik in the south and Pathein in the southwest.

A range of services operates on each of the major lines. Where possible, it's worth opting for the slightly faster "**express**" services, as these trains are given priority over slower **local** services, and are thus less likely to be delayed – tickets for the various classes cost the same, regardless of the train type. The express train from Yangon to Mandalay takes 14hr, while the local service takes 15–16hr over the same route.

Train classes and sleepers

All trains have **upper-** and **ordinary-class** carriages. Upper class has reservable reclining seats (which can be more of a curse than a blessing if the mechanism is broken), while ordinary class has hard seats that cannot be reserved – you may end up standing if the train is crowded. Some trains also have **first-class** carriages, which actually fall between upper and ordinary class in price and comfort, with seating usually on a padded wooden bench. **Upper-class sleeper carriages**, available between Yangon and Mandalay, Yangon and Bagan, and on some Mandalay–Myitkyina services, offer two- and four-berth lockable compartments with bedclothes provided. **Special sleepers** are available between Yangon and Mandalay, with self-contained compartments sleeping up to four passengers, a private toilet and sitting area as well as a private entrance. As yet, none of Myanmar Railways' rolling stock has air-conditioning – open windows are the order of the day – but the Yangon Circular Line and the Yangon–Mandalay line are due for air-conditioned carriages before long.

Express trains may have restaurant cars, and on all trains food vendors either come on board or carry out transactions through the windows at stops. Whatever the class of train, the bathrooms on board all services are basic and often unclean.

Fares and bookings

In April 2014, Myanmar Railways ended a system that saw foreign travellers charged substantially higher **ticket prices** than local people, and required them to pay in dollars. Now everyone pays the same price, denominated in kyat. By way of example, ticket prices between Yangon and Mandalay are as follows: ordinary class K4600; upper class K9300; upper-class sleeper K12,750. You will require your passport to buy train tickets.

It's almost mandatory to **book** sleeper berths well in advance (these tickets can be booked up to two weeks before you travel), and a good idea to book ahead even if you're planning to travel by upper class (generally tickets go on sale three days in advance for upper class and a day in advance for ordinary tickets). However, at intermediate stops between major stations tickets may only go on sale shortly before the train arrives. Foreigners are usually dealt with separately from local passengers, and you will find that station staff often invite you into their offices while they write out your ticket.

It's possible to buy tickets before you travel through a handful of Yangon **travel agents**, including Exotic Myanmar Travels & Tours (W exotic myanmartravel.com) and Myanmar Tour East (W myanmartoureast.com). Once you're in the country you'll need to head to the station yourself to buy a ticket direct from the booking office.

For the latest **information** on travelling by train in Myanmar (and timetables for the most popular services), The Man in Seat 61 (W seat61.com/Burma .htm) is the most comprehensive and reliable online resource.

By ferry

Myanmar offers some of Asia's great river journeys and travelling by boat is, in places, an excellent alternative to buses and trains. Boats connect some of the country's major destinations, most notably Mandalay and Bagan, and can be a good way to experience local life. The most popular routes are concentrated on the upper reaches of the **Ayeyarwady River**, but there are also interesting trips on the **Thanlyin** and **Chindwin rivers**, as well as from Sittwe to Mrauk U. Several sea routes link places that are difficult to reach overland, with ferries plying the waters of the Tanintharyi coast, and the trip from Sittwe to Taunggok.

Inland Water Transit or **IWT** (W www.iwt.gov.mm /en), a government-run service, operates the slow two-storey ferries that run regularly irregular services along the Ayeyarwady River between Mandalay and Bhamo, Nyaung U (for Bagan) and Pyay. Elsewhere IWT runs a few trips each week between Monywa and Kalewa along the Chindwin River and between Sittwe and Mrauk U in Rakhine State. Boats are often stacked high with cargo, leaving some covered deck space and a few cabins for passengers, with most locals setting up camp on deck for the duration of their voyage. Bring something comfortable to sit on and sleep under – if you're planning to travel on deck, take a mat and a blanket. Simple meals are available on board and vendors swarm onto the ship at each stop.

Privately run **"fast boats"** – usually long, thin motorboats carrying anywhere between thirty and eighty passengers – follow some of IWT's routes along the Ayeyarwady, and also cover the beautiful trip down the Thanlyin from Mawlamyine to Hpa-An, the journey down the Tanintharyi coast and the river voyage from Sittwe to Mrauk U. The comfort levels of the boats can vary wildly. Some vessels offer spacious seats and air-conditioning, while on others you'll have to make do with cramped wooden benches and a tarpaulin roof.

As with most forms of transport in Myanmar, journeys by boat can take far longer than advertised, particularly during the dry season (Dec–May) when water levels are low and the vessels – particularly the large, heavy IWT ferries – can get stuck on sand banks.

Fares for boat journeys are quoted throughout the Guide, with IWT ferries generally working out much cheaper than fast boats if you're prepared to travel on deck, rather than in cabin-bound comfort.

By car

As yet, self-drive holidays are not really a realistic prospect in Myanmar – current laws require that foreign drivers get permission from two different government departments and have a local driver on board at all times. Red tape aside, at the time of writing no international car rental companies had a presence in Myanmar, although this will surely change. Fortunately, it's relatively easy to

arrange a **car and driver** (from around $40/day) through your accommodation or a tour operator – it's best to work through the latter if you want anything more complicated than a day-trip. Straightforward as it may be to find a man with a car, do take care to specify exactly what is included. Useful questions to ask include how much mileage or petrol will be included, who will pay for the driver's food and accommodation, and whether you are expected to tip or not in addition to the daily rate.

By bike and motorcycle

Cycling is a brilliant way to explore parts of Myanmar, and bicycle tours of Bagan and Mandalay are a particular highlight for many visitors. Bikes are widely available to rent for around K2000 per day. In some parts of the country it is also possible to rent a **motorcycle**, typically for K8000–10,000 a day plus fuel. Note that motorcycles have been banned in central Yangon since 2003 when, rumour has it, a motorcyclist almost knocked over a senior general. Petrol can be bought at filling stations or, more commonly in the countryside, from stalls set up along the roadside selling one-litre bottles. Safety helmets may be provided, although not always – be aware that you can be fined for riding without one. Before renting a motorbike, check that your travel insurance covers you for such activities (see box, p.50).

There are numerous **hazards** for cyclists and motorcyclists: traffic can be very heavy in the cities, while in rural areas the roads are often in poor condition. Adding to these dangers is the fact that most cars are right-hand drive imports from Japan or Thailand even though Myanmar drives on the right (see p.358), meaning that cars have large blind spots.

Motorbike touring is relatively new in Myanmar. Mandalay Motorbike Rental (W www.mandalay motorbike.com) organizes group motorcycle tours as well as rentals, and Southeast Asia motorbiking site GT Rider (W gt-rider.com) also has some basic information on riding in the country. Cycling being more established, cyclists have a greater range of options, with several operators organizing multi-day tours of the country.

CYCLING TOUR OPERATORS

Grasshopper Adventures UK ☎ 020 8123 8144, US ☎ 1 818 921 7101, Australia ☎ 03 9016 3172; W grasshopperadventures.com. Specializing in cycling tours, Grasshopper organizes half-day tours around

Bagan and Mandalay, as well as longer trips (6–13 days) around Inle Lake, Bagan and Mandalay.

Myanmar Cycling Tours Myanmar ☎ 01 371105, ⓦ www .myanmarcyclingtours.com. The local branch of Indochina Bike Tours, this Yangon-based company organizes everything from half-day cycling tours of Yangon and Mandalay to 18-day countrywide fly-and-cycle tours.

Spice Roads Thailand ☎ 66 2 381 7490, ⓦ spiceroads.com. Southeast Asian cycling specialists, Spice Roads offer several multi-day bike tours of Myanmar, including a great 14-day trip from China's Yunnan province to Mandalay.

Veloasia US ☎ 1 415 731 4377, ⓦ veloasia.com. Organizing small-group trips on a single 12-day itinerary that takes in the "Big Four" sights, this firm also customizes cycling trips for couples and families.

Shared taxis, vans and pick-ups

Although not as common as in some Southeast Asian countries, **shared taxis** and **shared vans** are available on some routes, from Mandalay to Pyin Oo Lwin and Hsipaw for example. Prices are typically around fifty percent more than a seat on an air-conditioned bus, and you will generally pay the full fare regardless of where you get on or off. They will usually drop you wherever you like, however, which saves on transfer costs in towns where the bus station is inconveniently located. Vehicles can be arranged either through accommodation or at shared-taxi stands in town centres.

In addition to these routes between towns, which are primarily used by locals, there are a handful of services aimed specifically at foreigners. These are typically round trips, such as to Mount Popa from Bagan.

Local transport

Local transport in Myanmar is provided by a colourful mix of public buses, taxis, pick-ups, tuk-tuks, motorbike taxis and cycle rickshaws. **Public buses** run only in the largest cities, including Yangon and Mandalay, and are very cheap. Unless you read Burmese, it can be a challenge to work out the routes, and consequently we have not covered them in detail in the Guide, but if you aren't in a rush, riding on the buses is certainly an experience. The same can be said of **pick-ups** or *lain-ka* – adapted pick-up trucks with seating in the covered back portion – which cover set routes and pick up and drop people off on the way. They usually depart when full, which may include passengers riding on the roof. If you want the most comfortable seats, in the cabin, then you can pay a little extra; a seat in the

back (or on the roof) will seldom set you back more than K600.

Taxis are available in large towns and cities, and range from 1970s Toyotas to occasional new left-hand-drive Chinese imports. There are no meters but drivers tend not to overcharge as outrageously as in many other Southeast Asian countries. Expect to pay around K1500–2000 for a trip across town of a reasonable length, such as from a bus station on the edge of town to a central hotel. Burmese-style **tuk-tuks** (*thoun-bein*) – motorbikes with roofed flat-bed trailers attached behind them, with rows of wooden benches for seats – replace taxis in smaller towns and villages, and often work out slightly cheaper, starting at K500–1000 for a short ride. **Cycle rickshaws** (*saiq-ka*), also known as trishaws, are still in use in many towns, although these are being edged out by **motorbike taxis** (on which the passenger rides pillion). The latter are much faster and normally around the same price (starting from K500 per trip).

Most of these forms of transport can also be hired (with driver) for a day, and can be arranged direct, through accommodation or via travel agents; you'll need to bargain to get a good price. Motorbike taxis may not work out much more expensive than renting a self-drive motorcycle, while groups can often get a good deal on a pick-up or tuk-tuk for the day.

Finally, in small towns, **horse-drawn carriages** are used as a key form of transportation, and also ferry tourists around in a number of places, notably Bagan, Inwa and Pyin Oo Lwin. The horses are not always well looked after, however, and the lack of suspension on bumpy Burmese roads makes them uncomfortable for longer trips.

Accommodation

First, the bad news: accommodation in Myanmar is crazily expensive, and prices continue to rise dramatically thanks to the general shortage of rooms, the cost of taxes and licences, and the fact that the government itself encourages hotels to set artificially high tariffs in its attempt to maximize foreign-currency earnings. In many places quite ordinary rooms in a mid-range hotel can go for over $100 (in a country where many people earn less than $2 a day), while you're unlikely to find a reasonable en-suite budget room for much less than $25.

ACCOMMODATION PRICES

Rates quoted throughout this Guide are for the cost of the **cheapest double room** in high season (Nov–Feb), excluding peak-period spikes such as over Christmas and New Year and during Thingyan Water Festival. Rates at most places include all relevant **taxes and service charges**, although some top-end places quote pre-tax rates and then add on an additional fee – typically a ten percent service charge and a ten percent government tax. If in doubt, check when you book/check in. **Breakfast** is normally included (see below). **Single room** rates, where available, are normally around two-thirds the price of a double room.

Secondly, more bad news. Given the cost of accommodation, and the fact that so many of the better places are owned by businessmen with close **government links**, this is where you'll need to be especially careful if you don't want your money falling into the hands of the government's cronies (see p.43). Most hotels and hotel chains are locally owned, and international chains have yet to arrive, except for a couple of rare examples – you won't currently find any Burmese Hiltons, Hyatts, Marriotts or Sheratons. On the upside, although accommodation remains in generally short supply, the country's rapidly booming tourism industry means that new places are now opening all the time, in all price categories, and there's now a far wider choice of places to stay than ever before.

Be aware that not all guesthouses are **licensed to accept foreign guests**, so some places (particularly small guesthouses in remote towns that don't see many foreigners) may be forced to turn you away even if they have rooms.

National power shortages mean that **electricity** is only available in some towns for set periods (typically 6am–6pm, although in some places electrical cuts may happen in the middle of the night). Most, but not all, mid- and top-end places have their own generators – and therefore 24hr electricity. In budget places you'll have to do without electricity during outage hours.

Rates and reservations

Where you stay will depend a lot on where you are. In larger tourist centres (Yangon, Mandalay, Bagan) there's plenty of accommodation and you can afford to pick and choose (assuming you reserve ahead). In smaller and/or less touristed places there may be only a handful of options, if that. Given all this, it pays to **reserve in advance** – Yangon can be particularly tricky to find a cheap bed in, for example, while at the time of writing there were only seven rooms in the whole of Ngapali for under $100, making advance reservations more or less essential if you're travelling on any kind of budget. Equally, don't be amazed if your reservation isn't honoured – many places, particularly budget guesthouses, are rather good at losing bookings. It's also often worth **bargaining**, especially in budget guesthouses (although you may even have some joy at mid-range places), particularly in low season or if you're staying several days.

Different places give room rates in either dollars or kyat (sometimes both) – we've quoted prices throughout the Guide in the **currency** used by the establishment itself. Most places include some kind of **breakfast** in their room rates – all the prices quoted in the Guide include breakfast, unless specifically stated otherwise. The breakfasts themselves are usually fairly stereotypical offerings of processed bread, eggs and a cup of coffee, plus maybe a banana or other fruit. Bigger places may lay out a more interesting buffet spread, sometimes featuring Burmese dishes, although disappointingly few places offer *mohinga*, the delicious noodle soup eaten by most Burmese themselves to start the day (see p.34).

Budget accommodation

Many of the country's very **cheapest guesthouses** and hotels (under $15/night) are aimed squarely at locals and aren't licensed to accept foreigners – and those that do have a foreigners' licence are often pretty squalid. Rooms are often dirty cubicles with filthy bedding and flimsy walls covered with squashed insect remains and disintegrating paint.

TOP FIVE BUDGET GUESTHOUSES

Motherland Inn II, Yangon See p.84
Chan Myaye Guest House, Yangon See p.84
Soe Brothers Guesthouse, Hpa-An See p.148
Golden Lily, Kalaw See p.233
Lily the Home, Hsipaw See p.305

TOP FIVE BEACH RESORTS

Emerald Sea Resort, Ngwe Saung
See p.107
Amara Ocean Resort, Ngapali See p.110
Sandoway Resort, Ngapali See p.111
Coconut Guesthouse, Maungmagan
See p.162
Andaman Club, Thahtay Kyun Island
See box, p.165

And you'll most likely be sharing a grubby communal bathroom with cold water only.

Budget accommodation aimed at foreign visitors is mainly in **family-run guesthouses** or **smaller hotels**. Rooms typically cost between $15 and $30 per night for a double room. At the lower end of this price range you'll probably be sharing a bathroom and the room itself is likely to be pretty shabby. For around $25 per night you can usually find somewhere reasonably clean and comfortable with en-suite bathroom (possibly with hot water). Most rooms have air-conditioning, except in cooler upland areas of the north and east, where this often isn't necessary (and, where available, costs extra). Mosquito nets are only sporadically provided.

Mid-range and expensive accommodation

Most **mid-range accommodation** ($50–100/ night) is in functional concrete-box hotels. Rooms tend to be larger and with a few extra trimmings (perhaps a fridge, safe, satellite TV and writing desk), and there might be an in-house restaurant and 24hr reception, although all things considered you may find yourself paying $50–70 per night for a room not appreciably better than one costing $30.

Rates at **top-end accommodation** are similarly sky-high – and many are owned by individuals or companies with strong government links. A few places offer genuinely stylish and enjoyable lodgings for as little as $100 per night, though you can easily pay double that, and rates at the very best establishments run into the hundreds of dollars. Many upmarket hotels are attractively presented and very professionally run, although most follow an identikit template, usually with bungalow-style rooms with wooden floors and furniture (plus a few Burmese artefacts for decorative effect) set among lush gardens, usually with a swimming pool, and often a spa as well.

Food and drink

Sandwiched between gastronomic big-hitters India, Thailand and China, Burmese food is one of Asia's least-known cuisines. While Myanmar's food does absorb influences from its better-known culinary neighbours, it remains unique in many respects: Burmese cooks use fewer spices than their Indian counterparts; Thai cuisine's chilli and coconut milk are notably absent; and pulses and beans are used with an abandon that would be foreign to most Chinese chefs. As elsewhere in Asia, much of daily life in Myanmar revolves around food and mealtimes, and the phrase "Sa pi bi la?" or "Have you eaten?" is a common greeting.

Meals

Most Burmese people eat **breakfast** early in the morning, often stopping for a bowl of noodles or a fried snack at a teahouse. Although many hotels in Myanmar do include breakfast in their room rate, it's worth foregoing what is usually a fairly depressing offering of white bread, fried eggs and instant coffee, and venturing out to a nearby market or teashop for something tastier.

One of the Eight Buddhist Precepts (see box, p.34) states that good Buddhists ought to eat only after sunrise and before noon, and **lunch** in Myanmar is consequently taken rather earlier than is common in the West (although for all except the most devout, this precept is conveniently forgotten around dinnertime). Most people tuck into their lunchtime noodles or curry between 11am and 1pm. Make sure to eat your **evening meal** early too, as many restaurants will be closed by 9pm.

A wide variety of snacks and salads fill the gaps between meals, and there's usually some kind of deep-fried treat available if you're ever in danger of running low on calories. Cakes and sweets are often flavoured with coconut and palm sugar and eaten between meals rather than as a dessert, and it's common to just have a lump of t'ǎnyeq (jaggery, or unrefined palm sugar) at the end of a meal.

Burmese food

A brief look around any market in Myanmar will reveal the **key ingredients** of Burmese cuisine:

onions and shallots, rice and *ngăpí*, a pungent fermented fish paste that vendors often stick incense sticks into to take the edge off the smell. If you are at all interested in food, it's well worth seeking out **wet markets** on your travels. These colourful, messy markets reveal the huge range of exotic ingredients that go into Burmese cooking, and are often a focus of local life.

In Burmese cooking it's considered important to **balance flavours**, with sour, spicy, bitter and salty tastes combined in each meal; this is generally done across a series of dishes rather than on a single plate. For example, a mild curry might be accompanied by bitter leaves, dried chilli and a salty condiment such as *ngăpí*.

Noodles

A typical local breakfast is **noodle soup**, such as the national dish **mohinga** (catfish soup with rice vermicelli, onions, lemongrass, garlic, chilli and lime, with some cooks adding things like boiled egg, courgette fritters and fried bean crackers). Alternatives include *oùn-nó k'auq-s'wèh* (coconut chicken soup with noodles, raw onions, coriander and chilli) and Shan noodles or *Shan k'auq-s'wèh* (rice noodles in a thin savoury broth, topped with minced chicken or pork, spring onions and ground peanuts, served with pickled vegetables). Another tasty Shan noodle dish is *mi-shay*, thin rice noodles topped with minced chicken or pork, coriander, deep-fried shallots and soy sauce, which is served with clear soup and pickles.

Salads and snacks

Salads are a common snack, although they may not resemble salad as you know it – the Burmese term, *ăthouq*, simply means "mixed" – and they are usually cold dishes built around a single central ingredient mixed with raw onions, gram flour, chilli and coriander in a savoury dressing.

TOP FIVE BURMESE RESTAURANTS

999 Shan Noodle Shop, Yangon
  See p.87
Lucky Seven, Yangon See p.88
San Ma Tu, Hpa-An See p.149
Thirihayhar, Kalaw See p.234
Shan Mama, Mandalay See p.277

Common *ăthouq* are *nàn-gyì thouq* (thick rice noodle salad), *kayan-jin-dhi thouq* (tomato salad) and *myin-kwa-yuet thouq* (pennywort salad). It's also worth trying *samusa thouq* (samosa salad), a delicious dish of chopped-up samosas served with the same toppings.

Burmese **tea-leaf salad** (*lahpet thouq*) and ginger salad (*jin thouq*) are also worth trying, particularly the former, which is something of a national favourite. Fermented tea leaves (see box, p.302) are topped with vegetable oil, fried garlic and crisp broad beans, crushed dried shrimp and occasionally chopped tomato and whole green chilli. The end result is not unlike Italian pesto with a kick of caffeine, which makes it a popular afternoon pick-me-up with Myanmar's students.

Many other common Burmese **snacks** are deep-fried, ranging from familiar things like home-made potato crisps flavoured with dried chilli, to deep-fried insects sold in paper cones. In teahouses across the land you will have the chance to breakfast on greasy-but-delicious *cha kway* (Chinese-style doughnuts), best dipped in tea or coffee; French toast (*chit-u bamoq gyaw*), served with sugar; as well as **samosa** and various Indian-influenced breads (most commonly paratha – called *palata* in Myanmar – naan and puri), served with mild vegetable-based curries.

BUDDHISM AND FOOD IN BURMA

Happily, it's possible to be considered a devout Buddhist in Myanmar even if you only practise the **Eight Precepts** (which include bans on intoxicating drinks, dancing and eating after noon, among other good things) for two days a month. In daily life, however, Burmese Buddhists are more likely to abstain from eating **beef** than from drinking **alcohol**, the former being considered taboo, as cows are highly respected. That said, beef curries are still available in some Myanmar restaurants, but chicken, pork and fish are far more common.

Many Burmese people will be temporarily **vegetarian** at various points during the year, particularly during **Buddhist Lent**, which usually falls between July and October. Outside of this period meat is eaten freely, in apparent violation of yet another precept – to refrain from taking life – the thinking being that as long as one doesn't kill the animal oneself, it's a-okay to eat it.

VEGETARIAN FOOD IN MYANMAR

Despite the fact that many people in Myanmar are Buddhists, most are enthusiastic omnivores rather than strict vegetarians (see box opposite). There are plenty of **vegetarian** options out there for travellers, but at times – typically when faced with a meat-only curry spread – it might not feel like it.

One of the first things to learn is "*theq-thaq-luq*", a Burmese phrase meaning "without living things" that is widely used to describe vegetarian food. In many instances, it's possible to point at a dish and ask for it served *theq-thaq-luq*. Although this approach doesn't guarantee that the chef will hold back on the fish sauce or bone stock, it will produce the same dish served without obvious meat or fish.

For true vegetarian food, you may need to be slightly conservative in regard to what and where you eat. **Curries** (even the egg ones) are often prepared with either *ngăpí* fish paste or meat-based stock, and are best avoided if that concerns you. In Burmese curry restaurants fill up instead on lightly flavoured **side dishes and salads**, as these are often served *theq-thaq-luq* to begin with. Vegetable and tofu dishes in Chinese restaurants are generally vegetarian-friendly, and Indian and Western restaurants often serve a range of vegetarian dishes.

Vegan travellers will face similar challenges, although – thanks to the lack of dairy products used in Burmese cooking – the vast majority of Burmese dishes are dairy-free to begin with.

Curries

Curry and rice, or *t'ămìn hin*, is the quintessential Burmese meal, best sampled at lunchtime when the food is fresh – the curries are usually cooked in the morning and left in pots all day. (Although many good restaurants still attract crowds of evening diners, you may prefer to eat dinner in Chinese restaurants or teahouses where the food is cooked to order.) A meat, fish or prawn curry (*hin*) in a thin gravy will be accompanied by a hearty bowl of rice (*t'ămìn*), a clear **soup** (usually peppery *hin gyo* or sour *chinyay hin*) and dishes of fried vegetables. A great deal of oil is added to Burmese curries, supposedly to keep bacteria out, but like locals you can skim the oil off. At the best restaurants, the meal will also include a selection of up to a dozen small **side dishes**, including *balachaung*, a spicy mix of crisp deep-fried shallots, garlic, chilli and dried prawns, plus fresh vegetables and herbs with a dip (usually *ngăpí-ye*, a watery fish sauce). Chinese green tea will usually be thrown in, and sometimes you'll get a **dessert** such as tasty *lahpet thouq* (tea-leaf salad; see opposite) or jaggery.

While many people now use a fork and spoon to eat curry and rice in restaurants, traditionally the Burmese eat with their **hands**. In some places you will see people using their right hands to massage lumps out of the steamed rice, before ladling gravy onto the same plate and mixing it through with their fingers. When it's satisfactorily mixed, a small handful will be gathered in a pinching motion and pushed into the mouth using the thumb, with the diner taking bites of the meat and vegetables in between. Often, the quantity of rice seems ridiculous when compared to the small bowls of curry that are dished up, but these quantities make sense when eating with your hands – the gravy goes a lot further. People generally eat with their right hands, although the taboo against eating with the left hand is not as strong here as it is in India. Chinese-style spoons are used to serve from common dishes and for eating soup.

Regional cuisine

Thanks perhaps to the ubiquitous Shan noodles and *mi-shay*, **Shan cooking** has a higher profile inside Myanmar than the cuisine of many other ethnic minorities. While some dishes are similar to their Bamar counterparts, the Shan versions are often less oily and feature more fresh ingredients, often being served with a small dish of *mon-nyin jin* (pickled vegetables). Shan **tofu soup** (*tohu ngwe*) is a popular breakfast dish – the tofu is actually a gram flour paste, cooked with rice vermicelli and topped with coriander and chilli to serve. Shan-style **buffet meals** are common in Mandalay (perhaps more so than in Shan State itself), with big colourful spreads served all day – best eaten in the morning or at lunchtime.

TOP FIVE FOOD AND DRINK

Mohinga See opposite
Shan buffets See above
Teahouses See box, p.37
Toddy See box, p.156
Lahpet thouq (tea-leaf salad)
See box, p.302

Further north, the traditional food from **Kachin State** is also lighter than most Burmese cuisine, with many steamed dishes and some interesting salads, including *amedha thouq*, which comprises pounded dried beef flavoured with chilli and herbs, and *shat jam*, a dish of rice, diced vegetables, ground meat and herbs mixed together. Other cooked dishes include *chekachin*, a dish of chicken steamed with herbs in a banana leaf, and *sipa* – steamed vegetables with herbs topped with a vaguely sesame-flavoured sauce.

International food

While people in Myanmar take great pride in their cuisine, if you ask someone for a restaurant recommendation then there's a good chance that they will suggest a place serving **Chinese food**. This is partly because they worry that foreign stomachs can't cope with local cuisine, but also because most people rarely go to restaurants, so when they do they eat Chinese as a treat. Most towns will have at least a couple of Chinese restaurants, typically with large menus covering unadventurous basics such as sweet and sour chicken; dishes start at around K1000 for vegetables or K1500 for meat. **Indian restaurants** are also popular, particularly in Yangon, which had a very large Indian population during the British colonial era. In many such restaurants, Indian curries and dhal are served Burmese-style, accompanied by side dishes and fresh vegetables.

In the far south and in tourist hotspots across the country, you'll find **Thai dishes** make an appearance on many menus, thanks to the availability of similar ingredients in both countries, and the thousands of Burmese people who have brought a taste for Thai flavours home with them from working abroad. **Western food** of wildly varying quality is available in the main tourist destinations, with Italian cuisine being particularly popular.

Drink

Tap water isn't safe to drink in Myanmar; bottled water is available throughout the country for around K300 for a small bottle. Many businesses and homes will have large earthenware jars outside, which are provided – along with a common cup – for thirsty passers-by as a way of accruing good karma. The water ranges from clean, UV-treated water to stuff straight from the village well – it might be useful in a pinch, but drink it at your own risk.

Tea and coffee

In many restaurants, free jugs of **green tea** (*lahpet-ye-gyàn* or *ye-nwè-gyàn*) and cups are left on each table, with customers often rinsing their cups out with a little of the tea before drinking from them. **Black tea** (*lahpet-ye*) is served with lavish quantities of condensed milk. Burmese tea-drinkers are often quite specific about how they take their tea, ordering it *paw kya* (strong and not too sweet), *cho hseint* (milky and sweet) or *paw hseint* (milky and not too sweet) – drinking black tea without sugar is not an option.

A request for **coffee** (*kaw-p'í*) will get you a cup of hot water and a packet of coffee mix (pre-mixed instant coffee, creamer and sugar) for you to stir in yourself. If you want to try the good home-grown coffee or are just desperate for a change from coffee mix, ask for Burmese coffee (*Bamar kaw-p'í*), which will get you a cup of black coffee, served with sugar and lime on the side – unusual, but delicious.

A hot drink in a teahouse will cost around K300, far less than it would set you back in one of the Western-style coffee shops that are popping up in

---

STREET FOOD AND MARKETS

Street food isn't as abundant in Myanmar as elsewhere in Southeast Asia, but there are still plenty of street eats available – particularly in **Yangon**, where vendors sling entire stalls from shoulder yokes and set up shop in side streets across the city centre (see box, p.89). Outside the capital, the situation varies, though some towns offer a good variety of food stalls.

Markets – both wet markets selling fresh food and night markets – are perhaps a better bet for informal dining, and an excellent place to try authentic local dishes, from Shan tofu soup (see p.35) in markets across Shan State, to *bein moun* – rice flour pancakes smeared with jaggery syrup and shreds of coconut – in Hpa-An.

Whether in a market or on the street, most stalls will specialize in a small selection of dishes or drinks, with noodle dishes, curry and rice combos and barbecued skewers being particularly common.

TEAHOUSES

Wherever you are in the country, a trip to a Burmese **teahouse** is a great way to experience local life. These institutions are hugely popular places to meet friends, family and business acquaintances, with tables and low plastic chairs often spilling out onto the pavements. Most open early in the morning and serve up hot drinks and inexpensive meals all day – only closing when the last customers ebb away in the evening. The busiest times are usually early mornings and later in the evening, when many show live Premier League football matches at weekends.

Each teahouse has its own **specialities** and, given the rarity of English menus, your best bet is often to point and order. Common dishes include *mohinga*, Shan noodles, and deep-fried snacks, with prices starting at just K100–200 for a snack or K500 for a bowl of noodles.

When you sit down in a teahouse a tea-boy will bring a selection of snacks to your table unasked. When you come to leave – air kissing for your waiter's attention (see box, p.45) – you will only pay for what you've eaten. Noodle dishes and salads are generally only made to order.

Myanmar's larger cities and the main tourist hotspots, where an **espresso** will typically cost around K800.

Alcohol

Burma's only home-grown alcoholic drink is *t'àn-ye* – **toddy** or palm wine (see box, p.156), which is usually only available in low-key village toddy bars not far from where it's made, thanks to the drink's incredibly short shelf life (it turns to vinegar in a matter of hours). Although there are few places resembling Western bars or pubs outside of Yangon and Mandalay, most towns will have a couple of **beer stations** that can be identified by their obvious signs and predominantly male clientele. These places usually serve draught beer (around K600 for a glass) as well as bottles (from K1600 for 640ml), with the former usually restricted to the most popular brew, **Myanmar Beer** (produced by a government joint venture). Other local beers include Dagon, Double Strong (around 9 percent alcohol), and ABC Stout. Adventurous drinkers may want to try Myanmar Beer's Spirulina Beer, made with nutritional algae from Sagaing Region, which reputedly has an anti-ageing effect. Imported beers such as Tiger and Singha are also occasionally available on draught.

Mid-range and upmarket restaurants will often have a list of imported **wine**. There are even a couple of **vineyards** making wine in Shan State, and it's better than you might expect: look out for Red Mountain (see box, p.244) and Aythaya. Fruit wines are produced around Pyin Oo Lwin from plums and other fruit.

Locally distilled **spirits** are widely available and popular as a cost-effective alternative to beer, with a large bottle of whisky starting at K1200. Grand Royal Whisky and Mandalay Rum are both common brands. Imported spirits are only available in the larger cities and hotel bars.

Cold drinks

Due to Myanmar's unreliable electricity supply, refrigeration is not widespread and providing cold drinks is a specialist business. Ice factories deliver clear slabs of ice to cold-drink stores each morning, and the stores then use it to cool drinks and make ice cream. Although Myanmar's fruit is excellent, fruit shakes and smoothies aren't as widespread here as elsewhere in Southeast Asia, and the drinks owe more to South Asia with **falooda** (milk, ice and flavouring mixed together with jelly cubes, tapioca pearls and vermicelli) and various **lassi**-type drinks being particularly popular. Strawberry **pyo-yeh** (*p'yaw-ye* meaning juice) is a delicious drink to try if you're in Myanmar during strawberry season (Feb–April) – the crushed berries are mixed with sweetened milk and yogurt then poured over chunks of ice. **Sugar-cane juice** is another popular beverage – look for the hand-operated presses outside stalls or shops.

Health

The quality of healthcare in Myanmar is generally fairly abysmal. Routine advice and treatment are available in Yangon and Mandalay, but elsewhere the hospitals often lack even basic supplies. Minor injuries and ailments can be dealt with by pharmacists, but if you are seriously ill it's best to contact your

embassy for help. As always, it is important to travel with insurance that covers medical care and emergency evacuation – international-quality care is expensive and in certain situations you may need to be moved to Thailand or Singapore for treatment.

Vaccinations and prophylaxis

Besides ensuring that any routine **immunizations** are up to date, your doctor may recommend that you be vaccinated against hepatitis A and typhoid before travelling to Myanmar, as well as taking malaria prophylactics while in the country. Immunization against hepatitis B, cholera, Japanese encephalitis and rabies is often also suggested.

Malaria is a risk throughout Myanmar, except for in Yangon and Mandalay and areas above 1000m elevation. The strain of malaria found along Myanmar's eastern borders from Kachin State to Tanintharyi is resistant to chloroquine and proguanil (Malarone), and doctors may recommend that you take mefloquine or doxycycline instead, but preventing insect bites is important regardless of your anti-malarial regimen (see below).

Hepatitis A is a viral infection spread by contaminated food and water, whereas the rarer **hepatitis B** is spread through unprotected sexual contact, unscreened blood transfusions and dirty needles. Both diseases cause inflammation of the liver, with symptoms including lethargy, fever and pains in the upper abdomen, and lead to yellowing of the eyes and skin if left untreated.

Typhoid and **cholera** are infections spread by food and water that have been contaminated by bacteria from another infected person, typically in localized epidemics. Typhoid fever is the more common of the two, with symptoms usually appearing up to three weeks after exposure. They start with extreme fatigue, fever and headaches, with some people also suffering from constipation or diarrhoea. Travellers have a lower risk of contracting cholera, which begins with a sudden but painless onset of watery diarrhoea, later combined with vomiting, nausea and muscle cramps. Rapid and severe dehydration, rather than the infection itself, is the main danger, and patients should be treated with constant oral rehydration solutions.

Japanese encephalitis and **rabies** are both zoonoses – animal diseases that can spread to humans. Those living and working in rural areas in close proximity to farm animals are at particular risk of contracting Japanese encephalitis from mosquitoes that have bitten infected livestock. Rabies spreads to humans through the saliva of infected mammals, typically from feral dogs, as well as monkeys and bats, although all mammals are at risk. Both Japanese encephalitis and rabies can be fatal.

A yellow fever vaccination certificate is only required to enter Myanmar if you are travelling from a region where the disease is endemic (i.e. parts of Africa or South America) or if you have been in airport transit in such an area for more than twelve hours. For more information visit Ⓦwho.int /yellowfever.

Diarrhoea

The most common health hazard for visitors to Myanmar is **travellers' diarrhoea**, usually a mild form while your stomach gets used to the unfamiliar food and drink. In more serious cases, diarrhoea is accompanied by stomach cramps and vomiting, indicating **food poisoning**. In both cases, get plenty of rest, drink lots of water and use **oral rehydration salts** (ORS) to replace lost fluids – this is particularly important when treating young children. Take a few sachets of ORS with you, or make your own by mixing half a teaspoon of salt and three of sugar to a litre of bottled water.

While you're suffering from diarrhoea, avoid spicy and greasy foods, milk, coffee and most fruit in favour of plain rice, bananas and clear, bland soup. If symptoms persist, or if you notice blood and mucus in your stools, consult a doctor as you may have **dysentery**, which requires medication to cure.

To avoid upset stomachs, eat at places that look busy and clean, and stick – as far as possible – to fresh, thoroughly cooked food and only eat fruit that you have peeled yourself. Drink **boiled or bottled water** and hot drinks, and avoid untreated tap water. Ice is generally made with treated water in dedicated ice factories, but may not be transported or handled hygienically – travellers with sensitive stomachs may want to avoid ice cream and ice cubes in drinks.

Insect bites

Mosquitoes are not only responsible for spreading malaria and Japanese encephalitis (see above) – they also transmit **dengue fever**, for which there is no vaccination or cure. The symptoms of dengue fever include a high fever and severe headache, joint and muscle pain as well as a rash, nausea and vomiting. There is no specific treatment for the virus, save for resting and taking paracetamol – do not take aspirin, as this will increase the likelihood of haemorrhaging.

Because of the risks, in addition to taking malaria prophylactics, it is important to try and avoid insect bites while you are travelling. Whereas malaria is spread by a mosquito that bites between dusk and dawn, the dengue-carrying mosquito typically bites during the daytime and at any time of year – don't let your guard down in dry season – with occasional concentrated outbreaks.

Prevent mosquito bites by wearing **light-coloured clothes** that cover your arms and legs. Cover any exposed skin with an insect repellent containing a high percentage of **DEET** – around 30 percent. Use mosquito nets or screens when sleeping, and spray any holes in the netting with your insect repellent before going to sleep.

Heat problems

Most places in Myanmar are hot year-round. For visitors from cooler climates, it can take some time to adjust to the temperatures, especially when you are frequently walking outdoors. The most common heat-related complaint is **dehydration**, which should be dealt with immediately to avoid developing into **heat exhaustion**. Symptoms include weakness, headaches, vomiting and nausea, and a weak and rapid pulse. Dilute ORS in a litre of water, try to get out of the heat and rest with the legs elevated until the symptoms abate. The same measures can be taken to reduce swelling of the feet and ankles, another common irritation in this climate.

Heatstroke is a more serious medical problem. Symptoms include a sudden increase in body temperature, weakness, confusion, loss of coordination, fitting and – eventually, if left untreated – death. If you or anyone in your party is showing symptoms of heatstroke, seek medical help immediately, get out of the heat and apply cold, wet cloths and ice to the patient's body.

Hospitals, clinics and pharmacies

In Yangon there are several international-standard **medical centres** (see p.93), and large towns will often have several private medical centres that are used by wealthier locals. Conditions in these clinics are variable but generally better than those in **public hospitals**, which are best avoided where possible. Whichever type of hospital you use, you will typically be required to pay upfront in US dollars before receiving treatment.

Outside the main cities, **local pharmacies** are a good place to seek help for medical problems, and you'll often see queues of people waiting outside the better ones. In the major tourist destinations pharmacists will often speak English. Be aware that there are considerable problems with fake and **out-of-date drugs** in Myanmar – if you take regular medication ensure that you bring enough with you to last for your entire stay, and avoid buying over-the-counter drugs wherever possible.

MEDICAL RESOURCES

Canadian Society for International Health ☎ 613 241 5785, Ⓦ csih.org. Extensive list of travel health centres.
CDC ☎ 1 800 232 4636, Ⓦ wwwnc.cdc.gov/travel. Official US government travel health site.
International Society of Travel Medicine ☎ 1 404 373 8282, Ⓦ istm.org. A comprehensive list of travel health clinics in the US.
London Hospital for Tropical Diseases Ⓦ www.thehtd.org. The UK government's latest travel advice, as well as travel health information.
MASTA (Medical Advisory Service for Travellers Abroad) Ⓦ masta-travel-health.com. Information on UK travel clinics and health advice for travellers.
The Travel Doctor (TMVC) Ⓦ traveldoctor.com.au. Lists travel clinics in Australia, New Zealand and South Africa.

The media

Not surprisingly, Myanmar's media was kept in an iron-fisted grip under the country's military regime. Strict censorship was introduced following the military coup of 1962 and relaxed only in 2012, although controls remain tight to this day – the country was ranked a lowly 145 out of 179 in the 2014 worldwide Press Freedom Index produced by Reporters Without Borders (although even this is a major improvement on its 2010 position, when it ranked 174 out of 178 countries surveyed).

The 2012 reforms allowed at least a modicum of press freedom. Most importantly, it allowed the private ownership of daily newspapers and the lifting of pre-publication censorship, leading to the increasingly big spread of newspapers and magazines you'll see laid out on the pavements of Yangon and other cities. Online, international news and exiled Burmese websites were unblocked (along with YouTube). Even so, the government maintained control of most major media outlets, with pages and programmes full of worthy reports of the government and generals' latest activities, sycophantically reported.

Newspapers and magazines

There are four state-owned **daily newspapers**: three in Burmese plus the rather Orwellian English-language *New Light of Myanmar* (**W** www .moi.gov.mm/npe/nlm). The new clutch of privately owned dailies published since 2012 are all Burmese-language publications – the only daily in English, *Myanma Freedom Daily* (the country's first privately owned, English-language daily for half a century), ceased publication in April 2014, although it may resume in the future. For breaking news it's best to consult one of the news websites (see below). **Weekly publications** include the *Myanmar Times* (**W** mmtimes.com), published in both Burmese and English. Founded by Australian Ross Dunkley in 2000, this is privately owned but has always had close government links and has sometimes been criticized as upmarket propaganda given a Western gloss, although it is worth a look.

Easily the most interesting of the country's English-language **magazines** is monthly *The Irrawaddy* (**W** irrawaddy.org), run by a group of Burmese journalists based in Thailand and full of in-depth, independent articles on key political and economic issues. Their website is also an excellent source of breaking news.

NEWS WEBSITES

Burma News International **W** bnionline.net
Democratic Voice of Burma **W** english.dvb.no
Independent Mon News Agency **W** monnews.org
The Irrawaddy **W** irrawaddy.org
Mizzima News **W** mizzima.com
Shan Herald Agency for News (S.H.A.N.) **W** english
.panglong.org

Television and radio

The state-run **Myanmar Radio and TV** (MRTV) broadcasts in various languages including English and is as exciting as you'd expect, as is the state-run, English-language Myanmar International TV. Many rooms now come with a TV, although only upmarket places generally offer international satellite channels. **Radio** stations include the state-run Radio Myanmar and the most populist City FM (89.0FM).

Festivals and events

Myanmar's busy festival calendar still revolves almost exclusively around religious festivals marking the cycles of the Buddhist calendar (see box opposite). Each of the twelve months of the Buddhist lunar calendar has its own associated festival, although with the exception of the big three festivals – Thingyan, Thadingyut and Tazaungdaing – these are likely to pass largely unnoticed by casual visitors.

As well as the major national festivals, many towns have their own **pagoda festival** (*paya pwe*), a kind of Burmese equivalent of a country fair, with impromptu day and night markets and food stalls mushrooming around the pagoda, accompanied by performances of traditional dance, drama, comedy and music. Notable pagoda festivals are held at the Ananda Paya and Shwezigon Pagoda in Bagan; at the Shwedagon and Botataung pagodas in Yangon; at Kyaiktiyo (the Golden Rock); and at the Shittaung Paya (Mrauk U), Shwesandaw Pagoda (Twante) and Shwemawdaw Pagoda (Bago).

The second major type of traditional Burmese festival is the **nat pwè**. This is like a more raucous version of the homely pagoda festival, dedicated to the country's revered *nat* spirits (see p.356) and featuring copious drinking, dancing and music, as well as appearances by Myanmar's colourful *nat kadaw* (see box, p.49). Major *nat pwè* festivals are held at Mount Popa and at a number of places near Mandalay including Mingun, Taungbyone and Amarapura (see box, p.266).

Festival **dates** are set according to the Buddhist lunar calendar, typically shifting by a week or two year on year (with the exception of the Thingyan Festival, which has now been given fixed dates). **Public holidays** are listed under "Travel essentials" (see p.52).

A FESTIVAL CALENDAR

The following is a short list of countrywide festivals or local festivals of national significance; other local festivals are covered throughout the Guide.

Naga New Year Northwest Myanmar; Jan 15. A unique festival in Myanmar's remote Naga tribal districts during which all Naga tribes converge to celebrate the harvest and welcome in the new year with dancing and singing. A rare and remarkable glimpse into a vanishing world, to which some operators (see p.25) run tours.

Irrawaddy Literary Festival Mandalay; three days in Feb ⓦ irrawaddylitfest.com. Burmese and international writers descend on Mandalay for three days of talks and discussions – 2014 guests included Ian McEwan and Julian Barnes.

Shwedagon Pagoda Festival Yangon; two weeks in Feb/March. Myanmar's largest pagoda festival during which pilgrims descend on the great pagoda from all over the country to make offerings, accompanied by pwe dancing and theatre, robe-weaving competitions and more.

Thingyan Water Festival Countrywide; April 13–16. The mother of all national festivals, for which the entire country more or less shuts down for the duration. In theory it's a celebration of the Burmese New Year and a time to observe and reaffirm one's Buddhist beliefs. In reality the festival is more like an enormous water fight, with children and hormonal teenagers taking to the streets and dousing one another (and anyone else nearby, foreigners especially) with huge buckets of water, and special streetside platforms erected from which revellers hose down passing motorists, accompanied by deafening music.

Thadingyut Festival of Lights Countrywide; three days in Oct. After Thingyan, the second-biggest national festival, celebrating the end of Buddhist Lent and the descent of the Buddha from heaven after preaching to the gods. Events are held at pagodas across Myanmar (particularly in Yangon and at Inle Lake), along with food stalls galore and performances of traditional drama and dance, while locals fill their houses with lanterns and candles.

Tazaungdaing (aka Tazaungmone) Festival of Lights Countrywide; Nov. Held on the full-moon night of the Buddhist month of Tazaungmone and celebrating the end of the rainy season. Streets, homes and pagodas are brilliantly illuminated and offerings made to monasteries, with triangular wooden frames erected around towns and along roadsides to which devotees pin banknotes and attach other gifts to be handed over to local monks. In some places (particularly Taunggyi) hot-air balloons illuminated with candles are released, while special robe-weaving competitions (the biggest at Yangon's Shwedagon Pagoda) are also held at shrines across the land, with young ladies attempting to weave a new monastic robe in the course of a single night.

Taunggyi Fire-Balloon Festival Inle Lake; one week in Oct or Nov. A local offshoot of Tazaungdaing Festival (see above) during which the lake's Pa-O community release hundreds of giant paper balloons, often designed in the shape of animals such as ducks, dragons and elephants, amid a great barrage of fireworks (see box, p.250).

Outdoor activities and sports

With its wide-open spaces, lakes, hills, mountains and thousands of kilometres of coast, Myanmar is a potential gold mine of adventure tourism. It remains largely unexploited, although a few places in the hills lure visitors with well-developed trekking networks, and there's a decent selection of other outdoor activities available, from cycling to scuba-diving.

Trekking, rock-climbing and mountaineering

The most popular outdoor activity in Myanmar is undoubtedly **trekking**, which offers the chance to experience the country's superb landscapes while interacting with local people, particularly minority ethnic groups. The hike from Kalaw to Inle Lake remains enduringly popular (see box, p.232), while other memorable treks include the route from Kalaw to Pindaya, walks around Inle Lake, treks among the hill tribes around Kengtung (see box, p.254), and treks into the tea-swathed hills and villages of northern Shan State from Kyaukme (see box, p.301) and Hsipaw (see box, p.304). In the far north, challenging treks up into the high Himalaya can be arranged from Putao (see p.327), while the ascent of Mount Victoria in Chin State (see box, p.218) offers a real taste of Myanmar well off the beaten track. Unlike trekking, Myanmar's enormous potential for **rock-climbing** and **mountaineering** remains almost totally untapped. The Technical Climbing Club of Myanmar (find them on Facebook) is attempting to develop rock-climbing in the country and establish bolted routes.

Cycling

Cycling is another rewarding activity – much of the country is predominantly flat, although

---

THE BURMESE BUDDHIST CALENDAR

The **Burmese Buddhist calendar**, like the Western calendar, has twelve months, consisting alternately of 29 and 30 days (each equivalent to a lunar month), totalling 354 days. Leap years (of either 384 or 385 days, featuring a second Waso month) are inserted roughly every four years in order to keep lunar and solar cycles in sync. The twelve months (corresponding, extremely roughly, to the Western January, February and so on) are: Tagu, Kason, Nayon, Waso, Wagaung, Tawthalin, Thadingyut, Tazaungmone, Nadaw, Pyatho, Tabodwe and Tabaung.

CHINLONE

Somewhere between sport and dancing, **chinlone** is one of Myanmar's most distinctive pastimes. A non-competitive sport, *chinlone* is traditionally played by six people standing in a circle and kicking a rattan ball between themselves. The basic aim of the game is to stop the ball from touching the ground for as long as possible, although additional kudos is attached to the skill and style with which the ball is kept aloft – over 200 types of kick are recognized using five different parts of the foot, plus knees. A popular, competitive variant of the game, akin to Malaysian *sepak tawkraw* (kick volleyball), is also often played, with a net between opposing players/teams and rules similar to volleyball, except that the ball is kicked rather than punched.

potholed roads and heavy traffic can prove challenging. Biking around Bagan is one of Myanmar's classic experiences (see p.209), while the Mandalay (see p.274) and Inle Lake areas (see box, p.240) also offer some great riding opportunities. A few tour operators run multi-day bike tours and longer cross-country journeys if you don't fancy going it alone (see p.30).

Diving and watersports

There's very little **diving** compared to other nearby countries. There are basic dive centres at Ngapali (see box, p.112) and Ngwe Saung (see box, p.106), although serious divers head to the spectacular Myeik Archipelago in the far south, where you can also arrange snorkelling, kayaking and sailing trips (see box, p.165). Some **watersports**, though nothing very sophisticated, are available at Ngapali and Chaung Tha (see box, p.104), where you can also set up **fishing** trips, including deep-sea fishing.

Sport

Myanmar isn't an especially sporty country. **Football** is the most popular game. Premier League games are widely broadcast, as is the Myanmar National League, established in 2009 with eight teams, each owned by one of the government's crony capitalists (see box, p.350).

Golf is also modestly popular, although courses are relatively few. The best is probably the Gary Player-designed Pun Hlaing Golf Club in Yangon, and there are also courses at Mandalay, Bago, Bagan, Ngapali, Pyin Oo Lwin, Kalaw and Taunggyi.

Indigenous sports include **lethwei**, a Burmese martial art similar to Thai kick boxing featuring a mix of punching, kicking, head-butts and blows with the elbows and knees. Fights are held regularly around the country during pagoda festivals.

Responsible travel

Trying to be a responsible tourist in Myanmar is an unusually complicated business. Not only do you have to be aware of all the usual ground rules of ethical tourism in Asia but a major added twist is provided by the challenge (should you wish to accept it) of ensuring that as little of your money as possible goes to the country's government or government-linked businessmen.

Should you visit?

The question of whether or not you should visit Myanmar has long been an emotive issue. In 1995 Aung San Suu Kyi's National League for Democracy (NLD) called for an international **tourist boycott** of the country, arguing that foreign visitors were putting money directly into the pockets of the regime. Many foreigners respected this call to stay away. Others continued to visit, saying that with care it was possible to minimize the money given to the regime and to ensure that foreign cash still reached local communities – and also arguing that plunging the country into complete isolation simply caused further hardship for the long-suffering Burmese.

Following tentative **reforms**, in 2010 the NLD softened its stance, saying that it opposed only package and cruise tourism, while in May 2012 it dropped its suggested boycott entirely. Despite the NLD's shifting position, however, the ethical dilemma remains much as it always has been. Notwithstanding some quasi-democratic window-dressing, the government remains **repressive**, exploitative and deeply corrupt – while Aung San Suu Kyi and the NLD have also shown worrying signs of cosying up to the generals and their cronies, and exhibited a shamefully opportunistic silence regarding the fate of the horribly oppressed

Rakhine Rohingya (see box, p.116) in order to woo Burmese support.

The bottom line, therefore, is that Myanmar is still a deeply unjust society, and that, like it or not, at least a little of your money will end up in the wrong hands. On the other hand, the **positives** of visiting the country as it begins to re-enter the global mainstream can't be overstated. Your money, spent carefully, will be of enormous benefit to local communities, and your mere presence will also be massively appreciated by many, given the long decades of isolation suffered by the Burmese people. Perhaps most importantly, the growing contribution of tourist dollars to the national coffers makes it increasingly likely that a proper democracy will eventually be established as the military and their cronies come to appreciate the **economic benefits** of a fair and open society free of Western sanctions.

Where does your money go?

Like it or not, if you visit Myanmar you will at some stage be obliged to give money directly to the government. You pay the government for your visa fee, and also for the multi-sight entrance tickets in Bagan, Mandalay, Mrauk U and elsewhere – places that are probably the main reason you're visiting in the first place – not to mention many other sights and museums around the country, plus train tickets and permits to visit restricted areas.

Fees directly levied by the government are merely the tip of a much larger and messier iceberg, however. Large swathes of the Myanmar economy – including its banks, airlines and many top-end hotels – are owned by companies with close links to the regime and generally run by businessmen, the so-called **cronies** (see box, p.350), who have grown spectacularly rich through their links to the generals over the past two decades. Take a domestic flight, withdraw money from an ATM or stay in an upmarket hotel, and you'll be contributing to their coffers.

On the other hand, it's also possible to argue the case for crony-linked businesses such as airlines and hotels, unpalatable though it might sound. These employ thousands of ordinary Burmese untainted by the regime, and whose livelihood depends upon their continued employment, however unsavoury the companies they work for.

Establishing exactly who has fingers in which particular pie is not always easy, although excellent background on Myanmar's spider's web of crony capitalism and other ethical issues can be found at Ⓦ tourismtransparency.org.

Accommodation

No accommodation in Myanmar is entirely clean, from an ethical standpoint. All guesthouses and hotels require a **government licence** to accept foreign guests, meaning that even when staying in the cheapest family-run guesthouse available you will still be contributing (however modestly) to government coffers. Staying in top-end accommodation is particularly problematic. Many places are owned by crony businessmen, while some were

---

CRONY HOTELS

The biggest player in the hotel business among Myanmar's cronies (see box, p.350) is the infamous Tay Za who owns two major upmarket hotel chains, the **Aureum Palace** chain (branches in Bagan, Inle Lake, Ngwe Saung, Ngapali, Naypyitaw and Pyin Oo Lwin) and **Myanmar Treasure Resorts** group (branches in Ngwe Saung, Ngapali and Bagan), as well as the **Popa Mountain Resort** at Mount Popa, the **Kandawgyi Palace Hotel** in Yangon and the jaw-droppingly expensive **Malikha Lodge** in Putao. Other chains to watch out for include the Max Hotels Group, owned by Zaw Zaw, which runs the **Hotel Max** in Chaung Tha and **Royal Kamudra Hotel** in Naypyitaw, and the Shwe Taung Group, which owns the **Eskala** resort in Ngwe Saung and **Junction Hotel** in Naypyitaw.

Other notable hotels with strong government and/or crony connections (according to Tourism Transparency) include the **Inya Lake Resort**, the **Central Hotel** and the famous old **Strand Hotel** (all in Yangon), and the **Hotel Pyin Oo Lwin** in the town of the same name. Note, also, that all the hotels in **Naypyitaw** have government links.

Throughout the Guide we've listed hotels based on merit, rather than on who owns them (unfortunately, some of the country's nicest places to stay are crony-owned). Ultimately, the choice of where to stay is a personal decision, while it's worth bearing in mind that the ethical dilemma is not entirely cut and dried. Boycotting crony hotels may deprive government stooges of cash, but, equally, punishes the thousands of blameless Burmese who work in these places, and who might well struggle to find employment otherwise.

built on expropriated land using forced labour. Some upmarket establishments may claim to be ethically clean, although it's often impossible to determine exactly what has been paid and to whom in order to facilitate their construction and ongoing operation, and rates will include **government taxes** which go directly to the regime.

The best way of making sure your money goes to deserving Burmese is therefore to stay in small, family-run budget guesthouses. If you want to check the ethical credentials of more upmarket places, read the "Crony hotels" box (see p.43) and have a look at the listings at ⓦ tourismtransparency .org to identify places without government or crony links.

Transport

Bus companies are privately owned, and as ethically clean a means of getting from A to B as you can find in Myanmar (short of walking, or perhaps cycling). **Trains** are run by the government, although fares are so modest that you can at least feel that you're contributing the bare minimum to official revenues. The country's domestic **airlines** are where you're most likely to be pouring money into crony coffers. All have links with either the government or government-linked businesses, however murky.

Other considerations

Try to hire guides and transport as you go rather than booking a **package tour**. This helps spread your money among as many people as possible, while upmarket package tours and especially **cruises** are particularly likely to involve government- and/or crony-linked companies.

All Myanmar **banks** have crony or government links, while several are alleged to have been involved in money laundering and ties to the country's drug trade (Myanmar is the world's second-largest source of **opium** after Afghanistan, producing around a quarter of the global supply, mainly from Shan and Kachin states). Although it's a pain, bringing money in with you and changing it at local businesses is more ethical than using an ATM and paying the standard withdrawal fees levied for the privilege.

Given the massive social and environmental abuses connected with Myanmar's enormous **jade** trade (see box, p.326), you might prefer to avoid souvenirs incorporating this particular stone.

Finally, be extremely careful when **talking politics** with people you meet in Myanmar. Wait for others to broach the subject and don't try to make people say things that might land them in (possibly serious) trouble.

Culture and etiquette

In common with the people of other Southeast Asian Buddhist countries, the Burmese are a profoundly polite people, with a gentle, ceremonious culture and customs rooted in the country's Buddhist beliefs.

Burmese manners and social interactions are rooted in the notion of **āna**, a multi-faceted concept defined by the *Myanmar–English Dictionary* as "a tendency to be embarrassed by feelings of respect, delicacy; to be restrained by fear of offending". For the Burmese, *āna* applies particularly to the business of dealing with strangers, when the risk of causing accidental offence or embarrassment is greatest – hence the sometimes exquisite levels of politeness you will encounter anywhere from a local teahouse to a five-star hotel.

Compared to some of their less scrupulous cousins in neighbouring countries such as India and Thailand, it's worth noting that most of the Burmese you'll have dealings with during your travels – taxi and rickshaw drivers, shop and guest-house owners, and so on – are still refreshingly honest. Tourist **scams** are rare (although changing money on the street remains a risky business), and you'll generally be offered a fair price for whatever you're looking for. There's still some scope for **bargaining** in shops and perhaps when haggling over transport costs, but bear in mind that the cut-throat haggling that's more or less obligatory in some other Asian countries doesn't apply here, and given how impoverished most Burmese are it's worth reminding yourself what a difference even a handful of kyat can make to a local cycle-rickshaw-driver or market-stall owner.

The Burmese **dress** modestly. In some ethnic minority villages it's still the norm to wear traditional dress, and even in cities many men and women still wear longyi (see box, p.7), although Western-style clothes are increasingly common. People will be too polite to say anything, but they may be offended by the sight of tourists wearing revealing clothes including shorts cut above the knee, and – particularly for women – tops that are tight or show the shoulders.

TEAHOUSE KISSES

Sit in any local café or teahouse in Myanmar and you're bound to notice the distinctive **kissing sounds** which local men make when they want to attract a waiter's attention – a bit like the sound you might make when trying to make friends with a cat. The endless air-kissing may sound a bit flirty (or just plain rude) to Western ears, although for the Burmese it's all perfectly routine – and no one will mind if you attempt a bit of simulated kissing yourself when you want service. Burmese women don't usually air-kiss for attention, although Western women can generally get away with it.

Although most obvious in teahouses and cafés, kissy-kissy sounds are also used out on the street as a general call for attention – meaning anything from "Come into my shop" to "Watch out, I'm about to flatten you with my motorbike", so don't be surprised (or offended) if you attract a few puckered lips yourself when travelling around Myanmar.

Physical **demonstrations of affection** (particularly holding hands) are common between friends of the same sex and family members, but not between men and women. Couples will rarely even hold hands in public, although they can often be seen sitting very close together in parks under the shelter of a protective umbrella.

You should also avoid touching another person's head (considered the most sacred part of the body), and when sitting try to avoid pointing your feet (which are considered impure) at anyone. Always use your right hand when shaking hands or passing something to someone (the left hand is traditionally used for toilet ablutions). If invited inside a Burmese **house**, remove your shoes before going inside.

Greetings

There's no equivalent in Myanmar to the prayer-like **greetings** employed in other nearby Buddhist countries (such as the Thai *wai*, Cambodian *sampeah* or the Sri Lankan *ayubowan*). Men will shake hands on meeting; women meeting one another or a woman meeting a man will content themselves with a smile and a *min-gǎla-ba*. Men should not try to shake hands with women.

The standard Burmese greeting is the rather formal *min-gǎla-ba* (meaning roughly "blessings upon you"), although this only entered the language in the post-colonial period as a replacement for the colonial "Good morning/good afternoon". Given that there's no clear equivalent of "hello" in Burmese, foreign visitors have adopted *min-gǎla-ba* as an easy, all-purpose greeting, and the phrase has been embraced with gusto by the Burmese as a way of addressing foreigners.

Burmese speakers themselves rarely use *min-gǎla-ba*, preferring more informal greetings, typically *nei kaun la* ("how are you?") or just "hello". You might also hear *htamin sa pi bi la* – literally, "have you eaten rice?".

WHAT'S IN A NAME?

Traditional **Burmese names** are of one or two syllables only. There are no family surnames in Burmese, nor can names be shortened or divided – a man named Tin Moe, for example, can't be called "Tin" or "Mr Moe". In order to indicate the relative positions of two people talking, names are often combined with a further word: Tin Moe, for example, would be called U Tin Moe (where "U" signifies "Mr" or "uncle") in formal situations or Ko Tin Moe or Maung Tin Moe by his family and friends ("Ko" and "Maung" meaning "brother"). The female equivalents are "Daw" ("Mrs" or "aunty") and "Ma" (sister). Women do not change their names upon marriage.

Astrology also plays a major role, with children traditionally given a name reflecting the day of the week on which they were born. In addition, Burmese commonly change their names to reflect changing circumstances – Aung San, for example, was born Htein Lin but changed his name to Aung San (meaning "victory") when embarking upon his revolutionary career.

Traditional naming systems have been increasingly modified by **Western influences** with the incorporation of maternal, paternal and other names, although still not in any particularly consistent fashion – as demonstrated by Aung San Suu Kyi herself, who was named after her father (Aung San), grandmother (Suu) and mother (Khin Kyi), giving her a name which translates (loosely) as "a bright collection of strange victories".

LUCK BIRDS

Travelling around Myanmar you'll sooner or later notice the cages set up by roadsides and around towns (particularly outside temples) stuffed full of frantically fluttering and chirruping birds. These are so-called **luck birds**, the unfortunate victims of a popular Buddhist practice whereby birds are captured by local villagers and farmers to be purchased and set free by those seeking to acquire merit by saving a life. The act of buying and freeing a caged bird may appear selfless and spiritually fulfilling but the practice is far from humane. Many birds die (or are fatally injured) in captivity, while numerous endangered species are threatened by the luck bird trade – common-or-garden species cost a dollar or so, but this rises significantly for larger and more exotic captives. Lucky for seller and buyer, perhaps, but certainly not for the birds themselves.

Temple etiquette

Dress conservatively when visiting **temples** (some travellers carry a longyi for such situations) and make sure you take shoes and socks off before entering. Inside, try not to point your feet at any Buddha images – locals tend to sit with their legs tucked beneath themselves. It's traditional to walk around stupas in a clockwise direction, although no one will particularly mind if you go in the opposite direction.

Shopping

Myanmar isn't quite the shopper's paradise of neighbouring Thailand and India but has plenty of affordable traditional souvenirs and crafts worth looking out for. The best places to shop are Yangon (Bogyoke Market in particular), Mandalay and Bagan; elsewhere, pickings can be thin on the ground.

Bargaining is generally the order of the day except in more upmarket shops or places with clearly marked prices – although you could always try your luck. Note that the **export of antiques** is prohibited, although exactly what constitutes an antique is not entirely clear. If in doubt, ask the shop you're buying from if they can supply you with an export licence.

Traditional artefacts

Lacquerware is perhaps the most emblematic of all Burmese crafts: lacquerware vessels are still used in many homes and a lacquered bowl or plate makes a beautiful, if pricey, souvenir. Lacquerware is available all over the country, although Bagan offers the best selection and lowest prices, as well as the chance to visit local workshops and see pieces being made.

Another iconic Burmese collectible is the colourful, beautifully decorated **umbrellas** carried by the country's monks and nuns (see box, p.102). Pathein remains the main production centre for traditional cotton umbrellas, while silk parasols (originally from Bagan and Mandalay) can also be found here and elsewhere.

Carvings in sandalwood, stone, marble and other materials are also widespread. Buddha images are ubiquitous, although there are also more unusual statuettes to be found depicting *nats*, mythical beasts and other creatures. Mandalay, particularly the area near the Mahamuni Paya, is a major stone-carving centre.

Traditional Burmese **puppets** are another fun souvenir. Many are made in Mandalay, where you'll find the biggest selection and best prices. **Sand paintings** are a particular speciality of Bagan, and are sold by local artists and hawkers at all the major temples. Many feature copies of Bagan's ancient temple murals, although you'll also find pieces in a more contemporary style. The detail and workmanship are often superb, and prices are a snip, with smaller pieces going for just a few dollars. They're also easily transportable since you can roll them up without destroying them.

Look out, too, for the **pyit taing daung** (or *pyit taing htaung*). One of Myanmar's most distinctive traditional toys, these odd-looking dolls resemble a papier-mâché Easter egg with an oversized smiley face painted on it. They're also weighted inside, meaning that however much you bash them, they never fall down, rather like the Western Weeble – hence their name meaning "up whatever thrown".

Clothes, textiles and jewellery

Beautiful cotton and, especially, silk **fabrics and textiles** are widely available. Mandalay is again the main centre of production, although many of the country's ethnic minorities also produce their own distinctive weavings. A **longyi** (see box, p.7) makes a practical and portable souvenir, available either in inexpensive, functional cotton or more lavish silk. In addition, skirts, scarves, shirts and fabric shoulder bags can all make good buys.

Myanmar has an extraordinary wealth of natural minerals and precious stones. **Jade** (most of it from the far north of the country) is very much in evidence, from simple traditional bangles through to chintzy statuettes and other bric-a-brac – although note that buying jade is fraught with ethical complications (see box, p.326). There's also plenty of gold and silver **jewellery**, as well as precious stones including rubies and sapphires. Fakes are not unknown, though – buy from a reputable dealer or risk being ripped off.

Travelling with children

Few Westerners travel with children in Myanmar, but if you do you'll be guaranteed a very warm welcome, with locals going out of their way to make a fuss of your kids and help in any way they can.

Having said that, although you can be guaranteed plenty of social interaction, specific kids' attractions are pretty thin on the ground, given that most of the country's major draws are essentially cultural. The generally long journeys involved in getting from A to B are a further drawback, while parents of fussy eaters may also struggle, especially outside major tourist centres. Travelling with **babies and toddlers** is a real challenge. You'll struggle to find formula milk, nappies or baby food (although discreet breast-feeding is perfectly acceptable), and you'll also need to be aware of the potentially serious effects of heat, sunstroke, dehydration and the risk of malaria (and other diseases). And be aware that, should anything go wrong, medical facilities in the country are rudimentary at best.

Activities

Older kids may enjoy exploring the ruins of Bagan by **bike** or in a **horse-drawn carriage** (especially if you can dress it up in suitably Indiana Jones style) and might enjoy a **boat trip** on Inle Lake, and possibly a **day trek** through local villages. The **beaches** are another possible draw, although there's not a lot in terms of specific child-friendly activities apart from a few watersports (for older kids who are also confident swimmers). Visits to **elephant camps** at places like Ngwe Saung and Taungoo may also appeal, as will the **zoos** at Yangon and (especially) Naypyitaw. In Mandalay, kids may enjoy the **puppet performances** at Mandalay Marionettes or the Minta Theater, as well as the dances of the Moustache Brothers (though the satire at the latter will likely go over children's heads). Sporty youngsters will also get a kick out of just hanging out with the locals, maybe joining in an impromptu football match or trying a spot of **chinlone** (see box, p.42) – locals will be delighted to take them under their wing.

Travel essentials

Addresses

The words "road" and "street" are used interchangeably throughout Myanmar. In some towns streets are clearly signed, whereas in other places signage can be nonexistent. As elsewhere in Asia, directions are usually given in relation to local landmarks rather than using street names and house numbers.

Costs

Accommodation (see p.31) is likely to be your main cost in Myanmar, with even the cheapest rooms costing around $15–25 and upmarket lodgings going for $150 or considerably more. **Food** is much more affordable – you can get a meal on the streets or in local cafés for just a couple of dollars, with mains in more touristy places costing around $4–5 (although equally some top-end places charge prices on a par with Europe or North America). **Bus** and **train** tickets are also relatively (if not exceptionally) cheap – an express bus from Yangon to Bagan, for example, costs around $15. **Flying** is obviously much pricier but not prohibitively expensive, especially when you consider the time-saving involved – Yangon to Bagan, for example, will cost somewhere in the region of $70–100. Hiring your own car and driver is expensive, as are packaged trips, especially cruises – more upmarket river trips can cost thousands of dollars. **Admission fees** aren't too punitive – the week-long ticket covering the whole of Bagan costs a modest $15. Government museums typically charge a $5 entrance fee.

All things considered, if you're travelling around Myanmar as a couple you might conceivably be able to survive on a **daily budget** of $15–20/ £9–12/€11–15 per person (maybe even less), although $25/£15/€20 per day is a more realistic target. For $40/£25/€30 per person per day you can be pretty comfortable. Equally, it's perfectly easy to spend $200/£120/€150 a day if you're staying and eating in top-end hotels and travelling with a car and driver. Travelling on your own obviously bumps costs up considerably, given that you'll have no one to split pricey accommodation rates with.

Upmarket restaurants and hotels may add a ten percent service charge. Elsewhere, **tipping** in local restaurants, teahouses, taxis and so on isn't really expected (although of course is always appreciated). Caretakers and guardians will expect a tip for unlocking a temple, museum or other monument for you.

Crime and personal safety

Despite decades of military oppression, often grinding poverty and a string of local insurgencies, Myanmar remains an extremely safe place for foreign visitors. Violent crime against tourists is extremely rare, and even petty theft is relatively uncommon, although obviously it pays not to leave valuables lying around or rooms unlocked. If you are unlucky enough to suffer a theft you'll need to report it to the **police** to get a statement for your insurance claim. Taking a Burmese-speaking companion to translate is pretty much essential – ask at your accommodation. Major tourist centres have dedicated tourist police, although even so it's worth taking a Burmese-speaker with you if possible.

The biggest risk at present for foreigners travelling in Myanmar is the chance of becoming accidentally caught up in **political or ethnic violence** – particularly the increasing number of clashes between Buddhists and Muslims which have afflicted Sittwe, Meiktila, Lashio and Mandalay in recent years. One tourist was injured in Yangon in an explosion in October 2013, while in early 2014 the offices of Western NGOs were attacked by

mobs in Sittwe (although visiting tourists were left in peace). There are also ongoing clashes in various parts of the country between the army and various ethnic resistance groups, with occasional incidents in Kachin State around Myitkyina and Bhamo, for example. The government generally closes off any area where there's even a hint of danger, however, both to keep tourists safe and to stop them seeing things the rulers don't want Westerners to see.

Customs regulations

Arriving in Myanmar, you're allowed to bring in **duty free** up to 2 litres of liquor, 150ml of perfume and 400 cigarettes (or 50 cigars). You have to declare hard currency over $2000 or equivalent and fill in an FED (Foreign Exchange Declaration) form. The **export of antiques** is prohibited (see p.46). Details of import/export restrictions can be checked at Ⓦ www.myanmarcustoms.gov.mm.

Electricity

Myanmar mains electricity runs at 230 volts. Most **sockets** take two round-pin plugs (UK-style sockets with three square pins are occasionally found in upmarket hotels). Adaptors are cheap and readily available. **Power cuts** are a way of life; in many smaller towns electricity is cut off for a fixed number of hours every day, and outages are still common across the country, even in Yangon. Avoid leaving gadgets plugged in during a power cut, as there may be a surge when the supply is restored. Note that many air-conditioning units are fitted with special boxes to protect against power surges; there's often a delay of five minutes between turning the unit on and it actually beginning to work.

Entry requirements

All foreign nationals require a **visa** in order to visit Myanmar; for the latest information check the official Ministry of Foreign Affairs website (Ⓦ www.mofa.gov.mm – for some reason visa-related matters are listed under "Contact Us"). Note that your passport must be valid for at least six months from your proposed date of arrival, and allow as long as possible – ideally not less than a month. Tourist visas typically last for 28 days from the date of entry, which must be within three months of issue.

The government is currently introducing a **tourist e-visa** system, allowing visitors to purchase

---

EMERGENCY NUMBERS

Police ☎ 199
Ambulance ☎ 192
Fire ☎ 191

visas online, which should be up and running by the time you read this. Applications can be made at (Ⓦ www.myanmarevisa.gov.mm). E-visas are only available for visitors flying into Yangon and currently also cost two or three times the price of a visa obtained from your local embassy (at the time of writing, the quoted price for an e-visa for UK citizens was £50).

If the e-visa system has ceased working (or you prefer not to use it for any reason), then you'll need to apply either in person or by post at your nearest embassy or consulate, with visas currently costly around $20–30. Some embassies, such as the one in Bangkok, offer a same-day service for an extra charge.

Tourist visas cannot be extended, but it is possible to **overstay** them: a fee of $3 per day of overstay for the first thirty days, and $5 per day thereafter (plus, sometimes, an additional $3 "administration" fee) will be collected at the airport when you leave. Visitors have reported overstaying by three weeks or more without officials at the airport raising any objections. The only possible hitch is that guesthouses occasionally express concern with expired visas, although it's rare that people are actually refused a room.

MYANMAR EMBASSIES OVERSEAS

Australia 22 Arkana St, Yarralumla, ACT 2600, Canberra Ⓣ 02 6273 3811, Ⓦ mecanberra.com.au.
Canada 336 Island Park Drive, Ottawa, Ontario K1Y 0A7 Ⓣ 613 232 9990, Ⓦ meottawa.org.

China Embassy, 6 Dong Zhi Men Wai St, Chao Yang District, Beijing 100600 Ⓣ 010 6532 0351, Ⓦ myanmarembassy.com; Consulate-general, 99 Ying Bin Lu, Guan Du Qu, Kunming, Yunnan Province Ⓣ 086 871 6816 2804, Ⓦ mcgkunming.org.
South Africa 210 Leyds St, Arcadia, Pretoria Ⓣ 027 12341 2556, Ⓦ myanmarembassysa.com.
Thailand 132 Sathorn Nua Rd, Bang Rak, Bangkok 10500 Ⓣ 022 337 250, Ⓦ myanmarembassybkk.com.
UK 19A Charles St, London W1J 5DX Ⓣ 020 7499 4340, Ⓦ www.myanmarembassylondon.com.
USA 2300 S St. N.W. Washington D.C. 20008 Ⓣ (202) 332 3344, Ⓦ mewashingtondc.com.

Gay and lesbian travellers

Homosexuality is technically illegal in Myanmar and punishable by fines or imprisonment – anything up to life in theory (under the country's archaic penal code, which dates back to colonial times). Actual arrests are rare, however, and gay and lesbian communities are gaining more recognition and acceptance following the partial return to democracy. There is a discreet gay scene in Yangon – and the city even hosted its first **Gay Pride** event in 2012 – but little elsewhere. See Ⓦ en.wikipedia.org/wiki/LGBT_rights_in_Burma for detailed background on the situation and Ⓦ utopia-asia.com/tipsburm.htm for practical information.

For visitors, **discretion** is naturally advised – you're unlikely to encounter any problems unless you very clearly call attention to yourself. Note that

---

MYANMAR'S GAY SHAMANS

Despite being widely ignored or villified by conservative Burmese, gay men (as well as transgendered women and male transvestites) in Myanmar have found an unlikely niche in one of the country's most traditional religious settings through their role as **nat kadaw**. A kind of Burmese shaman, *nat kadaw* (literally "nat wives") serve as mediums for the country's revered pantheon of *nats* (see p.356), entering trances during which the spirit of any one of the various *nats* takes possession of their bodies.

Nat kadaw were traditionally women, with the profession being passed down from mother to daughter, but over the past thirty years their places have increasingly been taken by gay men. Male *nat kadaw* will dress either as a man or woman depending on the identity of the *nat* currently possessing them – and even when identifying with a male *nat*, they will typically wear sumptuous clothing, with considerable quantities of make-up. The fact that such overt gender-bending is generally accepted most likely derives from the nature of **nat pwè** themselves (see p.40). These are typically raucous, carnivalesque affairs during which large quantities of booze are consumed and things done which would not be considered entirely respectable in more workaday settings (*nat kadaw* themselves typically drink and smoke their way into a state of high intoxication in order to best communicate with the spirits of the *nats*).

The **Taungbyone Nat Pwè** (see box, p.266) is particularly well known in this respect. Although not in any sense a specifically gay festival, the *pwe* nowadays attracts large numbers of LGBT locals and travellers alike – and the *nat kadaw* are particularly flamboyant.

ROUGH GUIDES TRAVEL INSURANCE

Rough Guides has teamed up with **WorldNomads.com** to offer great travel insurance deals. Policies are available to residents of over 150 countries, with cover for a wide range of adventure sports, 24hr emergency assistance, high levels of medical and evacuation cover and a stream of travel safety information. Roughguides.com users can take advantage of their policies online 24/7, from anywhere in the world – even if you're already travelling. And since plans often change when you're on the road, you can extend your policy and even claim online. Roughguides.com users who buy travel insurance with WorldNomads.com can also leave a positive footprint and donate to a community development project. For more information, go to Ⓦroughguides.com/travel-insurance.

it's culturally acceptable for Burmese friends of the same sex to hold hands in public, although this is no indication of their sexual orientation.

Insurance

It's essential to take out **insurance** before travelling, to cover against theft, loss and illness or injury, although be aware that some insurance companies do not offer coverage for Myanmar, whether for the country as a whole, or for specific areas that your home government advises against visiting. A typical travel insurance policy usually provides cover for loss of baggage, tickets and – up to a certain limit – money, as well as cancellation or early curtailment of your journey. Most of them exclude so-called dangerous sports unless an extra premium is paid: in Myanmar this might mean scuba diving, trekking, rock-climbing and mountain expeditions. Many policies can be chopped and changed to exclude coverage you don't need – for example, sickness and accident benefits can often be excluded or included at will. When securing baggage cover, make sure that the per-article limit – typically under £500 – will cover your most valuable possession. If you need to make a claim, you should keep receipts for medicines and medical treatment, and in the event you have anything stolen, you must obtain an official statement from the police.

Internet and wi-fi

Until recently Myanmar had one of the world's lowest internet penetration rates, although all that is now rapidly changing. The country's **wi-fi** network, in particular, is growing at an exponential pace. Pretty much all mid-range and top-end hotels now offer wi-fi as standard, as do the majority of budget establishments, including even quite down-at-heel places, as well as many restaurants – although connections may be hit and miss.

Internet cafés are rather less widespread, although all major towns and cities have at least one or two places, typically charging around K500 per hour. Almost all have printers and many provide Skype, although connections are often agonizingly slow.

The formerly stifling levels of internet **censorship** have been radically scaled back since 2012, allowing unrestricted access to international news sites, dissident bloggers and the like. You probably won't be aware that there's any censorship at all unless you go surfing online for porn, poker, or Myanmar brides.

Laundry

Not surprisingly, you won't find any laundrettes in Myanmar. Upmarket (and some mid-range) hotels generally have a laundry service, usually pricey, while budget guesthouses may be able to wash clothes (or farm them out to someone who does). Alternatively, just look out for a convenient back-street laundry. These should be able to turn washing around overnight, charging in the region of K500 per item.

Mail

The postal service in Myanmar isn't known for its efficiency; sending postcards is cheap but they often do not reach their destinations. **Post offices** are typically open Monday to Friday 9.30am to 4.30pm and sometimes on Saturday mornings, and many have an EMS (Express Mail Service; Ⓦwww.ems.com.mm) counter offering faster and more reliable international delivery.

Maps

The best country maps of Myanmar currently available are the ones published by Reise Know-How (1:1,500,000) and by Freytag & Berndt

(1:1,200,000), although neither is generally available in Myanmar itself. The local fold-up maps of major tourist towns around the country produced for the Ministry of Tourism by DPS Maps (Ⓦ dpsmap.com) are also useful; they're widely available from local hawkers for $1–2, or you can download reasonably hi-res images of the maps direct from the website.

Money

Myanmar's currency is the **kyat** (pronounced something like "chat"), usually abbreviated as K or Ks (or, officially, as MMK). Notes are available in denominations of K1, K5, K10, K20, K50, K100, K200, K500, K1000, K5000 and K10,000, although the lowest value you are likely to encounter is the K50 note. There are no coins. The **US dollar** (again, notes only) is widely used alongside the kyat as a secondary currency to pay for more expensive items and services.

In the past, dollars were specifically needed to pay for things like train tickets, entrance tickets to certain sights and other items, although now it's possible to pay for just about everything in kyat. Note, however, that many touristy places (including hotels, restaurants, shops and tour operators) quote prices and prefer payment in dollars, and some more upmarket hotels and operators may insist on payment in dollars (it's certainly easier than counting out huge wads of kyat), although this is becoming increasingly rare. Note that if you do pay in local currency at such places where kyat are preferred, the kyat price will typically be calculated at a disadvantageous exchange rate (typically $1=K1000), making it slightly cheaper to pay with dollars – keep some low-denomination notes handy for such occasions. Change may be given in either dollars or kyat.

Changing money

At one time the official exchange rate for kyat was kept artificially low and most people changed money on the black market, but today banks and official moneychangers offer a realistic rate. Avoid changing money on the street, however good the rate you're offered, as scams are common. Kyat can't

> ### EXCHANGE RATES
> At the time of writing the **exchange rate** was roughly K975 to $1, K1660 to £1, and K1300 to €1.

be exchanged overseas – be sure to change all your leftover currency before leaving the country.

Dollars are the easiest overseas notes to exchange, although you should also be able to change euros, pounds and other major currencies. Note that you won't be able to exchange US dollars issued before 2006; high-value notes (particularly $100 bills) attract the best exchange rates.

It's imperative (this can't be stressed enough) that any notes that you intend to use in Myanmar are in **pristine condition** (ideally, ask if your home bank can get you mint condition notes). Banknotes that are creased, torn or marked in any way – however minor – may not be accepted in payment, or you'll be forced to sell them at a reduced rate if exchanging for kyat. Similarly, in the (slightly unlikely) event that you end up having to buy dollars in Myanmar, reject any note not in perfect condition.

ATMs and credit cards

Myanmar's economy has started changing rapidly over the past few years as the first internationally connected ATMs have appeared and more and more places have begun to accept credit cards. Western Union and MoneyGram services are also now available. There's now at least one **ATM** (usually several) in all major towns, and most accept both Visa and MasterCard (exceptions are noted in the Guide). They do tend to go out of service on a regular basis, however, and it's still best to bring all the cash you'll need in with you in dollars (ATMs currently dispense only kyat), treating ATMs as a backup. Note, too, that ATMs typically charge a $5 withdrawal fee (on top of whatever your bank at home might charge you), which goes straight into the pockets of crony businessmen (see box, p.350). **Credit cards** are now generally accepted in all top-end and some mid-range hotels, plus a few upmarket shops and restaurants.

Meditation

Myanmar is a good place to study or practise meditation – there's even a special, extendable three-month meditation visa for visitors with a letter of support from a recognized centre. Some centres will only take foreigners who commit to staying for several weeks, but there are also ten-day courses available in Yangon (see p.93) and near Mandalay (see p.281).

Opening hours and public holidays

Standard **business hours** are Monday to Friday 9am to 5pm; **banks** typically open Monday to Friday 9am to 3pm, although some close earlier and currency exchange counters may not open until 11am. Major **temples** may stay open 24 hours a day (especially during festivals and holidays), and will certainly be open (at minimum) from around 6am to 9pm. Opening times for **restaurants**, **teahouses**, **bars** and **shops** are given throughout the Guide.

PUBLIC HOLIDAYS

Several holidays (marked *) are based upon the lunar calendar and therefore change date each year.

January 4 Independence Day
January 10 Kachin New Year
February 12 Union Day
March 2 Peasants' Day
March/April* Tabaung full moon
March 27 Armed Forces Day
April 13–16 Thingyan (water festival)
April 17 New Year
May 1 Labour Day
May* Kasong full moon
July 19 Martyrs' Day
July* Waso full moon (beginning of Buddhist "Lent")
October* Thadingyut full moon (end of Buddhist "Lent")
November* Tazaungmone full moon
November/December* National Day
December/January* Kayin New Year
December 25 Christmas Day

Phones

Most guesthouses will let you make calls **within Myanmar** from a phone at reception (check the cost first), or may even be persuaded to make the call for you if you're worried that the phone will be answered by a non-English-speaker. Calls made from the in-room IDD phones found in some top-end hotels always come with a massive mark-up. There are also local call stands – often just a table with a telephone – in the streets and in some shops. The cheapest and easiest way to call **internationally** is through a VOIP (Voice Over Internet Protocol) service such as Skype or Voipfone. Otherwise you'll need to use public call centres (try asking at the post office), although international calls are expensive.

International **roaming** is in its infancy in Myanmar, and currently works only with some Asian SIM cards. Getting hold of a **local SIM card** in

Myanmar is a proverbial nightmare (in the mid-noughties cards were changing hands for over $1000). Foreigners were previously able to buy SIM cards lasting for a month for around $20, but these had been withdrawn at the time of writing. At the time of writing, your only option was to hire a SIM card plus phone at either Yangon or Mandalay airports, although this costs a rip-off $10/day. The situation changes frequently, however, so check the latest online before travelling. Mobile phone numbers start with 09.

To **call home from Myanmar**, dial the international access code (☎00), then the country code (UK ☎44; US & Canada ☎1; Ireland ☎353; Australia ☎61; New Zealand ☎64; South Africa ☎27), then the area code and subscriber number. Note that the initial zero is omitted from the area code when dialling the UK, Ireland, Australia and New Zealand from abroad.

To **call Myanmar from abroad**, dial your international access code then the country code for Myanmar (☎95), then the area code, minus the initial zero, then the subscriber number.

Photography

Most Burmese love having their photo taken, but it's polite to ask before shoving a lens in someone's face and, assuming you're using a digital camera, to show them the picture afterwards. To ask "Is it okay if I take a photo?" in Burmese say "*Daq-poun yaiq-teh, ya-deh naw?*". Don't photograph anything resembling a military installation, and it's probably best to avoid snapping police and soldiers as well.

The best photographic conditions are early in the morning, around 6–8am. Not only is the light at its best, but this is one of the busiest times of the day around local markets and also a good time to photograph temples and other attractions before hordes of tourists arrive.

Time

Myanmar time is 6hr 30min ahead of GMT (5hr 30min ahead of British Summer Time), 11hr 30min ahead of US Eastern Standard Time, 14hr 30min ahead of US Western Standard Time, and 3hr 30min behind Australian Eastern Standard Time. There are no daylight-saving time changes in Myanmar.

Tourist information

The government-run **Myanmar Travels & Tours** (**MTT**) maintains tourist offices in Yangon and

Mandalay, but in general the best sources of travel information are generally local travel agents or the staff at your guesthouse or hotel. There are no Myanmar tourist information offices abroad, although embassies and consulates may be able to help with information about which areas are currently restricted or off limits.

MYANMAR ONLINE

Good online news resources are listed in "The Media" section (see p.39).

Ⓦ **burmalibrary.org** Handy links to thousands of Myanmar-related websites and publications.

Ⓦ **myanmartourism.org** Official tourism website with general background information including a list of places that are off limits or require permits (although this may be out of date).

Ⓦ **myanmartourismwatch.org** Background information on abuses related to the tourism industry, particularly the use of forced labour to build tourism projects and the expropriation of land.

Ⓦ **seat61.com/Burma** The Myanmar page of this excellent website covering all things railway-related in Myanmar.

Ⓦ **tourismtransparency.org** Excellent background and unrivalled information on responsible travel in Myanmar.

Travellers with disabilities

Myanmar is poorly set up for travellers with disabilities, although with a bit of determination and pre-planning you can still enjoy much that the country has to offer. Getting around is the first challenge. Public **transport** by bus or train is a total non-starter for disabled travellers, meaning that you'll have to contact a local or foreign tour operator (see p.25) to arrange for suitable transport by private vehicle. The various domestic airlines should be able to take care of you, however, given appropriate notice of any special requirements. Specially adapted **accommodation** is also virtually nonexistent, although given that most accommodation outside Yangon and Mandalay is typically laid out in one-storey bungalow-style buildings, accessibility, at least, shouldn't be a major obstacle.

In terms of **sights**, many of the major ones in Yangon and Mandalay are relatively accessible, although the densely crowded pavements of downtown will present serious difficulties. Burmese temples are typically set at the top of long flights of steps, although some of the biggest (including the Shwedagon in Yangon) have lifts, making them easily accessible. Many of Bagan's temples are also relatively easy to visit, often with fewer steps (and, in any case, it's often the exteriors of these temples and the surrounding landscape that provide the main draw). **River cruises** should also be possible on dedicated tourist boats (but not public ferries), though this does not really extend to Inle Lake, where vessels are small, narrow and difficult to balance at the best of times – the lack of decent safety equipment makes things a little risky.

Yangon
and around

SHWEDAGON PAGODA

1

Yangon and around

Myanmar's largest city, Yangon (ရန်ကုန်), still perhaps better known by its old colonial name of Rangoon (which remains in widespread circulation to this day), is a city of startling contradictions. Decades of economic and cultural isolation are still very much in evidence, exemplified by the old downtown district with its endless streets of decaying colonial buildings, erratic electricity and sardine-packed rustbucket buses. The international chains and logos which are steadily consuming many other cities in the region are conspicuous by their almost complete absence, and the fabric of downtown city life – a dense honeycomb of pavement cafés, street hawkers, ramshackle markets and soaring stupas – looks, in places, strangely untouched by the modern world.

And yet the winds of change are already gusting through the city, with streams of late-model Japanese cars flooding the city streets, along with a rapidly growing number of swanky hotels, formica-clad local fast-food joints, illuminated billboards and shops flogging the latest smartphones, tablets and other digital accessories. All of which gives the strange impression of a city divided in time: at once thoroughly modern but also several decades out of date – which is perhaps the essence of the place's peculiar appeal.

For visitors, Yangon is very much a city of two halves. The old colonial city – or **downtown Yangon**, as it's often described – remains far and away the most absorbing area in this rapidly expanding megalopolis, a fascinating urban landscape of picturesquely decaying colonial architecture dotted with gilded Buddhist pagodas, Hindu and Chinese temples, mosques and markets. North of here stretch the endless suburbs of **modern Yangon**, a largely featureless urban sprawl dotted with a sequence of florid Buddhist shrines and the sylvan Inle and Kandawgyi lakes. Pride of place goes to the stupendous **Shwedagon Pagoda**, one of the world's most spectacular Buddhist temples, while it's also worth searching out some of the other pagodas and supersized Buddha statues that dot the area.

Brief history

A relative newcomer by Burmese standards, Yangon is a largely colonial creation, although its roots run deep into early Burmese history. A fishing village named **Dagon** was established here in the early eleventh century by the Mon, then the dominant power in Lower Burma, although it remained a relative backwater despite the presence of the revered Shwedagon Pagoda. In 1755, King Alaungpaya, founder of the Konbaung dynasty (see p.336), seized control of Dagon, renaming it **Yangon** and diverting trade here from nearby Thanlyin, previously the major port hereabouts. The British captured Yangon during the First Anglo-Burmese War (1824–26), but returned it to the Burmese in 1827 following the conclusion of hostilities.

COLONIAL ARCHITECTURE, YANGON

Highlights

❶ Sule Pagoda Landmark temple in the dead centre of Yangon, its soaring golden spire featuring in many of downtown's most memorable views. **See p.61**

❷ Colonial architecture Despite rapid development, downtown Yangon remains one of Asia's finest showpieces of British colonial urban planning, with streets full of majestically time-warped architecture in various states of atmospheric decay. **See box, p.62**

❸ Bogyoke Market Enjoyable British-era bazaar, home to dozens of shops piled high with gems, jade, handicrafts, slippers and more. **See p.65**

❹ Shwedagon Pagoda Myanmar's greatest temple, its unforgettable gilded stupa rising high above the city and packed with colourful shrines busy at all times of day and night. **See p.70**

❺ Ferry ride to Dalah Take the short ferry ride over the river to Dalah for memorable views of the Yangon waterfront and for a startlingly abrupt change of scenery, offering a glimpse of authentic rural Burmese life just ten minutes from downtown. **See p.79**

❻ Street food Eat your way around the city pavements, crammed with food stalls dishing up everything from exotic tropical fruits to deep-fried snakes. **See box, p.89**

HIGHLIGHTS ARE MARKED ON THE MAP ON P.68

1

Yangon's sudden and unexpected rise to national pre-eminence occurred following the **Second Anglo-Burmese War** of 1852, during which the British recaptured the city (along with the rest of Lower Burma). The formerly modest town was selected as the site of the new capital of British Burma thanks to its location at the meeting point of the Indian Ocean and Ayeyarwady River, navigable for almost 1600km into the heart of the country. The antique Mon riverside settlement was razed and a grandiose new urban design laid out, based on the gridiron plan created by army engineer Alexander Fraser.

British rule

Following the conquest of Upper Burma in the Third Anglo-Burmese War of 1885, colonial **Rangoon** (as it was known by the British) became the undisputed economic and commercial heart of Burma. Grandiose new buildings were raised in the fashionable Neoclassical and Indo-Saracenic styles, new hospitals, schools and colleges established,

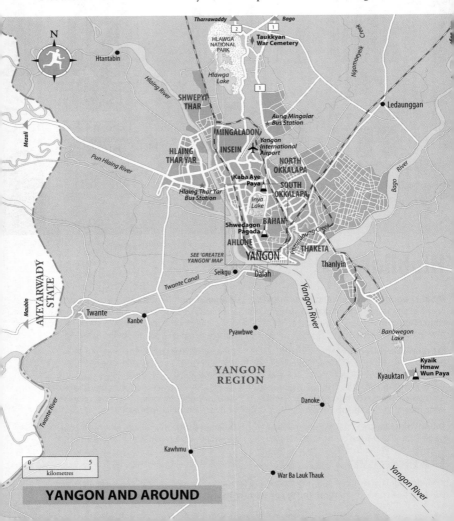

YANGON AND AROUND

YANGON FESTIVALS

As well as all the usual national events (see p.40), Yangon hosts a number of its own annual festivals.

Yangon Photo Festival Institut Français, 340 Pyay Rd ☎01 536900, ⓦyangonphoto.com. Exhibitions and talks by leading international photographers. Jan–Feb.

Shwedagon Pagoda Festival Myanmar's largest pagoda festival, banned by the military between 1988 and 2012, during which pilgrims descend on the great pagoda from all over the country to make offerings, accompanied by *pwe* dancing and theatre, weaving competitions and more. Two weeks in Feb/March.

Murugu Festival Colourful Hindu festival featuring processions and acts of ritual self-mortification in honour of the God Murugan, centred on downtown's Sri Kali and Sri Devi temples. March/April.

Shwesandaw Pagoda Festival Annual pagoda festival at the main temple in Twante, coinciding with Burmese New Year. April.

Tazaungdaing (Robe-Weaving) Festival Shwedagon, Botataung and other pagodas host robe-weaving contexts, during which young ladies attempt to weave a perfect Buddha's robe in the course of a single night. One night in November. See p.41.

parks laid out, a railway constructed and Inle and Kandawgyi lakes created to provide water for the new city. There was also substantial immigration to the new city from other parts of the British Empire, notably India, giving the city a pronounced subcontinental flavour which endures (in places) to this day.

Following World War I, Rangoon became the heart of the Burmese **independence movement**, led by students from the British-created Rangoon University and culminating in a series of national strikes (in 1920, 1936 and 1938). The British were finally ousted during **World War II**, during which the city fell under Japanese occupation (from 1942 to 1945), before being retaken by the Allies in 1945, after suffering heavy damage.

Independence

Rangoon became the capital of the new Union of Burma upon **independence** in 1948. The city continued to expand exponentially outwards, with new suburbs mushrooming to the north of the old colonial centre. At the same time, the city's demographic make-up changed substantially, with many Burmese of Indian descent, plus the city's once sizeable Jewish community and other ethnic groups, leaving following independence and later during Ne Win's isolationist rule of the 1960s. Many of the city's old colonial street names were changed, while in 1989 the country's military rulers changed the city's name from Rangoon back to **Yangon**, although the change was not recognized by many local and international organizations, and the old name continues sporadically in circulation right up to the present.

Yangon became a major hotbed of **pro-democracy protests**, particularly during the popular uprisings of 1974, 1988 and 2007. Further carnage ensued in 2008, when **Cyclone Nargis** devastated Yangon's industrial infrastructure – although human casualties were mercifully few. The city suffered a significant symbolic blow in 2005 with the founding of a new Burmese capital at Naypyitaw, but despite being stripped of capital-city status and losing a few ministerial privileges en route, Yangon remains very much the economic, cultural and political heart of the country, with a population now well over four million spreading over an area of over sixty square kilometres.

Downtown Yangon

The old colonial-era city – or **downtown Yangon** as it's now generally known – remains the heart of modern Yangon and far and away its most absorbing district. Laid out by

1

DOWNTOWN YANGON

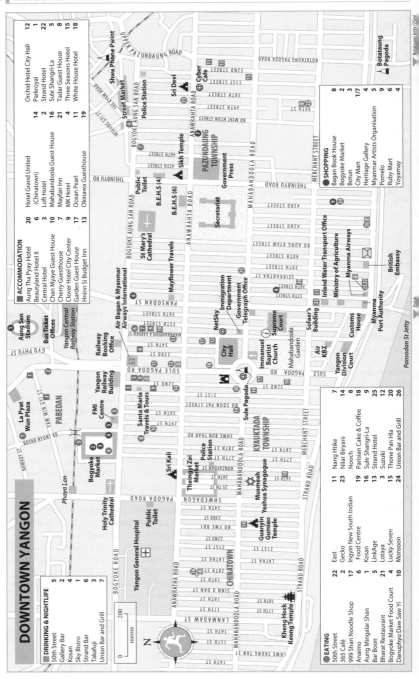

DRINKING & NIGHTLIFE

50th Street	5
Gallery Bar	2
Kosan	4
Sky Bistro	1
Strand Bar	6
Takafuji	3
Union Bar and Grill	7

ACCOMMODATION

Aung Tha Pyay Hotel	20	Hotel Grand United (Chinatown)	12
Beautyland Hotel II	6	Loft Hotel	1
Central Hotel	3	Mahabandoola Guest House	14
Chan Myaye Guest House	10	Mayfair Inn	22
Cherry Guesthouse	7	MK Hotel	5
Clover Hotel City Center	16	Ocean Pearl	16
Garden Guest House	21	Okinawa Guesthouse	15
Hnin Si Budget Inn	4	Orchid Hotel City Hall	8
	17	Parkroyal	11
	9	Strand Hotel	2
	19	Sule Shangri-La	18
	13	Tadar Guest House	
		Three Seasons Hotel	
		White House Hotel	

EATING

50th Street	22	Nang Htike	11
365 Café	2	Nilar Biryani	23
999 Shan Noodle Shop	17	Nooch	8
Anaimo	6	Parisian Cake & Coffee	19
Aung Mingalar Shan	1	Sule Shangri-La	16
Bar Boon	5	Strand Hotel	13
Bharat Restaurant	21	Suzuki	3
Bogyoke Market Food Court	4	Thone Pan Hla	15
Danuphyu Daw Saw Yi	10	Union Bar and Grill	24
East	22		
Gecko	2		
Ingyin New South Indian	17		
Food Centre	6		
Kosan	1		
LinkAge	5		
Lotaya	21		
Lucky Seven	4		
Monsoon	10		

SHOPPING

Bagan Book House	8
Bogyoke Market	2
Botun	3
City Mart	1/7
Heritage Gallery	4
Myanmar Artists Organisation	9
Pomelo	5
Ruby Mart	6
Yoyamay	4

the British in the 1850s, downtown comprises a geometrical gridiron of streets, almost 5km wide and 1km deep, although the original design has proved hopelessly insufficient to deal with the sheer weight of twenty-first-century vehicular and pedestrian traffic, and regularly descends into gridlock, on both the roads and pavements.

Rapid development notwithstanding, downtown remains one of Asia's great colonial-era cityscapes, with streets full of Neoclassical public buildings in various states of monsoon-stained, tropical-overload decay. Superimposed on the old-world fabric the bustling street life of Yangon goes on unabated, with roads and pavements crammed full of more food stalls, street hawkers, traffic, touts, shoppers and red-robed monks than you'd believe possible – this is very much a place where it pays to go slow and savour the detail. It's also the place where you'll get the best sense of Yangon's multicultural heritage, with a dense confusion of *thanaka*-smeared Burmese, bearded Muslims, dark-skinned Tamils and pale Chinese, all navigating their way slowly between innumerable street-side stalls and pavement cafés.

Sule Pagoda

ဆူးလေတ့ဘုရား• Sule Pagoda Rd • Daily 5am–9pm • $3

Rising out of the very heart of downtown Yangon, the **Sule Pagoda** is the most visible of all Burmese temples, its soaring golden stupa providing the old colonial city with its defining landmark, towards which all streets seem to converge. Placed at the centre of the British gridplan in the 1850s, the pagoda remains very much at the centre of downtown life, both physically and culturally (all distances to other parts of the nation are still measured from the pagoda, like a Burmese version of London's Charing Cross). The pagoda is particularly beautiful when illuminated at night, although it looks rather incongruous by day, marooned within a busy roundabout, surrounded by a constant swirl of traffic and with a string of small shops inserted into its outward-facing sides.

According to local tradition, the pagoda was built during the lifetime of the Buddha himself, although the more likely, albeit prosaic, explanation is that it dates back to the Mon era in the tenth century, or thereabouts. The 43m-high stupa was enlarged to its present size by Queen Shinsawbu (1453–72), and is said to enshrine one of the Buddha's hairs, given (it's said) by the Buddha himself to the brothers Tapissa and Balika, two itinerant merchants from Myanmar. More recently, the Sule Pagoda served as an important rallying point for pro-democracy activists during both the 1988 uprising and the 2007 Saffron Revolution – and was the scene of a brutal massacre during the latter, when the military opened fire on unarmed protestors, killing nine people.

Four staircases lead up to the pagoda from each of the cardinal points, with four matching shrines attached to the base of the stupa at the top of each flight of stairs, all topped with flamboyant gilded roofs. The stupa itself sits on an octagonal base (following the standard Burmese design) but is unusual in that both the bell and spire of the stupa continue the octagonal shape, rather than following the circular pattern adopted by virtually all other Burmese stupas.

Early evening is particularly busy and atmospheric, while you'll also see many people praying in the direction of the stupa in the streets outside as they pass.

Mahabandoola Garden

မဟာဗန္ဓုလပန်းခြံ • Between Sule Pagoda Rd and Mahabandoola Garden St • Daily 5.30am–6pm • Free

Providing a blissful square of open green space amid the super-compacted streets of downtown Yangon, **Mahabandoola Garden** is at once a peaceful city park and also a shrine to Burmese nationalism. Formerly named Fytche Square (in honour of Albert Fytche, Chief Commissioner of British Burma), the park was later renamed after the legendary General Mahabandoola (or Maha Bandula), leader of Burmese forces during the First Anglo-Burmese War (see p.338), and is also home to the soaring Independence Monument, commemorating Burmese independence in 1948. The garden itself, dotted

1

with little bonsai-like topiary trees, is a nice place to stretch your legs after the cramped downtown pavements, and also offers good views of the neighbouring City Hall and Sule Pagoda. A line of palmists ply their trade outside the railings along the gardens' west side, while it's also a popular spot for locals practising *t'ai chi* before and after work.

Around Mahabandoola Garden

Yangon's finest array of **colonial architecture** lies clustered in the area immediately to the east of Mahabandoola Garden and down Pansodan Street. Flanking the northern side of Mahabandoola Gardens is the sky-blue **City Hall** (1924), its Neoclassical outlines jazzed up with a riot of ersatz-oriental decorative motifs including pagoda-topped roofs, chintzy stone latticework and a pair of dragons suspended over the main entrance, with a peacock between.

The large, faintly French-looking building opposite was originally a department store before being turned into the **Immigration Department**. It's recently undergone a major restoration and has now re-emerged in pristine condition, an example of what these superb old buildings could look like, given sufficient time, love and money.

On the other side of Mahabandoola Road, a pair of distinctively spiky spires top the **Immanuel Baptist Church** of 1952 (the original church, commissioned by an American missionary in 1885, having been destroyed during World War II), while sprawling beyond down the east side of Mahabandoola Gardens is the former **Supreme Court** building (1911) in generic Neoclassical style with cream details, topped by a giant red-brick clocktower.

Pansodan Street

ပန်းဆိုးတန်းလမ်း

The southern end of **Pansodan Street** was once the city's most prestigious address, and today the street is still lined with a veritable beauty parade of fine old colonial edifices. Starting from the junction with Mahabandoola Road, the first major building is the **Government Telegraph Office**: a red-brick colossus with paired white ionic columns above its entrance, although the whole thing's looking a bit run-down, with a crumbling upper storey and a radio mast plonked unceremoniously on the roof.

South of here, on the east side of the road at the junction with Merchant Street, is the chintzy **Sofaer's Building**, built in 1906 by the Baghdad-born, Rangoon-educated

---

YANGON'S COLONIAL HERITAGE

Downtown Yangon boasts one of the world's greatest collections of **colonial architecture**, and is the last major city in Myanmar to preserve its original nineteenth-century core at least partially intact, with (in places, at least) entire streets still lined with their original buildings. Decades of neglect have taken a serious toll, however, with historic buildings subdivided into shops, flats or just abandoned to squatters, as well as being disfigured with adverts, satellite dishes, radio masts and mass air-conditioning units. Many structures are now in an advanced state of disrepair, while other landmark buildings once occupied by various ministries have all been left empty since the government upped sticks and moved to Naypyitaw in 2005.

The scale of the preservation required is immense (the cost of restoring the landmark Secretariat building alone has been costed at $100m-plus, for example), while the urgent need for land and new buildings in downtown means that many colonial-era structures face an uncertain future. The establishment in 2012 of the **Yangon Heritage Trust** (Ⓦyangonheritagetrust.org) by influential historian Dr Thant Myint-U is a major step in the right direction, with the aim of establishing a citywide plan for the conservation of historically significant buildings, although how much can be saved in this rapidly developing city remains to be seen.

Jewish brothers Isaac and Meyer Sofaer. This was once the epicentre of city life, home to the city's Reuters telegram office and shops selling German beer, Scottish whisky, Egyptian cigarettes and English sweets. Part of the ground floor has now been renovated as the excellent *Gecko* restaurant (see p.88), with the original Manchester-manufactured floor tiles and Lanarkshire steel beams preserved *in situ*, although the rest of the ground floor is now boarded up and looking sadly derelict.

Opposite Sofaer's stands the **Internal Revenue Department** (1936) with Art Deco flourishes (still sporting its original "Rander House" sign). Further down (on the left) is the large and rather plain **Inland Water Transport** office (1933), its corniche decorated with seashells. This was formerly the headquarters of the Irrawaddy Flotilla Company, a Scottish-owned enterprise which during the 1920s operated the world's largest fleet of river boats, with over six hundred vessels carrying some nine million passengers a year.

Next door is the **Ministry of Agriculture and Irrigation** with its solid-looking vaulted gold doors under a fancy silver canopy and quirky facade of green semicircles, with lion heads arranged along the roof corniche. At the bottom of the street stands the imposing **Myanma Port Authority** building with its landmark tower and huge arched windows, with roundels decorated with ships and anchors between.

A left turn along Strand Road leads to the *Strand Hotel* (see below). Alternatively, heading right brings you to the neat red-brick **Customs House**, complete with clock and cupola, and then the **Yangon Division Court**, impressively large but almost invisible under scaffolding at the time of writing.

The Strand Hotel

စတ္ရဲန်းဟိုတယ် • 92 Strand Rd • ☎ 01 243377, ⊕ hotelthestrand.com

Downtown Yangon's address of choice for the rich and famous is the **Strand Hotel**, looking like a staid elderly duchess amid the disreputable hubbub of Yangon's historic, but run-down, waterfront Strand Road. Opened in 1901, the *Strand* was the brainchild of Aviet and Tigran Sarkies, two of the four entrepreneurial, Armenian-descended Sarkies brothers, who established a string of luxury hotels throughout Southeast Asia including the *Raffles* in Singapore and the *Eastern & Oriental* in Penang. The whites-only hotel (Burmese were not admitted until 1945) was described as "the finest hostelry east of the Suez" by John Murray in his *Handbook for Travellers,* with guests including Rudyard Kipling, Somerset Maugham and Lord Mountbatten. It fell into disrepair following independence but reopened in 1993 after extensive renovations.

The Secretariat

ဝန်ကြီးများရုံး • Between Mahabandoola, Anawrahta, Bo Aung Kyaw and Theinbyu roads

The most impressive of all Yangon's colonial monuments is the gargantuan **Secretariat** (also known as the Ministers' Building), a vast red-brick Neoclassical structure occupying an entire city block, sprawling over sixteen acres and with 37,000 square metres of floor space – roughly two-thirds the size of the Paris Louvre. Completed in 1902 (with the east and west wings added three years later), this is the most famous and historically significant colonial building in Yangon: the former seat of British administrative power in Burma; the spot where Aung San and six cabinet ministers were assassinated on 19 July 1947; and also the place where the country's independence ceremony was conducted the following year. It later served as the national parliament building until the 1962 coup, since when it has been off limits. The entire building is currently wrapped in scaffolding and tarpaulin pending a decision about its future and, hopefully, restoration – a massive task, likely to cost at least $100m and "potentially one of the largest historic restoration projects in the world", as Al Jazeera recently described it.

1

St Mary's Catholic Cathedral and around

စိန်မေရီကက်သလစ်ဘုရားရှိခိုးကျောင်း • Junction of Bogyoke Aung San and Bo Aung Kyaw roads

The imposing **St Mary's Catholic Cathedral**, immediately north of the Secretariat, is the city's principal Catholic place of worship and the country's largest church. Designed by Dutch architect Jos Cuypers (son of Pierre Cuypers, creator of Amsterdam's Central Station and Rijksmuseum), the building was finished in 1899 in a neo-Gothic style not dissimilar to that of the rival Holy Trinity Anglican cathedral across the city (see opposite). Unfortunately it's generally locked except when services are being held, when you can appreciate the impressively tiled and vaulted interior.

On the south side of the cathedral is the impressive **B.E.H.S. (6) Botahtaung** of 1860 – just two of a number of old colonial-era B.E.H.S (Basic Education High Schools) which still dot the city. Formerly known as St Paul's English High School, this was once one of the most elite schools in Yangon. East of the cathedral, on Theinbyu Road, the all-girls **B.E.H.S. (4) Botahtaung** (formerly St Mary's Convent School) is another fine old colonial memento still in use today. A fine **Sikh temple** flanks the southern side of the school, while across the road is the former **Government Press** – yet another handsome red-brick Neoclassical edifice, now sadly derelict.

Sri Devi Temple

Anawrahta Rd, between 50th & 51st sts • Daily 6–11.30am & 4.30–8.30pm • Free

Dedicated to the Hindu mother goddess Devi, the **Sri Devi Temple** provides spiritual succour to the many Indian-descended Yangonites living in the subcontinental enclave around the eastern end of Anawrahta Road (the modern-day descendants of Yangon's once omnipresent Indian community who settled in the city during the era of British rule). The temple features the usual multicoloured *gopuram* plus red-and-white-striped walls and an inner shrine manned by a couple of a resident Brahmins.

Botataung Pagoda

ဗိုလ်တထောင်ဘုရား • Strand Rd (foreign entrance on east side) • Daily 6am–9.30pm • $3

Tucked away on the far eastern side of downtown is the **Botataung Pagoda**, the second of colonial Yangon's two major Buddhist pagodas – the name (literally "1000 officers") refers to the soldiers of the king who are said to have formed a guard of honour to celebrate the arrival here of precious Buddhist relics from India. The current complex dates from the Mon era, around the same time as the Shwedagon Pagoda, although it was largely obliterated by a stray RAF bomb in 1943 (they were aiming for the nearby Yangon wharves). Reconstruction work started on 4 January 1948 – the first day of Burmese independence. During rebuilding, a previously unknown relic chamber was uncovered containing an extraordinary treasure-trove of seven hundred items including precious stones, jewellery, gold, silver and brass statues and – most importantly – a pure gold stupa-shaped reliquary containing two tiny body relics ("each the size of a mustard seed", as it was reported) and what is believed to be a hair relic of the Buddha.

The temple's highlight is the 39m-high gilded **stupa**, particularly its hollow **interior** (a result of post-war rebuilding – the original stupa was solid). A sumptuously decorated little corridor runs through the inside of the stupa, its walls and ceilings covered in gilded panels, while at the stupa's centre is an even more spectacularly embellished miniature shrine containing the Buddha's hair relic, along with other items from the excavated relic chamber, showcased in fancy glass cabinets.

The terrace surrounding the stupa is unusually large, if slightly ramshackle. A **long hall** on the western side of the terrace houses several fine gilded Buddhas as well as a typical Myanmar-style temple-cum-fairground attraction, comprising a revolving table with several alms bowls on it, into which visitors attempt to throw folded-up banknotes.

In the southwest corner of the inner courtyard, look out for the temple's **nat shrine**, which includes an image of the pagoda's white-turbaned *nat* guardian, or Bo Bo Gyi ("great grandfather"), with a shrine to Shin Upagot (see p.356) beside. Close by, at the southern edge of the complex is a large but rather ugly Buddha of 2008, seated in a pavilion facing the river, with attractive views over the water.

There's a handy **short cut** around the back of Bogyoke Market, where a small footbridge near the *Lotaya* restaurant crosses the railway lines – useful if you're heading to the *Aung Mingalar* restaurant, *Park Royal* hotel or other locations just north of the tracks.

Bogyoke Market and around

ဗိုလ်ချုပ်အောင်ဆန်းဈေး • Bogyoke Aung San Rd • Tues–Sun 10am–5pm • ⓦ bogyokemarket.com

Bookending the northern side of downtown Yangon is the city's principal tourist honeypot, **Bogyoke Market** – or Bogyoke Aung San Market, as it's officially known – home to Myanmar's most diverse and foreigner-friendly collection of souvenir shops, jewellery-wallahs and other consumerist collectibles. Built in 1926, this colonial-era Burmese bazaar was formerly called Scott Market after the then municipal commissioner. The market was renamed Bogyoke ("General") Aung San Market after the country's beloved independence leader in 1948.

The modern market is an attractive and atmospheric place, albeit a million miles away from the ramshackle chaos of your average Myanmar bazaar, and also hosts the best collection of craft and souvenir shops (see p.92) under a single roof in the country. The most upmarket and touristy shops are the streetside places under the arcade fronting Bogyoke Aung San Road, many of them stuffed with huge quantities of Myanmar jade (including some spectacularly tasteless statues and assorted bric-a-brac aimed at visiting Chinese) plus considerable quantities of lacquerware, paintings and textiles. The main alleyway through the centre of the covered market is lined with dozens of jewellers selling gold, silver, rubies, emeralds and yet more jade, fashioned into bangles, pendants and necklaces, plus a few touristy souvenir places. Shops get gradually more downmarket as you move away from the central alleyway.

Along Bogyoke Aung San Road

East of Bogyoke Market, **Bogyoke Aung San Road** is usually busy with pavement hawkers selling an entertaining medley of stuff ranging from old coins and colonial-era bric-a-brac through to tropical fruit, original oil paintings and Aung San Suu Kyi T-shirts. At the end of the block, you can't fail to see the fine old **Yangon Railway Building** at the junction with Sule Pagoda Road, another of the city's colonial landmarks currently under restoration.

The extensive buildings of the **Yangon General Hospital** of 1899 are another of the city's British-era landmarks and scene of a particularly vicious massacre on 10 August 1988 when soldiers fired into the hospital, killing injured patients (who were assumed to have taken part in anti-government protests) along with doctors and nurses. Two weeks later, Aung San Suu Kyi made her first ever public speech in the hospital grounds.

Holy Trinity Cathedral

Corner of Bogyoke Aung San and Shwedagon Pagoda roads • Free • Daily 10am–5pm

The **Holy Trinity Cathedral** is one of the largest of the many colonial-era churches which still dot Yangon, and Myanmar's principal Anglican cathedral. The foundation stone was laid by the Viceroy of India, Lord Dufferin, in 1886,

1

although a lack of funds meant that it took eight years to complete, didn't acquire its spire until 1913 and had the indignity of being converted by the Japanese into a brewery during World War II. Designed by Madras-based architect Robert Chisholm in High Gothic style, the cathedral's soaring spire and strident red-painted, white-trimmed brick exterior are hard to miss, even if it does looks more like a giant piece of Lego than a place of worship. The whitewashed interior beneath a dark wooden roof is contrastingly plain, bar some fine stained-glass windows. A moving little Forces Chapel commemorates the many British and Commonwealth soldiers who died in the Burma Campaign of 1942–45.

Sri Kali

Anawrahta Rd • Daily 6–11.30am & 4–8pm • Free

The colourful **Sri Kali temple** is where the area's sizeable local Indian population come to pay their respects to the fearsome mother goddess Kali, whose black image sits in the temple's inner shrine, surrounded by shrines to Shiva, Ganesh, Laxmi and Karthik (more commonly known as Kartikeya or Murugan). Shiva and Parvati sit in a subsidiary shrine outside (on the right as you enter the inner building), with Shiva's bull Nandi carefully looking on.

Theingyi Zei Market

သိမ်ကြီးဈေး • In the block between Anawrahta and Mahabandoola roads, bounded by Shwedagon Pagoda Rd to the west and Kon Zay Dan St to the east • Daily 8am–5pm

A world away from the clean, calm and carefully manicured Bogyoke Market, **Theingyi Zei** is what a proper Burmese bazaar looks like, filling almost an entire city block with a chaotic crush of stalls, shoppers, sacks, boxes, bicycles, piles of rubbish and the occasional rat. The market is divided between two parallel buildings separated by a pedestrian alleyway that hosts one of Yangon's biggest and busiest vegetable markets. The western of the two buildings is insanely crowded, especially on its Mahabandoola Road side, usually rammed with crazed bargain-hunters and stuffed with huge quantities of cheap clothes piled up on the quaint wooden stalls (most of which appear to date back to colonial times, with an unusual design resembling large, two-storey cupboards). The eastern building is only fractionally less chock-a-block, although things become a little calmer as you head north, and the market acquires a distinctly Indian flavour as you approach Anawrahta Road and the Sri Kali temple, with shops full of sacks of spices, pulses, dried herbs, and mysterious bits of culinary and medicinal herb and root.

Musmeah Yeshua Synagogue

26th St • No official opening hours – stick your head into the courtyard to see if the synagogue's guardian is available to show you around

The self-effacing **Musmeah Yeshua Synagogue** is easily missed in one of downtown Yangon's busiest districts. The synagogue was constructed from 1893 to 1896 to replace an earlier building of 1854 and served colonial Rangoon's thriving community of Sephardic Jews from Baghdad and India (such as the Sofaer brothers; see p.63). Before World War II the city was home to as many as 2500 Jews, although most left either during the wartime Japanese occupation or later, following Ne Win's military coup of 1962. The synagogue lost its last rabbi in 1969; Yangon's current Jewish population now numbers fewer than twenty and much of the synagogue congregation comes from overseas visitors. The beautifully preserved interior is well worth a look, with its gold-railed *bimah* (the platform from which the Torah is read) flanked by a pair of *menorah* lamps, a finely decorated ceiling and high arches supporting a pair of wooden balconies – for women – on either side.

Chinatown

တရုတ်တန်း

Yangon's bustling **Chinatown** (roughly the area south of Anawrahta Road between Shwe Dagon Pagoda Road and Lanmadaw Street) is the major home for the city's Chinese-descended inhabitants, and one of the liveliest and most enjoyable parts of downtown.

Guanyin Gumiao Temple

Mahabandoola Rd • Free • Daily 24hr

At the heart of Chinatown, the imposing **Guanyin Gumiao Temple** (aka the Guangdong Guanyin Temple) is dedicated to Guanyin (the Chinese version of Avalokitesvara, the Bodhisattva of compassion), attracting a mainly Cantonese crowd. The original temple was built in 1823, and destroyed by a fire in 1855 before rising back up out of the ashes in 1864. The tiled interior is less impressive than the Kheng Hock Keong (see below), but still a fine sight, with red tables laden with incense pots, flower vases, and assorted fairy-lit shrines.

Kheng Hock Keong Temple

ခိန့်ဟုတ်ပုဒ္ဓဘာသာဘုရားကျောင်း • Strand Rd, between 17th and 18th sts • Free • Daily 24hr

The flamboyant **Kheng Hock Keong** Chinese temple ("Temple in Celebration of Good Fortune") is the city's largest and most impressive – a wooden temple was first erected here in 1861, replaced by the current brick structure in 1903. Standing close to the waterfront and docks, the temple is dedicated to the sea goddess Mazu and maintained by the local Hokkien clan association, attracting mainly Hokkien and Hakka worshippers. The central altar enshrines an image of Mazu within an intricate riot of gold decoration, flanked on her left by Guan Gong, god of war, and on her right by Bao Sheng Da Di, god of medicine.

Midtown Yangon

The suburbs of **midtown Yangon** immediately north of the old colonial centre are home to some of the city's leading attractions. Pride of place goes to the stunning **Shwedagon Pagoda**, Myanmar's greatest Buddhist place of worship, while there are further supersized Buddhas nearby at the **Chauk Htat Gyi** and **Nga Htat Gyi** pagodas, as well as the pick'n'mix attractions of the city's sporadically entertaining **National Museum**.

National Museum of Myanmar

အမျိုးသား ပြတိုက် • Pyay Rd • Tues–Sun 9.30am–4.30pm (last entry 4pm) • K5000 • No photography

Yangon's **National Museum of Myanmar** is a bit of a mixed bag. There are some outstanding artefacts here, although the badly lit rooms and erratic signage don't help, while parts of the five-storey museum's huge exhibition space are rather lacking in actual exhibits. Explore selectively, however, and it's worth at least an hour or two of your time.

Ground floor

The ground floor focuses on exhibits from **Mandalay (Yadanabon)**. The undoubted highlight, and the museum's most celebrated exhibit, is the splendid **Lion Throne**, in a room all of its own. Made for King Bodawpaya in 1816, this was originally one of nine similar thrones, models of which can also be seen here, but the only one to survive, despite being carted off to India in 1902 (it was returned by Lord Mountbatten after Independence in 1948).

The adjacent **Yadanabon gallery** showcases the artistry of Mandalay's court, with cabinets full of extravagant and finely worked artefacts including toy-sized wooden models of the Mandalay Royal Palace and assorted clothes and palanquins, although

1

the randomness of the exhibits and lack of signage means the overall effect is rather like browsing a superior handicrafts shop.

First floor

Top of the bill on the first floor is the magnificent, solid-gold **Royal Regalia**, comprising the royal helmet, fan, sash and sandals plus assorted betel containers, caskets, goblets, urns and an entertaining, vaguely Dalí-esque crayfish-shaped pitcher.

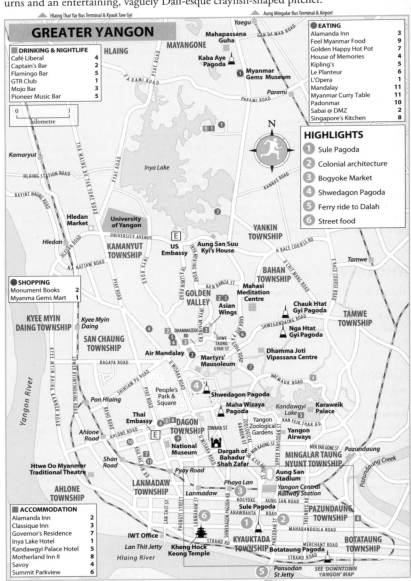

GREATER YANGON

DRINKING & NIGHTLIFE

Café Liberal	4
Captain's Bar	2
Flamingo Bar	5
GTR Club	1
Mojo Bar	3
Pioneer Music Bar	5

EATING

Alamanda Inn	3
Feel Myanmar Food	9
Golden Happy Hot Pot	7
House of Memories	4
Kipling's	5
Le Planteur	6
L'Opera	1
Mandalay	11
Myanmar Curry Table	10
Padonmar	10
Sabai @ DMZ	2
Singapore's Kitchen	8

HIGHLIGHTS

1. Sule Pagoda
2. Colonial architecture
3. Bogyoke Market
4. Shwedagon Pagoda
5. Ferry ride to Dalah
6. Street food

SHOPPING

Monument Books	2
Myanma Gems Mart	1

ACCOMMODATION

Alamanda Inn	2
Classique Inn	3
Governor's Residence	7
Inya Lake Hotel	1
Kandawgyi Palace Hotel	5
Motherland Inn II	8
Savoy	4
Summit Parkview	6

1

The grindingly dull **Natural History** gallery has the inevitable dishes of prehistoric bones and stone-age tools – a clump of fossilized poo is about as exciting as it gets – while the **Bronze Age Axes and Spearheads** gallery is as yawn-worthy as you'd suspect. Fractionally more absorbing is the **Burial Urns and Stone Carvings** gallery, with exhibits from Sri Ksetra (Thayekhittaya; see p.184), Hanlin (see p.318) and Beikthano, featuring some delicate metalwork and statuettes.

Second floor

The second floor is the most enjoyable in the museum, displaying a rich selection of distinctively Burmese craftsmanship at its extravagant best. The **Traditional Folk Art** gallery holds a wide range of crafts, from beautiful glass mosaic work and spectacular lacquerware through to fun and colourful toys and dolls, animal figurines, and wooden carts, plus a pumpkin-shaped alms bowl and a pair of ingenious chairs with antler horns for legs.

Equally fine is the **Performing Arts Gallery** – although it's frustrating that you can't hear what any of the musical instruments on display actually sound like. These include several quaint *mi-gyaung*, a crocodile-shaped, three-string zither (the strings are plucked with a plectrum), enormous Shan pot drums and a spectacular glass-mosaic xylophone in the shape of the *pancharupa*, one of Myanmar's many mythical beasts, made from a combination of five other animals. There are also two complete drum ensembles comprising gongs, bamboo clapper, oboe, "timing bell", a "drum circle" (a kind of traditional Burmese drum kit, with the performer sitting inside a ring of drums), and a big drum hung from a *pancharupa* stand. Other exhibits include some fabulous marionettes and assorted masks worn by actors during performances of the Yama Zatdaw, the Burmese version of the Ramayana.

Third floor

The third floor is the museum's least interesting, and easily skipped. Highlight of the **Art Gallery** is the work of U Ba Nyan (1897–1945), with a mix of dark and rather sombre portraits in a kind of generic post-impressionist style alongside cheerier watercolours and pencil sketches of natural scenes. An endless succession of watercolours and oil paintings by other national artists ensues, with the emphasis on chintzy landscapes and chocolate-box scenes of Burmese rural life.

Fourth floor

Few visitors see the museum all the way through to its bitter end on the deserted **fourth floor**. The **Buddha Images Gallery** houses numerous statues from the second century BC through to the eighteenth century – all impressive enough, although none is especially memorable.

Also on this floor, the **National Races Gallery** showcases the crafts and cultures of the nation's ethnic minorities. The mannequins in traditional dress are probably the highlight, but most of the other stuff here looks like unlabelled bric-a-brac – and exhibits like the "big bamboo spoon" are unlikely to set the pulse racing.

Dargah of Bahadur Shah Zafar

Ziwaka St • Donation • No fixed opening hours but usually open daily 8am–8pm

One of Yangon's most interesting curiosities is the *dargah* (shrine) of the last Mughal emperor of India, **Bahadur Shah Zafar**, or Bahadur Shah II (1775–1862). The peaceable and largely powerless emperor became the reluctant figurehead of the Indian Mutiny of 1857, during which many of his family were killed, including two of his own sons (the full and fascinating story of the emperor's role in the uprising is brilliantly told in William Dalrymple's *The Last Mughal*). Having surrendered to the British, Bahadur was exiled to Rangoon, where he lived out the rest of his days before being buried in

1

an unmarked grave which was only rediscovered in 1991. The tomb of the last Mughal emperor now lies in a crypt below ground, with three further tombs (including that of his wife Zinat, in the middle) above – each a simple rectangular block draped in copious green silks and scattered with rose petals. The emperor is still regarded as a Sufi saint by many Burmese Muslims, who come here to seek blessings at his shrine.

Shwedagon Pagoda

ရွှေတိဂုံစေတီတော် • Shwedagon Pagoda Rd • Daily 4am–10pm • K8000 or $9 • ⓦ shwedagonpagoda.com • Allow 2–3hr for a visit, best towards sunset • Guides can normally be found for hire at the top of the southern stairs

Myanmar's greatest temple, and one of the world's most majestic Buddha monuments, the **Shwedagon Pagoda** towers above Yangon like some kind of supersized spiritual beacon – a magically shimmering outline by day, a spectacular blaze of gold after dusk, when the lights come on. The pagoda is the most revered in Myanmar, said to enshrine eight strands of hair of the historical Buddha, Gautama, along with further relics of his three predecessors (see box opposite): the staff of Kakusandha, the water bottle of Konagamana, and a fragment of Kassapa's robe. The pagoda remains not only the holiest shrine in Myanmar but also a potent symbol of national identity and a major rallying point for the pro-democracy movement since colonial times. It remains magical at any time of the day or night, but is particularly beautiful around sunset, when locals come to pray and the great gilded stupa seems almost to catch fire in the last of the day's light.

Brief history

According to local legend, the Shwedagon dates back to around 588 BC, making it the oldest stupa in Myanmar, if not the world – although more likely it was originally built by the Mon between the sixth and tenth centuries. Mon king Binnya U of Bago (ruled 1348–84) had the stupa raised to a height of 18m, but the temple only really started taking shape a century later under **Queen Shinsawbu** (reigned 1453–72), who had the height of the stupa doubled to 40m and also laid out the terrace around the stupa and added the northern stairway, as well as assigning land and slaves for the pagoda's maintenance. She also began the tradition of gilding the stupa, donating her own body weight in solid gold.

By the beginning of the sixteenth century the pagoda had become Myanmar's most famous place of pilgrimage, as well as attracting the attentions (in 1608) of the Portuguese adventurer **Philip de Brito e Nicote** (see p.80), ruler of nearby Thanlyin, whose troops attacked the Shwedagon, carrying off the 300-tonne Great Bell of King Dhammazedi. De Brito's plan was to melt the bell down to make cannons, although sadly it fell into the Bago River in transit (curiously, exactly the same thing happened when the British attempted to make off with another of the pagoda's bells two centuries later). De Brito subsequently paid with his life for defiling the temple. The pagoda was also repeatedly rocked by various earthquakes – the worst, in 1768, caused the top of the stupa to collapse. A new and enlarged stupa was commissioned by King Hsinbyushin of the Konbaung dynasty, who raised the stupa to its present shape and height in the late eighteenth century.

The colonial era

Shwedagon suffered badly during colonial-era conflicts. It was seized by the British during the First Anglo-Burmese War in 1824 and held for two years (during which it was fortified and suffered the inevitable pillaging and vandalism, including the digging of a tunnel into the depths of the stupa in an attempt to discover if it could be used as a gunpowder magazine). It was reoccupied and refortified during the Second Anglo-Burmese War in 1852, although this time the British retained control of it until 1929.

The pagoda played a leading symbolic role in many of Myanmar's twentieth-century political upheavals. Burmese students met at the pagoda in 1920 to plan protests against the colonial University Act – a monument (see p.72) now marks the spot – while protesting students also camped out on the pagoda's terrace during the second university students' strike of 1936, followed by a similar strike-camp of protesting oil workers in 1938 during the so-called "1300 Revolution" (see p.340). General Aung San addressed a mass meeting at the stupa in 1946 demanding independence from Britain, while during the pro-democracy uprising of 1988 his daughter Aung San Suu Kyi spoke to another huge gathering at the pagoda, which was also a focal point of the 2007 Saffron Revolution, with huge demonstrations and protest marches featuring as many as twenty thousand monks and nuns.

The stairways

Four majestic covered **stairways** (*zaungdan*) lead up from street level to the pagoda above. Those at the north, south and west are guarded at the bottom by pairs of enormous chinthe, although these impressive guardian figures failed to prevent the destruction of the western stairway by fire in 1931, nor the British from badly damaging the eastern stairs when they attacked the temple during the Second Anglo-Burmese War. There are lifts on the north and south sides, although it's much more fun to walk. The **southern stairway** (with 104 steps) is perhaps the most impressive, its roof supported by rich red columns and lined with shops selling assorted religious artefacts – Buddha images, miniature paper umbrellas, incense sticks, flowers, religious tomes, and so on. Further shops line the almost equally impressive **eastern stairway** (118 steps), decorated with gilded columns with fancy woodwork. The chintzy, almost rococo-looking **northern stairs** (128 steps) look like something out of the interior of a French chateau. The **western stairs** are the longest (166 steps), and contrastingly plain, with white walls, golden columns, and an escalator down the middle.

The stupa

The stupa is 99m high, the entire gargantuan structure gilded using the metal from almost 22,000 gold bars. It's the iconic example of the classic Burmese stupa and has served as the prototype for hundreds of other stupas across the country (see p.360). The entire structure sits on a square white base encircled with a mass of colourful statues positioned at ground level, including dragons, chinthe, sphinxes and assorted figures ranging from gods and kings through to loin-clothed ascetics and dancing girls wringing out their hair – as well as a string of **planetary posts** (see box below).

THE FOUR BUDDHAS AND EIGHT PLANETS OF SHWEDAGON

In common with most Burmese temples, the Shwedagon has four principal shrines attached to the base of the stupa at each of the cardinal points and dedicated to the **four Buddhas** of the current *kalpa*. These include the historical Buddha, Gautama, along with his predecessors Kakusandha, Konagamana and Kassapa (a few temples have a fifth shrine, dedicated to the future Buddha Maitreya, the last of the Buddhas of the present *kalpa*).

Also found here (and at other Burmese temples) is the sequence of "**planetary posts**" encircling the base of the stupa, each representing **a day of the week**, along with its associated heavenly body and animal (although one curiosity of Burmese astrology is that Wednesday is divided into two, giving eight "days" in total). Astrology is still taken very seriously in Myanmar – particular importance is attached to the day of the week on which one is born, and locals come to pray at the relevant planetary shrine, each with its own little Buddha image set on a plinth, which worshippers wash reverently during the course of their devotions.

Starting from the southern stairs and heading clockwise, the pagoda's planetary posts are: Wednesday a.m. (Mercury; elephant with tusks); Saturday (Saturn; a *naga*, or snake); Thursday (Jupiter; rat); Wednesday p.m., or "Rahu" as it's known in Burmese (the moon, ascending; elephant without tusks); Friday (Venus; guinea pig); Sunday (Sun; a Garuda, the mythical bird-mount of the Hindu god Vishnu); Monday (the moon; tiger); and Tuesday (Mars; lion).

1

Rising up from its square platform, the first section of the stupa proper comprises three octagonal **terraces** (*paccaya*), ringed with 64 mini-stupas (eight on each of the eight sides) – only monks are allowed to ascend these terraces. Above rises the huge bell and spire, crowned with a **hti** (umbrella) said to be set with 5448 diamonds, 2317 rubies and 1065 golden bells, along with sapphires and other gems, the whole thing topped with a single 76-carat diamond designed to catch the first and last rays of the sun every dawn and dusk.

Around the terrace

The **terrace** surrounding the stupa is scarcely less eye-popping than the stupa itself, ringed with a veritable forest of shrines and pavilions topped with spiky golden roofs, like dozens of Buddhist antennae pointing towards heaven.

Between the southern and western staircases

Arriving at the top of the southern stairs you come out onto the terrace opposite the ornate shrine housing an image of the **Konagamana Buddha** (signed "Kawnagammana"), one of the four Buddhas of the present *kalpa* (see p.371) which sit at the stupa's cardinal points. All four were commissioned by King Singu (reigned 1776–82) using a five-metal alloy containing gold, silver, copper, iron and lead – a particularly auspicious metal (derived from the ancient Hindu tradition of *panchaloha*) favoured for sacred icons – although the Kassapa image (on the west side of the stupa) was subsequently damaged by fire and replaced.

Turning left and heading clockwise around the terrace brings you to the Chinese Merited Association pavilion housing a single **solid jade Buddha**, made in 1999 with 324kg of jade from Kachin in northern Myanmar and inlaid with 2.5kg of gold, 91 rubies and nine diamonds. Just behind here is the so-called **Sun–Moon Buddha**, flanked with images of a peacock and a hare (symbolizing the sun and moon respectively), while immediately behind that image stands a small square **Commemorative column** inscribed in Burmese, English, French and Russian and honouring the student leaders of the 1920 revolt (see p.340).

Continuing around the terrace, the exceptionally florid **Rakhaing Tazaung** (or Arakan Pavilion) was commissioned by a pair of wealthy Rakhine merchant brothers and houses a huge reclining Buddha almost 10m long, plus miniature sculptures showing the founding of the Kyaitktiyo temple.

Between the western and northern staircases

A **Kassapa Buddha** image (see box, p.71) stands in a shrine opposite the top of the western stairs. Just past the western staircase, a shiny-bright shrine with dazzling glass mosaic pillars houses a replica of the **Buddha's Tooth** (a copy of the original, held in Kandy's Temple of the Tooth in Sri Lanka). Diagonally opposite, on the base of the stupa, is a small golden statue of **King Okkalapa**, the ruler who is said to have helped establish the original Shwedagon Pagoda back in 588 BC, while behind the Buddha's Tooth pavilion a **museum** houses items gifted to the pagoda over the years.

Continuing around the terrace, a pavilion on the northwest side of the stupa holds the superbly decorated bronze **Bell of King Singu** (also known as the Maha Ganda Bell), commissioned by King Singu in 1778, weighing almost 25 tonnes and standing over 3m tall. An attempt by the British to steal the bell backfired when the boat carrying it sank in the Ayeyarwady; it was subsequently rescued and restored by the Burmese.

The large area of open terrace directly in front of the bell pavilion is known variously as the "**Auspicious Ground**" or "**Wish-fulfilling Place**" and is said to be particularly favourable for the granting of boons – hence the locals who can usually be found praying here. Behind here is the huge seated **Chanthargyi Buddha**, the temple's largest, and the small gilded **Shinsawbu Buddha** (to the left of the Chanthargyi Buddha),

1

donated by Queen Shinsawbu (see p.70) herself. A small **photo gallery** next to the Chanthargyi Buddha has some interesting shots of the pagoda including close-ups of details (including the extravagant *hti*) impossible to see with the naked eye.

Further around is the eye-catching **Sacred Hair Relic Washing Well** (signed "Hsandawtwin" [Hair Relic Well]), an odd-looking green and blue shrine with glass mosaic inlay, built in 1879 over the site of the spring in which the Buddha's eight hairs are said to have been washed before being enshrined in the pagoda.

Between the northern and eastern staircases

The terrace on the northern side of the stupa is much larger than on others, covered in a dense and disorienting maze of shrines. Facing the northern stairs, the shrine at the base of the stupa houses an image of the historical Buddha, **Gautama**. Diagonally opposite is the unusual **Mahabodhi Pagoda**, a garish parody of the great Mahabodhi Stupa at Bodhgaya in North India, looking as incongruous amid the surrounding Burmese architecture as a panda at a bishop's convention. Past here, and dominating the northeast corner of the terrace, is the brilliantly gilded **Naungdawgyi** ("Elder Brother") **Pagoda**, like a miniature of the main stupa, said to mark the spot where the eight hair relics were first stored.

A further sequence of revered images can be found close to the Mahabodhi Pagoda. These include the **Shin Izzagona Buddha** (signed "Shin Issa Gawna's Buddha Image" and flanked by images of holy men) and – in a colourfully painted little wooden shrine in front of the Boe Boe Aung Buddha – the small, golden and rather Chinese-looking **Pyidawpyan Buddha** (signed "Pyidaw Pyan Returned Buddha Image"), given back to the Shwedagon after having been removed to England in colonial times, and now protected by stout bars. Close by is **King Tharyarwady's Bell** (aka the Maha Tithaddha Gandha), cast in 1841 and even more massive than King Singu's bell, with a weight of 42 tonnes, a height of 2.6m and a diameter (at its mouth) of 3.3m.

Near the top of the eastern stairs is the celebrated **Dhammazedi Inscription**, erected by King Dhammazedi in 1485 and cataloguing the history of the pagoda in three languages (Burmese, Mon and Pali) on a trio of huge stone slabs.

Between the eastern and southern staircases

An image of the third of the four present-era Buddhas, **Kakusandha**, occupies the shrine opposite the top of the eastern stairs. Past here it's worth hunting out the tricky-to-find but exceptionally finely costumed **Padashin Buddha** (signed "Magic Ruby Enshrined Buddha Image"), just in front of the bridge to the southern lift.

Almost back at the southern staircase, set against the base of the stupa just past the Tuesday Planetary Post, is the **Child-clutching Brahma** (signed "Child holding Brahma Image"), showing the Indian god holding an infant and popular with devotees hoping to have children of their own. Directly opposite, a glass case holds a solid-gold miniature **Replica of the Shwedagon**.

Maha Wizaya Pagoda

မဟာဝိဇယစေတီ • Corner of Shwe Dagon Pagoda and U Htaung Bo roads • Daily 6am–9pm • Free

Built in 1980, the **Maha Wizaya Pagoda** was officially constructed to commemorate the unification of all Theravada orders in Burma, although unofficially it stands as a monument to its creator, military ruler Ne Win (not to mention the king and queen of Nepal, who also contributed various Buddhist relics). Sitting virtually in the shadow of the Shwedagon, from the outside the Maha Wizaya Pagoda looks like a modest miniature sister of its huge neighbour. Inside the hollow stupa it's a completely different story, with a bizarre interior done up to look like a miniature forest with a night sky above, decorated with myriad symbolic animals and other objects.

1

Martyrs' Mausoleum

အာဇာနည်ဗိမာန် • Ar Zar St (entrance roughly opposite the bottom of the Shwedagon Pagoda's northern staircase) • Daily 8am–5pm • K3000

The striking **Martyrs' Mausoleum**, immediately north of the Shwedagon Pagoda, is a vaguely Soviet-looking mausoleum-cum-monument shaped rather like a skateboarding ramp, painted bright red and decorated with a single white five-pointed star (the same as appears on the national flag, symbolizing the union of Myanmar). The mausoleum holds the remains of General Aung San and the eight cabinet ministers assassinated alongside him in 1947 at the city's Secretariat (see p.63), as well as his spouse, Khin Kyit, and the graves of Queen Supayalat, wife of Burma's last king, Thibaw, and former UN Secretary-General U Thant. The original mausoleum was largely destroyed in a 1983 bomb blast carried out by North Korean agents in an attempt to assassinate South Korean president Chun Doo-hwan during a visit to the mausoleum – the president escaped, but 21 others were killed in the explosion. The monument was subsequently rebuilt but kept closed to the public until 2013 for fear that it would serve as a rallying point for pro-democracy campaigners thanks to its association with General Aung San and his family.

Yangon Zoological Gardens

ရန်ကုန် တိရိစ္ဆာန် ဥယျာဉ် • There are three entrances to the gardens: the Southern Gate, at the junction of Zoological Garden and Bo Min Khaung roads; the Northern Gate (off Lake Rd); and the Museum Gate (at the junction of Upper Pansodan and Bo Min Khaung roads) • Daily 6am–7pm • $2

Yangon's old-fashioned **Zoological Gardens** (opened in 1906) aren't exactly state of the art but, equally, aren't as bad as some Asian zoos. The fact that many of the animals formerly held here have now been moved to the new zoo in Naypyitaw (see p.178) means that overcrowding isn't a problem, although the handful of tigers which remain are still confined within wretchedly small pens, and the monkey cages are pretty medieval too. Otherwise it's a pleasant place, with a good range of fauna scattered around attractive wooded parkland, even if there are rather more free-range crows on view than any other sort of wildlife. Star exhibits include a red panda, a white tiger, white rhinos, black bears and the unusual binturong (bear-cat). Visitors are also allowed to feed some of the animals (including elephants, bears, hippos and monkeys) with selected foods bought next to the pens in question (sugar cane for the elephants, for example). Needless to say, such unregulated feeding runs contrary to all good zoological and veterinary practice, although it does at least save the zoo the cost and bother of feeding the animals itself.

Kandawgyi Lake

ကန်တော်ကြီး • Boardwalk $2 for foreigners

Much of the area immediately east of the Shwedagon Pagoda and north of Yangon Zoo is occupied by the attractive **Kandawgyi Lake**, a crinkly-edged expanse of water wrapped up in attractively landscaped gardens and surrounded by some of the city's prime real estate. The "Great Royal Lake" (as the name translates) was created by the British using water channelled from Inya Lake – it's around 8km in circumference, but not much more than 1m deep at any point. The best views of the water are from Yeik Thar Road on its southern side, either from an attractive boardwalk or from the adjacent public road (which the government generously allows overseas visitors to use free of charge, although there's an ugly fence between you and the lake).

FROM TOP KANDAWGYI LAKE; RECLINING BUDDHA, CHAUK HTAT GYI PAGODA (P.76) >

1

Karaweik Palace

ကရဝိက်နန်းတော်

Impossible to miss on the east side of the lake is the striking **Karaweik Palace**, a chintzy pagoda-style hall built in 1974 and set on a pair of barges pointing out into the water, each with the head of an enormous karaweik (a mythical bird famous for its melodious song) on its prow. The design echoes the *pyigyimun*, or royal barge, commonly used for ceremonial purposes by Burmese monarchs of the past. It's a nice place to watch the sun set over Shwedagon, while the lavish interior now houses a restaurant staging a touristy nightly dinner buffet-cum-cultural show (see p.92).

Chauk Htat Gyi Pagoda

ခြောက်ထပ်ကြီးဘုရား • Shwegone Rd • Daily 6am–8pm • Free

Even in a land of big Buddhas, the giant reclining figure at the **Chauk Htat Gyi Pagoda** (also spelt "Kyauk Htat Gyi") is an unquestionable show-stopper: almost 66m long, with a 7.3m-long face, 2.7m worth of nose, and 50cm-high eyes. The figure was begun in 1959 but not completed until 1974 (there's a photo of it, labelled "Wingaba, Rangoon", in front of the reclining image). The name of the pagoda, meaning "Six-storey Pagoda", refers to this impressively huge but now-vanished seated statue – the present reclining figure being more of a three- or four-storey affair.

Housed within a huge corrugated iron shed propped up on glass mosaic columns, the Buddha has a delicate, rather feminine-looking face complete with blue eye shadow and supersized eyelashes (each 33cm long). A stylish little bindi, diamond-encrusted crown and golden robes decorated with glass mosaics complete the look, while the soles of the image's huge feet are covered in auspicious golden markings. A gilded statue of the ubiquitous Shin Upagot (see p.356) sits in a small shrine opposite the feet.

Nga Htat Gyi Pagoda

ငါးထပ်ကြီးဘုရား • Shwegone Rd (turn right out of the Chauk Htat Gyi Pagoda, head down Shwegone Rd for 100m then go left through the arch signed "Nat Htat Gyi Paya" and down this side road for 100m, then head up the covered staircase on your right) • Free, although a donation (in US$) may be requested

The **Nga Htat Gyi Pagoda** ("Five-storey Pagoda") is home to another of Yangon's supersized Buddhas – not quite the equal of the nearby Chauk Htat Gyi in size at a mere 9m high, although the super-intricate, hyperactive decoration makes the Chauk Htat Gyi Buddha look positively boring in comparison. Seated in the earth-witness mudra, the figure – one of the country's most flamboyant images – brushes the ground lightly with enormous pink fingernails and sports riotously decorated golden robes plus a jewel-encrusted crown, the whole thing set against a magnificent wooden backdrop.

Northern Yangon

The featureless suburbs of **northern Yangon** straggle all the way up to the airport and beyond. None is of any particular interest, although they are dotted with a few further Buddhist monuments including the fanciful **Kaba Aye Pagoda** and the grand **Lawka Chantha Abhaya Labha Muni Buddha** statue, the latter easily combined with a trip to the suburb of Insein on the city's popular **Circle Line** railway. **Inya Lake**, **Myanma Gems Museum** and **Kabe Aye Pagoda** can easily be seen together as a single day-trip; a taxi out from downtown should cost around K5000.

Inya Lake and around

အင်းယားကန်

Centrepiece of northern Yangon is the extensive **Inya Lake** (formerly Lake Victoria), created by the British in 1883 to provide water for the city. It's now one of the city's favourite pleasure-spots with attractive (and free) lakeside walkways along its eastern and western sides, usually busy with couples smooching under umbrellas.

The area around the lake is home to some of Yangon's premier real estate, particularly along **University Avenue**, on the south side of the lake. Here, at no. 54, you'll find the **house of Aung San Suu Kyi**, where Myanmar's most famous dissident was kept under house arrest for fifteen years, although there's not much to see apart from the large walled compound topped with metal spikes, razor wire, many National League for Democracy flags and a photo of General Aung San over the main gate. Further down the road is the former home of Aung San Suu Kyi's long-term adversary Ne Win, who lived here until his death in 2002.

Myanma Gems Museum

မြန်မာကျောက်မျက်ရတနာပြတိုက် • Third floor, 66 Kaba Aye Pagoda Rd • Tues–Sun 9.30am–4pm • K5000 • No photography

If you want to fully understand Myanmar's incredible mineral wealth, the government-run **Myanma Gems Museum** offers a good introduction (shame about the rip-off entry fee). Start off with the fun illuminated map which helps you locate where everything comes from at the press of a button, then explore the miniature royal regalia (modelled after that in the National Museum, complete with a tiny replica of the Lion Throne). There are also plenty of other gems and artefacts, some of considerable beauty, others veering into tat. Myanmar's ubiquitous jade is very much in evidence, with exhibits including assorted jade teapots, dinner services, various animals, a diminutive General Aung San and a pair of similarly minuscule golfers. You'll also see huge pearls, rubies, sapphires, lots of cut and uncut stones and intricate jewellery – look out for the lovely sapphire peacock, a miniature harp made of jade and jewels, and a chintzy "flowering gem tree".

If you fancy shopping for some precious stones of your own, the three floors of shops below the museum, comprising the **Myanma Gems Mart** (see p.93), are a good place to start.

Kaba Aye Pagoda

ကမ္ဘာအေးစေတီ • Kaba Aye Pagoda Rd • 9km north of downtown (roughly $5 by taxi) • Daily 6am–9pm • Free

The cartoonish **Kabe Aye Pagoda** (meaning "World Peace Pagoda" and pronounced *k'bah AY* with the stress on the last syllable, pronounced like the letter "A") is one of the first great landmarks of independent Myanmar, commissioned by U Nu and completed in 1952 in time for the Sixth Buddhist Synod of 1954–56 (celebrating the 2500th anniversary of the Buddha's enlightenment). The first prime minister of independent Myanmar, U Nu was also a devout Buddhist who succeeded in having Buddhism declared the official state religion of Myanmar in 1961, complete with a ban on the slaughtering of cows – although just a year later Ne Win reversed the ruling and, despite the country's militant Buddhist leanings, there is still no official state religion.

Shop-lined stairs (including a number of palmists) lead up to the unusual stupa (measuring precisely 34m high and 34m around the base). The odd, chintzy-looking pagoda comprises a relatively small stupa-spire above and a circular shrine below, with (unusually) five entrances rather than the customary four in order to accommodate an additional shrine to the future Buddha Maitreya (see box, p.71). Inside, five large seated Buddhas face each of the five doors, with statues of the 28 previous Buddhas seated around the huge central column. At the very centre of the pagoda, a small shrine, protected by bank-vault-style doors, houses a further, splendidly costumed, silver Buddha and numerous other precious artefacts donated to the temple.

1

Mahapasana Guha

မဟာပါသာဏလှိုင်ဂူ သိမ်တော်ကြီး • Kaba Aye Pagoda Rd • Daily 6am–9pm • Free

Built at the same time as the adjacent Kaba Aye Pagoda, the **Mahapasana Guha** ("Great Stone Cave") was constructed to host meetings of the Sixth Buddhist Synod in 1954, during which 2500 monks descended on the cave to recite the entire Tripitaka in Pali. The Mahapasana Guha is a modern remake of the Sattapannin Cave in India, where the First Buddhist Synod was held shortly after the Buddha's death. From the outside it resembles a huge rocky hillock; inside, the "cave" is actually just a huge conference hall, capable of holding up to ten thousand people, supported on six enormous pillars and with a single small illuminated Buddha flashing crazily on a shelf at the far end.

Insein

အင်းစိန်

Several of northern Yangon's most interesting attractions are clustered in the northern suburb of **Insein** – home of the city's notorious Insein Prison – and easily visited in combination with a partial circumnavigation of the city's Circle Line (see box opposite).

Kyauk Daw Kyi Pagoda

ကျောက်တော်ကြီးဘုရား • Min Dhamma Rd • Daily 6am–9pm • Free

Insein's major attraction is the **Kyauk Daw Kyi Pagoda** (pronounced "Chow *daw* gee", with the final syllable said like the letter "g"), home to the revered **Lawka Chantha Abhaya Labha Muni Buddha**, an 11m-high seated Buddha carved from a single gigantic piece of marble discovered near Mandalay in 1999. The military, always keen to deflect attention from their repressive regime by spectacular acts of religious merit-making, commissioned the statue and had the 500-tonne image conveyed with great ceremony to Yangon by barge and a specially constructed railway track – murals showing the transfer and arrival of the image can be seen over the two sets of staircases leading up to the statue, with assorted generals very much to the fore. The image is fine enough, although not as impressive as others in Yangon, while the glass case it's encased in makes it frustratingly difficult to see.

Hsin Hpyu Daw Elephant Park

ဆင်ဖြူတော်ဥယျာဉ် • Min Dhamma Rd (turn left out of the Kyauk Daw Kyi Pagoda and walk down the road for about 3min; the park – no sign – is on the opposite side of the road) • Daily 9am–5pm • Free

A companion piece to the nearby Kyauk Daw Kyi Pagoda, and offering further subtle propaganda on behalf of the ruling military, the **Hsin Hpyu Daw Elephant Park** is home to a trio of rare white elephants (plus a normal grey elephant) discovered in Rakhine State and brought to Yangon in 2001–02. White elephants are traditionally regarded as a symbol of good fortune and prosperity in Myanmar and the junta has been keen to collect as many as possible – further specimens can be found at the Uppatasanti Pagoda in Naypyitaw (see p.177). So-called "white" elephants are actually albinos and not really white at all, but rather a pale reddish-brown (or pink when wet). This may be regarded as lucky for their military owners, but has proved less so for the poor elephants themselves, who now find themselves miserably chained up for the greater part of every day in a small pavilion.

INSEIN ORIENTATION

To reach the places listed under Insein on foot, go straight ahead out of Insein Station, ignoring a couple of large roads left and right and continuing straight on down the leafy little Insein Butaryon Road until you hit the junction with Lanthit Road, where you'll find the **Arlein Ngar Sint Pagoda** (just over 1km from the station). Continue right down Lanthit Road and straight on at the junction with Pyay Road after a further 250m, then right again down Min Dhamma Road shortly afterwards, where you'll see the **Kyauk Daw Kyi Pagoda** rising on its hillock ahead.

THE CIRCLE LINE

A popular excursion with many visitors, the **Circle Line** – or the **Yangon Circular Railway** as it's officially known – describes a huge loop around the city, running for 46km and stopping at 39 stations on the way. Admittedly, it's not the world's most exciting rail journey, although the train's slow, ambling pace, with glimpses of house backs, gardens and trackside life en route, is pleasant enough, and makes a change from yet more pagodas. The complete circuit takes around three hours, which is probably a bit long for most tastes. A good plan is to ride the train as far as Insein (1hr) then hop off to explore local attractions (see opposite).

PRACTICALITIES

Circle Line trains leave Yangon Central Railway Station from platforms 6 and 7 (where there's also an office from where you buy tickets). There are currently fourteen services daily (nine travelling clockwise, five anticlockwise), running at irregular intervals between 6.10am and 5.10pm – it's a good idea to check latest times the day before travel. There are three types of train: busy local services and fancier "special" and a/c services; foreigners pay a flat fee of $1 for a ticket valid all day. Note that if you're not completing the full circuit you'll need to produce your passport when buying a train ticket back to central Yangon, which also involves the sort of form-filling normally associated with visa applications – an entertaining or maddening insight into Burmese bureaucracy, depending on whether you're about to miss your train or not.

Arlein Ngar Sint Pagoda

အာလိန်ငါးဆင့်ဘုရား • Lanthit Rd • Daily 6am–9pm • Free

A short walk from Insein station, the **Arlein Ngar Sint Pagoda** is well worth a look, and easily combined with a visit to the Kyauk Daw Kyi Pagoda. This is without doubt one of Yangon's kookiest temples, particularly the strange central shrine, topped with what looks like a large pineapple and surrounded by a miniature maze arranged around dozens of little golden pavilions. A large, green, rather Chinese-looking pagoda-tower stands behind, guarded by pairs of horses, tigers and elephants.

Around Yangon

Despite the city's size, it's surprisingly easy to get out of Yangon (assuming you don't head north through the endless suburban sprawl). The quickest escape is by hopping on the ferry south over the Yangon River to **Dalah**, from where you can continue to the pottery and temple town of **Twante**, with perhaps a visit to the weird **Snake Temple** en route. Heading east, the oil-based boomtown of **Thanlyin** is home to another fine temple, while the gorgeous **Ye Le Pagoda**, memorably islanded in the middle of a lake, is also close by.

Dalah

ဒလ • Ferry $2 one way • Boats depart every 20min from the Pansodan St Jetty (at the end of Pansodan St); the crossing takes 10min

On the far side of the Yangon (Hlaing) River, the tumbledown little village of **DALAH** offers a truly surreal contrast between the crowded streets of downtown on the one side and the rural landscapes of the Delta on the other. The ten-minute ferry ride is an experience in itself, usually packed with both passengers and hawkers and offering fine views of Yangon's waterfront. You'll probably be approached on the boat itself with offers of onward transport to Twante. There's not much to Dalah itself, although the flyblown little market and dusty streets offer an interesting snapshot of rural life in the Delta, seemingly a million miles away from the densely packed buildings of the city rising just over the river.

Twante

တွံတေး • Horribly crowded and uncomfortable pick-ups (K1000; 1hr) run between Dalah and Twante, leaving when full; alternatively, a motorbike taxi will cost in the region of K6000, a taxi around K8000

For an instant taste of small-town rural life in the Burmese Delta (see p.96), within an hour of downtown Yangon, **TWANTE** is the place to go. Twante is known within Myanmar for its cotton-weaving and, especially, as a major **pottery centre**, with workshops scattered all over town, including the well-known Oh-Bo Pottery Sheds – most workshops are happy for visitors to drop in and have a look around at the workshops' pottery wheels, kilns and great stacks of bowls. The town was badly damaged by Cyclone Nargis in 2008 but has largely been patched up now.

Shwesandaw Pagoda

ရွှေဆံတော်စေတီ • 1km southwest of the centre along the Dalah Rd • K2000

Twante's main attraction is the fine **Shwesandaw Pagoda**, dating back to the eleventh century and one of four identically named temples scattered around the country (the others being at Taungoo, Pyay and Bagan), each of which enshrines a hair relic of the Buddha.

Entered via a broad flight of steps on its southern side, the temple is centred around a 76m-high Shwedagon-style stupa, gilded above but rather crudely gold-painted below. Numerous shrines dot the terrace, including fine glass-mosaic shrines at the stupa's south, north and west sides, and with an unusually impressive crop of Buddhas in both marble and bronze.

Baungdawgyoke Pagoda (Snake Temple)

ဗောင်းတော်ချုပ် (မြွေဘုရား) • 6km east of Twante • Daily 8am–8pm • Free

Local motorbike taxi drivers in both Twante and Dalah will also probably try to get you on the back of their bike for a trip to the **Baungdawgyoke Pagoda**, commonly described as the **"Snake Temple"**, just east of Twante. An interesting alternative to your usual Burmese pagoda, the temple comprises a small shrine in the middle of a square lake, connected to the shore by four long wooden walkways. The real surprise is inside, however, where a couple of dozen huge (but harmless) Burmese pythons roam, sliding around Buddhas and dangling from windows. The snakes are cared for by the temple's nuns, who consider them holy – not so surprisingly, given that they're one of the world's five largest snake species, with an average length approaching 4m.

Thanlyin and around

သန်လျင်မြို့ • 15km southeast of Yangon • K35 by taxi

Southeast of Yangon, across the confluence of the Yangon and Bago rivers, the city of **THANLYIN** (formerly known as "Syriam") has been one of Myanmar's principal ports for centuries, pre-dating the much younger city over the water. The town first rose to prominence in the fifteenth century and was controlled successively by the kingdoms of Hanthawaddy and Taungoo before (in 1599) falling to a Rakhine attack led by Portuguese soldier-of-fortune **Filipe de Brito e Nicote**. Appointed the city's new governor, de Brito subsequently declared independence from his Rakhine masters, ruling over Thanlyin until he was overthrown by soldiers from Taungoo in 1613. De Brito was executed by impalement, a gruesome punishment reserved for those who had defiled Buddhist shrines.

Kyaik Khauk Pagoda

ကျိုက်ခေါက်စေတီ • Kyaik Khauk Pagoda Rd • Daily 6am–9pm

The imposing **Kyaik Khauk Pagoda**, on a small hill on the southern side of town, has fine views over the Yangon River. The current stupa is thought to date back to around 1300 and is claimed to enshrine two Buddha hair relics. It's an impressive structure in generic Shwedagon style, with the usual large gilded stupa on an octagonal base.

Ye Le Pagoda

ရေလယ်ဘုရား: • Kyauktan, 15km south of Thanlyin • Daily 6am–8pm • $2 • Boat crossing $5

South of Thanlyin in the town of **KYAUKTAN** is the superb **Ye Le Pagoda**, built on an island in Hmaw Wun Creek and appearing to float miraculously in the water. The pagoda's elaborate collection of shrines includes structures dedicated to Shin Upagot, a moustachioed, white-turbaned Bo Bo Gyi, and a marble Buddha seated on an extraordinarily detailed golden Lion Throne-style affair, while you can also buy food to offer to the catfish that splash around the temple. Unfortunately, the fees levied on foreigners for entrance and the thirty-second boat crossing to the temple are a complete rip-off.

Taukkyan War Cemetery

 တောက်ကြံစစ်သချိုင်း: • Bago Rd, Taukkyan, 15km north of Yangon airport (take any bus heading towards Bago) • Daily 7–11am & 1–4.30pm • Free

North of Yangon, in the town of **TAUKKYAN**, the immaculately maintained **Taukkyan War Cemetery** (the largest of three such sites in Myanmar) provides a moving and sombre monument to the many thousands of Allied and Commonwealth soldiers (including large numbers from India and Africa) who lost their lives fighting the Japanese in Burma and Assam during World War II. There are 6374 named soldiers buried here, with a further 867 graves containing unidentified bodies, as well as the cemetery's Rangoon Memorial, inscribed with the names of 27,000 further soldiers whose bodies were never recovered.

ARRIVAL AND DEPARTURE

YANGON

BY PLANE

Yangon's airport (ⓦygnia.com) is around 15km north of downtown Yangon, with separate domestic and international terminals right next door to one another. You'll find a couple of ATMs as you exit the building, plus several moneychangers offering identical rates.

Transport to/from the city A taxi into town costs a fixed K7000 if booked through the taxi counter in the international terminal, or K8000 at the domestic terminal; alternatively, you can probably negotiate a slightly cheaper fare with one of the freelance drivers outside. The journey to downtown usually takes around 45min, although it can be considerably longer during rush hours. Bus #51 (K200; 1–2 hourly; 1hr) runs into downtown; the stop is close to the terminals – turn left out of the airport building and head along the road outside (600m from the international terminal, 250m from the domestic terminal) and look for the bus stop where the road curves around. Alternatively, more frequent services can be found by turning right out of the international terminal; walk down the airport approach road for 1.3km to reach the junction with Pyay Rd, take a right and then cross the road to catch a southbound bus. Buses back to the airport (K200; 1–2 hourly; 1hr) leave from one block south of Sule Paya.

Airlines Air Bagan, 56 Shwe Taung Gyar St, Bahan (ⓣ01 513422); Air China, *Yangon International Hotel*, cnr Pyay and Kaba Aye Pagoda roads (ⓣ01 655882); Air KBZ, cnr Bank St and Mahabandoola Garden St, Kyauktada (ⓣ01 373766); Air Mandalay, 146 Dhammazedi Rd, Bahan (ⓣ01 525488); Asian Wings, 34 Shwe Taung Kyar St,

Bahan (ⓣ01 516654); Golden Myanmar Airlines, Ground Floor, Sayar San Plaza, New University Ave, Bahan (ⓣ01 533272); Malaysia Airlines, 335/337 Bogyoke Aung San Rd, next to *Central Hotel* (ⓣ01 241007); Myanmar Airways International, Sakura Tower, 339 Bogyoke Aung San Rd (ⓣ01 255260); Qatar Airways, Room 345, *Parkroyal Yangon Hotel*, 33 Alan Pya Phaya Rd (ⓣ01 250 388 ext. 8345); Thai Airways, Sakura Tower, 339 Bogyoke Aung San Rd, Kyauktada (ⓣ01 255499); Yangon Airways, 166, Level 5, MMB Tower, Upper Pansodan Rd, Mingalar Taung Nyunt (ⓣ01 383100).

Destinations Bagan (4 daily; 1hr 20min); Daweil (1 daily; 1hr); Nyaungshwe (4–5 daily; 1hr 15min); Kalaw (4–5 daily; 1hr 15min); Kawthaung (3 daily; 3hr); Lashio (1 daily; 1hr 45min–3hr); Mandalay (19 daily; 50min–2hr 5min); Mawlamyine (2 weekly; 30min); Myeik (daily; 2hr); Myitykyina (7 weekly; 2hr 20min); Naypyitaw (5 daily; 1hr); Ngapali (5 daily; 40min); Sittwe (6 daily; 1hr 20min); Tachileik (5 weekly; 1hr 35min).

BY BUS

Most buses to and from Yangon arrive/depart from one of the city's two enormous bus stations: Hlaing Thar Yar terminal, in the northwest of the city, which is the starting point for buses to the Delta; and Aung Mingalar terminal in the city's north, which is where most other services depart. Both terminals are around 20km from the centre – the journey to either can take anything from 40min to over an hour depending on traffic, so allow plenty of time. Most companies also require you to check

1

in for your bus half an hour beforehand. Given how large both terminals are, make sure your taxi driver takes you to the relevant bus office. Failing this you'll have to put yourself in the hands of one of the touts working the terminals, who will expect a tip in return for walking you to your bus. A taxi to either terminal from downtown should cost around K8000–10,000; arriving in Yangon you'll have to bargain hard to get a reasonable fare since the cab drivers who work the terminal are (by Yangon standards) an unusually rapacious and pushy bunch – you might be asked $15 or more for the ride downtown. Special bus #43 (and other slower services) runs from Sule Pagoda to Aung Mingalar terminal and there are also local services to Hlaing Thar Yar.

Tickets Many guesthouses and travel agents (see opposite) can book bus tickets for you for a small commission. Alternatively, you can save yourself a dollar or two by booking directly at the cluster of bus company offices just north of the railway station.

Destinations from Aung Mingalar Bagan (10 daily; 10hr); Bago (6 daily; 2hr); Dawei (11 daily; 12hr); Hpa-An (6 daily; 7hr 30min); Hsipaw (3 daily; 16hr); Kalaw (at least 5 daily; 10hr); Kinpun for Kyaiktiyo (7 daily; 5hr); Kyaukme (1 daily; 15hr); Lashio (2 daily; 18hr); Magwe (1 daily; 12hr); Mandalay (frequent; 8–10hr); Mawlamyine (5 daily; 7hr); Meiktila (6 daily; 7–10hr); Mrauk U (1–2 daily; 30hr); Myeik (11 daily; 22hr); Naypyitaw (10 daily; 6hr); Ngapali (2 daily; 16hr); Nyaungshwe (at least 5 daily; 12–14hr); Pyay (6 daily; 6–7hr); Pyin Oo Lwin (daily; 12hr); Sagaing (1 daily; 11hr); Shwenyaung for Inle Lake (1 daily; 11hr); Sittwe (1 daily; 30hr); Taungoo (4 daily; 5hr); Thaton (3 daily; 7–8hr).

Destinations from Hlaing Thar Yar Chaung Tha (2–4 daily; 6hr); Ngwe Saung (2 daily; 6hr); Pathein (4 daily; 5hr).

BY TRAIN

Yangon Central Railway Station is just north of downtown. The entrance is on the north side of the station, although there's a clever little short cut down to platform 6 (for the Circle Line) from the flyover at the top of Pansodan St. **Tickets** for inter-city journeys must be booked in advance at the (surprisingly easy to miss) Myanmar Railways Booking Office on Bogyoke Aung San Rd (daily 7am–3pm). Unfortunately, everything is in Burmese and staff don't speak much English, which can make getting information a bit tricky (timetables are also posted in the lobby of the railway station itself). Tickets must be paid for in kyat, not dollars.

Destinations Bagan (1 daily; 19hr); Bago (10 daily; 2hr); Dawei (daily; 25hr); Kyaikhto for Kyaiktiyo (3 daily; 5hr); Magwe (1 daily; 12hr) Mandalay (3 daily; 15–16hr); Mawlamyine (3 daily; 9hr 30min); Naypyitaw (3 daily; 9–10hr); Pyay (1 daily; 8hr 30min); Shwenyaung (1 daily; 27hr); Taungoo (3 daily; 7hr); Thanbyuzayat (1 daily; 12hr 15min); Thaton (3 daily; 7–8hr); Thazi (3 daily; 12hr).

BY BOAT

The old government slow-boat from Yangon across the Delta to Pathein was once one of Myanmar's classic journeys, although at the time of writing they were running only as far as Myaungmya (2 weekly at 4pm; 22hr; deck $7, cabin $35) with buses (K1500) making the final 1hr journey to Pathein; there are rumours that the entire service will be discontinued due to falling demand and improved road transport. If running, boats depart from Lan Thit jetty, 2.5km west of the *Strand Hotel* on Strand Rd; check at the IWT office (see below) or the tourist office (see opposite) for the latest information. **Tickets** are available from the IWT office at the jetty – it's in Building 63 (no sign) next to Building 64 (signed), on the right-hand side of the main road into the port area.

GETTING AROUND

Despite its size, Yangon is reasonably easy to get around. **Downtown** is relatively compact, making it possible to walk between most of the major sights, although narrow pavements and dense crowds can make for painfully slow going in the very centre. **Outside the centre**, distances between attractions are significantly longer, although there are plenty of inexpensive taxis available. Note that motorbikes and tuk-tuks have been banned from the city centre, meaning that traffic in the city, while often dense, is generally relatively orderly by Burmese standards.

By taxi The easiest way to get around Yangon is by catching one of the city's plentiful taxis (mostly white Toyota Corollas; all clearly identified by the yellow "TAXI" sign on their roofs). None are metered, although the city's drivers are a generally honest and helpful bunch – unless arriving at one of the city bus stations (see p.81) – and you'll most likely be offered a fair price without the need for strenuous bargaining (although of course it pays to haggle if you feel you're being asked for a fare that's over the odds, and, equally, you should *always* agree a fare being setting off). Fares are generally a bargain: around $2 for a trip around downtown, for example; $2–3 from downtown to

the Shwedagon; $5–6 from downtown up to the Kaba Aye Pagoda; and $7–8 out to the airport. Booking a taxi through your accommodation is the easiest way to get hold of a cab and get a fair fare, although they can also be flagged down on the street. If you get stuck, there are usually plenty of empty vehicles hanging out at the front of Bogyoke Market, or try in front of the *Sule Shangri-La Hotel*.

By train The city's famous Circle Line (see box, p.79) is worth taking just for the fun of the ride, and also offers a cheap and convenient way of reaching Insein (see p.78).

By bus The heart of the city's extensive bus network is the eastern side of Sule Pagoda roundabout, downtown,

CABBIES OF CONSCIENCE

For an interesting alternative to your average Yangon taxi, consider hiring one of the cabs run by the **Golden Harp Taxi Service** (☎09 7304 0615 or ☎09 4490 04810), established in 2010 by three former political prisoners – Shell, Bobo and Talky (their prison nicknames) – looking to earn a living after regaining their freedom. The taxi service now offers former prisoners of conscience the micro-finance needed to establish themselves as city cab drivers, while visitors using their services get the opportunity to meet some of those involved at the sharp end of the pro-democracy struggles of recent years.

although buses are of minimal use to casual visitors – routes are difficult to work out and vehicles are signed and numbered in Burmese only.

By cycle rickshaw Cycle rickshaws are still fairly common throughout the city and, although not particularly fast, offer a pleasant respite from slogging along crowded downtown streets as well as the chance to experience a quintessential but rapidly vanishing slice of old Asian life. Count on around K500–1000 for a short journey around downtown.

TRAVEL AGENTS AND TOUR OPERATORS

There are plenty of travel agents around town, and many guesthouses can also arrange bus and plane tickets, as well as taxis and simple sightseeing tours.

AIR TICKETS

Most travel agents can arrange plane tickets, although the two following places are particularly well set up for organizing air travel.

Danna Moe Air Ticket Centre Next to City Hotel, Bogyoke Aung San Rd ☎01 383655.

May Flower Travels and Tours 240 Pansodan Rd ☎01 377495, ⓦmayflower-travels.com.

BUS AND OTHER TRAVEL ARRANGEMENTS

Delta Travels 33rd St (next door to Beautyland II Hotel).

Global Myanmar Glory 256/257 Upper Mahabandoola Garden St ☎01 389769.

Min Thaw Khant Travels & Tours 179–181 Botahtaung Pagoda Rd ☎01 397880, ✉mtkhant.ygn@gmail.com.

Tay Thi Yar Travels and Tours 256 Mahabandoola Garden St ☎01 375009.

TOUR OPERATORS

Exotissimo 47 Shwegonedaing St, Bahan ☎01 8604933. Yangon HQ of leading Asia specialists (see p.25).

Good News Travels Room 18, Building no. 204, Yanshin Rd, East Yankin ☎09 511 6256, ⓦmyanmargoodnewstravel.com.

Myanmar Delight 899 Kyaung Lane, Insein Township ☎01 651833, ⓦmyanmardelight.com.

Myanmar Shalom 70 31st St ☎01 252814, ⓦmyanmarshalom.com.

Santa Maria Travels & Tours 2nd Floor, 233–235 32nd St ☎01 256178, ⓦmyanmartravels.com.

Seven Diamond Express Cnr of U Wi Zar Ya & Dhammazedi Rd, Kamaryut Township ⓦsevendiamondtravels.com.

Tango Tour & Trek Ground Floor, 62 19th St ☎01 382394, ⓦtangotours.webs.com.

INFORMATION

Tourist information The official MTT tourist office (signed "Information Service"; ☎01 252859; daily 8.30am–5.30pm) is on the eastern side of Mahabandoola Gardens at 122 Mahabandoola Rd. Staff here are helpful and informative, although they don't book transport or accommodation, issue permits, or in fact do anything apart from provide info.

Online ⓦyangonite.com and ⓦmyanmore.com/yangon both have good listings of upcoming events around the

YANGON RIVER CRUISES

Sunset cruises along the Yangon River are offered by several local operators, departing from Botataung Jetty, on the river close to the Botataung Pagoda.

Royal Green River (ⓦroyalgreenriver.com) run sunset cruises on Fridays (5pm; $25 including snack and drink) and weekend dinner cruises (Sat & Sun 5.30pm; $30 including buffet).

RV King Whale Sunset cruises (Fri–Tues 4.30pm; $20; ☎09 520 0747, ⓦyangonrivercruise.com); morning and general sightseeing cruises can also be arranged on request.

1

city, plus plenty of reviews, articles and other info. Myanmore also publish a leaflet, the *Weekly Guide to* *Yangon*, with details of upcoming events, sporadically available from hotels and other outlets around the city.

ACCOMMODATION

As you'd expect, there's a good spread of accommodation in Yangon, from backpacker guesthouses to five-star palaces – although few bargains. The overall shortage of accommodation means that places can get booked solid days or weeks in advance; reserve as far ahead as you can whenever possible. The downtown area is where you'll find almost all the city's **budget** accommodation, as well as many **mid-range** places (although very few upmarket options). Staying here has the obvious benefit of putting you right in the thick of things, although pressure of space means that rooms can be smaller, while cheaper places often lack windows and are located up many flights of stairs. Most of the city's more **upmarket** options are found scattered around the city's modern suburbs north of downtown; the majority are cast in the generic international five-star mould and singularly lacking in character, although there are a few honourable exceptions including a trio of fine old colonial piles: the *Strand*, *Savoy*, and *Governor's Residence*. All the places listed have a/c, free wi-fi and include breakfast in their rates unless otherwise stated.

DOWNTOWN
BUDGET
Beautyland Hotel II 188/192 33rd St ☎01 240054, ✉beautylandtwo@gmail.com; map p.60. Enjoyably time-warped guesthouse, with good service and plenty of old-time atmosphere (if you don't mind the weird electrics, erratic hot water and plastic undersheets). Rooms are small, although some have windows, and there's a nice first-floor lounge and breakfast restaurant. Overpriced at current rates, however. $45

★**Chan Myaye Guest House** 256 Mahabandoola Garden St ☎01 380855 or ☎01 382022, ✉chanmyaye .gh@gmail.com; map p.60. Excellent new guesthouse right in the thick of the downtown action with super-friendly and very professional service and ultra-competitive rates. Rooms are bright, modern and relatively spacious (some en suite with hot water and some sharing unusually clean and spacious bathrooms; more expensive ones have balconies and windows). Excellent single rates too ($20, or $18 with shared bath), plus two state-of-the-art dorms with single and double ($20) beds, all of which are individually curtained and come with their own a/c units and plug sockets. Rooms are spread between the fourth and seventh floors (no lift). Dorm $14, double $28

Cherry Guesthouse 278/300 Mahabandoola Garden St ☎01 255946 or ☎09 534 0623, ✉cherry.gesthouse @gmail.com; map p.60. One of Yangon's better budget options, on the fourth and fifth floors of a characteristically tall and skinny downtown building, with the bonus of an (oversubscribed) lift. The largely windowless tiled rooms (all en suite; hot water $3 extra) are small but spotlessly clean, and service is friendly and professional. $27

Garden Guest House 441–445 Mahabandoola St ☎01 253779; map p.60. You'll not get more central than this old favourite, right next to Sule Pagoda. Rooms resemble wooden boxes and are a bit shabby but comfortable enough; all are en suite (although with cold water only in cheaper rooms) and rates are competitive. $18

Hninn Si Budget Inn 213–15 Botataung Pagoda Rd ☎01 299941, ⊛hninnsibudgetinn.com; map p.60. Neat, clean and quiet little guesthouse (entrance upstairs on the first floor next to some seriously impressive plumbing). Rooms (all sharing a clean and spacious common cold-water bathroom) are boxy and windowless, and relatively pricey for what you get, but OK for a night or two. $25

Mahabandoola Guest House 453/459 Mahabandoola St ☎01 248104; map p.60. Very basic, but as cheap as it gets in Yangon (and with singles for just $6). Accommodation is in tiny cubicle rooms (with a/c) – shabby but reasonably clean, and all sharing a grubby bathroom. No breakfast. $12

Mayfair Inn 57 38th St ☎01 253454, ✉inn@myanmar .com.mm or ✉maytinmg@gmail.com; map p.60. Long-running guesthouse in a quiet side street in the heart of Yangon's finest colonial district. Scores highly for its homely atmosphere, peaceful location and spacious tiled rooms (all en suite; hot water $5 extra), although lousy service (don't expect reservations to be honoured or emails answered) spoils what would otherwise be one of the city's top budget choices. No breakfast. $25

★**Motherland Inn II** 433 Lower Pazundaung Rd ☎01 291343, ⊛myanmarmotherlandinn.com; map p.68. Downtown Yangon's best budget option – if you don't mind the inconvenient location a 20min walk (or short taxi ride) from the centre. Rooms are unusually large, bright and peaceful, and there's a well-equipped internet café, free airport pick-up for international arrivals (plus free morning and afternoon airport bus shuttles), and an excellent range of travel services, including efficient bus and plane ticketing. The cosy little in-house restaurant serves up good food, and rates include an excellent breakfast, either Western or Burmese – order the night before for *mohinga*, *onnoth khawk hswe* (noodles with coconut milk gravy) or *nan gyi thoke* (thick noodle salad). $30

Ocean Pearl 125 Botataung Pagoda Rd ☎01 297007, ⊛oceanpearlinn.com; map p.60. Long-running guesthouse, a decade or two past its best, although rooms (all en suite; a few with windows) are bigger than average and kept spotlessly clean. Friendly and efficient staff, and they also offer free airport pick-up – a major bonus. **$30**

Okinawa Guesthouse 64 32nd St ☎01 374318; map p.60. Unusual-looking place with a distinct touch of Japanese style in its minimalist wooden rooms with hardly any furniture and mattresses on the floor under big mosquito nets. A characterful, if not especially comfortable, option, and very gloomy lighting and pricier than it should be. They run a second place, the *Okinawa Guesthouse 2*, just down the road with similar rooms at similar rates. **$26**

Tadar Guest House 278 Mahabandoola Garden St ☎01 255649; map p.60. There's not much ta-dah! about the *Tadar*, but it does OK if the adjacent *Chan Myae* and *Cherry* are both full. All rooms have a/c, but bathrooms are cold water only and breakfast isn't included in the, admittedly quite low, rates. Cheaper rooms share a nice clean communal bathroom. **$16**

Three Seasons Hotel 83–85 52nd St ☎01 901 0066, ✉threeseasonshotel7@gmail.com; map p.60. One of Yangon's most appealing guesthouses (not a hotel, whatever the name says) in a characterful wood-panelled house full of old-fashioned character and with a charming proprietress. Rates are a bit higher than elsewhere, although standards are too, with good-sized rooms all with a/c, hot water and a window. **$35**

White House Hotel 69–71 Konzaydan St ☎01 240780, ✉whitehouse.mm@gmail.com; map p.60. Cheerful Chinese-owned place with friendly service and quirky mosaic decor – it feels like being inside an enormous seashell. Rooms (all en suite with hot water; pricier ones give you a window as well) are smallish and rather minimally furnished – those with fan only are significantly better value than those with a/c ($35). **$22**

MID-RANGE AND EXPENSIVE

Aung Tha Pyay Hotel 38th St ☎01 378663, ✉aungthapyayhotel.com; map p.60. Dated but comfortable mid-range place in an attractive old colonial building. Rooms are bigger than in many other similar hotels and well equipped with tea-and-coffee-making facilities, fridge and flatscreen TV, while the location on a very central but relatively quiet side-street is good too. **$65**

Central Hotel 335–37 Bogyoke Aung San Rd ☎01 241001, ✉central.ygn@mptmail.net.mm; map p.60. Long-running three-star (popular with visiting Chinese), dowdy and dated but in a good location and at a very reasonable price. Rooms are frumpy but spacious and well equipped with tea-and-coffee-making facilities, flatscreen TV and minibar; those on higher floors also have good city views. **$80**

Clover Hotel City Center 217 32nd St ☎01 377720, ✉info@clovercitycenter.asia; map p.60. Tucked away

behind the *Sule Shangri-La Hotel*, this small hotel makes the most of a very cramped location, with eight floors of slightly capsule-like but surprisingly chic rooms, with pure-white minimalist decor and mod cons including TV, safe, fridge and in-room wi-fi. **$75**

Hotel Grand United (Chinatown) 621 Mahabandoola Rd (on corner of Bo Ywe St; reception on 4th floor) ☎01 372257, ✉grandunited.chinatown@gmail.com; map p.60. Decent mid-range option in the middle of Chinatown – slightly better (albeit a bit pricier) than other choices in this category, with small but neatly furnished modern rooms equipped with minibar, tea-and-coffee-making facilities and flatscreen TV; superior rooms ($10 extra) have good bird's-eye views of the streets below. **$80**

Loft Hotel 33 Yaw Min Gyi St ☎01 372299, ✉theloftyangon.com; map p.60. This funky new boutique hotel has brought a dash of style to Yangon's downtown accommodation options, with loft-style decor featuring lots of hardwood floors and brick walls, with splashes of white and red. Rooms are stylishly kitted out with white linen, pink armchairs and cool contemporary furniture and artworks, and well equipped with writing desks and big flatscreen TVs. **$180**

MK Hotel 1 Wut Kyaung St ☎01 297274, ✉mkhotelyangon.com; map p.60. Above-average mid-range option at a competitive price. Rooms are well equipped with an eclectic mishmash of furniture alongside a fridge, kettle, writing desk, hairdryer and in-room wi-fi. Less dated and drab than many other places in this price range, complemented by friendly, efficient service. **$65**

Orchid Hotel City Hall 169–71 Mahabandoola Garden St ☎01 370920, ✉orchidhotelcityhall.ygn.myanmar @gmail.com; map p.60. Efficient mid-range place tucked away behind City Hall in a very central but relatively quiet location. Rooms are a bit dated but a decent size and pleasantly furnished – some also come with minuscule balconies. The competitive rates currently make this one of the best deals in this price range in town. **$60**

Parkroyal 33 Alan Pya Phaya Rd ☎01 250388, ✉parkroyalhotels.com; map p.60. One of Yangon's swankiest five stars, in a conveniently central location and with a host of facilities including pool, spa, gym, sauna and a trio of restaurants (international, Chinese, Japanese). Rooms are kitted out in generic five-star plush style – comfortable if characterless – and rates are good value compared to other similar places in town. **$215**

Strand Hotel 92 Strand Rd ☎01 243377, ✉hotel thestrand.com; map p.60. Yangon's finest old colonial pile (see p.63), still going strong after a century in business and with plenty of atmosphere, although overzealous restorations have robbed the place of some of its old-world character, and parts of the hotel don't look very different to any of the city's modern five-star hotels. The 31 huge,

1

high-ceilinged suites are nicely furnished although the faux-colonial decor borders on bland – disappointing, especially given the price tag. Facilities include a pair of restaurants (see p.88), a popular bar (see p.91) and spa – but no pool. **$490**

Sule Shangri-La (formerly the Traders Hotel) 223 Sule Pagoda Rd ☎01 242828, ⊕shangri-la.com; map p.60. Swanky five-star in a prime central location between Sule Pagoda and Bogyoke Market. Accommodation is in spacious if rather unexciting rooms with all the usual mod cons, and facilities include two decent restaurants (see p.88), the pleasant *Gallery Bar* (see p.91), and an upstairs outdoor pool, all backed up by the city's smoothest service. **$250**

OUT OF THE CENTRE

★**Alamanda Inn** 60b Shwe Taung Gyar Rd ☎01 534513, ⊕hotel-alamanda.com; map p.68. Compared to most of Yangon's humdrum accommodation offerings, this place is a real find, occupying a homely colonial-style villa set amid lush gardens in the exclusive Golden Valley area – all very peaceful, and feeling a long way from the hubbub of the city centre. The spacious, old-fashioned rooms are nicely kitted out with colonial-style furniture and the occasional artwork – a little worn around the edges but full of character and charm. There's also an excellent restaurant (see p.89) in the garden out the front. A taxi from here to Sule Pagoda costs around K4000. **$100**

Classique Inn 53b Shwe Taung Kyar St (Golden Valley Rd) ☎01 525557, ⊕classique-inn.com; map p.68. Guesthouse-style accommodation in an attractive modern villa in the smart Golden Valley suburb, with eight stylishly furnished rooms with wooden floors and crisp white linen (plus another three in the adjacent family house). A taxi from here to Sule Pagoda costs around K4000. **$80**

Governor's Residence 35 Taw Win Rd ☎01 229860, ⊕belmond.com/governors-residence-yangon; map p.68. An oasis of calm in one of Yangon's most superior suburbs, occupying a lovely old 1920s two-storey mansion with wrap-around wooden balconies, gorgeous gardens and plenty of period charm. The 49 spacious suite-size rooms are attractively decorated in colonial style with teak and silk furnishings, while facilities include a pair of good (though pricey) restaurants (see p.90) plus a spa and a big fan-shaped garden pool. Rates are seriously steep, although special offers and low-season discounts can

sometimes reduce prices by a third or more. **$550**

Inya Lake Hotel 37 Kaba Aye Pagoda Rd ☎01 9662866, ⊕inyalakehotel.com; map p.68. Huge grounds and a fine setting on Inya Lake make this place feel more like a country resort than an uptown hotel – an impression unfortunately spoilt by the ugly, vaguely submarine-shaped hotel building itself, resembling a badly converted multistorey car park. Rooms are arranged along possibly Myanmar's longest corridor (complete with squeaky parquet), functionally furnished in bland and dated international generic with all the mod cons. Surprisingly few rooms have lake views, although there's a nice waterside bar and a large lakeside pool. **$180**

Kandawgyi Palace Hotel Kan Yeik Tha Rd ☎01 249255, ⊕kandawgyipalace-hotel.com; map p.68. This long-running tour-party favourite (now owned by notorious government crony Tay Za) isn't very politically correct but is also one of Yangon's best upmarket options, in an attractive location by Kandawgyi Lake. Built around the old Rangoon Rowing Club of 1934, the hotel's handsome traditional architecture, palm-filled gardens and the Shwedagon views are a pleasure. Rooms are full of attractive Burmese touches, and the excellent facilities include good French and Chinese restaurants plus a beautiful waterfront pool and spa. **$265**

★**Savoy** 129 Dhammazedi Rd ☎01 526289, ⊕savoy-myanmar.com; map p.68. The third of Yangon's trio of old colonial hotels: less grand than the *Strand*, less luxurious than the *Governor's Residence*, but with more genuine old-world character than either. Unassuming from the outside, the interior has heaps of charm, with a pair of fine restaurants (see p.90), the cosy *Captain's Bar* (see p.91), plus a spa, a neat little garden pool with loungers, and gorgeous rooms, beautifully furnished with faux-colonial wooden and rattan furnishing. Pricey in high season, but good low-season discounts ($200). **$350**

Summit Parkview 350 Ahlone Rd ☎01 211888, ⊕summityangon.com; map p.68. Run-of-the-mill four star in a rather shabby concrete block attempting (and failing) to hide behind fancy wooden pagoda-style porticoes. Rooms are spacious and well furnished, if bland; some at the front have fine views of the Shwedagon. Facilities include pool and gym, and it's very handy for the Shwedagon and National Museum, while there are several passable restaurants nearby, plus plenty of nightlife at the neighbouring *Yangon International Hotel*. **$225**

EATING

Yangon's eating scene offers a striking reflection of the country's years of isolation, with a surprising lack of Western-style cafés and restaurants for a place of well over four million people. This is one of the few cities of its size in Asia where you'll find not a single *McDonald's* or *Starbucks* (although local fast-food chains and modern cafés are beginning to spread through the city) – instead, most Yangonites still eat on the streets, perched on tiny plastic chairs amid the endless **food stalls** which mushroom on many of downtown's pavements, especially after dark. Eating your way around some of the city's food stalls remains Yangon's quintessential foodie experience (if you don't mind the dodgy hygiene), while there are

COFFEE SHOPS

Yangon's **café culture** still remains firmly rooted in the traditional tea shop, although there's also a burgeoning number of modern coffee shops springing up around the city, not to mention the upmarket *Strand Café* (see p.88) in the landmark *Strand Hotel*, proud purveyor of the country's finest afternoon tea.

365 Café Thammada Hotel ☎01 243047; map p.60. Cool contemporary café, serving up good coffee plus a big menu of reasonably priced (mains mostly K4000–5000) pan-Asian food, plus pasta and steaks. Daily 9am–10pm.

Bar Boon Bogyoke Aung San Rd; map p.60. This chic urban "Dutch Deli & Espressobar" (as it calls itself) is as smart as it gets in Yangon, with indoor seating plus an outdoor terrace overlooking busy Bogyoke Aung San Rd. The coffee's not bad (although not cheap either at around K3000 per cup), and there's

also a short menu of light meals (baguettes, soups and salads; K5000–7000), plus assorted cakes. Daily 8am–9pm.

Parisian Cake & Coffee 132 Sule Pagoda Rd ☎01 387298; map p.60. This lively place is what you get if you cross a French patisserie with a slightly raucous Burmese teashop. The coffee's pretty good, and there are also fancy cakes (K1200–1500), ice cream and fruit juices. Popular with Yangon's bright young things. Daily 7am–10pm.

also plenty of little local noodle cafés and *mohinga* joints for cheap eats and local colour. More upscale venues remain thin on the ground, although a rash of recent new openings (including *Gecko* and the *Union Bar and Grill*) suggests that Yangon is finally beginning to catch up with other, more cosmopolitan, Asian destinations.

DOWNTOWN

★**50th Street** 50th St ☎01 397060, ⍟50thstreet yangon.com; map p.60. The most enjoyable of downtown Yangon's small handful of upscale Western venues, looking a bit like a superior European pub, with a lively bar area downstairs and slightly more sedate restaurant seating upstairs. The excellent (though pricey; most mains K9000–12,000) food includes top-notch pizzas, pasta, burgers and sandwiches, plus some slightly cheaper salads and Asian-style tapas (K4500–8500) and seriously pricey Australian steaks (K29,000–33,000). There's also a good drinks list (25 percent off during the daily 3–7pm happy hour), a pool table and regular live music. Daily 10am–3/4am.

★**999 Shan Noodle Shop** 130B 34th St ☎01 389363; map p.60. Shoebox café serving up some of the best Shan noodles in town at rock-bottom prices along with assorted other noodle soups, salads and stir-fries. Mains K1000–1500. No beer. Daily 6am–7pm.

Anaimo 300 Mahabandoola Garden Rd ☎01 378022, ⍟facebook.com/anaimo.yangon; map p.60. Cosy and very cheerful little restaurant with bright modern decor and a decent range of authentic and well-prepared Japanese food (mains around K5000) – maki, noodles, teriyaki dishes and so on, plus big, good-value set meals (K6500–7500). Mon–Fri 11.30am–2pm & 5.30–10.30pm, Sat 5.30–10.30pm.

Aung Mingalar Shan 34 Boyarnyunt St, on the corner of Nawady St ☎01 385185; map p.60. One of the best known of Yangon's many Shan noodle joints, serving up a good range of noodle soups and salads, plus

dumplings, tofu and claypot dishes. Mains K1500–2000. Daily 7am–9pm.

Bharat Restaurant Mahabandoola St, between 38th and 39th St; map p.60. No-frills local restaurant offering an enjoyable and authentic taste of India in the middle of downtown Yangon. The South Indian thali-style set meals (veg K1500, meat K2500, including free refills) are tasty and good value, and there are also smaller meals and snacks including masala dosas, vadais and potato curry served with a chapati or puri. Classic subcontinental sweets like *Mysore pak* and *gulab jamun* are also on offer. Daily 6.30am–8.30pm.

★**Bogyoke Market Food Court** West side of Bogyoke Market, behind Bambi Hot and Cold Drink; map p.60. A great place to refuel during a shopping expedition into Bogyoke Market, this little covered courtyard of colourful cafés looks like a real slice of Burmese life, with the various resident chefs dishing up simple fried noodles, rice dishes and curries (around K1500–2000). Most places have English menus, although few show prices – check before you order. It's also a good place for an iced coffee or fresh juice, with unusual beverages including freshly squeezed avocado, plum and black seaweed. Tues–Sun 10am–5pm.

Danuphyu Daw Saw Yi 175–177 29th St ☎01 248 977; map p.60. Neat little no-frills restaurant popular both with locals and tourists wanting a taste of authentic Yangon food life. There's no menu – food is laid out behind the counter and the helpful staff will talk you through what's available, which might include anything from simple chicken and veg dishes through to butterfish and lobster. Food is good, although prices are above

1

average – expect to spend around K4000 for a main course plus rice, soup and veg side dish. Daily 10am–9pm.

East East Hotel, 234–240 Sule Pagoda Rd ☎ 09 7313 5311; map p.60. Smart hotel restaurant – zero atmosphere, but a comfortable retreat if you fancy a break from the streets. The wide-ranging menu (most mains around $6) features plenty of Asian classics – pad thai, nasi goreng, various Malaysian and Chinese options – as well as pizzas, pasta, burgers, salads and soups, and they also do a decent Myanmar curry. Daily 11am–9.30pm.

★Gecko 535 Merchant St, between 37th and Pansodan sts ☎ 01 286986; map p.60. This swanky new restaurant deserves a bouquet for having restored and reinvigorated a section of the magnificent but dilapidated old Sofaer Building (see p.62). It also serves up some of the best food in town, with excellently prepared pan-Asian dishes, mainly Japanese, with a couple of Korean and Indonesian options; expect okonomiyaki, kimchi rolls, chicken tonkatsu, spicy Korean beef and ramen tonkatsu. Pricey (mains K11,000–13,000) but worth it. Daily 9am–midnight.

Ingyin New South Indian Food Centre Corner Bo Sun Pat and Anawratha; map p.60. Lively little place dishing up good, cheap South Indian food. Choose from veg, chicken, mutton, prawn, fish and crab curries served with puri or chapati; they also do a good dosa. Mains K1200–2000 – and they'll keep on topping up your plate until you can eat no more. Daily 5am–10pm.

Kosan 108 19th St ☎ 01 503232, ⊕ facebook.com /kosan.myanmar; map p.60. One of the liveliest of 19th St's bustling restaurants, and also one of the few serving food other than Burmese or Chinese, with an eclectic selection of burgers, kebabs, quasi-Mexican and Japanese – the sesame shabu chicken is a treat. Most mains around K2500. A good place just for a drink, too, with cheap beer and bargain cocktails (K1700–1800). Daily noon–midnight.

LinkAge 1st floor, 221 Mahabandoola Garden Rd – above Audionet near the south end of the block, almost on Anawrahta Rd; follow stairs signed up to SNA Gallery ☎ 09 4305 2916; map p.60. Tucked away inside a neat little art gallery, this place is easy to miss, but well worth seeking out for its good, reasonably priced Burmese food including lots of Myanmar-style fish and seafood curries, salads and soups – the green papaya and pickled mango salad is a treat. Most mains K1500–2500. Daily 11am–10pm.

Lotaya Bogyoke Market (turn right out of the principal exit at the back of the main market building); map p.60. This unpretentious little café provides a useful pit stop behind Bogyoke Market, attracting a mixed tourist and local crowd. Shan noodles are the speciality, with assorted Thai and Chinese dishes thrown in for good measure (mains K2000–3500). Tues–Sun 9am–5pm.

★Lucky Seven 130 49 St ☎ 01 292382; map p.60. If you want to know what a traditional Burmese teashop looks like, this is the place to come, packed most hours of the day with a lively local crowd enjoying tea, noodles and buns. The big picture menu is full of good things (mains K5000–1500) – an excellent breakfast *mohinga*, noodles and dumplings galore, Indian-style curries with puris or parathas, spare ribs and tasty samosa salads. Seating is either inside or on the pretty little outdoor terrace smothered in plants. Daily 6am–8pm.

★Monsoon 85–87 Theinbyu Rd ☎ 01 295224; map p.60. One of downtown's smartest and most attractive restaurants, in a high-ceilinged old colonial building with fans twirling overhead. There's a good selection of Western food available, but it's *Monsoon's* Southeast Asian cuisine which really hogs the limelight, with oodles of Thai, Lao, Vietnamese and Cambodian dishes plus excellent Burmese food – try the Ayeyarwady butterfish, or the "Bachelor's curry" with chicken and gourd (mains K6000–8000). Good drinks list too, with half-price cocktails during happy hour (daily 5–7pm). Daily 10am–10.30pm.

Nang Htike Bogyoke Aung San Rd, between 46th and 47th sts; map p.60. No-frills restaurant serving up decent Shan noodles (K1000), plus various other noodle and rice dishes, with seating either in the cramped interior or on the pavement outside. Handy if you're staying in the area, but not worth a special trip otherwise. Daily 7am–11pm.

Nilar Biryani Anawratha Rd; map p.60. Bright, busy and cheerfully scruffy modern café with giant curry-filled tubs set out along the front. As the name suggests, this place does one thing – biryani – but does it very well, with chicken, mutton and veg options (K1900–2200) served in big, inexpensive portions, and the meat slow-cooked to perfection (although served with a positively foul Burmese-style soup rather than the Indian-style sauce). Also has a big selection of juices, lassis and ice cream, but no beer. Daily 10am–10pm.

Nooch 387/397 Upper Shwe Bonthar Rd ☎ 01 378166, ⊕ noochbar.com; map p.60. Cheery café-style restaurant with chirpy lime-green decor and a good range of pan-Asian dishes (mains around K5000), particularly Thai. Daily 11am–11pm.

Strand Hotel 92 Strand Rd ☎ 01 243377, ⊕ hotelthestrand.com; map p.60. Old-world-style dining in Yangon's most famous colonial hotel (see p.63). Afternoon tea in the *Strand Café* (served either European- or Burmese-style; 2.30–5pm; $20) is everlastingly popular, and they also do a range of international mains ($15–20) including an upmarket take on traditional *mohinga*. Alternatively, there's European-style fine dining in the posh *Strand Grill* with a short menu of fish and meat mains ($24–46). Strand Café daily 7am–10.30pm; Strand Grill daily 6.30–10.30pm.

Sule Shangri-La 223 Sule Pagoda Rd ☎ 01 242828; map p.60. The restaurants at this plush hotel offer an upmarket alternative to local café and street dining. Downstairs, the bright *Café Sule* serves up classy buffets (lunch $22, dinner $30) plus a big selection of à la carte European and Asian mains (around $10). Upstairs, the *Summer Palace* restaurant specializes in pan-Chinese fine dining (mains $10–13), including lavish dim sum. Café Sule daily 6–10am, 11.30am–2.30pm & 6.30–10pm; Summer Palace daily 11am–2.30pm & 5.30–10pm.

Suzuki 182 Sule Pagoda Rd ☎01 392686; map p.60. A popular backpacker hangout, this long, skinny café squeezed in along Sule Paya Rd serves up a reasonable selection of Thai and Chinese food (mains K3000–5000) – nothing fancy, but tasty enough, and reasonably priced, with cheery foreigner-friendly service, cheapish beer and decent coffee thrown in for good measure. Daily 9am–10pm.

Thone Pan Hla 454 Mahabandoola Rd; map p.60. Archetypal local Yangon teahouse, good for breakfast *mohinga* (available until around 10am; K400) and other affordable standards like Shan noodles (K700). Daily 6am–7pm.

Union Bar and Grill 42 Strand Rd ☎09 3101 8272, ⓦunionyangon.com; map p.60. This buzzing new bistro has added some welcome pizzazz to Yangon's moribund Strand Rd. The funky interior has plenty of urban chic (the clientele just as much as the decor) while the mainly Western menu serves up good pizza, pasta, burgers, sandwiches and fish and chips (most mains K11,000–13,000) plus more expensive seafood and steaks. Daily 10am to midnight.

OUT OF THE CENTRE

Alamanda Inn 60b Shwe Taung Gyar Rd ☎01 534513, ⓦhotel-alamanda.com; map p.68. Idyllic restaurant

---

YANGON STREET FOOD

Large parts of downtown Yangon often resemble an enormous outdoor café, especially after dark, when every available piece of pavement seems to fill up with **food stalls** and crowds of locals perched around low-slung tables on tiny child-sized plastic chairs. Burmese curries and noodles are ubiquitous, while hotpot (*kyay-oh*) is another local favourite, with diners seated around vats of bubbling water in which they cook their own slivers of meat and vegetables. Also worth seeking out is the local *samusa thote* – slices of samosa served in a minty salad. Food stalls are often interleaved with market stalls piled high with vegetables and colourful tropical fruit, plus mobile vendors sitting behind enormous mangling machines selling glasses of freshly crushed cane sugar – a popular local beverage.

The most popular street-food experience among tourists is on **19th Street** in Chinatown where you can snack to your heart's content on everything from pig's ears and glutinous sausages to chicken wings, crunchy tofu and lots of seafood. Most of the pavement venues here are actually extensions of the various cafés lining the road rather than proper food stalls, although the grub is excellent and the beer's cheap and plentiful (unlike the city's traditional food stalls, which only serve tea and soft drinks). The cafés here now spill out into Mahabandoola Road, which is lined with further food stalls and market stands offering up some of the city's more outlandish foodstuffs – including deep-fried locusts, deep-fried snakes, severed duck heads and assorted pieces of pig.

Elsewhere in the city, **Anawrahta Road** is arguably the king of food streets, particularly around the junction with Sule Pagoda Road (which also boasts dozens of food stalls after dark in the area north of the pagoda – the cluster of stalls outside *Takafuji* (see p.91) serve up a good spread of local curries and are well used to dealing with blundering foreigners). The sections of Anawrahta Road around the Sri Devi and Sri Kali temples also boast stalls selling Indian nibbles including the inevitable samosas and other deep-fried snacks, as well as shops loaded with traditional Indian sweets, including *rasmalai*, *jalebi* and *gulab jamun*. A few places (such as *Shwe Bali*, on Anawrahta Road just west of Sule Pagoda) also sell delicious lassis, while elsewhere you might find another classic subcontinental cocktail, falooda – a kind of fluorescent milky concoction loaded with bits of fruit and jelly.

One major caveat applies, however: **hygiene**. A study in early 2014 revealed that over a third of food tested from Yangon street stalls contained *Staphylococcus aureus* and *Bacillus cereus* bacteria, both of which can lead to food poisoning (and a quarter of the samples contained these bacteria in dangerously high levels). Choosing busy stalls where food appears to be hot and freshly prepared may help reduce risks, as does patronizing stalls where vendors use plastic gloves rather than scooping food up with their bare hands. The major underlying factors – utensils washed in dirty water and poor food hygiene and storage – are more difficult to spot, however. You may prefer to save your street food sampling for the end of your trip, meaning that if you do get ill, it at least won't wreck your holiday.

1

attached to one of Yangon's most appealing small hotels (see p.86), set beneath a sweeping pavilion in the garden in front. Food features a good selection of light meals and snacks – sandwiches, salads, crepes and baguettes (K2500–6500) – plus European steaks, meat and fish mains, and (surprisingly) a selection of tagines and couscous (most mains K8000–10,000). Daily 6.30am–9.30pm.

★ **Feel Myanmar Food** 124 Pyihtaungsu Avenue St ⊕09 7320 8132, ⍟feelrestaurant.com; map p.68. Plenty of Yangonites vote this the city's best place to sample Burmese food, as proven by the queues which form most lunchtimes and evenings outside its doors – arrive early or expect to wait (and don't come at all if you're looking for a quiet romantic meal). The restaurant occupies an attractive bamboo-lined, jungle hut-style construction, with food laid out in a big buffet spread at the back – the helpful, English-speaking staff will guide you around and explain what's on offer, typically including all sorts of Burmese veg and meat curries, quite delicately spiced. Expect to pay around K5000 for one dish plus vegetables, soup and rice. Daily 6.30am–8am.

Golden Happy Hot Pot 18 Ko Min Ko Chin Rd ⊕01 559339; map p.68. A fun, authentically Burmese eating experience, and handy for a meal before or after a visit to Shwedagon Pagoda. Help yourself to what you want from the colour-coded dishes (K800–1800 each) in the fridges at the back and then take it to your seat where you cook it yourself in the little steaming hotpots with which each table is provided – staff are on hand if you need assistance. Daily 10.30am–10.30pm.

House of Memories 290 U Wizara Rd (on a small side road just past the Edo Zushi restaurant) ⊕01 534242, ⍟houseofmemoriesmyanmar.com; map p.68. A real taste of colonial Yangon, set in a chintzy old half-timbered house (once home to the office of General Aung San) and with an interior last updated in around 1930. There's good Myanmar food – including chicken *chet* curry, beef yoghurt curry with raisins, prawn and coconut curry (mains K5750–8000) – plus some Thai and Chinese options, and a pianist tinkles the ivories every Fri and Sat evenings. Daily 11am–11pm.

Kipling's Savoy Hotel 129 Dhammazedi Rd ⊕01 526289; map p.68. Appealing colonial-style restaurant in the lovely old *Savoy Hotel* (see p.86) with plenty of white linen and wickerwork chairs, plus views of nearby Shwedagon and seating either inside or on the pool-facing terrace. The resident French chef rustles up a mix of Western and Myanmar cuisine (mains $12–15), backed up by a good drinks list and wine selection, all at relatively affordable prices. Daily 6–10.30pm.

Le Planteur 22 Kaba Aye Pagoda Rd ⊕01 541997, ⍟leplanteur.net; map p.68. Generally considered Yangon's top foodie destination, this beautiful fine-dining garden restaurant combines French finesse with strong

Asian influences under the leadership of Michelin-starred chef Felix Eppisser. It's pricey, even by European standards (mains $28–43; six-course set menu $78), although the business lunch ($30) offers a more affordable alternative. There's also a huge (mainly French) wine list, with bottles from around $30. Daily noon–2pm & 6–11pm.

L'Opera 62d U Htun Nyein St ⊕01 665516, ⍟operayangon@gmail.com; map p.68. Idyllic little backstreet restaurant, with Italian owner and chef providing Yangon's best Italian food either in the attractive a/c dining room or on a gorgeous lakeside terrace outside. Pasta and pizza go for $11–16, with meat and fish mains double that. It's also a nice spot to have just a drink. Reservations recommended. Daily 11am–2pm & 6–10.30pm.

Mandalay Governor's Residence, 35 Taw Win Rd ⊕01 229860; map p.68. Set on the ground floor and terrace of the beautiful *Governor's Residence* (see p.86), this is one of the city's most alluring (and expensive) restaurants, using top-notch local ingredients to serve up fine international cuisine (mains $30–50) – Chilean sea bass, filet mignon and the signature Ngapali lobster – plus cheaper sandwiches, burgers and lunchtime mains ($23–28). Noon to 2.30pm & 6–10.30pm.

Myanmar Curry Table Governor's Residence, 35 Taw Win Rd ⊕01 229860; map p.68. A slightly cheaper alternative to the fancy *Mandalay* downstairs, on a beautiful first-floor veranda, offering a daily evening buffet ($48 including beer and soft drinks) that features excellent Myanmar cuisine freshly cooked for you on the spot. Daily 6–10pm.

Padonmar 105/107 Kha Yae Bin Rd ⊕01 538895, ⍟myanmar-restaurantpadonmar.com; map p.68. Another of Yangon's time-warped restaurants, set in an atmospheric old colonial house and serving a huge selection of Myanmar and Thai food (mains K5000–9000) both classic and more offbeat – banana bud salad, Inle tofu curry and so on. Handy for the National Museum, but can get busy with tour parties. Daily 11am–11pm.

Sabai @ DMZ Mya Kyun Tha Park (opposite the Sedona Hotel), Kaba Aye Pagoda Rd ⊕01 8605178; map p.68. One of Yangon's better Thai restaurants, in an eye-catching two-storey glass box cantilevered out over Inya Lake. The wide-ranging menu features good, authentic Thai food (mains K5000–6000) plus a good vegetarian selection too (K3500). Daily 11am–2pm & 5–9.30pm.

Singapore's Kitchen 330 Ahlone Rd ⊕09 7301 6788; map p.68. Cheerful if not especially cheap Asian restaurant handy for the National Museum and the nearby clubs at the *Yangon International Hotel* (with late-opening hours to match). The huge picture menu features all sorts of mainly Chinese food, plus a few dishes from Myanmar, Singapore, Thailand, Malaysia and Hong Kong. Cheaper fried rice and noodle dishes go for around K3500, although most mains are around K5500. Daily 10am–3am.

SELF-CATERING

For self-catering and food shopping, try **Market Place by City Mart** (daily 9am–9pm), a well-stocked little supermarket with imported goods, a bakery and a deli in the basement of the FMI Centre (Parkson Building; go in between the escalators) on Bogyoke Aung San Road. **City Mart** is the main city supermarket, with branches across Yangon including a big branch on Gyo Phyu Street (near the Aung San Stadium and bus company ticket offices just north of the centre) plus smaller downtown branches on Anawrahta Road (east of the centre near the *Lucky Seven* teashop), and at the junction of Mahabandoola Road and Pongyi Street west of the centre. **Ruby Mart** (daily 9am–9pm), at the junction of Bogyoke Aung San Road and Pansodan Street is conveniently central, but utterly manic.

DRINKING AND NIGHTLIFE

There's a distinct lack of Western-style **pubs** and **bars** in Yangon, and although there are a fair number of local cafés-cum-beer stations they tend to get packed, and aren't always the nicest places for a quiet tipple. If you want to drink with off-duty Yangonites the best plan is to head out to **19th Street** in Chinatown, lined with cafés and food stalls all serving up cheap beer, and with a permanent party atmosphere. Yangon's nightlife is getting livelier, but still has a long way to go before it's anything close to that of somewhere like Bangkok. Check ⓦyanmore.com and ⓦyangonnite.com for events listings. With a few exceptions, **nightclubs** in Yangon tend to involve little dancing; many have nightly "fashion shows" (in which fully clothed young women walk up and down on a stage) or karaoke. You may encounter sexpat-oriented prostitution in some places, but it's low-key compared to many other large cities in the region. The major hub for Western-style nightlife is the compound at the Yangon International Hotel (ⓦhoteljapanyangon.com) on Ahlone Rd, which is where you'll find two of the city's better clubs, the *Flamingo Bar* and *Pioneer Music Bar* (see p.92), as well as a couple of other modern Western-style bars and the slightly sleazy *MBOX* karaoke joint.

BARS

50th Street 50th St ☎01 397060, ⓦ50thstreetyangon.com; map p.60. This lively pub-restaurant (see p.87) is as good for a drink as it is for food, with a big drinks list (25 percent off during the daily 3–7pm happy hour), pool table and regular live music. A bottle of Myanmar Beer costs K4000. Daily 10am–3/4am.

Captain's Bar Savoy Hotel, 129 Dhammazedi Rd ☎01 526289; map p.68. Yangon's nicest colonial-style bar, in its most characterful old hotel, with an extensive drinks list and live piano music some evenings. Daily 10.30am–1am.

Gallery Bar Sule Shangri-La Hotel, 223 Sule Pagoda Rd ☎01 242828; map p.60. A pleasant retreat in the heart of Yangon – lacking any particular character besides the usual five-star bland, admittedly, but does the job after a hard day pounding pavements and pagodas, with a pool table, live sports on TV and a daily two-for-one happy hour (5–8pm) during which drinks become surprisingly affordable (two glasses of beer for K3000, for example). They also do decent bar meals (around $7–9) if you're in for the long haul. The hotel also boasts a small upstairs pool bar if the *Gallery* doesn't appeal. Daily 1pm–1am.

Kosan 108 19th St ☎01 503232; map p.60. This popular little restaurant (see p.88) is also a good place for a drink, serving up bargain beer (big bottles cost just K1400) alongside cheap mojitos (K800) and cocktails (K1800). Daily noon–midnight.

Sky Bistro 20th floor, Sakura Tower, 339 Bogyoke Aung San Rd ☎01 255277; map p.60. This bistro bar atop the Sakura Tower has all the atmosphere of an airport lounge but compensates with stunning city views through wraparound floor-to-ceiling windows, with the Shwedagon Pagoda magnificently floodlit after dark. There's an extensive but expensive drinks list (draught beer K2500, glass of wine K5000) with prices slightly discounted during the daily 6–9pm happy hour. Daily 9am–10.30pm.

Strand Bar Strand Hotel, 92 Strand Rd; map p.60. Renovations have robbed the old *Strand Hotel* bar of much of its musty old colonial character, but it remains a pleasant, if slightly anonymous, place for a drink. It can be somnolent verging on moribund some evenings except during the weekly two-for-one happy hour (Fri 5–11pm), a popular social event among local expats. Drinks include draught beer (K3000), cocktails (from K7000) and a signature range of single-malt whiskies (K9000–12,000). Daily 10am–11pm.

Takafuji 176 Sule Pagoda Rd ☎09 7303 6638; map p.60. Lively little place, with seating either in the small, smoky interior or on the pavement outside, attracting an unusually eclectic mix of local boozers and foreign backpackers. It's nominally a restaurant (with oil-soaked Chinese and Burmese mains for K3000–4000) but most people come for the beer, sold in considerable quantities at rock-bottom prices, with glasses of draught beer for under K1000. Daily 10am–midnight.

Union Bar and Grill 42 Strand Rd ☎09 3101 8272, ⓦunionyangon.com; map p.60. This busy new restaurant is also a decent place for a drink, especially during daily happy hour (5am–7pm, featuring $3 cocktails). At other times a big bottle of Myanmar Beer will set you back K4500. Regular live DJs also spin their stuff – check wfacebook .com/UnionBarAndGrill for forthcoming events. Daily 10am–midnight.

NIGHTCLUBS

Café Liberal Natmauk Rd (next to the Chatrium Hotel), Bahan ☎09 642 0930; map p.68. Long-running Yangon club on the north side of Kandawgyi Lake with good-sized large dance floor plus chill-out area. Fri & Sat 11pm–5am.

Flamingo Bar Yangon International Hotel Compound, 330 Ahlone Rd (downstairs from MBOX) ☎09 7304 8544, wfacebook.com/flamingobaryangon; map p.68. Yangon's biggest dance club, this big, bare warehouse-like venue hosts resident and visiting DJs (mainly of the house and hip-hop persuasion) most weekends. Aimed more at hardcore clubbers than casual drinkers.

GTR Club 37 Kaba Aye Pagoda Rd, in the Inya Lake Hotel complex ☎09 7309 0680, wfacebook.com /GTRClub; map p.68. Aimed mainly at well-heeled locals, this is one of the most fashionable clubs in the city, playing mostly electro house. Entry is free, but even soft drinks cost K3000. Daily 9pm–3am.

Mojo Bar 135 Inya Rd (corner of Inya and Dhammazedi roads) ☎01 511418, wfacebook.com/mojoinnya; map p.68. One of the city's more upmarket venues, with fancy Art Deco-inspired decor and regular DJs and other events. Free entry. Daily 11am–1am.

Pioneer Music Bar Yangon International Hotel Compound, 330 Ahlone Rd ☎09 7309 0680, whoteljapan yangon.com; map p.68. Long-running Yangon nightlife institution offering fun, no-frills clubbing with a cheesy but enjoyable soundtrack, reasonably priced drinks and lots of lasers and working girls. Free entry. Daily 10pm–3am.

ENTERTAINMENT

CULTURAL SHOWS

Htwe Oo Myanmar Traditional Puppet Theatre 12 Yama St, Ahlone ☎09 5127271, whtweoomyanmar.com. A more unusual (and a lot less touristy) alternative to the shows listed below, featuring displays of traditional Burmese puppetry in the owner's front room. Enquire ahead to check when the next show is scheduled and to reserve a place.

Kandawgyi Palace Hotel Kan Yeik Tha Rd ☎01 249255, wkandawgyipalace-hotel.com. A slightly cheaper and more low-key alternative to the shows at the Karaweik Palace (see p.76), comprising a similar mixture of dance, puppets and Burmese music. Tickets cost $20, payable in dollars and including buffet meal. Buffet from 6.30pm, show 7.30pm.

Karaweik Palace Kandawgyi Lake ☎01 290546,

wkaraweikpalace.com. Traditional cultural variety shows (usually comprising a mix of dancing, music and puppetry) are staged every evening at the landmark Karaweik Palace (around $30 including buffet dinner). Touristy and pricey, but fun and with expert performers – although the food won't win any awards. Buffet from 6.30pm, show 7.30pm.

CINEMA

Yangon is a cinema-crazy city, with dozens of movie theatres screening Hollywood blockbusters (with English subtitles) along with the latest Bollywood offerings. The Nay Pyi Taw Cinema and the Shae Saung Cinema, either side of *East* hotel and restaurant on Sule Pagoda Rd, are both modern and central. Tickets cost K1500 downstairs, K2500 upstairs.

SHOPPING

Bagan Book House 100 37th St ☎01 377227; map p.60. Long-running little bibliophile's treasure-trove, stuffed full of books on Myanmar, including some rare old titles. Daily 9am–6pm.

Bogyoke Market Bogyoke Aung San Rd; map p.60. Yangon's pre-eminent market and shopping attraction (see p.65), stuffed full of artefacts from every corner of the country including heaps of jade and jewellery, antique curios, contemporary artefacts and more run-of-the-mill items. It's also worth browsing the stalls of the pavement hawkers outside, stretching east along Bogyoke Aung San Rd almost to the junction with Sule Pagoda Rd and selling everything from old coins and banknotes through to contemporary paintings. These stalls are also a great place to pick up Aung San Suu Kyi memorabilia including T-shirts and mugs emblazoned with the Burmese icon's ubiquitous portrait – images of which were banned until just a few years ago. Tues–Sun 10am–5pm.

Botun 149 Central Arcade (near the rear entrance to the main market building), Bogyoke Market ☎01 384573; map p.60. Established in 1936, this quaint little shop usually has a good range of unusual Burmese artefacts, curios and colonial bric-a-brac for sale – anything from old coins and banknotes to antique wooden *nat* statuettes. Daily except Mon 10am–5pm.

Heritage Gallery Bogyoke Market (around the east side of the market's upstairs front floor, next to Yoyomay) ☎01 10527, enostalgia.arts@gmail.com; map p.60. Beautiful antique artefacts including some particularly gorgeous lacquerware. Sadly, most items are far too big to fit in your luggage, although shipping can be arranged. Daily 9.30am–4.30pm.

Monument Books 150 Dhammazedi Rd ☎01 536306; map p.68. The city's best general bookshop, with a decent selection of titles on Myanmar and other bits of Southeast Asia, plus some Western fiction and other books. Daily 8.30am–8.30pm.

Myanma Gems Mart Kaba Aye Pagoda Rd ☎01 665115; map p.68. The three floors of shops below the Myanma Gems Museum (see p.77) are the city's best place to shop for gems, jewels and, especially, jade, with a huge array of stuff on offer and lower prices than downtown, and with some scope for bargaining. Tues–Sun 9.30am–4pm.

Myanmar Artists Organisation East side of Bogyoke Market ☎09 4200 27304; map p.60. A blast of fresh air compared to the lame landscapes and cheesy paintings of monks that fill most of the city's galleries, showcasing a diverse, inventive and affordable range of work by upcoming local artists, plus small, cheap unframed paintings and greetings cards. Tues–Sun 9am–5pm.

Pomelo (formerly known as Loft) 2nd floor, 89 Thein Pyu Rd ⓦpomeloyangon.com; map p.60. Fun little boutique supporting local social projects. The shop's signature brightly painted papier-mâché animals make a nice souvenir, and they also sell unusual and ingenious knick-knacks and bric-a-brac – keyrings fashioned from old coins, bottle openers made from recycled tyres and so on – plus some lovely, if pricey, fabrics. Daily 10am–9pm.

Yoyamay Bogyoke Market (around the east side of the market's upstairs front floor, next to Heritage Gallery) ☎01 256411, ⓦyoyamay.com; map p.60. This unusual "ethnographic textile gallery" specializes in traditional Burmese textiles, sourced from across Myanmar (particularly Chin state) and made into bags, cushion covers, table runners, decorative hangings and so on, plus elegant (but pricey) silk and lotus clothes and scarves. Tues–Sun 10am–5pm.

DIRECTORY

Banks There's a growing number of ATMs around the city (although only about fifty percent of them ever seem to be working at any particular time); most accept both Visa and MasterCard. Useful machines can be found by the main entrance to Bogyoke Market; by the entrance to the Sakura Tower at the junction of Sule Pagoda and Bogyoke Aung San roads and inside the nearby Nay Pyi Taw Cinema on Sule Pagoda Rd; in the basement of the FMI Centre (Parkson Building); opposite the west side of Mahabandoola Gardens; inside the *Strand Hotel*; and at the main railway station. Moneychangers are also easy to find. The most convenient place in the city centre is Bogyoke Market, where many shops double as moneychangers; there's another handy moneychanger opposite the western side of Mahabandoola Gardens. In eastern downtown, try Swan Htet Yee, a few doors south of the *Hninn Si Guesthouse*, or Farmer Phoyarzar moneychanger opposite the *Eastern Hotel* on Bo Myat Htun St.

Embassies Australia, 88 Strand Rd (☎01 251810, ⓦwww .burma.embassy.gov.au); China, 1 Pyidaungsu Yeiktha Rd (☎01 221280, ⓦmm.china-embassy.org); New Zealand, c/o Embassy of New Zealand, M Thai Tower, 14th Floor, All Seasons Place, 87 Wireless Rd, Pathumwan, Lumpini, Bangkok, Thailand (☎+66 2 254 2530, ⓦnzembassy.com/Thailand); Republic of Ireland, c/o Embassy of Ireland, 2nd floor, Sentinel Place, 41A Ly Thai To, Hoan Kiem District, Hanoi, Vietnam (☎+84 4 3974 3291, ⓦembassyofireland.vn); South Africa, c/o South African Embassy, 12th A Floor, M Thai Tower, All Seasons Place, 87 Wireless Road, Lumpini, Bangkok, Thailand (☎+66 2 659 2900, ⓦdirco.gov.za/Bangkok); Thailand, 94 Pyay Rd (☎01 222784, ⓦthaiembassy.org/yangon/en); UK, 80 Strand Rd (☎01 380322, ⓦgov.uk/government /world/organisations/british-embassy-rangoon); USA, 110 University Ave (☎01 536509, ⓦburma.usembassy.gov).

Golf The Pun Hlaing Golf Club (☎01 687660, ⓦpunhlaing golfestate.com) is probably the best course in Myanmar, with eighteen immaculate holes laid out to a Gary Player design. It's located around 15km northwest of the centre.

Hospitals and health clinics Standards of healthcare are abysmally low in Myanmar. The city's main hospital, the Rangoon General on Bogyoke Aung San Rd, is one of the best in the country, but still worth avoiding if possible. In an emergency you're better off contacting either the Myanmar branch of International SOS, *Inya Lake Resort*, 37 Kaba Aye Pagoda Rd (Mon–Fri 8.30am–5.30pm, Sat 8.30am–12.30pm; ☎01 657922, ⓦinternationalsos .com), or the private Asia Royal Hospital (14 Baho St; ☎01 538055, ⓦasiaroyalmedical.com).

Internet There's a decent number of internet cafés around town, most charging around K500/hr. In the centre, the best place is NetSky (158 Mahabandoola Garden St; daily 8am–10pm; K600/hr), a huge, a/c place with around forty machines with (by Myanmar standards) speedy connections. There's a further trio of small internet cafés inserted into the base of the Sule Pagoda on the northwest side of Sule Pagoda roundabout. In eastern downtown, try CyberCafé, opposite the Sri Devi Temple.

Laundry Ava Laundry Service, 305 Mahabandoola Rd, between Pansodan and 37th streets (on north side of road).

Meditation The well-regarded Mahasi Meditation Centre (16 Thathana Yeiktha Rd; ☎01 541971, ⓦmahasi.org.mm) runs courses in Vipassana meditation for committed meditators (minimum seven-day stay, although for full benefit the centre recommends courses lasting six to twelve weeks). Alternatively, the Dahmma Joti Vipassana Centre, near the Chauk Htat Gyi Pagoda on Nga Htat Gyi Pagoda Rd (☎01 549290, ⓦjoti.dhamma.org; donation), offers ten-day courses. Courses at both centres are free, although donations towards costs are welcomed.

Pharmacies AA Pharmacy, 146 Sule Pagoda Rd (☎01 242651; daily 8am–9pm); City Care Pharmacy (daily 9am–9pm), basement of the FMI Centre (Parkson Building; go in between the escalators) on Bogyoke Aung San Rd.

Post office The main post office is at the corner of Strand Rd and Bo Aung Kyaw St (Mon–Fri 8am–6pm).

The Delta and western Myanmar

WOMEN DRYING FISH NEAR NGAPALI

The Delta and western Myanmar

West of Yangon stretches Myanmar's Delta region, an endless swathe of pancake-flat, emerald-green paddy fields irrigated by the waters of the Ayeyarwady and its innumerable tributaries, which empty through thousands of mangrove-fringed creeks into the waters of the Andaman Sea. Lying just a few metres above sea level, the Delta's rich alluvial soils are among Myanmar's most agriculturally productive, while its rivers provide much of the country's fishing catch.

Despite its economic importance, most of the region remains firmly off the tourist trail, with hardly any foreign visitors getting past the region's enjoyable capital, **Pathein**, and its two nearby beach resorts – the cheerful, local-leaning village of **Chaung Tha** and the more upmarket and foreigner-friendly **Ngwe Saung** – although a few visitors also make it to Twante (see p.80). Further north up the coast, remote **Rakhine State** (also spelt "Rakhaing") was formerly the independent kingdom of **Arakan** (see box, p.115) and preserves a strong sense of its own identity, culture and history quite separate from the Bamar mainstream. As with the Delta, the state remains largely unexplored by foreigners save for a pair of headline attractions: the seductive beach of **Ngapali** and the remarkable temple-town of **Mrauk U** (reached from boat via the absorbing but troubled city of **Sittwe**).

Much of the Delta was devastated in 2008 when **Cyclone Nargis** (see p.348) ripped through the densely populated flatlands, leaving around 130,000 people dead and at least a million homeless, although surprisingly little physical evidence of the cyclone's destructive passage now remains.

Pathein

ပုသိမ်

The largest settlement in the Delta, breezy **PATHEIN** is one of Myanmar's more enjoyable provincial capitals, and although most foreign visitors pass straight through, is well worth an overnight stop for its colourful array of temples, including the landmark **Shwemokhtaw Pagoda**, and the chance to visit one of the workshops where the brightly coloured cotton and silk **umbrellas** for which the city is famous are made.

Historically, Pathein was part of the **Mon kingdom**, although the modern city now has few ethnic Mon residents, the majority being Bamar and Kayin, along with sizeable Karen and Rakhine minorities. The city has long been an important port, enjoying close links with India – its name is said to derive from the Burmese word for "Parsi", *Pathi*, due to the large number of Arab and Indian traders who once lived here. It was also a major centre of **British** rule (during which it was known as "Bassein"), when a fort was built and a garrison established in 1826 following the First Anglo-Burmese War.

MRAUK U

Highlights

❶ Pathein Capital of the Delta, with a breezy riverfront and plenty of colourful temples – and even more colourful traditional parasols. **See opposite**

❷ Ngwe Saung Enjoyable west-coast beach, still refreshingly unspoilt despite its relative accessibility and number of good places to stay and eat. **See p.105**

❸ Ngapali Escape to one of Myanmar's ultimate beach boltholes, with idyllic sands, beautiful resorts, and the general sense of being a long, long way from anywhere else. **See p.108**

❹ Strand Road, Sittwe Faded colonial architecture, gorgeous marine views and one

of the country's most absorbing local markets offer a memorable slice of old-world Myanmar. **See p.115**

❺ Ferry from Sittwe to Mrauk U Take a fast or slow boat down the tranquil Kaladan River to Mrauk U for tantalizing glimpses of deepest rural Myanmar. **See p.117**

❻ Shittaung Paya, Mrauk U A magical grotto of medieval Burmese art, packed with spectacular sculptures and carvings. **See p.122**

❼ Htukkanthein Paya, Mrauk U Perhaps the most iconic of all Mrauk U temples, with its fortress-like exterior and richly decorated subterranean corridors within. **See p.123**

HIGHLIGHTS ARE MARKED ON THE MAP ON P.98

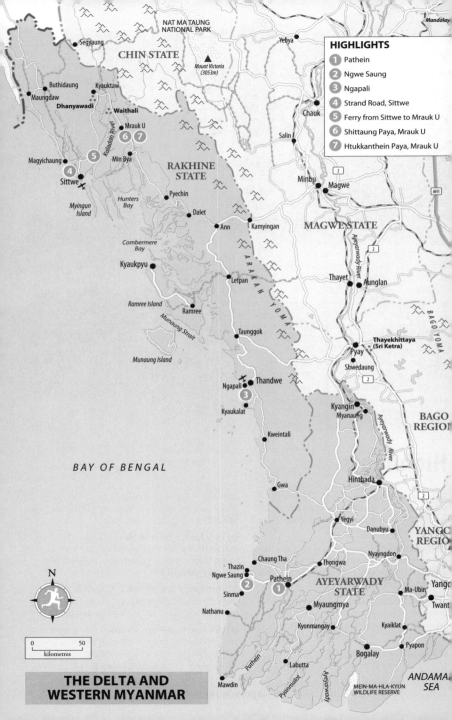

HIGHLIGHTS

1. Pathein
2. Ngwe Saung
3. Ngapali
4. Strand Road, Sittwe
5. Ferry from Sittwe to Mrauk U
6. Shittaung Paya, Mrauk U
7. Htukkanthein Paya, Mrauk U

Mandalay

Yebya

NAT MA TAUNG
NATIONAL PARK

CHIN STATE

Segyaung

Mount Victoria
(3053m)

Chauk

Buthidaung
Kyauktaw

Maungdaw

Dhanyawadi

Waithali

Salin

Kaladan River

Mrauk U
6 7

Magyichaung

Min Bya

RAKHINE
STATE

Minbu   Magwe

Sittwe

Pyechin

AH1

Myingun
Island

Hunters
Bay

Dalet

Ann   Kamyingan

MAGWE STATE

2

Combermere
Bay

Letpan

Thayet   Aunglan

Kyaukpyu

ARAKAN YOMA

Ayeyarwady River

BAGO YOMA

Ramree Island

Ramree

Taunggok

Thayekhittaya
(Sri Ketra)

Pyay

Munaung Strait

Shwedaung

2

Munaung Island

Thandwe

Ngapali
3

BAY OF BENGAL

Kyaukalat

Kyangin
Myanaung

BAGO
REGION

Kweintali

Ayeyarwady River

Gwa

Hinthada

2

N

Yegyi

Danubyu

YANGO
REGIO

Nyayngdon

Thazin   Chaung Tha

Thongwa

0   50
kilometres

Ngwe Saung
2

Pathein
1

AYEYARWADY
STATE

Ma-Ubin   Yango

Sinma

Myaungmya

Twant

Nathanu

Kyonmangay

Kyaiklat

Bogalay   Pyapon

THE DELTA AND
WESTERN MYANMAR

Mawdin

Labutta

Pyonmalot

Ayeyarwady

MEIN-MA-HLA-KYUN
WILDLIFE RESERVE

ANDA
SEA

Pathein

> **TRAVEL RESTRICTIONS**
> All the areas covered in this chapter are fully open to foreign visitors except for a few extremely remote areas in the far north of **Rakhine State** close to the border with Bangladesh, which require a permit to visit.

Modern Pathein is now the fourth-largest city in Myanmar, with a population of around 350,000, capital of the Ayeyarwady Region and (despite lying slightly inland, up the broad Pathein – or Bassein – River) still the most important port in the country after Yangon, serving as the main conduit for the Delta's huge rice exports.

Shwemokhtaw Pagoda

ေ႐ႊမုေ႒ာေဆာ္တီ · Main entrance from Pagoda Rd · Daily 6am–9pm · Free

Pathein's main sight is the **Shwemokhtaw Pagoda**, squeezed tightly into the very centre of town between Pagoda, Merchant and Panchan streets. Local legend claims that it was built at the order of a Muslim princess named Onmadandi, who challenged each of her three Buddhist suitors to build her a stupa in order to discover who could furnish her with the most impressive erection. Fables aside, dull historical fact suggests that what you see now is largely the work of Bagan's King Alaungsithu (in 1115) and the Mon King Samodogossa (in 1263), who raised the stupa to something approaching its current height of 47m. The crowning *hti* is said to be made of 6kg of solid gold set on tiers of silver and bronze and encrusted with over 1600 diamonds and rubies – although you can't really see anything from the ground.

Inside, the courtyard is one of Myanmar's more architecturally harmonious temple complexes, and while the stupa itself isn't particularly huge, it compensates with its elegantly slender outline. Surrounding the stupa you'll find eight shrines dedicated to the various **days of the week**, as at the Shwedagon in Yangon (see box, p.71), plus a ninth shrine representing the ruling sign, Ketu – each is equipped with its own Buddha seated on a tiny circular garden plinth, complete with its own tap for watering.

On the south side of the pagoda, a shrine houses the revered **Thiho-shin Phondawpyi** Buddha image, said to have been made in ancient Sri Lanka and then set adrift on a raft, after which it floated over to Pathein. On the opposite, northwest, side of the terrace is a shrine to Shin Upagot (see p.356) set in the middle of a small pond. Close by are a couple of small *nat* shrines with an image of the elephant-headed Hindu god Ganesh (incorporated into the Burmese *nat* pantheon under the name of Maha Peinne) between.

The northern entrance frames fine views of the Shwezigon Pagoda's giant seated Buddha.

Shwezigon Pagoda

ေ႐ႊစည္းခုံ · Kozu Rd · Daily 24hr · Free

Due north of the Shwemokhtaw, the **Shwezigon Pagoda** is hard to miss thanks to its huge, open-air seated Buddha. The rest of the temple comprises a fairly cursory and haphazard collection of shrines including a series of decaying sculptures in rusty cages (a procession of monks, Brahma mounted upon on a *hamsa* and the ubiquitous Shin Upagot among them) along with further assorted *nats*.

The market and riverfront

Daily 8am–6pm

Pathein's **market** is spread over two blocks. The newer southern block is relatively humdrum, with lots of stalls selling cheap clothes. The older northern block looks fairly sedate from the outside but is typically congested and borderline chaotic within, with old-fashioned wooden stalls, like enormous, two-storey cupboards.

North and south of here, **Strand Road** runs along the breezy Pathein River waterfront. Facing the river just north of the market is the attractive old colonial **Customs House**. The area along Strand Road north of here is home to the city's busy **night market**.

Dani Tan Monastery

ဓနိတန်းဘုန်းကြီးကျောင်း • Mahabandoola Rd

It's difficult to miss the modern **Dani Tan** (aka Tikekyi) **Monastery**, the roof of its main hall topped with outlandish models of the Shwedagon and Golden Rock at Mount Kyaiktiyo, appearing (at least from certain angles) to float miraculously in midair.

28 Pagoda

၂၈ဆူဘုရား

Directly behind the Dani Tan monastery, the long, low **28 Pagoda** is contrastingly self-effacing. The rustic-looking shrine is named for the 28 standing Buddhas, with 28 further Buddhas sitting in niches behind them – the standing figures are posed in the characteristic Mandalay style with hands holding the hems of the outer robe open around the knees, as though about to step through a puddle. The building is usually kept locked, although you can get a decent view in through the windows even if you can't locate a keyholder to open it for you.

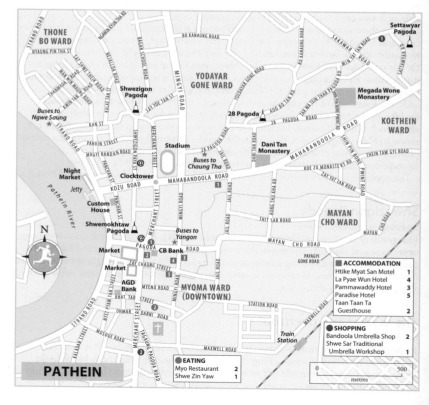

PATHEIN

ACCOMMODATION
Htike Myat San Motel	1
La Pyae Wun Hotel	4
Pammawaddy Hotel	3
Paradise Hotel	5
Taan Taan Ta Guesthouse	2

SHOPPING
Bandoola Umbrella Shop	2
Shwe Sar Traditional Umbrella Workshop	1

EATING
Myo Restaurant	2
Shwe Zin Yaw	1

0 ——— 500 metres

Eastern monasteries

The area east of the centre along Mahabandoola Road is dotted with further temples and monasteries – none is of any particular antiquity, although the various clusters of often colourful and quirky buildings make an attractive backdrop to a walk out to the Shwe Sar Traditional Umbrella Workshop (see p.102), which is also in this part of town. Most attractive is the large **Megada Wone Monastery** at the end of 28 Pagoda St, while further east (and just around the corner from Shwe Sar) is the **Settawyar Pagoda**, one of the largest in town.

2

ARRIVAL AND DEPARTURE
PATHEIN

By plane There are sometimes a couple of flights weekly to Pathein in high season with Air Bagan (or possibly other airlines) but details change regularly and flight info is difficult to come by – ask at a reputable ticketing agency or travel agent in Yangon.

By bus There's no central bus station in Pathein – different services arrive and depart in various places in town (see map opposite). Clapped-out minibuses run to Ngwe Saung and Chaung Tha, and comfortable express buses to Yangon. Destinations Chaung Tha (6 daily; 2hr); Ngwe Saung

(3 daily; 2hr); Yangon (4 daily; 4hr).

By train Pathein lies on a branch line off the main Yangon–Bagan route, connecting to the mainline at Pyay. There are rumours that a direct train to Yangon will be introduced in the future, although at present services are of little practical use to foreign travellers, however, and to reach even Pyay you'll have to change en route at Kyangin (2 trains daily; 14–18hr), making for a journey of at least 24hr in total.

By boat The future of the ferry from Yangon to Pathein is currently wrapped in uncertainty (see p.82).

ACCOMMODATION

Accommodation in Pathein is generally good value, although unusually for Myanmar none of the following include breakfast in their rates, unless specifically stated otherwise. Note that the electricity supply is decidedly erratic. Power is pretty much guaranteed from 6pm to 6am, but goes off fairly regularly during the day.

Htike Myat San Motel 8 Mahabandoola Rd ☎042 22742, ✉htikemyatsan@gmail.com. Smart new hotel run by a charming Chinese family and with pleasant modern rooms – but avoid those close to the noisy main road. Cheapest rooms have shared bathrooms ($5 extra for en suite); all come with a/c and wi-fi (more expensive ones with hot water). Unusually for Pathein, rates include breakfast on the breezy rooftop with views of the quirky Dani Tan Monastery. $20

La Pyae Wun Hotel 30 Mingyi Rd ☎042 24669. Comfortable if somewhat lifeless hotel which appears to have fallen into a coma sometime in the mid-1990s and never quite woken up again. The decent-sized rooms come with a/c, TV, fridge and wi-fi. Top-floor rooms (same price) are brighter and quieter but have cold water only. $30

Pammawaddy Hotel 14a Mingyi Rd ☎042 21165, ✉newpammawaddy@gmail.com. Functional concrete-box hotel with zero atmosphere but providing pleasant a/c

rooms equipped with TV, fridge, hot water and wi-fi. Rooms, bizarrely, get cheaper the higher you go – those on the third floor are brighter, quieter and cost $10 less than those on the first floor. Try to get a room away from the road. $25

Paradise Hotel 14 Zay Chaung Rd ☎042 25582. Bright tiled rooms with a/c, TV and fridge in a biggish modern building right in the centre. Cold water only, and no wi-fi (or breakfast), but excellent value, if you don't mind the slightly moribund atmosphere. $15

Taan Taan Ta Guesthouse Merchant St ☎042 22290, ✉taantaanta25@gmail.com. Welcoming and well-run backpacker favourite – don't be put off by the shabby paintwork and grubby appearance, rooms are actually much cleaner and more comfortable than they immediately appear, and at an excellent price, including singles for just $10/12 with fan or a/c. All come with a/c (apart from cheapest singles) and attached bathroom. $15

EATING

Eating options in Pathein are strictly limited. As well as the two places listed here there's also a decent **night market** on Strand Rd, although it's rather crammed in alongside the road and not the most relaxing place to eat. A number of other restaurants can be found along the waterfront hereabouts, although they mainly serve as local drinking dives.

Myo Restaurant Bwat Kyi Tan Rd ☎042 24338. This scruffy local drinking hole doesn't look like much but serves up a big selection of surprisingly good (if rather oily) meat and seafood mains in the usual Chinese-y style (most

mains around K2000), plus cheap beer and Premier League footie on the TV. Daily 10am–11pm.

Shwe Zin Yaw Pagoda Rd. Cheery local café with a short English menu offering a range of tempting and

2

PATHEIN PARASOLS

Pathein is famous for its colourful **umbrellas**, perhaps Myanmar's most iconic handicraft – you'll often see both monks and nuns carrying them and looking absurdly picturesque, as though dressed up specially for some Burmese photoshoot. Umbrellas have always served as a symbol of distinction in Burmese life. They once formed part of the royal regalia, while an architectural umbrella (*hti*) crowns the top of the spire of all the country's most important stupas, often richly decorated with precious stones.

Strictly speaking, the items made in Pathein are **parasols** rather than umbrellas, since they're designed to protect against sun rather than rain (although they're also claimed to be waterproof – not that you'll want to test this theory if you buy one yourself). There are two styles of umbrella: the traditional Pathein-style **cotton hti**, and the rather Chinese-looking Mandalay/Bagan-style **silk umbrella**. Umbrellas take around a week to make. Handles, stems and spokes are crafted from bamboo, with intricate geometrical and floral designs hand-painted on the top. An extract from the *tae* fruit (persimmon) is used to waterproof the umbrellas, and also boiled to create the glue which holds them together. Umbrellas come in a wide range of colours – rich reds and intense oranges are perhaps the most traditional, although many other colours can also be found. Monks traditionally carry dark-red umbrellas (pink for nuns), with no decoration on the underside.

There are a number of workshops in Pathein around the **28 Pagoda** – owners are always pleased to see visitors and happy to explain the umbrella-making process, while prices for umbrellas bought straight from the maker are a snip compared to what you'll pay elsewhere.

well-prepared dishes (K1000–1500) including citrus, pennywort and grilled prawn salads, Malay soup and various curries including duck, goat's liver, mutton, catfish and sardine – although don't expect everything on it to be available at any one time. Daily 7am–9pm.

SHOPPING

Bandoola Umbrella Shop Merchant St. Charmingly antiquated shop, and a good place to pick up a cut-price Pathein-style silk umbrella, which sell here for as little as K2000–2500. Daily 7am–9pm.

Shwe Sar Traditional Umbrella Workshop 653 Tawyakyaung Rd ☎ 042 25127. Pathein's best-known umbrella workshop, run by the same family for more than a century (some of their earlier work can now be seen in museums around the country). They make a mix of silk and cotton umbrellas, created using top-quality traditional ingredients including persimmon glue and bamboo from the Rakhine mountain. The smallest umbrellas cost just K2000, rising to K70,000 for the largest – way less than you'll pay for the same umbrella elsewhere in the country. Daily 7am–6pm.

DIRECTORY

Banks The CB and AGD banks have ATMs; there's also a moneychanger at the AGD Bank.

Internet There are several internet cafés around town. Try the well-equipped Lynn Internet Cafe on the way to the Shwezigon Pagoda, or the Internet Cafe & Network Game Centre right in the town centre.

Chaung Tha

ချောင်းသာ

If you're looking for a picture-postcard tropical beach with deserted sands, unspoilt coastal scenery and nothing to break the silence save the sound of a distant cocktail being discreetly mixed, then **CHAUNG THA** definitely isn't the place to come. The beach is none too clean, and despite its considerable size fills up quickly (at weekends especially) with vast hordes of visiting Yangonites playing football and *chinlone*, splashing around in inner tubes, and consuming astonishing quantities of grilled seafood and beer. Opportunities for peaceful swimming, sunbathing and contemplation of the waves are strictly limited, but as a place to observe Myanmar's middle classes at play, there's probably nowhere better, and if you take Chaung Tha for what it is – a kind of miniature Burmese Bognor Regis, with a determinedly bucket-and-spade ambience – you might find the place surprisingly enjoyable.

Chaung Tha ("Pleasant Stream") is situated on a promontory between the Bay of Bengal and the Chaung Tha River. The main beach road runs roughly northwest to southeast for about 2.5km, passing a burgeoning straggle of restaurants and hotels before terminating in Chaung Tha **village**, where you'll find the biggest concentration of guesthouses, cafés and souvenir shops, catering to a determinedly local crowd, and always lively after dark. The **beach** itself is extremely wide, dotted with barbecue stalls and plastic chairs under parasols at its far end towards *Hotel Max* and becoming quieter and emptier as you head away from the village, passing a lumpy-looking pagoda built on top of a small limestone outcrop on the way.

2

White Sand Island

သဲဖြူကျွန်း • Boats to the island leave from the jetty in the village every hour or so (15–20min; K3000)

To escape the crowds your best bet is to head out to the tiny speck of land known as **White Sand Island** (Thel Phyu), which is good for swimming and snorkelling (you can rent snorkelling gear from Mr George; see p.104), although there are no facilities, and not much shade either.

ARRIVAL AND DEPARTURE
CHAUNG THA

Arriving at the beginning of the main road through Chaung Tha you'll almost immediately past *Sea & See* guesthouse (on your right), followed shortly afterwards by the *Belle Resort* and *Shwe Ya Minn* (on the right and left respectively). The bus/minibus "station" (an open space in the middle of a small square of shops) is about another 750m down the road, and the *Hotel Max* a further 250m or so beyond, just before Chaung Tha village proper.

By bus It's best to buy bus tickets at least a day in advance, particularly in peak season. Tickets can be bought at the bus station, via Mr George (see p.104), or possibly through your hotel.
Destinations Pathein (6 daily; 2hr); Yangon (2–4 daily; 6hr).
By motorbike It's possible to travel directly from Chaung Tha to Ngwe Saung by motorbike (K12,000; 2hr), a fun if bumpy ride through the wild and hilly coastal hinterlands, with three short ferry crossings en route. Ask at Mr George's

or your accommodation. Another cost-effective alternative is to visit the Ngwe Saung Elephant Camp (see box, p.104) and then ask to be set down at Ngwe Saung afterwards.
By boat Travelling to Ngwe Saung, a more comfortable (but considerably more expensive) alternative to motorbike taxi is to charter a boat (K40,000–50,000 for up to five people; 2hr). Note that at present it's a lot cheaper (for no obvious reason) to do this trip starting in Chaung Tha compared to Ngwe Saung (see p.106) – ask at Mr George's or the *Shwe Ya Minn* hotel.

ACCOMMODATION

There are loads of places to stay in Chaung Tha, but most are drab and poor value. Weekends can get insanely busy; things are slightly quieter, and rates more negotiable, during the week. As with other places along the coast, the government **electricity** supply operates only from 6pm to 6am. More upmarket places have their own generators, although even then additional power may only be available from around 1pm to 4pm. Most places slash rates or close entirely during the rainy season.

Belle Resort Main Rd (opposite Shwe Ya Minn) ☎ 042 42112, ⊕ belleresorts.com. Chaung Tha's most appealing place to stay, rather more stylish than pretty much anywhere else in the village and at a very competitive price, with attractive bungalows set around peaceful gardens overlooking the sea, plus a spa and smallish pool. $76
Hill Garden Hotel Outside the village ☎ 09 4957 6072, ⊕ hillgardenhotel.com. Peaceful retreat from the beachside hubbub, set amid fields a 10min bike ride from the village. The rustic wooden cabanas come with either

shared bathroom (cold water only) or en-suite (hot water extra $10); fans are provided on request, but sea breezes mean you don't really need them. There's a small beach nearby, and bikes available for K1500/day. $15
Hotel Max Main Rd ☎ 042 42346, ⊕ maxhotelsgroup .com. A cut above everywhere else in town bar the *Belle Resort* – although bizarrely at a cheaper price than many other less appealing places, and excellent value overall. Accommodation is in a cluster of white chalets set amid Chaung Tha's attractive gardens close to the beach, all

2

CHAUNG THA ACTIVITIES AND EXCURSIONS

There's a small selection of tours and activities to keep you occupied in Chaung Tha, including various thrills-and-spills-style **watersports**, aimed mainly at visiting Burmese. More interesting are local river and sea **boat trips**, perhaps in combination with a spot of snorkelling at the small coral reef just offshore.

TOUR OPERATORS

Mr George Main Rd near Shwe Hin Tha hotel, towards the northwest end of the beach ☏ 09 4973 4562, ✉ mrgeorgeprince292@gmail.com; daily 7am–10pm. Chaung Tha's long-serving Mr Fixit. Services include bus ticket sales, bike (K2000/day) and motorbike (K10,000/day) rental; snorkelling equipment rental (K2000/day) and a small book exchange. Also arranges tours and activities including snorkelling from shore (K1500pp), mangrove, river and fishing-village boat trips (K30,000 for up to 5 people); all-day sea-fishing trips (K150,000 for up to 5 people); and cooking classes (K12,000/person), starting with a 7am visit to market followed by four hours of cooking and eating. He also arranges trips to Ngwe Saung elephant camp (K18,000/person, not including entrance and riding fees)

– you could ask to be dropped off at Ngwe Saung on your way back, which is a good way of reaching the place. Alternatively, a day-trip to Ngwe Saung costs K60,000 (for up to 5 people) by boat, or K13,000 by motorbike.

Shwe Ya Minn Hotel Main Rd ☏ 042 42126. Runs a wide range of boat trips featuring fishing, snorkelling, river, mangrove and village tours. Half-day tours cost K25,000–30,000 for a boat seating 1–5 people.

Water Sport Entertainment c/o the Lai Lai, Max, Golden Beach and New Chaung Tha hotels ☏ 09 4480 27521. Providing splashtastic entertainment to Chaung Tha's Burmese visitors including jet skiing, banana boating and various other activities involving being dunked in the waves on various kinds of inflatables – wildly popular with locals.

---

spacious and attractively kitted out with plenty of wooden furniture. Facilities include a spa, medium-sized pool, and a nice restaurant complete with billiards table. **$70**

Sea & See Main Rd ☏ 042 42399. Near the top end of the village, this place is as cheap as it gets in Chaung Tha, offering simple but clean and bright rooms with shared bathroom (cold water only) – although the mattresses are uncomfortably thin. Friendly service, but not much English spoken. No breakfast. **K15,000**

Shwe Ya Minn Main Rd (opposite the Belle Resort)

☏ 042 42126. Chaung Tha's only real budget guesthouse for foreign visitors, which fortunately is pretty good. Rooms (a/c $10 extra) are small and simple but perfectly comfortable, with decent mosquito nets and not too hot, and there's also reliable wi-fi and a good breakfast included in the price (K2000 for non-guests). There's also a good attached restaurant (see below), and the professional staff can arrange a wide range of boat trips and excursions. **$25**

EATING

As you'd expect, Chaung Tha majors in seafood, with a string of restaurants down the road with identical signs and near identical menus (although hardly any of them ever have prices on – check before you order). Food isn't particularly cheap (around K4000–5000 for a whole fish) but ingredients are fresh and portions consistently huge. If you fancy eating **on the beach**, there's an enjoyable little mini-village of wooden shacks under massed umbrellas on the beach just north of *Hotel Max* with dozens of small stalls selling freshly grilled fish and seafood alongside traditional curries.

★Pasta Fresca 30 Khine Shwe War St ☏ 09 4224 45138 (turn inland off Main Rd down the track past the Alliance Resort and follow the signs). A very unexpected find in determinedly local Chaung Tha, this little garden restaurant is run by a charming Italian mother-and-son team with excellent, authentic pizza and home-made pasta at bargain prices (most mains K5500). Daily from around 7pm; also open for lunch if people show up.

Shwe Pyae Aung Main Rd ☏ 09 4972 1897. One of the

string of identikit seafood restaurants along the main road serving up well-prepared fish, prawns, crab, squid, octopus, oysters and abalone, plus a few meat dishes. Daily 10am–11pm.

Shwe Ya Minn Shwe Ya Minn Hotel, Main Rd ☏ 042 42126. Chaung Tha's best-looking restaurant, with smooth service, cheap beer and well-prepared versions of all the usual seafood dishes plus one of the village's biggest selections of meat and veg curries, noodles and so on (mains K4000–5000). Daily 7am–11pm.

DIRECTORY

Banks There are no banks or ATMs in Chaung Tha, although you might be able to change money at one of the larger hotels. Bring all the cash you'll need.

Internet A few hotels (including *Shwe Ya Minn*) have wi-fi, and there's internet access at the *Hotel Ayeyarwady*

(K1000/hr; open until 11pm).

Swimming pools The nicest pools open to non-guests are those at the *Hotel Max* and *Belle Resort* (both K5000/day, although the latter is open to non-guests only if hotel occupancy levels aren't too high).

Ngwe Saung

ငွေဆောင်

Crashed-out **NGWE SAUNG** ("Silver Beach"; pronounced, approximately, "Nway Song") sees far more foreign visitors than nearby Chaung Tha, and with good reason thanks to its fine swathe of wide golden sand stretching north and south of the small village for kilometre after kilometre, with a series of mainly upmarket resorts (plus a couple of good budget places) hidden at discreet intervals among the endless palms backdropping the beach. Ongoing development is steadily changing the face of the village, while road improvements mean that the journey from Yangon can now be made in less than five hours, putting the beach firmly on the map both of foreign tourists and wealthy Burmese fleeing the congested capital. But for now, at least, Ngwe Saung retains its somnolent atmosphere and feeling of a place where the clock is stuck permanently at four o'clock on a Sunday afternoon.

Towards the northern end of the beach, compact **Ngwe Saung village** is as lively as things ever get hereabouts, stuffed with a good collection of restaurants, handicrafts shops and stalls piled high with huge mounds of dried fish. The coast **north of the village** has been mainly gobbled up with a collection of generally lacklustre resorts enclosed within fortress-like walls; the beach **south of the village** is much more attractive, with its endless swathe of sand, generally peaceful and pretty clean, and often deserted entirely. Best of all is the area around **Lover's Island** (offshore roughly opposite *Shwe Hin Tha* hotel, about 4km south of the village), which you can wade out to at low tide. There's also a bit of snorkelling around here – you may be able to rent equipment from *Shwe Hin Tha* hotel.

Elephant camp

Off the Pathein road, around 45min east of Ngwe Saung • Daily 6am–noon • $5 • Local tour operators (see box, p.106) can arrange transport to the camp by motorbike taxi (K10,000) or car (K30,000)

East of Ngwe Saung, the small **elephant camp** near the road to Pathein is a tourist venture rather than a proper working camp, with five (sometimes more) elephants currently in residence. It's pretty low-key: you watch the elephants being washed in a stream/pond and can feed them sugar cane (K1000 per portion). It's also possible to go for a ride on one ($10 for around 30–45min) – although as with all elephant rides the experience is uncomfortable, unexciting and, most importantly, cruel to the poor animals themselves, who are forced to clank miserably about in their chains.

Thazin and Sinma

သာဇင် / ဆင်မ • Count on around K10,000 for the trip to Thazin by motorcycle taxi, slightly more to Sinma

Local excursions offered by Ngwe Saung's tour operators (see box, p.106) are to a couple of local fishing villages just down the coast. The village of **THAZIN** (the first village you reach on the way to Chaung Tha; around 30min by motorbike) offers the chance to see (depending on the time of year) locals fishing off the beach using enormous nets worked by teams of up to thirty or (if you visit early) the local fleet of night-fishing boats returning to shore at around 6–8am bringing in a catch of tiger prawns, barracuda, squid, tuna and mackerel.

2

2

NGWE SAUNG TOURS AND ACTIVITIES

Both the **guides** listed below can provide bikes and motorbikes, arrange **transport** (boat or overland) to Chaung Tha (or just a return boat trip to Chaung Tha – count on around $100 return), plus **tours** to the local elephant camp, Bird Island and the nearby fishing villages of Thazin and Sinma. Ko Toe is also planning to launch **cookery** classes in 2015. **Diving** can be arranged through Myanmar Subsea (see below).

TOUR OPERATORS

Ko Toe Bike-rental stall opposite Myanmar Subsea/ Wine Wine Le Restaurant ☎ 09 4225 08473, ✉ kotoe.toegyi@gmail.com. Bike rental, tours and (hopefully by the time you read this) Ngwe Saung's only cookery classes. If he's not at his home base opposite Myanmar Subsea, try asking at the nearby *Jasmine* restaurant.

Tom Tom Village ☎ 09 4224 62904, ✉ tom.tunlin @gmail.com. Full range of local tours, including an unusual trip south to Gaw Yan Gyi Island (4hr each way by motorbike, best done with an overnight stay at the village of Ngayokekaung), offering visits to local villages and a taste of deep rural life in the Delta (around $45 plus meals for overnight trip). He was in a temporary office at the time of writing but should have opened a new base in the village by the time you read this, signed "Sandalwood" (he is also occasionally found at his second office at the *Shwe Hin Tha* hotel).

DIVING

Myanmar Subsea Village, next to Wine Wine Le Restaurant ☎ 09 4965 3076, 🌐 myanmarsubsea .com. Disinterested dive operator offering one-day trips with two dives for $80 including all equipment. They may or may not have a qualified PADI teacher in residence, depending on whether they've had a better offer from elsewhere.

Slightly further away (around 45min by motorbike, with one ferry crossing en route), **SINMA** village is another good place to see the morning's catch being landed, as well as vast quantities of fish drying on the beach.

Bird Island

ငှက်ဥပျာဥ်ကျွန်း • The trips costs around $75 for a boat seating five or more people arranged through a tour operator, or you might be able to negotiate a cheaper per-person rate (as little as $20) from a boatman on the beach

The ride out to **Bird Island**, about one hour offshore, makes for an interesting half- or full-day excursion. Despite the name, the island is best for snorkelling rather than birdwatching, with plenty of colourful fish and live coral, while the boat ride out through the crashing waves is also fun.

ARRIVAL AND DEPARTURE   NGWE SAUNG

Ngwe Saung lies at the end of a twisty little side road from Pathein, winding its way through jungle-covered hills as you approach the coast – signs of rampant deforestation can be seen on the way (even more so than along the similar road to Chaung Tha).

By bus Old and cramped minibuses make the journey from Pathein to Ngwe Saung, and there are also comfortable express buses direct from Yangon's Hlaing Thar Yar bus terminal. Buses tend to drop off passengers all along the main road before terminating at the bus station.
Destinations Pathein (3 daily; 2hr); Yangon (2 daily; 6hr).
By motorbike/boat from Chaung Tha It's also possible to get to Ngwe Saung directly from Chaung Tha overland by motorbike taxi (K20,000), a fun, if bumpy, 2hr ride involving three small ferry crossings en route, or by hiring a boat (K80,000–100,000) for a boat seating five-plus people – a great way to arrive if you can get a group together to share the cost, although prices for this trip are currently a lot cheaper in Chaung Tha, so you may prefer to take the trip starting there. Transfers by boat and motorbike can be organized through local tour operators (see box above).

GETTING AROUND

The beach area is very spread out – it's almost 5km from the village to the *Silver Coast Beach Hotel*, for example. Some guesthouses/hotels have **bikes** for rental, while bikes (K3000/day) and **motorbikes** (K10,000/day) can also be rented from Ko Toe and Tom Tom (see box opposite). A few **motorbike taxis** and **rickshaws** tend to meet arriving buses, but other than this, transport is thin on the ground.

ACCOMMODATION

Hotels and guesthouses are strung out at discreet intervals along the beach. Most are located **south of the village**, although there's a further cluster of large and more upmarket resorts **north of the village** too. Pretty much all Ngwe Saung's restaurants and shops are concentrated **in the village** itself, which also boasts a few decent places to stay if you want to be in the thick of things and don't mind being a walk or bike ride away from the sands. Note that the government **electricity** supply only runs from 6pm to 6am. More upmarket places have their own generators, but in budget establishments expect to be powerless during the day.

IN THE VILLAGE

Hotel Lux 40 Myoma Rd ☎ 042 40252, ⓦ hotellux.com .mm. Attractive mid-range resort in the middle of the village, set in a minimalist modern white and cream building backing onto the beach and with a smallish infinity pool right above the sands. Rooms are spacious and attractively furnished – oddly, they become cheaper the higher up the building you go. Those at the top are very good value; those downstairs (costing almost double) less so. There are also a few fancier suite-sized bungalows ($130) almost on the beach, with private verandas overlooking the sand. Wi-fi. **$50**

Luxer Deluxe Hotel Myoma Rd ☎ 09 2305 84925. Attractive modern hotel set in a vivid yellow building right in the heart of the village – not particularly beachy, but very pleasant, and at a good price. The neat tiled rooms are well equipped with a/c, flatscreen TV, with slight sea views from higher floors at the back (same price). Friendly service and erratic wi-fi complete the deal. **$40**

NORTH OF THE VILLAGE

Aureum Palace Myoma Rd, 1.5km north of the village ☎ 042 40217, ⓦ aureumpalacehotel.com. One of Ngwe Saung's best-looking resorts, from the stylish thatched lobby through to the immaculately manicured gardens and delicious swathe of sand beyond. Accommodation is in a cluster of spacious wooden villas ($190) plus cheaper rooms in a two-storey block behind – nice enough, but lacking the wow factor you might expect at this price. Facilities include a spa, a nice restaurant and decent-sized pool. **$160**

SOUTH OF THE VILLAGE

★ **Emerald Sea Resort** 2.5km south of the village ☎ 042 40247, ⓦ emeraldseahotel.com. One of Ngwe Saung's most attractive and affordable resorts, set around a palm-studded lawn backing onto the beach. Accommodation is in thatched chalets ($110), spacious and attractively furnished with traditional artworks and textiles (some also have outdoor showers); there are also some slightly cheaper rooms at the back in two-storey blocks with quirky temple-style staircases. Facilities include a decent-sized pool, a very affordable spa and an attractive pavilion restaurant. **$100**

Eskala 1km south of the village ☎ 042 40341, ⓦ eskala.com. Brand-new upmarket resort in cool, slightly severe, minimalist style – the huge pavilion lobby alone could swallow up several smaller hotels. Accommodation is in a mix of stylish cream and wood bungalows ($145) spread around spacious beachfront gardens, and some slightly cheaper and less appealing rooms in a two-storey block behind. There's also a spa and a lovely big pool. **$110**

Myanmar Treasure Resort 250m south of the village ☎ 042 40224, ⓦ myanmartreasureresorts.com. This village-style resort is one of Ngwe Saung's most upscale options, with lush gardens and buildings almost buried under huge thatch roofs. Rooms come with stylish wooden furniture, four-poster beds and big bathrooms with film-star mirrors. Facilities include a decent-sized pool, spa, business centre, games room (pool and table tennis) **$135**

Palm Beach Resort 2km south of the village ☎ 042 40233, ⓔ palmbeachngwesaung@gmail.com. Peaceful, village-style beach resort, with wood and white thatched chalets arranged around magnolia-shaded walkways. Rooms are stylishly furnished with wooden sofas, desk and four-poster beds and well-equipped bathrooms (sea-view rooms come with a $20 surcharge). Facilities include a spa and T-shaped infinity pool, with a cute bar and restaurant spreading out around it. **$130**

Shwe Hin Tha 4km south of the village ☎ 042 42118, ⓔ info@shwehinthahotel.com, ⓦ shwehinthahotel.com. Ngwe Saung's most popular budget option, towards the southern end of the beach and with Lover's Island rising out of the waters opposite. Choose between the rather plain bungalows ($55) right on the beachfront (with a/c, hot water, TV and fridge) or the cheaper and more characterful but less comfortable wooden cabanas behind (with wall fan and cold water only). Wi-fi and an attractive beachfront restaurant. Cabanas **$30**

Silver Coast Beach Hotel 4.5km south of the village ☎ 042 40324, ⓔ htoo.maw@mptmail.net.mm. Close to Lover's Island at the sleepy southern end of the beach, this place has a slightly Robinson Crusoe atmosphere, with little to disturb the peace apart from the occasional falling coconut. The simple but large and comfortable bungalows (a/c, TV and fridge; hot water $5 extra) come with sea views and big verandas to enjoy them from. There are also some good-value economy rooms ($25, with table fan and cold water only) in a little building at the back – plain but spacious and adequately furnished. Simple attached restaurant, but no wi-fi at present. **$40**

EATING

As at neighbouring Chaung Tha, restuarants in Ngwe Saung major in seafood, offering largely generic menus featuring the same dishes, mainly prepared in pseudo-Chinese style (sweet and sour, hot and spicy, and so on), along with a couple of Burmese curry-style variations. What's actually available will depend on what the local fishermen have recently hauled in – you might ask to have a look in the kitchen to see what's in stock, and to check how fresh it is.

Golden Myanmar Restaurant Village ☎ 042 40241. This lively local restaurant is usually one of the village's most enjoyable places to hang out over a meal or beer, with decent food and cheery service. The menu features a good range of seafood and meat dishes (mains around K4500) plus cheaper noodles and salads. Daily 6am–9/10pm.

Jasmine Seafood Restaurant Village ☎ 042 40262. Generic menu of seafood and meat mains, although a fraction pricier than elsewhere (mains mostly K3500), well prepared and served in generous portions. The crispy fish in orange sauce is good and something a bit different, and they also dish up some good salads including seaweed, seafood, papaya and jelly noodles. Daily 7am–9pm.

Royal Flower Village ☎ 042 40309. One of the village's most popular hangouts among visiting Westerners thanks to its cooler-than-average decor and ambience. Mains (mostly K4000) feature all the old seafood and meat favourites in generic Chinese style, with a pinch of Thai. Welcoming service, although the occasional live music acts can seriously mess with your digestion. Daily 7am–10pm.

Ume 3km south of the village, next to the main road between the Silver View and Yamonnar Oo resorts. One of the few independent restaurants outside the village, this friendly little place dishes up a short menu of simple Japanese dishes (mains K4000–6000) plus a few assorted light meals and snacks accompanied by nightly "fire dancing" at 7.30pm. Daily 10am–10pm.

DIRECTORY

Banks There are no ATMs or banks at present in Ngwe Saung – bring whatever cash you need with you.

Internet A number of hotels and guesthouses have (erratic) wi-fi. Otherwise the only place to get online currently is Nbine Nbine Internet (daily 10am–9.30pm), in the village opposite the *Golden Myanmar* restaurant, which has a few dodgy terminals plus more reliable wi-fi (both K500/30min).

Swimming pools Hotels in Ngwe Saung tend to charge exorbitant rates for non-guests to use their pools. The most affordable is the medium-sized pool at the *Bay of Bengal Resort* (K5000/day). The lovely pool at the *Eskala* resort (K7000/3hr) is another possibility. *Myanmar Treasure Resort* charges an eye-watering $10/hr, while the *Aureum Palace* comes in at a mere $20/day (or free if you spend at least $30 on food and drink).

Ngapali

ငပလီ

Asked to vote for their favourite Burmese beach, nine out of ten travellers will most likely plump for **NGAPALI**. Named, according to folklore, by a homesick Italian in memory of his native city, Ngapali (pronounced "Napoli") has just about everything you'd expect of the perfect tropical getaway: kilometres of idyllic and still largely untouched beach, with powder-fine white sands backdropped by endless palms and fringed with a discreet line of upmarket resorts. The perfect bolthole, it feels a long way from anywhere but is easily accessible via a short flight from Yangon (although reaching it overland remains an unquestioned slog). The only real downside is the exorbitant cost of accommodation here, even by skyrocketing Myanmar standards – up to double the cost of similar places down the coast in Ngwe Saung.

The beach

"Ngapali" is a rather loose umbrella term used to cover several former fishing villages now all but linked up into a long necklace of hotels and resorts. At the north end of

TRIPS TO THANDWE

Around 10km inland from Ngapali (around K7000 one way by tuk-tuk), the town of **THANDWE** provides a low-key but enjoyable reminder of Burmese life beyond the beach – and sees quite a few visitors from the resorts looking for a slice of the "real" Myanmar. Thandwe has a long history. Minbin himself (see p.335) served as governor here for a decade before launching his bid for power, while the British (who called it **Sandoway**) established a garrison here. It's now the largest town in southern Rakhine, although there's nowhere for foreigners to stay, and food is limited to the usual noodle and curry stalls around the market.

Thandwe's intensely atmospheric **market**, housed (bizarrely) in the old colonial jail, is worth a look, and there are also three rhyming temples, each said to enshrine a bodily part of the Buddha. Just over 1.5km northwest of the market, the **Nandaw Paya** is said to have one of the Enlightened One's ribs, while to the east of the market the **Sandaw Paya** has a hair and the **Andaw Paya** a tooth.

the beach, the area **around the airport** is home to a burgeoning number of large resorts, while south of here the villages of **Lin Thar** and **Mya Pyin** (aka "Myabin") are where you'll find most of Ngapali's other hotels.

South of Mya Pyin (just past the *Pleasant View Resort*), the larger village of **Gyeiktaw** (aka Jade Taw) remains determinedly local, with lots of little thatched wooden huts and a pervasive smell of drying seafood – there's a lively fish market here, best in the early morning (around 6–7am). The next village south is **Lon Tha**. A small hilltop temple here offers superb views over the area – guides for the walk can be arranged at the *Silverfull* restaurant (see p.111).

There's nothing much to distract you from the beach here, although there are a few tours and water-based activities on offer (see box, p.112). For something more cultural, check out Ngapali Art Gallery (⊛ngapaliartgallery.com) and Htein Lin Thar Art Gallery, next door to one another at the northern end of Lin Thar village.

ARRIVAL AND DEPARTURE
NGAPALI

By plane Flights arrive at Thandwe Airport at the northern end of Ngapali beach. The hotels stretch from just outside the airport all the way down the coast to the *Pleasant View Resort*, around 10km south. Most hotels provide free airport transfers – check when you book. There are regular flights to Thandwe Airport with KBZ, Yangon Air, Air Bagan, Air Mandalay and Asian Wings. Most flights stop at Thandwe as part of longer circular routes, including Yangon–Thandwe–Sittwe and Nyaung U–Heho–Thandwe, meaning that although you can fly direct from Yangon to Thandwe (for example), travelling from Sittwe to Thandwe you might have to go all the way back to Yangon. Many flights cease running in the rainy season. You can buy plane tickets from Caravan travel agent (☎ 043 44044) on the road to the airport.

Destinations Bagan (daily; 1hr 20min); Sittwe (3 daily; 40min); Yangon (5 daily; 40min).

By bus Approaching by bus, you might end up in the nearby town of Thandwe (see box above), from where it's a short (around K7000) ride by tuk-tuk to Ngapali. There are services direct to Ngapali from Yangon via Pyay and then 1 nightly (12hr) from Pyay to Thandwe – these pick up/drop off passengers at hotels along the beach (some hotels also sell bus tickets). There may be additional services to Yangon, travelling down the coast via Gwa, which are sometimes slightly quicker, depending on the latest road conditions.

Destinations Pyay (1 daily; 12hr); Yangon via Pyay (1 daily; 18hr); Yangon via Gwa (1 daily; 16hr).

By boat Boats run from Sittwe (see p.118) to the small town of Taunggok, around 80km north of Thandwe, from where pick-ups (4hr) run on to Thandwe. You'll most likely have to either spend the night in Taunggok (pick-ups tend to all run in the mornings) or splash out on a taxi to Ngapali, assuming you can find one. There are a couple of basic guesthouses in Taunggok – the *Khant Guesthouse* is probably preferable to the *Royal*.

SOUTH ALONG THE COAST TO GWA

The beautiful swathe of coastline south of Ngapali is open to foreigners but remains largely unexplored. A few adventurous travellers village-hop up or down the coast, stopping off in **Maw Shwe Chai**, **Kanthaya** and **Gwa** (all of which have basic accommodation) en route.

GETTING AROUND

Ngapali is very spread out, and transport is in short supply. Occasional **tuk-tuks** and **pick-up** trucks ply the main road, but it's probably easiest to arrange something through your accommodation. **Bicycles** are also hard to find – try the *Royal Beach Motel* (K2500/day) or the *Jade Marina Resort* (K5000/day), just south of the *Aureum Palace*.

ACCOMMODATION

AROUND THE AIRPORT

★**Amara Ocean Resort** 3km north of airport ☎01 652 191, ⊛amaragroup.net. Well away from the hoi polloi, this is one of Ngapali's more exclusive addresses, with just 24 luxurious bungalows scattered discreetly around a stretch of drop-dead gorgeous beach. The cool dark-wood architecture is very easy on the eye, as is the superb infinity pool, and boating, hiking, biking and bird-watching trips can be arranged, in the unlikely event that you fancy venturing outside. **$290**

Amazing Ngapali 1km south of the airport ☎043 42011, ⊛amazingngapaliresort.com. Not as designer-perfect as some places in Ngapali, but scores highly for its fine stretch of beach, ultra-attentive staff and reasonable

rates. Accommodation is in rather chintzy villas, all with sea view as standard, and facilities include the usual pool and spa. **$150**

LIN THAR VILLAGE

Bay View Beach Resort Main Rd ☎043 42299, ⊛bayview-myanmar.com. One of Ngapali's better-value options, with accommodation in spacious bungalows crisply furnished in cool contemporary style. Facilities include the in-house *Catch* restaurant and the attractive (but expensive) *Sunset Bar* on the beach. There's also a big pool, plenty of loungers on the beach, plus spa and a billiards and darts room. Guests also get free bikes, and kayaking and catamaran trips can be arranged. **$170**

Memento Resort Main Rd ☎043 42441, ✉ngapalimementoresort@gmail.com. A rare sort-of budget option, with a good location on a prime stretch of beach and helpful, professional service. The four budget rooms at the back ($35) are basic but comfortable enough (with floor fan and cold water only), and there are also various more expensive rooms along the resort's extensive beachfront ($40–90), far and away the cheapest sea view to be had anywhere in Ngapali. Electricity runs 5.30pm–7am only, except in the most expensive rooms, which have 24hr power. The pleasant stilted restaurant right over the beach makes a nice spot for breakfast or a sundowner – and a lot cheaper than other hotels along the beach. Free wi-fi in reception. **$35**

Silver Beach Hotel Main Rd ☎043 42266, ⊛silverbeachngapali.com. Old-fashioned mid-range place with accommodation in plain cabanas topped with corrugated-iron roofs and set amid scrubby gardens – small and dated inside, but cosy enough, and all close to the beach. Some cheaper rooms ($75) in a newly constructed building set slightly back from the beach should have opened by the time you read this and may prove decent value, by Ngapali standards at least. Nice beachfront restaurant. **$100**

Thande Beach Hotel Main Rd ☎043 42278, ⊛thandebeachhotelmyanmar.com. One of Ngapali's best-value places (not saying much, admittedly), set amid lush and gorgeously manicured palm-studded gardens. The stylish rooms are attractively kitted out with antique-repro wooden furniture and there's a decent-sized (albeit shallow) pool, plus spa. Sea-view surcharges are less crippling than at other places. **$125**

MYA PYIN VILLAGE

Amata Resort & Spa ☎043 42177, ⊛amataresort .com. Ngapali's most original-looking resort, from the

Golf Course (3.5km), **1** (4km), Airport (6km), **2** (8km) & Thandwe (10km)

Htein Lin Thar Gallery

Ngapali Art Gallery

LIN THAR

N

MAIN ROAD

MYA PYIN

MAIN ROAD

GYEIKTAW (JADE TAW)

NGAPALI

0   500
metres

Gwa

■ **DRINKING**
| Memento Resort | 1 |
| Ye Hlay Bar | 2 |

■ **ACCOMMODATION**
Amara Ocean Resort	2
Amazing Ngapali	1
Amata Resort & Spa	9
Bay View Beach Resort	4
Memento Resort	5
Ngapali Bay Villas	7
Pleasant View Resort	12
Residence by Sandoway	10
Royal Beach Motel	11
Sandoway Resort	8
Silver Beach Hotel	3
Thande Beach Hotel	6

● **EATING**
Excellence	2
Htay Htay's Kitchen	1
Pleasant View Restaurant	5
Silverfull	4
Two Brothers	3

stunning wooden lobby (topped by a kind of abstract boat) through to the cute two-storey villas, set amid dense trees and constructed in a mix of wood and concrete and topped with bits of thatch and curiously shaped pitched roofs sticking out at quirky angles. Inside, big windows illuminate stylish rooms decorated with colourful fabrics and artworks. Facilities include an excellent spa and a rather undernourished pool. Fancier rooms with sea view come with a massive mark-up. $220

Ngapali Bay Villas ☎ 043 42301, ✆ ngapalibay.com. This super-chic resort looks like something straight out of a designer magazine. Rooms come with huge picture windows and giant mosquito nets cascading from high wooden ceilings, while bathrooms feature roll-top baths and gilded washbasins – and special sea-view windows from *inside* the showers (some rooms also have their own plunge pools). There are also beautiful gardens, a well-equipped spa, medium-sized pool and upmarket restaurant, and guests also have their own numbered loungers on the beach, so there's no squabbling with towel-dropping Germans. Closed May–Sept. $305

Pleasant View Resort ☎ 043 42251, ✆ pvrngapali .com. One of Ngapali's better-value resorts – if you don't mind the stylish but rather severe, quasi-industrial design. Rooms in the two-storey block at the back are also a bit too minimalist for the setting; the bungalows at the front are right on the beach and are more attractively furnished – and excellent value this close to the waves in Ngapali. There's a spa but no pool (although one is planned), and the attractive *Pleasant View Restaurant* (see below) is right

next door. Room $130, bungalow $180

Residence by Sandoway ☎ 043 42233, ✆ sandoway resort.com. Squeezed between the buildings of the *Amata Resort*, this easily missed little outpost of the *Sandoway Resort* has just fourteen beautiful rooms in a very quiet location very close to the waves – the six beachfront rooms ($40 extra) are as close to the sand as you'll get in Ngapali, and guests can use all the *Sandoway Resort* facilities, a 200m walk up the beach. Good value. $140

Royal Beach Motel ☎ 043 42411, ✆ royalbeachngapali .com. Along with the *Memento Resort*, this is Ngapali's only budget option at present, with just three basic budget rooms ($40) in what look like converted wooden sheds, although they do at least have attached bathrooms (cold water only) and 24hr electricity. There are also some more expensive wood and brick cabanas ($75–100) in a mishmash two-storey block on the beach, but they're darkish and unappealing given the price. $40

★ **Sandoway Resort** ☎ 043 42233, ✆ sandowayresort .com. One of Ngapali's longest-running places, open fifteen years but still looking minty fresh. The resort feels like a miniature self-contained village, full of twists and turns amid the densely tree-studded grounds. There's a range of attractively furnished rooms (as usual, sea-view rooms come with a hefty surcharge, and there are no in-room TVs), while the superb facilities include one of the biggest and nicest pools in Ngapali; an attractive library, spa and beachfront restaurant; and a superb little in-house cinema. Good value, given the quality. Closed May–Oct. $190

EATING

Seafood so fresh it practically jumps out of the bucket is the main draw at Ngapali, as elsewhere along the coast. There are plenty of **restaurants** along the main road, mostly small, family-run affairs, although without much to distinguish one from another. Alternatively, try the cluster of impromptu beach-bar shacks and little wooden cafés strung out on the beach between the *Memento Resort* and *Thande* hotel – particularly pretty after dark.

Excellence Lin Thar Village ☎ 043 42249. Big, attractive wooden pavilion restaurant with friendly service and a typical Ngapali menu focusing on fish, mainly Burmese style, along with a few Thai-style dishes plus a few token Western options (mains around K3000). The coconut fish curry is a guaranteed crowd pleaser. Daily 7am–10pm.

Htay Htay's Kitchen Lin Thar Village ☎ 043 42081. A bit more stylish than other places hereabouts, complete with romantically moody lighting and flowers on tables. The seafood-leaning menu features the usual Thai and Chinese dishes along with a good selection of Burmese options ranging from smoked-fish soup through to fishball salad with lemon leaves and assorted coconut-flavoured curries. Mains K3000–4000. Daily 8am–10pm.

Pleasant View Restaurant Mya Pyin Village ☎ 043 42251, ✆ pvrngapali.com. Ngapali's most appealing restaurant, set on a little rocky islet just offshore, connected

to the beach by a short wooden bridge (sometimes involving wading through a few centimetres of water when the tide is coming in, while a free boat is provided when the water gets sufficiently high). Food is a bit pricey (most mains K5500–8000) but generally good, featuring a mix of Burmese, Thai, Chinese and Western (fish and seafood only). Daily 9am–9pm.

Silverfull Mya Pyin Village ☎ 09 4965 3790. Run by three local brothers and serving up a wider than usual choice of food (mains mostly K3000–4000) including a good range of salads, pasta, tempura, sashimi and good-value set menus, plus cheap beer and cocktails. Also runs short cookery classes and can arrange tours (see box, p.112). Service is attentive, although sometimes verging on the pushy. Daily 9am–10pm.

Two Brothers Mya Pyin Village (opposite the Amata resort) ☎ 09 4965 3655. Cute little rattan-roofed

2

NGAPALI ACTIVITIES

Watersports can be arranged through Ngapali Water Sport Center (see below) and you can also arrange **snorkelling** through some of the hotels (around K20,000 for two people for half a day) – the best area is reckoned to be around Pearl Island, at the south end of the beach, which has good tropical fish (although hardly any coral). Some hotels – and also the *Silverfull* restaurant (see p.111) – can arrange other activities including kayaking, boat trips and fishing, while boatmen offering trips out to sea also hang out on the stretch of beach between the *Memento* and *Thande* hotels, where you'll also find various **massage shacks** (around K8000/hr), if you don't mind the lack of privacy. The main on-land activity is the local nine-hole **golf course**, between Lin Thar village and the airport. There are also short **cookery workshops** at the *Silverfull* restaurant.

OPERATORS

Ngapali Water Sport Center Airport Rd ☎ 09 4957 7070, ⊛ ngapaliwatersport.com. Arranges diving trips ($110–150/day plus $25 equipment rental), plus snorkelling, kayaking, fishing and local tours.
Silverfull Restaurant Mya Pyin Village ☎ 09 4965 3790. Runs daily, 30min cookery classes at 5pm

an item from the menu and they'll teach you how to prepare it. You pay the price of the dish from the menu plus K1500 per person. They also arrange combined fishing and snorkelling trips (4hr; K15,000 for 2 people) and walks to the Lon Tha temple and viewpoint (3hr; K10,000 for 2 people).

restaurant with friendly service and a menu bursting with assorted seafood, including lobster, crab, oyster, squid, prawns, octopus and other fruit of the waves, along with

the usual fish and meat dishes. Mains K3000–4000, plus some more expensive seafood options. Daily 6am–9pm.

DRINKING

Memento Resort Main Rd ☎ 043 42441. The breezy little café here (raised on stilts over the beach) is a pleasant spot for a drink – and a lot cheaper than many other places along the beach. Daily 8am–10pm.
Yé Hlay Bar Aureum Palace Hotel, Main Rd

☎ 043 42412. Cute bar in an old wooden boat right next to the sand. The drinks list features cocktails only, for a pricey K7000, although you can get two-for-one deals during the daily 5–7pm happy hour. Daily 2–10pm.

DIRECTORY

Banks There are no banks or ATMs in Ngapali, although there is a currency exchange desk at the airport. There's a KBZ bank with ATM in Thandwe on Bayintnaung Thitsar St.
Pharmacy Main road, opposite the *Sandoway Resort*.

Swimming pools Non-guests can use the lovely, serpenting pool at the *Aureum Palace* hotel for free if they take a meal in the hotel restaurant; alternatively, the big pool at the *Bay View Beach Resort* costs $10/day for non-residents.

Sittwe

စစ်တွေ

Capital of Rakhine State and gateway to Mrauk U, the remote town of **SITTWE** is one of western Myanmar's most absorbing – and disquieting – destinations. Landing here (or arriving after the arduous bus journey from Magwe), you'll feel a long way from the rest of Myanmar, and less than 100km from Bangladesh as the crow flies (not that you'd notice it). The town occupies a superb natural setting, at the point where the Kaladan River and other inland waterways drain into the Bay of Bengal, with views of endless water and distant hills in every direction, while the battered traces of old colonial architecture, *thanaka*-smeared Rakhine and lively market make the town one of Myanmar's more personable provincial capitals.

That, at least, is the surface. Less savoury is the town's recent history as the major flashpoint for clashes between the Rakhine and the town's **Rohingya Muslims** (see box, p.116), who once made up half the town's population but have now been driven out of

their homes and forced into refugee camps in the surrounding countryside – ethnic cleansing, by any other name. The character of the town has now significantly changed, and little evidence of the Rohingya's centuries-long presence in Sittwe now survives, save for the beautiful old Friday Mosque (see p.116), currently fenced off and watched over by armed police. The town wears a largely peaceful air following the upheavals of 2012–13, although an undercurrent of tension persists, with further riots erupting in early 2014 against local Western NGOs. Even in periods of calm, you may be confronted by locals spouting vicious racist nonsense concerning the brutalized Rohingya minority, which leaves a very sour taste.

Brief history

Formerly known as **Akyab**, Sittwe ("Sit-way" according to Burmese pronunciation, or "Sigh-tway" in Rakhine) is a largely colonial creation. Originally a small fishing settlement, the town was occupied by the British during the First Anglo-Burmese War and then chosen as the administrative capital of the annexed kingdom of Arakan (modern Rakhine State) in preference to the historic capital of Mrauk U. Sittwe grew exponentially during the following years, developing into an important port and major colonial centre, with direct steamers plying the route between here and Calcutta (its progeny including British short-story writer Hector Hugh Munro, better known under his pen name Saki, who was born here in 1870). The city's maritime importance is set to be revived following the 2011 bilateral agreement between Myanmar and India during which the two countries agreed to invest $120 million in developing a new

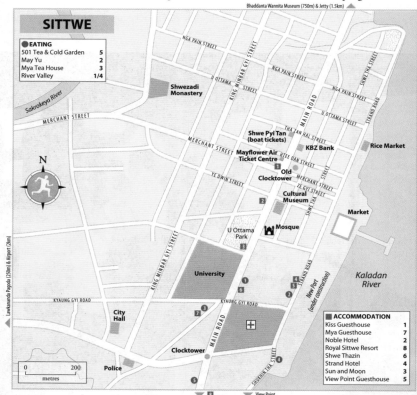

SITTWE

EATING
501 Tea & Cold Garden	5
May Yu	2
Mya Tea House	3
River Valley	1/4

Bhaddanta Wannita Museum (750m) & Jetty (1.5km)

NGA PAIN STREET
KING MINBAR GYI STREET
U OTTAMA STREET
NGA PAIN STREET
SHWE THA STREET
Sakrokeya River
MERCHANT STREET
Shwezadi Monastery
NGA PAIN STREET
MAIN ROAD
U OTTAMA STREET
STRAND ROAD
THA ZAN HAL STREET
Shwe Pyi Tan (boat tickets)
KBZ Bank
Rice Market
MERCHANT STREET
Mayflower Air Ticket Centre
HTEE DAN STREET
Old Clocktower
MERCHANT STREET
SE GYI STREET
SHWE THA
YE DWIN STREET
Cultural Museum
Market
U Ottama Park
Mosque
Lawkananda Pagoda (250m) & Airport (2km)
University
KING MINBAR GYI STREET
New Port (under construction)
Kaladan River
KYAUNG GYI ROAD
City Hall
KYAUNG GYI ROAD
MAIN ROAD
Clocktower
SHUKHIN THA STREET
Police
View Point

0 200 metres

ACCOMMODATION
Kiss Guesthouse	1
Mya Guesthouse	7
Noble Hotel	2
Royal Sittwe Resort	8
Shwe Thazin	6
Strand Hotel	4
Sun and Moon	3
View Point Guesthouse	5

2

KINGS AND CROCODILES: A BRIEF HISTORY OF ARAKAN

The history of the kingdom of **Arakan** (modern-day **Rakhine State**) is claimed to date back nearly five thousand years, and the Rakhine preserve a genealogy of 227 native kings lasting until the Konbaung conquest in 1784. At its height, it covered large parts of what is now modern Myanmar and Bangladesh, stretching from the Ganges to the Ayeyarwady. According to tradition, the first Rakhine kingdom emerged around the northern town of **Dhanyawadi** in about 3400 BC, lasting until the founding of Waithali in 327 AD – the Buddha himself is alleged to have visited the kingdom, with the famous Mahamuni Buddha image (see p.271) being cast at around the same time.

The capital subsequently shifted to **Waithali** (aka Vesali), which grew prosperous on trade with India and China. In around 818 a new dynasty arose on the Laymro River, ushering in the **Lemro** period. The final Rakhine kingdom was founded in 1429 by Min Saw Mon at **Mrauk U** – the golden age of Rakhine history (see p.334 & p.335). Mrauk U was conquered by the Konbaung dynasty in 1784, and then passed to the British in 1826 following the First Anglo-Burmese War, after which the capital was transferred to Sittwe, where it remains to this day.

Rakhine saw fierce fighting during World War II, including the Arakan Campaign of 1942–43 and the notorious **Battle of Ramree Island**, during which almost a thousand Japanese soldiers are said to have been eaten by crocodiles – listed by the *Guinness Book of World Records* as the "Worst Crocodile Disaster In The World".

Arakan became part of the newly independent Union of Burma in 1948, although the 1950s saw increasing calls for a restoration of Arakanese independence, and nationalist feelings remain high.

---

port complex to facilitate trade between India's northeastern states, as well as direct large-scale shipping between Sittwe and Kolkata (Calcutta).

Sittwe also has a long tradition of radical Buddhism (most notably as the birthplace of radical monk **U Ottama**, a leading figure in the colonial-era independence movement), while the city's monks also played a leading role in the so-called Saffron Revolution (see p.348). Religious belligerence has also shown an uglier face in recent years during repeated clashes between the city's Rakhine population and the increasingly brutalized **Rohingya** minority (see box, p.116).

Strand Road

ကမ်းနားလမ်း

Sittwe's most interesting street, **Strand Road** runs along the east side of the centre, dotted with some of the town's best surviving colonial architecture including a couple of fine old wooden garden villas down near the *May Yu* restaurant. Close by, a large expanse of cleared ground announces the location of Sittwe's new **port**, designed to bolster trade with India.

The street's major landmark is the fine old **market** building, stuffed with marine creatures both fresh and preserved including eye-catching bundles of enormous air-dried fish tied up by their tails, while further north along the road a second building provides a home for local rice dealers, with huge piles of rice sacks laid out on the road.

On the far side of the main market building the **jetty** offers beautiful views across the smooth waters of the Kaladan estuary to the hills opposite, of myriad boats, and of Sittwe's low-slung waterfront houses nestling amid the palms.

Main Road

လမ်းမကြီး

Heading a block inland from the market brings you out on **Main Road** close to the old **colonial clocktower** – a chintzy, falling-to-bits old Victorian relic set on top of a large pylon.

A short walk south, just past the Cultural Museum (see below), is the town's main **mosque**, a fitting symbol of Sittwe's oppressed Muslim minority, its entrance now blocked off with barbed-wire-festooned crash barriers and guarded by gun-toting soldiers. It's difficult to see much of the mosque now, shielded by high walls and dense trees, although you can catch a few glimpses of the florid – if semi-derelict – colonial-era building, its chintzy Neoclassical ground floor complete with incongruous Doric columns topped with a flamboyant mass of diminutive domes and miniature minarets.

A further block south, the trees opposite the *Shwe Thazin* hotel are home to an enormous colony of **fruit bats**, hanging spookily from the trees in big black clusters by day, then waking at dusk and swirling above the streets before setting off to hunt through the night.

Cultural Museum

ယဉ်ကျေးမှုပြတိုက် • Main St • Tues–Sun 9.30am–4.30pm • K2000

Sittwe's lacklustre **Cultural Museum** serves to fill an hour – just. Ground-floor exhibits focus on Rakhine culture and crafts, plus an introduction to the moves of Rakhine wrestling – handy if you find yourself in a spot of bother with a bear, or suchlike. Rakhine history (see box, p.115) takes over on the **first floor**. Most impressive is the 3m-tall Anandacandra Pillar, commissioned by King Anandacandra in 729 and recording the achievements of the previous 37 Rakhine monarchs in faded Sanskrit – the only surviving historical record of the entire Wethali (Vesali) period.

ROHINGYA REPRESSION IN RAKHINE

One of the world's most persecuted minorities (according to the UN), the **Rohingya Muslims** of Myanmar are currently facing a titanic battle not just for basic political rights, but for their very survival. Around 800,000 Rohingya live in Rakhine State, with a further million spread across Bangladesh, Pakistan, Thailand and Saudi Arabia. Most Burmese regard them, bizarrely, as illegal immigrants (despite the fact that they have been in the country since at least colonial times, possibly much longer) and insist they should all be sent back to Bangladesh (which doesn't want them, and in which the vast majority of Rohingya have never set foot). They are also **stateless**, having been stripped of their citizenship in 1982 – while despite their large numbers the Rohingya ethnicity was not even recognized in the national census of 2014.

Tensions between the Burmese and Rohingya have simmered for decades – particularly since the withdrawal of the British – and the government has routinely discriminated against the Rohingya. As well as stripping them of citizenship, Rohingya have also been forbidden from travelling even locally without permission or from having more than two children. Forced labour, extortion, arbitrary taxation, land seizures and chronic food shortages have also been common facts of life.

And then, in 2012, things got even worse with the outbreak of major riots throughout Rakhine State following the rape and murder of a Buddhist woman and the retaliatory killing of ten Rohingya. Dozens, perhaps hundreds, of Rohingya were killed, and thousands displaced – more than 100,000 continue to languish in **camps** in Myanmar (along with many thousands more similarly detained in Bangladesh, and in areas around the Myanmar–Thai border). Efforts by international organizations to ease the plight of those living in the camps have been strongly resisted – the Buddhist clergy have been particularly noisy in condemning organizations working with the Rohingya.

Myanmar's desire to ethnically cleanse itself of the Rohingya appears to permeate all levels of society. Members of the National League for Democracy, whilst loudly protesting their own lack of political freedom, have been equally dismissive of the Rohingya's plight, while even Aung San Suu Kyi – the one figure in Myanmar with the standing and moral authority to possibly shift entrenched racist attitudes – has been shamefully silent on the issue.

Lawkananda Pagoda

လောကနန္ဒာဘုရား • Airport Rd • Daily 6am–9pm • Free

A short walk southwest of the centre is the imposing **Lawkananda Pagoda**, Sittwe's principal temple. The huge Shwedagon-style pagoda (the gift of military ruler Than Shwe in 1997) sits on a vast empty terrace covered in jazzy blue and white tiles, with four faux-antique stone doorways leading into the opulent interior, painted in wall-to-wall gold and red and with many gilded pillars supporting the domed ceiling.

From the west side of the terrace, steps lead down to a small octagonal pavilion topped with a many-tiered gilded roof, like a very fancy hat. This is home to the exquisite **Sakyamuni Buddha**, a 45cm-high bronze Buddha said to be more than two thousand years old. The statue is seated in the earth-witness pose, holding a star-shaped *dharmachakra* ("wheel of dharma") and clad in a robe and hat covered with more than a thousand finely carved mini-Buddhas.

View Point

ရှုခင်းသာ • K2000 by tuk-tuk – although it's also perfect for a late afternoon walk

The best place to appreciate Sittwe's superb natural setting is at the beautiful **View Point** (or just "The Point"), 3km south of town along the peaceful waterfront road. There's also a small café here (daily 6am–9pm) – great for a beer while watching sunset over the waves.

Bhaddanta Wannita Museum

ဘဒ္ဒန္တဝဏ္ဏိတပြတိုက် • Main St, 1.5km north of the centre • No fixed opening hours, although there's likely to be someone around to let you in at most hours of the day or evening • Free, but donations appreciated

Housed in a fine old colonial mansion north of the centre, the Maha Kuthala Kyaung Tawgyi monastery is home to the **Bhaddanta Wannita Museum**, showcasing (if that's the right word) the great heaps of bric-a-brac collected by the late Venerable U Bhaddanta Wannita. The museum's dusty display cases are stuffed full of coins, notes, Buddhas, pipes, bits of coral and a couple of golfing trophies – nothing's actually labelled, although most of it is obviously junk. Resident monks often hang around wanting to practise their English – their conversation is likely to be a lot more interesting than the exhibits on display.

ARRIVAL AND DEPARTURE | SITTWE

BY PLANE

The airport is 2.5km west of town (K3000 by tuk-tuk). The best local source of air tickets and other flight info is the Mayflower Air Ticket Centre (☎043 23452), on Main Rd opposite the KBZ Bank. Thandwe (for Ngapali beach) is just 40min away by air, although airlines typically travel a circular Yangon–Thandwe–Sittwe route, meaning you might have to travel back to Yangon first.

Destination Yangon (6 daily; 1hr 20min).

BY BUS

Foreigners were previously banned from taking the road out of Sittwe, due to the large number of military bases along the route. The road was opened to foreigners in 2013 but may conceivably close once more in the event of trouble. Check the situation locally and book tickets at least a day ahead. Reaching Sittwe by bus remains a hard slog. The closest jumping-off point is Magwe, although direct buses also run from as far afield as Meiktila and Mandalay.

All these services go via Mrauk U, but it's not generally faster than the boat (except the slow government ferry), and a lot less enjoyable. The bus station is 4km west of town, around K3000 by tuk-tuk from the centre.

Destinations Magwe (1 daily; 15hr); Mandalay (1 daily; 30hr); Meiktila (1 daily; 26hr); Mrauk U (3–4 daily; 5hr); Yangon (1 nightly; 30hr).

BY BOAT

TO MRAUK U

There is one ferry daily to Mrauk U, run by different operators on different days – all boats depart at 7am from the jetty at the end of Main Rd, around 2km north of the centre (K2000 by tuk-tuk).

IWT ferry The slowest option is the government boat (Tues & Fri; 6hr 30min–7hr 30min; K7000). Tickets for this can be bought at the jetty from 6am on the morning of departure. The boat can get pretty packed, so arrive in good time. You'll have to pay an extra K1000 for a seat – usually a deckchair.

2

Aung Kyaw Moe boat Faster is the thrice-weekly Aung Kyaw Moe boat (Mon, Thurs & Sat; K10,000; 4–5hr); either buy your ticket when you turn up or in advance from their office at the jetty.

Shwe Pyi Tan Quickest of all is the Shwe Pyi Tan boat (Sun & Wed; K20,000; 2hr 30min) – twice as fast and twice as expensive. Tickets are available from the Shwe Pyi Tan office (☎ 09 4959 2709) just north of KBZ Bank on Main Rd – there's no English sign, although the big banner of a boat over the door rather gives it away.

Private boats You could also arrange a private boat (up to four people; 5–6hr; K150,000 return) at the airport and leave the same day, so long as you arrive by about 2.30pm. Make sure you agree on how many days they'll wait for you in Mrauk U.

TO TAUNGGOK
The ferry to Taunggok leaves from the jetty at 6.30am on Wed, Sat and Sun, arriving in Taunggok at around 4pm. Tickets (K35,000) can be bought from the Shwe Pyi Tan office (see above).

GETTING AROUND

Central Sittwe is pretty compact, although you'll need transport when travelling to/from the airport and boat jetty, and out to the View Point. There are plenty of Rakhine-style **tuk-tuks** (a kind of pick-up truck attached to a motorbike) cruising the streets, and you may also be able to rent a **bicycle** from the *Shwe Thazin* hotel.

ACCOMMODATION

The increasing number of tourists, business travellers and aid workers passing through Sittwe means that accommodation can often be surprisingly difficult to find – this is definitely one place where it pays to book ahead. The shortage is compounded by the fact that many of the guesthouses along Main Rd (including the *Golden*, *Mercedes* and *Prince* guesthouses) aren't licensed to accept foreign guests. In addition to the places below, the long-running *New Palace Hotel* at the north end of town (5 Main Rd; ☎ 043 21996, ⓦ newpalacehotelsittwe.com) may have reopened by the time you read this, following renovations. Breakfast is included at most places below (unless specifically stated), but nowhere except at *Kiss* and *Royal Sittwe* currently has wi-fi, or any other kind of internet.

Kiss Guesthouse 145 Main Rd (opposite the old clocktower) ☎ 043 23451. Simple but cheap option, with basic but reasonably clean and comfy tiled rooms with attached bathroom (cold water only), although rooms close to the road are a bit noisy. Currently has the only wi-fi in the town centre. $20

Mya Guesthouse 51/6 Bowdhi St ☎ 043 23315. Sittwe's best-known budget guesthouse, although one that's grown increasingly fat and lazy thanks to an easy flow of foreign customers. The simple rooms, with a/c and attached cold-water bathrooms, are adequate but overpriced (although single rates are decent value at just $20), while service is indifferent and reservations aren't always honoured. $30

Noble Hotel 45 Main Rd ☎ 043 23558, ⓔ anw.noble @gmail.com. So-so mid-range hotel bang in the heart of town. All rooms come with a/c, TV minibar and safe, although they're looking dated and aren't great value for money. Acceptable, but not as nice as the nearby *Shwe Thazin*. $50

Royal Sittwe Resort 3km south of town ☎ 043 23478, ⓦ royalsittweresort.asia. Sittwe's most upmarket option – although the workaday resort-style complex hardly sets the pulse racing. The old-fashioned and rather plain rooms aren't particularly good value, and the restaurant is humdrum, although a fine location overlooking the Bay of Bengal and a priceless (but erratic) wi-fi connection partly compensate. Free transfers from airport/boat jetty included. $105

Shwe Thazin 250 Main Rd ☎ 043 23579, ⓦ shwethazin hotel.com. Central Sittwe's plushest option, with comfortable and well-furnished a/c rooms at a fairly reasonable price, plus decent service and a good breakfast buffet. $55

Strand Hotel Strand Rd ☎ 043 22881. Not quite open at the time of writing, this new place promises a handful of bright modern rooms for a price most likely in the region of $75

Sun and Moon Main Rd (no phone). Fallback option right in the middle of town, with dilapidated and not particularly clean rooms with attached cold-water bathrooms, but not much else. $15

View Point Guesthouse Strand Rd ☎ 043 23689. Filthy, mosquito-plagued cubicle-style "rooms" (with private bathroom for $5 extra, and free cockroaches). No breakfast. Strictly for use in an emergency only. $15

EATING

501 Tea & Cold Garden Main Rd. Attractive local garden restaurant – and a quieter alternative to the nearby River Valley, with friendly service and well-prepared versions of all the usual Chinese and seafood dishes (mains K1500–4000). Nice place for a beer, even if you don't eat. Daily 8am–10pm.

May Yu Strand Rd, opposite the new port. Pleasant seafront restaurant (although the new port construction opposite blocks out the waves) in a cheery wooden building painted yellow and blue outside and pink within, and with a nice terrace in front. Food includes a smallish selection of local seafood plus all the usual Chinese staples (mains K1500–4000), competently if unexceptionally prepared. Daily 8am–10pm.

Mya Tea House Next to the Mya Guesthouse. Cheery garden tea shop, dishing up simple, inexpensive meals including big bowls of nourishing *mohinga* (K500). Daily 6am–7pm.

River Valley 5 Main Rd ☎ 043 23234. Convivial, foreigner-friendly restaurant with seating in a pleasant garden illuminated with fairy lights after dark and a long list of mainstream but well-prepared Chinese dishes (mains K3500–4000). There's a second branch on the seafront nearby with an identical menu and attracting more of a local crowd. Daily 7.30am–10pm.

DIRECTORY

Banks There's an ATM and moneychangers at the big branch of KBZ on Main Rd (but not at the smaller KBZ on Strand Rd).

Internet Sittwe was seriously offline at the time of writing, with no internet or wi-fi access anywhere in the town centre apart from wi-fi at the *Kiss Guesthouse*.

Mrauk U and around

 မြောက်ဦးမြို့

Hidden upriver amid the watery labyrinths of the Kaladan River, the remote and decidedly rustic town of **MRAUK U** was once the last and greatest capital of the kingdom of **Arakan** (see p.115 & p.334), its 49 kings ruling for 350 years over an empire stretching, at its apogee, from the Ayeyarwady to the Ganges and controlling large areas of what is now Myanmar and Bangladesh. Mrauk U also served as a unique medieval melting pot of foreign influences. Its Buddhist rulers adopted Islamic titles and customs influenced by the nearby Sultanate of Bengal, while the city also faced off Portuguese incursions and later served as a major pan-Asian trading base. The conquest and sack of the city at the hands of the Konbaung dynasty in 1784 brought Mrauk U's glory days to an end, while the British decision to move the provincial capital to Sittwe in 1826 further hastened its decline. Lasting mementoes of Mrauk U's glory days survive, however, in the shape of a unique collection of remarkable fortified **temples** – among Asia's weirdest Buddhist monuments.

For the traveller, Mrauk U has always had a peculiar allure, and nowadays pulls in a steadily growing number of foreign visitors, notwithstanding the difficulty of reaching the place or recent troubles in Rakhine (the town has frequently been off limits in recent years due to local unrest). Few people who make the effort of reaching the place regret it, even if the town is now increasingly entering the tourist mainstream and has now lost much of its final-frontier allure – a new airport and railway line are planned, while there are also rumours that the government plans to evict inhabitants from their old houses among the temples (as happened in Old Bagan) in order to develop it as a tourist attraction.

Around Mrauk U, interesting day-trips along the Lemro River offer a rare opportunity to visit **Chin villages** and see some of the famous tattooed ladies who live there, while the slight remains of the former Arakanese capitals of **Dhanyawadi** and **Waithali** can also be seen.

Central Mrauk U

For all its historical significance, the centre of Mrauk U still looks like the archetypal one-horse Burmese country town, with its busy market, potholed streets, and makeshift shops and rustic cafés lined up along dusty **Minbar Gyi Road**, which is usually as busy as Mrauk U ever gets. In complete contrast is the expansive, largely empty swathe of land

One popular theory holds that the **name** Mrauk U is a corruption of *myauk u*, meaning "Monkey Egg", said to have been offered to the Buddha by a monkey as a sign of his devotion. It's pronounced "Mrow-Oo" by the Rakhine, or as a rather feline-sounding "Meow-Oo" by the Burmese.

2

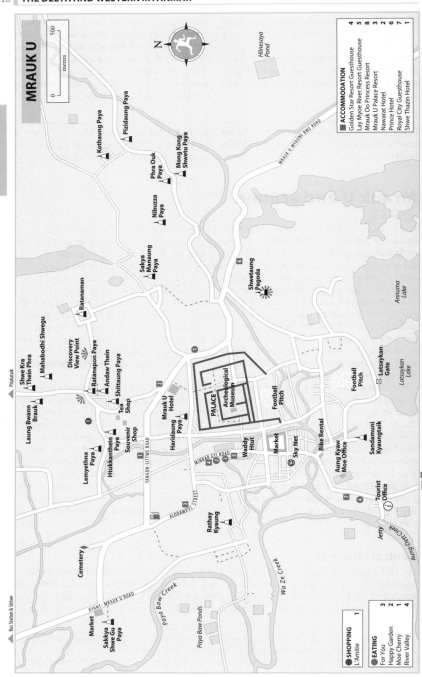

MRAUK U

N

0 metres 500

▲ Pitakataik

◀ Bus Station & Sittwe

ACCOMMODATION
Golden Star Resort Guesthouse	4
Lay Myoe River Resort Guesthouse	5
Mrauk Oo Princess Resort	8
Mrauk U Palace Resort	3
Nawarat Hotel	2
Prince Hotel	6
Royal City Guesthouse	7
Shwe Thazin Hotel	1

SHOPPING
| L'Amitie | 1 |

EATING
For You	3
Happy Garden	2
Moe Cherry	1
River Valley	4

Hlinesaya Pond

Kothaung Paya
Pizidaung Paya
Phra Ouk Paya
Mong Kong Shwetu Paya
Nibuzza Paya
Sakya Manaung Paya
Ratanaman
Mahabodhi Shwegu
Discovery View Point
Shwe Kra Thein Phra
Batanapon Paya
Andaw Thein
Shittaung Paya
Laung Bwann Brauk
Lemyethna Paya
Htukkanthein Paya
Souvenir Shop
Tea Shop
Haridaung Paya
Mrauk U Hotel
PALACE
Archeological Museum
Shwetaung Pagoda
MRAUK U–MYAUNG BWE ROAD
Latsaykan Gate
Football Pitch
Football Pitch
Annuma Lake
Latsaykan Lake
Sandamuni Kyaungtaik
Aung Kyaw Moe Office
Bike Rental
Market
Waddy Htut
Sky Net
Tourist Office
Jetty
Aung Dott Creek
Wa Ze Creek
Rathay Kyaung
ALODAWPYI STREET
MINBAR GYI ROAD
YANGON–SITTWE ROAD
Cemetery
Market
Sakkya Shwe Gu Paya
KYAWT–MRAUK U ROAD
Poyo Baw Creek
Paya Baw Ponds

just northwest which formerly housed Mrauk U's magnificent, but now entirely vanished, royal **palace**.

The Palace and Archeological Museum

နန်းတော်နှင့် / ရှေးဟောင်းသုတေသနပြိုတိုက် • **Palace site** open 24hr • Free **Museum** Tues–Sun 9.30am–4.30pm • K5000

There's not much left of the original **Palace** complex, bang in the middle of town, apart from its impressively long walls arranged in three concentric squares around a trio of successively rising terraces – the actual pal ace would have stood on the highest terrace at the centre, which now provides good views over the site. The original royal residence was commissioned by King Minbin in 1430 and rebuilt at least two times subsequently, providing a home for 49 kings over a period of 350 years, although the magnificent wooden palace building itself was destroyed when the city was sacked by the forces of the Konbaung dynasty in 1784.

On the western side of the complex, the overpriced government **Archeological Museum** is about as exciting (or not) as you'd expect, collecting together assorted finds from around the site plus some artefacts from the previous Arakanese capital of Waithali (see p.127), just down the road.

Haridaung Paya

ဟာရိတောင်ဘုရား

On a small, steep hill just north of the Palace area, the tiny **Haridaung Paya** is little more than a simple gold-painted stupa but offers one of Mrauk U's finest views, with dozens of stupas crowning the hills all around and glimpses of water between the trees. It's not signed: look out for the white steps (which can get appallingly hot under bare feet) next to the road, from where it's a few minutes' walk to the top.

Market

Mrauk U's little tree-studded **market** is an appropriately rustic affair, with the usual stalls full of fruit, vegetables and herbs alongside piles of traditional Rakhine-style pointed bamboo hats, heaps of *chinlone* balls, anchors, enormous saws and a surprising quantity of pharmacies, including one alleyway stuffed entirely with little shops selling either pills or beer. The west side of the market is where you'll find the town's tailors, lined up at a row of tables behind heaps of cloth and old-fashioned sewing machines.

Northern Group

Mrauk U's **Northern Group** of temples is the undoubted highlight of the ancient city, centred on the landmark **Shittaung** and **Htukkanthein** temples. Both are classic examples of the city's unique style of fortified temple, set upon impregnably high bases

---

EXPLORING MRAUK U'S TEMPLES

The two main groups of temples are to the **north** and **east of the centre**; most are open daily 7am–5.30pm, with entry covered by a single ticket (K5000) issued at the Shittaung Paya (although ticket checks at other temples were virtually nonexistent at the time of writing).

Although Mrauk U is often described as the "new Bagan", comparisons are misleading. Aside from the "big three" temples – **Shittaung**, **Htukkanthein** and **Kothaung** – Mrauk U doesn't really have Bagan's landmark monuments and must-see sights, and in some ways rather than ticking off temples it's more fun just to cycle or walk at random among the thickly wooded, stupa-studded hills.

Easily the best introduction to ancient Arakan and Mrauk U is Pamela Gutman's *Burma's Lost Kingdoms: splendours of Arakan* (Bangkok: Orchid Press; 2001), although it's difficult to come by. *Famous Monuments of Mrauk U* by Myar Aung (K5000) is widely available locally, but is mainly unintelligible gibberish.

and with thick, almost windowless walls. The design offers an apt reflection of medieval Arakan's turbulent history, during which the city was attacked on numerous occasions – the temples themselves possibly served as refuges for the embattled population. Later and more decorative monuments such as the nearby **Ratanapon** and **Laung Bwann Brauk** offer a notable contrast in style.

Shittaung Paya

ရှစ်သောင်းဘုရား • K5000 for ticket collected at Shittaung along with a more or less obligatory K2000 "donation" to light the corridors of three temples (Shittaung, Htukkanthein and Andaw Thein) for one hour

The usual starting point for tours of Mrauk U is the landmark **Shittaung Paya**, built by the founder of Mrauk U, King Minbin, in 1535 to celebrate his reconquest of "the twelve towns of the Ganges" (roughly half of modern Bangladesh) – the name refers to the 80,000 (*shittaung*) images said to be housed here. The temple is set on a huge fortified terrace and surrounded by numerous small stupas in Mrauk U's distinctive style, topped not by the usual spire but with a truncated finial vaguely resembling a stone mushroom. Some faint reliefs can also be seen in places around the outer walls (including a couple of vaguely erotic scenes on the southern side). Unfortunately the exterior is now a complete mess following the addition of a modern prayer hall and stairway in the mid-twentieth century, while in 2003 (following the discovery of cracks in the main stupa) the Archeology Department decided to encase the temple's upper terrace in eyesore concrete in order to stop water leaking into the temple below.

The Shittaung Pillar

At the bottom of the steps up to the temple stands the **Shittaung Pillar** (set inside in a green barred shelter), with inscriptions in badly eroded Sanskrit recording the genealogy of the Arakan kings. The three sides (the fourth is blank) are thought to have each been carved two hundred years apart, in the sixth, eighth and tenth centuries respectively.

The prayer hall and central shrine

At the top of the stairs, entrance is via a small vestibule where tickets are issued and guidebooks sold (walking straight through the vestibule and exiting via the rear door brings you out right next to the Andaw Thein). Turn left into the colourful modern **prayer hall**, with gilded Buddhas stacked up around the walls and bright ceiling paintings overhead. An elaborate stone door directly ahead of you (as you enter the hall) leads into a **central shrine** with a large gilded Buddha, its body patterned with squares of gold leaf applied by worshippers.

The corridors

Shittaung's real highlights, however, are the pair of marvellously atmospheric corridors reached via doors in the far left corner of the prayer hall. The **inner corridor**, walled with roughly hewn sandstone and lined with dozens of Buddhas, coils round on itself before reaching a dead end, with tiny openings in the walls offering glimpses of the main prayer hall and outer corridor.

Even more impressive is the **outer corridor**, however, more than 100m-long and lined with a spectacularly intricate stone frieze decorated with more than a thousand sculptures. The frieze is divided into six levels, alternately projecting and recessed, with faded paint covering many surfaces. Carvings depict the usual Jataka scenes and miscellaneous mythical monsters along with figures from Rakhine life (musicians, dancers, soldiers). Larger projecting sculptures include King Minbin himself (in the southwest corner), Indra mounted on his three-headed elephant Erawan, and Brahma astride his *hamsa*.

Htukkanthein Paya

ထုက္ကန်သိမ် • Daily 7am–5.30pm • Entry covered by main temple ticket

The **Htukkanthein** (or "Dukkanthein") **Paya** is the most memorable of all Mrauk U's temples, and the perfect example of the town's distinctive architectural style: a huge mass of brick and stone virtually unrelieved by any kind of decoration and looking more like a fortress, high-security prison or nuclear bomb shelter than anything remotely religious. The temple's defensive qualities are enhanced by its setting on a high, almost sheer-sided, terrace, with just a single entrance – even the tiny square windows look like embrasures for cannon rather than sources of light.

Built in 1571 by King Min Phalaung, the U-shaped temple itself is linked to a small rectangular shrine at the back and topped with five "mushroom" stupas in a quincunx pattern (or almost). Most of the interior is occupied by a remarkable **corridor**, which loops around on itself twice and connects two interior chambers before climbing up to the barn-like rooftop shrine. Lining the corridor are 179 seated Buddha images in niches each flanked by carved male and female figures said to represent the donors who financed construction of the temple. The figures are famous for modelling all 64 of medieval Mrauk U's **traditional hairstyles**, most of which seem to involve big topknot and turban-style arrangements – not a million miles away from the mushroom-shaped caps on the stupas outside.

Lemyethna Paya

လေးမျက်နှာဘုရား • Daily 7am–5.30pm • Entry covered by main temple ticket

Next to the road just past the Htukkanthein, the small **Leymyethna Paya** was built in 1430 by King Min Saw Mon. Outside, it's another of Mrauk U's characteristically impregnable constructions: a windowless bunker topped with a stupa with cut-off spire. Four entrances lead into the circular interior, with eight seated Buddhas placed around the central octagonal pillar beneath a vaulted ceiling.

Andaw Thein

အံတော်သိမ်ဘုရား • Immediately north of the Shittaung's Paya (exit the rear side of Shittaung's antechamber leading to the main prayer hall) • Daily 7am–5.30pm • Entry covered by main temple ticket

The **Andaw Thein** was original built as an ordination hall (*thein*) in 1521 by King Thazata and subsequently expanded into a temple by King Raza II to house a tooth relic (*andaw*) of the Buddha brought back from a visit to Sri Lanka in around 1600. Fourteen stupas (each hollow, and with a small seated Buddha inside) are arranged around three sides of the octagonal **main shrine**, built in the usual bunker style and topped with further stupas. Two concentric corridors penetrate the inside, lined with niched Buddha statues.

Attached to the shrine is a rectangular **prayer hall** still boasting a fine stone doorway on its eastern side, although the original roof has gone, now replaced with a corrugated iron shelter.

Ratanapon Paya

ရတနာပုံ ဘုရား • Open access 24hr • Entry covered by main temple ticket

Immediately past Andaw Thein is the **Ratanapon** (aka "Yadanpon") **Paya**. Built in 1612 by King Min Khammoung (or possibly his wife), this is one of Mrauk U's later and less militaristic-looking monuments, centred on an unusually tall (if rather bottom-heavy) stupa. A necklace of seventeen mini-stupas encloses the main stupa, set on an octagonal terrace decorated with a few lion sculptures, now badly eroded. The temple's name translates as "Pile of Jewels", referring, it's said, to the precious stones enshrined in the central stupa, although none has ever been found despite the best efforts of bounty hunters, while a direct hit from a Japanese bomb in World War II also failed to reveal any buried treasure (the damage has since been restored).

Mahabodhi Shwegu

မဟာဗောဓိရွှေဂူ • Daily 7am–5.30pm • Entry covered by main temple ticket • To reach the Mahabodhi Shwegu, go north along the road from the Ratanapon towards the Laung Bwann Brauk; just before you reach the latter you'll see a covered well on your right – follow the steep path up the hill behind this to reach the temple

Dating from the latter half of the fifteenth century, the tiny **Mahabodhi Shwegu** is one of Mrauk U's more unusual monuments, with a quaint little octagonal domed shrine connected to a narrow antechamber. Its main interest, however, is the intricate, albeit very eroded, carvings decorating the antechamber walls and the throne of the central Buddha image. These include representations of the Buddhist heaven and hell along with some erotic images – although you'll have to look very closely to make anything out.

Laung Bwann Brauk

လောင်ပွန်းပြောက်ဘုရား • Open access 24hr • Entry covered by main temple ticket

The slightly leaning stupa of Mrauk U, **Laung Bwann Brauk** temple is characterized by its fractionally tilted outline (more obvious from some angles than others), the stupa having crumpled slightly under its own weight. The base of the octagonal stupa is ringed with elaborately carved niches, some still containing Buddha images, or what's left of them, while the front of the terrace is decorated with unusual flower-shaped glazed tiles, although many are now sadly crumbling into dust.

Just north of here on the other side of the road stands the diminutive **Shwe Kra Thein Phra**: a pretty little stupa raised high on a finely carved six-tier base.

Pitakataik

ပိဋကတ်တိုက် • Daily 7am–5.30pm • Entry covered by main temple ticket

Mrauk U's smallest and prettiest monument, the quaint **Pitakataik** is the only one of the city's original 48 libraries to have survived – although it looks far too small to have stored more than a handful of books. The building was commissioned by King Mong Phaloung in 1591 to house a set of the Buddhist Tripitaka and is unusual in being constructed of solid stone rather than the usual brick, elaborately decorated with abstract geometrical shapes, a fancy door and a spiky zigzag roof in four tiers, now sagging slightly under its own weight. The tiny vaulted interior is contrastingly bare.

Eastern group

Mrauk U's **eastern group** of monuments is rather more scattered and low-key than the northern group, barring the massive **Kothaung Paya**, one of the town's stand-out sights. Many date from the kingdom's middle years and include a trio of fine stupas – at the **Mong Khong Shwetu**, **Sakyaman Aung** and **Ratanaman** temples – exemplifying Mrauk U's later and lighter architectural style.

Phra Ouk and Mong Khong Shwetu

ဘုရားအုပ်/မင်းခေါင်ရွှေတူ • Open access 24hr • Entry covered by main temple ticket

Set atop a small hillock next to the road, the pint-sized **Phra Ouk Paya** is said to have been erected as a talisman by King Phalaung in 1571 when warned of external threats against his kingdom. The building comprises an unusually shaped, angular little brick stupa-shrine, with a disproportionately large stone doorway (probably a later addition) and a chain of Buddhas set in niches around the base, looking out in all directions over the surrounding countryside, perhaps in order to face off approaching invaders.

The **Mong Khong Shwetu Paya** (1629) on the opposite side of the road is a good example of Mrauk U's later style, with a tall and elegant sandstone stupa (although parts of the stonework are beginning to sag with age) topped with a distinctive star-shaped finial and finely carved double niches arranged around each of its four sides.

Pizidaung Paya

ပိစိတော်ဘုရား • Open access 24hr • Entry covered by main temple ticket

The **Pizidaung Paya** is said to contain a testicle (*pizi*) relic of the Buddha – although this sounds suspiciously like another Burmese cock-and-bull story, and the site's main attraction is its gorgeous view of the nearby Kothaung. There's not much left of the temple itself, situated on a hillock right next to the road junction but surprisingly easy to miss. Much of the shrine has collapsed, leaving one Buddha sitting lone and proud at the top of the hill, with four more Buddhas seated in the remains of the ambulatory below, also now open to the sky.

Kothaung Paya

ကိုးသောင်းဘုရား • Daily 7am–5.30pm • Entry covered by main temple ticket

Built between 1554 and 1556, the gigantic **Kothaung Paya** is the result of a piece of shameless one-upmanship by King Dikkha, who ordered a building large enough to store 90,000 (*kothaung*) Buddha images, just that little bit bigger than his father King Minbin's landmark temple, which could hold just 80,000 (*shittaung*). Dikkha's vainglory did him little good: he reigned just three years and his vast temple fell rapidly to pieces (its marshy location causing the foundations to subside) and had to be meticulously put back together again in a massive restoration programme starting in 1997.

Even by Mrauk U's outlandish standards it's a singularly strange structure, looking like some kind of huge Buddhist bomb shelter, its stepped sides stacked with hundreds of mini-stupas. There's nothing else like it in Myanmar, although it does bear a certain (probably fortuitous) resemblance to the great stupa-mountain of Borobodur in Java.

Entrance is from the east. Inside the walls (which are sandstone on the outside, and faced with brick within), most of the temple is actually open, split on two levels, with corridors, now largely roofless, around each level and a large stupa on the higher section. The **outer corridor** (on the lower level) is particularly fine, its walls finely carved with thousands of identikit miniature mosaic-style Buddhas interspersed with larger Buddhas seated on plinths. The **inner corridor** (on the upper level) is more fragmentary, lined with hundreds of small seated Buddhas, while two quaint ogre guards flank the entrance to the corridor on the northern side opposite the stupa.

Sakya Manaung Paya

သကျမာန်အောင်ဘုရား • Open access 24hr • Entry covered by main temple ticket

The **Sakya Manaung Paya** was built at the same time as the similar Mong Khong Shwetu Pagoda nearby. Two huge, brightly painted ogres stand guard over the entrance, facing outwards, while behind them two more supersized figures stand praying towards the temple – the statues are revered in their own right, with squares of gold leaf applied to their bases (although some people content themselves with offering strips of gold-coloured adhesive tape rather than the real thing).

The **main stupa** is a classic example of the later Mrauk U style, set inside a ring of eleven mini-stupas and rising from a quasi-octagonal, zigzagging base which has now expanded to many levels, making up almost half the height of the entire structure. Elaborate two-storey niches decorate the stupa's four faces, with *makara*-like finials at the corners of the three main base terraces.

Ratanaman

ရတနာမာန် • Open access 24hr • Entry covered by main temple ticket

Halfway between the northern and eastern groups, the **Ratanaman** is another elegant, late-period stupa set on a many-tiered octagonal base. Eight colourful little figures representing the days of the week (see box, p.71) stand around the base of the stupa, along with a modern prayer hall and a pair of old brick shrines.

South of the centre

The area south of the centre is relatively devoid of ancient monuments, although you can still see the modest remains of the old **Laksaykan Gate**, leading through to the gorgeous **Laksaykan Lake**.

Sandamuni Kyaungtaik

စန္ဒာမုနိကျောင်းတိုက် • Approaching from the town centre, turn off the road running south from the bike rental shop through a yellow arch (signed, but in Burmese only) and continue to the end of the road and turn left up the steps at the sign saying "Sanda Muhni Phara Gri Kyang Tak" • No fixed opening hours; entrance is free (although you might want to give a donation)

The extensive **Sandamuni Kyaungtaik monastery** (aka the Bandoola Kyaung) spreads up a hillside just west of Laksaykan Lake. It's best known as the home of the **Sandamuni Buddha**, said to date from 308 BC. The image had been covered in cement – possibly to hide it from marauding British troops in the 1850s – then forgotten about until one of the eyes fell out in 1988, revealing the original statue hidden within. There's also a small museum here – the metal table-top on the right as you enter is actually an original copper roof tile from the old Mrauk U palace, one of the few pieces of the royal residence to have escaped being looted when the city was sacked in 1784.

Shwetaung Pagoda

ရွှေတောင်ဘုရား: • Open access 24hr • Entry covered by main temple ticket

It's worth climbing the hill up to the **Shwetaung Pagoda** not for the temple itself (which is just an average-sized, bog-standard stupa) but for what is probably the definitive view of Mrauk U – particularly memorable at dusk, and around dawn, with the mysterious outlines of myriad stupas emerging from the early-morning mists in every direction, and flashes of water between.

To **reach the temple** head for 100m down the side road which runs south off the main road between the centre and the *Prince Hotel*, looking for a pink archway (leading to a small monastery complex) on your left. Turn left off the road, go up to the arch (but not through it) and turn left again along the wide dirt track immediately in front of the archway skirting the monastery boundary wall. Follow this for around 20m, just past the end of the wall, and you'll see a small steep path on your right snaking its way up the hill. Follow this to reach the temple at the top – a brisk ten-minute walk.

Around Mrauk U

The remains of two more of ancient Arakan's former capitals – **Dhanyawadi** (former home of the revered Mahamuni Buddha) and **Waithali** – can be visited close to

---

CHIN VILLAGE TRIPS

With Chin State mostly off limits (see box, p.218), a day-trip from Mrauk U along the sylvan Lemro River to a series of nearby Chin villages is the easiest way to meet people from this large ethnic minority group, best known for the practice of tattooing the faces of their womenfolk. The practice was outlawed during the 1960s, although in most villages you'll see at least one or two old women with the tattooed faces. Local stories suggest that this painful procedure (using a mix of soot and buffalo liver) was intended to make girls less attractive to raiders, but more likely it was as a mark of identity for the various Chin tribes. The **tattooed ladies** are used to attracting attention: some of them produce handicrafts for sale while others charge a small fee to be photographed. Many visitors find the experience uncomfortably voyeuristic, although money from tourism helps fund community projects such as schools and water pumps (you may be asked for a donation) and provides much-needed income to one of Myanmar's most impoverished ethnic groups. Day-trips to the villages typically cost $70–80 for a boat seating up to four people (including guide).

Mrauk U, while trips down the scenic Lemro River to visit the nearby **Chin villages** are also popular, thanks to the presence of the famous old ladies with tattooed faces – a vanishing relic of old Burmese culture and customs past.

Waithali
ဝေသာလီမြို့

Hidden among rolling hills some 9km north of Mrauk U are the remains of the ancient city of **WAITHALI** (also spelt "Wethali" and often referred to by its Pali name, **Vesali**), founded in the fourth century and capital of Arakan (see box, p.115) from around 327 to 794. According to the Anandacandra pillar (see p.116), its subjects practised Mahayana Buddhism, although its monarchs considered themselves descendants of the Hindu god, Shiva – a characteristically Arakanese syncretism.

Much of the former city has now fallen into ruin, although you can still make out the remains of a few temples and fragments of the city's brick walls and the palace within. The main attraction is the **Great Waithali Payagyi**, a huge seated Buddha image more than 5m tall and said to be made from a single piece of boulder. One of Myanmar's oldest Buddhas, legend claims that it was a gift of the chief queen of King Maha Taing Candra, who founded the city in 327 AD – although the original features have been altered somewhat by modern restorations.

Dhanyawadi
ဓညဝတီ

Around 40km northwest of Mrauk U are the remains of the first of Arakan's four capitals, **DHANYAWADI**. As at Waithali, the ruins of the old city are fragmentary and the site is best known nowadays as the original home of the enormously revered **Mahamuni Buddha** statue (see p.271). Ancient Arakanese chronicles claim, perhaps a little ambitiously, that the Buddha himself visited the city in 554 BC, during which a statue – the Mahamuni – was made. Worshipped for centuries by Rakhine's monarchs, the statue was regarded as a symbol and protector of the country, although it couldn't prevent the sack of Mrauk U in 1784, after which the Mahamuni was carried off by King Bodawpaya to Mandalay, where it remains to this day.

The temple (much modernized) in which the image was once housed survives, however, along with three ancient Buddhas which still attract many worshippers, particularly the 1.5m-high central image, known as "Mahamuni's Brother". There's also a small **museum** here, with some fragments of stone carvings and inscriptions found around the site.

ARRIVAL AND DEPARTURE	MRAUK U AND AROUND

By bus Foreigners are now allowed by road to Mrauk U, although few currently do so, and it remains something of an adventure – while lousy roads mean that the bus back to Sittwe is actually slower (and a lot more uncomfortable) than the faster ferries, so there's not much incentive to travel this way. Leaving Mrauk U, buy your ticket at least one day in advance. You may also need copies of the information pages of your passport to hand out at government checkpoints en route – check the latest situation locally.

Destinations Magwe (1 daily; 10hr); Mandalay (1–2 nightly; 24hr); Sittwe (3–4 daily; 5hr); Yangon (1–2 nightly; 24hr).

By boat Most visitors still come by boat from Sittwe (see p.117). Services dock at the jetty close to the town centre within walking distance of most accommodation. A tuk-tuk to outlying hotels will cost K1000–2000. Leaving Mrauk U, there is currently one boat daily back to Sittwe. The fastest is the *Shwe Pyin Tan* (Mon & Thurs; K20,000; 2hr 30min; buy tickets in advance from the *Hay Mar* restaurant by the jetty); slightly slower is the *Aung Kyaw Moe* (Tues, Fri & Sun; K10,000; 4–5hr; tickets available in advance from their office near the jetty, or buy them as you board the boat); the slow government boat (Wed & Sat; $6 or K7000, plus K1000 for a seat; 6hr 30min–7hr 30min) fills in one of the remaining days. All boats leave at 7am. You can also charter a boat from Sittwe (see p.118).

2

INFORMATION AND TOURS

Tourist information The tourist office (signed "Regional Guides Society"; ☎09 4217 20168, ✉rgs.mrauku@gmail .com) is opposite the ferry jetty, although it's not often manned. If you want to arrange a local guide to show you round the temples it's best to call or email in advance.

Tours Tours (to local Chin villages and elsewhere) can be arranged through most guesthouses and hotels, or try Aung Zang ("Mr Fix-It"; ☎09 4217 22241), who can usually be found hanging out at the *Lay Myoe River Resort Guesthouse*.

GETTING AROUND

The roads in Mrauk U are some of the worst in Myanmar – more pothole than actual road in many places – just riding a bike can be a bit of a rattle, while even a kilometre in a tuk-tuk can turn into a bone-shatteringly bad trip.

By bike The town centre is very compact, although exploring the temples is best done by bike. Than Tun Bicycle Rental (closed Sun), between the town centre and the jetty, has loads of gearless bikes for K2000/day.

Alternatively, ask at your guesthouse.
By tuk-tuk Rakhine-style "tuk-tuks" – a motorbike with a mini pick-up-style attachment bolted to the back – meet all incoming ferries.

ACCOMMODATION

The government currently only supplies electricity to Mrauk U from 5am to midnight – more upmarket places have their own generators; budget options leave you in the dark.

Golden Star Resort Guesthouse 116 Minbar Gyi Rd ☎09 4967 4472. Friendly and competitively priced guesthouse (with singles for just $13). The whole place feels a bit makeshift and tumbledown, but rooms are comfy enough and the communal garden is also pleasant, while rates include an above-average breakfast. **$20**

Lay Myoe River Resort Guesthouse Minbar Gyi Rd ☎09 852 2139. Mrauk U's cheapest accommodation, with simple boxy little rooms with fan and attached bathroom (cold water only). Basic but reasonably clean, and at a very fair price. **$12**

Mrauk Oo Princess Resort Riverfront ☎043 50232, ⓦmraukooprincessresort.com. The town's only upmarket option at present – attractive enough, but spectacularly overpriced in the absence of any competition. Accommodation is in 33 rather stern-looking black-wood "village houses" lined up next to a gorgeous lotus pond – although the corrugated iron roofs, slightly tatty rooms and minimal facilities (no pool, no wi-fi, no TVs – but there is a spa) make this one of Myanmar's most shameless rip-offs. They can also arrange a private boat from Sittwe for a modest $550 – although this does include lunch. **$330**

Mrauk U Palace Resort Alotawpyi St ☎09 853 2277, ⓦmraukupaceresort.com, ✉mraukupalaceresort @gmail.com. Recently opened place with so-so wood-and-stone cabanas equipped with a/c, hot water, fridge, 24hr electricity, wi-fi and some of Rakhine's ugliest bedspreads. It all looks like a bit of a work in progress (and the gardens currently resemble a building site) but a reasonable option at this price. **$45**

Nawarat Hotel Yangon–Sittwe Rd ☎09 852 2264. Functional chalets resplendent in sickly green shades of paint (looking like a slightly toned-down version of the eyesore *Mrauk U Hotel* opposite), although if you can get over the colour scheme the rooms are OK – dated but comfortably furnished with kettle, fridge, safe, plus wi-fi and 24hr electricity. **$65**

Prince Hotel Myaung Bwe Rd ☎043 50174, ⓦmraukuprince.com. In a pleasant rural setting a 10min walk from town. Accommodation is in large but overpriced and decidedly shabby cabanas, none too clean and with plenty of holes through which local insect life is wont to come visiting. Plus points include the charming owners and good breakfasts. Wi-fi and a generator are promised. **$25**

Royal City Guesthouse Near the ferry dock ☎043 24200. Spreading over both sides of the road conveniently close to the town and ferry dock. The cheaper rooms (fan and cold water only) on the reception side of the road are one of Mrauk U's better deals – neat, tiled and clean, with writing desk. The handful of fancier bungalows opposite (with a/c, hot water and TV) are tiled, spacious, clean and nicely furnished, although right next to the road. Wi-fi is promised – and the disinterested service could do with an upgrade too. Room **$25**, bungalow **$40**

Shwe Thazin Hotel Yangon–Sittwe Rd ☎043 50168. Mrauk U's best mid-range option, with attractive stone-and-wood chalets decorated with fancy traditional carvings and equipped with wi-fi, 24hr electricity and fridge. **$65**

EATING

For You Minbar Gyi Rd. A decent lunch stop in town, serving up a short menu of tasty fried rice, noodles and

soups (most featuring either chicken or pork) at bargain prices K1000–2000. Daily 8am–8pm.

Happy Garden Minbar Gyi Rd. Cheery little local café-cum-beer station set in a cute little wooden building on stilts (although the "garden" below is just a sandy space under a large awning). The inexpensive mains (K2000–4000) include no-frills noodles and fried rice dishes plus grilled fish and the usual Chinese staples. Daily 7am–11pm.

Moe Cherry Northeast corner of the palace complex ☎09 4217 33711. Deservedly popular with visiting foreigners, with a short selection of noodle and proper Myanmar curries (around K4000), nicely cooked and served with a decent selection of vegetable side dishes, plus soup. Daily 8am–11pm.

River Valley Near the ferry dock ☎043 50257. An offshoot of the popular Sittwe restaurant, set on a pleasant terrace hung with multicoloured lanterns and serving up an identical menu (mains K3500–4000) to its Sittwe sister, with a big and competent if unremarkable selection of Chinese-style seafood and meat dishes. Daily 7.30am–10pm.

SHOPPING

L'Amitie Just north of the Shittaung Paya ✉artsmtmu@yahoo.com. This art gallery is the home base of the father-and-son painting team of Shwe Maung Tha (who has had his work shown overseas) and Khine Minn Tun, one of whom can usually be found around the place. Daily 7am–dusk or later.

DIRECTORY

Banks There are no banks or ATMs yet in Mrauk U, so bring all the cash you'll possibly need, plus a bit more. There's a currency exchange at the *Nawarat Hotel*.

Internet Try Sky Net, Mrauk U's only internet café at present (daily 8am–9pm; K1000/hr), well equipped but with connections usually slower than a fossilized tortoise – and oppressively hot as well.

Southeastern Myanmar

KYAIKTIYO (GOLDEN ROCK)

Southeastern Myanmar

Stretching for a thousand kilometres from the turbid waters of the Gulf of Mottama to the sun-drenched islands of the Myeik Archipelago, Myanmar's panhandle is often overlooked by visitors in the rush to head north from Yangon. However, with Tanintharyi and the region's Thai border crossings now largely open to foreign visitors, this lush and beautiful region – peppered with intriguing sights and fringed with the least developed beaches in Southeast Asia – is poised to enter the mainstream.

3

Generations of devout Buddhist monarchs have left **Mon State**, the northernmost of the region, a gold-coated legacy. Not far from Yangon, the countryside around the historical Mon capital of **Bago** is full of golden *zedi* and dreamy reclining Buddhas. Further east, **Kyaiktiyo**, or the Golden Rock, is the most revered of the southeast's religious monuments, the precariously balanced pagoda-crowned boulder floating high above the Eastern Yoma Mountains.

With its drawn-out coastline and sheltered natural harbours, the southeast played an important role in Indian Ocean trade for centuries, exporting pottery, teak and other exotic products from the Burmese interior. While the port city of **Mawlamyine** came to prominence only under nineteenth-century British rule, it's the best place to get a sense of this mercantile heritage, with bustling markets and peeling godowns dotting the town centre. The countryside nearby is full of fascinating day-trips, from **Thanbyuzayat**'s sombre war cemetery to **Win Sein Taw Ya**, a crumbling 180m-long reclining Buddha.

East of Mon State, **Kayin State** was the site of one of Myanmar's most violent **ethnic conflicts** (see p.352), with decades of fighting between Kayin nationalists and government troops leaving hundreds of people dead and tens of thousands more living as refugees in neighbouring Thailand before a ceasefire was signed in 2012. Today, the peaceful countryside around state capital **Hpa-An** belies the violence of the recent past, and the small town is a great place to stay while exploring the dramatic mountains and Buddha-filled caves nearby.

In the far south, newly accessible **Tanintharyi Region** is home to a string of dazzling deserted beaches around **Dawei**, and **Myeik** is a fascinating hub for all sorts of tropical industries, from cashew-nut factories to malodorous workshops fermenting fish for *ngăpí* fish paste. Off the coast, along the difficult-to-access **Myeik Archipelago**, sea gypsies still ride the waves, and fishermen perch on bamboo platforms plucking fish from the rich waters of the Andaman Sea.

SHWEMAWDAW PAGODA, BAGO

Highlights

❶ Bago A backwater today, Bago has a rich and fascinating history, the remnants of which lie scattered around this low-key town. **See p.134**

❷ Kyaiktiyo (Golden Rock) Buddhists flock to this gravity-defying pile of gold-covered boulders, purportedly held in place by a few extra-strong strands of Buddha's hair. **See p.140**

❸ Hpa-An Clamber up jungle-shrouded mountains, explore holy bat caves and soak in cool, clear pools amid the limestone karst landscape of Kayin State's laidback capital. **See p.143**

❹ Mawlamyine Filled with crumbling colonial architecture and set against a backdrop of pagoda-topped hills,

Mawlamyine makes a great base for exploring nearby sights. **See p.150**

❺ Bilu Kyun A short boat ride away from Mawlamyine, buffalo carts and ancient buses rumble down palm-lined roads on Bilu Kyun, home to a plethora of interesting cottage industries. **See p.156**

❻ Dawei Beach-hop on the beautiful Dawei Peninsula – from endless stretches of sand to tiny beachside fishing villages, there's something for beach bums of all stripes. **See p.159**

❼ Myeik to Kawthaung Thread your way through the Myeik Archipelago waters teeming with flying fish and past mangrove-edged islands. **See box, p.161**

HIGHLIGHTS ARE MARKED ON THE MAP ON P.134

HIGHLIGHTS

1. Bago
2. Kyaiktiyo (Golden Rock)
3. Hpa-An
4. Mawlamyine
5. Bilu Kyun
6. Dawei
7. Myeik to Kawthaung

Bago

ပဲခူးမြို့

While **BAGO** is a quiet provincial town today, its outskirts retain hints of a magnificent and turbulent past. Formerly known as Pegu, the town was the capital of several Mon and Burmese kingdoms, and flourished as a bastion of Theravada Buddhism in the fifteenth century, and as a regional trade entrepôt in the sixteenth. Each period of dominion brought with it a new layer of gilded **pagodas** and languorous **reclining Buddhas**, and today the small town makes a fine place to spend a day or two cycling between its gold-coated sights.

Some 80km from Yangon, Bago sits astride the Yangon–Mandalay railway and the old highway, making it a convenient stopoff between the two cities. Having been chosen as the location for Yangon's new **Hanthawaddy International Airport**, the town will become even more easily accessible, should the project – which broke ground in 1994 – ever reach completion.

Brief history

According to Buddhist legend, the newly enlightened **Siddhartha Gautama** made a flying trip to Lower Burma, which at that time was covered by sea water. Seeing a female *hamsa* sitting on the back of a male, perched on a tiny island of dry land, Buddha foretold that this spot would become the centre of a prosperous kingdom 1500 years later. Roughly on schedule, the waters having receded, two Mon princes founded the town, known as Hanthawaddy to the Mon, in 825 AD. The **double hamsa** motif can be seen all over Bago today.

After centuries sandwiched uncomfortably between the armies of Bagan and Ayutthaya, the Mon kingdom moved its capital from Mottama, near Mawlamyine, to Bago in 1369. The town became a major religious centre under the fifteenth-century reign of devout Queen Shin Sawbu, who passed her throne to an alchemist monk named **Dhammazedi**, to whom the queen had married her

TRAVEL RESTRICTIONS

At the time of research it was possible to travel overland as far south as Myeik. Between **Myeik and Kawthaung**, foreigners were still required to travel by boat or by plane. Travel in the **Myeik Archipelago** was strictly limited to those on organized diving trips (see box, p.165), and the **interior** – home to several nature reserves – was, at the time of writing, still off limits.

daughter. During his 32-year reign, Dhammazedi entrenched Bago's position as a centre of Buddhist orthodoxy, expanding pagodas, funding pilgrimages and holding mass ordinations.

After the Hanthawaddy kingdom collapsed in 1539 (see p.334), **King Bayinnaung** (also known as Bayintnaung) sacked the city in his struggle to annex Lower Burma. The energetic monarch then set about rebuilding Bago as his capital, digging a moat filled with crocodiles (the crocodiles are long gone, but weed-choked fragments of the moat remain), and building the Kanbawzathadi Palace (see p.137). However, after just fifty years at the centre of national affairs, Bago was razed again in 1599, continuing a pattern of destruction and reconstruction that has continued almost to the present – the town was last levelled by an earthquake in 1930. After the Bago River silted up in the sixteenth century, Bago lost access to the sea and ceded its position as a trade centre to Thanlyin (then called Syriam), and the town slowly slipped back into obscurity.

Shwemawdaw Pagoda

ရွှေမောတော်ဘုရား• Pagoda Rd • Daily 5am–10pm • Bago Archeological Zone ticket (see box, p.137), although ticket checks are less zealous from late afternoon onwards; camera fee K300

Visible for many kilometres around, **Shwemawdaw Pagoda**'s vast golden dome dominates Bago's skyline. Buddhist legend has it that a pair of merchant brothers built the monument to enshrine two of Buddha's hairs in 582 BC, with successive generations adding relics and extending the spire to its current height of 114m – taller than even Shwedagon in Yangon – and covering it with 1.5 tonnes of gold leaf.

The *zedi* has fallen victim to numerous **earthquakes** over the years. A large chunk of brickwork that collapsed in 1917 is dramatically embedded in its western side, sprouting incense sticks from cracks in its mortar. After the most recent earthquake in 1930, the pagoda lay in ruins for twenty years, until unpaid volunteers built the structure you see today in the early 1950s.

The four staircases leading to the pagoda are flanked by large chinthe with tiny golden Buddhas in their open mouths; the western staircase leads east to Hintha Gon Paya (see below) along a covered arcade. Shwemawdaw is the site of a major ten-day pagoda festival around the Tagu full moon, which falls in March/April each year.

Hintha Gon Paya

ဟသာ်ကုန်းဘုရား• Off Thanat Pin Rd, 500m east of Shwemawdaw Pagoda • Daily 5am–10pm • Free; camera fee K300

Its name meaning "Hamsa Hill", **Hintha Gon Paya** was once the only point of land above sea level around Bago, and the hill is believed to be the place where Buddha spotted the two *hamsa* that gave rise to his prophesy about Bago. King Bayinnaung constructed the complex in 1567, but the current tiered shrine is the creation of the hermit monk **U Khanti**, and dates from 1924.

In addition to decent views of the pagoda-stippled surroundings, the main reason to climb up here is for the chance to witness one of the **nat ceremonies** for which Hintha Gon is known. Transvestite *natdaws* (mediums) energetically channel the *nat* to the frenetic accompaniment of a traditional orchestra, purportedly bringing good luck to

3

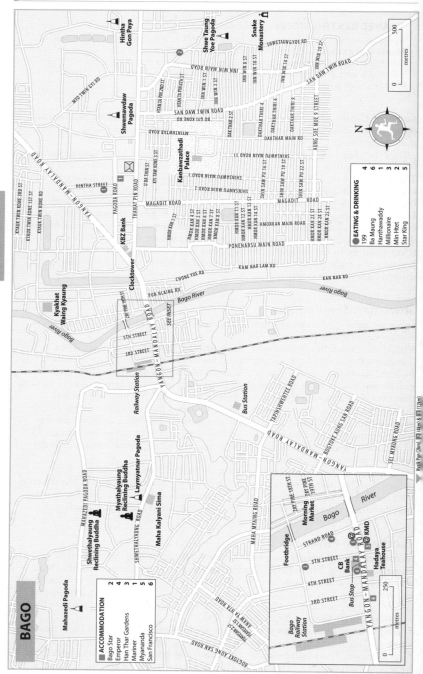

BAGO

■ **ACCOMMODATION**

Bago Star	2
Emperor	4
Han Thar Gardens	3
Mariner	1
Myananda	5
San Francisco	6

● **EATING & DRINKING**

199	4
Ba Maung	6
Hanthawaddy	1
Millionaire	3
Min Htet	2
Star King	5

Mahazedi Pagoda

Shwethalyaung Reclining Buddha

MAHAZEDI PAGODA ROAD

Myathalyaung Reclining Buddha

SHWETHALYAUNG ROAD

Laymyatnar Pagoda

Maha Kalyani Sima

Kyakhat Wang Kyaung

Bago River

Clocktower

KBZ Bank

Thant Pin Road

Pagoda Road

HINTHA STREET

YANGON–MANDALAY ROAD

MYO TWIN GYI RD

KYAUK TWIN KONE 3RD ST
KYAUK TWIN KONE 1ST ST
KYAUK TWIN KONE RD
KYAUK TWIN KONE 2ND ST

Shwemawdaw Pagoda

Hintha Gon Paya

Shwe Taung Yoe Pagoda

Snake Monastery

SHWETAUNGYOE RD

INN WIN MAIN ROAD

INN WIN 13 ST
INN WIN 11 ST
INN WIN 8 ST
INN WIN 10 ST
INN WIN 3 ST
INN WIN 14 ST
INN WIN 19 ST

SAN DAW TWIN ROAD

HEIKTA PIN 2ND ST
HEIKTA PIN 1ST ST
HEIKTA PIN 6TH ST

BO GYI KONE RD

SAN DAW TWIN ROAD

Kanbawzathadi Palace

MYINMYATKAR ROAD

SHINSAWPU MAIN ROAD 11

OAKTHAR 2 ST

OAKTHAR MAIN RD
OAKTHAR THIRI 4
OAKTHAR THIRI 6
OAKTHAR THIRI 9

AUNG SOE MOE 9 STREET

SHINSAWPU MAIN ROAD

U BA THIN ST
KITTAW KONE 1ST ST

SHINSAWPU MAIN ROAD 1
SHINSAWPU MAIN ROAD 2

SHIN SAW PU 16 ST
SHIN SAW PU 19 ST
SHIN SAW PU 22 ST

MAGADIT ROAD

MAGADIT ROAD

HMOR KAN 1ST ST

HMOR KAN 3 ST
HMOR KAN 5 ST
HMOR KAN 6 ST
HMOR KAN 7 ST
HMOR KAN 8 ST

HMOR KAN 11 ST
HMOR KAN 13 ST
HMOR KAN 14 ST

HMORKAN MAIN ROAD

HMOR KAN 21 ST
HMOR KAN 23 ST
HMOR KAN 24 ST
HMOR KAN 25 ST

PONENARSU MAIN ROAD

KAM NAR LAM RD

CHONE YOE RD

KAN NAR RD

Bago River

Bago River

PUN HLAING ST

2ND PINE ST

5TH STREET

3RD STREET

Railway Station

YANGON–MANDALAY ROAD

SEE INSET

Bus Station

TAPINSHWETTEE ROAD

BOGYOKE AUNG SAN ROAD

YANGON–MANDALAY ROAD

SEL MYAUNG ROAD

MAHA MYAING ROAD

Koak Pun (2km), ► (14km) & ► (12m)

N

0   500
metres

INSET:

2ND PINE 18TH ST
JAY PINE 19TH ST

Morning Market

Bago River

Footbridge

STRAND ROAD

5TH STREET

4TH STREET

3RD STREET

CB Bank

@ ROAD
@ KMD

Hadaya Teahouse

YANGON–MANDALAY ROAD

Bus Stop

Bago Railway Station

BOGYOKE AUNG SAN ROAD

ANAW YA HTA ROAD

YERASAN ST
YERASAN 2 ST

0   250
metres

BAGO ARCHEOLOGICAL ZONE

Entrance to the Shwemawdaw Pagoda, Kanbawzathadi Palace, Shwethalyaung Reclining Buddha and Kyaik Pun is covered by the **Bago Archeological Zone ticket**, which costs K10,000 and is valid for a week from purchase. While you can see all these sights from the street, you won't be able to get up close without stumping up the cash – particularly worthwhile at Shwemawdaw Pagoda. Tickets can be purchased at any of the covered sights.

---

worshippers. Several *nats* are represented here, but foremost among them is **Bago Medaw**, a local Mon *nat* depicted as a woman wearing a buffalo skull.

Kanbawzathadi Palace

ကမ္ဘောဇသာဒီရွှေနန်းတော် • Myintawtar Rd, 400m south of Shwemawdaw • Daily 9am–5pm • Entry fee covered by the Bago Archeological Zone K10,000 ticket

Built in 1553 at the heart of King Bayinnaung's Bago, the original **Kanbawzathadi Palace** survived for less than fifty years before it was looted and razed by Rakhine troops in 1599. The palace lay in ruins for four centuries, until it was excavated and restored in the mid-1990s under General Khin Nyunt's sponsorship.

Today, the poorly maintained concrete throne halls are photogenic enough from a distance, but give little sense of the original scale of the palace buildings. More interesting are the jagged remains of the original teakwood columns, sent to Bayinnaung from around the country, and a few artefacts discovered during the excavation that are housed in a small **archeological museum** on the same site.

Snake Monastery and around

မြွေဘုရား: • Off Shwetaungyoe Rd, 1.5km south of Hintha Gon Paya • Daily during daylight hours • Free

One of Bago's less orthodox religious sites, **Snake Monastery**, also known locally as Mwei Paya, is home to a venerable Burmese python. Estimated to be an incredible 120 years old, the 5m-long female snake is believed to be the reincarnation of an abbot from a monastery in Hsipaw, who now divides her time between sleeping (or meditating, depending on your view) and eating chickens. The banknotes tucked by followers into her scaly folds have funded the rapid expansion of the monastery, which also hosts exciting **nat ceremonies** on full moon days.

Some 300m to the north of the monastery is the hilltop **Shwe Taung Yoe Pagoda**, or Sunset Pagoda, worth visiting for its great views over Bago.

Kyakhat Waing Kyaung

ကြိခတ်ဝိုင်းကျောင်းတိုက် • 100m north of the market • Daily 7am–noon • Free

Sandwiched between the northwest corner of the moat and the Bago River, **Kyakhat Waing Kyaung** is Bago's biggest monastery. It formerly housed 1200 monks, though many were forced to return to their home communities after the crackdown that followed 2007's Saffron Revolution (see p.348) and today around five hundred remain. The monastery is best known for its 11am **lunchtimes**, where busloads of Thai tourists descend to give packets of instant noodles as alms to a long line of straight-faced monks.

Shwethalyaung Reclining Buddha

ရွှေသာလျောင်းဘုရား: • Mahazedi Pagoda Rd • Daily 5am–dusk • Entry fee covered by the Bago Archeological Zone K10,000 ticket; camera fee K300

The tenth-century **Shwethalyaung Reclining Buddha** lies 2km west of Bago. Built by King Migadepa in 994 AD to celebrate his conversion to Buddhism (a series of paintings on the back of the statue tells the full story), the 55m-long statue shows Buddha resting his head on an ornate pillow on the eve of his enlightenment. The statue was abandoned after Alaungpaya sacked Bago in 1756, lying forgotten and overgrown with jungle until it was rediscovered by British railway contractors in 1880.

Like many of Bago's religious buildings, few traces of Shwethalyaung's antiquity remain, and the site is covered with a rather obtrusive canopy. Photographers may prefer to walk a few minutes south to the similarly proportioned **Myathalyaung Reclining Buddha**, built in 2002, which remains uncovered.

Maha Kalyani Sima

မဟာကလျာဏီသိမ် · Shwethalyaung Rd · Daily 5am–dusk · Free

It's easy to overlook this dilapidated monastery on your way to the other sights west of town, but **Maha Kalyani Sima** is the site of Myanmar's first **ordination hall**. Built in 1476 by King Dhammazedi, the hall celebrates the return of 22 monks he had sent to Sri Lanka, the orthodox home of Theravada Buddhism, in hope of reinvigorating his country's *sangha* (monastic community). Find your way to the rear of the scruffy monastery buildings and you'll discover ten stone tablets with inscriptions in Pali and Mon, which describe the early history of Buddhism in the region. Like most of Bago's historic buildings, the hall has been rebuilt several times, with its latest incarnation reopened in 1953 by U Nu, then Prime Minister of Burma.

Mahazedi Pagoda

မဟာစေတီဘုရား · Mahazedi Pagoda Rd · Daily 5am–dusk · Free; camera fee K300

On the western edge of Bago, white and gold **Mahazedi Pagoda** is one of the most striking religious buildings in Bago, with steep whitewashed staircases leading to the base of the pagoda itself (although it's a men-only zone beyond the main terrace), and a few attractive shrines nearby. King Bayinnaung built the original structure in 1561 and he enshrined a fake tooth relic thought to be the sacred Tooth of Kandy in Sri Lanka here in the 1570s. When it was later discovered to have been an ox bone fake sent by the king of Kotte, Bayinnaung regally dismissed the tooth's sceptics and today it is a venerated relic in Sagaing's Kaunghmudaw Paya (see p.286).

Kyaik Pun

ကျိုက်ပွန်ဘုရား · Kyaik Pun Rd · Daily 8am–dusk · Entry fee covered by the Bago Archeological Zone K10,000 ticket; camera fee K300

Around 4km south of the railway station, just west of the main Yangon road, **Kyaik Pun** consists of four 30m-high Buddhas representing Siddhartha Gautama and his three predecessors, all shown at the moment of their enlightenment, in *bhumisparsha* mudra with one hand touching the earth. The back-to-back arrangement of the statues, which can also be seen at the **Laymyatnar Pagoda** near Maha Kalyani Sima, seems to have originated with the Mon before spreading to Bagan and Thailand.

ARRIVAL AND DEPARTURE

BAGO

By bus The bus station is 1km southwest of the town on the Yangon–Mandalay road. Tickets are available both from here and the bus company offices on the main road between the *Myananda* and *San Francisco* hotels. Most buses will stop at both the bus station and in town by *Three Five* restaurant, but do check this when you buy your ticket. *Hadaya Teahouse* sells tickets to destinations in Upper Burma for a small mark-up, as do most hotels for a larger one.

Destinations Hpa-An (6 daily; 6hr); Kinpun (for Kyaiktiyo,

hourly; 3hr); Mandalay (4 daily; 10–12hr); Mawlamyine (5 daily; 5hr 30min); Pyin Oo Lwin (daily; 10hr 30min); Taunggyi (for Inle Lake, daily; 12hr); Taungoo (2 daily; 4hr); Yangon (6 daily; 1hr 30min–2hr).

By train Bago's railway station is just west of the town centre, on the north side of the main road. For Kyaiktiyo, take a Mawlamyine-bound train and get off at Kyaikhto. For Inle Lake, change at Thazi.

Destinations Dawei (daily; 22hr 30min); Kyaikhto (3 daily;

3hr); Mandalay (3 daily; 14hr); Mawlamyine (3 daily; 7–8hr); Naypyitaw (5 daily; 7–8hr); Taungoo (3 daily; 4hr 30min); Thaton (3 daily; 5hr); Thazi (3 daily; 10–11hr); Yangon (8 daily; 2hr); Ye (daily; 14hr).

GETTING AROUND

By motorbike taxi A short journey around town ought to cost no more than K500, and full-day tours can be arranged for a reasonable K3000 through the budget hotels, although most drivers do not speak English. Former Inle trekking guide Win Naing, who speaks good English and can be contacted through the *Myananda* hotel, charges K7000 for a guided one-day motorbike tour.

By bicycle Bikes are available to rent from the *San Francisco* and *Emperor* hotels for K2000/day.

ACCOMMODATION

Bago Star 11–21 Kyaik Pun Rd 4km out of town ☎ 052 30066, ⓦ bagostarhotel.googlepages.com. Owned by a friendly local family, this hotel has thirty wood-panelled rooms arranged in rows of concrete bungalows. It has a decent-sized pool, a restaurant that serves simple meals, and is located down the quiet street that leads to Kyaik Pun. Free wi-fi. **$43**

Emperor 8 Main Rd ☎ 09 4282 02757, ⓔ nyeinchanbgo @gmail.com. One of the nicer budget options in town: the small rooms are clean and colourful and all come with a/c, hot water and wi-fi. Another bonus is that you can check out at any time – handy if you're on the late bus to Mandalay. Single rooms are $10; breakfast not included. **$20**

★ Han Thar Gardens 34 Bullein Tar Zone Village, 12km south of Bago on the Yangon–Mandalay Rd ☎ 09 4281 77217, ⓔ hanthargardens@gmail.com. Several classes above anything else in Bago, this place has airy and beautiful deluxe rooms in the eco-friendly main building, with vast bathrooms and plenty of local touches. The cheaper superior rooms are less exciting, but still attractive and spacious, and there is a small pool and sundeck. The only downside is the out-of-town location, but with a pretty on-site café serving excellent Burmese food, you may not need to leave anyway. Free wi-fi. **$125**

Mariner 330 Pagoda Rd ☎ 052 201034, ⓔ hotel mariner.hm@gmail.com. Close to Shwemawdaw, this is one of the few foreigner-friendly hotels in the eastern part of town, with thirty bright standard rooms and a shiny new elevator. It's housed on the top three floors (you can expect to pay a little more for a pagoda view) of a building that also contains a shopping centre, hair salon and a doughnut café. **$40**

Myananda 10 Main Rd ☎ 052 22275. The cheapest rooms here are simple boxes with shared bathrooms and thin dividing walls, but all have a/c and there's even rumoured to be wi-fi. **$15**

San Francisco 14 Main Rd ☎ 052 22265. With twenty fan-cooled rooms, the cheapest single starting at K6000 and knowledgeable (if somewhat bossy) staff, *San Francisco* is understandably popular with backpackers. The rooms are acceptable, although some at the back bear more than a passing resemblance to caves. Breakfast not included. **K13,000**

EATING AND DRINKING

199 Strand Rd. In a quiet spot facing the river just off the main road, this beer station is one of the few places in Bago to offer riverside seating. It serves up basic Burmese and Chinese dishes, icy draught beer and incredibly moreish onion rings. Just remember to bring your mosquito repellent. Daily 10am–10pm.

Ba Maung 13 Main Rd ☎ 052 21447. *Ba Maung* is one of the better Chinese restaurants along Bago's main strip. The standard fried dishes on the cute English menu start from K2000, with bottles of Myanmar beer costing a reasonable K1300. Daily 8am–9pm.

Hanthawaddy 192 Hintha St ☎ 09 4921 7309. Bago's most upmarket dining option, *Hanthawaddy* is housed in a villa with good views of Shwemawdaw from the upstairs balcony. The menu covers Burmese, Thai and Chinese dishes – the Burmese dishes being the best executed – for K4000–6000. It's popular with tour groups, and if it's busy you may be directed to their nearby sister restaurant, *Century*. Daily 11am–9pm.

Millionaire 5th St. Bago is home to a few branches of a local teashop chain. The 5th Street branch is busy throughout the day, making it one of the more interesting places to stop for a bowl of *mohinga* or a cup of sweet tea. Look out for their Burmese-only sign – white characters on a blue and red oval. Daily 6am–9pm.

★ Min Htet Shwetaungyoe Rd, just north of Shwe Taung Yoe Pagoda. Locals flock to this simple restaurant at lunchtime for tasty Burmese-style curries (usually with one vegetarian option on offer), accompanied by the usual trappings of salad, *ngāpí* and vast quantities of rice. Expect to pay K1200 for a meal with tea. Mon–Sat 9am–6pm.

Star King Yangon–Mandalay Rd ☎ 052 21298. It may be a bit dingy inside, but the young owners serve up simple Western food, plus ice cream and drinks (their coffee with lime is particularly good), and the wi-fi is the fastest in town. Daily 9am–9pm.

DIRECTORY

Banks CB Bank on the main road between *Three Five* restaurant and the *Emperor* hotel has an ATM and currency exchange, as does the KBZ Bank near the clocktower.

Internet If you get fed up waiting for your hotel wi-fi, head to KMD Internet Bar (daily 9am–9pm; K400/hr) or Star King (daily 9am–9pm; K500/hr for a computer, wi-fi free with a purchase), which are on opposite sides of the main road just west of the river.

Post office Bago's post office is tucked away in an unassuming bungalow south of Shwemawdaw – be prepared to ask for directions.

Kyaiktiyo (Golden Rock)

ကျိုက်ထီးရိုးဘုရား

One of the holiest places in the country, **Kyaiktiyo** is a major draw for Buddhist pilgrims, with thousands visiting every day during the November to March pilgrimage season. The site also pulls substantial numbers of non-believers, attracted by the pagoda's spectacular location, rising out of a huge gold-covered boulder – the **Golden Rock** – which is itself perched rakishly on a granite slab high up in the Eastern Yoma Mountains.

A Mon name, Kyaiktiyo means "pagoda on a hermit's head", a reference to its legendary back story. Burmese Buddhists believe that Buddha gave a strand of his hair to a hermit, who tucked it into his own topknot for safekeeping. The hermit later presented the hair to the king of Thaton on the condition that it be enshrined in a rock shaped like the hermit's own head. After a long search, the king managed to find a suitable rock at the bottom of the ocean and, with some supernatural help, transported it to its current location, where the hair has been holding it in place ever since. It's rumoured to be possible to pass a thread between the rock and its base by rocking the boulder gently back and forth, and yet the Golden Rock has managed to withstand several large earthquakes in its long history. Whether you believe the legend or not, it's clear that something unusual is keeping the rock up there…

Ascending Kyaiktiyo

Trucks run from Kinpun to the mountaintop plaza (K2500 uphill/K1500 down) and Yathetaun truck stop (K1500 uphill/K1000 down) 6am–6pm, departing when full and less frequently as the afternoon wears on; sedan chairs cost K20,000/person

The stony **trail** to the Golden Rock starts from the small town of **KINPUN**, from where a well-marked path leads 11km to the mountaintop. While the hike starts relatively gently, it's a long and sweaty climb – Kyaiktiyo sits at 1100m, 1000m above Kinpun itself – and takes at least four hours. The trail is well shaded by day, but poorly lit after dark, and it is not advisable to climb overnight. Villagers have set up bamboo stalls along the track, and water and snacks are widely available on the walk up, as are small children shouting "*mingalaba!*".

Most visitors to Kyaiktiyo, however, settle for taking an open **truck** up the mountain from Kinpun, either to the mountaintop plaza or to **Yathetaun truck stop** – the fares explicitly include life insurance, which may give a sense of how exciting the drive can be. From Yathetaun truck stop it's a 45-minute walk up a steeply switch-backed path to the Golden Rock, but if it all proves too much, sedan chairs are available. On descent, be aware that trucks from Yathetaun to Kinpun are far less frequent than those from the mountaintop – unless you are travelling with a group you may end up waiting for hours for the truck to fill up.

On the mountain

Ticket office daily 7am–9pm • Two-day pass K6000 • Dress appropriately (no shorts or revealing clothing)

Once at the top of the mountain, foreigners are required to pay a **government fee**, which buys a two-day pass. From the ticket office it's a short walk to the main complex, an expanse of tiles and minor shrines surrounding the Golden Rock itself. Men are allowed to cross the **footbridge** to the Rock to add to its lustre (a tiny sheet of gold leaf; K1700), but women must stay a short distance away.

Pilgrims throng Kyaiktiyo both day and night, but activity is greatest early in the morning and at dusk, with people praying, lighting candles and making offerings. Among the **stalls** that crowd the mountaintop, keep an eye out for one decked with spotlights – donate K20,000 and you can have the pagoda illuminated in your name for a night.

It is worth taking time to explore beyond the crowded main plaza, where several quiet trails lead across the mountains. For a short, sharp walk follow the path down past *Yoe Yoe Lay* hotel to a T-junction. The left-hand path leads 2.5km downhill to **Moe Baw Waterfall**, while the right-hand path leads past a small **cave shrine** and dozens of macabre traditional medicine stalls, decorated with centipedes and goat skulls, up to **Kann Pa Sat**, a small pagoda with a large loudspeaker that broadcasts blessings. From Kann Pa Sat you can head straight back to the plaza (making a 1.5km loop), or continue along the ridge, past a row of helipads and through attractive wooded scenery to a series of smaller improbably shaped rock-and-stupa combinations. One of the more striking places to aim for is **Bodhi Taw Kaw**, 1.5km along the ridge from the plaza, where ranks of small Buddha statues seated on pedestals cover the hillside. The 3km trail ends in a winding set of steps that lead down to **Kyauk Ta Gyi**, a small shrine set deep in a wooded valley; from here you'll need to retrace your steps to the plaza.

ARRIVAL AND INFORMATION KYAIKTIYO (GOLDEN ROCK)

By bus Some buses run direct to Kinpun, stopping outside *Sea Sar* restaurant, while others stop 15km away in Kyaikhto and transfer passengers to Kinpun by truck (included in the bus ticket). Bus tickets can be purchased in Kinpun at the booths opposite *Sea Sar*, with most services finishing by mid-afternoon.
Destinations Bago (7 daily; 3hr); Hpa-An (3 daily; 4hr); Mawlamyine (4 daily; 4hr); Yangon (daily; 5–6hr).
By train The nearest railway station to Kyaiktiyo is in Kyaikhto. All trains between Yangon and Mawlamyine stop

here, most passing through inconveniently early in the morning, although there is one train in each direction around noon each day. From the station it's a 30min pick-up (K500) or motorbike (K1500) ride to Kinpun.
Destinations Bago (3 daily; 3hr); Dawei (daily; 20hr); Mawlamyine (3 daily; 5hr); Thaton (3 daily; 2hr); Yangon (3 daily; 5hr).

Services The KBZ Bank on Kinpun's central junction has an unreliable ATM and offers currency exchange.

ACCOMMODATION

Those travelling on a budget are best off abandoning hope of a mountaintop stay – while **Kinpun** has some decent cheap accommodation, hotels **on the mountain** charge a robust premium. At the time of research, foreign travellers were not allowed to stay in the inexpensive pilgrims' hostels at the top.

IN KINPUN
Golden Sunrise Golden Rock Rd ☏ 09 872 3301, ⊚ goldensunrisehotel.com. Located in a peaceful garden a 10min walk down the road to Kyaikhto, *Golden Sunrise's* sixteen pretty rooms make it Kinpun's classiest hotel. The bungalows come with small verandas overlooking the garden, and there's a pleasant, rustic-looking restaurant on site. $58
Pann Myo Thu Kyaiktiyo Rd ☏ 057 60285. On the road that leads up the mountain, *Pann Myo Thu's* cheapest rooms are small and noisy, with dingy shared bathrooms, but the owners are helpful and there are nicer rooms available for just a few dollars more. $9
Sea Sar Just off the main road ☏ 09 872 3288. Tucked away behind *Sea Sar* restaurant and set around a lawn, the bungalows here are better value than some of the budget

competition. The cheapest rooms have fans and cold-water-only bathrooms, but there's a good range of more comfortable options available (up to $35). No discount for single occupancy; free wi-fi $10

ON THE MOUNTAIN
Golden Rock Near Yathetaun truck stop ☏ 09 871 8391, ⊚ goldenrock-hotel.com. Set in lush grounds a 45min walk downhill from the mountaintop, this hotel offers the same level of comfort and service as its sister property, *Mountain Top*, but with a less convenient location and correspondingly lower prices. Free wi-fi; closed May–Oct. $85
Mountain Top Near the Foreigners' Registration Office ☏ 09 871 8392, ✉ grtt@goldenrock.com.mm. With comfortable, nicely designed rooms arranged on a steep slope, sunrise views and a pretty garden restaurant, this hotel

is understandably popular with well-heeled foreign travellers. The owner lives in California, which may account for the un-Burmese look and feel of the place. Free wi-fi. **$100**

Yoe Yoe Lay Mountaintop plaza ☎ 09 872 3082, ⓦ yoeyoelayhotel.com. On the opposite side of the plaza to the main approach, close to the Golden Rock itself, this is the cheapest foreigner-friendly accommodation up here. The least expensive doubles are laughably small with shared bathrooms and no windows. A basic room with en-suite will set you back $65, although discounts may be available. Closed May–Oct. **$30**

EATING AND DRINKING

Kinpun has plenty of eating options, most of them touristy Burmese–Chinese places lining the road to the trail. Locals gravitate towards the small restaurants away from the main junction. As you might expect, food options **on the mountain** are more expensive and limited than in Kinpun. The cheapest are the canteens that cluster between the Golden Rock and Kann Pa Sat, but there are one or two more interesting options around.

IN KINPUN

Kaung San Kyaiktiyo Rd ☎ 057 23671. On the path leading to the mountain, *Kaung San* serves up tasty Burmese and Chinese dishes. Although the service can be a bit brusque, their *jin thouq* (ginger salad) is excellent. Prices for hot dishes start at K1500. Daily 6am–9pm.

Mya Yeik Nyo Overlooking the truck terminal. One of Kinpun's more atmospheric restaurants (thanks to their romantic lighting), with friendly staff and good food. A Burmese curry and rice set costs K3000, with other dishes starting from K2000. Daily 4am–9pm.

ON THE MOUNTAIN

A1 Opposite the Foreigners' Registration Office. With tables dotted around a pleasant tree-filled yard, *A1* serves up decently priced Burmese soups and salads, along with Chinese stir-fries. A meal will set you back around K3000. No alcohol. Daily 6am–9pm.

★Mountain Top Restaurant Mountain Top Hotel ☎ 09 871 8392. With white tablecloths, candles and a wine list, the patio here may feel a tad incongruous with the setting, but it's the most appealing place to eat on the mountain. The dishes on their Burmese–Western menu start at $3, with set menus from $13. Daily 6am–10pm.

Thaton

သထုံမြို့

Formerly an important Indian Ocean seaport and capital of a tenth-century Mon kingdom (see p.330), **THATON** is a sleepy little place today. With the port silted up for centuries and the city walls long gone, all that remains of Thaton's past is a collection of inscribed tablets discovered in the precincts of the main pagoda, **Shwe Saw Yan Pagoda**. Nonetheless, Thaton is still a rewarding place to spend the day wandering through its neat streets and poking around the lively **market**, part of the attraction being that very few foreigners stop here. Energetic types may wish to climb up the covered staircase to **Mya Thapaint Pagoda**, 1.5km due east of the market, for beautiful views over ranks of palm trees to the shimmering sea – now almost 16km to the west.

ARRIVAL AND DEPARTURE
THATON

By train Thaton's railway station is a short walk west of the market, with tickets going on sale just before each departure.

Destinations Bago (3 daily; 5hr); Kyaikhto (3 daily; 2hr); Mawlamyine (3 daily; 2hr 30min–3hr); Yangon (3 daily; 7–8hr).

By pick-up Frequent pick-ups to Hpa-An (1hr) and Mawlamyine (2hr) leave regularly from the car park outside Shwe Saw Yan during daylight hours, with the last one leaving around 4pm. Both destinations cost K1500, or K4000 if you want to sit up front.

ACCOMMODATION AND EATING

Aung Shwe Saw Yan Rd. This typical Burmese restaurant, just north of Shwe Saw Yan's north gate, is the most popular in a small row of similar restaurants serving up excellent curries and mounds of rice. Vegetarian options available, Burmese-only sign. Daily 8am–7pm.

First Café Mountain Mya Thapaint Pagoda Rd ☎ 09 872 0904. On the road towards hilltop pagoda Mya Thapaint, this big café is popular with local young people and Thaton's businessmen. It produces good Burmese curries, Chinese dishes plus real coffee and juices. A curry meal costs around K2500 and there's good, fast wi-fi available. Daily 9am–9pm.

Tain Pyar Guesthouse 381 Hospital St ☏ 057 40036. This guesthouse is as good as it gets in Thaton: the cheapest rooms have fans and cold-water-only shared bathrooms, but there's a (foreigners-only) hot shower (ask for the key), and more expensive rooms ($35) have a/c and en-suite bathrooms. **$15**

Hpa-An and around

ဘားအံမြို့

Just outside the capital of Kayin State, **HPA-AN**, a sheer limestone ridge pokes through the brilliant green rice paddies that surround the town, lending a sudden drama and beauty to the landscape. There's not much to see in the understated town itself, although the **markets** are bustling and **Shweyinhmyaw Paya** boasts wonderful views of the **Thanlyin River** sliding past. The main attraction here is the opportunity to get out into the countryside, where it's possible to poke around **caves**, climb up jungle-draped **Mount Zwegabin** and swim in spring-fed pools. **Kyauk Kalat Pagoda**, perched on a vertiginous finger of rock, will amaze even those suffering from pagoda overexposure, and there are numerous **Kayin villages** to explore as well. Many people come here for a few days and end up staying longer, but when you do manage to tear yourself away, there's the fun option of catching a **riverboat** down the Thanlyin to Mawlamyine (see box, p.154). Visit in December/January, and you may catch the lively **Kayin New Year** celebrations, when Hpa-An hosts dancing and kick-boxing competitions.

Shweyinhmyaw Paya

ရွှေယင်မျှော်ဘုရား် • Thida St • Daily 5am–10pm • Free

For the best views of the Thanlyin River and Mount Hpar-Pu's distinctive silhouette (see p.144), head down to the petite **Shweyinhmyaw Paya** at dusk to watch the sun set

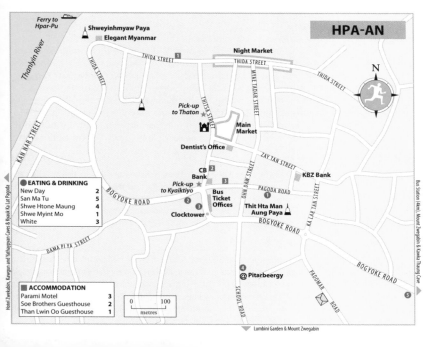

over the riverbank. The pagoda is also home to a statue of a giant green frog (frogs are an important symbol for the Kayin) and a *naga* – a reference to the story behind Hpa-An's name, which means "Frog Vomit". Kayin legend tells of a *naga* swallowing a frog that had a gem in its mouth. The gem magically stopped the *naga* from keeping his dinner down, and it vomited the frog onto the banks of the Thanlyin where Hpa-An stands today – immediately bestowing Myanmar's most memorable and least poetic place name upon the town.

Mount Hpar-Pu

ဟား့ပုတောင် • Ferry across the river K500/person (every 30min: daily 6am–6pm)

The nearest limestone peak to downtown Hpa-An, **Mount Hpar-Pu**, is a quick boat trip across the Thalwin River from Shweyinhmyaw Paya. Once on the opposite bank it's a short walk through vegetable fields to a village where there's an English sign pointing the way. The road leads to the foot of Hpar-Pu, before swinging right towards the river. Follow the road around to the bottom of the steps up the mountain – a sweaty twenty-minute climb from here ought to see you close to the summit. Note that after a landslide swept away a chunk of the hill during the 2013 rainy season it is no longer

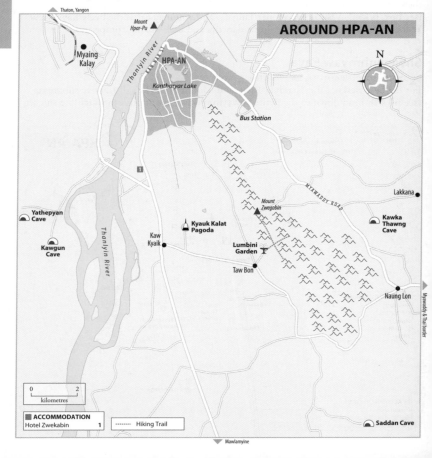

AROUND HPA-AN

ACCOMMODATION	
Hotel Zwekabin	1

------- Hiking Trail

safe to climb to the very top, but it is still possible to get high enough for wonderful views of the river and out towards Mount Zwegabin.

Mount Zwegabin

ဇွဲကပင်တောင် • 10km south of Hpa-An • Tuk-tuk from Hpa-An K5000; motorbike taxi K2500

From certain angles, the limestone bulk of **Mount Zwegabin** erupts from the landscape like a giant molar tooth. While it may look impossibly steep from downtown Hpa-An, there are two beautiful paths to the summit of the 725m-high mountain, making it a rewarding half-day hike.

Most people ascend the less direct and more scenic western side of the mountain, along a trail starting from **Lumbini Garden**, 3km east of Kyauk Kalat Pagoda, where 1100 Buddha statues have been arranged in picturesque rows. From here it takes around two hours to climb the steep and winding path to the summit, with water and drinks available from a single stall en route and plenty of **macaques** for company. The trail down the eastern flank of the mountain is more direct, with relentless staircases leading to a small restaurant at the foot of the mountain, from where it's a straight, flat 1km walk to the Myawaddy road. Whichever way you cross the mountain, it's advisable to arrange a pick-up at the other end to avoid a long wait.

For many people, staying overnight at the mountaintop monastery to watch sunrise is the highlight of a trip to Hpa-An. At the time of writing it was possible to sleep on mats in a basic **dormitory** (donation expected), but Hpa-An's immigration department periodically clamps down on the practice – check at the *Soe Brothers Guesthouse* before you drag your backpack up here.

Kyauk Kalat Pagoda

ကျောက်ကလပ်ဘုရား • 10km south of Hpa-An, between Kaw Kyaik and Taw Bon villages • Daily during daylight hours; closed noon–1pm • Free • Motorbike taxi from Hpa-An K2500, tuk-tuk K5000

Balanced on a bizarrely shaped limestone pinnacle with frangipani trees sprouting from cracks in the rock, **Kyauk Kalat Pagoda**, 7km south of Hpa-An, is the area's most arresting sight. On an island in the centre of an artificial lake, the site is part of a working monastery and a shoe-free, vegetarian zone that closes for an hour each lunchtime to allow the monks to meditate in peace. Revered monk **U Winaya** (see box below) was a novice here in the 1920s before he founded a monastery at Thamanya, 40km southeast of Hpa-An.

THE THAMANYA SAYADAW: U WINAYA

Years after his death, **U Winaya**, *sayadaw* of Thamanya Monastery, remains one of Myanmar's most respected religious figures – pictures of him decorate taxis across the country. A spiritual adviser and supporter of Aung San Suu Kyi, U Winaya was renowned for his humanitarian work. During decades of vicious fighting between the Karen National Liberation Army and government forces, the area surrounding Thamanya Monastery was a sanctuary of non-violence until the abbot passed away in 2003 at the age of 93.

Shockingly, in 2008 U Winaya's **tomb** was broken into and his body disappeared. Four days later, the monastery received an anonymous phone call notifying them that the abbot's body had been burned, and his remains left outside a small *zedi* near the edge of the monastery grounds. Many believe that this violation was part of a **yadaya** inspired plot to help the government win a crucial referendum on constitutional reform that was held a few weeks later. *Yadaya* is a uniquely Burmese practice where steps taken now on the advice of an astrologer are believed to prevent future bad luck – a practice that senior generals in Myanmar's military government have been known to indulge in for years.

Saddan Cave

ဆဒ္ဒန်ဝု • Daily Nov–April only • Free; boat trip K1500/person • Motorbike taxi from Hpa-An K3500, tuk-tuk K5000–7000

In a hard-to-find spot 28km south of Hpa-An, at the southern end of the jagged limestone ridge, lies **Saddan Cave**, the most dramatic of the region's caverns. A complete golden *zedi* sits inside the cave entrance but the Buddhist statuary quickly gives way to natural rock formations – stalactites drip from the ceiling like molten wax and mushroom-like stalagmites emerge from the earthen cave floor. Bats roost in the erratically lit main cavern (take a good torch), which takes around fifteen minutes to walk through barefoot. On the far side, the path emerges beside a limpid forest pool, from where (between November and February only) you can take a short boat trip back towards the entrance. Note that the entire complex is off limits during the rainy season.

The cave's name comes from an elaborate Jataka story about one of Buddha's previous incarnations, in which he was the elephant king Saddan – keep an eye out for the elephant statues flanking the entrance.

Kawgun Cave

ကော့ဂွန်းဝု • Daily 7am–dusk • K3000 • Motorbike taxi from Hpa-An K2500, tuk-tuk K5000

Its walls covered in rippling mosaics of terracotta votive tablets, with fragments of aged stucco reliefs visible in the gaps, **Kawgun Cave**, 12km southwest of Hpa-An in Kawgun village, has been used by local Mon Buddhists since the seventh century, with each generation scraping away some of the old to make room for the new. While the shallow cave's walls are an impressive sight, many of the oldest statues have been destroyed by tremors resulting from work at the nearby cement factory, leaving only a few sandstone tablets of late Bagan-style carving and the rather average modern statuary intact.

Yathepyan Cave

ရသေ့ပြိန်ဝု • Daily 7am–dusk • Free • Motorbike taxi from Hpa-An K2500, tuk-tuk K5000

Near Kawgun village, 12km southwest of Hpa-An, the small **Yathepyan Cave** is filled with newish statues and a few timeworn reliefs and has good views of Mount Zwegabin. Its most notable feature is a hole in the cavern roof, with a pagoda covered in bird droppings directly below it. During King Anawrahta's eleventh-century campaign in Lower Burma, a hermit took refuge here with a golden Buddha statue. Newly converted to Theravada Buddhism, Anawrahta coveted the statue and tried to wrest it from the hermit, who burst up through the cave roof with the statue under his arm and flew to safety, supposedly creating the hole you see today.

Kawka Thaung Cave and around

ကျောကသောင်ဝု • Daily 8am–5.30pm • Free • Motorbike taxi from Hpa-An K2500, tuk-tuk K5000

Ten kilometres southeast of Hpa-An, a short distance east of the road to Mae Sot, is **Kawka Thaung Cave**. The cave itself is a shallow affair, its single chamber narrowing to a cramped meditation space for monks, with a shrine containing some tiny fragments of bone relic. The area beyond the cave is likely to hold your attention for longer – a photogenic row of monk statues leads to a second Buddhist cave (usually locked), a creepy-looking **nat shrine** and a swimming hole filled with cool, clear spring water, surrounded by teahouses.

Lakkana village

လက္ကဏာရွာ

Near Kawka Thaung Cave, set among vivid green ricefields across a slender concrete bridge, is **Lakkana village**. It's an attractive, diffuse little place, where you can drink

toddy and explore the pretty village lanes to your heart's content. In the countryside beyond you'll find diminutive hamlets where traditional Kayin life continues little-changed.

ARRIVAL AND DEPARTURE · HPA-AN AND AROUND

By bus The bus station is 4km southeast of the central clocktower on the Myawaddy road. Many buses stop at both the bus station and near the clocktower, but check this when you buy your ticket. Bus tickets are available from the bus station, at the bus company offices near the clocktower, and in most hotels. All Yangon-bound buses make stops at Bago and Kyaikhto (for Kyaiktiyo). Buses to Mawlamyine run hourly from the bus station and every 2hr from town until 4pm.

Destinations Bago (6 daily; 6hr); Kyaikhto (for Kyaiktiyo; 6 daily; 4hr); Mandalay (12 daily; 15hr); Mawlamyine (1–2 hourly; 2hr); Naypyitaw (2 daily; 9hr); Taungoo

(2 daily; 7hr); Yangon (6 daily; 9hr).

By pick-up Pick-ups to Thaton (frequent; 1hr) leave from a small lane just north of the mosque. A pick-up to Kyaiktiyo (stopping in Kinpun) leaves from Zay Tan St daily at 7am.

By shared taxi Cars to Myawaddy (every other day; 5–6hr) leave when full from the clocktower when the narrow road between Kawkareik and Myawaddy is open in the right direction (see opposite) – check this at your hotel.

By boat The boat journey between Hpa-An and Mawlamyine is one of southern Myanmar's most attractive journeys (see box, p.154).

GETTING AROUND

By tuk-tuk and motorbike taxi Taking a tuk-tuk to the sights further afield is K5000 each way, although the drive to Saddan Cave may be a little more expensive. A motorbike taxi will cost half that each way.

By motorbike Motorbikes can be rented from

Soe Brothers, Than Lwin Oo and a small shop directly south of Soe Brothers, the going rate at all three places K8000/day.

By bicycle Bikes are available to rent from Soe Brothers (K2000/day) and Than Lwin Oo (K1500/day).

INFORMATION AND TOURS

Maps Both Soe Brothers and Than Lwin Oo offer decent photocopied maps to guests. There's a fancier English map available from bookstores around town, but it's less useful than either of the free ones.

Tours Soe Brothers has cornered the market in day-trips around Hpa-An, with most people joining one of their tuk-tuk tours. The trips cost K30,000 per vehicle per day, so the more people you manage to squeeze into your tuk-tuk the

cheaper it will be – K5000 each is usual. Be aware that few of the drivers speak English. If you would like an English tour, the Soe Brothers' manager, La Shu, is an excellent guide, and a day scooting around on the back of his motorbike will cost around K15,000. Elegant Myanmar (☏ 09 3156 7303, ⌨ elegantmyanmartours.com) have an office near Shweyinhmyaw Pagoda and offer a full-day sightseeing tour by tuk-tuk ($10) and a sunset cruise on the river (1hr; $5).

ACCOMMODATION

Parami Motel Pagoda Rd ☏058 21647; map p.143. Close to the centre of town, Parami has pleasant staff and spacious, high-ceilinged rooms – those on upper floors have wonderful views over Hpa-An to Mount Zwegabin. The decor is rather odd in places (some rooms are decorated with huge posters of tropical islands), but common areas are nice and it's one of the better-value hotels in this price range. **$35**

★ Soe Brothers Guesthouse 2/146 Thitsa St ☏058 21372; map p.143. The rooms are decent in this long-time budget favourite – small but cool and clean – but the main draws are the staff, who are expert at dealing with travellers' needs, and the common areas which add to the fun and friendly atmosphere. There's a small sleeping-mat dormitory upstairs. No breakfast. Dorm **$4**, double **$12**

Than Lwin Oo Guesthouse Thida St ☏058 21513; map p.143. At the time of research this guesthouse had

only just been licensed for foreign guests. While it's not as foreigner-savvy as the Soe Brothers, it's a good alternative, as long as you can handle the intense purple paint job both outside and in. Rooms are very clean and there's a great little roof terrace and free wi-fi, the only downside being that none of the bathrooms has hot water. **K8000**

Hotel Zwekabin Hpa-An–Mawlamyine Rd, 6km south of Hpa-An ☏058 22556, ✉hotelzwekabin.zkb@gmail .com; map p.144. A 10min drive from Hpa-An, this resort-style hotel sits at the foot of a limestone outcrop with partially obscured views of Mount Zwegabin. The more expensive bungalows are very spacious with small verandas, but the cheaper rooms are in a small multistorey block. All rooms are pleasantly decorated, with a/c, and there's a restaurant on-site, though the location might be too quiet for some. Free wi-fi. **$70**

EATING AND DRINKING

Hpa-An's **markets** are the most interesting and low-cost places to eat, although the offerings at both the morning and night markets are somewhat noodle-centric. Sweet-toothed travellers should seek out *bein moun* – crispy rice-flour pancakes smeared with jaggery syrup and sprinkled with coconut shreds.

New Day Bogyoke Rd ☎ 058 21325; map p.143. Bright and canteen-like, this bakery is possibly the only place in Myanmar where you can have cappuccino with a potato curry and puris for breakfast. Cheesecake and other baked treats are also on the menu. Daily 6am–6pm.

★**San Ma Tu** Bogyoke Rd ☎ 058 21802; map p.143. This place has a well-deserved reputation for great Burmese food, which means that it's often full of foreigners. Choose a vegetarian (K500) or meat (from K1500) curry from their wide selection, and it will be served with ten side dishes, soup and tea. Rice is an additional K500. Daily lunch and dinner.

★**Shwe Htone Maung** School Rd; map p.143. This bustling teahouse serves up delicious bowls of noodles, hot drinks, juices and sinful fried snacks throughout the day

– prepare to get addicted to the banana fritters they serve at breakfast. English menu available. Daily 6am–10pm.

Shwe Myint Mo 2 Pagoda Rd ☎ 058 21362; map p.143. Serving Burmese food with Indian undertones as well as particularly tasty soups and salads, *Shwe Myint Mo* also has three beers on tap and a handwritten English menu, featuring the hopefully mistranslated "Bird's Rump (Human Nose)". Daily 7am–10pm.

White Bogyoke St; map p.143. This scruffy-but-charming teahouse serves up great sugar parathas and crispy naan bread all day long. They also do a wonderful samosa *thouq*, but you'll need to get here early to sample it before they run out of samosas. Daily 6am–10pm.

DIRECTORY

Banks Both CB Bank on Thitsa Rd and KBZ on Zay Tan St offer currency exchange, but neither has an ATM yet. If you need kyat outside of banking hours, it's possible to change US dollars at the dentist's office on the south side of Zay Tan St.

Internet While wi-fi is widely available in Hpa-An's hotels

and guesthouses, it's often terribly slow. The most central internet café is Pitarbeergy (daily 8am–9pm; K500/hr), just south of Shwe Htone Maung on School Rd.

Post office Hpa-An's post office is on Padomar Rd, about 400m south of the roundabout. There's no English sign – look for the Myanmar flag outside.

Myawaddy

မြဝတီမြို့

One of the more convenient checkpoints on the Thai–Myanmar border, the border crossing between **MYAWADDY** and Mae Sot in Thailand is relatively accessible from major cities on either side. However, despite the volume of traffic, the narrow road from Myawaddy to Kawkareik snakes over the Dawna Mountains in a single lane, and traffic is strictly one-way – westbound one day, eastbound the next. You'll need to check in advance in which direction traffic is flowing unless you plan to spend the day watching the frenetic border-town activity in Myawaddy.

Migyaung Gon Pagoda

မိကျောင်းကုန်းဘုရား • Just off Nat Shin Naung St, 400m south of the main road • Daily 5am–10pm • Free

Just 1km southwest of the border, the central shrine at **Migyaung Gon Pagoda** rests on the back of a vast concrete crocodile, making it one of the more bizarre photo opportunities in Myawaddy, and the only one worth searching out if you're stranded here for a day. Women aren't allowed on the crocodile itself, where the chapels hold a collection of Burmese- and Thai-style Buddhas, and murals relating the story of the pagoda's construction – a princess hid her jewels in a crocodile's nest for safekeeping, apparently, later donating the jewels to the monastery – line the walls.

ARRIVAL AND GETTING AROUND
MYAWADDY

By shared taxi Minivans to Mawlamyine (6hr) and Hpa-An (6hr) leave from the main road just beyond the border post

when full and when the road is open in the right direction. It costs K10,000 per person to either destination. A branch of

---

MYAWADDY–MAE SOT BORDER CROSSING

Since the Myanmar government removed a rule requiring foreigners to leave their passports at the **Myawaddy–Mae Sot border crossing** in 2013, numbers of overland travellers using this border have increased dramatically. The Myanmar border post (daily 6am–5.30pm) is on the west side of the Moei River. Foreigners can use a small immigration office, rather than queuing with the locals. From here, it's a short walk over the Friendship Bridge to the Thai side of the border (6.30am–6.30pm Thai time) and a 50 *baht* pick-up ride to Mae Sot's bus station, from where there are direct buses to Bangkok (6 daily; 8hr) and Tak (hourly; 1hr 30min). From Tak there are direct buses to Chiang Mai, Chiang Rai, Lampang and Mae Sai.

Vega Travel (☎ 09 0440 9590), inside the immigration office, also arranges minivans to Yangon for K45,000/person.

By motorbike taxi A motorbike taxi costs K500/person for a ride anywhere in town.

ACCOMMODATION AND EATING

River View Guesthouse By the river ☎ 058 51061 or ☎ 08 2774 4006 (Thailand). Visible from the bridge, *River View* is an adequate mid-range option with spacious, clean rooms scented with mothballs and furnished with the usual assortment of orphaned furniture. It's also one of the most popular places to eat and drink in Myawaddy. The menu has a good selection of fried dishes, salads and cold draught beer, but it's on the expensive side, starting at

K2000 for a salad. Decent wi-fi and a good breakfast in the riverside restaurant included. **K20,000**

Yuzana Guesthouse Yuzana St ☎ 09 312 23912. The only budget option in town, *Yuzana* is tucked away down a side street just south of the border post – look for its blue walls. The cramped fan-cooled rooms are the cheapest option, and a/c rooms start from K15,000 (or 500 baht); all have shared bathrooms. Breakfast not included. **K8000**

DIRECTORY

Banks The KBZ Bank has an ATM as well as currency exchange upstairs – the rates are better than the branch of CB Bank opposite, but neither bank will exchange Thai

baht. To change baht you'll need to stop in at the Vega Travel desk inside the immigration office, or take your chances at one of the roadside booths.

Mawlamyine

မော်လမြိုင်မြို့

Sandwiched between a ridge of pagoda-topped hills and the island-filled estuary of the Thanlyin River, **MAWLAMYINE** is an absorbing place to spend a few days. With the town centre dominated by a series of fascinating markets, the neighbourhoods beyond dotted with neat churches and extravagantly crumbling **colonial mansions** (even by 1904 Mawlamyine's atmosphere was already described as being "one of decay" by a British travel writer, V.C. Scott O'Connor), the town is a diverting place to explore. However, it would be a shame not to venture into the surrounding region, whether to the picturesque island of Bilu Kyun or to visit one of the unusual religious sites nearby (see p.156). Finally, good travel connections make Mawlamyine an excellent starting point for forays south to Tanintharyi, or north along the Thanlyin River to Hpa-An in Kayin State (see box, p.154).

Brief history

For much of its history, Mawlamyine was overshadowed by nearby Mottama (formerly known as Martaban), which was a major Indian Ocean trade entrepôt until the mid-sixteenth century. When the **British** annexed Tanintharyi (Tenasserim) after the First Anglo-Burmese War, Mawlamyine – then little more than a fishing village known to the British as Moulmein – was made capital of Lower Burma from 1827 to 1852. Located at the confluence of the Thanlyin, Gyaing and Ataran rivers, with a sheltered harbour on the Andaman Sea, the city became a wealthy teak port and home to a substantial British and Anglo-Burmese population.

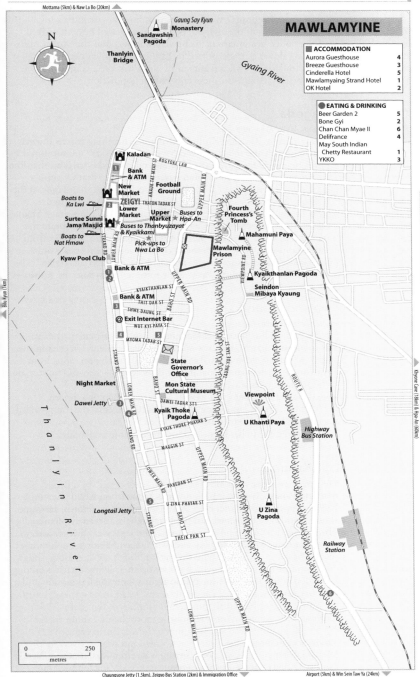

Mottama (5km) & Naw La Bo (20km)

Gaung Say Kyun Monastery

Sandawshin Pagoda

Thanlyin Bridge

Gyaing River

MAWLAMYINE

■ ACCOMMODATION	
Aurora Guesthouse	4
Breeze Guesthouse	3
Cinderella Hotel	5
Mawlamyaing Strand Hotel	1
OK Hotel	2

● EATING & DRINKING	
Beer Garden 2	5
Bone Gyi	2
Chan Chan Myae II	6
Delifrance	4
May South Indian Chetty Restaurant	1
YKKO	3

3

Kaladan

BOGYOKE LAN

Bank & ATM

New Market

Football Ground

UPPER MAIN RD

Boats to Ka Lwi

ZEIGYI

THATON TADAR ST

Lower Market

Upper Market

Buses to Hpa-An

Fourth Princess's Tomb

Surtee Sunni Jama Masjid

Boats to Nat Hmaw

Buses to Thanbyuzayat & Kyaikkami

Mahamuni Paya

Pick-ups to Nwa La Bo

Mawlamyine Prison

Kyaw Pool Club

Bank & ATM

VIEWPOINT RD

Kyaikthanlan Pagoda

KYAIKTHANLAN ST

Bank & ATM

THIT DAR ST

Seindon Mibaya Kyaung

SHWE DAUNG ST

@ Exit Internet Bar

WUT KYI PAYA ST

MYOMA TADAR ST

TAUNG TOE TAN ST

State Governor's Office

Night Market

BAHO ST

Mon State Cultural Museum

DAWEI TADAR ST

Viewpoint

Dawei Jetty

Kyaik Thoke Pagoda

ROUTE 8

KYAIK THOKE PHAYAR S

U Khanti Paya

Highway Bus Station

MAGGIN ST

UPPER MAIN RD

LOWER MAIN RD

T h a n l y i n R i v e r

Bilu Kyun (1km)

STRAND RD

PABEDAN ST

Longtail Jetty

U ZINA PHAYAR ST

BAHO ST

U Zina Pagoda

THEIK PAN ST

Railway Station

0	250
	metres

Chaungsone Jetty (1.5km), Zeigyo Bus Station (2km) & Immigration Office

Airport (5km) & Win Sein Taw Ya (24km)

Khayone Cave (18km) & Hpa-An (60km)

Several generations of writer **George Orwell**'s (see p.316) family – including his mother – were born and grew up in the city, but by the time Orwell himself arrived here in 1926 to staff the police headquarters, its heyday was over and the timber mills and shipyards were closing down as trade shifted to Yangon. The town became a popular retirement spot for British civil servants until Ne Win's 1962 coup d'état led to an exodus of the British, Anglo-Burmese and Indian population.

Kyaikthanlan Pagoda

ကျိုက်သန်လန်ဘုရား • Viewpoint Rd • Daily 5am–10pm • Free

One of the few places visited by Rudyard Kipling during his three-day trip to Burma in 1889, **Kyaikthanlan Pagoda** is the self-same "old Moulmein Pagoda" immortalized in the opening lines of his poem, *Mandalay*. The oldest and tallest of the pagodas that line Mawlamyine's eastern ridge of hills, Kyaikthanlan has a tiled terrace that's a popular spot from which to watch the sun set over Bilu Kyun (see p.156) and the islands of the Thanlyin estuary; it also offers good views of the 1908 prison, which is still in use.

The pagoda's name is thought to be a corruption of "Kyaikshanlan", meaning "Shan defeating pagoda", the earliest brick structure having been built here to celebrate the routing of a Siamese army in 875. The most pleasant way to reach the complex from town is along Kyaikthanlan Road, which becomes a covered staircase just east of its junction with Upper Main Road, passing several monasteries. Another attractive walkway joins Kyaikthanlan to Mahamuni Paya, a few hundred metres to the north.

Mahamuni Paya and around

မဟာမုနိဘုရား • Viewpoint Rd • Daily 5am–9pm • Free

The densely mirrored powder-blue interior of **Mahamuni Paya** is particularly beautiful at dusk. A replica of the Buddha at Mandalay's Mahamuni Paya (see p.271) sits in the central shrine, flanked by curved elephant tusks. Built in 1905 with donations from a wealthy local lady, the original tiles – hand-painted with peacocks – can still be seen on the walls of the corridor that circles the main chapel.

A few minutes' walk downhill from here, just west of Mahamuni Paya, is a forlorn, crumbling white stupa that marks the last resting place of **Fourth Princess**, the strong-willed and intelligent youngest daughter of King Thibaw and Queen Supalayat (see p.339), who was born in exile in India and came to her homeland for the first time as an adult.

Seindon Mibaya Kyaung

စိန်တုံးမိဖုရားကျောင်း • Viewpoint Rd • Daily during daylight hours • Free

The century-old **Seindon Mibaya Kyaung** (also known as Yadanarbon Myint Kyaung) looks terribly dilapidated from the outside, even by Mawlamyine's standards. However, the main hall contains a wealth of lively red and gold teak reliefs, carved elephants' tusks and a cobweb-festooned period replica of a throne, the legacy of the monastery's royal connections. One of King Mindon's many widows, Queen Seindon, took refuge here after her husband's death in 1878 and paid for the building's construction. Today, the monastery is home to just nine monks, who have set up their living quarters among the faded finery – they'll turn on the lights for you in return for a small donation and a signature in their visitors' book.

U Zina Pagoda

ဦးဇိနဘုရား • Viewpoint Rd • Daily during daylight hours • Free

At the southern end of Mawlamyine's hills, a long, sweaty walk from Kyaikthanlan Pagoda, is the nineteenth-century **U Zina Pagoda**. The eponymous monk U Zina founded the monastery after discovering a cache of gemstones on this spot, having been shown the location in a dream. At the time of research, the pagoda was being re-gilded, and the fabulously jewelled *hti* was on display in the hall at the southern end of the complex, along with a collection of life-size teak statues of the "four sights" – an old man, a sick man, a dead body and an ascetic – that led Siddhartha Gautama to renounce his princely status.

The markets

Daily 6am–5pm

While local people differentiate between the various markets that sprawl between Strand Road and Upper Main Road, for visitors they may all blur into one. The whole area is known as **Zeigyi** (not to be confused with Zeigyo, a separate part of the city, 6km to the south) and divided into Upper and Lower markets. The **Lower Market** is made up of a characterless modern complex on Lower Main Road (built after a two-day fire raged through its predecessor in 2008) and the dark, atmospheric and much more interesting covered **New Market** just to the north. In the latter, porters pad barefoot down the aisles and entire sections are devoted to betel leaves and *ngăpí*; there's also the odd market bar, with stallholders nursing glasses of whisky and watching television. A small alleyway lined with gold and *longyi* shops links the Lower Market with the **Upper Market**, largely devoted to stalls selling gold, cosmetics and Chinese-made toys.

Mon State Cultural Museum

မွန်ပြည်နယ်ကေး္မွုပြတိုက် • Corner of Baho St and Dawei Tadar St • Tues–Sun 10am–4.30pm, closed on public holidays • K2000

The modest collection on display at the two-floor **Mon State Cultural Museum** may be confusingly organized and poorly lit, but it's still well worth a visit – just remember to bring a torch. The highlights include a Mon crocodile-shaped harp, an eighteenth-century teak palanquin, and a beautiful palm-leaf fan set with gold and glass patterns, along with an informative series of displays about local industries.

Gaung Say Kyun

ခေါင်းဆေးကျွန်း • Daily during daylight hours • Free • Boat from Mawlamyine K1000 return

A short boat trip from the northern end of Mawlamyine, the pretty island of **Gaung Say Kyun** is forested with almost equal numbers of palm trees and pagodas. The island's name, meaning "Shampoo Island", dates from the Ava period, when the water for the king's annual hair-washing ceremonies was drawn from a **spring** here and transported to Inwa, 800km away. The spring is now covered by a pavilion that is usually kept locked, but a small tank at the side of the pavilion is accessible – local people sometimes still use the water for rinsing their hair, as it's thought to bring good luck.

You'll need to explore Gaung Say Kyun barefoot, leaving your shoes by the jetty. The nineteenth-century Mon-style **monastery** buildings are home to a small convent, a monastery and a meditation centre (although with the 2006 Thanlyin Bridge just 50m away, meditation is presumably far more challenging than it used to be), and the outlying *zedi* represent several different Buddhist traditions from Nepal to China, although the centrepiece is the Burmese-style **Sandawshin Pagoda**.

ARRIVAL AND DEPARTURE	MAWLAMYINE

By plane Some 8km southeast of town, Mawlamyine's small airport is served by a weekly Myanma Airways (☎ 057 21500) flight from Yangon, which continues south to Kawthaung after a brief stop. Nok Air operates a daily flight to Mae Sot in Thailand, although the runway at Mae Sot was closed for repairs at the time of research.

Destinations Kawthaung (weekly; 2hr); Mae Sot (daily; 1hr); Yangon (2 weekly; 30min).
By bus There are several bus stations in Mawlamyine. Buses to Yangon and Upper Burma leave from the highway bus station on the eastern side of the hills, while southbound services depart from the Zeigyo bus station 6km south of the

3

MAWLAMYINE TO HPA-AN BY BOAT

The three- to four-hour boat ride along the **Thanlyin River** from Mawlamyine's bustling harbour, past bucolic villages of palm-thatch huts, to the dramatic limestone scenery around Hpa-An is one of the most memorable journeys in southern Myanmar. Most people choose to go from Mawlamyine to Hpa-An, leaving the best of the scenery to the end of the trip. The most popular boat service (K7000), organized jointly by the *Soe Brothers Guesthouse* in Hpa-An and *Breeze Guesthouse* in Mawlamyine (see below), makes the round trip from Mawlamyine to Hpa-An and back in a day – if there aren't enough people to run the first leg, then the boat will not do the second leg either. Elegant Myanmar (see p.148) operates the more expensive *Thanlwin Princess* (3–4hr; $12–15) that departs Hpa-An for Mawlamyine each morning at 8.30am, and sets out from Mawlamyine for the return journey at 2pm. The boat service stops between June and October.

market. Buses to Hpa-An depart from just south of the football ground, near the Upper Market, and services to Thanbyuzayat and Kyaikkami depart from the southern end of the Zeigyi Market on Lower Main Rd until 4pm. For Inle Lake take the Mandalay bus and change at Meiktila (10hr).
Destinations Bago (5 daily; 5hr 30min); Dawei (11 daily; 9hr); Hpa-An (1–2 hourly until 4pm; 2hr); Kinpun (for Kyaiktiyo, 4 daily; 4hr); Kyaikkami (hourly; 3hr); Mandalay (2 daily; 12hr); Myeik (11 daily; 16hr); Naypyitaw (2 daily; 11–12hr); Thanbyuzayat (hourly; 2hr); Yangon (2 daily; 8hr).
By shared taxi Minivans depart for Myawaddy (6hr; K10,000) from the Zeigyo bus station every other day (traffic can only run in one direction at a time along the narrow mountain road) between 8 and 10am. Book a seat in advance through your accommodation and you'll qualify

for a free pick-up.
By train Mawlamyine's railway station is located 4km southeast of the market area on the eastern side of the ridge. At the time of writing, foreigners required permission from the immigration office on Taung Waing Rd near the Zeigyo bus station in order to travel to Dawei by train – oddly, permission is not necessary for those travelling along the same route by bus, and the requirement will hopefully disappear soon.
Destinations Bago (3 daily; 7–8hr); Dawei (daily; 15hr); Kyaikhto (for Kyaiktiyo, 3 daily; 5hr); Thaton (3 daily; 2hr 30min–3hr); Yangon (3 daily; 9hr); Ye (daily; 6hr).
By boat Chugging upstream along the Thanlyin River to Hpa-An (4hr) is a popular way to depart Mawlamyine (see box above). Boat services to Bilu Kyun are covered in the "Around Mawlamyine" section (see p.156).

GETTING AROUND

By motorbike taxi A short trip around town ought to cost K500. Longer trips start from K1000 (from the market area to the Zeigyo bus station), up to K7000 for the return journey to Nwa La Bo.
By bicycle Bikes are available to rent from *Breeze*

Guesthouse (K2000/day).
By motorbike Motorbikes can be rented from *Breeze Guesthouse* and Kyaw Pool Club, one block north of *Breeze*. Both charge around K10,000/day.

INFORMATION AND TOURS

Maps Most of the hotels can provide city maps, although the *Cinderella Hotel*'s version is a cut above the rest with photographs and information about local sights on the reverse – you can pick these up from the hotel reception.
Tours *Breeze Guesthouse* runs reasonably priced day-trips to Bilu Kyun (see p.156) and Nwa La Bo (see p.156). Local tour

operator, Thiri Hanthar (☏09 3176 9249, ✉thirihanthar15 @gmail.com), also organizes a range of tours around Mon State and to Hpa-An. If you require an English-speaking guide during your stay, you can either find one through your accommodation or call Mr Myo (☏09 4252 60072), an experienced official guide, although he charges a rather steep $40/day.

ACCOMMODATION

Aurora Guesthouse 277 Lower Main Rd ☏057 22785. This neat little guesthouse has a selection of cheap partitioned rooms with spotless shared bathrooms, as well as a few with en-suite ($20). There's a pleasant shared balcony and the owner is gruff but helpful, making this a great budget option if you want to escape from *Breeze*. No wi-fi or breakfast available. **$12**
Breeze Guesthouse 6 Strand Rd ☏057 21450, ✉breeze.guesthouse@gmail.com. This backpacker

favourite looks promising at first glance, but the majority of the grubby cell-like rooms are crammed into one small corner of the elegant colonial building. There are a few more attractive rooms available (K25,000), but you'll need to reserve online if you want to stay in one, as these are perennially booked up. However, the staff are knowledgeable and the location is great. Free wi-fi. **K14,000**
★**Cinderella Hotel** 21 Baho St ☏057 24411, ⊛cinderellahotel.com. A few blocks east of Strand Rd,

Cinderella has a small army of staff who provide excellent service, from the welcome drink to the enormous breakfasts. Rooms are pleasant, the beds are comfortable, and the hallways display a treasure-trove of Burmese handicrafts. The huge breakfasts are particularly good and there's fast free wi-fi. $45

Mawlamyaing Strand Hotel Between Lower Main Rd and Strand Rd ☏ 057 25624, ⊛ mawlamyaingstrand hotel.com. As you'd expect from Mawlamyine's fanciest hotel, the spacious rooms here are attractive and comfortable, though they're somewhat bland. There are two hotel restaurants (one inside and one open-air, the latter with nightly karaoke) and an excellent buffet breakfast is included, as is free wi-fi. $90

OK Hotel 11–12 Thaton Tadar St, on the corner with Strand Rd ☏ 057 24677, ⊛ okhotel-mlm.com. The tiled rooms here may not be particularly stylish, but they are clean and comfortable, and each one comes with a/c and en-suite bathroom, some with bathtubs. Since it's close to the market, rooms facing Thaton Tadar St can be very noisy – try to get one of the quieter rooms overlooking Strand Rd and the river. $35

EATING AND DRINKING

Every day from 5pm onwards, a strip of **open-air food stalls** sets up along Strand Rd, just north of Dawei Jetty, making this an excellent place to watch the sunset. The food on offer is predictable (barbecued skewers, fried rice and noodles dominate the menus) but it smells and tastes good, and there's more atmosphere than many other places in town.

Beer Garden 2 Strand Rd. This beer station close to the river serves up great barbecued food and icy-cold beer. Take your pick of the skewers from the fridge, and they'll be served up accompanied by a delicious tamarind-based sauce and your beverage of choice. Daily lunch and dinner.

Bone Gyi Strand Rd ☏ 057 26528. Dishing up good Chinese food, this popular restaurant stays full of well-to-do Mawlamyiners until late in the evening, although as many come here to drink as to dine (there's even a wine list). Vegetable dishes from K1800, meat from K3500. Daily lunch and dinner.

Chan Chan Myae II Route 8 ☏ 09 4015 9131. Rather inconveniently located just south of the railway station – look for the English sign proclaiming "Thai Noodle and Food" – *Chan Chan Myae II* serves tasty and authentic Thai food in a bright barn-like restaurant. There's a limited English menu, but the friendly staff will help to translate if you need it. Daily 11am–9pm.

Delifrance Strand Rd, south of Dawei Jetty ☏ 09 566 0192. In imitation of the international chain, this small café serves decent coffee (cappuccino K1200), cake and sandwiches, with a small patio overlooking Strand Rd and the river. Daily 8am–9pm.

★ **May South Indian Chetty Restaurant** Strand Rd. This low-key restaurant is at its best (and busiest) around lunchtime, when it fills with market porters and office workers who come for the delicious Indian-inspired curries and biryani, served Burmese-style with fresh vegetables and side dishes. You'll pay around K1400 for a filling meal. Daily 10am–8pm.

YKKO Dawei Jetty, Strand Rd ☏ 09 4015 91212. Clean and bright, with good views of the river, upmarket *YKKO* serves Thai food, barbecue and *kyay-oh* (noodle soup), along with juices and coffee in its a/c dining room. Prices are higher than elsewhere in town – a plate of barbecued skewers will set you back K2000. Wi-fi available. Daily 10.30am–10.30pm.

DIRECTORY

Banks Mawlamyine has plenty of banks and ATMs, with several on Strand Rd just south of the *Mawlamyaing Strand Hotel*, and more just north of *Breeze Guesthouse*. There is also an ATM at the *Cinderella Hotel* and even *Breeze* changes US dollars at rates that aren't terrible. Note that the ATM at the Strand Road branch of Ayeyarwady Bank doesn't accept MasterCard.

Internet Exit Internet Bar (8am–10pm, K400/hr), on Lower Main Rd between Shwe Daung St and Wut Kyi Paya St, is Mawlamyine's most central internet bar.

Post office Mawlamyine's large post office is housed in a building directly north of the State Governor's offices on Baho St.

Around Mawlamyine

The countryside around Mawlamyine is full of quirky side-trips – Buddhist **Khayone Cave** moonlights as a lively *nat* shrine; **Bilu Kyun** ("Ogre Island") contains nothing more fearsome than some really bad roads; and the vast, unfinished **Win Sein Taw Ya** reclining Buddha seems more like a monk's bid for immortality than a holy shrine. Further afield, there's the **Thanbyuzayat war cemetery** and the remains of the infamous World War II "Death Railway", and a seaside pagoda at **Kyaikkami**.

Bilu Kyun

ဘီလူးကျွန်း

Despite its disquieting name, Ogre Island – **Bilu Kyun** – is actually something of a rural idyll, rather than the haunt of man-eating giants. The largely Mon villages that dot this bucolic 32km-long island are linked by a web of rutted tracks, with more buffalo carts than cars. Islanders divide their time between fishing, growing rice and working in one of many **cottage industries**, and it's the chance to watch the latter that makes a visit here so absorbing.

There are several stories behind the island's name, the most likely being that the head-hunting aboriginal people who originally populated this area were pushed onto the island by the arrival of the more sophisticated Mon, who – fearing their neighbour's proclivities – called it "ogre island".

Workshops on the island produce a wide range of home-grown products, from bamboo or banana-leaf hats to toddy (see box below) and even rubber bands. The small factories generally welcome visitors and there's little pressure to buy, but as most places are hard to find, joining a tour is the best way to get the most out of a day on the island (see below).

3

ARRIVAL AND DEPARTURE
BILU KYUN

Tours At the time of writing it was not possible to stay on the island overnight, added to which the unreliable ferry timetable and slow island transport all become serious incentives to sign up for the *Breeze Guesthouse*'s popular day-trip (K15,000–19,000 per person, depending on group size), which takes in a good selection of the workshops, and stops at a swimming hole; all transport and food are included. Most of the mid-range hotels will be able to organize more flexible private trips along the same lines.

By ferry If you're determined to do-it-yourself, check the return ferry times in Mawlamyine before you hop on a boat. Government ferries depart from one of the two jetties on Strand Rd next to the market. Ferries to Ka Lwi (Mon–Sat 2 daily; 1hr) at the northern tip of the island depart from the northernmost of the two, while boats from the southern jetty head to Nat Hmaw (Mon–Sat 3 daily; 2hr; K1000), halfway down the island's eastern shore. A private ferry service operates every day between the inconveniently located Chaungsone Jetty and Nat Hmaw.

By long-tail boat There's also a long-tail boat straight across the channel to the island (daily 6am–6pm, departing when full; 20min; K3000) from a jetty on Strand Rd, near *Beer Garden 2* – the drawback here being that it drops you off at an isolated section of shore, rather than in a village, so you'll need your own transport.

Nwa La Bo

နွားလပို့တောင်ပို • Daily during daylight hours; closed during rainy season • Free

High up in the hills 20km north of Mawlamyine, **Nwa La Bo** – a stack of three slender gold-covered granite slabs, balanced end-on-end and crowned with a small pagoda – stands proudly overlooking the far-off Thanlyin River. Despite its creation purportedly pre-dating the Golden Rock at Kyaiktiyo, and despite its more precarious placement, the rocks at Nwa La Bo are far less revered than their more famous cousins, mainly because they contain less distinguished hair relics. Pilgrim numbers peak during the **pagoda festival** held in the second half of the Thingyan

---

PALM WINE AND TODDY TAPPERS

Toddy, or palm wine, is responsible for hangovers from Nigeria to Papua New Guinea. All over Myanmar, where it's known as *tan-ye*, you'll see spindly bamboo ladders leading up spiky palmyra palms – a sure sign that a toddy collector is at work nearby. A collector, also known as **tapper**, will fasten a bamboo tube around the cut stem of the tree's flowers, and gather the sweet, white sap that drips out. The sap is then left to ferment naturally for a few hours, producing a cloudy, lightly alcoholic beverage. Sweet and lightly sour, toddy must be drunk on the day it is produced, before it turns into vinegar. Happily for the toddy tappers, however, leftover toddy can be evaporated and turned into delicious and exceedingly addictive lumps of caramel-coloured **jaggery**, often served at the end of a meal and jokingly called "Burmese chocolate".

water festival each year. There are a few further outcrops of rock nearby, but the hiking is limited – it's basically a pleasant, peaceful place to sit and watch swifts flitting above the shrine.

ARRIVAL AND DEPARTURE   **NWA LA BO**

By pick-up Pick-ups to Kyonka village (K1000), at the foot of the mountain, leave when full from outside the market on Mawlamyine's Lower Main Rd.

By motorbike and tuk-tuk A motorbike taxi to Kyonka costs K7000 for the return trip, and *Breeze Guesthouse* can arrange tuk-tuks to Kyonka (K14,000/vehicle).

Kyonka to the summit Once in Kyonka, the entrance is marked by a golden archway, but there's no obvious sign. A

truck departs at 11am every day for the top of the mountain (K2000 return), leaving from just inside this entrance – unless there are enough visitors to fill subsequent trucks, you're faced with a long (7km), unshaded walk to the top with no water available en route, although there is a small teahouse at the top. The 11am truck usually returns to Kyonka around noon, though it's best to confirm this with the driver.

Khayone Cave

ခရုံဂူ • Daily 6am–dusk • Free • Hpa-An-bound buses pass the road to the cave, from where it's a 10min walk

Around 18km northeast of Mawlamyine on the road to Hpa-An, the otherwise flat landscape suddenly gives way to a single sheer-sided limestone karst hill. At its base is **Khayone Cave**. There are two small cave systems here, one reached by a road lined with a picturesque queue of life-sized monk statues, the other reached by a straight access road; the main cave is at the end of the latter.

While Khayone Cave is nominally Buddhist, arrive around 7–9am and you will coincide with the crowds of locals who come to pray to the local *nats* whose images stand alongside rows of golden Buddhas. Inside the entrance is the statue of a *zawgyi*, which visitors rub in the hope of driving away sickness; nearby is the effigy of an education-promoting *nat* riding on a *hamsa*, where students leave hopeful bunches of flowers before their exams. Like a sort of cave-bound clinic, Khayone is also the site of faith-healing sessions and regular morning seances, during which one of the three *nats* depicted sitting in a row by the cave's exit possesses a medium, and local women wait patiently for its counsel.

Win Sein Taw Ya

ဝင်းစိန်တောရ • Daily 7am–dusk • Free • Take a bus or pick-up towards Thanbyuzayat from outside the market on Mawlamyine's Lower Main Rd, and get off at Win Sein Taw Ya (hourly; 40min) – the junction marked by a golden gateway topped with two large cranes – from where it's a 2km walk to the Buddha

Even if you've visited enough reclining Buddhas to last a lifetime, do make time to visit **Win Sein Taw Ya**, which lounges across a series of hillsides 22km south of Mawlamyine en route to Mudon. The eight floors inside this 180m-long reclining Buddha figure are neither complete nor structurally sound (some of the stairwells on the three floors open to the public have chalk crosses on the walls to indicate that they're not safe for public use), but it's still fascinating to wander among the unfinished dioramas of Buddhist hells (the women being punished inexplicably wearing jeans shorts) or scenes from Jataka stories that fill the giant concrete shell.

The ninety-something-year-old monk who dreamt up this bizarre project is busy supervising construction of an even larger statue on the opposite side of the narrow valley, which will be even larger, if it's ever finished.

Thanbyuzayat

သံဖြူဇရပ်မြို့ • Buses to Thanbyuzayat (hourly 6am–4pm; 2hr) run from Lower Main Rd beside Mawlamyine's market

THANBYUZAYAT, 64km south of Mawlamyine, was the end point of World War II's infamous "Death Railway" (see box, p.158), constructed by the Japanese using forced

3

> ## THE DEATH RAILWAY
>
> When Japan seized control of Burma in 1942, the supplies and troops needed to maintain their forces had to be shipped here by sea. The battles of the Coral Sea and Midway that spring reduced Japanese naval strength, and the long voyage to Burma was judged to leave the precious fleet vulnerable. An alternative was required, and the **Burma–Siam railway** – a route previously surveyed by the British government of Burma in the 1880s – was revived. In July 1942 construction started simultaneously from in Thailand and Thanbyuzayat in Burma.
>
> The Japanese aimed to complete the 420km-long railway in just fourteen months, despite the difficulties posed by the mountainous, jungle-covered terrain. It is estimated that 60,000 Allied POWs and 180,000 *rômusha* (Asian civilian labourers, primarily from Indonesia) worked on the project, hacking through the Tenasserim Hills with primitive tools. By the time the railway was completed in October 1943, 12,399 POWs and around 90,000 *rômusha* had died from maltreatment, sickness and starvation.
>
> In the end, the railway was in operation for just over twenty months before an Allied bombing raid put it out of action. A 130km-long stretch is still in use in Thailand, but inside Myanmar the tracks have been slowly reclaimed by the rainforest. The Myanmar government periodically announces plans to rebuild the railway, but as yet, none has been able to move beyond the drawing table.

labour at appalling human cost. Some 1.5km south of Thanbyuzayat's clocktower, a **steam locomotive** (painted with the Myanmar Railways insignia) sits on a section of track to commemorate the railway.

Thanbyuzayat War Cemetery

သံဖြူဇရပ်စစ်သချုႋင်း・ Daily during daylight hours・Free

The neat **Thanbyuzayat War Cemetery**, maintained by the Commonwealth War Graves Commission, is a moving memorial to the Death Railway. A kilometre west of the clocktower, the cemetery contains the graves of four thousand Commonwealth and Dutch soldiers who died during the construction of the railway and in air raids after its completion. Bronze plaques, often with heart-breaking inscriptions from bereaved mothers and wives, mark each grave.

Kyaikkami

ကျိုက္ခမီမြို့

Some 24km northwest of Thanbyuzayat, the tidy little coastal town of **KYAIKKAMI** juts into the murky waters of the Gulf of Mottama. The British annexed the town after the First Anglo-Burmese War, renaming it **Amherst**, and it became a popular seaside resort for Mawlamyine's expatriate and Anglo-Burmese community.

Yele Paya

ရေလယ်ဘုရား・Open daily・Free

Today, most visitors come to Kyaikkami to visit **Yele Paya**, a picturesque seaside pagoda, situated 1km from town at the tip of a small peninsula. Local Buddhists believe that the pagoda, reached along a covered causeway, contains a Buddha image that floated here from Sri Lanka, as well as several hair relics. These treasures are covered with an unusual tiered shrine encircled by rows of Mandalay-style Buddhas. Note that women are not allowed to enter the main chapel, and must instead use a designated "Lady Worship Area" to the side of the main one.

ARRIVAL AND DEPARTURE   KYAIKKAMI

By bus and pick-up Buses to Kyaikkami depart from outside Mawlamyine's main market, on Lower Main Rd (hourly; 3hr). From Thanbyuzayat, pick-ups leave from the clocktower (K500).

ACCOMMODATION

Ka Day Kywe Guest Villa Bogyoke Rd ☎ 057 75019. If you get stranded in Kyaikkami, this is the only accommodation in town, offering decent fan-cooled singles (K8000) and farcically overpriced doubles with a/c in a quaint colonial-style villa. K90,000

Tanintharyi Region

တနသၤာရီတိုင်းဒေသကြီး

Off limits to foreign visitors for almost fifty years, **Tanintharyi Region**, Myanmar's southernmost territory, finally opened to travellers in 2013. Having spent decades in isolation, Tanintharyi's coastline is tantalizingly undeveloped – something it has in common with the region's infrastructure. From the beaches outside laidback **Dawei** to the bustle of **Myeik** and the idyllic **Myeik Archipelago** beyond, Myanmar's Andaman coastline will be a huge draw for beach bums and hotel developers alike. For now, while travel between Dawei and Myeik is permitted, access to the archipelago is limited only to divers on organized tours, and some travel restrictions remain on the stretch between Myeik and Kawthaung.

Dawei and around

ထားဝယ်မြို့

While it's eclipsed by its better-known neighbour, the Myeik Archipelago, the isolated coastline around **DAWEI** conceals some of the region's best **beaches**. Fishing villages spill right down to the gloriously clear water around **San Hlan**, a lone gold pagoda looks out over the Andaman Sea at **Shin Maw**, and unlikely-looking sandy tracks lead to gorgeous stretches of sand everywhere. And, save for the fishermen, there's seldom another person in sight. The only shadow on the horizon for Dawei is the question of how long its temptingly undeveloped shoreline will remain intact. The Myanmar government has grand plans to develop the area (see box, p.160), but these had ground to a halt at the time of writing. If ongoing attempts to revive the project succeed, Dawei's days as a beautiful backwater may be numbered.

Dawei (formerly Tavoy) itself is an attractive, relaxed town that is thankfully bereft of major things to see – there's little to distract you from heading to the seaside – but it makes a convenient base, with plenty of good hotels and decent transport connections. Should you lose track of time completely and overstay your visa, the **Htee Kee–Phu Nam Ron border crossing** (see box, p.162) with Thailand is a few hours' drive away.

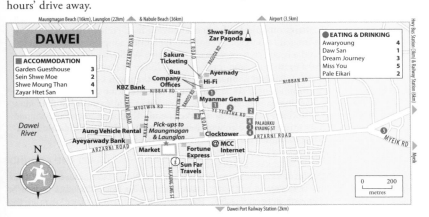

DAWEI'S MEGAPORT

Along the northern edge of Nabule Beach, 30km northwest of Dawei, a wide, sandy road leads to the isolated shoreline. Either side of it a series of signs stands in front of scrubby, deserted plots, proclaiming ambitiously "LNG Terminal – 35 Acres" and "Main Port 2km". This is the **Dawei Special Economic Zone (SEZ)**.

In 2008 the Myanmar and Thai governments signed a deal to develop this stretch of coast into a huge industrial estate and **deep-sea port**. With a highway, railway and pipeline leading directly to Bangkok, 350km to the east, the development would allow firms from across Southeast Asia to bypass the busy waters of the Straits of Malacca.

Local people, fearing that they stand to lose their land and livelihoods, and that the benefits will accrue to overseas businesses rather than local ones, have established an NGO, the Dawei Development Association, to monitor the SEZ. Before ground has even been broken for the project there have been accusations that farmers have been forced to give up their cashew and betel nut plantations without fair compensation, and complaints of land grabs have surged as developers rush to find a foothold in the area.

In 2013 the Thai developer was booted off the project after failing to attract sufficient investment, and the Japanese government was approached for help. While a Japanese firm has shown interest in resuscitating the project, the port is in limbo for the time being. It's possible to visit the project **showroom** near Nabule to get a flavour of what the future here might look like but, for now, just off the beach local men continue to fish these waters, as they have done for generations.

Maungmagan Beach and around

မောင်းမကန်

The best known of Dawei's beaches, **Maungmagan**, 16km north of town, is the only one that's even vaguely set up for visitors, with a string of restaurants lining the beach and an excellent guesthouse or two nearby (see p.162) – strange, then, that it's also one of the less attractive beaches in the region, with darker sand and more rubbish than elsewhere.

That aside, it's a good place from which to explore the surrounding area, which includes the site of the proposed **megaport** (see box above), pretty villages set among groves of cashew trees and a 12km-long beach at **Nabule** (pronounced Nabu-lay), 36km north of Dawei. Head south along the coast road from Maungmagan, and after 11km you'll reach **Myaw Yit Pagoda**, a collection of *zedi* at the end of a causeway on a rocky section of shore.

Launglon and the Dawei Peninsula

လောင်းလှ

Some 22km southwest of Dawei, the small town of **LAUNGLON** is the closest to a string of fantastic beaches that scallop the coastline – if only you can find them. Most of the access roads are little more than sandy or rocky paths leading over the hills to the coast, so be prepared to ask directions and for fairly challenging road conditions.

SAN HLAN is a palm-fringed fishing village 5km southwest of Launglon, with a harbour full of wooden boats and a beach covered with drying racks. While the village is rather rubbish-strewn, it's still a pretty spot, and there's the possibility of hiring a fishing boat to one of the nearby beaches – **Pa Nyiq** or **Shan Maw**, both to the north of San Hlan, make good targets, although you may need some Burmese to communicate what you're after.

From Launglon the peninsula stretches for a further 50km, until you reach **Shin Maw** (not to be confused with Shan Maw) at the southern end. This open horseshoe-shaped bay has a pagoda on its southeastern tip, with beautiful open views over the Andaman Sea beyond. The nearest foreigner-friendly accommodation is in Dawei.

ARRIVAL AND DEPARTURE

DAWEI AND AROUND

By plane Dawei's small airport has daily flights to Yangon, Myeik and Kawthaung (the latter stopping briefly in Myeik). The terminal is 3.5km north of the town centre (K1500 by motorbike taxi, K4000 by tuk-tuk). Tickets are available from Sun Far Travels, 298 Padauk Shwe Wa St (⊕ 059 21110, ⊛ sunfartravels.com), and Sakura Ticketing

Centre, at the junction between Pagoda Rd and Ye Rd (☎ 059 22444).

Destinations Kawthaung (daily; 1hr 45min); Myeik (daily; 45min); Yangon (daily; 1hr).

By bus Buses stop at Dawei's Highway bus station, a 15min drive east of the town (K4000 by tuk-tuk or K1500 on a motorbike taxi). Tickets are available from the bus company offices that are concentrated on Ye Rd, just north of the junction with Nibban Rd. Minibuses to the Htee Kee–Phu Nam Ron border crossing (see box, p.162) depart from Dawei daily, although the road is often impassable after heavy rain – don't count on this route during rainy season. Book a seat in advance through your accommodation.

Destinations Htee Kee (daily; 4hr); Mawlamyine (11 daily; 9hr); Myeik (7 daily; 9–10hr); Yangon (11 daily; 12hr).

By train Dawei has two railway stations: the main one, 6km east of the main market (K2000 by motorbike or K4000 by tuk-tuk), and Dawei Port, 2.5km south of town – it's best to get off at the main station (the first one you arrive at southbound), as the shunt between stations takes eons. A single train departs each day for Ye (rumoured to be the slowest train in the country), where everyone switches trains before heading on to Mawlamyine and Yangon.

Destinations Bago (daily; 22hr 30min); Mawlamyine (daily; 15hr); Yangon (daily; 24hr 30min); Ye (daily; 9hr).

By boat Dawei's jetty is a 1hr 45min bus ride away, which is included in the boat ticket price (see box below).

Destinations Kawthaung (daily; 11–12hr); Myeik (daily; 4–5hr).

GETTING AROUND

By motorbike taxi A trip to the airport or bus station will set you back K1500, while the long ride out to Maungmagan costs around K5000.

By pick-up Pick-ups to Maungmagan and Launglon (both K1500) leave from around the market on Arzarni Rd.

By tuk-tuk A short trip around town will cost K1000–1500. A tuk-tuk to Maungmagan will cost a fairly steep K15,000.

By motorbike Given the excellent potential for day-trips around Dawei, renting a motorbike is a useful option. Myanmar Gem Land (Ye Rd, just north of the junction with Ye Yeiktha Rd; ☎ 09 4100 4311) rent out motorcycles from their tiny office for K6000–8000/day, as do Aung Vehicle Rental (145 Anauk St; ☎ 09 4509 94525) for a similar price.

INFORMATION AND TOURS

Online Run by a locally based expat, the Southern Myanmar website (ⓦ southernmyanmar.com) is regularly updated with information about the region.

Tours Motorcycle taxi driver and Dawei native, Tin Naing (☎ 09 4509 94118), speaks decent English – a day out beach-hopping with him costs around K30,000.

DAWEI TO KAWTHAUNG BY BOAT

Three companies, Fortune Express, Ayernady and Hi-Fi, operate fast **boats** along the coast from **Dawei** to **Myeik** and on to **Kawthaung**. The boats seat around fifty passengers and have two classes, "upper" and ordinary, with foreigners usually only allowed to buy upper-class tickets. The long, thin boats can get cramped, but if claustrophobia sets in it's usually possible to escape to sit on the roof or foredeck to enjoy the beautiful seascape, complete with palm-fringed islands and flying fish.

Southbound boats depart Dawei around 4am each morning, arriving in Myeik around 8–9am and getting to Kawthaung mid-afternoon. Northbound boats leave Kawthaung around 3.30–4.30am, stopping at Myeik around noon and arriving in Dawei mid-afternoon. The three operators all charge similar prices: $25 for Dawei–Myeik, $45 for Myeik–Kawthaung and $65 for the whole journey between Dawei and Kawthaung. There's no food or water available on board, so do make sure to bring provisions.

The boat service often stops temporarily in rainy season (usually June–Sept), and during and after bad weather at any time of year.

MOTORBOAT OPERATORS

While boat company offices are spread out around Dawei, all three companies have offices on Chinthe Thone Kaung Street in Myeik and Strand Road in Kawthaung, near each town's jetty.

Ayernady Pagoda Rd, Dawei ☎ 059 22444; Myeik ☎ 059 41142; Kawthaung ☎ 059 51400.

Fortune Express Arzarni Rd, Dawei ☎ 059 22144;

Myeik ☎ 059 41579; Kawthaung ☎ 059 51718.

Hi-Fi Ye Rd, Dawei ☎ 059 22177; Myeik ☎ 059 41836; Kawthaung ☎ 059 51500.

> ### HTEE KEE–PHU NAM RON BORDER CROSSING
>
> Opened in August 2013, the border crossing between **Htee Kee** in Myanmar and **Phu Nam Ron** in Thailand is one of the least used crossings, despite being the closest to Bangkok, largely due to Tanintharyi's inaccessibility from the rest of Myanmar. Minibuses have a monopoly on the route between Dawei and Htee Kee (4hr; K30,000), which at the time of writing was still a dirt road and impassable during rainy season. Once you're stamped out of Myanmar at Htee Kee, it's 5km through no-man's-land to the Thai border post at Phu Nam Ron, which you can cover either on foot or by hitchhiking. From Phu Nam Ron there are buses to Kanchanaburi (2hr; 70 baht), and thence to Bangkok.

ACCOMMODATION

DAWEI

Garden Guesthouse 88 Ye Rd ☏ 059 22116. Housed in an 1842 villa, this hotel is much larger than it looks from the street. The high-ceilinged rooms range from cramped $10 singles with fans and shared bathrooms to attractive (though still a/c-free) $35 rooms. Wi-fi throughout. Breakfast not included. **$15**

Sein Shwe Moe 577 Ye Yeiktha Rd ☏ 09 874 0208. While the owners may be a little unfriendly, this small, lemon-yellow hotel is extremely clean, and though the rooms are small, they're reasonably priced – the four single rooms with fans are just K7000. Breakfast not included. **K12,000**

★ **Shwe Moung Than** 665 Pakaukku Kyaung St ☏ 059 23764, ✉ shwemaungthan22@gmail.com. This newish hotel is excellent value. The comfortable rooms are bright and decently sized, and the staff are terribly helpful. Free wi-fi in the lobby. **K15,000**

Zayar Htet San 566 Ye Yeiktha Rd ☏ 059 23902, ✉ hotelzayarhtetsan@gmail.com. Reminiscent of a Cubist painting from outside, *Zayar Htet San* stands out a mile on this quiet street. Once inside, the rooms are comfortable and nicely designed, with wood floors and tasteful decoration, and very good value overall. Free wi-fi available. **$40**

MAUNGMAGAN

★ **Coconut Guesthouse** Maungmagan village ☏ 09 4237 13681, ✉ cocoguesthouse95@gmail.com. While there are a few places to stay in Maungmagan, this is the pick of the bunch, with ten simple, fan-cooled rooms in bungalows a short walk from the beach. Run by the charming Zinmar – a Burmese Halle Berry lookalike – with a chilled-out restaurant on-site (breakfast not included), it's a good enough reason to stay in Maungmagan in itself, even if the beach itself doesn't tickle your fancy. **$25**

EATING AND DRINKING

Awaryoung Corner of Arzarni Rd and Pakaukku Kyaung St ☏ 059 21887. A popular teahouse with outdoor seating, *Awaryoung* produces a good range of snacks and excellent noodle salads. English menu. Daily 7am–10pm.

★ **Daw San** 560 Nibban Rd ☏ 09 4987 2584. A low-key Burmese restaurant, which dishes up delicious curries all afternoon. The beef curry is particularly good, but there are plenty of vegetarian options available too. A meal with side dishes will cost around K2000. Daily 10am–8pm.

Dream Journey 661 Pakaukku Kyaung St ☏ 09 500 7091. This café serves up reasonably priced doughnuts and coffee (espresso K500) – the latter particularly popular with fatigued

teachers from the school opposite. The helpful young owner, Zin Wai, speaks excellent English. Daily 7am–10pm.

★ **Miss You** Myeik Rd. Although it's out of the town centre, it's worth making the trip to *Miss You* to sample their delicious Thai–Burmese food – the seafood is particularly good. The eminently cool owner spent years working in Thailand. Daily 9am–10pm.

Pale Eikari 572 Ye Yeiktha Rd ☏ 059 21282. A kind of upmarket beer station, this garden restaurant is a popular nightspot with well-to-do locals dining on fairly average Chinese and Thai food and enthusiastically drinking draught beer. Daily 6am–10pm.

DIRECTORY

Banks KBZ Bank (Nibban Rd) and Ayeyarwady Bank (Arzarni Rd) both have ATMs; the former also offers currency exchange. Neither ATM currently accepts MasterCard.

Internet MCC Internet at 68 Arzarni Rd (daily 8am–11pm; K400/hr) has a good connection and also sells international calling cards.

Myeik
မြိတ်

Surrounded by pearl-filled tropical waters and home to floating villages of Salone sea gypsies, **MYEIK** – Tanintharyi's largest city – enjoys a rather exotic reputation.

Inevitably, however, the reality falls somewhat short. The town sprawls around the estuary of the Tanintharyi River, its Strand Road looking out over a rubbish-littered bank to the **Twin Islands** (Padaw Taung and Pathet Taung), now linked by reclaimed land and home to a large fish factory. And the Myeik Archipelago, of which the town stands at the northern end (see box, p.165), is largely off limits, as are the resident Salone.

However, Myeik is still an interesting place to explore, mainly for the opportunity to see an impressive range of exotic industries in action. Entire neighbourhoods are given over to drying fish and making *ngăpí* (fermented fish paste), and there's the chance to poke around nearby shipyards and cashew nut factories, although you'll need a guide to find most places. There's also plenty of attractive colonial architecture, and an interesting hilltop pagoda, **Theindawgyi**, from where you can watch the sunset.

Note that at the time of research all overland travel south of Myeik was off limits to foreigners.

Brief history

Like most of Tanintharyi, Myeik (formerly known as Mergui) was part of the Bagan Empire until its collapse in 1287. From then until the mid-eighteenth century, the town belonged to Siam, with a few short interludes of Burmese rule. The port flourished as result of its location, poised between the Indian Ocean and the South China Sea. Traders would travel from Myeik up the Tanintharyi River to Tanintharyi town (the town, river and region all share the same name), 80km to the southeast, and across the hills to Siam proper. After the Konbaung dynasty sacked Ayutthaya in 1787, Myeik returned to Burmese rule, until the British annexation of Tanintharyi in 1826.

3

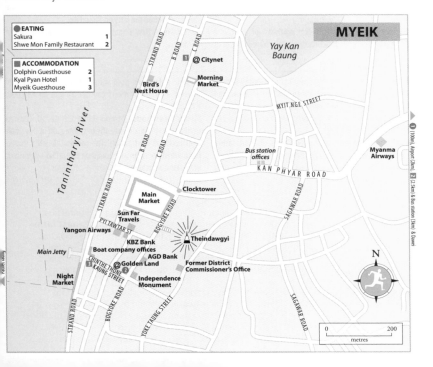

Theindawgyi and around

သိမ်တော်ကြီး • Between Bogyoke Rd and Yoke Taung St • Daily 5am–10pm • Free

At the top of a modest hill, **Theindawgyi** is Myeik's oldest and most important pagoda. It's particularly lively in the evening, when locals visit in the hope of catching a rare breeze. Of particular architectural interest is the **ordination hall**, its teak ceiling carved with hermits and parrots.

Just south of the compound, on the road that runs along the hilltop, is the British-era **District Commissioner's office**, still in government service, and opposite a small building that was formerly the town's arsenal.

Twin Islands

Daily during daylight hours • Free • Long-tail boats (K1000) head out to either island from just south of the main jetty

In theory, Myeik's **Twin Islands** are off limits to foreigners, but in practice it's possible to visit, as long as you get out here before the immigration officers clock on each morning. The northernmost island, **Padaw Taung**, is home to a standing Buddha statue and several small stupas, while **Pathet Taung**'s resident Buddha is a large reclining version. It's not possible to walk from one to the other.

ARRIVAL AND DEPARTURE   MYEIK

By plane Myeik's airport, 4km to the east of the town, has daily flights to Yangon (stopping briefly in Dawei) and Kawthaung. Tickets are available from the Sun Far Travels office on Pyi Tawtar St (☎ 059 41160, ⊕ sunfartravels.com) – the Yangon Airways office is near here too. Air KBZ, Air Mandalay, Myanma Airways and Yangon Airways operate daily flights to Yangon, Dawei and Kawthaung.
Destinations Dawei (4 daily; 45min); Kawthaung (4 daily; 45min); Yangon (4 daily; 2hr).
By bus The bus station is 4km northeast of the centre (K1000 by motorbike); tickets can be purchased here or at

offices near the fire station on Kan Phyar St. On the drive to Dawei, buses stop 26km north of town to take a vehicle ferry across a small river between the villages of Lutlut and Tamok, continuing north from there.
Destinations Dawei (7 daily; 9–10hr); Mawlamyine (11 daily; 16hr); Yangon (11 daily; 22hr).
By boat The boat companies' offices, for trips north to Dawei and south to Kawthaung (see box, p.161), are clustered around the jetty on Strand Rd.
Destinations Dawei (daily; 4–5hr); Kawthaung (daily; 7–8hr).

ACCOMMODATION

Dolphin Guesthouse 139 Kan Phyar Rd ☎ 059 41523. This French-run hotel is in rather an awkward location, well out of town near the bus station. The rooms may be rather bland, but they're decent and very clean. Singles from $25 and wi-fi is included. **$40**
Kyal Pyan Hotel 58 C Rd ☎ 059 41427. A rather unprepossessing option, Kyal Pyan is the only vaguely budget option in town, with plenty of grubby twins with

en-suite bathrooms (cold water only) in a fairly central location – single travellers can get a room for K15,000. **K25,000**
Myeik Guesthouse Strand Rd ☎ 059 42758. Located right next to the main jetty, the best thing about this small guesthouse is its location. The rooms (all with shared bathrooms) are clean and adequate but rather overpriced. Breakfast not included. **$25**

THE BIRDS

At dusk each day, clouds of swiftlets stream into an anonymous house on Strand Road. The suburban-looking home, its windows boarded over, is home to a **bird's-nest farm** – one of Myeik's weirdest industries. The story goes that a flock of swifts moved into the roof of the house. The entrepreneurial owner, realizing the value of his new tenants, moved out and turned his house into a man-made "cave", where the swifts could build their valuable nests, and he could sell them to Chinese gourmands keen to enjoy a bowl of bird's-nest soup.

Landlords hoping to repeat his success have in some places built structures without windows to replicate the darkness of the birds' natural homes, and play recordings of swifts' calls each day around dusk, which you'll hear throughout Myeik and Kawthaung, in the hope of attracting the birds.

THE MYEIK ARCHIPELAGO

The islands of the Myeik Archipelago are the stuff of legend. Between the hundreds of gorgeous, uninhabited islands fringed with white-sand beaches, hidden military bases and the **Andaman Club**'s island casino, the archipelago sounds more like the set of a James Bond movie than a holiday destination.

The islands were opened to dive boats in 1996. Since then, access has been limited to those on **live-aboard boat tours** and guests of the crony-owned luxury *Andaman Club* and the low-key *Myanmar Andaman Resort* – the only two **hotels** on the islands (see below). Rumours of future hotel developments are rife, and it's surely only a matter of time before the situation here begins to change dramatically. For now, though, you'll need to book well in advance through a recognized operator to enjoy a slice of this particular paradise.

Despite the marketing spiel, the islands are not quite as untouched as they might first appear. Widespread dynamite fishing has killed many of the reefs, and the **Salone sea gypsies** are increasingly being resettled on land in scruffy villages. Whether they will be subjected to "human zoo"-style ethnic tourism, a fate that has befallen their Moken cousins in Thailand, remains to be seen.

TOURS AND ACTIVITIES

A One Diving ☎ 00 66 81 891 5510, �🌐 a-one-diving .com. Ranong-based operator offering live-aboard dive tours and also runs the *Andaman Resort*'s dive centre. Dive trips to the archipelago start from $850/ person for a five-day trip, including all expenses except park and visa fees.

Asia Whale ☎ 012 26069, �🌐 asiawhale.com. Based in Yangon, Asia Whale organizes diving, sailing and snorkelling trips, sharing the same fleet and diving operation as A One Diving. Four-day, twelve-dive trips around the archipelago start at $980, not including equipment rental or park and visa fees.

Moby Dick Adventures ☎ 012 02064, �🌐 island safarimergui.com. With offices in Phuket, Yangon and Kawthaung, Moby Dick specializes in "island safaris" where the focus is on kayaking and snorkelling rather than diving. A five-day trip will set you back $1110/ person, while a day-trip costs $150.

HOTELS

Andaman Club Thahtay Kyun Island ☎ 00 66 2 287 3031, �🌐 andamanclub.com. A 15min motorboat ride from Kawthaung, this island resort has an 18-hole golf course, casino and in-house zoo. The staff are keen and the rooms perfectly comfortable, with great views from the seafront ones, though the hotel is frequently empty and doesn't quite realize its potential for Bond-style glamour. No Myanmar visa necessary. $110

Myanmar Andaman Resort Macleod Island ☎ 059 51046, �🌐 myanmarandamanresort.com. Designed along eco-lodge lines, this attractive small hotel and its established dive centre were closed for major renovations at the time of writing, and were expected to open again in October 2015. Closed May–Oct.

EATING AND DRINKING

Each evening from 5pm to 10pm, a **night market** sets up on Strand Road south of the boat jetty. With views out to the Twin Islands, it's an attractive place to eat, with the food focused on skewers, fried rice and salads – a meal will cost around K1800. There's also a small **morning market** (daily 6–11am) off C Rd, just south of the *Kyal Pyan* hotel. Dodge your way past the fish-sellers at the entrance and you'll find a range of delicious snacks on sale – try the *kawb moun*, a coconut-heavy batter cooked in an iron bowl until the edges are crispy and the centre still moist.

Sakura U Myat Lay St, 1km east of the clocktower ☎ 09 876 0488. *Sakura* specializes in fish and seafood dishes, but there are also hamburgers, sandwiches and omelettes on the menu – expect to pay K2000–4000 for a meal. Dining room with a/c and outdoor seating available. The friendly Burmese owner spent years in Singapore. Lunch and dinner.

Shwe Mon Family Restaurant Chinthe Thone Kaung St. A traditional Burmese curry buffet is on offer all day, every day, but you'll need to get there early to have much of a choice. Their pennywort salad is excellent, and a curry and rice combo will cost around K2000. Lunch and dinner.

DIRECTORY

Banks There's a branch of AGD Bank on Bogyoke Rd, near the Independence Monument, with ATM and foreign exchange. KBZ Bank on Pyi Tawtar St also has an ATM. Neither ATM accepts MasterCard.

Internet Citynet, opposite the *Kyal Pyan* hotel, has slow internet and wi-fi for K400/hr, as does Golden Land (K500/hr) on Chinthe Thoun Kaung St.

Tours Eccentric septuagenarian, U Chit Ko Ko

(☎ 09 4222 26088) – who also goes by the English name of James Lable – can arrange motorbike tours of Myeik and the surrounding area, charging K20,000 with transport not included.

Kawthaung

ကော့သောင်းမြို့

By the time you reach **KAWTHAUNG**, in the extreme south, you are likely to be focused either on getting to Thailand or starting the long journey north to Yangon. The small town isn't especially exciting, but there are a few things to see if you find yourself stuck here between connections.

While Kawthaung's outskirts sprawl along the coastline, the centre of town is compact and easy to navigate on foot. As you arrive at the jetty you'll see the **clocktower**, 100m inland – Airport Road curves uphill southwest of here, and the main market sits a block to the north. It's possible to stroll around the southernmost point of mainland Myanmar at **Bayinnaung Point** (originally named Victoria Point by the British, and provocatively renamed after the Burmese king that sacked Ayutthaya in 1564) and to the north of town is the **555 Viewpoint**, which offers great views of the islands and away across the border to Ranong.

Further afield, **Maliwan Waterfall** lies 40km overland to the northeast, and you can sunbathe at **Palutonetone Beach** on Thane Island 7km northwest, which is reached across a bridge from the mainland.

ARRIVAL AND DEPARTURE   KAWTHAUNG

By plane Kawthaung's airport is 11km north of town (K3000 by motorbike taxi, K7000 in a tuk-tuk). Air KBZ, Air Mandalay and Yangon Airways all operate daily flights to Yangon that stop briefly in Myeik and Dawei. Friendly ticket booker U Zaw Min Oo (☎ 09 4100 5428), who works out of a booth 50m south of the clocktower, has the best prices.
Destinations Dawei (3 daily; 1hr 45min); Myeik (3 daily;

45min); Yangon (3 daily; 3hr).
By boat Kawthaung's jetty, for motorboats to Myeik and Dawei (see box, p.161), and immigration office are towards the southern end of Kawthaung's Strand Rd. Boats to Ranong in Thailand depart from a temporary-looking jetty just north of where the fast boats arrive.
Destinations Dawei (daily; 11–12hr); Myeik (daily; 7–8hr).

GETTING AROUND

By motorbike taxi and tuk-tuk A motorbike taxi around town will cost K1000, while the return trips out to Palutonetone Beach or 555 Viewpoint will cost K3000–3500 with waiting time. The longer journey out to Maliwan

Waterfall costs K8000–10,000, depending on your haggling skills. Tuk-tuks will cost at least double the motorbike taxi fare. Drivers gather on the street between the jetty and clocktower, and outside *J-Bon Coffee and Cold* on Airport Rd.

ACCOMMODATION

Honey Bear Hotel Strand Rd ☎ 059 51352. Right on Strand Rd, the noisy front rooms here have partially obscured sea views (there's an island in the way). It's pleasant enough inside, and the most conveniently located of Kawthaung's hotels, but the pricey en-suite rooms don't

have hot water. $45
Kawthaung Bosonpat St ☎ 059 51474, ⓦ mount pleasanthotelmyanmar.com. Located a 10min walk west of the jetty, just off the airport road. The superior rooms ($45) have nice sea views, there's a range of services on

---

KAWTHAUNG–RANONG BORDER CROSSING

The **Kawthaung–Ranong border crossing** straddles the Kra Buri or Pakchan River. Boats (100–150 baht one-way) cruise from one side to the other while the crossing is open (daily 6am–5.30pm, Myanmar time). There's one short stop close to Kawthaung for Myanmar passport control, and another closer to Ranong for citizens of ASEAN member states, before you reach Thai passport control. Once outside the Thai border post, there are ATMs and it's a 20 baht pick-up ride to Ranong bus station.

offer and the staff are pleasant, but overall the rooms are average and the hefty foreigner mark-up makes them feel like rather poor value. Free wi-fi. $35

★**Penguin** 339 Sabel St ☎ 059 51145, ✉ penguin hotelkt@gmail.com. This extravagantly tiled guesthouse is tucked away in a backstreet, a sweaty 10min walk uphill from the jetty. Rooms are clean and neat, and there's a small restaurant downstairs. There's free wi-fi, and the hotel accepts US dollars, baht and kyat, with baht prices offering best value for money. $30

EATING AND DRINKING

J-Bon Coffee and Cold Airport Rd, 200m uphill, southwest of the clocktower. This excellent teahouse, near the northern entrance to Bayinnaung Point and set in a leafy yard, offers a better-than-usual selection of cold drinks and teahouse snacks – their noodle salad is delicious – as well as a fine cup of Burmese coffee and lime. Daily 6am–6pm.

Love Coffee Shop Opposite the jetty. The first place you'll see as you get off at the jetty, this little coffee shop has been serving good iced coffee and fried rice to visa-runners for years. English menu. Daily 9am–9pm.

★**Penguin** Near the clocktower. Down an anonymous side street (one block away from the clocktower towards the jetty, on the south side of the road), *Penguin* is the busiest restaurant on Kawthaung's dining scene – it's best to get here early before they run out of their delicious curries and side dishes. Vegetarian options available. Daily 9am–9pm.

DIRECTORY

Banks Despite the bank buildings that dot the town centre, the KBZ Bank on Airport Rd near the *Kawthaung* hotel is the only one that actually offers banking services; there's no ATM, but they'll change US dollars and euros for you. To change baht you'll need to chance it at one of the counters along Strand Rd.

Internet Myanmar Info Tech, south of the jetty on Strand Rd, has a decent connection, which is just as well, because it's rather pricey at K900/hr.

3

Bagan and central Myanmar

BAGAN

Bagan and central Myanmar

Stretching between the Shan hills to the east and the Ayeyarwady River to the west, the plain of central Myanmar (which includes parts of Bago, Mandalay and Magwe divisions) comprises a flat and relatively featureless expanse of countryside whose modern-day somnolence belies its pivotal role in the history of the nation. The heartland of Bamar identity, the region is home to three of the country's former capitals – Pyay, Bagan and Taungoo – each of which successively controlled empires stretching across large parts of Myanmar, and sometimes beyond. Attempts to re-create the region's former glory can also be found at Myanmar's surreal new capital, Naypyitaw, strategically situated midway between Yangon and Mandalay.

Highlight of the region is undoubtedly **Bagan**, heartland of the first great pan-Burmese empire, whose legendary temples blanket the surrounding plains in an astonishing profusion of Buddhist architecture. Bagan is also the jumping-off point for visits to the quirky *nat* shrines at **Mount Popa**, while slightly further afield the workaday town of **Monywa** provides a convenient base for exploring the eye-crackingly huge Buddhas of **Maha Bodhi Tataung** and the endearingly kitsch pagoda of **Thanboddhay**.

For the majority of visitors, shuttling post-haste between Yangon, Mandalay and Bagan, the remainder of the region is a place to be traversed as painlessly as possible, though there are several other interesting destinations en route that offer a quintessential taste of provincial Burmese life. Heading north from the capital along the Yangon–Mandalay Expressway, the moated town and former capital of **Taungoo** is worth a stop for its clutch of temples, fine lake and hints of former glory, while further north personable **Meiktila** has plenty of small-town charm, a beautiful lakeside setting and a further sprinkling of colourful shrines. Midway between the two, the nation's bizarre new capital, **Naypyitaw**, is essential viewing for students of Myanmar at its most brazenly outlandish. Alternatively, taking the slow road north from Yangon along National Highway 2, it's worth overnighting at lively **Pyay**, home to another major temple complex and the enigmatic remains of the ancient Pyu capital of **Thayekhittaya** (Sri Ksetra).

Yangon to Mandalay

The modern **expressway** between Yangon and Mandalay offers a swift and relatively painless route to both Mandalay and Bagan, although the personable towns of **Taungoo** and **Meiktila** offer an enjoyable slice of traditional Burmese small-town life if you fancy breaking the journey. Halfway between Yangon and Mandalay, the nation's new capital of **Naypyitaw** is required viewing if you're interested in the consummate madness of

TAUNG KALAT (MOUNT POPA)

Highlights

❶ **Shwezigon Pagoda, Bagan** One of the oldest, grandest and more revered of all Bagan's temples, still busy with worshippers after almost a thousand years. **See p.192**

❷ **Ananda Paya, Bagan** A massive mountain of stone, embellished with terraces, stairways and stupas, and topped with a soaring spire. **See p.196**

❸ **Sunset over Bagan** Climb to the top of one of Bagan's ancient monuments and watch the sun set over the innumerable temples dotting the plains below. **See p.201**

❹ **Sulamani Paya, Bagan** A fiery red-brick jewel of a temple – perhaps the most perfect of all Bagan's myriad monuments. **See p.202**

❺ **Taung Kalat (Mount Popa)** A colourful cluster of shrines and temples, perched dramatically on top of an ancient volcanic outcrop and celebrating the weird and wonderful world of the Burmese *nat* spirits. **See p.216**

❻ **Thanboddhay Pagoda** Modern Myanmar temple architecture at its kitsch best, with golden stupas, zany statues and clashing colours galore. **See p.220**

❼ **Maha Bodhi Tataung** This bizarre complex includes the world's second-biggest Buddha statue, towering in surreal splendour above quiet rural backlands near the town of Monywa. **See p.221**

HIGHLIGHTS ARE MARKED ON THE MAP ON P.172

TRAVEL RESTRICTIONS

All the areas covered in this chapter are fully **open to tourists** without prior permission, with the exception of a few high-security areas around Naypyitaw and the elephant camp outside Taungoo. Permits are also required for boat trips north of Kalewa on the **Chindwin River** (see box, p.222), and for any trips into **Chin State** (see box, p.218).

Myanmar's ruling military junta and the surreal excesses of modern urban planning gone wrong, although it doesn't have a lot to recommend it otherwise.

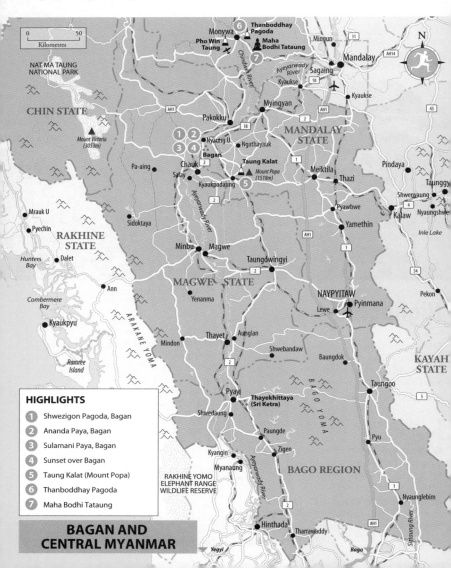

HIGHLIGHTS

1. Shwezigon Pagoda, Bagan
2. Ananda Paya, Bagan
3. Sulamani Paya, Bagan
4. Sunset over Bagan
5. Taung Kalat (Mount Popa)
6. Thanboddhay Pagoda
7. Maha Bodhi Tataung

BAGAN AND CENTRAL MYANMAR

Taungoo

တောင်ငူမြို့

Just off the old Yangon–Mandalay road (National Highway 1), and only 10km east of the newer (and faster) Yangon–Mandalay Expressway, the bustling little provincial city of **TAUNGOO** (aka Toungoo) has a cluster of low-key sights as well as one of the region's most appealing guesthouses. Taungoo's engagingly small-town atmosphere belies its considerable significance in the history of Myanmar as the centre of the **Taungoo dynasty** (see p.334), for a time one of the largest empires in the history of Southeast Asia. Little remains of the city's glory days, however, the royal palace having been obliterated by Japanese bombers during World War II.

The heart of Taungoo is the original **moated city** – parts of the original moat survive, along with a few fragments of the original city walls. Imposing new eastern and western **gates** were built in 2010 to celebrate the city's five-hundredth birthday, with a large statue of Taungoo's founder, King Mingyinyo, erected just outside the east gate for good measure. In the southwestern corner of the walled city, the fine **Kandawgyi Lake** is a pleasant spot for a bike ride or stroll, with an attractive string of cafés along its eastern side and the fanciful temple-style roofs of the *Royal Kaytumadi* hotel rising across the water.

Shwesandaw Pagoda

ရွှေဆံတော်ဘုရား• Daily 6am–9pm • Free

The most impressive of Taungoo's various temples, the **Shwesandaw Pagoda** sits more or less in the centre of the old walled city, its large gilded stupa rising high above the surrounding streets. The stupa was built in 1597 on a sight of a much older structure which is said to have contained hair relics of the Buddha (the temple's name means "Golden Sacred Hair Relic").

The most interesting approach is from the east, via a long covered walkway, initially lined with shops selling assorted religious items before passing through a pretty jumble of stupas and monastic quarters. From here, a short flight of steps leads up to a stupa, which is very similar in outline to the Shwedagon in Yangon, with eighty-odd miniature stupas stacked up around its lower two terraces. Various statues in glass cabinets stand around the terrace, showing scenes from the life of the Buddha and processions of kings and monks, and murals depict the gory punishments awaiting sinners in hell. A striking Mandalay-style Buddha sits in the shrine on the west side of the stupa, gifted to the temple in 1912 by a retired civil servant who donated his own body weight in silver and bronze. On the opposite (eastern) side of the stupa, a large reclining Buddha is under construction.

Myasigon Pagoda

မြစည်းခဲ့ဘုရား• Daily 7am–8pm • Free • The museum is usually locked, although you can ask someone to unlock it for you (around K1000)

Close to the southern edge of the walled city centre, the glitzy **Myasigon** (or Mizagon) **Pagoda** offers a complete contrast to the traditional Shwesandaw. The temple's small stupa seems almost an afterthought to the adjacent shrine, with its huge gilded Buddha ensconced in a shiny-bright pavilion covered in dazzling glass mosaics. Outside, the terrace surrounding the stupa is home to an unusually kitsch model of Kyaiktiyo (the Golden Rock; see p.140), complete with miniature steps and shrines rising out of sculpted forest, plus a couple of tiny, doe-eyed elephants.

In the northwest corner of the terrace a cream-coloured building houses a small **museum** containing various Buddhas and other religious artefacts, a statue of the three-headed elephant Erawan (the mount of Indra), plus a few old colonial-era notes and coins and a very dusty old soda bottle. Though the museum's usually kept locked, you can get a decent look through the window slats if you don't fancy finding someone with a key.

4

4

Kaunghmudaw Pagoda

ကောင်းမှုတော်ဘုရား • 1.5km west of town (follow the road out of the west gate)

Set in beautiful countryside west of Taungoo centre, the pretty rural **Kaunghmudaw Pagoda** makes a good target for a leisurely out-of-town bike ride. Flamboyantly roofed stairways lead from the north and east up to the terrace and the small but elaborately sculpted gold stupa, with leering chinthe standing guard at each corner, surrounded by the usual impressive bo tree, bell, prayer pole and inevitable model of the Kyaiktiyo.

ARRIVAL AND DEPARTURE
TAUNGOO

By bus Buses stop at various bus company offices along National Highway 1. A motorbike taxi to *Myanmar Beauty Guesthouse* or *Mother's House Hotel* costs K1500.
Destinations Bago (2 daily; 4hr); Hpa-An (2 daily; 7hr); Kalaw (1 nightly; 10hr); Mandalay (2 daily; 7hr); Meiktila (4 daily; 5hr); Naypyitaw (5 daily; 2hr 30min); Pyin Oo Lwin

(daily; 10hr); Thazi (3 daily; 5hr); Yangon (4 daily; 5hr).
By train The railway station is on the south side of the centre, just inside the city walls.
Destinations Bago (3 daily; 4hr 30min); Mandalay (3 daily; 8–9hr); Naypyitaw (3 daily; 2hr 30min); Thazi (3 daily; 6hr); Yangon (3 daily; 7hr).

GETTING AROUND

By bicycle Central Taungoo is compact enough to be covered on foot, although renting a bicycle from *Myanmar Beauty* is a nice way to explore, especially if you want to go

out to Kaunghmudaw temple.
By motorbike taxi A motorbike taxi from one of the out-of-town guesthouses to the centre costs around K1500.

ACCOMMODATION

Amazing Kaytu Off Yangon–Mandalay Rd ☎ 054 23977, ⓦ amazing-hotel.com. Neat, modern little hotel set slightly off from the main road. Standard rooms upstairs (with TV, a/c, hot water and fridge) are pokey and old-fashioned; superior rooms downstairs cost just $6 extra and are much more attractively decorated – albeit also on the small side,

and with an overwhelming smell of mothballs. **$43**
Mother's House Hotel 501 Yangon–Mandalay Rd, 3km south of town ☎ 054 24240, ✉ mhh@baganmail.net .mm. A passable fallback if the nearby *Myanmar Beauty* is full, although slightly too close to the main road for complete comfort. Cheaper rooms (with hot water, a/c, TV

TRUNKS AND TIMBER

Interesting, albeit expensive, day-trips to a working **elephant camp**, three hours away in the foothills of the Bago Yoma mountains, can be arranged (ideally with a few days' notice) through the *Myanmar Beauty Guesthouse* or *Mother's House Hotel* (see below). The camp is home to some sixty elephants, usually divided into working groups of six to eight animals. Elephants are used to help transport logged timber out of the mountainous jungle, and visits generally involve watching one of the various groups at work, after which you might be given the chance of taking a ride on one of the elephants or feeding them some bananas.

Visits by car or pick-up leave at 5.30am and cost around $125 per person in a group of two (with per-person prices falling for larger groups). You may be able to arrange a slightly cheaper ($90–100pp) trip through *Mother's House* by taking a motorbike instead – though it's a long slog on the back of a bike (and not much more comfortable by pick-up). Prices include permit, lunch and guide.

and fridge) are pleasant enough, although it's worth paying an extra $5 for one of the larger and more attractive wood-panelled bungalows around the back. There's also a small restaurant attached, though it's right on the road. $30

★ **Myanmar Beauty Guesthouse II, III & IV** 3km south of town, just off the east side of the Yangon–Mandalay Rd ☎054 25073 or 25074. Overlooking fields south of town, this lovely guesthouse justifies a stopover in Taungoo all by itself. Rooms are spread over three separate wooden buildings. Those in building *II* (en-suite, cold water only) are simplest and cheapest but perfectly adequate; those in *III* ($30; with hot water) are more attractively furnished; while those in *IV* ($50) have a/c and balconies with fine countryside views (but no TVs to spoil the peace). All rates include a spectacular breakfast featuring a huge spread of local fruits, samosas and all sorts of wonderful sticky-rice concoctions. They also have creaky old bikes for rent (K2000/day). $20

Royal Kaytumadi Hotel Taw Win Kaytumadi Rd ☎054 24761, ⊛kmahotels.com. Taungoo's fanciest hotel (although owned by a company with strong government links) occupies a string of quaint pagoda-style bungalows dotted around extensive gardens in a beautiful location right next to the lake. Rooms (try to get one facing the water) are nicely decorated with wooden floors and chintzy furniture, and facilities include a big pool, plus gym and spa. $134

EATING

Yangon Food Villa Bo Hmu Po Kun Rd ☎054 23707. With its low-slung red and orange sofas and (sort of) booths, this place bears an unlikely but compelling resemblance to a Burmese diner. Food comprises a biggish selection of Asian (mainly Thai- and Chinese-style) dishes, and they can also produce sandwiches, burgers and a decent plate of fish and chips. Mains mostly K2000–2500. Daily 8.30am–9.30pm.

DIRECTORY

Amusement park The Kyet Minn Nyi Naung Amusement Park (daily 2–10pm), next to the *Royal Kaytumadi Hotel* on the west side of the lake, has bumper cars, a playground, a couple of tennis courts and pedalos.

Banks There are ATMs at the AGD Bank and Ayeyarwady Bank on the main Yangon–Mandalay road just east of town, and at the AGD Bank and CB Bank close to one another on the same road just south of the market.

Internet There are internet cafés all over town – try the well-set-up Arena or T.com, conveniently situated on Bo Hmu Po Kun Rd just inside the east gate (daily 9am–10pm; both K300/hr).

Swimming Non-guests can use the lovely pool at the *Royal Kaytumadi Hotel* for a modest K3000. There's also a small pool at the *Evergreen* café on the east side of the lake (K500/2hr), although its pea-green waters look suspiciously murky.

Naypyitaw

နေပြည်တော်

Quite possibly the world's weirdest capital, the newly created city of **NAYPYITAW** (aka Nay Pyi Taw, Nay Pyi Daw or Naypyidaw – meaning "Abode of the Kings") was unveiled in 2005 as the brainchild of Myanmar's military government (see box, p.177) and occupies a strategic location roughly midway between Yangon and Mandalay. The official reason given for the sudden relocation was a lack of space in Yangon, although rumours suggest that the decision to move the capital was taken by General Than Shwe after his personal astrologer had warned him of the possibility of an invasion from the sea. (Quite who would wish to invade Myanmar, by sea or by any other route, remains unclear.) The location of the new capital – complete with a substantial military presence – close to the historically turbulent Shan, Kayah and Kayin states may also have been a factor in the decision.

For the visitor, Naypyitaw is interesting mainly as a study in contemporary urban planning at its most OTT – and for the gaping disconnect between the city and the rest of Myanmar. Spreading over a vast area of still largely empty countryside, the new capital is simultaneously outlandish, brazen and faintly lunatic – a vast wilderness of eight-lane highways (largely deserted, except when the motorcade of a passing general or visiting dignitary shatters the silence), supersized roundabouts, grandiloquent government buildings and overblown hotels more reminiscent of the modern cities of the Arabian Gulf than anything remotely Burmese. City life, such as it is, is confined to a few stringently demarcated market zones plus a couple of modern malls, while specific sights, barring the vast **Uppatasanti Pagoda**, are few.

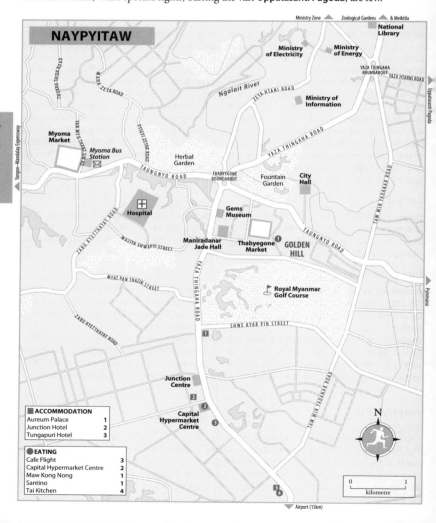

MINISTRIES IN MOTION

Myanmar's new **capital** was constructed amid cloak-and-dagger secrecy between 2002 and 2005 at an estimated cost of around $4 billion on a greenfield site between the old Yangon–Mandalay highway and the small towns of Pyinmana and Lewe. Following its unveiling, government ministries were moved en masse from Yangon, with staff being given 48 hours to relocate (though their families were banned from following). Meanwhile, the foreign diplomatic community remains stubbornly entrenched in Yangon – so far the only embassy to have moved into the city's designated International Zone is that of Bangladesh.

The city's long-suffering bureaucrats, summarily transferred from Yangon, now occupy Lego-like swathes of dormitory suburbs, their roofs colour-coded to signify the status of the officials within, while the ruling elite have ensconced themselves in the city's fiercely guarded **military zone** (strictly off limits to casual visitors), complete, it's alleged, with many kilometres of tunnels and bunkers, plus a vast military parade ground overseen by statues of kings Anawrahta, Bayinnaung and Alaungpaya – Myanmar's three greatest empire-builders, and greatly beloved of the army bigwigs – often featuring in militaristic propaganda, though inaccessible to the average citizen.

Surprisingly, Naypyitaw's population is already nudging the million mark, making it Myanmar's third-largest city, and one of the world's fastest-growing urban centres, although you'd hardly guess this, given the largely deserted and decidedly moribund atmosphere, and the entire place still feels very much like a work in – perhaps permanent – progress.

Uppatasanti Pagoda

ဥပ္ပါတသန္တိစေတီတော် • Yaza Htarni Rd, around 9km from Thabyegone Roundabout • Daily 6am–9pm • The $5 foreigner's entrance fee which formerly applied was not being asked for at time of writing • A taxi/motorbike taxi from the Yaza Thingaha Rd hotels will cost around K15,000/K8000 return, including an hour's waiting time

Naypyitaw's major monument, the **Uppatasanti Pagoda** (although local pronunciation makes it sound more like "Uppatadaani") looms above the city's largely flat and featureless hinterlands, visible for many kilometres in every direction. Completed in 2009, the pagoda was offered as a merit-making act by the man responsible for the city, General Than Shwe, and his wife (displaying a distinct parallel with Burmese kings). The name, roughly translating as "protection against calamity", derives from a sixteenth-century Buddhist sutra designed to be recited at times of crisis, and particularly when confronted with the threat of foreign invasion – a telling allusion to Naypyitaw's founding *raison d'être* and the prevailing paranoid fear of invasion.

A near-copy of the Shwedagon in Yangon (although it comes in at a symbolic 30cm shorter), the Uppasanthi is impressively huge from a distance, although less remarkable close up, when the shoddiness of the workmanship, including lots of cheap gold paint with red and white smears (only the topmost section of spire is properly gilded), becomes apparent. Three grand staircases lead up to the **terrace** (although only the eastern stairs are usually open, and most visitors take the lift). The terrace itself is huge, windswept and depressingly bare, with only a couple of token Buddha statues and a single huge prayer pole to relieve the emptiness, although the sweeping views partly compensate.

The pagoda's chief peculiarity is that it's hollow. A huge square pillar stands in the centre of the green-and-gold **interior**, as if carrying the weight of the stupa on its shoulders. Fine carvings showing scenes from Buddhist mythology, history and the life of the Buddha are arrayed around the sides.

In a small pen near the bottom of the eastern stairs you'll find the pagoda's celebrated menagerie of five **white elephants** (see p.78), which can often be seen here munching on bamboo (although they're sometimes taken off for exercise elsewhere), plus a couple of even smaller and cuter ordinary elephants, providing an interesting colour contrast. Locals regard these rare creatures as being extremely auspicious. Sceptical foreigners may feel that the animals provide an apt symbol of Naypyitaw itself – given that it's essentially nothing but an enormous white elephant of a slightly different kind.

Fountain Garden

Taungnyo Rd • Daily 9am–8pm • K500

Just east of Thabyegone Roundabout, and providing a pleasant change of scene from the concrete wasteland outside, is the pretty ornamental **Fountain Garden**, set either side of the small Ngalait River; a pair of small bridges traverse the river, including an enjoyably wobbly, jungle-style construction. Lush clumps of bougainvillea, palms and topiary trees abound, along with assorted pavilions, a playground with water slide, and a musical clock, none of whose four faces can agree on the correct time. The signature fountains, sadly, are fired up only for special occasions.

Gems Museum

Yaza Thingaha Rd, 400m south of Thabyegone Roundabout • Tues–Sun 9.30am–4pm • K5000

Next to the distinctive, flying-saucer-shaped Maniradanar Jade Hall exhibition centre, the modest, one-room **Gems Museum** serves up a decent overview of Myanmar's gem production. On show are assorted rubies, sapphire, lots of jade and the country's largest pearl, although few visitors find it worth the inflated admission price.

Zoological Gardens and Safari Park

တိရစ္ဆာန်ဥယျာဉ်နှင့် ဆာဖာရီဥယျာဉ် • Zeyar Thiri, a 45min drive northeast of the centre • **Zoological Gardens** Tues–Sun 8.30am–8pm • $10 **Safari Park** Tues–Sun 8.30am–4.30pm • $20 • A taxi to the zoo will cost around $25–30 return

Naypyitaw's modern **Zoological Gardens and Safari Park** make for a surprisingly enjoyable half-day trip, though since it's more or less in the middle of nowhere few people make the effort. The twin attractions were opened in 2011, with animals housed in Yangon's crumbling old zoo being located to the new facility. A Burmese comedian, hearing that Yangon's zoological attractions were following in the steps of the city's government officials, joked that "All the animals are going to Naypyitaw" – and promptly found himself jailed for his pains.

Occupying a sixty-acre complex, the **Zoological Gardens** are home to over six hundred animals, with a good selection of international wildlife including white tigers, leopards, elephants and kangaroos. The **Safari Park** next door offers tours in electric buggies and the chance to spot further wildlife in three separate zones showcasing the fauna of Asia, Africa and Australia.

ARRIVAL AND DEPARTURE   NAYPYITAW

By plane Naypyitaw's shiny new airport (⊙nptia.com) is 16km southeast of the centre. A taxi from here into town (there are no buses) will cost around K10,000.
Destinations Heho (1 daily; 40min); Mandalay (3 daily; 50min); Yangon (5 daily; 1hr).
By bus The main Myoma Bus Station is on Yan Myo Thant Sin Rd, around 6km northwest of the hotel zone. Approaching from the south you may be able to hop off on Yaza Thingaha Rd, where most of the city's hotels are located.
Destinations Hpa-An (2 daily; 9hr); Hsipaw (3 daily; 12hr);

Kalaw (1 daily; 5hr); Lashio (daily; 13hr); Mandalay (7 daily; 4hr); Mawlamyine (2 daily; 11–12hr); Meiktila (7 daily; 3hr); Pyin Oo Lwin (2 daily; 8hr); Taungoo (5 daily; 2hr 30min); Yangon (10 daily; 6hr).
By train The huge railway station is in a massively inconvenient location 14km north of Uppatasanti Pagoda, a $15 taxi journey from town.
Destinations Bago (5 daily; 7–8hr); Mandalay (2 daily; 6–7hr); Taungoo (3 daily; 2hr 30min); Thazi (3 daily; 3hr); Yangon (3 daily; 9–10hr).

GETTING AROUND

By motorbike taxi Naypyitaw is way too big to even think about walking around. Motorbike taxis hang out around many of the hotels, Capital Hypermarket Centre, Junction Centre and Myoma Market – count on around

K2000 for the trip from Myoma Market to the Yaza Thingaha hotels or around K10,000 for a half-day tour of the city.
By taxi There are usually taxis for hire outside the Capital Hypermarket Centre, or book one through your hotel.

ACCOMMODATION

Accommodation is concentrated in the string of huge new hotels lining **Yaza Thingaha Road**, many of them still fresh out of their wrappings, although the lack of visitors can make some places feel decidedly moribund – the entire strip has all the atmosphere of a motorway service station. There are no real budget places to stay, although the massive glut of accommodation at least means that most places are excellent value for money, with rooms here going for around half the price or less of equivalent-standard establishments in Yangon.

Aureum Palace Yaza Thingaha Rd ☎ 067 420746, ⓦ aureumpalacehotel.com. Idyllic resort, with appealing contemporary Asian styling and super-attentive service. Accommodation is scattered around extensive grounds overlooking a small lake; rooms are bright and spacious – more expensive ones come with all mod cons and fancy furnishings. Facilities include a big (although shallow) pool, gym and spa. Excellent value. $67

Junction Hotel Yaza Thingaha Rd ☎ 067 422011, ⓦ www.junctionhotelnpt.com. A small place looking a bit like a rather cosy little motel, with bungalows arranged around the parking spaces at the front. Rooms are very comfortably furnished and well equipped (although with rather dim lighting). One of the better-value places, and handy for mall facilities, since it's just between Capital Hypermarket and Junction Centre. $55

Tungapuri Hotel 9/10 Yaza Thingaha Rd ☎ 067 422020, ⓦ tungapurihotel.com. Feeling more lived-in that most along Yaza Thingaha, this hotel has some of the city's cheapest rooms, plus good attached Thai (see below) and Chinese restaurants. $40

EATING AND DRINKING

Cafe Flight Sky Palace Hotel, Yaza Thingaha Rd ☎ 067 422122. Easily the most comfortable flight you'll ever take in Myanmar, located in a grounded Myanma Airways jet parked in front of the *Sky Palace Hotel* and converted into a lounge restaurant and bar. There's an extensive selection of mainly Chinese (plus a few Thai and Western) dishes (mains mostly K4500–7000), plus some cheaper noodles, burgers and sandwiches, and a good selection of coffee, juices and booze. Daily 10.30am–10.30pm.

Capital Hypermarket Centre Yaza Thingaha Rd. There's a good range of eating options in the modern mall attached to the Capital Hypermarket. The neat little *Korn Thai* restaurant has a big selection of Thai classics (mains K3000–4000), while *Tasmania* has inexpensive Asian fast food, burgers, fried chicken and fish and chips (mains K2000–2500). For coffee and snacks there's the workaday *Overfresh Bakery* and a brand of Yangon's upmarket *Bar Boon* coffee shop (see p.87). A further cluster of (slightly less inspiring) eating places can be found in the Junction Centre (daily 10am–9pm) just down the road. Daily 9am–9pm.

Maw Kong Nong Golden Hill, near Thabyegone Market. This big and cheery hilltop beer station is one of the few places in central Naypyitaw resembling a local Burmese restaurant and has decent traditional food dishes (with an English menu) including the usual Shan noodles plus dishes like fried chicken with green mustard, fried pork with bamboo shoots, and traditional Shan meat and vegetable salads. Choose from what's shown in the cabinet (two meat plus one veg dish for K1500) or go à la carte (mains around K1400). Daily 6am–7pm.

Santino Golden Hill, near Thabyegone Market. Bright, modern restaurant serving up a huge selection of Western, Thai, Japanese and Burmese dishes (mains K4000–6000), plus good Western and Burmese breakfasts. There's also a small in-house bakery, good coffee and wi-fi. Daily 7am–10pm.

Tai Kitchen Next to the Tungapuri Hotel, Yaza Thingaha Rd ☎ 067 422282. Large and pleasantly lively (at least for Naypyitaw) modern restaurant serving up a big menu of authentic Thai cuisine, plus a few traditional Shan dishes – the *pad thai* (K2500) is as good as you'll get in Burma, and there's a good drinks list and coffee selection too. Mains K2500–5000. Daily 8am–10pm.

DIRECTORY

Bank There are several ATMs at both the Capital Hypermarket Centre and Junction Centre, as well as at several of the hotels. There's also a moneychanger in the Capital Hypermarket.

Internet All our recommended hotels have (reasonably reliable) wi-fi.

Swimming pool Non-guests can use the nice pool at the *Aureum Palace* for $7.

Meiktila
မိတ္ထီလာမြို့

The attractive lakeside town of **MEIKTILA** is one of the most enjoyable places to break the journey north from Yangon to Mandalay. The town stands at something of a crossroads, with connections west to Bagan, east to Lake Inle and north to Lashio, as well as to Mandalay and Yangon. It's also one of central Myanmar's prettiest and most enjoyably low-key destinations, with its shrine-studded lake, bustling market and

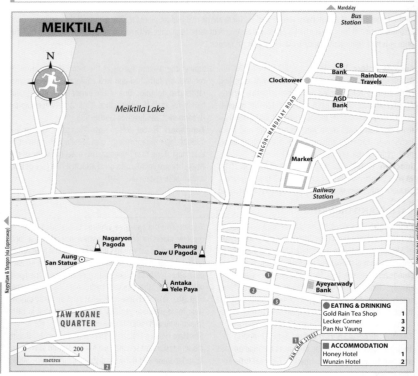

4

tree-lined streets, although present appearances belie the town's turbulent past. The town is famous as the site of one of Southeast Asia's bloodiest conflicts when, between February and March 1945, British forces killed 20,000 Japanese soldiers in a final battle for the control of Burma, devastating the town. Catastrophic fires enveloped Meiktila in 1974 and 1991, while in March 2013 the town hit the international headlines when **Buddhist mobs** went on the rampage against their Muslim neighbours (formerly comprising around thirty percent of the population), killing over forty people and forcing an estimated 12,000 others from their homes while government security forces, it's alleged, stood by and watched. In the Muslim district, along the road east from the clocktower, the burnt-out and bulldozed remains of numerous houses, plus a pair of gutted mosques, could still clearly be seen at the time of writing.

The lake

In the middle of town is Meiktila's beautiful **lake**, fringed with shrines and stupas and crossed by two bridges. Next to the southern bridge you'll immediately notice Meiktila's most memorable landmark, the striking **Phaung Daw U Pagoda**, constructed in the form of a large boat, with soaring stern and the head of a mythical karaweik (aka *karavika*) bird. Inside, the temple's single wood-panelled hall is largely bare, save for a single gold stupa and a few entertaining paintings illustrating moral fables from Burma ancient and modern.

Crossing the bridge you'll see (on your left) the diminutive **Antaka Yele Paya**, comprising a small stupa and shrine perched amid the waters of the lake, connected to the shore by a long wooden footbridge. Continuing along the main road just past here you'll reach the striking **Nagaryon Pagoda**, built in honour of the Japanese soldiers killed in Meiktila during World War II. A gilded statue of Aung San stands outside.

The market

Just east of the Yangon–Mandalay road, north of the train station • Most stalls open daily around 8am–6pm

It's worth having a wander through Meiktila's sprawling and enjoyably ramshackle **market**, where hundreds of hawkers sit beneath lopsided parasols selling piles of leaves and other country produce and shopkeepers measure rice, pulses, tea and spices out of cut-down oil drums. A dilapidated (and currently locked) temple stands buried in the middle of the throng, its small cluster of stupas rising (but not by much) above the surrounding stalls.

ARRIVAL AND INFORMATION

MEIKTILA

By bus and pick-up The bus station is just northeast of the clocktower at the northern end of town, although services usually also drop off passengers along the main road. Arriving, there are plenty of motorbike taxis available to ferry you across town, although the place is small enough that you could just walk. Agents selling bus tickets can be found all along the road running east from the clocktower – Oscar at Rainbow Travels (☎ 064 26093) is a helpful source of information.

Destinations Bagan (1 daily at 10.30pm; 3hr 30min); Lashio (5 daily; 10–11hr, with some services continuing on to the Chinese border at Muse); Magwe (2 daily; 4hr 30min); Mandalay (7 daily; 3hr); Naypyitaw (7 daily; 3hr);

Sittwe (1 daily; 26hr); Taungoo (4 daily; 5hr); Taunggyi (3–4 daily; 4hr); Yangon (6 daily; 7hr via the new Expressway, 9–10hr via old highway).

By train The railway station is more centrally located than the bus station, just southeast of the market, although it's situated on a small branch line with limited services. To reach Yangon, Mandalay or Lake Inle it's much easier to go to nearby Thazi – regular pick-ups run from the bus station (45min), leaving when full – and pick up a train there.

Services There are ATMs at the CB Bank, next to Rainbow Travels, at the AGD Bank opposite, and the Ayeyarwady Bank. Both the hotels listed have wi-fi, as does the *Pan Nu Yaung* restaurant.

GETTING AROUND

By motorbike taxi Meiktila is easily walkable, although there are plenty of motorbike taxis (identifiable by their drivers' official jackets) around town. Count on K500–1000 per journey.

ACCOMMODATION

Honey Hotel Pan Chan St, near the lake ☎ 064 25755. Medium-sized hotel in a peaceful spot overlooking the lake. Rooms (all large with a/c and – in theory if not always in practice – hot water) are a bit grubby but perfectly ok for a night, if you don't mind the rock-hard mattresses and feral dogs in the street outside. $5 extra gets you a TV and minibar. $25

Wunzin Hotel Taw Koane Quarter ☎ 064 23848 or ☎ 064 23559, ⍬ mountpleasanthotelmyanmar.com. In a quiet location just across the lake (and next to the one and only court of the Meiktila Tennis Club), this seriously overpriced place is only really worth considering in the unlikely event that the *Honey* is full. The tatty rooms (some of which actually appear to slope downhill) come with a/c, hot water (in not very clean bathrooms) and some spectacularly random furniture. $45

EATING AND DRINKING

There's a convivial little cluster of teahouses and cafés along the street around the *Gold Rain Tea Shop*, while towards dusk dozens of food stalls set up here, creating one of the region's most appealing **night markets**. For breakfast *mohinga*, there's a good stall about five buildings west of the *Pan Nu Yaung* restaurant.

Gold Rain Tea Shop Just off the main Yangon–Mandalay road. One of a cluster of lively teahouses along this side street, with tables set out on the broad pavements and serving up tea, coffee and enormous Chinese-style buns stuffed with minced chicken or pork. Daily 6am–8pm.

Lecker Corner Just off the main Yangon–Mandalay road. This smart, new, modern restaurant has taken Meiktila's limited eating scene several notches upmarket. The menu includes a big list of authentic Thai dishes plus a

slightly shorter and less interesting Chinese selection, backed up by a long drinks list. Mains K2000–5000. Daily 10am–9pm.

Pan Nu Yaung Yangon–Mandalay road. Popular local restaurant dishing up cheap rice and noodle snacks, including *mohinga* (K500–800), alongside Thai, Burmese and Chinese mains, with most dishes going for K1500–3500. Daily 7am–9pm.

4

Thazi

သာစည်

The crossroads town of **THAZI** sees a certain amount of tourist traffic due to its location at the intersection of the Yangon–Mandalay railway and the roads east to Lake Inle and west to Meiktila and Bagan. You might find yourself overnighting here depending on how your transport connections work out, although there's no real incentive to linger, especially with the far more attractive Meiktila so close to hand.

ARRIVAL AND DEPARTURE   THAZI

By bus There's no bus station in Thazi – services drop off and pick up passengers along the main road. Regular pick-ups (45min) run from Thazi to Meiktila, from where there's a wider range of bus services heading north, south and west. Destinations Kalaw (3–4 daily; 2hr); Naypyitaw (2 daily; 3–4hr); Taunggyi (3–4 daily; 3hr 30min); Taungoo (2 daily; 5–6hr).

By train Thazi is on the main Yangon–Mandalay line. The railway station is a couple of minutes' walk north of the main road through town.
Destinations Bago (3 daily; 10hr); Mandalay (3 daily; 3hr); Naypyitaw (3 daily; 3hr); Shwenyaung (2 daily; 11hr 30min); Taungoo (3 daily; 6hr); Yangon (3 daily; 12hr).

ACCOMMODATION

Moonlight Guesthouse Main Rd ☎ 064 69056. Simple guesthouse on the main road about 500m from the railway station. Rooms are simple and a bit run-down (cheaper ones have fan only and shared bathroom), but the owners are friendly and there's good food available on request. $20

Wonderful Guesthouse Main Rd ☎ 064 69068. Newer and smarter alternative to the *Moonlight*, a 5min walk from the station and with pleasant modern rooms, although with government links. $25

Yangon to Bagan

Journeying between Yangon and Bagan, most travellers nowadays either fly or take an express bus via the Yangon–Mandalay Expressway. With more time on your hands you could follow the slower route along the old Yangon–Bagan highway via the riverside city of **Pyay**, one of the country's oldest settlements and also the starting point for the long bus journey to Ngapali. Further north, **Magwe** sees few visitors but has bus connections west to Sittwe and Mrauk U, although these are still the preserve of the adventurous few.

Pyay and around

ပြည်မြို့

The largest city on the old Yangon–Bagan highway, **PYAY** lies around 275km north of Yangon (and 350km south of Bagan), sitting next to the Ayeyarwady midway between the Rakhine Yoma and Bago Yoma mountains. Pronounced variously as either "Pyay" or "Pea", the city makes a convenient and enjoyable stop, with one of central Myanmar's finest temples, the **Shwesandaw Pagoda**, and the ruins of ancient **Thayekhittaya (Sri Ksetra)** nearby.

One of the oldest settlements in Myanmar, Pyay's history stretches back to the days of ancient Sri Ksetra (see p.330). The town subsequently developed into a major centre during the colonial era after being captured by the British first in 1825 (who named it "Prome") and then retaken in 1852 during the Second Anglo-Burmese War. Burma's first railway line was completed here in 1877, connecting colonial Prome with Rangoon, while at the end of the colonial period the city was the scene of major fighting between British and Japanese forces during World War II.

All roads in Pyay lead sooner or later to the gilded **statue of Aung San**, standing at the junction of Bogyoke and Main roads and the Yangon highway. Just west of here, leafy **Strand Road** runs along the Ayeyarwady, with gaps between the houses and trees revealing views of water, boats and temples rising from the wooded hills on the far shore including the huge gilded stupa of the **Shwe Bontharmuni Pagoda**.

The market

Strand Rd, 10min walk north of the centre • Most stalls open daily 8am–6pm

North of the centre is Pyay's large, interesting and slightly anarchic **market**. A long row of *thanaka*-wood vendors sit lined up along the waterfront at the front of the market – the Shinmadaung *thanaka* tree (one of several used to produce *thanaka* paste; see box, p.7) grows abundantly in the Pyay district, and although mass-produced *thanaka* creams are widely available, many Burmese still prefer to grind their own. There's a large **Chinese temple** on the corner of Ta Yoke Tann Street on the south side of the market.

Shwesandaw Pagoda and around

ရွှေဆံတော်စေတီ • Bogyoke Rd • Daily 6am–9pm • Free

The main sight in town is the **Shwesandaw Pagoda** ("Golden Hair Relic Temple"), which rises high above the southern side of Bogyoke Road, to which it's connected by 160 steep stairs lined with shops (there's also a lift, although – as ever – it's much more fun to walk). The majestic central stupa, said to contain a couple of the Buddha's hairs, is one of the largest in the country – a metre taller than the Shwedagon in Yangon itself, with every surface gilded and polished to a dazzling sheen. The spire, topped (unusually) with not one but two *hti*, is uncharacteristically large in relation to the bell below, giving the whole thing a distinctively slender and narrow-waisted outline – particularly spectacular when floodlit at night.

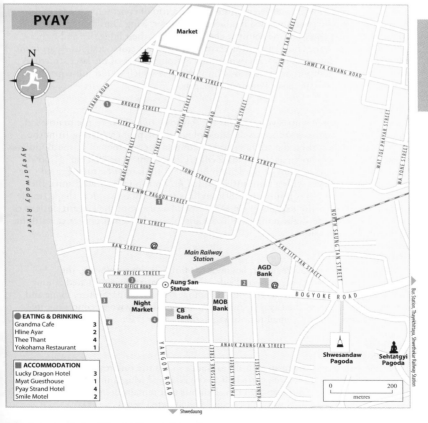

PYAY

4

Market

TA YOKE TANN STREET
PAN PAE TANN STREET
SHWE TA CHUANG ROAD
STRAND ROAD
BROKER STREET
PANTAN STREET
MAIN ROAD
LONG STREET
SITKE STREET
SITKE STREET
WAT OE PHAYAR STREET
WA YONE STREET
MARCHANY STREET
MARKET STREET
YONE STREET
SWE NWE PAGODA STREET
TUT STREET
KAN STREET
@
PW OFFICE STREET
OLD POST OFFICE ROAD
Main Railway Station
SAR TITE TAN STREET
NORTH SAUNG TAN STREET
AGD Bank
@
Aung San Statue
BOGYOKE ROAD
Night Market
CB Bank
MOB Bank
ANAUK ZAUNGTAN STREET
Shwesandaw Pagoda
Sehtatgyi Pagoda
YANGON ROAD
TIKYITSONE STREET
PHAYANI STREET
PHONEGYI STREET

Ayeyarwady River

Bus Station, Thayekhittaya, Shwethekar Railway Station

0   200
metres

● EATING & DRINKING
Grandma Cafe	3
Hline Ayar	2
Thee Thant	4
Yokohama Restaurant	1

■ ACCOMMODATION
Lucky Dragon Hotel	3
Myat Guesthouse	1
Pyay Strand Hotel	4
Smile Motel	2

Shwedaung

In the northeast corner of the courtyard the small and dusty **Pyay Shwe San Daw Museum** (donation) houses assorted monastic artefacts, including a beautiful miniature karaweik and a couple of intricately carved ivory tusks. Also on display are a few interesting old photos, including shots of the Gurkha Rifles entering Prome in 1945.

Slightly further around (heading clockwise) a tiny model of the stupa sits in what looks like a giant birdcage, with good views of the Sehtatgyi Pagoda (see below) to the rear. On the south side of the terrace a shrine holds a replica of the Buddha's Tooth Relic from Sri Lanka – the replica is said to have been stored alongside the original tooth in Kandy and thus to have being similarly charged with spiritual power.

Just east of the temple you can't fail to see the enormous **Sehtatgyi Pagoda** ("Big Ten-Storey") Buddha, seated in the earth-witness mudra facing the Shwesandaw, his eyes more or less level with the temple terrace, and clearly visible from it.

Thayekhittaya (Sri Ksetra)

သရေခေတ္တရာ • Pyay Rd • Daily 9am–4pm • $5; the museum attracts an extra charge (see below) • Ox-cart tours of the site cost around $5–8 per cart, depending on the number of people • A motorbike taxi to the site costs around K2000 each way

Some 8km east of Pyay lie the scant remains of ancient **Thayekhittaya** – or **Sri Ksetra**, as it was known in its heyday – the great Pyu city which held dominion over large swathes of central Myanmar between the fifth and ninth centuries (see p.330). The faint aura of desolation that hangs over the impressively large site is haunting, hinting at a once great city now virtually erased from the map.

Thayekhittaya's most impressive monuments are a trio of enormous **stupas**, said to be three of the nine commissioned by the city's founder, King Duttabaung. These are among the oldest stupas in the country, characterized by their huge size and rather primitive shapes – the complete antithesis of later Burmese stupa designs. Apart from the stupas, the ruins are fairly underwhelming, although some of the later structures offer tantalizing glimpses of the glorious Burmese style which would subsequently flower in Sri Ksetra's successor kingdom of Bagan.

Payagyi Stupa

The first of the three stupas you reach is the **Payagyi**, right next to the main road about 1km before the entrance to the archeological site proper. Dating from the sixth or seventh century, the stupa is said to contain the big toenail of the Buddha's right foot; it's also known as the Maha Zedi ("Great Stupa") or "Sai Sai" ("Slowly Slowly") Pagoda on account of the length of time it took to construct. Seated on three circular terraces with a diminutive gilded *hti* on top (a later addition), the sheer size of the thing is impressive, although its rudimentary conical shape (made slightly lopsided by the ravages of time) is a world away from the elegant designs of Bagan and later. The slight remains of some discoloured original plaster can still be seen clinging to its sides.

Payamar Stupa

A second huge stupa, the **Payamar**, lies about 100m past the entrance to the archeological site, off on the left-hand side of the road, attractively situated among paddy fields. Also attributed to King Duttabaung, it's very similar in size, shape and date of construction to the Payagyi stupa, although in slightly worse condition, its brickwork now sprouting small tufts of vegetation.

The museum

Tues–Sun 9.30am–4.30pm • $5

The small and expensive **museum** at the entrance to the site isn't really worth the money – many finds have been carted off to the National Museum in Yangon, which has extensive displays on the ancient city. Exhibits that remain *in situ* include a few old Pyu inscriptions and burial urns, silver coins and assorted beads,

---

THAYEKHITTAYA (SRI KSETRA) ORIENTATION

Most of Thayekhittaya's remains are contained within a designated **archeological park**, although two of the three big stupas – **Payagyi** and **Payamar** – lie outside it, and can be visited for free. The fragmentary ruins cover a sizeable area. Bikes and cars aren't allowed into the site, so you can either **walk** (although really it's too big to cover comfortably on foot) or charter an **ox-cart**, which are hired out for a set period of three hours. These are fun for about the first ten minutes, but also tediously slow and pretty uncomfortable for the next two hours and fifty minutes. You might prefer to go for a shorter circuit instead, even if you can't negotiate a discount on the full fare. If you do walk, there are plenty of signs and strategically placed maps to point you in the right direction.

---

plus statues of a couple of Hindu deities and other Indian-influenced figures – proof of the strong cultural contact between Sri Ksetra and the subcontinent.

The archeological park

Immediately beyond the museum lie the extensive, carefully reconstructed walls of the former **palace** area, more or less in the middle of the old city. A ten-minute cart ride southwest brings you to the **Rahanda** (or "Yahanda") **Gate**. The actual gate has pretty much disappeared, although you can still see the collapsed, earth-covered remains of the original brick **city walls** on either side. Just past the gate, outside the walls, is the narrow **Rahanda Cave Pagoda**, with a triangular, brick-vaulted roof and eight small seated Buddhas looking back towards the city inside the walls.

Continuing southeast around the outside of the walls brings you to the (probably) fifth-century **Bawbawgyi Stupa**, the most impressive of Thayekhittaya's three giant stupas and one of the oldest Buddhist monuments in the country – and indeed anywhere else in Southeast Asia. Standing 46m tall with almost sheer sides and a flattish top, it looks quite unlike any other such structure in Myanmar, although it bears a passing resemblance to the famous Dhamek Stupa at Sarnath in India, from where inspiration for this prototypical Burmese stupa may have come.

A couple of minutes further east is the quaint tenth-century **Bei Bei Pagoda**. Dating from the twilight years of Sri Ksetra, this diminutive square brick shrine shows clear evidence of the emerging Bagan style, with characteristic flamed-shaped door pediments and the remains of a tall stupa-spire on top. Just south of here is another small square brick shrine, the **Lay Myet Hna**, its collapsing walls held together in a cage of big red girders.

Re-entering the walls and heading north you'll reach the small eighth-century **East Zegu Pagoda**, with its four entrances (all now bricked up) and heavily moulded brick doorways and pilasters, although the original roof has now been replaced by a large concrete daub. One final hop north brings you to the **Payahtaung Pagoda**, just east of the museum. Dating from the tenth or eleventh century, this is the largest and finest of Thayekhittaya's shrines: a big square brick box, each of its four sides penetrated by a solitary undersized door. A mini-stupa sits on one corner of the roof next to three superimposed terraces which look as if they once supported a rooftop stupa-spire, although no trace of this remains.

Shwedaung

ေ႐ႊေတာင္ · Regular pick-ups run from Pyay to Shwedaung

A popular day-trip from Pyay is to the **Shwemyetman Pagoda** in the town of **Shwedaung**, 15km south of Pyay on the Yangon highway. The temple is famous for its bespectacled Buddha: a huge seated image wearing a natty pair of round spectacles and bearing a faint but unmistakable resemblance to John Lennon. One tradition holds that the statue was first equipped with eyewear by King Duttabaung in the fourth century after he went blind – whereupon the monarch promptly regained his sight; another, that the glasses were added to the statue to provoke local interest in the Buddhist faith (although the statue's original spectacles were stolen long ago and the image now wears modern replacements). Whatever its origins, the statue is believed to have the power to cure poor eyesight and other ocular diseases – a case near the statue is full of glasses discarded by visitors who claim to have had perfect vision restored during a visit to the temple.

ARRIVAL AND DEPARTURE
PYAY AND AROUND

By bus The bus station is 4km east of the centre along Bogyoke Rd – to get there from the centre either catch one of the pick-ups that shuttle up and down Bogyoke Rd or catch a motorbike taxi (K1000). The only bus to Bagan currently leaves in the late afternoon; alternatively, catch a bus to Magwe and pick up a connection there. If you're tackling the adventurous overland route to Sittwe and/or Mrauk U by bus you'll most likely also have to change at Magwe, but it's worth asking just in case any direct services have become available.

Destinations Magwe (4 daily; 5hr); Mandalay (2 daily; 13hr); Nyaung U (1 daily; 8hr); Ngapali (1 nightly; 12hr); Yangon (6 daily; 6–7hr).

By train Nightly services to Yangon leave from the main station right in the middle of town. There's also an overnight service to Bagan departing from Shwethekar station, around 10km east of the centre.

Destinations Bagan (1 nightly; 10hr); Yangon (1 nightly; 8hr 30min).

By boat Twice-weekly IWT government ferries call at Pyay on their way up- and downriver between Yangon, Bagan and Mandalay, offering one of Myanmar's slowest riverine journeys (taking two days to Yangon, three to Bagan, and four to Mandalay). Current uncertainty over all IWT services means the future of the ferry is uncertain, while even if it's running they may not be prepared to sell tickets to foreigners. Check the latest situation at your hotel.

GETTING AROUND

Central Pyay is compact enough to cover easily on foot, although you'll need transport to get to and from the bus and railway stations. The *Myat Guesthouse* has **bicycles** to rent for K2000/day – handy for getting out to Thayekhittaya, although you're not allowed to cycle around the site itself.

ACCOMMODATION

★ **Lucky Dragon Hotel** 772 Strand Rd ☎ 053 24222, ⊚ luckydragonhotel.com. Unexpectedly upmarket little mini-resort in the heart of Pyay, with accommodation in attractive white chalets spread out down a long thin garden, plus a smallish pool. Rooms are surprisingly stylish, with parquet floors, cool white decor and smart, modern bathrooms. Excellent value. $45

Myat Guesthouse Market St ☎ 053 25695. Long-running budget stalwart. "Rooms" downstairs are little better than squalid cubicles (with shared bath and wafer-thin mattresses); those upstairs – with ($18) or without ($32) bathroom – are simple but far nicer, if you don't mind the peeling paint, old-fashioned a/c units and bits of lino and wallpaper held together with masking tape – they come in various shapes, sizes and prices, so have a look at a

few before deciding. There's also wi-fi, and the madly exuberant Chinese owner is a delight. $12

Pyay Strand Hotel 6 Strand Rd ☎ 053 25846. Pleasantly old-fashioned hotel, with large, bright, high-ceilinged rooms kept in decent nick, although some of the mattresses appear to be made of concrete and rates are on the high side, especially given the lack of wi-fi and hot water – and there are no single rates either. $30

Smile Motel 10–11 Bogyoke Rd ☎ 053 25142, ⊚ smilemotel333@gmail.com. Slightly battered-looking place on the main road. Rooms are old-fashioned and pretty worn, but spacious enough and more or less clean. Hot water (with some seriously surreal plumbing) is included, but there's no wi-fi. $24

EATING AND DRINKING

Pyay has an above-average range of eating options compared to most places in Myanmar of a similar size, and the centre tends to stay lively until relatively late – particularly the busy string of restaurants along the Yangon road south of the Aung San statue. There's also a small but excellent **night market** spreading along Old Post Office Rd west of the statue with stalls dishing up everything from freshly grilled meat skewers to exotic fruits.

Grandma Cafe Old Post Office Rd ☎ 09 4950 0737. Functional little modern café, not nearly as atmospheric as the food stalls of the night market outside but serving up above-average meals (mains K1500–2200), including an

excellent range of Korean dishes (which the owner learned to cook when working in Malaysia) plus burgers, pasta, salad and sandwiches. Daily 11am–9pm.

Hline Ayar Khittaryar Ayar Park, Strand Rd

☎053 29398. Lively restaurant and local boozer in an attractive riverside setting, with nice views from its waterside terrace area. Food is Chinese (mains K3000–4000, plus more expensive seafood dishes) and there are also singing and "fashion" shows nightly at 7pm on the restaurant's small stage. Daily 10am–11pm.

Thee Thant Yangon Rd. One of a cluster of lively restaurants-cum-beer stations hereabouts, serving up a big menu of passable if unexciting Chinese-style mains

(K1500–4000), although some of the menu translations don't give much away, and you probably won't be tempted by the "Under-done slice of potato". Daily 8am–11pm.

Yokohama Restaurant Strand Rd, near the market ☎09 4236 70456. Bright, modern restaurant offering authentic Japanese fare (small dishes K1500–2000, larger set meals K3000–5000) – *tonkatsu, tori teriyaki, ebi* tempura and so on. Daily 11.30am–2pm & 5–10pm.

DIRECTORY

Banks There are plenty of ATMs around town including the CB Bank, AGD Bank and MOB (the last of these doesn't take MasterCard); there's also a second CB Bank ATM at the *Lucky Dragon* hotel.

Internet Reliable places include Cosmic, near *Myat Guesthouse*, and Lazer Zone, on Bogyoke Rd near the Shwesandaw Pagoda (daily 8am–10pm or later; both 500k/hr).

Magwe

မကွေး

Sprawling along the east bank of the Ayeyarwady some 240km north of Pyay and 175km south of Bagan, **MAGWE** (or "Magway" as it's often spelt) is a busy provincial centre and the capital of Magwe Region, home to a large university and an impressive 2.5km bridge over the river. There's not much to interest the casual visitor, although if you're travelling between Bagan and Pyay with your own vehicle you might want to stop for an hour to have a look around the dusty market and the landmark **Mya Tha Lun** ("Jade Throne") pagoda, perched on a hilltop north of the centre. The only reason you might end up overnighting in Magwe is if you're heading by bus along the little-travelled (at least by foreigners) overland route from Pyay or Bagan to Sittwe or Mrauk U, in which case you'll most likely have to change buses here.

ARRIVAL AND DEPARTURE

MAGWE

By bus The bus station is around 2km east of the centre down Pyi Taw Thar Rd (around K1000 by motorbike taxi, or a little less in a shared pick-up).

Destinations Bagan (3 daily; 4hr); Mandalay (1 daily; 8hr); Meiktila (2 daily; 4hr 30min); Mrauk U (1 daily; 10hr); Pyay (4 daily; 5hr); Sittwe (1 daily; 15hr); Yangon (1 daily; 12hr).

ACCOMMODATION

Htein Htein Tar 17th St ☎063 23499. Comfortable but seriously overpriced rooms – although singles for $30 are much better value – with a/c, TV, fridge. No wi-fi. **$60**

Nan Htike Thu Hotel Strand Rd, south of the bridge ☎09 56328597, ⊕facebook.com/nanhtikethumagway.

Smart, modern and competitively priced 68-room hotel with well-equipped rooms plus pool and wi-fi. **$45**

Rolex Guesthouse Near the bridge ☎063 23536. Well-maintained and reasonably priced guesthouse with a mix of cheap fan rooms with shared bathroom and pricier en-suite rooms with a/c (K30,000). No wi-fi. **K15,000**

Bagan

ပုဂံ

BAGAN is unquestionably one of Asia's – indeed the world's – great sights: a vast swathe of temples and pagodas rising from the hot flat plains bordering the Ayeyarwady River, the landscape bristling with uncountable shrines and stupas which carpet the countryside in an almost surreal profusion and stretch as far as the eye can see in every direction. Over two thousand temples lie scattered over an area of almost seventy square kilometres, constructed in one of history's most extravagant extended building booms over the two-and-a-bit centuries between around 1050 and 1280. As an architectural showpiece Bagan (or "Pagan" as it's also sometimes Romanized) is rivalled only by the roughly contemporaneous temples of Angkor in Cambodia, although while the major monuments of Angkor have now disappeared under a flood of coach parties, the temples of Bagan remain relatively free from crowds, and still retain much of their prevailing magic and mystery – for the time being at least.

The sheer scale and density of Bagan's monuments are almost guaranteed to overwhelm – its riches are such that superb temples which almost anywhere else would be headline attractions often fail to merit even a mention in most tourist literature. Despite the super-abundance of monuments, Bagan's architecture comprises an extended variation on a few basic themes, with a handful of recurrent styles and structures that evolved over time, and much of the pleasure of exploring the myriad temples is in unravelling the underlying motifs and meanings that underpin the thousands of monuments.

The greater Bagan area divides into three main areas. The lively town of **Nyaung U**, where you'll find most of Bagan's cheap accommodation, is the main centre, while around 5.5km down the road the historic walled city of **Old Bagan** is home to a cluster of upmarket resort-hotels and the greatest concentration of historic monuments. Around 4.5km further south, somnolent **New Bagan (Bagan Myothit)** has further (mainly mid-range and upmarket) accommodation options. There are a few further places to sleep, eat and shop in the villages of **Wet Kyi Inn** (midway between Nyaung U and Old Bagan) and **Myinkaba** (between Old and New Bagan). Stretching inland from here away from the river, the **Central Plain** is where you'll find many of Bagan's finest temples (but no facilities). The entire area (covering around forty square kilometres) is protected as the **Bagan Archeological Zone**, although there's no physical evidence of a demarcated area on the ground.

Nyaung U

ညောင်ဦးမြို့

The heart of the busy if unremarkable small town of **NYAUNG U** looks surprisingly untouched by the thousands of tourists who descend on it every year. The centre of town is marked by the roundabout at the junction of Anawrahta and Main roads (both of which lead down to Old Bagan), next to which you'll find the town's attractive **market** (see p.215). There are also a few temples in the town itself, most notably the superb **Shwezigon**, one of Bagan's finest monuments, and the mural-covered **Kyansittha Umin** nearby.

Thiripyitsaya 4 Street

သီရိပစ္စယာ

The tourist centre of Nyaung U lies southwest of the town centre proper, centred on **Thiripyitsaya 4 Street** (aka as "Restaurant Row", for obvious reasons). At the top of the street, the Shwe Pyi Nann shopping complex houses a couple of low-key museums.

BAGAN ENTRY FEES

All foreign visitors are theoretically required to pay a **$15 entry fee** on arrival in Bagan in exchange for a ticket valid for one week. Buses will usually stop at a government post, and the fee is also collected at the airport and the jetties. The system isn't waterproof, however, and a few people manage to slip through the net without paying. Equally, if you stay more than a week you're unlikely to be required to purchase a new ticket, unless you leave Bagan and then come back again. Note that a few attractions, such as the Bagan Archeological Museum, charge an additional admission fee.

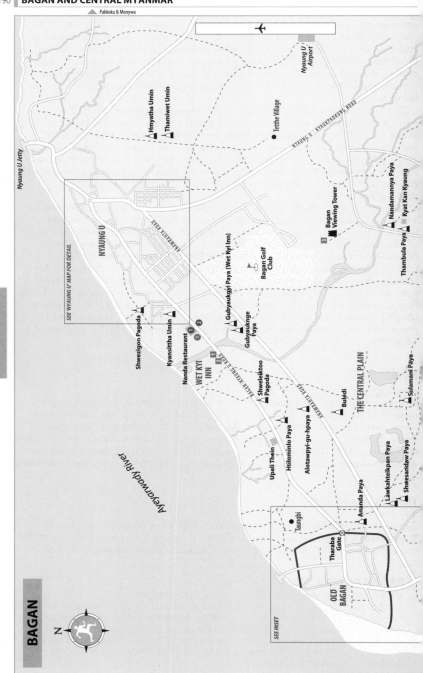

4

BAGAN

▲ Pakkoku & Monywa

Nyaung U Jetty

Ayeyarwady River

Nyaung U Airport

SEE 'NYAUNG U' MAP FOR DETAIL

NYAUNG U

ANAWRAHTA ROAD

NYAUNG U – KYAUKPADAUNG ROAD

Ietthe Village

Hmyatha Umin

Thamiwet Umin

Nandamannya Paya

Kyat Kan Kyaung

Thambula Paya

Bagan Viewing Tower

Bagan Golf Club

Gubyaukgyi Paya (Wet Kyi Inn)

Gubyauknge Paya

Shwezigon Pagoda

Kyansittha Umin

Nanda Restaurant

WET KYI INN

BAGAN–NYAUNG U OLD

ANAWRAHTA ROAD

Shwelaiktoo Pagoda

Buledi

Sulamani Paya

THE CENTRAL PLAIN

Upali Thein

Htilominlo Paya

Alotawpyi-gu-hpaya

Lawkahteikpan Paya

Shwesandaw Paya

Ananda Paya

Taungbi

Tharaba Gate

OLD BAGAN

SEE INSET

N

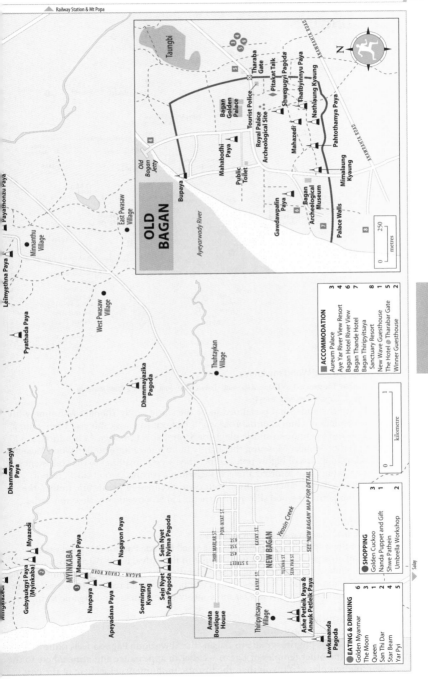

Taungbi

Tharaba Gate

Pitakat Taik

Shwegugyi Pagoda

Thatbyinnyu Kyaung

Nathlaung Kyaung

Pahtothamya Paya

Bagan Golden Palace

Tourist Police

Royal Palace Archeological Site

Mahazedi

Mahabodhi Paya

Public Toilet

Bagan Archeological Museum

Mimalaung Kyaung

Gawdawpalin Paya

Palace Walls

Bupaya

Old Bagan Jetty

Ayeyarwady River

OLD BAGAN

East Pwasaw Village

Payathonzu Paya

Minnanthu Village

Leimyethna Paya

West Pwasaw Village

Pyathada Paya

Thuhtaykan Village

Dhammayazika Pagoda

Dhammayangyi Paya

Myazedi

Gubyaukgyi Paya (Myinkaba)

MYINKABA

Manuha Paya

Nagayon Paya

Nanpaya

Sein Nyet Nyima Pagoda

BAGAN – CHAUK ROAD

Apeyadana Paya

Seemingyi Kyaung

Sein Nyet Ama Pagoda

Amata Boutique House

Thiripyitsaya Village

Ashe Petleik Paya & Anauk Petleik Paya

Lawkananda Pagoda

THIRI MARLAR ST.

POK-NYAT ST.

KAYAY ST.

THIRI MARLAR ST.

OZANA ST.

SS ST.

639

KAYAY ST.

3 STREET

KAYAY ST.

SEIN PAN ST.

NEW BAGAN

Yeoin Creek

SEE 'NEW BAGAN MAP FOR DETAIL'

■ ACCOMMODATION	
Aureum Palace	3
Aye Yar River View Resort	4
Bagan Hotel River View	6
Bagan Thande Hotel	7
Bagan Thiripyitsaya	8
Sanctuary Resort	
New Wave Guesthouse	1
The Hotel @ Tharabar Gate	5
Winner Guesthouse	2

● EATING & DRINKING	
Golden Myanmar	6
The Moon	3
Queen	1
San Thi Dar	2
Star Beam	4
Yar Pyi	5

● SHOPPING	
Golden Cuckoo	3
Nanda Puppet and Gift	1
Shwe Pathein	
Umbrella Workshop	2

0 250 metres

0 1 kilometre

4

Salay ▶

N

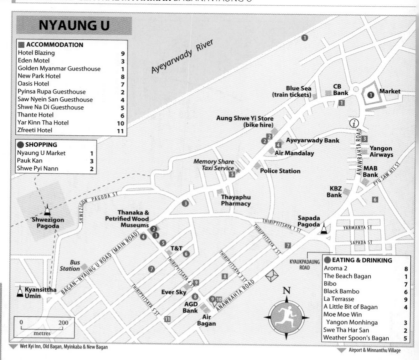

NYAUNG U

ACCOMMODATION
Hotel Blazing	9
Eden Motel	3
Golden Myanmar Guesthouse	1
New Park Hotel	8
Oasis Hotel	7
Pyinsa Rupa Guesthouse	2
Saw Nyein San Guesthouse	4
Shwe Na Di Guesthouse	5
Thante Hotel	6
Yar Kinn Tha Hotel	10
Zfreeti Hotel	11

SHOPPING
Nyaung U Market	1
Pauk Kan	3
Shwe Pyi Nann	2

EATING & DRINKING
Aroma 2	8
The Beach Bagan	1
Bibo	7
Black Bambo	6
La Terrasse	9
A Little Bit of Bagan	4
Moe Moe Win	
Yangon Monhinga	3
Swe Tha Har San	2
Weather Spoon's Bagan	5

Map labels: Ayeyarwady River; Blue Sea (train tickets); CB Bank; Market; Aung Shwe Yi Store (bike hire); Ayeyarwady Bank; Air Mandalay; Yangon Airways; ANAWRAHTA ROAD; MAB Bank; Memory Share Taxi Service; Police Station; KBZ Bank; PYU SAW HTI ST; Thayaphu Pharmacy; Shwezigon Pagoda; SHWEZIGON PAGODA ST; Thanaka & Petrified Wood Museums; THIRIPYITSAYA 1ST; Sapada Pagoda; YARMANYA ST; SAPADA ST; T&T; THIRIPYITSAYA 3 ST; KYAUKPADAUNG ROAD; Bus Station; BAGAN–NYAUNG U ROAD (MAIN ROAD); Kyansittha Umin; THIRIPYITSAYA 5 ST; Ever Sky; AGD Bank; Air Bagan; ANAWRAHTA ROAD; N; 0 200 metres; Wet Kyi Inn, Old Bagan, Myinkaba & New Bagan; Airport & Minnanthu Village

Thanaka and Petrified Wood museums

Shwe Pyi Nann complex, Thiripyitsaya 4 St • **Thanaka Museum** • Daily 8.30am–9pm; **Petrified Wood Museum**
အင်ကြင်းကျောက်ဖြုတုိက် • Daily 9am–9pm • Free

Next to the street stands what is claimed to be the world's only **Thanaka Museum**, with unedifying displays of chunks of *thanaka* wood laid out in glass cabinets. There's not a lot else bar a couple of not-so-subtle plugs for Shwe Pyi Nann *thanaka* products.

Adjacent to the Thanaka Museum, the slightly more interesting **Petrified Wood Museum** features colourful lumps of highly polished petrified wood, fossilized to the consistency and texture of stone, plus assorted artefacts including a petrified-wood clock, teapot, mirror and so on. If you fancy acquiring your own specimen of prehistoric timber, the Shwe Pyi Nann petrified-wood showroom (see p.215) is conveniently close to hand.

Sapada Pagoda

ဆပဒဘုရား• At the junction of Anawrahta and Kyaukpadaung roads

Marooned in the middle of a roundabout, the small **Sapada Pagoda** is a good example of the Sri Lankan-style stupa which was popular in the early days of Bagan, with its distinctive box-like *harmika* (relic chamber) separating the slightly bulbous dome and the top-heavy spire above – later Burmese stupas (see p.360) would replace the *harmika* with a lotus-shaped *amalaka*, achieving a far more satisfyingly seamless and organic form.

Shwezigon Pagoda

ရွှေစည်းခုံဘုရား• Shwezigon Pagoda St • Daily 6am–9pm

The most important pilgrimage site in Bagan, the **Shwezigon Pagoda** feels quite different from the other temples of Bagan – closer in appearance and atmosphere to the great working temples of Yangon than the historic monuments elsewhere in the city, with its enormous gilded stupa surrounded by a colourful complex of subsidiary shrines. Despite its relatively modern appearance, the Shwezigon is one of Bagan's oldest monuments, begun by King Anawrahta (ruled 1044–77) to enshrine (it's said) a collarbone and a tooth of the Buddha brought from Sri Lanka, although it wasn't finished until the reign of his son Kyansittha (ruled 1084–1112) in around 1089.

Long covered passages, each flanked by a huge pair of white chinthe, lead into the temple from the south and east (beware the shopkeepers on the southern side, where most tourists enter, who are probably the most cut-throat in Bagan). Inside, the complex is dominated by its vast **stupa**, set atop three battlemented terraces, with elaborate red-carpeted staircases flanked with lions rising to the summit. The stupa is actually built mainly of sandstone rather than the usual brick, although you can't see this since the whole thing (including terraces) is dazzlingly gilded right down to the pavement. Fine glazed tiles depicting various Jataka scenes are set around the base (although many are now missing), while double-bodied lions guard each corner.

EXPLORING BAGAN

The **architectural background** to the temples of Bagan is covered in detail in Contexts (see box, p.360), which provides a fuller overview of the various styles and features of the myriad monuments and their historical context. The **history** of Bagan is also covered in Contexts (see p.331).

ITINERARIES

There are endless different ways of tackling the temples of Bagan, with monuments clustered so thickly on the ground that fixing on a particular itinerary is a matter of personal taste rather than practical necessity. It's best to take your time – rush at Bagan, and you're likely to become rapidly templed out and terminally stupa-fied. You'll need at least **three days** to get to grips with the major monuments, and getting on for **a week** to properly explore all the places covered below. A thorough investigation of the whole site could take the best part of a year.

Having said which, a few pointers may prove useful. The monuments of **Old Bagan** make a logical starting point, the site's densest and most diverse collection of temples including the landmark Thatbyinnyu and Gawdawpalin along with a host of other fascinating buildings. The temples of the **Central Plain** – including the stunning Shwesandaw, Dhammayangyi and Sulamani – will fill a second day, perhaps with the Mingalazedi and Dhammayazika Pagoda included, while a third day can be spent exploring the area **between Nyaung U and Old Bagan**, particularly the magnificent Shwezigon Pagoda and Htilominlo Paya, and the mural-covered Upali Thein and Gubyaukgyi Paya. A further string of temples stretches south of Old Bagan through **Myinkaba** village to **New Bagan**, and there's another cluster of absorbing little monuments around the village of **Minnanthu**, somewhat off the beaten track, and a perfect place to escape the (admittedly quite modest) crowds.

It's also worth remembering that there are **around two thousand further temples** not covered in the accounts below, and it's also fun to leave your guidebook in your hotel room and go off exploring where the fancy takes you – and you're more or less guaranteed to have most places entirely to yourself.

PRACTICALITIES

Many of Bagan's less-visited temples are kept **locked**, particularly those containing delicate murals or valuable artefacts. In most places someone will magically appear to unlock the temple for you; occasionally you might have to ask around to find the keyholder. A tip of around K500 generally suffices.

A decent **torch** is pretty much essential if you want to properly appreciate Bagan's many remarkable temple murals. If you don't have one, you can sometimes borrow one from the temple keyholder or resident hawker. A tip is obviously expected – again around K500 is fine.

Note that **photography** of Bagan's fragile murals is expressly forbidden inside the more popular temples. In less-touristed temples you might be allowed to take photographs, although given the damaging effects of flash on the temple's delicate, centuries-old paintings the responsible thing to do is to keep your camera in your bag.

4

THE NATS OF SHWEZIGON

The Shwezigon is interesting historically for its role in the development of Burmese Buddhism. Aware of his people's love of the old **nat spirits** (see p.356), the savvy King Anawrahta decided to encourage interest in the new Theravada Buddhist faith by placing images of the 37 most revered nats on the lower terraces of the stupa, believing that people would be won over to the new Buddhist faith more easily if it incorporated aspects of their traditional beliefs – and thus setting a precedent for the combined *nat* and Buddhist shrines that can still be found throughout Myanmar to this day (nowhere more so than at nearby Taung Kalat and Mount Popa).

The *nats* of Shwezigon, meanwhile, having fulfilled their original function, are now relegated to a subsidiary shrine – signed "**Shrine of Bodaw Indra and 37 Nats**" – tucked away in the far southeast corner of the temple compound. You may be able to find someone to open it for you for a tip, offering you a surreal glimpse of the 37 small gilded images of assembled *nat* notables lined up solemnly in glass cases – and looking decidedly neglected compared to their glory days sitting enthroned upon King Anawrahta's magnificent stupa.

Large shrines sit at the bottom of the four staircases, each containing an impressive standing **gilded bronze Buddha** (the four largest in Bagan), modelled after the Indian Gupta style, although they're rather difficult to see behind their protective grilles. Exiting the northern side of the temple, the path leads down to the water, with fine river views.

The temple is the site of a major **festival** during the Burmese month of Tazaungmone (Oct/Nov), during which pilgrims from all over the country converge on Nyaung U, and Shwezigon transforms into an enormous country fair complete with puppet shows, open-air theatre, dance performances and so on, plus handicraft and food stalls aplenty.

Kyansittha Umin

ကျန်စစ်သားဥမင် · Signed off Main Rd a few metres past the entrance to the Shwezigon Pagoda's southern covered terrace · Daily 8am–6pm

Almost in the shadow of the Shwezigon Pagoda, the modest **Kyansittha Umin** is easily missed but worth a look for its unusual murals. The name means "Cave of Kyansittha" in honour of King Kyansittha, although the building most likely dates back to the rule of his father, Anawrahta. The small rectangular brick building (not actually a cave) was apparently used as a monastic residence, although it's difficult to see how anyone would have managed to live in the cramped interior, bisected by a grid of narrow passages which are now propped up with steel frames following earthquake damage in 1975.

Virtually every interior surface is covered with fine **murals** in subdued whites, browns and yellows depicting various scenes from daily life and Buddhist mythology. Particularly interesting are the paintings of Mongol soldiers (on the rear wall roughly opposite the entrance) – a memento of the repeated Mongol incursions into Myanmar in the late thirteenth century. The invaders are instantly recognizable thanks to their distinctive hats, like upturned fruit bowls decorated with fancy plumes.

Nyaung U to Old Bagan

Myriad monuments dot the area between Nyaung U and Old Bagan, although relatively few are of sufficient interest to feature on most tourist itineraries. They do, however, include two of Bagan's finest temples – the flamboyant **Htilominlo Paya**, midway between Nyaung U and Old Bagan, and the magnificent **Ananda Paya**, just outside the latter.

Gubyaukgyi Paya (Wet Kyi Inn) and around

ဂူပြောက်ကြီးဘုရား · Off Anawrahta Rd · Daily 8am–6pm

Not far from Nyaung U is the thirteenth-century **Gubyaukgyi Paya** ("Great Painted Cave Temple" – not to be confused with the identically named temple in Myinkaba), signed off Anawrahta Road as "Nge Gu Pyauk Gyi". Traces of fine plasterwork can still be seen on the exterior, which has an unusual pyramidal spire above – perhaps inspired by that at the Mahabodhi temple in Old Bagan. Inside are many fine murals showing assorted Jataka scenes, arranged mosaic-like within dozens of small square panels. Sadly, many of the paintings were removed by a certain Dr Thomann from Germany, who visited in 1899 and proceeded to ransack the temple – the holes where the naughty German removed large sections of plaster are still gapingly obvious.

Around 250m past the Gubyakgyi, the **Gubyauknge Paya** (signed off Anawrahta Rd as "Gu Byauk Nge – Wet Kyi Innn") is very similar both in style and name, with further fine exterior plasterwork and some well-preserved murals within.

Htilominlo Paya

ထီးလိုမင်းလိုဘုရား • Main entrance off the Bagan–Nyaung U road • Daily 8am–6pm

Roughly halfway between Nyaung U and Old Bagan, the **Htilominlo Paya** is one of the last and finest of Bagan's temples, and a perfect example of the city's late-period architecture. The temple was constructed by King Htilominlo (aka Nantaungmya, ruled 1211–35), the youngest of the five sons of King Narapatisithu. According to legend, the five princes were placed around a white umbrella and Htilominlo elected ruler when the umbrella fortuitously tilted in his direction. The grateful young king subsequently commemorated the event by building a temple on the site of the decisive ceremony. History suggests that the umbrella's judgement may have been flawed, however, since Htilominlo turned out to be one of Bagan's less effectual rulers, more interested in temple-building than in overseeing affairs of the realm.

His temple is undeniably impressive, even so, built in the characteristic double-cube structure reminiscent of the Sulamani and Thatbyinnyu temples (even if the entire inner courtyard has been transformed into a miniature tourist bazaar packed with assorted shops and stalls). The exterior is notable for its exceptionally fine stucco carvings, featuring dozens of ferocious *kirtimukha* arranged around the cornice, spewing upside-down lotuses out of their gaping, fang-filled mouths. Four large gilded Buddhas sit inside, with extensive geometrical murals covering the walls.

Upali Thein

ဥပါလိသိမ် • Next to main road, 250m west of the Htilominlo Paya • Daily 8am–6pm

Erected during the reign of King Kyazwa (ruled 1235–50), the small but striking **Upali Thein** is one of Bagan's few surviving ordination halls (*thein*). The building looks unlike any other in Bagan – its steeply ridged roof and lean-to aisles possibly modelled after now-vanished wooden buildings of the period, with two tiers of quaint lozenge-shaped battlements (an eighteenth-century addition) and a tiny spire on the top.

A steel frame supports the lopsided **interior**, damaged during the 1975 earthquake, with a single Buddha statue at the end. The walls are decorated with intricately detailed murals depicting various Jataka scenes in pale greens, dark reds and whites. These are not original, however, having been added in the eighteenth century, and the figures are much larger than those in traditional Bagan paintings.

Alotawpyi-gu-hpaya

အလိုတော်ပြည့်ဂူဘုရား • About halfway between Nyaung U and Old Bagan, right next to Anawrahta Rd • Daily 7am–9pm

The eye-catching **Alotawpyi-gu-hpaya** is one of the few temples between Nyaung U and Old Bagan still in daily use, normally busy with locals (although relatively few tourists stop by) and offering a lively contrast to the time-warped monuments surrounding it on all sides. Built in the twelfth century by King Kyansittha, the ancient shrine with latticed brick windows is pure early-period in style, while the incongruously glitzy gilded stupa above has a distinct touch of Hollywood about it, giving the building the air of a very elderly lady in an outrageously loud hat. The modern tiled **interior** is very much that of a working temple rather than an archeological monument, its walls decorated with crude but colourful orange and brown murals of identikit Buddhas lined up in rows. A large stupa stands directly behind the temple, with traces of green glazed tiles still visible on its bell.

Ananda Paya

အာနန္ဒာဘုရား • Daily 8am–6pm

Completed in 1090 during the reign of King Kyansittha, the **Ananda Paya** is one of the largest and most stunning of all the Bagan temples, its landmark spire rising 52m high above the surrounding plains. The Ananda is generally considered the culminating masterpiece of early-period Bagan architecture, although it also hints at the city's later architectural style, with its six rooftop terraces and soaring spire giving it an upwardly mobile profile quite unlike earlier, horizontally challenged designs. The ground plan (a Greek cross embedded in a square) is also innovative, with four entrances rather than the customary one, while the absence of the usual brick-latticework fill inside the window frames allows far more light inside compared to the atmospheric gloom which had previously been the norm in Bagan shrines.

The exterior

Before plunging inside, it's worth circumambulating the temple to have a look at the building's superb **exterior**. The four imposing entrances are richly decorated with miniature stupas and extravagant flame-shaped door and window pediments, while above, the corners of the six terraces are crowded with assorted miniature stupas and statues of lions and Buddhas. Fine glazed tiles depicting various Jataka scenes (the largest such collection in Bagan) run around all six terraces; those adorning the base of the temple depict (on the western side of the building) the Buddha's victory over Mara and his monstrous army and (on the eastern side) *devas* holding auspicious symbols. Look out, too, for the unusual double-bodied chinthe which sit at ground level guarding the corners of the structure.

The interior

The Ananda boasts one of Bagan's finest **interiors**. The four entrances are each protected by a pair of door guardians seated in niches. Beyond, there's an unusual double ambulatory (one ambulatory enclosed within the other), with huge teak doors hung at each of the four entrances to the outer ambulatory and numerous ornate niches lining the ambulatory walls, with small carvings within including Buddha figures and scenes from his life.

Four enormous **Buddhas** stand on each side of the temple's central core, with further pairs of guardian figures in front. The Buddha statues on the north and south sides are original (in the *dharmachakra*, or teaching, mudra). The other two are replacements in the later Konbaung style for original statues destroyed by fire in the 1600s. Sitting at the feet of the western Buddha (in the *abhaya* – "have no fear" – mudra) are two lacquer figures said to depict King Kyansittha and Shin Arahan (see p.355). The eastern Buddha – with arms by its side and hands outstretched – is unusual in that it doesn't conform to any recognized mudra. The small object between the image's fingertips is said to be a herbal pill, perhaps symbolizing the cure from suffering offered by the Buddha's teachings. Quirkiest of all is the face of the southern Buddha, which changes from a pensive pout to a cheesy grin as you walk away from it.

Old Bagan

ပုဂံမြို့ဟောင်း

The monuments clustered within the old walled city of **OLD BAGAN** are without doubt the finest in Bagan, and an excellent place to start exploring the archeological zone. The sights here are also remarkably diverse, covering all the various periods and styles of Bagan, from the ancient **Bupaya** and bunker-like **Pahtothamya Paya** through to the flamboyant late-style **Gawdawpalin Paya**, as well as several curiosities including the *nat*-inspired **Tharaba Gate**, the ersatz-Indian **Mahabodhi Paya**, the **Pitakat Taik** library and the Hindu **Nathlaung Kyaung** shrine – not to mention the magnificent **Thatbyinnyu Paya**, one of Bagan's greatest temples.

Tharaba Gate

သရပါ တံခါး

Approaching from Nyaung U, the entrance to the formerly walled city of Old Bagan is via the quaint **Tharaba Gate**, the only one of Old Bagan's twelve former gateways to survive. Sections of the original city walls, constructed by King Pyinbya (ruled 846–76) in 849, can still be seen on either side. Casting aside Buddhist orthodoxy, the gate is dedicated to the two Mahagiri (see box, p.217) **nat spirits**, popularly known as Maung Tinde ("Mr Handsome"), whose image stands in a niche on the left-hand side of the gate, and his sister Shwemyethna ("Golden Face") opposite.

Bagan Golden Palace

ရွှေနန်းတော် • Daily 6.30am–10pm • $5

A shameless eyesore in the heart of historic Bagan, the **Bagan Golden Palace** complex claims to re-create the royal splendour of former Bagan kings, complete with overblown pseudo-traditional architecture, extraneous quantities of gilded paint and other stylistic nonsense – although it's really just an OTT shopping and entertainment venue designed to squeeze easy dollars out of the passing coach-party trade. The inflated entrance price gives you full access to the complex's overpriced souvenir shops and so-called "bazaars", but not much else.

Royal Palace Archeological Site

ဆာဒဘုရား:

Opposite the ersatz Bagan Golden Palace, the **Royal Palace Archeological Site** protects the uninteresting remains of Bagan's original palace complex. It's not currently open to visitors, which is no great shame, and you can in any case get a decent view of the modest excavations by peering through the roadside fence.

Mahabodhi Paya

မဟာဗောဓိဘုရား: • Daily 8am–6pm

Looking like an exotic foreign stranger amid the surrounding Bamar- and Mon-style temples, the **Mahabodhi Paya** is built in imitation of (and named after) the great Buddhist temple at Bodhgaya in North India, erected on the site of the bodhi tree under which the Buddha gained enlightenment. Built during the reign of Htilominlo, the temple is dominated by its mighty pyramidal tower, subdivided into horizontal niches filled with hundreds of small seated Buddhas gazing placidly down at the passing tourists below. It all looks very Indian, although in fact the temple is a far from exact copy of the Bodhgaya original – whether this was the result of an intentional redesign or the consequence of dodgy building contractors remains unclear.

On the north side of the Mahabodhi, the fragmentary brick ruins of the **Ratana-Gara** ("Gem House") house Bagan's only extant examples of glazed painted tiles, although they're so badly worn as to be virtually indecipherable.

Bupaya

ဗူးဘုရား: • Daily 7am–9pm

Commanding the Ayeyarwady from atop a high bluff overlooking the water, the **Bupaya** ("Gourd Stupa") is Old Bagan's most popular place of local worship, with an atmosphere of cheerful Burmese hustle and bustle quite different from other temples hereabouts. The small complex's major feature is its unusual **gilded stupa**, raised above the water on a crenellated white terrace, with steps leading down to the river below. Said to date back to the reign of the semi-legendary third king of Bagan, Pyuswati

(162–243), the stupa's distinctively bulbous, gourd-shaped outline is typical of early Pyu architecture – although what you see now is actually a reconstruction, the original having been toppled during the 1975 earthquake.

Gawdawpalin Paya

ကန်တော့ပလ္လင်ဘုရား• Daily 8am–6pm

A skinny supermodel amid the venerable monuments of Old Bagan, the **Gawdawpalin Paya** was begun during the reign of Narapatisithu (ruled 1174–1211), completed by his son, Htilominlo, and then seriously damaged in the 1975 earthquake, although it's now been patched up. A superb late-period double-cube structure, it looks like a taller, slimmed-down version of the Thatbyinnyu, with a slender spire reaching a height of 55m – one of the loftiest in Bagan. Fine stuccowork showing the usual *kirtimukha* with pearls and garlands decorates the exterior, although the interior is disappointingly plain, save for some traces of floral murals around the four main entrances.

Bagan Archeological Museum

ရှေးဟောင်းသုတေသနပြိုတိုက်• Daily except Mon 9am–4pm • K500 • No photography

Given the wealth of attractions in Bagan, you might consider skipping the largely lacklustre **Bagan Archeological Museum**, housed in a large and unforgivably ugly building in ersatz-traditional Burmese style plonked right in the heart of historic Old Bagan.

Entering the museum, the main hall on the **ground floor** has some fine sandstone Buddhist carving from the Gubyaukgye and Nagayon temples in Myinkaba and a pair of fine pillar inscriptions erected by Kyansittha. The attached "Showroom of Bagan Period Literature" is full of pillar inscriptions recording the various buildings donated by local notables to Bagan's monastic community, along with accompanying lands, slaves and the occasional cow. Here you'll also find the museum's most important exhibit, the **Myazedi inscription**, one of a pair of identical carvings, the other being at the Myazedi temple in Myinkaba (see p.206). Also on the ground floor, the "Bagan Period Arts and Crafts" showroom is worth a quick look for its rare cloth painting and models of outlandish Bagan-era hairstyles, plus a mishmash of other artefacts including some interesting stone carvings and the inevitable pots.

Pickings are thinner up on the **first floor**, although the "Buddha Images" room is worth a quick peek, including further images from the Nagayon Paya; an eleventh-century Buddha fashioned from an alloy of five metals (now protected by stout golden bars); and some fine wooden, stone and lacquer Buddha images.

Mimalaung Kyaung

မီးမလောင်ကျောင်း• Directly behind the drink stalls opposite the Bagan Archeological Museum • Daily 8am–6pm

The engaging **Mimalaung Kyaung** ("The Temple Which Fire Cannot Burn") is one of Old Bagan's prettiest monuments. Built in the reign of Narapatisithu, the small temple acquired its soubriquet after surviving a devastating conflagration in 1225. Its fire-resistant qualities are enhanced by the unusually high platform on which it's built, reinforced with huge buttresses and ascended via a small staircase lined with a large pair of cheerfully grinning chinthe. The small **shrine** on the platform at the top is similarly unusual, topped with a fancifully sculpted roof and slender spire, while its elevated position also provides one of the finest **views** in Old Bagan, with the monumental Thatbyinnyu close by, the Ananda temple rising behind and various other monuments dotted below.

Pahtothamya Paya

ပုထိုးသားများဘုရား• Follow the dirt road in front of the Mimalaung Kyaung for around 250m • Daily 8am–6pm

Built sometime in the tenth or eleventh century, the brooding **Pahtothamya Paya** is a low-set, heavy structure in classic early-period style, with tiny latticed-brick windows and an incongruously slight and inconsequential Sri Lankan-style stupa plonked on top – typical of the city's oldest temples before the curved shikhara-style tower became the superstructure of choice. Entrance to the **interior** is through an arched antechamber which looks rather like the inside of a capsized ship. Blackened mosaic-style murals line the walls, while a brooding Buddha sits in near-darkness in the central shrine. Past here, a gloomy and intensely atmospheric **ambulatory** leads around the shrine. Shine a torch, and the walls come alive with marvellously detailed murals – some of the oldest in Bagan – captioned in Mon and including scenes showing Prince Siddhartha on a boating trip and a fine panel depicting the legendary visit of Kaladevila to the infant Buddha-to-be, the sage splendidly bearded and clad in an extravagant red cloak, holding the tiny Prince Siddhartha aloft in one hand.

Nathlaung Kyaung and around

နတ်လျောင်ကျောင်း • Daily 8am–6pm

The modest **Nathlaung Kyaung** is one of the oldest temples in the city, possibly dating from the reign of Anawrahta, or perhaps as much as a century earlier. It's also notable for being Bagan's only Hindu temple, built for Indian merchants visiting the city and dedicated to Vishnu (the name means "Temple Where The Nats Are Confined" – perhaps a reference to the foreign Hindu deities contained within). The compact square structure, topped with an elaborately moulded spire, is now somewhat reduced from its former dimensions, the original entrance hall having disappeared. Niches lining the exterior formerly housed images of the ten incarnations of Vishnu, although only seven survive, all pretty battered. Note, also, the dramatic flame-shaped pediment over the entrance, perhaps the oldest of its kind in Bagan and marking the first appearance of what would become one of the city's most distinctive architectural motifs.

Inside, a small ambulatory surrounds a single shrine. Facing the entrance is a modern sculpture of Vishnu reclining on the cosmic serpent Anata-Sesha, whose successive coilings and uncoilings are said to alternately move time forward and instigate creation, and then reverse it, causing the universe to end. Smaller images of the three major gods of the Hindu pantheon – Brahma, Vishnu and Shiva – hover above. Further images of Vishnu adorn the three other sides of the shrine, each holding a disc, mace, trident and lotus.

Standing directly opposite the Nathlaung Kyaung is the **Ngakywenadaung Pagoda**, a small, unusually bulbous stupa looking like a miniature version of the nearby Bupaya. Traces of the green glazed tiles that originally covered it can still be seen.

Thatbyinnyu Paya and around

သဗ္ဗညုဘုရား • Daily 8am–6pm

Dominating the skyline of Old Bagan is the monumental **Thatbyinnyu Paya**, one of the largest temples anywhere in Bagan. It's also the tallest, rising to a height of around 66m, although it's the sheer mass of the building that really impresses. Built by King Alaungsithu (ruled 1112–67), the temple marks an important transitional point between Bagan's early and late styles. This was Bagan's first fully fledged "double-cube" two-storey temple, with the main shrine placed on the upper storey and the traditional ground-floor shrine replaced with a "solid-core" structure in order to support the extra weight of the additional storey above. Each of the two storeys is topped with three terraces (now with flat roofs rather than the pitched lean-to roofs of earlier temples) and adorned with crenellations and corner stupas. Entrances are placed at each of the cardinal points – the so-called "four-faced layout" (with a slightly larger eastern portico) typical of late-period Bagan style and which, unlike earlier temples, typically only had a single entrance. The **interior** has nice traces of geometrical floral murals inside the west entrance, but is otherwise disappointingly plain.

On the northeast side of the temple, look out for the small "**tally temple**" (*gayocho*). One brick out of every ten thousand used in the construction of Thatbyinnyu was set aside for counting purposes and a whitewashed temple built with the resultant bricks – the surprising scale of the resultant structure gives a good idea of quite how many bricks were consumed by the mother temple.

4

ALAUNGSITHU AND NARATHU

The Shwegugyi Paya stands on an unusually high brick platform. According to one (particularly implausible) legend, this rose spontaneously from the ground in tribute to **King Alaungsithu**'s accumulated spiritual merit prior to the temple's construction in 1140. Twenty-three years later, it is said, the elderly and ailing king was brought back to Shwegugyi and left to die. When the king began showing unwelcome signs of recovering from his illness, his son and heir-apparent **Narathu** decided to hasten him on his way by smothering him to death in his own bedclothes, thereby murdering Alaungsithu in the temple which his own merit had helped to create. The moral of the story remains unclear.

Around 100m south of the temple, a small surviving stretch of Old Bagan's crumbling **city walls** offers fine views over the surrounding monuments.

Shwegugyi Paya

ရွှေဂူကြီး • Daily 8am–6pm

Built in 1140 during the reign of Alaungsithu, the **Shwegugyi Paya** is one of Old Bagan's most elegant temples, relatively small but perfectly formed. Like the nearby Thatbyinnyu, the Shwegugyi exemplifies the transition between Bagan's weighty Mon- and Pyu-influenced early style and the lighter, airier and more upwardly mobile late style, with its graceful curvilinear tower and stupa finials rising needle-like from the temple's roof.

Unusually, the main entrance is on the north side (rather than the customary east), presumably in order to face the nearby royal palace. A large Buddha sits facing the main entrance, opposite which (on your right as you enter) stands a pair of ancient Pali **inscriptions** recording, among other details, the temple's construction, which it is claimed took just seven months. Elsewhere traces of fine plasterwork decoration are still visible, along with three smaller Buddha figures in the ambulatory, roughly caked in gold leaf applied by dutiful worshippers.

The temple is also one of Bagan's most popular **sunset-viewing spots** (see box opposite), offering splendid views from its narrow upper terraces, although space is at a premium, and the crowds unrelenting.

Pitakat Taik

ပိဋကတ်တိုက် • Daily 8am–6pm

The unusual **Pitakat Taik** is thought to be the library built by King Anawrahta (ruled 1044–78) to house the thirty sets of the Tripitaka (the major sacred texts of the Buddhist canon) seized during the loot of the city of Thaton in 1057, and which Anawrahta is said to have borne home in triumph on the 32 white elephants of the vanquished King Manuha. The basic plan of the building is similar to that of the traditional Bagan temple with the addition of three small staircases leading up to the low platform on which the building is set. The crowning spire and extravagant peacock-style finials adorning the five-tiered roof were added by King Bodawpaya in 1783.

The Central Plain

The **CENTRAL PLAIN** is Bagan at its most iconic: untrammelled by human habitation, hundreds of temples rise out of the sandy, scrub-covered plains like the archetypal remnants of some fabulous lost civilization. The scale of the temples and stupas here are nothing short of astounding. They feature several of Bagan's most majestic monuments, including the landmark **Shwesandaw Pagoda**, the super-sized **Dhammayangyi Paya**, and the exquisite **Sulamani Paya**, perhaps the most perfect of all Bagan temples.

Shwesandaw Pagoda

ရွှေဆံတော်ဘုရား • Off Anawrahta Rd, roughly opposite the Ananda Paya • Daily 8am–6pm

Built around 1057 during the reign of Anawrahta, the **Shwesandaw Pagoda** ("Golden Sacred Hair Relic") was the very first of Bagan's great monumental stupas. It was constructed to enshrine a hair relic of the Buddha presented to Anawrahta by the king of Bago in gratitude for his military assistance in fending off a Khmer invasion. The design of the stupa established a model subsequently followed throughout Bagan, with a series of square terraces (decorated with rounded battlements) supporting a huge bell-shaped stupa (*anda*). The stupa itself sits on an octagonal base, providing a structural transition between the square terraces and round superstructure. Steep staircases lead up all four sides of the structure, providing access to the various terraces; these were formerly lined with glazed tiles illustrating the Jatakas, although most have now vanished. The stupa is one of Bagan's most popular **sunset-viewing spots** (see box below), although the marvellous views over Old Bagan are slightly compromised by the eyesore Archeological Museum, and the relatively narrow terraces get horribly packed come sundown.

Right next to the stupa, inside the temple compound, look out for the **Shinbinthalyaung Temple**, a long, low, brick building housing Bagan's largest reclining Buddha (18m long) in *parinibbana* pose.

Lawkahteikpan Paya

လောကထိပ်ပန် • Around 150m north of the Shwesandaw Pagoda • Daily 8am–6pm

The diminutive **Lawkahteikpan Paya** is easily missed but worth a look for its fine murals. Black-and-white Jataka strip paintings decorate the sides of the entrance hall, with two Buddha footprints on the ceiling above, while the shrine's gilded Buddha image is framed by a series of larger and more colourful painted scenes showing the usual events from the life of the Buddha, including the ever-popular Temptation of Mara (at the top of the arch behind the image on the right-hand side); Mara himself is seated grandly on top of a white elephant.

Dhammayangyi Paya

ဓမ္မရံကြီးဘုရား • Follow the dirt track off Anawrahta Rd opposite the track leading to the Ananda Paya • Daily 8am–6pm

A brooding presence amid the monuments of Bagan's Central Plain, the huge **Dhammayangyi Paya** is cloaked in sombre legend. Built by the homicidal **King Narathu**

SUNSET-VIEWING TEMPLES

Sitting high on the terrace of an ancient temple watching the sun set over the plains below is one of Bagan's essential experiences, although the decision in 2013 to close many of the temples' upper terraces for conservation purposes means that the choice of sunset-viewing perches is now somewhat limited, and the most popular places can get unbearably crowded. Horse-drawn carriage drivers can often point you in the direction of lesser-known viewing spots.

The classic place to watch the sun go down is the **Shwesandaw Pagoda** (see above), which is strategically located close to many of Bagan's landmark monuments, though it can get appallingly busy – arrive early. The same can be said for the almost equally popular **Shwegugyi Paya** (see opposite) in Old Bagan; nearby, largely crowd-free alternatives include the Mahazedi stupa and the **Mimalaung Kyaung** (see p.198). Another popular spot is the well-positioned **Buledi**, a large stupa off Anawrahta Road between Nyaung U and Old Bagan, although again space is at a premium (to reach it, take the dirt road just east of the Alotawpyi-gu-hpaya following the sign to "Bulethi/Sulamani"). The nearby **Shweleiktoo Pagoda** offers equally good views, and is usually a bit less crowded. In the Central Plain, the spacious terrace atop the **Pyathada Paya** (see p.202) offers plenty of room and fewer crowds, although it's now being steadily discovered by the coach-party brigade.

One final option is the government's eyesore **Bagan Viewing Tower** (daily 6am–10.30pm; K5000). It's overpriced, rather too far from the major landmarks and not nearly as atmospheric as the temples, although it does have the advantage that, being on it, you won't have to look at it.

(ruled 1167–71), the Dhammayangyi's construction was planned as a grandiose act of royal merit-making which, Narathu apparently hoped, would be sufficient to wipe out the bad karma accumulated following the murder of his father (see box, p.200), brother and wife. In the event, Narathu himself was assassinated just two years after taking the throne by an eight-man hit squad despatched from India by the unhappy father of his murdered bride.

Modelled after the Ananda Paya, the Dhammayangyi is instantly recognizable not only for its sheer size but also for its distinctive outline. The temple is unique among later Bagan monuments in that it lacks an upper storey, compensating instead with a series of no fewer than six steep terraces (rather than the usual three) placed on top of the shrine, giving it a uniquely ziggurat-like appearance. The collapse of the original shikhara-style spire that formerly crowned the edifice further accentuates the building's pyramidal profile.

The **exterior** is notable for its superb masonry – it's said that Narathu ordered the bricks to be fitted together so tightly that not even a needle could be inserted between them (and lopped off the hands of any workmen who failed to achieve the necessary close-fitting finish). The stark **interior** boast a few traces of murals around the four entrance porches but is otherwise bare and faintly melancholy, with high corridors and the squeaking of bats and cooing of doves in the darkness overhead. There was originally a double ambulatory, although the entrances to the inner ambulatory have been mysteriously sealed up. One tradition says that this was an act of revenge against the godless Narathu, although a more prosaic explanation is that the inner corridor was bricked up in order to prevent the huge structure from collapsing. A pair of Buddhas sit opposite the western entrance, with the historical Gautama and the future Maitreya placed next to each other – Bagan's only example of two major Buddha images placed side by side. Two stone inscriptions in Pali recording the temple's construction can be seen directly behind the paired images.

Sulamani Paya

စူဠာမဏိဘုရား: • Turn left along the dirt track at the fork just before you reach the Dhammayangyi Paya, or take the earlier dirt track off Anawrahta Rd signed to "Bulethi/Sulamani" • Daily 8am–6pm

Sitting in splendid isolation more or less at the dead centre of the archeological zone is the magnificent **Sulamani Paya**, built by King Narapatisithu in around 1183. The Sulamani isn't the biggest or tallest of the archeological zone's myriad temples but for many people it's the most beautiful of all Bagan's monuments, and the iconic example of the city's late-style architecture in all its flamboyant finery. The double-cube structure was perhaps modelled on that of the Thatbyinnyu (and subsequently copied by other temples such as the Gawdawpalin and Htilominlo), although none quite matches the Sulamani's perfect proportions, with two storeys of equal height, each topped by three terraces, striking a delicate balance between the vertical and horizontal. The graceful shikhara above is actually a reconstruction following the 1975 earthquake – close up you can see how much newer the bricks are compared to the rest of the building, although from a distance it looks fine.

The **exterior** boasts fine plasterwork along with unusual green and yellow glazed decorative tiles (also visible above some of the doors). **Inside**, the temple's entertaining murals are an eighteenth-century Konbaung-era addition, with large figures (including a couple of huge reclining Buddhas) painted in an engagingly naïve style.

Pyathada Paya

ပြိဿဒါး:ဘုရား: • Follow the dirt road past the Sulamani Paya for around 750m • Daily 8am–6pm

Buried away amid a labyrinth of dirt tracks in the depths of the Central Plain, the **Pyathada Paya** is a singularly odd-looking late-period temple, with a large lower level and a small and decidedly cursory rooftop shrine – it actually looks as if only the lower half was finished, and a much large upper storey originally intended. Whatever the reason, by serendipitous chance this has resulted in an unusually large and spacious rooftop terrace, almost as if expressly designed for sunset viewing (see box, p.201), which is what the temple is now best known for.

Dhammayazika Pagoda

ဓမ္မရာဇိကာဘုရား · 3km northeast of New Bagan, off the Minnanthu Rd · Daily 8am–6pm

Stranded way out at the very edge of the archeological zone, a considerable distance from any other major monument, the **Dhammayazika Pagoda** is a bit of a hike to reach but well worth the effort. Sitting in an attractive garden-style compound, the impressively large gilded pagoda was built during the reign of Narapatisithu in 1198 to enshrine holy relics presented by the ruler of Sri Lanka. The complex is notable mainly for its unusual **pentagonal layout**, a design which can also be found at a few other Bagan temples, but nowhere else in the Buddhist world. It's thought that the five-sided structure resulted from the desire to provide a shrine to the future Buddha Maitreya alongside the four Buddhas of the present world cycle – Kakusandha, Konagamana, Kassapa and Gautama (see box, p.71) – who are commonly found in most Bagan temples, one at each cardinal point. Five gateways lead into the five-sided enclosure, with the central stupa sitting on a pentagonal terrace. Standing around the base of the stupa are five large and beautifully decorated shrines, each with a gilded Buddha and traces of Konbaung-era murals inside, while four lions and a pair of seated guardian figures keep watch on the roofs above, topped with intricately carved little shikhara-style towers. Fine stucco decoration and glazed Jataka panels can be seen around the stupa terraces, which are also studded with an unusual number of dragon-mouthed waterspouts.

Around Minnanthu

The cluster of low-key monuments between the Bagan Viewing Tower and the small village of **MINNANTHU** isn't the most exciting in Bagan, although it's the quietest area within the archeological zone and you'll most likely have many of the temples here largely to yourself. Small examples of late-period architecture predominate, with some superb murals.

Nandamannya Paya and around

နန္ဒမညာဘုရား · 1km north of Minnanthu · Daily 8am–6pm (if the temple's locked, ask at the Payathonzu Paya for someone to let you in)

The modest little **Nandamannya Paya**, built in 1248 during the reign of Kyazwa, is of interest mainly for its murals – some of Bagan's most famous. These include a fine painting of the **birth of the Buddha** showing Prince Siddhartha emerging from the hip of his mother, Queen Maya, and a well-known depiction of the **Temptation of Mara**, in which scantily clad nymphs attempt vainly to rouse the Buddha from his meditation (face the shrine's Buddha statue and the Mara mural is behind you in the left corner at around waist height, while the birth of the Buddha is on your right, to the left side of the window).

Behind the Nandamannya look out for the odd little **Kyat Kan Kyaung**, a modern monastic building placed in a large hole in the ground in order to minimize outside distraction.

Thambula Paya

သမ္ဘူလဘုရား · 200m south of the Nandamannya Paya · Daily 8am–6pm (If the temple's locked, ask at the Payathonzu Paya for someone to let you in)

Similar in appearance to the nearby Nandamannya, the pretty little late-style **Thambula Paya** (1255) is home to another superb tranche of murals – and for once the airy interior, with its high ceilings and tall pointed arches, is sufficiently light that you probably won't need a torch to see them. A profusion of densely detailed paintings covers virtually every surface, and includes floral decorations, miniature mosaic-pattern Buddhas and, in the west portico and elsewhere, several intricately painted inscriptions. The murals in the north porch are especially fine, and look out too for the unusual painting of a boat race inside the south porch.

Payathonzu Paya

ဘုရားသုံးဆူ • 300m south of the Thambula Paya • Daily 8am–6pm

A true curiosity, the unique **Payathonzu Paya** ("Temple of Three Buddhas") comprises three identical small tower-topped shrines joined together in a line and connected by a single corridor. The shrines house some of Bagan's most unusual **murals**, which are light enough to see without a torch. Entrance is via the middle shrine; this and the shrine to your left (the eastern shrine) are richly decorated in unusual paintings showing a pronounced Mahayana or possibly even Tantric Buddhist influence, with many-armed figures, embracing couples, strange mythological animals and (in the eastern shrine) a small picture of a three-headed Brahma. At the opposite end of the temple, the walls of the western shrine are entirely bare, suggesting that the temple wasn't finished.

Leimyethna Paya

လေးမျက်နှာဘုရား • 200m south of the Payathonzu Paya • Daily 8am–6pm

Sitting on a platform reached by a rustic stairway roofed in corrugated iron, the **Leimyethna Paya** ("Temple of the Four Faces") is a fine late-period temple, built in 1223 by a minister of King Htilominlo. The intricately designed shrine features a mass of decorative pediments, miniature corner-stupas and moulded terraces, with a fine shikhara above. Inside, the light, airy interior is brightly decorated, with many mosaic-pattern black and gold Buddhas in the four porches and colourful, engagingly naïve-style murals on the interior walls and central cube, quite different from those at other temples nearby.

Myinkaba to New Bagan

The monuments stretching south of Old Bagan through the village of **MYINKABA** and on into **NEW BAGAN** are a bit of a mishmash, lacking the stellar attractions of other parts of Bagan but offering an interesting cross section of Bagan architecture through the ages. They include the small but architecturally significant shrines of **Nanpaya** and **Apeyadana Paya**, as well as the majestic **Mingalazedi**.

Mingalazedi

မင်္ဂလာစေတီ • Bagan–Chauk Rd, just south of Old Bagan • Daily 8am–6pm

Just south of the Old Bagan city walls, the **Mingalazedi** ("Blessing Stupa") was built during the reign of King Narathihapate (ruled 1256–87) – the last major monument to be constructed in Bagan before the Mongol incursions of 1287 sent the kingdom plummeting into decline. One of the finest of all Bagan's late-style stupas, the Mingalazedi is reminiscent in outline of the famous Shwedagon in Yangon, whose proportions it is said to have copied. Fine glazed tiles depicting Jataka scenes are arrayed around the base of the stupa (there were originally 1061, of which 561 remain), while staircases (now closed) lead up through three terraces, their corners decorated with Indian-style *kalasa* (nectar pots).

The stupa's creator, **Narathihapate**, is remembered chiefly for his notorious gluttony (three hundred dishes per meal were considered obligatory) and for his subsequent headlong flight from the invading Mongols, which earned him the sobriquet of *Tayok-pyay-min*, roughly translated as "The King who ran away from the Chinese".

Gubyaukgyi Paya (Myinkaba)

ဂူပြောက်ကြီးဘုရား • Bagan–Chauk Rd • Daily 8am–6pm • To reach it, turn left on the road downhill just at the beginning of Myinkaba village (if you reach the *Sar Pi Thar* restaurant you've gone too far) – it's directly in front of the Myazedi, easily spotted thanks to its distinctive gilded stupa

Colourful murals – some of the oldest in Bagan – can be found at the small but florid **Gubyaukgyi Paya** (not to be confused with the identically named temple in Wet Kyi

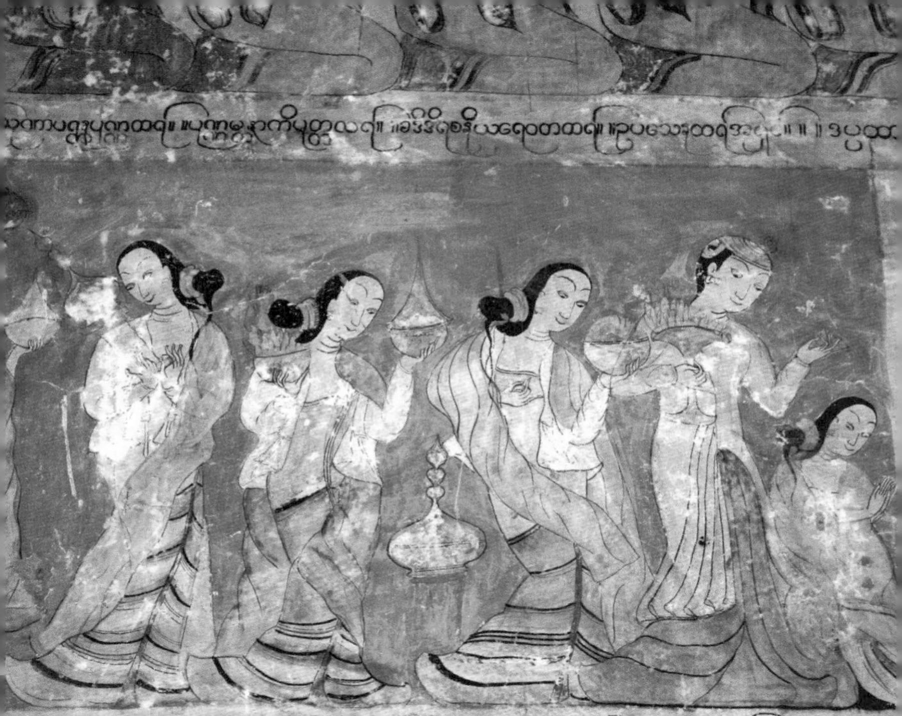

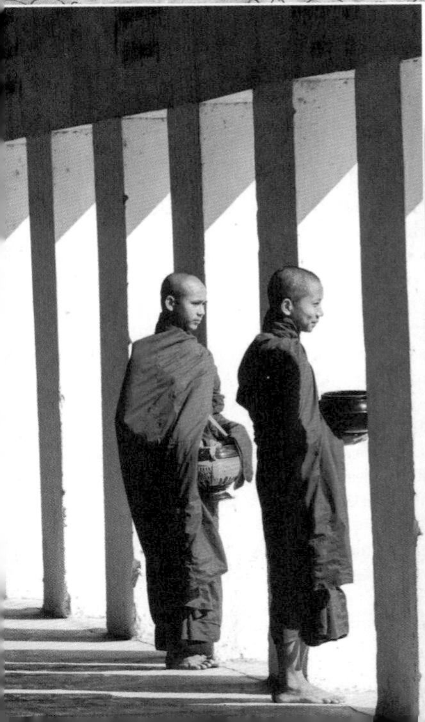

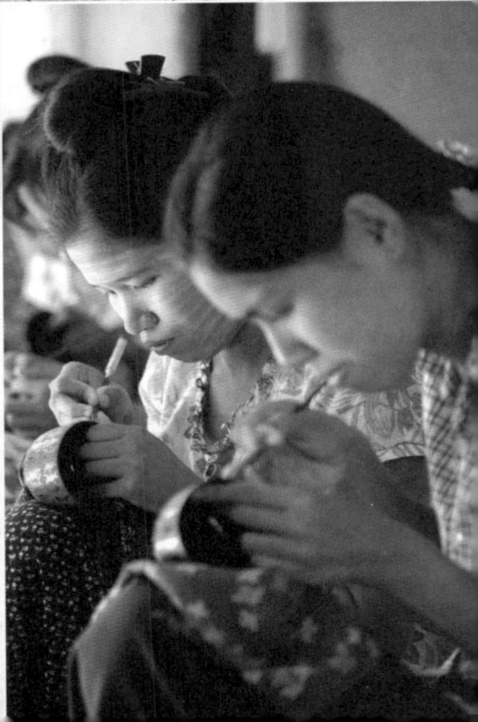

Inn), built around 1113 by Prince Rajakumar (aka Yazakumar), a son of King Kyansittha, in honour of his recently deceased father. The temple also offers an intriguing snapshot of Bagan architecture in evolution. Early-period hallmarks – the low-set, single-storey structure with an interior kept deliberately dark thanks to the almost completed bricked-up windows (carved here into unusual geometrical designs) – dominate, although there are hints of the emerging late-period style in the large shikhara and small rooftop shrine; the latter would subsequently develop into the fully fledged second storey characteristic of Bagan's later "double-cube" temples.

The **exterior** features some exceptionally fine stuccowork and carving, particularly around the elaborate window frames and pediments. Not much light gets into the gloomy **interior**. The best paintings – showing various Jataka scenes captioned in Mon – are in the ambulatory around the shrine, although it's very dark and you won't see anything without a torch.

Myazedi

မြေစေတီဘုရား• Bagan–Chauk Rd • Daily 8am–6pm

Immediately behind the Gubyaukgyi stands the contrasting **Myazedi** ("Jade Stupa"), centred around a large, brilliantly gilded stupa. A busy, modern, working temple, it's of minimal architectural distinction but is notable as the home of one of the two so-called **Myazedi inscriptions** (the other one being in the Bagan Archeological Museum). Carved onto a large pillar on the south side of the stupa (now protected behind bars in an ugly little concrete shelter), the inscription records the creation of the adjacent Gubyaukgyi temple by Prince Rajakumar, with the text repeated in four different languages – Pyu, Mon, Pali and Burmese – on each side of the square pillar. It's the longest extant inscription in Pyu ever discovered, while the parallel translations on the pillar's four faces served (like a kind of Burmese Rosetta Stone) as the basis for the deciphering of the previously untranslatable Pyu script in the early twentieth century.

Manuha Paya

မနုဟာဘုရား• Bagan–Chauk Rd • Daily 7am–9pm

Bang in the centre of Myinkaba village, the large and always lively **Manuha Paya** actually dates all the way back to 1059, despite its relatively modern appearance. According to legend, the temple was endowed by the captive Manuha, the former king of the Mon city of Thaton (see p.331), who had been brought back to Bagan by the all-conquering King Anawrahta and held prisoner in Myinkaba.

The temple itself is one of the earliest two-storey structures in Bagan, looking a bit like the Thatbyinnyu but smaller and more dumpily proportioned. A huge golden alms bowl stands in the entrance hall, with three huge Buddhas squeezed into a trio of tiny shrines behind – their cramped living quarters are said to symbolize the captivity and reduced circumstances of Manuha himself. A large reclining Buddha occupies a fourth, slightly larger, shrine at the back of the temple.

Nanpaya

နန်းဘုရားကျောင်း• Directly behind the Manuha Paya • Daily 8am–6pm • To reach it, exit the courtyard of the Manuha Paya via the steps in the southwest corner (i.e. the rear left-hand side as you look at it from the entrance), turn left and it's right in front of you; alternatively, follow the small track around the Manuha Paya wall on the left side of the temple through the red and gold arch and you'll see it almost immediately on your left

Like the adjacent Manuha Paya, the **Nanpaya** ("Palace Temple") is closely associated with Manuha, the deposed king of Thaton. One legend states that Manuha lived here during his years of exile; another, that it was built on the site of Manuha's former residence by his grandson during the reign of Narapatisithu, although the temple's distinctively low and heavy-set early-period design style suggests that it's at least a century too old for this particular theory to be true.

Whatever its provenance, the Nanpaya is one of Bagan's more offbeat structures. It's unusual chiefly for being constructed largely of sandstone rather than the customary brick, while the stumpy little shikhara-style curvilinear tower on top may have been the first of its kind in Bagan, setting a trend for rooftop towers rather than stupas which would henceforth be the city's defining style. Note too the finely carved floral frieze running around the base of the windows, with tiny *hamsa* inserted within each swirl of leaves.

The **interior** is similarly interesting, with a unique open-plan arrangement featuring four massive sandstone pillars. Etched onto the pillars are some of Bagan's finest carvings. Gape-mouthed *kirtimukha* are shown on two sides of each pillar, while the other sides sport three-headed images of the Brahma (often co-opted into Buddhist mythology) holding a pair of lotus flowers. A now-vanished Buddha statue originally stood in the centre.

Apeyadana Paya

အပေါ်ယံရတနာဘုရား• Bagan–Chauk Rd, just south of Myinkaba village • Daily 8am–6pm

Named after (and possibly commissioned by) King Kyansittha's first wife, the diminutive **Apeyadana Paya** (or Abeyadana) is a superb example of Bagan's early-period architecture, its exterior decorated with fine brick-lattice windows and with a Sri Lankan-style rooftop stupa above (very similar to the one at the Pahtothamya in Old Bagan, which was built at roughly the same time). Inside sits an image of the Buddha flanked by his two chief disciples, Sariputra and Mogallana, while many beautiful **murals** adorn the entrance hall and very dark ambulatory (bring a torch). Queen Apeyadana, originally from Bengal in India, was possibly a Mahayana Budhist, which perhaps explains the presence of murals depicting assorted Mahayana Bodhisattvas and Hindu gods including Vishnu, Shiva, Brahma and Indra.

Nagayon Paya

နဂါးရုံဘုရား• Bagan–Chauk Rd, 200m south of the Apeyadana Paya • Daily 8am–6pm

Built during the reign of Kyansittha, the **Nagayon Paya** is a superb example of Bagan's early style at its most flamboyant. The entire temple has a slightly theatrical look, raised on an eye-catchingly high terrace and done up with a showbiz super-abundance of mini-stupas, pretty geometrical lattice windows and lots of the characteristic flame-shaped pediments so beloved of Bagan's architects – the steeply pitched double pediment over the main entrance is particularly *de trop*. Best of all is the fine curved central tower, raised up on three high terraces and looking like a trial run for the great tower of the Ananda Paya, the crowning masterpiece of Kyansittha's reign.

Inside, there's the usual shrine-plus-ambulatory layout, with a large gilded standing Buddha, his head protected by the hood of the *naga* snake-king Mucalinda (the temple's name means "Protected by the Naga Serpent"), with two smaller images standing to either side. Badly eroded paintings line the dark ambulatory (torch needed) along with finely carved Buddha statues in niches, although many of the images formerly located here have now been carted off to the Bagan Archeological Museum.

Soemingyi Kyaung

စိုးမင်းကြီးကျောင်း• Bagan–Chauk Rd, roughly midway between Myinkaba and New Bagan • Daily 8am–6pm

Built in the early thirteenth century, the **Soemingyi Kyaung** is one of the few surviving monastic buildings in Bagan, most such foundations having been constructed in wood, and long since vanished. Not much remains of the original monastery bar a small courtyard with cells on its north and south sides and a small shrine. The bases of two staircases (at the courtyard's southeast and southwest corners) can also be seen. These would originally have led up to a now-vanished wooden roof, and offer impressive views over nearby temples, including a huge stupa immediately to the north.

Sein Nyet Ama and Sein Nyet Nyima pagodas

စိန်ညက်အစ်မ၊/စိန်ညက်ညီမ • Daily 8am–6pm

The so-called "Seinnyet Sisters" – Sein Nyet Ama and Sein Nyet Nyima – are an impressive pair of contrasting late-period structures standing next to one another close to the main road. The towering **Sein Nyet Ama Pagoda** (the *ama*, or elder, sister) is said to have been built in the eleventh century by Queen Seinnyet, although stylistically it looks much later, with its fine curvilinear spire set at the top of four steep terraces.

The adjacent **Sein Nyet Nyima Pagoda** (*nyima* meaning "younger sister") is slightly smaller, with a massive conical spire decorated with deeply incised rings and traces of fine carvings and stucco *kirtimukhas* around the bell below, with Buddha statues sat in niches on each side.

Ashe Petleik Paya and Anauk Petleik Paya

အရှေ့ဖက်လိပ်ပိပ်ဘုရား၊/အနောက်ဖက်လိပ်ပိပ်ဘုရား၊ • Next to the road running down to the Lawkananda Pagoda • Daily 8am–6pm • To reach it, follow the road through the big red arch on the right a few metres past the *Floral Breeze Hotel* (with an easily missed sign to the Lakwapanada)

The twin Anauk ("Western") Petleik and Ashe ("Eastern") Petleik temples are thought to date from the reign of Anawrahta, making them two of the oldest buildings in Bagan. Both have suffered massively from the ravages of time, however, and were largely rebuilt in 1905.

The first temple you'll see, the **Anauk Petleik Paya**, is the slightly better preserved of the two, with a Sri Lankan-style bell-shaped stupa which is missing the top of its spire. The adjacent **Ashe Petleik Paya** is even more fragmentary, topped by a large stupa which is now little more than a hunk of shapeless brick. The shrines are of interest principally for their remarkable collection of **unglazed tiles** stored within and depicting the usual Jataka scenes (these formerly comprised a complete cycle of all 547 Jataka stories, although many of the tiles are now missing). The prototypes for the later glazed tiles which decorate the exteriors of many other Bagan temples, these originals were too delicate to be exposed to the elements, and thus had to be kept indoors.

Lawkananda Pagoda

လောကနန္ဒစေတီတော် • Daily 7am–9pm • Accessed by continuing past the Ashe Petleik Paya and Anauk Petleik Paya to the end of the road

Set majestically above the river, the large and dazzlingly gilded stupa of the **Lawkananda Pagoda** ("Joy of the World") dates back to the reign of Anawrahta, making it one of Bagan's oldest such structures, although it's been much rebuilt since. Enshrining a replica of the Buddha's tooth presented to Anawrahta in 1059, the pagoda remains a popular place of local worship. The temple stands close to what was once Bagan's main harbour and still commands beautiful Ayeyarwady views, although the river's somewhat quieter now than it was in Anawrahta's heyday, when the docks below would have been busy with shipping from the Mon provinces, Rakhine, Sri Lanka and elsewhere.

ARRIVAL AND DEPARTURE | **BAGAN**

BY PLANE

Bagan airport The airport is around 4km southeast of town. A taxi into town will cost around K7000; heading to the airport there's more opportunity to wangle a cheaper fare, with prices staring from around K4000 from Nyaung U, or K6000 from New Bagan.

Routes Air Bagan (☎061 60588), Yangon Airways (☎061 60475) and Air Mandalay (☎061 60774) all have daily flights leaving in the morning to Mandalay (around $60) and Yangon (around $120); Air Mandalay also operates an evening flight to Yangon. There's a K1000 departure tax on all flights. Tickets can be bought either from the airline offices in town or from many local travel agents.

Destinations Mandalay (3 daily; 30min); Ngapali (daily; 1hr 20min); Yangon (4 daily; 1hr 20min).

BY BUS

Bus station The bus station is on the Main Rd in Nyaung U, close to the Shwezigon Pagoda and not far from Thiripyitsaya 4 St and some of the Main Rd guesthouses. If you're heading on to Wet Kyin Inn, Old Bagan or New Bagan you'll need to hire a taxi or pick-up (around K5000 to Old

Bagan or K7000 to New Bagan) or hop on a (slightly cheaper) motorbike taxi. Shared pick-up trucks also run from Nyaung U market down to New Bagan.

Tickets Tickets for express buses can be bought from any of the myriad tour operators in Nyaung U, plus a couple in New Bagan (see p.210).

Routes For Pakokku (1hr) and Monywa (4hr) you'll need to catch one of the two minibuses that depart daily (7am & 9pm), or alternatively catch a pick-up (5hr) from near the market.

Destinations Kalaw (3 daily; 7hr); Magwe (3 daily; 4hr); Mandalay (hourly until 9.30pm; 7hr); Magwe (3 daily; 4hr); Meiktila (1 daily; 3hr 30min); Nyaungshwe (3 daily; 8hr 30min); Pyay (1 daily; 8hr); Taunggyi (3 daily; 9hr); Yangon (10 daily; 10hr).

BY TRAIN
Railway station The railway station is 5.5km southeast of Nyaung U, past the airport (around K7000 by taxi).
Tickets The only licensed ticket seller anywhere in Bagan is located, rather improbably, at Blue Sea (☎061 60949 or ☎09 204 0135), a frozen-food and fish wholesaler on Main Rd in Nyaung U.
Destinations Mandalay (1 daily; 8hr); Pyay (1 daily; 10hr); Yangon (1 daily; 19hr).

BY TAXI
If you can get a group together, taxis (seating three, or four at a squeeze) are a convenient and reasonably affordable option for travel further afield. Count on around $120 to Mandalay, or $150 to Inle Lake.

GETTING AROUND

Bagan's sights are spread out over a considerable distance and you'll need some kind of transport to explore all the temples.

BIKES

Cycling is an enjoyable way to explore Bagan, although most of the bikes available for rent lack gears and are often not in the best mechanical shape, which can make pedalling even fairly modest distances hard work: the sandy backroads between outlying temples can snag wheels and sap strength with surprising rapidity. If you're cycling between Nyaung U and Old Bagan, note that the wider and relatively traffic-free Anawrahta Rd offers a more peaceful ride than the narrower and busier Nyaung U–Bagan road via Wet Kyi Inn.

Bike rental There are bikes for rent all over the place in Nyaung U and New Bagan for K1500/day (although in Old Bagan you're limited to the stand outside the *Bagan Hotel River View*, which charges a rip-off K4000/day). Slightly battered six-gear bikes are available from Aung Shwe Yi Store on Main Rd in Nyaung U, and from the *San Carlo Restaurant* (see p.214) in New Bagan (K2000/day at both places).

4

BAGAN TO MANDALAY AND PYAY BY BOAT

TOURIST BOATS

A popular way of travelling between Bagan and Mandalay (or vice versa) is by taking a **cruise boat** along the Ayeyarwady – some people find this a rewarding experience, although the size of the river means that for significant parts of the route the riverbanks are far distant and you don't actually see much save water on either side. Boats depart either from the jetty in Nyaung U (northeast of the market) or in Old Bagan (outside the old walls, to the north), depending on water levels. Services leave at around 6am, taking roughly 10–12hr to reach Mandalay.

The two main operators are **Malikha River Cruises** (☎09 7314 5748, ⓦmalikha-rivercruises .com) and **Shwe Keinnery** (☎09 7314 5748, ⓦnmaihka.com); both operators charge $35 for a one-way trip including breakfast. The Malikha boats are slightly more spacious and comfortable, although there's not much in it. More expensive trips are offered by the **Myanmar Golden River Group** (MGRG; ⓦmgrgexpress.com), costing $42 but including breakfast and lunch, and with more comfortable seating. The three operators offer at least one departure daily between them, although the vagaries of the various schedules mean that it's impossible to generalize about exactly which leave when. Tickets are most easily booked either through your accommodation or through a local tour operator.

IWT FERRIES

As well as the tourist-oriented services covered there are also local **overnight IWT ferries** to Mandalay, departing Monday and Thursday at 7am and arriving in Mandalay the following day at around 4/5pm. These cost just $10 and offer a great chance to get a worm's-eye view of local life on the water, although you'll have to sleep on deck. There are also little-used (by tourists at least) boats downriver to **Pyay** ($9; 2 weekly; 2–3 days), though their future is uncertain.

E-BIKES

Tourists aren't allowed to ride motorbikes in Bagan, although renting an e-bike (electric bicycle) offers a reasonable (if slightly slower) alternative, and saves you the effort of cycling. Chinese-made e-bikes are available to rent from many places in Nyaung U and New Bagan – small electric motors (operated via a moped-style handlebar throttle) give you a cruising speed of around 20–30km/hr, depending on the size of the bike, while spinning the pedals offers a quick turbo-charge as needed, useful on hills and dirt tracks. You might want to take your bike for a test drive before committing to it.

E-bike rental E-bikes generally cost around K8000/day, or K9000/day for slightly larger and more powerful models. The cheapest bikes are available at the Aung Shwe Yi Store on Main Rd in Nyaung U, with small e-bikes for just K5000, and larger ones K7000.

HORSE-DRAWN CARRIAGE

The classic way to tour Bagan is by horse-drawn carriage – a romantic, if not terribly comfortable, way of exploring the sights, saving you the bother of navigating your own way and allowing you to cut along sandy backroads which are hard work on two wheels.

Horse-drawn carriage rental Rates start from as little as K25,000 per day/K15,000 per half day, and you can book either through your hotel or a local tour operator, or approach a driver directly – in Nyaung U they can often be found hanging around at the top end of Thiripyitsaya 4 St and around the bus station.

TAXI

For maximum speed and comfort hiring a taxi is the way to explore the temples, although you'll miss out on a lot of the atmosphere of the archeological site while stuck inside a vehicle. Rates are around K35,000/day, or K20,000/half day.

INFORMATION AND TOURS

Tourist offices There are tourist offices in both Nyaung U, on Anawrahta Rd, and New Bagan on Bagan–Chauk Rd (daily 9.30am–4pm in theory if not always practice; ☎061 65040 for both offices). There's not much actual information available, although staff can arrange taxis to tour Bagan and to the airport (K5000/6000/7000 from Nyaung U/Old Bagan/New Bagan respectively). They can also provide guides (see below).

Guides Guides can be hired through Bagan's two tourist offices or through most tour operators around town. Professional licensed guides cost $35/day. Local guides can be hired for $20/day, although their services are likely to be considerably more hit and miss.

TOUR OPERATORS AND TRAVEL AGENTS

In addition to the operators listed below, major international outfits Exotissimo and Grasshopper Adventures (see p.25 & p.30) have offices in New Bagan, though neither local branch is particularly efficient.

Ever Sky Thiripyitsaya 4 St, Nyaung U ☎061 60895, ✉everskynanda@gmail.com. Helpful and reliable general tour operator.

Tourist Information & Travelling Services (T&T)

Thiripyitsaya 4 St, Nyaung U ☎09 4037 19542, ⊖sm .somkiat@gmail.com. Good general travel agent and a good place to arrange car hire, bus tickets and local tours.

ACCOMMODATION

Bagan is no bargain, thanks to the number of visitors and relative shortage of places to stay (particular in lower price brackets). Budget accommodation is clustered in **Nyaung U**, although there's a paucity of really inexpensive accommodation – most rooms under $20/night are little better than basic cubicles with shared bathroom and decrepit decor. Many Nyaung U guesthouses have now constructed newer and much more attractive buildings behind their original buildings, offering far superior lodgings for around $30/night – well worth the extra cash. Similar places stretch down the main road into the village of **Wet Kyi Inn**, about 1km south. **New Bagan** has a decent range of mid-range options (plus some seriously overpriced guesthouses, which offer similar standards to those in Nyaung U at significantly higher rates), while **Old Bagan** is home to a cluster of upmarket resorts – attractive, if rather pricey for what you get, and mostly generic, though there are a couple of more appealing exceptions. Rooms at the places listed below come with a/c and include breakfast. All have some sort of wi-fi (in theory, at least, if not always in practice) unless specifically stated otherwise.

NYAUNG U AND AROUND

Aureum Palace Near the Bagan Viewing Tower ☎061 60046, ⊛aureumpalacehotel.com; map pp.190–191. Bagan's biggest resort hotel, and also one of its nicest, occupying a swathe of stylish red-brick buildings with plenty of fancy Burmese decorative touches spread across 27 acres of attractively landscaped grounds. Rooms are spacious and stylishly furnished with traditional teak decor, while facilities include a spa and fitness centre – and the palm-studded infinity pool, framing a view of nearby temples, is perhaps

NEW BAGAN

EATING & DRINKING
Black Rose	2
Nooch	3
San Carlo	1
Star Beam	4

SHOPPING
Tun Handicrafts/ Moe Moe	1

ACCOMMODATION
Bagan Central Hotel	6
Kaday Aung Hotel	2
Kumudara Hotel	1
Mya Kan Thar	5
N.K. Betelnut Hotel	4
Shwe Yee Pwint Hotel	7
Thazin Garden Hotel	8
Thiri Marlar Hotel	3

Lawkanada Pagoda

the nicest in Bagan. It's not cheap, however, and rooms with enhanced views command a seriously hefty premium. **$299**

Hotel Blazing Thiripyitsaya 4th St ☎061 60864, ✉hotelblazing.hyu@gmail.com; map p.192. Newly opened hotel in a plum position on Restaurant Row. Accommodation is in a couple of two-storey buildings arranged around a small garden, with comfortable, well-appointed rooms (although some of the fixtures are already showing signs of wear). Good value, and staff might be susceptible to bargaining, especially if you're staying more than a night or two. **$55**

Eden Motel Anawrahta Rd, near the market ☎061 60639; map p.192. Reliable if unexciting budget option with competitively priced en-suite rooms with hot water – basic, but better than many other places in this price range. No wi-fi, however. There are similar rooms at a similar price in the *Eden Motel II* block over the road. **$20**

Golden Myanmar Guesthouse Main Rd ☎061 60901, ⓦgoldenmyanmarguesthouse.com; map p.192. Long-running and very friendly guesthouse. Rooms are bright and clean but showing their age, and a mite overpriced compared to other places along the road. **$30**

New Park Hotel Off Thiripyitsaya 4 St ☎061 60322, ⓦnewparkmyanmar.com; map p.192. Popular budget option in an excellent location on a quiet backstreet, with accommodation in a functional-looking one-storey block behind pleasant gardens. Rooms (of various prices and standards) are a mixed bunch – ask to look at a few before choosing. **$30**

Oasis Hotel Anawrahta Rd ☎061 60923, ⓦoasishotelbagan.com; map p.192. Appealing hideaway hotel, with a string of thatched concrete bungalows arranged along a narrow but very peaceful garden. Rooms are cool and comfortable, with rustic brown-brick bathrooms, and there's also a small pool. **$80**

Pyinsa Rupa Guesthouse Main Rd ☎061 60607; map p.192. One of the best budget guesthouses along Main Rd. Rooms with shared bathroom (cold water only) are basic but competitively priced, while the spotless en-suite rooms (with hot water) in the bright modern building around the back are one of the best deals in Bagan at this price ($25). **$15**

Saw Nyein San Guesthouse Main Rd ☎061 60651, ✉kolwinminzee@gmail.com; map p.192. Newly opened guesthouse, with ultra-friendly and attentive service and bright, spacious and very comfortable modern rooms at a reasonable price. **$35**

Shwe Na Di Guesthouse Main Rd ☎061 60409; map p.192. Not the most inspiring place, although rates are a reasonable deal by Bagan standards. Cheaper rooms with basic shared bathrooms (cold water only) are little more than a/c boxes, although cleaner than those in most other nearby establishments – if you don't mind the pervasive smell of fish sauce. There are also smarter and pricier en-suite rooms around the back ($30). **$15**

Thante Hotel Pyu Saw Hti St ☎061 61116; map p.192. Long-running option close to the centre of Nyaung U, with accommodation in spacious, old-fashioned bungalows spread around pleasant gardens complete with a good-sized (albeit very shallow) pool. Rooms are comfortable but so dated they're almost retro. A passable choice, although rates are on the high side. **$65**

Yar Kinn Tha Hotel Anawrahta Rd, at Thiripyitsaya 4 St ☎061 60051, ⓦyarkinnthahotelbagan.com; map p.192. Simple, modern hotel in a good location at the foot of Thiripyitsaya 4 St. Cheaper rooms are simple wood-panelled affairs, but decent value given the location and price; alternatively, there are also larger and pricier (although rather bare) bungalows set around the attractive gardens to the rear ($65). The excellent rooftop *La Terrasse* restaurant (see p.213) is a major plus. **$35**

Zfreeti Hotel 407 Thiripyitsaya 5th St ☏061 61003, ⓦzfreetihotel.com; map p.192. Set in a pair of good-looking brick buildings, this recently opened place is Nyaung U's most stylish hotel – and is very reasonably priced. Standard rooms are white, bright, neat and clean; deluxe rooms ($15 extra) come with a bit more style and chic. A small pool and gardens complete the package. **$70**

WET KYI INN

New Wave Guesthouse Main Rd ☏061 60731, ⓔnewwavebagan@gmail.com; map pp.190–191. One of Wet Kyi Inn's more appealing options, at a reasonable price, with bright and comfortable (if slightly bare) whitewashed, parquet-floored rooms. A pool is planned. **$50**

Winner Guesthouse Main Rd ☏061 61069; map pp.190–191. The best of Wet Kyi Inn's modest array of budget options. Cheaper rooms are bare but clean, sharing tolerable communal bathrooms with hot water. Smarter en-suite rooms ($30) are significantly brighter and more appealing, if you don't mind the strange metal beds, which look like they're been pilfered from a local intensive care unit. **$20**

OLD BAGAN

Aye Yar River View Resort Near the Bupaya temple ☏061 60313, ⓦbaganayeyarhotel.com; map pp.190–191. Another of Bagan's numerous generic upmarket resort-hotels – although despite the name it makes surprisingly little of its riverside location. Accommodation is set around pleasant gardens and a big clover-shaped pool, and there's also a spa. Rooms are relatively ho-hum, with anonymous decor and dark-wood finishes, although some come with nice temple views. **$190**

Bagan Hotel River View Behind the Gawdawpalin Paya ☏061 60316, ⓦkmahotels.com; map pp.190–191. In a superb location right behind the Gawdawpalin Paya, this rustic resort-style complex – formerly the *Bagan Hotel* – rivals *The Hotel @ Tharabar Gate* as Old Bagan's top address. Accommodation is in a cluster of low-slung red-brick buildings decorated with traditional touches, although rooms are a little humdrum given the price, and facilities including a nice banana-shaped pool plus spa. **$180**

Bagan Thande Hotel Behind the Bagan Archeological Museum ☏061 60025, ⓦbaganthandehotel.net; map pp.190–191. The cheapest accommodation in Old Bagan (though hardly a bargain), with accommodation in comfortable if uninspiring wooden and concrete bungalows with old-fashioned furnishings and dated bathrooms; pricier rooms come with slightly fancier decor and garden or river views. There's also a decent-size pool and spa. **$85**

Bagan Thiripyitsaya Sanctuary Resort Just south of Old Bagan, off Anawrahta Rd ☏061 60048, ⓦthiripyitsaya-resort.com; map pp.190–191. Top-dollar resort-hotel occupying a plum position in a very peaceful location just outside the old city walls, and with magnificent river views to boot. Unfortunately, it doesn't quite live up to its setting, with uninspiring rooms set in functional bungalows spread over bare gardens – and those with river views come with a hefty $70 surcharge. A pleasant spa and splendid riving-facing pool partly compensate for the overall drabness, while cooking and meditation classes are also available. **$190**

★**The Hotel @ Tharabar Gate** Tharaba Gate ☏061 60037, ⓦtharabargate.com; map pp.190–191. The most stylish – and expensive – of Old Bagan's various hotels, with bungalow-style accommodation scattered around exquisite gardens. The spacious, wooden-floored rooms come with all mod cons and are decorated with an attractive blend of modern chic and traditional paintings and artefacts. Facilities include a spa and a pretty (albeit shallow) pool surrounded by miniature stone elephants. **$225**

NEW BAGAN

Bagan Central Hotel 15/16 Kayay St ☏061 65057; map p.211. Dated hotel with a design so seriously odd it verges on retro-chic, although somehow it all works, in a weird kind of way. Accommodation is in a cluster of bungalows (faced with knobbly bits of petrified wood) set around a "garden" cobbled with black brick, while rooms come with heaps of gloomy wood panelling and quasi-Victorian furnishings like some kind of Gothic film set. Oddly comfortable, even so, and very reasonably priced. **$50**

Kaday Aung Hotel 3rd St ☏061 65070, ⓦhotelkadayaung.com; map p.211. Borderline eccentric hotel, occupying a kind of ersatz Neoclassical ruin. Rooms are a mixed bag: the cheapest, in the bungalows at the back, are acceptable if unremarkable; pricier rooms ($75) overlooking the hotel's decent-sized pool are smarter, if you don't mind the odd brick-and-wood decor, reminiscent of a sauna gone slightly wrong. Nonetheless, it's decent value and perfectly comfortable. **$45**

Kumudara Hotel 5th St, at Daw Na St ☏061 65142, ⓦkumudara-bagan.com; map p.211. Long-running establishment on the edge of New Bagan, with a hotchpotch of rooms. The functional cabins set around the small and rather bleak-looking pool are dated and depressing, despite the views of nearby temples. Newer rooms in a couple of modern two-storey blocks further back are significantly nicer (and some of them no more expensive), with attractive decor and smart bathrooms. Ask to have a look around before you check in. **$56**

Mya Kan Thar Kayay St ☏061 65014, ⓔuzawweikbgn @gmail.com; map p.211. One of New Bagan's cheapest options (for what it's worth) with accommodation in a pair of uninspiring concrete buildings – functional but comfortable enough, although no bargain. **$30**

N.K. Betelnut Hotel Kayay St ☏061 65054; map p.211. Attractive guesthouse-style hotel with simple but well-equipped wood-panelled rooms, including pretty cabanas at the front faced with split betel tree trunks (hence the name). It's a bit overpriced for what you get, although the genuinely warm welcome at least partly compensates. $45

Shwe Yee Pwint Hotel Kant Kaw St ☎061 65421, �ⓦ shweyeepwinthotel.com; map p.211. Attractive hotel arranged around a pair of walled garden courtyards (with a further selection of rooms in a less attractive block on the other side of the road). Rooms are well equipped, if uninspiring, and there's also a good-sized pool plus spa. Reasonable value, though unlikely to set the pulse racing. $100

Thazin Garden Hotel 22 Thazin Rd ☎061 65035, ⓔ thazingardenbagan@gmail.com; map p.211. One of New Bagan's nicest options, in a very peaceful location on the edge of town and with accommodation in pleasant bungalows set around a square of lush garden. The spacious, wood-panelled rooms are attractively decorated with Pathein parasols and other local artefacts and come with either garden or temple views. Decent value given the quality. $130

★ **Thiri Marlar Hotel** Thiri Marlar St ☎061 65229, ⓔ thirimarlarhotelbagan@gmail.com; map p.211. One of the best deals in New Bagan, set around a pretty little garden-patio and offering a genuine touch of class at sensible rates. Standard rooms are quiet, clean and nicely furnished (if you don't mind the peeling paint on the corridor outside), while superior rooms ($50) are decorated with stylish modern fittings, wooden floors and attractive bathrooms. $35

EATING AND DRINKING

There's a decent spread of **places to eat** in Bagan, although most are fairly humdrum, offering generic menus of pseudo-Western, sort-of Thai, insipid Burmese and plodding Chinese, often at above-average prices. Look out, though, for the delicious little local tamarind flakes wrapped in paper, a local speciality, which are served free at many places after meals as a digestive aid. The main cluster of restaurants is in **Nyaung U** along Thiripyitsaya 4 St (aka "Restaurant Row"), with further places spread along Main Rd and down into the nearby village of **Wet Kyi Inn**. In **New Bagan** a bunch of similar-style places flanks the roundabout right in the middle of town about halfway up Kayay St, while in **Old Bagan** there's a fun little group of vegetarian-leaning restaurants near Tharaba Gate. There are no real Western-style **bars**, although many of the restaurants are also nice places to drink.

NYAUNG U

Aroma 2 Thiripyitsaya 4 St ☎09 204 2630; map p.192. Specializing in Indian food, with seating on a large but rather gloomy terrace which many lanterns fail to quite illuminate. Food is average, and a humble chapati will cost you an extra K3000, although meals come with a nice spread of home-made chutneys (including an excellent tamarind pickle). Mains K5000–6000 (meat), K2500–3500 (veg). Daily 11am–3pm & 6–10/11pm.

The Beach Bagan 12 Hmang Kyo Yat ☎061 60126; map p.192. It's all about location location location at this upmarket restaurant, set in a gorgeous riverside position on a high terrace overlooking the Ayeyarwady. Food (mains K7000–1100) is decent but decidedly pricey, with the usual mix of Chinese, Thai and Western staples – or just come for a sundowner and then head off elsewhere to eat. Daily 8am–9pm.

★ **Bibo** Off Thiripyitsaya 4 St ☎09 4025 55241; map p.192. Super-friendly service from owner Thant Zaw Aung and his wife makes eating here a real pleasure. The menu covers Myanmar salads, soup and curries, plus a few Western dishes and a good selection of Thai curries and soups (mains K2000–3000) – not terribly authentic, but tasty enough, and competitively priced. Drinks include a good cocktail selection: a snip at K1500 each, and a positive give-away during the two-for-one happy hour (5.30–7.30pm). Daily 8am–9pm or until the last customer leaves.

Black Bambo Off Thiripyitsaya 4 St ☎061 60782; map p.192. This cool garden restaurant is the best-looking place to eat in Nyaung U, although food (and for that matter service) don't live up to the setting, with the usual mishmash of Asian and Western cuisines (mains K4000–6000) competently prepared, although a bit disappointing given the above-average prices. There's also decent coffee, a good drinks list and fresh home-made ice cream. Daily 9.30am–10pm.

★ **La Terrasse** Yar Kinn Tha Hotel, Thiripyitsaya 4 St ☎09 2590 10913; map p.192. If you're hankering after olive oil, balsamic vinegar, Parmesan, pancetta and home-baked foccacia, head for this newly opened restaurant under Swiss–Italian management hidden away on the rooftop of the *Yar Kinn Tha Hotel*. The short but well-chosen menu (mains K4400–6400) offers delicious and authentic Italian fare, including pasta, risotto, lasagne and a couple of fish and meat *secondi*, plus excellent salads – the *insalata Siciliana* is a joy. Daily 11.30am–9.30pm (last orders).

A Little Bit of Bagan Thiripyitsaya 4 St ☎061 60616; map p.192. One of the biggest and busiest places along Restaurant Row, in a large thatched pavilion attractively lantern-lit by night, although sometimes let down by lousy service. Food (mains K3000–6000) is a reliable mix of European and Asian: the Indian food (set meals K3500–5000) is probably the best in town, although portions are small, and the passable pizza and pasta, along with all the usual Chinese favourites and a few Myanmar curries, are also on offer. There's a second (usually much quieter) branch at the bottom of Thiripyitsaya 4 St sporting an ornate wooden facade and with an identical menu. Daily 7.30am–9.30/10pm.

Moe Moe Win Yangon Monhinga Main Rd; map p.192. For a break from the usual tourist breakfast of fried eggs and toast try this shoebox café specializing in excellent morning *mohinga* (K1000). Daily 6am–9pm.

Swe Tha Har San Main Rd ☎09 4026 48252; map p.192. Pretty little restaurant, handy for the guesthouses along Main Rd and lit up after dark with a blaze of candles and fairy lights – although road noise slightly spoils the romantic atmosphere. Chinese and Thai (most mains K2500) are the main offerings, far from authentic but palatable enough and at a good price. Daily 10am–10pm.

★**Weather Spoon's Bagan** Thiripyitsaya 4 St ☎09 4309 2640; map p.192. This unpretentious little café is far and away the nicest place to eat in Bagan (and much better than the British chain whose name the UK-returned owner has nostalgically adopted). The superb and entirely authentic Thai cuisine (mains K2000–3000) would put many a Bangkok restaurant to shame, while the Western food, including excellent burgers (K3500), is equally good, and there's also an above-average selection of international vegetarian dishes, plus assorted Chinese fare, all at super-competitive prices. Also has the best wi-fi connection in Bagan. Daily 9am–10pm.

WET KYI INN

★**Queen** Main Rd ☎061 60176; map pp.190–191. The best and liveliest of Wet Kyi Inn's various restaurants, in a pleasant open-air thatched pavilion decorated with the obligatory (for Bagan) fairy lights and hanging lanterns. The generic menu (most mains K4000–6000) includes the usual Chinese selection with a handful of Thai and assorted Western dishes (pizza, pasta, grills), although the real stars of the show are the splendid, delicately spiced Myanmar curries, presented on big lacquerware dishes (like a kind of Burmese thali) and served up with a good spread of accompanying side dishes and condiments. Daily 10am–10pm.

OLD BAGAN

Golden Myanmar Near Tharaba Gate, opposite Pyi Yar; map pp.190–191. A haven of local-style dining amid the touristy restaurants which surround it on all sides. There's no menu, but set meals (K3500) offer a huge spread of fifteen or so dishes including pork, chicken, beef and fish and come with assorted vegetable sides (and condiments) such as tasty tofu, crunchy tea-leaf salad and other Burmese delicacies. Daily 10am–8.30pm.

The Moon Near Tharaba Gate ☎09 4301 2411; map pp.190–191. The original of the cluster of homespun little vegetarian cafés just outside Tharaba Gate. The veg-only menu (mains K1500–2500) features all sorts of Asian and Western options including soups, salads, curries and stir-fries – anything from mung bean soup and gazpacho through to deep-fried gourd, tamarind-leaf curry and

papaya soup with yoghurt. Daily 9am–9.30pm.

Star Beam Near Tharaba Gate, close to The Moon café; map pp.190–191. The original branch of this well-regarded local restaurant, although most people now go to their newly opened premises in New Bagan (see below). Same menu (and prices) at both branches. Daily 11am–9pm.

Yar Pyi Near Tharaba Gate ☎09 2590 51436; map pp.190–191. Very similar to *The Moon* opposite, serving up a big selection of vegetarian dishes (mains K1500–2500) with plenty of curries, salads and unusual soups including banana, bean curd, and pumpkin and coconut. The guacamole and pappadums (K2500) get good reviews although the signature hot-and-sour bamboo shoots are a bit of a bore. Daily 7am–9pm.

MYINKABA

San Thi Dar Bagan–Chauk Rd, just past the entrance to the Gubyaukgyi Paya ☎09 3314 8397; map pp.190–191. Amid fierce competition, *San Thi Dar* carries off the prize for Bagan's most welcoming café. The mainly vegetarian menu features all sort of well-prepared local delicacies – pumpkin curry, tamarind-leaf salad, pickled tea salad, lemon salad – and there are also a few meat options, all at ultra-competitive prices, with mains going for just K1500–2000. Daily 9am–9.30pm.

NEW BAGAN

Black Rose Kayay St ☎061 65081; map p.211. Friendly little café (one of a lively little cluster around the small pagoda-roundabout halfway up Kayay St). The menu (mains K2000–3500) covers all the usual Thai, Chinese and Burmese bases including a few slightly unusual offerings like Ayeyarwady butter fish and river prawn curries, competently if not spectacularly done. Daily 10am–10pm.

Nooch Kayay St ☎09 4211 29920; map p.211. A slightly funkier alternative to New Bagan's other budget cafés, with seating either outside or in the faintly surreal purple dining room. The big picture menu features a good selection of Asian cuisine (mains K2500–3000) turned out by the resident Thai chef, plus evening barbecues. Daily 9am–10.30pm (last orders).

San Carlo 3rd St ☎061 65253; map p.211. Above-average Western food from an Italian-trained Burmese chef, including a big selection of pizza and home-made pasta (K3000–6500) using proper mozzarella, Parmesan, salami and so on. Also dishes up an extensive range of all the usual Chinese favourites (K3000–4000). Daily 8am–10pm.

Star Beam Near New Bagan Market, behind NLD Party Office ☎09 4015 23810; map p.211. Internationally trained chef Myo Myint turns out a short but well-chosen menu (mains K3500–6000) of superior local and international dishes including Rakhine fish and Myanmar prawn curries alongside a few Western dishes – the freshly baked baguettes with fries are a guaranteed hit. Daily 11am–9pm.

CULTURAL SHOWS

Several places around Bagan run nightly cultural shows featuring traditional puppets and/or dancing.

Amata Boutique House Thiripyitsaya Quarter, New Bagan ☎061 65099, ⓦamatabtqhouse.com. Performances nightly from Oct to March starting with a 30min puppet show followed by an hour of traditional Shan and Karen dancing. Free with a meal in the restaurant (with Asian mains for around K6000–7000). Daily 7–8.30pm (Oct–March only).

Bagan Golden Palace Main Rd, Old Bagan. Nightly shows of traditional dancing; $24 with dinner buffet or $10 entrance plus à la carte meal. Daily 7–9pm.

Nanda Restaurant Bagan–Chauk Rd, Wet Kyi Inn ☎061 60790. Enjoyable 40min puppet shows, free with a drink or meal at the restaurant (although the pedestrian Chinese food is expensive, with mains at around K5500–7000). Daily at 6.30pm, 7.15pm and 8pm.

SHOPPING

As with accommodation and eating, there are plenty of shops in Bagan, though few places that really get the pulses racing. **Lacquerware** is the main local craft, particularly in Myinkaba village, which is stuffed to the gills with lacquer workshops and showrooms. There are a few **woodcarving** shops in Nyaung U along Thiripyitsaya 4 St. For **books**, there's a small selection of secondhand novels at Ever Sky on Thiripyitsaya 4 St, while for material on Bagan and Myanmar try the bookstalls at the Shwezigon and Ananda temples.

Golden Cuckoo Myinkaba village (follow the dirt road down the right-hand side of the Manuha Paya) ☎061 65156; map pp.190–191. The most enjoyable of Myinkaba's many lacquerware workshops, run by the same family for four generations and offering absorbing workshop tours without any sales patter or pressure to buy. Cheaper items (with seven layers of lacquer; from around K10,000) are displayed in the showroom at the front, while the top-quality fourteen-layer pieces are kept in two rooms at the back (check out the lacquer iPhone cover, motorbike helmet and guitar). Daily 7.30am–10pm.

Nanda Puppet and Gift Nanda Restaurant, Main Rd, Wet Kyi Inn ☎061 60790; map pp.190–191. Small selection of attractive traditional wooden puppets plus a few other fine woodcarvings. Daily 9am–9.30pm.

Nyaung U Market Main Rd; map p.192. Nyaung U's surprisingly calm and pleasant local market is home to a good little cluster of tourist shops (on the market's north side, parallel to Main Rd) selling a decent selection of lacquerware, woodcarvings, bags, textiles and clothes —a good place to pick up a longyi if you fancy going native. Daily 9am–6pm.

Pauk Kan Thiripyitsaya 4 St ☎065 01143; map p.192. One of several woodcarving workshops along Restaurant Row. Most of the modern carvings on display are fairly stereotypical (the inevitable elephants and boring Buddhas) although they also have a small selection of far more attractive antique pieces on display – mostly on the large size. Daily 7am–10pm.

Shwe Pathein Umbrella Workshop Wet Kyi Inn ☎09 4934 0854, ⓦmyanmarhandmade.com; map pp.190–191. It's difficult to miss this shop thanks to the spectacularly large and colourful Pathein-style parasols (see box, p.102) laid out in front of it next to the road – the resident artisans can also usually be seen at work inside. Cotton parasols range from K8000 up to K150,000, and they also do colourful silk parasols for around K5000–8000. Daily 7am–9pm.

Shwe Pyi Nann Thiripyitsaya 4 St ☎061 60179; map p.192. Small shopping complex with little boutiques selling *thanaka*, jade and assorted souvenirs. The petrified wood outlet is worth a look: the large and expensive carvings may not appeal, but they also do some nice petrified wood jewellery, including bangles, necklaces and earrings, from as little as K1000 – an unusual and attractive souvenir. Daily 9am–9pm.

Tun Handicrafts/Moe Moe Bagan–Chauk Rd, New Bagan ☎061 65063; map p.211. Upmarket showroom devoted to high-quality but expensive lacquerware. Smaller pieces start at around K15,000, while larger pots run into the hundreds of dollars – although they might be susceptible to bargaining. Daily 8am–9pm.

DIRECTORY

Banks All the banks marked on our Nyaung U map (see p.192) have ATMs (note that the MAB bank only takes Visa). There's a foreign exchange counter at the AGD Bank on Thiripyitsaya 4 St, at the CB Bank on Main Rd, and at the MAB Bank on Anawrahta Rd.

Golf There's a fine 18-hole course at the Bagan Golf Club, on the edge of Nyaung U (☎09 4026 30885, ⓦbagangolfresort.net).

Internet Virtually all our recommended hotels (and many restaurants) offer free wi-fi, although connections are generally erratic and brain-crushingly slow – the enhanced wi-fi connection at *Weather Spoon's Bagan* (see p.192) is

4

BALLOONING IN BAGAN

There's perhaps no better way to see the temples of Bagan than from the air by balloon – although trips don't come cheap. Two operators run trips, though trips get booked up quickly, and in high season particularly it's a good idea to reserve as far in advance as possible. Flights cost from $320 per person and last around 45 minutes to an hour.

Balloons over Bagan Next to the Nanda Restaurant, Wet Kyi Inn ☎ 061 60347, ⓦ easternsafaris.com /balloonsoverbagan_home.html or ⓦ facebook.com /balloonsoverbagan.

Oriental Ballooning Amata Boutique House, New Bagan ☎ 061 65099, ⓦ orientalballooning.com.

---

generally reckoned the fastest and most reliable in town. There are also plenty of internet cafés, although again you might die of old age before you manage to get properly online. In Nyaung U try the Cyber Café at *A Little Bit of Bagan* (daily 7am–10pm; K600/hr) or the Shwe Pyi Nann centre directly opposite (daily 9am–10pm; K600/hr); in New Bagan, the well-equipped Step on Kayay St (daily 8am–9pm; K600/hr) is as good as anywhere.

Post office Anawrahta Rd, Nyaung U (signed "Telecommunications Centre"; Mon–Fri 9am–5pm, Sat 9am–noon).

Spas Spa treatments are available at many of the more upmarket hotels and also at the Blossom Spa at the *Amata Boutique House* in New Bagan (☎ 061 65099, ⓦ amatabtqhouse.com).

Swimming pools All Bagan's hotels allow non-guests to use their pools for a fee. The two nicest pools are at the *Aureum Palace* ($10/day) and the *Bagan Thiripyitsaya Sanctuary Resort* ($12). Other alternatives include the *Thazin Garden Hotel* in New Bagan and *The Hotel @ Tharabar Gate* in Old Bagan (both $10); cheaper options include (in Old Bagan) the *Bagan Hotel River View* and the *Bagan Thande Hotel* (both $5), and the *Thante Hotel* in Nyaung U ($6).

Around Bagan

There's an interesting crop of attractions in the area surrounding Bagan. Pick of the bunch is the dramatic **Taung Kalat** rock, the epicentre of Burmese *nat* worship, dotted with shrines to the unruly lords of the spirit realm. Visits to Taung Kalat can be combined with hikes up the adjacent **Mount Popa** or, alternatively, with a visit to **Salay**, south of Bagan, with its superb wooden monastery and cluster of Bagan-era monuments. Heading north, the riverside town of **Pakokku** is home to a colourful trio of modern temples, while continuing past Pakokku you can just about take in a couple of sights around Monywa (see p.220) in a single, albeit very long, day's excursion from Bagan.

Taung Kalat (Mount Popa)

တောင်ကလပ်

Easily the most interesting excursion from Bagan is the half-day trip to **Taung Kalat** ("Pedestal Hill"), a dramatic little sheer-sided, temple-topped plug of volcanic rock around an hour's drive from Nyaung U (it's usually, if erroneously, referred to as **Mount Popa**, although strictly speaking the mountain itself is the adjacent 1518m-high massif with its summit 4km to the east). Taung Kalat (and Mount Popa) are famous throughout Myanmar as the home of the **nat spirits** (see p.356), attracting thousands of pilgrims to come and pay their respects to (and perhaps request a cheeky favour of) the resident *nats*. Things are particularly busy during the full moon festival seasons of Nayon (May/June) and Nadaw (Nov/Dec).

According to tradition you shouldn't wear red, black or green when visiting the mountain, nor should you bring meat, especially pork – possibly in deference to the Muslim sensibilities of Byatta (see box opposite), one of the *nats* said to be resident upon the mountain.

Entrance to the shrines is **free**. It takes around fifteen minutes to climb to the summit of the rock, and an hour (or maybe slightly longer) is sufficient to explore the site.

Nat Temple

Before heading up the steps, be sure to visit the quirky **Nat Temple**, directly opposite the main stairway. Slightly kooky near life-size mannequins of assorted *nats* can be found here, standing along the back wall of the shrine inside a glassed-in corridor, many with banknotes stuffed into their hands. More or less at the centre of the gallery stands **Mai Wunna** (see box below), the "Queen Mother of Popa", flanked by her sons **Min Gyi** and **Min Lay**. A few figures down to the right is the eye-catching **Min Kyawzwa**, the "Drunken Nat", mounted on a horse and festooned with rum bottles and packets of cheroots in honour of his misspent life drinking, cockfighting and hunting. Further along is an image of the elephant-headed **Ganesh**, one of several Hindu gods inducted into the Burmese *nat* pantheon (where he is known as Maha Peinne).

To the summit

From the temple, head between the pair of large white elephants opposite and up the main steps. There are 777 steps up to the top, covered all the way. The lower third of the stairway is lined with numerous shops, beyond which is a footwear stall where you'll have to leave your shoes. The climb is punctuated by the incessant requests for "donations" for cleaning by locals who keep the stairs clean of monkey poo and other rubbish, while the monkeys themselves are very much in evidence, and fond of snatching food from the unwary.

Further *nat* shrines dot the steps on the way up. The most interesting is the one just above the footwear stall, signed "**Nat Nan**", featuring a parade of *nats* with helpful

---

THE MAHAGIRI NATS

Mount Popa is associated with many spirits, but particularly with the four **Mahagiri** ("Great Mountain") *nats* – Mai Wunna and her husband Byatta, and Maung Tinde and his sister Shwemyethna – all of whom are popularly believed to live on the mountain.

MAUNG TINDE AND SHWEMYETHNA

The first of the Mount Popa legends concerns **Maung Tinde** – aka Nga Tin De, Min Mamagiri ("Lord of the Great Mountain"), Eindwin Nat or simply "Mr Handsome" – and his sister **Shwemyethna** (aka Hnamadawgyi, Saw Me Ya, Myat Hla and "Golden Face" – although another version of the tale says that the sister was actually Thonbanhla, a different *nat* entirely). Legend recounts that the king of Tagaung, fearful of Maung Tinde's supernatural powers (which included the ability to snap the tusks of an elephant with his bare hands), wed Shwemyethna in order to lure her brother to the palace, whereupon he was promptly tied to a tree and burnt to death – only for his sister to leap into the flames with him. The expired siblings subsequently reappeared as malevolent spirits, haunting the tree where they had died, until the king ordered it cut down and flung into the Ayeyarwady, along which it floated down to Bagan. The two spirits then appeared in a dream to the king of Bagan asking him for a place to dwell and offering in return to guard the city. The king had the remains of the tree carried to Mount Popa, where the spirits of Maung Tinde and Shwemyethna are said still to reside, while shrines to the *nats* were erected at Tharaba Gate in Bagan (see p.197), where they remain to this day.

MAI WUNNA AND BYATTA

The second legend relates to **Mai Wunna** ("Miss Gold" – aka Popa Mai Daw, the "Queen Mother of Popa") who is said to rule over Mount Popa, on which her spirit dwells. Mai Wunna was a flower-eating ogress who became enamoured of **Byatta**, an Indian Muslim with supernatural powers who had been ordered by King Anawrahta to collect flowers ten times daily from the mountain. Mai Wunna's advances resulted in Byatta neglecting his duty and being executed by the king, but not before she had produced two sons, **Min Gyi** and **Min Lay** (aka Shwe Hpyin Naungdaw and Shwe Hpyin Nyidaw).

Mai Wunna, it is said, subsequently died of a broken heart, while her sons were taken away by the king, and were later themselves executed for dereliction of duty while in his service, becoming *nats* in their turn – their shrine at Taungbyone, near Mandalay, is now the site of one of Myanmar's biggest *nat pwè* (spirit festivals; see box, p.266).

4

CHIN STATE

Squeezed in between Myanmar, Bangladesh and the Indian states of Mizoram and Manipur, remote and impoverished **Chin State** is one of Myanmar's least explored regions, with thick jungles, mountainous terrain and only rudimentary infrastructure. The state's 500,000 or so Chin inhabitants are among Myanmar's most persecuted minorities. Large numbers converted to Christianity during colonial times, and have suffered widespread oppression from the 1960s through to the present day, with forced labour, torture, rape, acute food shortages and extra-judicial executions widely reported – as well as attempts to forcibly reconvert Chin Christians to Buddhism.

Foreigners require a **government permit** (see box, p.26) and the services of a **licensed guide** to visit any part of the state – allow at least a month to arrange the necessary paperwork. Inside Chin State, the only place even slightly on the tourist radar is **Nat Ma Taung** (aka **Mount Victoria**), most easily accessible from Bagan. Rising from dense forests, the upper reaches of the mountain form a so-called "sky island", with alpine plant and bird species characteristic of the Himalaya, along with other local endemic flora and fauna. Trips cost a minimum of around $1000 for two people for a four-night visit – the minimum timescale you'll need to make the long drive from Bagan and then tackle the all-day trek up to the 3053m summit and back down again.

Easier ways of meeting Chin people include visiting the Chin villages in **Rakhine State** near Mrauk U (see box, p.126), or flying into the half-Bamar, half-Chin town of **Kalaymyo** (aka Kalay), in Sagaing Province, served by intermittent flights from Yangon and Mandalay. The Chin people are covered in more detail in Contexts (see p.354).

English signs. Figures here include (from left to right) Myin Phyu Shin (aka Aung Zawmagyi, "Lord of the White Horse"), a messenger said to have been executed for delivering an important royal communiqué too slowly, along with a family group showing Byatta (see box, p.217) plus two images of his wife and sons.

The **summit** of the rock (737m) is covered in a dense cluster of Buddha and *nat* shrines, often crammed together shoulder to shoulder in the same shrine.

Mount Popa

ပုပ္ပားတောင် • The quickest way to access Mount Popa is along the road past the *Popa Mountain Resort*. Any of the Bagan tour operators (see p.210) should be able to arrange trips up the mountain, and guides are also usually available for hire through the *Popa Mountain Resort*

Rising immediately to the east of Taung Kalat, the thickly forested slopes of the **Mount Popa** massif (1518m) comprise the eroded remains of a massive, extinct stratovolcano, topped with an enormous caldera some 1.6km wide and 850m deep. Often described as Myanmar's Mount Olympus, the massif is still considered the spiritual home of the country's four Mahagiri *nats*, and the *nat* shrine about halfway up the mountain remains a popular place of pilgrimage.

Assorted trails snake through the forest swathing the mountainside, which is home to profuse vegetation and numerous orchids – the name Popa is believed to come from the Pali/Sanskrit *puppa*, meaning flower, and flowers also loom large in the local legend of Mai Wunna and Byatta (see box, p.217). It takes around four hours to reach the summit – guides can be arranged through the *Popa Mountain Resort*, halfway up the mountain.

ARRIVAL AND DEPARTURE   TAUNG KALAT (MOUNT POPA)

By pick-up Reaching Taung Kalat from Bagan by public transport, a pick-up leaves the bus station in Nyaung U daily at 8am (2hr 30min), returning at 1.30pm – although you might have to change to another pick-up at Kyaukpadaung, just over halfway to the mountain, if there aren't enough passengers. It drops you in the village at the foot of the rock.

By car/taxi It's far preferable to either hire your own car (around K35,000; 1hr) or take a seat in a shared taxi. Memory Share Taxi Service (Main Rd, Nyaung U ☎ 09 204 3579, ✉ kohtaybgn@gmail.com) runs daily shared taxis to Mount Popa at 9am for K10,000/person, or alternatively ask at the *Eden Motel* in the centre of Nyaung U.

ACCOMMODATION

Popa Mountain Resort 1km east of Taung Kalat (4km by road) ☎ 01 399 334, ⓦ myanmartreasureresorts .com. A neat little mountain retreat, affordably priced and offering the perfect base for treks up Mount Popa.

Accommodation is in a string of individual bungalows, nicely furnished with wooden floor and wicker furniture; some have stunning views of Taung Kalat below. $90

Salay

ဝေလ

Around 50km south of New Bagan, just south of the town of Chauk on the banks of the Ayeyarwady, **SALAY** (aka "Sale") developed as a satellite of Bagan in the twelfth and thirteenth centuries and remains an important religious centre. It's home to around fifty active monasteries, as well as over a hundred Bagan-era monuments and some interesting, if dilapidated, colonial buildings.

Yoke Sone Kyaung

ရုပ်စုံကျောင်း · Daily 9am–4pm · $5

Salay's main attraction is the impressive **Yoke Sone Kyaung** (aka "Youqson Kyaung"). Built in 1882, the unusual wooden structure consists of a large platform, raised on pillars, with a cluster of intricately carved wooden shrines on top. Flamboyant woodcarvings along its outer walls show scenes from the Jataka and Ramayana. The monastery is also home to the small **U Pone Nya Museum**, named after the celebrated nineteenth-century Burmese writer and containing assorted exhibits from other sites in Salay including further fine woodcarvings.

Other monuments

A couple of minutes' walk from the Yoke Sone Kyaung is a cluster of temples dating back to Bagan times. These include the **Payathonzu**, an unusual tripartite temple similar to its namesake in Bagan (see p.204). Close by, the **Man Paya Pagoda** is home to the 7m-tall Shinbin Maha Laba, the largest lacquer Buddha image in Myanmar, said to date back to the thirteenth century.

Around 6km south of town, the **Shinpinsarkyo Pagoda** boasts some fine murals and a thirteenth-century wooden Buddha, while a further 1.5km beyond, so-called **Temple 99** has further excellent Jataka murals in its small thirteenth-century shrine.

ARRIVAL AND DEPARTURE

SALAY

By car A trip by car to Salay from Bagan costs around $35–40 for a half-day, or around $75 for a day-long tour also including Mount Popa.

Pakokku

ပခုက္ကူ

A large, leafy town on the north bank of the Ayeyarwady around 30km northeast of Bagan, **PAKOKKU** hit the international headlines in 2007 when local monks took to the streets to protest against skyrocketing fuel prices, kick-starting the nation's ill-fated "Saffron Revolution" (see p.348). Things are a lot quieter now, while the opening of a huge new **bridge** (the longest in Burma) over the river in 2011 resulted in the demise of the old ferry service to Bagan, meaning that most travellers now pass straight through. The town is still a worthwhile destination for a half-day trip, however, offering a trio of temples and an interesting slice of traditional life compared to touristy Nyaung U down the river.

Thihoshin Pagoda

သိဟိုရ်ရှင်ဘုရား

The glittery **Thihoshin Pagoda**, in the centre of town, is instantly recognizable thanks to the large clocktower next to the main entrance, while its interior is dazzling, with virtually every surface covered in multicoloured glass mosaics. The large courtyard at the back is home to a modest **museum** (free), piled high with assorted exhibits in glass cases including the usual old Buddhas, banknotes, bells, palanquins, lacquerware and a considerable quantity of dust.

Shwegugyi Pagoda

ရွှေဂူကြီးဘုရား • Just under 1km down the road from Thihoshin Pagoda

Like the Thihoshin Pagoda, the **Shwegugyi Pagoda** is a study in Burmese kitsch, its main shrine decorated with abundant white-and-orange frills and flourishes, with a slender golden stupa on top. The interior is contrastingly plain, save for the temple's prized **Tangetawgyi Buddha**, framed against a hundred-year-old woodcarved backdrop, its mass of intricate filigree populated by 136 little people along with various birds and animals. The top of the carving depicts the Buddha's descent from the Tavatimsa (aka Trayastrimsha) heaven to earth after preaching to the gods above, accompanied by Indra and Brahma – a favourite subject of Burmese artists.

Shwe Mo Htwa

ရွှေမိုးထွာ

The town's third major temple is the **Shwe Mo Htwa**, a pretty little complex with a dense cluster of spiky-roofed shrines painted in various shades of gold and green, all arranged around a large courtyard dotted with prayer poles and planetary posts. The temple stands on the edge of town overlooking the Ayeyarwady, with sweeping views up- and downriver.

ARRIVAL AND DEPARTURE
PAKOKKU

By minibus/pick-up Two minibuses (1hr) depart daily at 7am and 9pm for Pakokku from Nyaung U, dropping near the market; alternatively, catch a pick-up (1hr 30min), also from near the market. Heading to Monywa (3hr), there are a couple of daily minibuses plus regular but slower and uncomfortable pick-ups. There are also buses to Shwebo (daily; 6hr).

By car A half-day trip to Pakokku from Bagan costs around $35/40 by jeep or car.

Monywa and around

မုံရွာမြို့

Sitting on the Chindwin River around 130km west of Mandalay and a similar distance north of Bagan, the large town of **MONYWA** (pronounced as two syllables something like "Moan-ywa") is of minimal interest in itself but makes a handy base for visits to several fine attractions in the surrounding countryside. These include the gigantic Buddha figures at **Maha Bodhi Tataung**, the quirky **Thanboddhay Pagoda** and the hillside cave shrines of **Pho Win Taung**.

Thanboddhay Pagoda

သမ္ဗုဒ္ဓေဘုရား • 11km southeast of Monywa, 1.5km northeast off the Mandalay road • Temple complex open 24hr • Free **Main shrine** daily 6am–5pm • $3

Built between 1939 and 1952, the zany **Thanboddhay Pagoda** is one of Myanmar's wackiest temple complexes: a technicolour riot of cartoon shrines, fairytale pagodas and shameless super-kitsch – enough to make even the most lavish Hollywood film set blush with embarrassment. Two huge white stone elephants, each with a small temple on its back, flank the entrance, setting the tone for what lies inside.

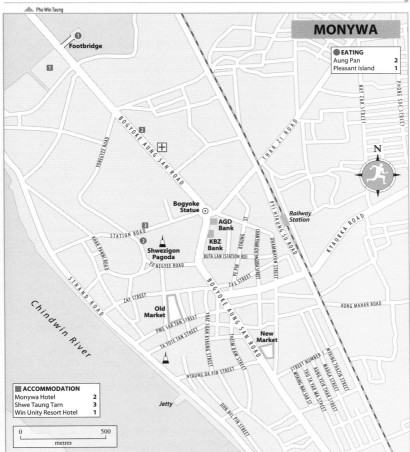

MONYWA

Bus Station (500m), Thanbodhay Pagoda (10km), Bodhi Tataung (18km), Pakokku, Bagan & Mandalay

The **main shrine** is an eye-popping, blood-red affair, surrounded by a riot of obelisks, lions, sphinxes and shrines, its roofs spiked with 864 needle-thin mini-stupas, like an architectural pincushion. Its vaguely Neoclassical-looking **interior** is a maze of dark-red arches, with walls covered in a dense mosaic of (it's claimed) over five hundred thousand tiny Buddha statues.

Further shrines and structures surround the main building on all sides, including a pea-green bathing pool surrounded by elephant carvings; a string of monastic buildings painted in vivid pastel blues, reds, pinks and greens; and a truly bizarre tower, looking like a cross between a minaret and a helter-skelter, with a small stupa on top.

Maha Bodhi Tataung

မဟာဗောဓိတစ်ထောင် • 8km east of Thanboddhay Pagoda • Daily 6am–5pm • Free

Even more surreal than the Thanboddhay Pagoda is the nearby **Maha Bodhi Tataung**, a sprawling religious complex founded in 1960 and dominated by two of the world's biggest Buddha statues. The name Maha Bodhi Tataung translates as "One Thousand Bodhi [Bo] Trees" (although there are now over nine thousand in total), and approaching the complex you'll pass swathes of these trees, each with a seated Buddha below.

It's the two giant Buddhas that really hog the attention, however, particularly the superhuman **Laykyun Setkyar** standing Buddha image, bestriding the landscape like some Brobdingnagian colossus and visible for many kilometres in every direction. Built between 1996 and 2008, this is the world's second-tallest statue, rising a massive 116m (or 130m if you include the base) – getting on for three times the height of Nelson's Column in London and outstripped only by the 153m-tall Spring Temple Buddha in Henan, China. The statue is actually hollow, with a 25-storey building concealed inside, each floor decorated with vivid murals. The bottom five or so storeys show the gruesome punishments awaiting sinners in hell, while paintings on higher levels become gradually more exalted in subject matter, with depictions of the various Buddhist heavens at the top of the statue – although visitors are allowed only as far as the sixteenth floor, some way short of nirvana (and slightly below where the Buddha's belly button would be, if he had one). There's no lift, either, so it's a bit of a climb.

The **reclining Buddha** (completed in 1991) directly in front is only a little less huge, measuring 95m in length. It's also hollow, with entrance via the Buddha's rear (as it were), although there's not much to see inside the gloomy interior bar a hall full of rather battered-looking Buddhist bas-reliefs. Nearby is the huge gilded **Aung Sakkya Pagoda** (1979), with fine views of the two statues and surrounding countryside from its terrace. Plans to construct a third supersized Buddha, to be seated on a nearby hillside, are also apparently in the pipeline.

Pho Win Taung and around

ဖိုဝင်တောင် • Open access • $2 • Jeeps from Nyaungbin village cost around $20 including waiting time; boats from Monywa to Nyaungbin cost K2500 each way

Buried deep in the countryside around 25km west of Monywa, **Pho Win Taung** (also transliterated as "Hpo Wing Daung") displays Burmese piety at work upon the landscape – it's more understated than the nearby Maha Bodhi Tataung but equally memorable. Hundreds of cave-shrines were cut into the hillside here between the

---

CHINDWIN RIVER TRIPS

Monywa is the major port on the **Chindwin River**, the main tributary of the Ayeyarwady, which runs north from here for almost a thousand kilometres (see map, p.294). Cruises along the Chindwin offer a chance to see a part of Myanmar still virtually untouched by tourism, striking deep into Sagaing Region and following the river as it runs close to the Indian border.

A number of **luxury cruises** run regularly along the Chindwin, particularly in later July/August, directly after the monsoon, when water levels are high. The main vessel is the **RV Pandaw** (ⓦpandaw.com), a luxury colonial-style vessel; seven-day cruises are run year-round between Monywa and Homalin, flying into Homalin and then heading back downriver. It's a memorable experience, although expensive, with prices starting at around $3000 per person (including flight). Longer (ten- to eleven-night) and even pricier cruises are also available on other vessels – such as the *Orcaella* (ⓦbelmond.com), *Paukan* (ⓦpaukan.com) and *Ananda* (ⓦsanctuaryretreats.com), which start from Mandalay and include a trip up and down the Chindwin before depositing passengers at Bagan. Cruises typically stop at (heading north) the riverside towns of Kani, Mingin, Moktaw, Kalewa (Kalay), Mawleik and Sittaung before reaching Homalin; journeys ending in Bagan usually visit Kani and Mingin on their way back down the river.

An alternative to an organized cruise is to arrange an **independent trip**, staying in local guesthouses and travelling on local IWT ferries (see opposite), which stop at all the main riverside settlements. You'll need to arrange the necessary permits and reservations through a travel agent in Yangon or Mandalay (allow several weeks), however, and the week-plus trip is still likely to cost in excess of $1000 per person, with costs varying depending on exactly how far upriver you plan to go.

fourteenth and eighteenth centuries – some sources put the number of shrines at exactly 492, although others claim there are actually more than double that. Many of the "caves" are tiny, with room for just a single Buddha image; others are larger, decorated with fine Jataka murals (bring a torch) rivalling anything in Bagan and still retaining much of their original colour after two hundred-plus years.

Getting to the caves is part of the fun. Visiting by hired car from Monywa you'll pass the chintzy **Shwetaung U Pagoda**, worth a stop for its sweeping river and countryside views. Alternatively, hire a boat from the jetty on Strand Rd to cross the Chindwin to bustling **Nyaungbin** village from where you can pick up a jeep to take you to the caves.

ARRIVAL AND INFORMATION   MONYWA AND AROUND

Monywa is now a lot easier to reach by from the south following the opening of the new Ayeyarwady bridge (see p.219), although it's still a bit of a dogleg. If you want to visit without the bother of catching public transport and overnighting in Monywa it's just about possible to visit the town plus Pakokku as a (very) long day-trip from Bagan or Mandalay – count on around $90 from the former, and $60–70 from the latter.

By bus The bus station is about 1km south of the centre. Count on around K1000 for the ride by motorbike taxi into town. Heading to Pakokku (3hr) and Nyaung U (4hr) there are a couple of daily minibuses plus regular but slower and uncomfortable pick-ups.
Destinations Hsipaw (daily; 11hr); Mandalay (hourly; 3hr 30min); Pyin Oo Lwin (daily; 3 daily; 7hr); Shwebo (hourly; 9hr).
By train The railway station is just east of the centre, though there's only one slow daily service from

Mandalay (5hr).
By boat IWT ferries run up the Chindwin River as far as Kalewa, with occasional ferries all the way up to Khamti in Kachin State – an adventurous journey with minimal facilities. Boats dock on the river at the jetty a short walk southwest of the centre.
Destinations Kalewa (2 weekly; at least 2 days); Khamti (monthly; at least a week).
Services The ATM at the AGD Bank accepts foreign cards and there's a money exchange counter at the KBZ Bank.

TOURS

A half-day trip combining Thanboddhay Pagoda and Maha Bodhi Tataung by **motorbike taxi** costs around K8000. Alternatively, your hotel may be able to arrange a **car** – the *Win Unity* hotel can arrange these and other local trips including taxis to Pho Win Taung and Maha Bodhi Tataung/Thanboddhay for around $25–30 each, although you might be able to find a cheaper deal elsewhere.

ACCOMMODATION

Monywa Hotel Bogyoke Aung San Rd ☎071 21581, ✉ monywahotel071@gmail.com. Decent mid-range option, and better value than the nearby *Win Unity*. Standard rooms, in some rather grubby-looking chalets, are definitely past their best; the large and bright (if rather bare) superior rooms, in a separate modern block, are much nicer and cost just $5 extra. All rooms come with a/c, hot water and wi-fi. __$40__
Shwe Taung Tarn Station Rd ☎071 21478. Centrally located cheapie on a quiet side road, with basic but bearable rooms in the main building, plus so-called "bungalows" (although they're actually just bog-standard

rooms) for $5 extra in a two-storey block behind – fractionally nicer if you can ignore the grimy exterior and faint smell of sewage outside. All rooms come with a/c and attached bathroom. __$20__
Win Unity Resort Hotel Bogyoke Aung San Rd ☎071 22438, ⊛inunityhotel.com. Monywa's top option – pleasant enough, but pricey for what you get, with functional and dated bungalows (more expensive ones have views of the adjacent lake) spread around dull grounds and a smallish pool. There's also a small spa offering inexpensive traditional massages (from $15) plus wi-fi. __$75__

EATING

Aung Pan Just off Station Rd. Popular local café dishing up passable curries (around K2000) served with an above-average spread of side dishes and accompaniments, although there's no English menu so you'll have to point. Daily 10am–9pm.
Pleasant Island Bogyoke Aung San Rd ☎071 21324.

Directly opposite the *Win Unity Resort*, this attractively rustic garden restaurant is set on its own tiny island, reached via a small footbridge. The exclusively Chinese menu is good, if pricey, with most mains at around K6000, plus more expensive seafood dishes. Daily 7am–10pm.

4

Inle Lake and the east

FISHERMEN ON INLE LAKE

5

Inle Lake and the east

A land of rolling mountains, idyllic lakes and umpteen minority peoples, Shan State is by far the largest in the country, and deservedly one of the most popular with foreign travellers. In a giant place with only three major cities, it's perhaps inevitable that the primary attractions are of the natural variety – Inle Lake is a swoon-worthy postcard picture come to life, and many of the independent travellers who visit do so at the end of a multi-day hike through fields and across gentle hills. Throw in a collection of superb cave-temples and some hot spring action, and you've a recipe for at least a week of travel. The Shan (see p.351) are the most prominent of the area's many ethnic groups, but you'll find Pa-O and Danu villages around Kalaw; Intha and (occasionally) long-necked Padaung living in stilt-houses on and around Inle Lake; and Akha, Lahu and longhouse-loving Loi way out east around Kengtung.

The area's main attractions are all located in a tight area (though some awful public transport can make it feel very large) to the southwest corner of the state. Furthest west is **Kalaw**, a small town beloved by colonialists for its altitude and accordingly cool climate. It's a pleasant place to hole up for a few days, though most head off as soon as they've been able to organize a **hiking trip** to Inle Lake – this is one of the most stupendous experiences that Myanmar can throw at you, and also one of the best opportunities you'll have to delve into local minority culture. North of Kalaw is **Pindaya**, an even smaller town set around a pretty lake; the main attraction here is the fantastic Shwe Oo Min Cave, filled with thousands upon thousands of golden Buddhas. To the east is the delightful town of **Nyaungshwe**, which functions as the main base for **Inle Lake** – the most popular attraction in Shan State by far, and one of Myanmar's foremost highlights. The overwhelming majority of those who visit go on a boat tour of some description, but other drawcards include a charming winery, a soothing hot spring resort and scores of great restaurants. East again is the state capital, **Taunggyi**, rarely visited by foreign travellers yet home to one of Myanmar's most spectacular festivals. Foreigners are not allowed to take overland transport east to **Kengtung**, but this town and its surrounding hill tribes may justify the cost of a plane ticket, especially if you're heading to or from Chiang Mai and other destinations in northern Thailand.

Note that Pyin Oo Lwin, Hsipaw, Lashio and other parts of northern Shan State are featured in the Northern Myanmar chapter (see p.294).

KENGTUNG MARKET

Highlights

❶ **Shan State markets** Every day's a market day in Shan State; after figuring out which one's about to take its turn on the rotating five-day schedule, head along and pick up some minority handicrafts. **See box, p.230**

❷ **Hiking from Kalaw to Inle** The best way to arrive at Inle Lake is at the end of a one- or two-night hiking trip from Kalaw, a route dotted with wonderful minority villages. **See box, p.232**

❸ **Shwe Oo Min Cave** Overlooking the pleasant town of Pindaya, and accessed by lengthy covered staircases, this cave is filled almost to bursting point with thousands of golden Buddha statues. **See p.236**

❹ **Wine-tasting** Just outside Nyaungshwe, and overlooking Inle Lake, the Red Mountain winery is up there with the most visually arresting places to drink in all Myanmar. **See box, p.244**

❺ **Boat trips on Inle Lake** You can't leave the Inle Lake area without taking a boat trip – stilt-house villages, long-necked Padaung ladies and floating tomato farms are all part of the picture. **See p.247**

❻ **Kengtung** Way out east, this scruffy town has some serious hiking potential – the hills surrounding it are home to a colourful assortment of ethnic-minority villages. **See p.252**

HIGHLIGHTS ARE MARKED ON THE MAP ON P.228

TRAVEL RESTRICTIONS

The main closed-off area in this chapter is the wide swathe of land **between Taunggyi and Kengtung**. Foreigners are not permitted to visit this area, but can take flights between these two cities. In addition, to get anywhere at all from Kengtung, you'll need government permission, though this is free and fairly simple to arrange. **Kayah State** comes with its own particular litany of clauses and sub-clauses – in theory part of it is now open to independent travellers, though in practice it's still best to take a tour (see box, p.251).

Kalaw and around

ကလော

One has to feel a little sorry for **KALAW**. Most tourists to this quarter of Myanmar overlook the place in favour of Inle to the east, and of those who do actually stay here, the vast majority are only doing so to start a **trek** to the lake – undoubtedly one of the highlights of a visit to Myanmar (see box, p.232), and a wonderful way in which to get a handle on local **minority culture**. Bar a few religious monuments, there's not much of sightseeing interest in Kalaw itself, though its lazy, carefree air often tempts visitors to stay on for a couple of extra days, taking a few leisurely walks on the hill-tracks surrounding the town, and making full use of some pleasing culinary opportunities.

Part of Kalaw's appeal is its invigorating **climate** – this is one place in which you won't need air-conditioning in your room. In fact, winter evenings can get decidedly chilly, and you'll likely need to don something with long sleeves. The town lies a full 1300m above sea level, and like similarly lofty places across Southeast Asia, it was used as a **hill station** retreat by overheated Europeans during the colonial period; a

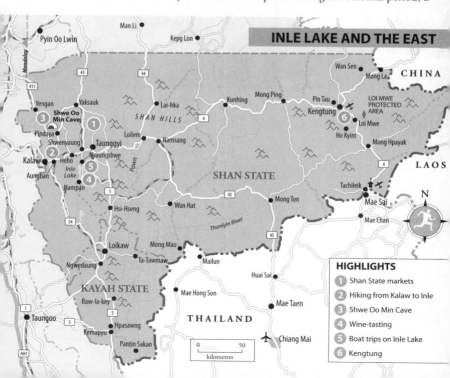

INLE LAKE AND THE EAST

CHINA

LAOS

THAILAND

SHAN STATE

KAYAH STATE

HIGHLIGHTS
1 Shan State markets
2 Hiking from Kalaw to Inle
3 Shwe Oo Min Cave
4 Wine-tasting
5 Boat trips on Inle Lake
6 Kengtung

0   50
kilometres

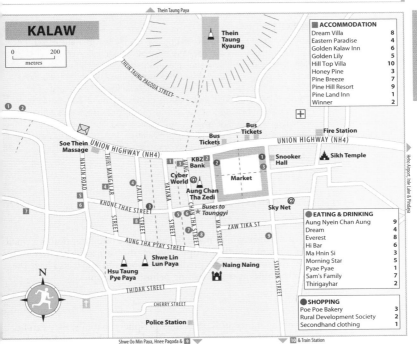

small population of Nepalis and Indians, used as road- and rail-builders at that time, remains in the town.

Aung Chan Tha Zedi

အောင်ချမ်းသာစေတီ • Kone Thae St • Daily 4am–9pm • Free

Poking up from the very centre of town, the **Aung Chan Tha Zedi** is Kalaw's most conspicuous stupa by far. It makes a fancy grab for attention, covered from tip to toe in tessellated mirrors which glint delightfully during the sunrise and sunset hours. All this said, there's no real need to step inside the rusty gates guarding the complex; the view from *Morning Star* teahouse (see p.234) is good enough.

Kalaw market

ကလောဈေး • Entrances on Union Highway and Kone Thae St • Daily 6am–5pm • Free

Right next to the Aung Chan Tha Zedi, Kalaw's **market** is worth popping into on any day of the week. It is of course best visited when Shan State's rotating market circus comes to town every fifth day (see box, p.230), on which occasions the stalls spill out onto neighbouring streets.

Thein Taung Kyaung

သိမ်တောင်ကျောင်း • Accessed from Union Highway • Daily 24hr; museum open on request • Free

For a bit of gentle exercise, take a walk up the covered staircase leading to the **Thein Taung Kyaung**, a small monastery overlooking the town. Aside from some friendly monks, a few sleeping or barking dogs and the obligatory "foot-wearing prohibited"

5

SHAN STATE MARKETS

A number of markets in Shan State operate on a rotating five-day cycle, with three or four markets taking place simultaneously on each day. With the possible exception of the very touristy Ywama "floating market", they're fascinating places – particularly early in the morning – where people from remote villages sell their produce or livestock and buy essential goods. The schedule given below was correct at the time of research, with the last listed place for each day either on or around Inle Lake, but tour operators, guides and hotel staff should know of any alterations. The products on sale at most markets are mostly geared to locals – fruit, veg, clothing, fishing equipment and the like. However, you'll certainly find fabrics aplenty, including longyi and the headscarves used by local minority ladies, and the more tourist-oriented markets will have silver implements and cheesy souvenirs too.

Day 1 Kalaw/Shwenyaung/Indein
Day 2 Nyaungshwe/Pindaya/Nampan
Day 3 Than Taung/Heho/Kyone/Taung To
Day 4 Aungban/Taunggyi/Ywama
Day 5 Pwe Hla/Maing Thauk/Phaung Daw Oo Paya.

signs, there's not much to see once you've made the ascent; the one exception is a small "museum" featuring examples of Buddhist scripts, though this isn't terribly interesting. However, the views from the monastery are predictably good, and you'll also have the option of taking off into the hills on tracks leading behind the complex.

Around Kalaw

There are a couple of diverting sights on Kalaw's hilly periphery; happily, they can be easily visited in just a couple of hours, even on foot. The loop can be done clockwise or counter-clockwise, though it's easiest to head for the **Shwe Oo Min Paya** first, via the otherwise unremarkable **Christ the King Church**, and the **Hnee Pagoda** last. A series of walls, gates and barbed wire will indicate that much of the area between the cave and the pagoda is a **military zone** – it is, in fact, one of only two venues in the land (Pyin Oo Lwin being the other) where lucky Burmese brass can make the quantum leap to the level of general. The aforementioned gates are almost always open, though they're occasionally closed so that an inevitably tubby general can play the final hole of the eerily deserted **golf course** in peace.

Shwe Oo Min Paya

ရွှေဥမင်ဘုရား • Shwe Oo Min Rd • Cave daily 5am–7pm • Free • From town, take Min St south and turn right onto University Rd, then right again after 500m

Just over 1km south of town, the **Shwe Oo Min Paya** is well worth the trouble of getting to, especially if a visit to Pindaya is not on your schedule. Like the eponymous complex in that town (see p.236), the most interesting part of this complex is a cave stuffed to the gills with golden Buddha statues. With hundreds and hundreds of them here already, and more being added all the time, it's almost like a Buddha warehouse; the path snakes around 150m into the hill, with glittering, golden views at every turn.

Hnee Pagoda

နီးဘုရား • Hnee Pagoda Rd • Daily 24hr • Free • From town, take Min St south and turn right onto Damasatkyar Rd, then follow signs at the main junction after 1.3km; from Shwe Oo Min Paya, continue west along Shwe Oo Min Rd, turn right at the end, then left after 500m

The charming **Hnee Pagoda** sits around 2.5km southwest of central Kalaw, amid rolling countryside that simply begs to be delved into. The "Bamboo Pagoda" is named after a Buddha statue fashioned from such material (and now, of course, heavy with gold leaf); it's said to be more than 500 years old. Otherwise, the complex is a fairly modest affair, though one boasting good views. Hang around for long enough and you'll likely be offered some tasty green tea, and quite possibly some edible tea leaves to take it with; do some walking around the area, and you'll see the tea itself being grown.

ARRIVAL AND DEPARTURE KALAW AND AROUND

By plane Heho airport is around 35km east of Kalaw. The vast majority of those landing there are heading towards Inle Lake, which makes it hard to find people to share a cab to Kalaw (1hr); cabbies will typically start the bidding at K30,000, though K22,000 is a fairer amount for the distance, and lucky souls may be able to get it down to K18,000 or so. The only cheaper alternative is to walk the 2km or so to the main road, and wait for a passing bus – this can take a while to arrive, and even if you're lucky enough to get a seat you'll likely have to change in Aungban. From Kalaw back to the airport, taxi prices are often a little cheaper; plane tickets can be purchased from agencies on Kalaw's Union Highway.

Destinations (Heho) Kengtung (1 daily; 55min); Lashio (daily; 50min); Mandalay (7 daily; 35min, though sometimes routed via Nyaung U); Nyaung U (for Bagan, 2–4 daily, sometimes routed via Mandalay; 40min–1hr 25min); Naypyitaw (1 daily; 40min); Tachileik (1–2 daily; 50min, though sometimes routed via Lashio); Yangon (4–5 daily; 1hr 15min).

By bus Kalaw is located on the Union Highway connecting Meiktila and Taunggyi. Almost all long-distance services start or terminate in the latter, meaning that, when taking these, you're going to have to pay the full ticket price to or from Taunggyi. Such buses can, however, be booked and boarded in Kalaw – head for the rank of agencies lining the Union Highway north of the market. The same stretch also forms the bus pick-up area, though since no services actually start in Kalaw, you may be waiting around for a while. The lone exceptions to this rule are decrepit buses to Taunggyi, which leave 6–7.30am from a spot on Kone Thae St, southwest of the market; these services are a cheap way to get to Shwenyaung, the jumping-off point for Inle Lake (1hr 30min–2hr). Lastly, note that foreigners are still prohibited from using overland transport to get out east to Kengtung.

Destinations Bagan (2–4 daily; 7–8hr); Hsipaw (3 daily; 11–13hr); Kyaukme (2 daily; 12hr); Lashio (3 daily; 15hr); Mandalay (up to 7 daily; 6–8hr); Naypyitaw 1 daily; 5hr); Taungoo (at least 1 daily; 8hr); Thazi (3–4 daily; 2hr); Yangon (frequent from 4.30–9.30pm; 10hr).

By pick-up and motorbike taxi Those heading west to Thazi (4hr) or east to Shwenyaung (for Inle Lake; 2hr) could try to hunt down one of the pick-ups that rumble along the Union Highway. They're also one way to make the first leg of the trip to Pindaya; it takes around 25min to get to Aungban (K700), where you'll have to change, though the distance is far more easily covered by motorbike (K2000). Once in Aungban, find a pick-up (K1000) or motorbike (K7000). Aung Yedana runs shared taxis between Mandalay and Inle Lake (around K30,000), though to book a seat you'll have to call their Mandalay office.

By taxi The slightly annoying public transport connections to Inle and Pindaya tempt some to bite the bullet and splash out on a cab: it'll be a minimum K35,000 to either destination, or more like K55,000 to visit the caves and head to Nyaungshwe.

By train Kalaw's station, just over 1km south of the centre, sits on an extremely slow train line heading east from Thazi, a small town on the main Yangon–Mandalay line. The views on this route are quite superb – some of the best in the land, indeed – though the wooden seating and bumpy journey (how can train lines have potholes?) will leave you with buns of steel. If you're prepared to trade comfort for this beautiful and truly local experience, there are two daily trains to and from Thazi (6hr 30min); they're also an alternative way of getting to Inle Lake, since the line continues east to Shwenyaung (3hr 30min).

GETTING AROUND

Bike rental Naing Naing (see below) rent out city bikes for K2000 per day, and mountain bikes for K10,000 per day; they're also able to supply decent maps of the area, and even lead full cycle tours.

TOUR AGENCIES

Agencies offering treks to Inle Lake have mushroomed in recent years, but in general it's still best to go with one of the few long-standing operators – the added security accrued from years of experience is worth the extra couple of bucks per day.

Holiday Union Highway ☎ 094 2833 8036. Reliable agency run by the jolly, bearded brothers from the *Golden Lily* guesthouse (see p.233). Most of their hikes operate off the main routes, which makes for fewer tourists, and friendlier villagers to boot. Their treks to Inle cost $12 per person per day in a group of five.

Naing Naing Min St ☎ 094 2831 2267. Agency offering a few nice alternatives to the standard Inle packages (K14,000 per person per day in a group of five). Their treks to Pindaya are highly recommended (certainly a lot harder than the Inle stroll, but with even better scenery; K25,000 per person per day in a group of four), while the energetic

5

manager often runs great bike tours ranging from half-day to overnight.

Sam's Family Aung Chan Tha St ☏ 081 50377. Operated from the dining tables of the eponymous restaurant (see p.234), this is another seasoned Inle Lake trek operator, though the affable Sam doesn't lead as many treks as he used to. Their fees (K14,000 per person per day in a group of five) include everything bar the Inle entrance fee.

ACCOMMODATION

There's a decent enough range of accommodation in Kalaw, with establishments often featuring a certain tree in their names – the town is locally famed for its pine trees, which grow on the surrounding hills and often end up in hotel rooms in the form of cladding and furnishings. At the time of writing, a few large, higher-end complexes were being

---

TREKKING TO INLE LAKE

If there's one must-do activity in Eastern Myanmar, it's taking a **multi-day trek** from Kalaw to Inle Lake. Even more enjoyable than taking a boat ride on the lake itself, it'll give you a gentle workout, striking countryside views and a peek into minority culture, all in one. While it's quite possible to walk from the lake to Kalaw, almost nobody does it this way – heading from west to east, it's downhill most of the way, and you get the lake as a reward at the end.

ARRANGING A TRIP

Given the distance, you'll have to arrange your trek through an agency (see p.231), whose trips always come with a guide, super-simple village or farmhouse accommodation (the monastery many operators once used gets way too busy these days, and is no longer a pleasant place to sleep), and three meals per full day. Your main choice will be whether to plump for a **two-** or **three-day** trip; these are essentially identical bar the first day of the three-day course, with those on two-day trips usually taken by vehicle to the trailhead. Some operators have four-day options, though three is enough for most travellers. Also think about where you'd like to **finish** the trip; there are numerous termination points on the western side of Inle Lake.

   Prices vary depending upon how many there are in your group; agencies will usually be able to lump you in with others, or you could try hunting trek-mates at your hotel or Kalaw's restaurants. Figure on K12,000–16,000 per person per day, and ask whether your fee includes the boat ride across the lake (K15,000–18,000, depending on places visited on the way across), the transport of baggage (typically K3000 per person) and the Inle entrance fee (K10,000). The walk is long but pretty easy, so all you need is decent **footwear** – in the dry season, it's just about possible to make the trek in flip-flops. Also useful are a **hat**, **sunblock** and **mosquito repellent** (the area was malaria-free at the time of writing, but better safe than sorry). Lastly, a **torch** comes in handy when making night-time toilet visits, and you'll need a **towel** to dry yourself after what passes for a shower in these parts.

THE WALK

Those on three-day courses will spend their **first day** on a semicircular route around town. This contains the only real forest on the trail, a small section that's only ever tricky after rain. Once through this, you'll emerge into a swathe of tea plantations, and weave from village to village along country trails – **Pa-O** and **Danu** people are most numerous in this area. The **second day** (or the first, if you're on a two-day trip) is mostly flat, with more villages to visit and plenty of agricultural activity to spot: rice, chilli, sesame and potato are among the crops grown in these parts, though if you're lucky you may be able to cull your own tasty treat from a tamarind tree or sugar-cane patch. The **final day** sees the big drop down into Inle, with water buffalo visible along the dusty trails, and the lake itself visible for some of the walk.

SHORTER OPTIONS

If you'd like to know what to expect of a multi-day trek, or simply can't afford one, it's quite possible to take a shorter walk around Kalaw. The town's many travel agencies (see p.231) can organize day-trips for around K15,000, or half-day trips from K7000, though it's quite easy to take off on safe routes yourself. For a little taster, try walking uphill to the west of town, past the *Pine Breeze* hotel (see opposite); turn right at the junction, then left to wrap around the pagoda on a dirt path. A mere fifteen minutes from Kalaw, you're already in the countryside, with easy paths leading to small villages and across the hills beyond.

built on the outskirts, a good omen for a town more accustomed to hosting wealthy day-trippers from Inle. Wi-fi is patchy across the board.

Dream Villa Zatila St ☎081 50144, ✉dreamvilla @myanmar.com.mm. One of the nicer places in the town centre, this guesthouse boasts a quiet, backstreet location, and wood-panelled rooms with minibar. It is, however, a little dear for what you get. $45

Eastern Paradise Thiri Mangalar St ☎081 50315, ✉easternmotel@gmail.com. Poor value since a recent doubling in price, this guesthouse has well-sized rooms, with carpeting of a sort, and staff able to organize tours and the like. You'll pay $10 more for an upstairs room. $25

Golden Kalaw Inn Natsin Rd ☎081 50311, ✉golden kalawinn1@gmail.com. In near-direct competition to the *Golden Lily* just down the road, this guesthouse has its adherents, but its grungy vibe, weak-framed beds and prison-cell rooms often see guests moving out after their first night. Best viewed as a back-up option. No wi-fi. $12

★**Golden Lily** Natsin Rd ☎081 50108, ✉goldenkalaw inn1@gmail.com. A long-time backpacker magnet, run by a charming Sikh family adept at organizing hiking tours to Inle Lake (see box opposite). The cheap rooms and their shared facilities are decent enough, but do think about stumping up double for one of the comfy, nicely decorated en-suite rooms in the new block, some of which have cute bathtubs. $7

Hill Top Villa Ward 3 ☎081 50346. Higher-end, chalet-style accommodation out past the train station – just aim for the red triangles on the adjacent hillside. The views are predictably good, and the rooms nice enough, though breakfasts are unfortunately mediocre – a pity when there's next to nowhere else to eat nearby. $80

★**Honey Pine** Zatila St ☎081 50728, ⊕honeypine hotel.blogspot.com. There's pine all over the place at this small guesthouse, whose carpeted rooms are up there with the best value in town, all en-suite, and featuring telly and minibar. Service isn't up to much, however, and the windowless single rooms aren't worth going for. $25

Pine Breeze Thittaw Rd ☎081 50459, ✉pinebreeze hotel@gmail.com. One of the town's newer options, occupying a lofty position up a side-street just west of the centre – there are great views from most rooms (some of which have balconies) and the top-level breakfasting hall, while the walk up and down will provide a nice workout for your legs. $35

Pine Hill Resort Oo Min Rd ☎081 50459, ⊕myanmar pinehill.com. Overpriced for sure, but this is about as good as accommodation gets in little Kalaw. Pine-clad rooms are par for the course in this town, but this hotel's manicured gardens and colonial-era architecture feel genuinely special. Do bear in mind that it's located in a quiet area 2km south of the town centre – a plus for some, a minus for others. $95

Pine Land Inn Union Highway ☎081 50020, ✉pineland .inn@gmail.com. Forget the gloomy reception area: rooms here are surprisingly large for the price, even if it does sometimes feel as though the floor is about to give way beneath you: do your morning star-jumps somewhere else. It's certainly worth paying the extra $4 for an en suite, though go for a room away from the main road unless you fancy hearing truck horns all night. No wi-fi. $10

Winner Union Highway ☎081 50025, ✉winner hotel.kalaw@gmail.com. A decent choice just off the main road, with clean, carpeted rooms and amiable staff. It's an extra $5 for an en-suite room, though those in the basement are often offered at a discount – not a bad idea, considering the occasionally noisy location. No wi-fi. $15

EATING AND DRINKING

A small town hosting a disproportionate number of tourists, it should come as little surprise to learn that Kalaw has a decent range of places to eat. As well as the places listed here, you'll find plenty of street shacks selling Shan noodles from the morning through to mid-afternoon.

Aung Nyein Chan Aung Station Rd ☎081 50662. If you fancy eating in a place where locals are guaranteed to outnumber tourists, this is your spot. There are no prices on the menu for their mix of Burmese, Shan and Chinese dishes, but it'll generally come to K2000 or so for a set of rice, main and sides. The Burmese food is served from 10.30am; as ever, the earlier in the day you eat it, the less time it has had to sit around acquiring germs. Daily 8.30am–10pm.

★**Dream** Zatila St ☎081 50554. Surprisingly elegant for central Kalaw, this is great little spot for Chinese food, served up in the lovely garden area, or set back from the road in a pretty house. If you're eating with someone else, dine in Chinese style by getting a combination of meaty main (K3500) and a veggie one (K2500) to share, possibly with some soup too if your belly's a-rumbling. Daily 10am–9pm.

Everest Aung Chan Thar Rd ☎081 50348. A long-time backpacker favourite, selling fare redolent of the Himalayas – try their filling *paneer masala* (K3000) or *dhal bhat* (K2500), both of which are served with rice, chapati and side-dishes, and finish up with a lassi (K1000) or chocolate banana chapati (K2000). Daily 9am–9pm.

★**Hi Bar** Kone Thae Rd ☎094 2837 0163. Amazingly, this place is actually a bona fide bar – a hugely pleasant

5

CHEWING BETEL, KALAW-STYLE

Kalaw is one of the better places in the land to give the chewing of **betel nut** parcels (see box, p.10) a go. While most travellers find the taste diabolical (and it's also carcinogenic), the fare on offer in Kalaw can be surprisingly pleasant to munch on. Sweeter, tastier ingredients such as **green papaya** and **coconut** are often added to the regular mix, while locals like the betel nuts themselves lightly roasted, adding yet another nuance to the taste. Dozens of shacks and tiny shops will sell you this local oddity, with the stretch south of the market a particularly happy hunting ground; figure on around K100 per parcel and, as ever, remember to spit out the first few times your mouth starts to fill with saliva, as the slaked lime can destroy your liver, as well as your teeth.

change from the typical Burmese beer-station night out, right down to the fact that most people will be drinking rum sours (K1000). There are only a dozen or so seats around its tiny, U-shaped bar, so the vibe is entirely dependent upon who's drinking here on any particular night; staff and visitors often give the atmosphere a stir with a bash on the house guitar. Daily 4.30–11pm.

★**Ma Hnin Si** Butar Rd ☏ 081 50727. Understated yet gorgeous little teahouse – with its mocha-coloured tables and kindergarten-size chairs, forest-green wooden doors, mint-coloured interior and hand-painted signs, it's like a little work of art that simply begs to be photographed. The tea (K250) is best taken with deep-fried Indian savouries (K100 for three). Daily 6am–8pm.

Morning Star Kone Thae Rd ☏ 081 50443. With its mauve tables, lime chairs and sky-blue doors, this teahouse is decorated more like a Belizean beach shack. The fare, however, is pure Indian; take your tea (K250) with super-sugary Indian sweets (K100 and up). They serve delectable *chapati puri* (K300) in the morning; sitting outside with a view of the glittering glass stupa is a mesmerizing way to start the day. Daily 6am–7pm.

Pyae Pyae Union Highway ☏ 081 50798. A cute little venue on the main road, popular with young locals on account of its excellent Shan noodles (K500); take them in soup or with salad, and with a choice of chicken or pork. There's also good curry (K1000), and a range of cheap noodle and meat dishes. Give the curiously grey "home-made" coffee a miss, though. Daily 6am–9pm.

Sam's Family Aung Chan Thar St ☏ 081 50377. Though it doesn't look all that welcoming from outside, this is a relaxed and popular place to eat before or after discussing trekking options with one of the town's most reliable operators (see p.231). Most of their curries cost K2000 and come with roti or chapati; veggie dishes are usually K1000, with the pumpkin recommended. Daily 7am–8pm.

★**Thirigayhar** Union Highway ☏ 081 50216. Also known as the "Seven Sisters", this is the most luxurious eatery in Kalaw, with dining conducted in a beautiful house lined with dark-wood furnishings, or outside in the pretty garden area. It's unfortunate that very few locals come here, though the cheery all-female staff more than make up for this. The menu bursts with a winning combo of Burmese, Shan, Chinese and European food, all of it very well done; a local recommendation is the *zat byat byat* (K4000), a Shan dish made from spiced, minced meat mixed with chopped tomato and basil. Try a papaya lassi (K2000) for dessert. Daily 10am–10pm.

SHOPPING

Poe Poe Bakery Kone Thae Rd. This bakery has been a lovely little addition to the town, and makes a perfect place to source some trekking snacks. The vast majority of what's on offer is sweet, rather than savoury; their banana bread (K400) is particularly good, while Western sweeties such as Toblerone and Ferrero Rocher will certainly tempt those who've been chocolate-lite Myanmar for a while. Daily 8.30am–6.30pm.

Rural Development Society Myoma Rd ☏ 081 50747, ✉ sdr1992@gmail.com. Fair-trade shop whose little space is filled with all sorts of goodies, including postcards (K500), hats (K4000) and longyi (K3000 and up), as well as all sorts of minority beads, bands and the like. All profits go towards development projects in surrounding minority villages. Daily 9am–5pm.

Secondhand clothing Butar Rd ☏ 093 6025 5111. Now, this is handy. Kalaw is one of the few places across the land where you may find yourself shivering at night – at this small, no-name shop, you can pick up a secondhand coat or windbreaker for as little as K2000. These can also come in handy on hikes to Inle Lake – many of the villagers you meet on the way would be grateful for a garment that you'll no longer need. Daily 8.30am–6.30pm.

DIRECTORY

Bank There's a branch of KBZ Bank (Mon–Fri 9am–3pm) on Min Rd, part of a large banking group whose owners have been subject to international sanctions (see box, p.350). Its ATM and currency exchange come in pretty handy, however. **Internet** Cyber World on Aung Chan Tha St (daily 8.30am–10pm) can get you online for K1000/hr; Sky Net

on Kone Thae St (daily 8am–midnight) isn't as reliable, though cheaper at K500/hr.
Massage Soe Thein offers traditional Pa-O massage for K7000/hr, from a first-floor room on the Union Highway

(daily 9.30am–6pm).
Post office Union Highway, Mon–Fri 9.30am–4.30pm.
Snooker There's a popular hall on Butar Rd (daily 9am–9pm), which also sells beer. Tables K2000/hr.

Pindaya

ပင်းတယ

Set around the pretty **Pone Taloke Lake**, PINDAYA is a typical Shan State town, a small, relaxed affair with a bustling market and friendly locals. Many visitors find themselves here for one reason alone – the fantastic **Shwe Oo Min Cave** above town, which is filled with thousands upon thousands of gleaming Buddha statues. Most see the cave, eat lunch and then zoom straight back to Inle or Kalaw, but it's certainly worth sticking around for the night – not only will you be one of very few travellers staying here, but you'll be able to see the cave at the crack of dawn, before the tour buses arrive.

Keep your peepers peeled on the journey into Pindaya, for the countryside hereabouts can be pretty spectacular. Regular potholes, detours and other interruptions to the bumpy road will provide ample evidence that the area is made

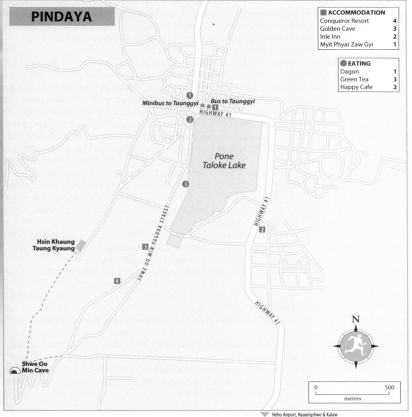

5

Note that there's a K2000 **entry fee** to Pindaya, levied at a booth as you approach from the south. Whether you arrive by bus, taxi or pick-up, your driver will pull over (he'll get into trouble otherwise), and the process is over quick as a flash. Those hiking in from Kalaw probably won't have to pay, and in any case you almost certainly won't be required to show your entry ticket at any time after purchase.

from earth of a deep red hue: this can seem unforgivingly arid during the dry season, but it explodes into a patchwork of green after the rains, making this one of Shan State's most important agricultural zones. Also keep a lookout for the people you'll see on the way – groups of **Danu** and **Pa-O** resplendent underneath colourful headdresses.

Shwe Oo Min Cave

ရွှေဥမင်ဂူ • Daily 6am–6pm; elevator 9am–noon & 1–4pm • K3000 • Accessible on a variety of paths from Shwe Oo Min Rd, about a 30min walk south of town, or take a motorbike or taxi to the elevator

In cave systems across East Asia, locals will delight in pointing out rock formations which look – from a certain angle, in a certain light or with a certain leap of the imagination – like Buddhist images. How delightful, then, to find the **Shwe Oo Min Cave**, which is filled with bona fide Buddha statues – more than nine thousand of them, in fact. There has apparently been a pagoda at the cave's entrance since the third century BC, and townsfolk like to regale visitors with the legend that the grotto was inhabited by a giant spider which took a fancy to local princesses and imprisoned them here – perhaps one reason why the statues inside the cave only date back to the late eighteenth century. More are being added all the time by Buddhist pilgrims, and an assortment of international organizations.

The cave is located way up on a limestone escarpment above town; you'll see several covered stairways making their way up from nearer to ground level, and the views just keep on getting better the higher up you go. Those lacking the necessary time or energy can make use of a lift, which heads from the top of the road to the cave level (though note that, for some reason, it takes a lunch break). It's wise to head up as early as you can, for the site is at its magical best, and most refreshingly tourist-free, around dawn. Another little tip: take a picture of the mountainside before you head on up, since this will aid navigation once you're there and when you're coming back down.

The **cave** itself is rather spectacular. On your way to its depths, you'll note that the statues are made of various different materials – wood, marble, cement and more. Both the temperature and the CO_2 level increase suddenly as you enter the largest of the grotto chambers, a muggy place which, it's tempting to believe, may well contain breath and sweat from the colonial period.

There are a couple of other things to see while you're up by the cave. One is the delightful **monastery** just alongside; a combination of whitewashed walls and rarefied air makes it feel almost Tibetan. Then there's **Alegu**, the biggest Buddha on the mountainside at over 12m in height, sitting in a side-hall a little further along.

Hsin Khaung Taung Kyaung

ဆင်ခေါင်းတောင်ကျောင်း • Daily 24hr • Free • Accessible on a variety of paths from Shwe Oo Min Rd, about a 15min walk south of town

This large, captivating **monastery**, made from carved teak wood, is well worth tracking down if you're in Pindaya for more than just a few hours. It's quite easy to visit this on your way to or from Shwe Oo Min – it's downhill to the north of the cave, along a dirt track from one of the covered arcade exits. Few visitors make it this way, so expect a bit of attention from local monks and children.

TREKKING AROUND PINDAYA

The three-day route from Kalaw to Inle Lake is absolutely fantastic (see box, p.232), but there are also **trekking** opportunities around Pindaya itself; best is the five-hour hike up to Yazagyi, a Padaung village up in the mountains. Ask at the *Golden Cave* hotel (see below), or the Old Home Tour Information Centre (☎081 66188) on the crossroads beside the market. Both charge around $15 per person per day including food, plus a small donation for accommodation at a monastery.

Pone Taloke Lake

ပုန်းတလုတ်ကန်

Pindaya life revolves around this pretty **lake**, and given the lack of much else to do, you're pretty much guaranteed to find yourself wandering along its banks if you're overnighting in Pindaya. It's best appreciated from *Green Tea* restaurant on its western bank, and there's a nice monastery at its northern end; in addition, the lake also makes a lovely sight during the silence of night-time, when twinkly lights are turned on around the shoreline.

ARRIVAL AND DEPARTURE
PINDAYA

By plane Heho airport (see p.231) is 65km from Pindaya; a taxi will set you back at least K45,000. If that's too steep, you could walk the 2km south to the main road and find a bus or pick-up heading west to Aungban; from there, it's easy to find a pick-up (K1000) or motorbike (K7000) for the remaining 1hr 30min to Pindaya. Heading from Pindaya to the airport, you could make use of the few daily buses to Taunggyi (see p.250), though obviously these may not depart at times appropriate for you.

By bus Pindaya doesn't crop up on many schedules, though there are two daily buses (5.30am and 5.45am), and two daily minibuses (6am and 2pm), to Taunggyi (3hr 30min), departing from the junction outside the *Dagon* restaurant/beer station (see p.238). These are useful if heading to Inle Lake; they'll drop you off in Shwenyaung (3hr into the trip). Coming from the lake it's harder for sure; be at the Shwenyaung junction by 2pm, and hope against hope that there's still a seat for you.

By pick-up and motorbike taxi These are the cheapest ways to hit Pindaya from Kalaw. There are no direct pick-ups; heading from Kalaw, first get yourself to Aungban (K700 by pick-up, K3000 by motorbike), then change to another pick-up (K1000), or motorbike (K7000) if you can brave 1hr 30min on a dusty, bumpy (though scenic) road.

By taxi Since Pindaya isn't the easiest place to reach on public transport, do think about taking a taxi: it'll be a minimum K35,000 to Kalaw, or more like K55,000 to visit the caves and head to Nyaungshwe.

ACCOMMODATION

Pindaya is not the most wi-fi-friendly destination – don't count on it at any of the following accommodation options, though they may have internet-ready terminals in the common areas.

Conqueror Resort Shwe Oo Min Rd, southwest of the lake ☎081 66355, ⍟conquerorresorthotel.com. Located near the caves, this large, resort-like complex was pretty enough when it was first built, but has been allowed to fall into disrepair since – even a recent drop in prices has failed to tempt customers back. Rooms are OK, though; choose from bamboo bungalows, Danu-style stilt houses or stone chalets. There is also a swimming pool (not always open) and restaurant on site. **$77**

Golden Cave Shwe Oo Min Rd, southwest of the lake ☎081 66166, ⍟goldencavehotel.com. The town's mid-range choice, with OK rooms, OK-ish service, and an OK-ish breakfast. The pleasant compound that the place calls home is located within walking distance of the caves – a definite plus-point. **$40**

★**Inle Inn** Maha Bandoola Rd, off east side of lake ☎081 21347, ⍟pindayainleinn.com. By far the most pleasant place to stay in town, set in a complex that's apparently attempting to imitate an "ethnic" village. Choose from stilted bamboo huts, or pricier two-level chalets; the former have huge beds and surprisingly large bathrooms, while the latter also have a fireplace in their suite-like layout. A gym, spa and decent restaurant round out the picture. Hut **$75**, chalet **$120**

Myit Phyar Zaw Gyi Zaytan Qtr, on north side of lake ☎081 66403. This dingy place is about as cheap as you're going to get in Pindaya. Rooms are way overpriced, though some have a lake view, and all have small tellies and decent beds. The real bonus here is for single travellers, since they'll give you a room for $15. **$30**

5

EATING AND DRINKING

Dagon Shwe Oo Min Rd, off northwest corner of lake. Either a restaurant or a beer station, depending upon whether you're looking at the signboard or the menu, but it functions pretty well in both regards. As well as selling draught beer (K700), it's one of the town's more reliable places for food, with simple dishes such as fried rice (K1500) or noodle soup (K1500). If you're in luck, you may spot a few customers wearing ethnic headdresses. Daily 7am–10pm.

★**Green Tea** Shwe Oo Min Rd, on west side of lake ☎081 66344. Come lunchtime, this lakeside venue is teeming with tour groups descending for post-cave luncheon – no real surprise, since this is by far the best place to eat in town. Their wide-ranging menu contains pasta, sandwiches and the like if you're missing Western food, though for something more interesting have a crack at local fare such as the sweet pumpkin soup with shallots (K1800), the filling veggie curry (K2400), or Danu-style mashed rice with potato and fish (K1800). Daily 9am–9pm.

Happy Cafe Shwe Oo Min Rd, on west side of lake ☎093 623 3738. Not the best-looking teahouse in town (those are a little further north), though the only one with an English sign and a lake view. The tea's OK (K300), and in contrast to most such places across the land, it gets a surprisingly high amount of female custom. Daily 6am–5.30pm.

DIRECTORY

Banks Though you might get lucky with currency exchange at the hotels, there's no ATM in Pindaya – arrive with all the cash you need.

Internet The hotels are your best bets for surfing the web, though service regularly goes down in the *Golden Cave*, and it doesn't exist at all at the *Myit Phyar Zaw Gyi*.

Nyaungshwe

ညောင်ရွှေ

The small town of **NYAUNGSHWE** is the de facto base for visitors to **Inle Lake**, whose waters begin just a few kilometres to the south. This has been one of the most visible beneficiaries of Myanmar's recent boom in tourist numbers and the sudden inflow of cash has brought jolting change to the town, as made evident by the mushrooming number of hotels and restaurants, as well as the multistorey buildings which poke incongruously from the dirt. However, Nyaungshwe has so far ridden these changes well, and with its lazy charm barely diluted it remains one of Myanmar's most pleasant places to stay, particularly for independent, backpackery sorts – head to the bars or night market and you'll meet travellers who arrived with the intent of staying one night, yet ended up basing themselves here for a week. Be warned: you may well find yourself doing the same.

In fairness, besides the diverting **Cultural Museum** and some pretty **monasteries**, there's not all that much to see in Nyaungshwe itself. It's best used as a place to unwind – and perhaps fill up, since its range of fantastic restaurants will come as a pleasant change to those who've been in the sticks for a while. However, a little effort can bring great rewards: just get on a bicycle and you'll be able to roll through fantastic countryside to bathe in **hot springs** (see p.248), or sample local **wines** at a vineyard (see box, p.244).

Nyaungshwe gets particularly busy during the Fire Balloon Festival in nearby Taunggyi (see box, p.250), which takes place in November, and during the Phaung Daw Oo Paya Festival (September/October).

There's a K10,000 **entry fee** to the Inle Lake area; this is most commonly levied at a booth as you approach Nyaungshwe from the north. Your bus, taxi or pick-up driver will pull over (he'll get into trouble if he doesn't), and you may not even have to leave your seat during the purchase process. Those hiking in from Kalaw probably won't have to pay, and in any case you almost certainly won't be required to show your entry ticket at any time after purchase.

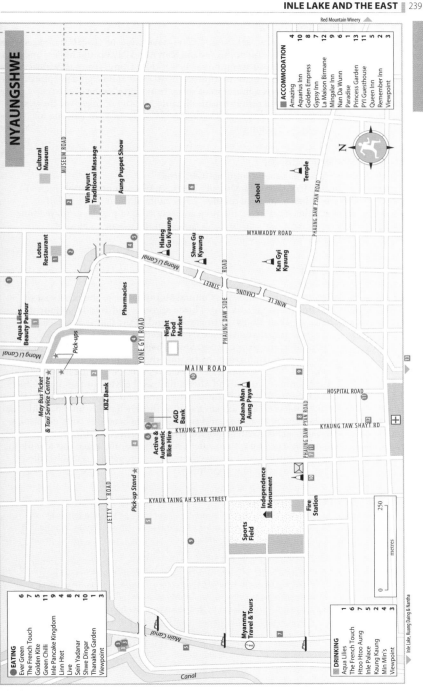

5

Yadana Man Aung Paya

ရတနာမာန်အောင်ဘုရား • Entrances on Main Rd & Phaung Daw Side Rd • Daily 6am–9pm • Free, though small donation expected

A distinctive stepped, golden stupa, the **Yadana Man Aung Paya** is the holiest and most interesting of the Buddhist monuments protruding from Nyaungshwe's very centre. Its shape is unique in Myanmar (quite a boast in a land of golden spires), while the interior functions as a museum of sorts, featuring a cache of dusty ceramics, clocks, carvings and other treasures hoarded by the monks over the years. Just to the west of the stupa, it's possible to climb the ruins of a similar one for superlative views out over Nyaungshwe.

The Monastery Quarter

ဘုန်းတော်ကြီးကျောင်းရပ်ကွက် • East bank of Mong Li canal • Daily 24hr • Free

Hugging the east bank of the small Mong Li canal is a trio of **monasteries**, each of them housing more than a hundred monks. While none of them is particularly interesting in an architectural sense, it's quite an experience to pass by at prayer-time (early morning being your best bet) in order to take in the ethereal sound of monotonous, synchronized chanting.

Cultural Museum

ယဉ်ကျေးမှုပြတိုက် • Museum Rd • Tues–Sun 10am–6pm • K2000

The most intriguing sight in town is the **Cultural Museum** out to the northeast of the centre. An odd mishmash of teak ruins, brick add-ons and Buddhist flourishes, supposedly modelled on the palaces of Amarapura and Mandalay, it has passed through several different incarnations since its completion in 1923. The main hall here was originally built as the palace of **Sao Shwe Thaik**, the last *saopha* (sky lord) of Nyaungshwe; an ethnic Shan himself, he became the first president of a newly independent Burma in 1948. The Shan, of course, went on to become marginalized under the subsequent military junta, and after a time as the Museum of Shan Chiefs the building was transformed into a Buddha Museum, its Shan identity erased. The times are a-changing, however, and a Shan flag now flutters happily outside; old Shan accoutrements such as the royal throne and furniture have been put back on display in the creaky interior, together with elaborate, sequinned royal costumes and some evocative photographs of the latter Shan rulers. All this said, the place was a work in progress at the time of writing, with many empty halls – hopefully set to be filled with something both interesting and appropriate.

NYAUNGSHWE BY BICYCLE

Nyaungshwe is surrounded by delightful countryside, and taking a **bicycle trip** is highly recommended (see opposite). There are a number of appealing options, including the Red Mountain winery (see box, p.244) and the Khaung Daing hot springs (see p.248); you can actually work both into a circular route by taking a boat (around K6000 after haggling) between Khaung Daing and Maing Thauk. It's easy to find the road heading east, then south, from Nyaungshwe, though since this is not entirely pleasant, it's far better to take minor paths. One highly recommended course starts south of Nyaungshwe at Nantha village (see opposite). You'll enter the village immediately after passing the Buddha statue; take a left turn at the tiny T-junction. After passing through an almost tunnel-like thicket of bamboo, the road veers left; turn right instead, onto a dirt track just before the small bridge. This path heads through bucolic farmyard scenery to a charming village, after which you'll be spat out onto the main road to Maing Thauk. If you'd like to head this way back to Nyaungshwe too, the paths starts almost opposite *Aung Thit Sar*, a tiny juice bar just north of a distinctive pink-painted building.

Nantha

ချော • 1km south of town

It's well worth the short walk south to the small village of **Nantha**, a charming place that provides an Inle Lake vibe without the need to leave dry land – stilt-housing, friendly locals and a rural atmosphere whose tranquil air is broken only by the regular put-putting of boat engines. Look hard enough and you'll find a tiny teahouse and small shop; far easier to spot is the huge **Buddha statue** sitting at the village's north end.

ARRIVAL AND DEPARTURE
NYAUNGSHWE

By plane Heho airport is 30km northwest of Nyaungshwe. Taxis will ask for K25,000 from the airport, and given the fact that most landing at Heho are heading that way, it's pretty easy to share the fare; hotels and agencies will be able to lump together those heading back to the airport, while even by yourself the fare should be much cheaper that way (as low as K12,000). Things are far trickier by public transport: from the airport, walk 2km south to the main road, find something heading east towards Taunggyi, get off at Shwenyaung, then hop on a cab (K2000 per seat) or pick-up (K1000) the rest of the way.

Destinations (Heho) Kengtung (1 daily; 55min); Lashio (2 weekly; 50min); Mandalay (7 daily; 35min, though sometimes routed via Nyaung U); Nyaung U (for Bagan; 40min); Tachileik (1–2 daily; 50min, though sometimes routed via Lashio); Yangon (4–5 daily; 1hr 15min).

By bus There are now a few direct buses to Nyaungshwe from other destinations in Myanmar, avoiding the need to change in Shwenyaung, or wait there on the way out of Inle for a service starting in Taunggyi (foreigners not being allowed to take overland transport to areas east of that city). Leaving Nyaungshwe, some tickets will also include pick-up at your hotel; there are gazillions of places selling bus tickets all over town, and your hotel will probably be able to arrange them too.

To Bagan (9hr). You've a choice of daytime or night-time buses (3 daily; 9hr; K11,000 including hotel pick-up).

To Mandalay (7–8hr). There's a choice of express or ordinary bus; there are various departures through the day, most including hotel pick-up.

To Pyin Oo Lwin, Hsipaw and Lashio (11hr, 15hr & 17hr). There are two daily departures to Hsipaw, while Golden Shuttle Express runs an afternoon departure to all three towns (pick-up 3pm). You'll pay the full Lashio price whichever your destination for the latter services.

To Pindaya (3hr from Shwenyaung). There are two daily buses and two daily minibuses linking Pindaya and Taunggyi. This is a far easier trip when heading from Pindaya (see p.237), but heading west you'll have to wait at Shwenyaung junction (2pm is the best time) and hope that there's still a seat (not likely).

To Yangon (12–14hr). The best options are the JJ and Thit Sar Oo overnight express buses, which start from in front of *Ever Green* café; both have toilets and TVs on board, and will give you dinner and even a toothbrush. Regular buses are a bit cheaper.

By pick-up and motorbike taxi To Kalaw it's a tricky trip involving a pick-up ride to Shwenyaung (K1000), then a bus or pick-up west to Kalaw (K2000; around 2hr); you may have to change in Aungban on the way. Note that the practicalities are a little different when making the same journey from Kalaw (see p.231).

By taxi Cabs are by far the easiest means of travel to or from Kalaw; figure on K35,000 one-way, or K55,000 including a stop at Pindaya's Shwe Oo Min Cave (see p.236).

By train There are two daily trains between Shwenyaung and Thazi (11hr 30min), passing Kalaw (3hr 30min) on the way – exceptionally scenic, yet exceptionally hard on your bottom.

GETTING AROUND

By bicycle Nyaungshwe is small and easily navigable on foot, though it's best to strike out into its rural environs by bicycle (see box opposite), rentable from places all over town (K2000/day). Bar the kick-ass bikes at Active & Authentic (see below), these are pretty much all the same;

just be sure to check the state of the tyres and brakes before handing over your cash.

By boat For advice on boat trips from Nyaungshwe, see the Inle Lake section (see box, p.247).

TOURS AND ACTIVITIES

★**Active & Authentic** Kyaung Taw Shayt Rd ☎094 2102 8796, ✉aat.toursmyanmar@gmail.com. There are umpteen places in which to rent a bike in town, but this one is simply a cut above the rest. For a start, they have bikes which would make a Dutchman go weak at the knees:

a little pricey at K12,000 for the day, but worth it if you're planning a long trip. They also rent out glasses and helmets, while the cheery, English-speaking staff can arrange excellent full-day trips (K25,000). Daily 8am–9pm.

5

Lotus Restaurant Museum Rd ☎094 2831 3717. Though this restaurant is not the best of places to eat, its staff can rustle up excellent half-day to two-day treks around Nyaungshwe (K5000–25,000/person), including the reverse-of-norm route all the way to Kalaw (around K35,000 in a group of three).

ACCOMMODATION

Nyaungshwe has by far the best and widest range of accommodation in Eastern Myanmar – no real surprise, since it has by far the most tourists too. Also note that if you're prepared to make a greater Inle outlay, there are higher-end options dotting the lakeshore (see p.249). Wi-fi is surprisingly good for an out-of-the-way Burmese location, but don't count on it working at all hours, or indeed on all days.

Amazing Yone Gyi Rd ☎081 209477, ⓦamazing -hotel.com. Rooms here aren't quite as amazing as you'd expect for the price, and service standards occasionally leave something to be desired. Nevertheless, it's one of the comfiest options in town, with a pleasing canalside location and an excellent on-site restaurant. $150

★**Aquarius Inn** Phaung Daw Pyan Rd ☎081 209352, ⓔaquarius352@gmail.com. Up there with the best places to stay in the town, this friendly guesthouse has a wide range of places to lay your head – from simple boxes with shared facilities to comfy en-suite rooms ($55). The intriguing layout is almost like a budget resort, while the staff are friendly and good at doling out travel advice. $18

Golden Empress Phaung Daw Pyan Rd ☎081 209037, ⓔgoldenempresshotel@gmail.com. The largest rooms you're going to get at this price level. Staff are friendly, the breakfast is decent and the location is both quiet and convenient – a good, safe choice. $35

Gypsy Inn Kann Nar Rd ☎081 209084. So close to the river that you'll be hearing the jagged motor sounds from dawn to dusk, this is one of the cheapest options in town, and a pretty good one to boot. You'll pay a few dollars more for a room upstairs, and around $10 extra for an en suite. No wi-fi. $12

La Maison Birmane Mingalar Quarter ☎081 209901, ⓦlamaisonbirmane.com. A good example of a place that's way too small – there are only ten rooms here (choose from bungalow, chalet or villa), and in high season you may have to book weeks, even months, in advance. Such popularity is justified, as it's a great boutique choice with comfy facilities, a pleasant garden area and a great little restaurant, but being constantly sold out has resulted in rather stuck-up management. $75

★**Mingalar Inn** Phaung Daw Pyan Rd ☎081 209198, ⓦmingalarinn.blogspot.com. This reliable choice is a tale of two wings, with tremendous price and quality differentials between the old and the new. Rooms in the old one are well sized, all en-suite and make perfectly decent places to stay; those in the new are beautiful affairs with coffee tables, bathtubs and balconies with deck chairs. Whichever you're staying in, you'll benefit from generous breakfasts and better-than-average service. Old wing $25, new wing $70

Nan Da Wunn Yone Gyi Rd ☎081 209211, ⓔnandawunn@gmail.com. With its creaky floorboards, this feels like an old mansion of some kind. Rooms are decent, with tubs and bathrooms that can be very large indeed. Do consider shelling out $5 extra for a superior room in the teak building. $35

Paradise Museum Rd ☎081 209321, ⓦinleparadise .com. Once the de facto higher-end choice, but still popular despite new competition. The large, peaceful complex hides rooms of varying standards, and many of them have pleasant verandas; try for one in the new wing at the rear, since these have the best bathrooms. Free tea and coffee; generous breakfasts. $130

★**Princess Garden** Mine Li Rd ☎081 209214. An excellent choice in a gorgeous, semi-rural area just south of the centre. As well as excellent rooms and friendly, knowledgeable staff, there's an inviting pool that's kept in decent nick, as well as a truly lovely breakfast area with views out over the fields. For $15 extra, you can get yourself a bungalow – recommended. $40

PYI Guesthouse Phaung Daw Pyan Rd ☎081 209076, ⓔpyi.nsmm@gmail.com. An odd complex of newish, red-brick houses, whose interiors are rendered almost suite-like on account of the separated bathroom and toilet areas. While they're comfy enough, it has to be said that the bedding isn't as good as one would expect at this price level. $65

Queen Inn Win Quarter ☎081 209544, ⓔqueeninle @gmail.com. This neat little guesthouse boasts a nice location on the opposite side of the canal, and the noise that such proximity to said waterway brings. Management is friendly, the rooms are quite large for the price (if a little bare) and the nearby area is splendidly rural. A new wing was under construction at the time of writing. $35

Remember Inn Museum Rd ☎081 209257, ⓦrememberinn.jimdo.com. Out near the museum, this is an enduringly popular budget choice; even the cheapest rooms get the job done, though the bathrooms could use a little love. Despite its size, the place does often fill up, so it's wise to book ahead. $25

★**Viewpoint** Taik Nan Bridge ☎081 209062, ⓦinleviewpoint.com. The most luxurious place in town by far, its superb rooms boasting all sorts of frills: think yellow *thanaka* face-paint in the bathrooms; natural shampoo, soap and exfoliants; and rice-straw insulation in the walls. Do try to look at a few, however, as some have better views than others. One negative point, for some, is the noise emitted from the hundreds of boats which zip by during the day – for others, it can sound quite pleasant after a while. $105, suites $190

EATING

From humble beginnings, Nyaungshwe is now up there with the best places to eat in all Myanmar, and international treats such as Thai curries, freshly made pasta, delectable dim sum or locally influenced tapas make it mouthwateringly tempting to let your tastebuds take a break from curries, rice and noodles. At the other end of the scale, the town's night market is a grand place to eat; while it would be unfair to single out any particular stall for attention, you'll easily find good places for chapati and curry, barbecued chicken sticks and Shan noodles. The fun starts just after sundown.

Ever Green Cnr Yone Gyi Rd & Kyaung Taw Shayt Rd ☎094 4801 6338. Tiny place selling decent Shan coffee and a range of juices (almost all K1500). Also notable for their surprisingly yummy fish and chips (K4000), made with fish from the lake. Daily 8am–10pm.

★**The French Touch** Kyaung Taw Shayt Rd ☎094 936 0030. An artsy, loungey place that doubles as a gallery of sorts. It's a great place for breakfast (sets K7000), or a quick coffee and pain au chocolat, though there are plenty of decent choices on the menu. Also makes a good drinking spot (see p.244). Daily 7am–10pm.

Golden Kite Yone Gyi Rd ☎081 209327. Still the best of the town's ever-increasing array of faux-Italian eateries. Plus points here are that they have a real wood oven for the pizzas (from K6000), and that the pasta is freshly made every day (dishes from K4000); you can't really go wrong with the choices. Daily 9am–10pm, sometimes later.

★**Green Chilli** Hospital Rd ☎095 214101. Elegant little place with balcony seating and the faint air of a colonial abode. The menu's almost entirely Thai – not completely authentic, but acceptably close. Meaty or fishy mains start at K4200, while the few veggie dishes are cheaper at around K2500. Try a *larb* salad – spiced, minced meat with shallots and mint. Though the place fills up in the evening, it's actually a lovely, quiet spot for coffee during the day (K2000 per pot, serves two). If you like it here, consider hitting their second venue when making your rounds of Inle Lake (see p.250). Daily 10am–10pm.

★**Inle Pancake Kingdom** Win Quarter ☎081 209288. This place has been around since the 1990s. It was originally a milkshake café, and these are still the best things on the menu (from K1000); try their chocolate-banana shakes, made with von Houten cocoa if they've been able to source some from Yangon. The pancakes are pretty good too (also from K1000), with plenty of fruity, savoury and sweet options. Daily 7am–9pm.

Linn Htet Yone Gyi Rd ☎081 209360. Friendly, deceptively simple-looking restaurant that's a favourite with foreigners and locals alike, on account of some incredibly filling curry sets. Just K2500 will buy you curry, rice and sides, and if you can finish the lot you must have been pretty hungry. Daily 8am–10pm.

★**Live** Yone Gyi Rd ☎094 2813 6964. This small dim sum restaurant has been a great addition to the town, and is a little treat to tastebuds which have had one too many bowls of Shan noodles. Try one of their platters (K3500), with a choice between fried or steamed dim sum; there are also some good Chinese and Thai dishes on the menu. Daily 8am–9pm.

Sein Yadanar Museum Rd ☎095 514 8918. Local barbecue joint opposite the *Paradise* hotel (see opposite), with better fare than you'll find at the night market – perhaps apart from the mystery-substance Angry Birds sticks. The rest cost K100–300 each; go for chicken strips, quail eggs, tofu blocks and more, or splash out on a grilled fish (K1500). Daily 2.30–9.30pm.

Shwe Dingar Off Main Rd ☎099 102 4411. If you fancy going local, you could do worse than heading to this amiable teahouse. The tea (K250) is served with a platter of Chinese dumplings, donuts, samosas and the like, though all of these cost a little extra. Open later on weekends if there's football on TV. Daily 6am–7.30pm.

★**Thanakha Garden** Tharzi St ☎094 2837 1552. The most pleasant venue for local food, situated on a charming dirt track near the *Paradise*; it's especially pleasant during the evening, when lit by candlelight and illuminated parasols. The best Shan option is the fish; try it served steamed, in a mildly spicy tomato sauce (K4500). International and fusion options include veggie tempura in tamarind sauce (K2000), all-day breakfast (K3500) and good burgers (K3500); they also have shisha pipes to puff on (K9000). Daily 11am–9.30pm.

Viewpoint Taik Nan Bridge ☎081 209062. The town's top hotel (see opposite) also makes a surprisingly affordable place to eat over the chatter of boats – choose your seat carefully, as from some tables you can see both mountain ranges at the same time, as well as the river. They specialize in "Shan tapas"; this sounds terrifying, but the end result is actually rather nice, and the dishes (from K2000; you'll need at least three for any kind of feed) are served in a cute canoe-shaped dish. Mains are more like K6000, while a big pot of coffee is yours for K2000. Daily noon–9.30pm.

5

INLE WINE

One of the most enjoyable side-trips from Nyaungshwe is to the **Red Mountain** winery (🌐 redmountain-estate.com; daily 9am–6pm; free), less than an hour southeast by bicycle off the road to Maing Thauk. Following harvest time in February and March, a range of wines is produced – Cabernet Sauvignon, two varieties of Shiraz, a rosé, and even a muscat and tawny port. Bottles cost from K7500, though you can drink over wonderful views from their outdoor pavilion with a bargain four-glass sampler set for K2000. The best form of access is by bicycle; it's not far by motorbike taxi, though since it's hard to find another one for the return journey, you may be looking at a fare of up to K8000, including waiting time.

DRINKING

Nightlife in Nyaungshwe is actually pretty good for a town of this size – though you can forget about dancing, there's a pleasing variety of places to drink. Do note, however, that everything's shut and shuttered by around 11pm.

Aqua Lilies Museum Rd ☎ 094 2836 3584. Though their meals and baked goods are merely so-so, this rooftop venue (connected to the spa of the same name; see below) is, though west-facing, a grand place for sunset cocktails (K3000). Daily 8am–9pm.

The French Touch Kyaung Taw Shayt Rd ☎ 094 936 0030. This loungey café (see p.243) is a decent place for cocktails (K4200). If you fancy people-watching, sit out front; for a more secluded drink, head to the garden area at the rear. Daily 7am–10pm.

Htoo Htoo Aung Phaung Daw Pyan Rd ☎ 093 610 1629. A wonderfully chilled place whose garden-like outdoor area is up there with Nyaungshwe's most inviting places to drink. Bottles of Myanmar beer cost K2000, and food is also available. Daily 4–9pm.

Inle Palace Yone Gyi Rd ☎ 094 2834 4972. Fresh-looking, two-level cocktail bar with long happy hours (6–9pm); cheap drinks (cocktails from K1500) and fun staff. The atmosphere is entirely dependent upon who's here on any particular night: it can be rocking one evening, then near-silent the next. Daily 10am–11pm.

Kaung Kaung Main Rd ☎ 081 209063. This local bar is one of very few local places selling draught beer (K600); other choices include small bottles of local rum (K800) and, oddly, Korean *soju* (K2500). The clientele swings between all-Burmese and majority-Western from night to night, but whoever's doing the drinking it's usually one of the more raucous venues in town. Daily 7am–10pm.

Min Min's Yone Gyi Rd ☎ 094 5804 1043. Perhaps this place possesses some sort of foreigner-attracting magnet – they're there drinking every single night, and nobody really knows why. The beer isn't the cheapest (K2200), the food's so-so, but all in all this is the best place in town in which to meet other travellers. Daily 9am–10pm.

Viewpoint Taik Nan Bridge ☎ 081 209062. Yes, this hotel (see p.242) and restaurant (see p.243) is a decent place to drink, too. Though proudest of their wine selection, they've a good range of spirits (from K3000), as well as great cocktails split into those that "won't kill you" and those that "might". Daily noon–9.30pm.

ACTIVITIES

ENTERTAINMENT

Aung Puppet Show Ahletaung Kyaung Rd. Traditional 30min puppet shows from a family which has been doing this for decades; the "theatre" is absolutely tiny, which makes for a truly intriguing atmosphere. Interestingly, they also sell the puppets used for the show (K10,000–20,000). Nightly 7pm & 8.30pm.

COOKING CLASSES

Inle Heart View North of Myatheintan Village ☎ 094 2831 4979. Way out southeast on the road to Maing Thauk, this remote restaurant runs cooking classes (K15,000) on request – a winning mix of Shan, Padaung and Intha dishes. If you so desire, you can even head out to the fields to pluck some of the ingredients yourself.

Myo Myo Cooking Class Museum Rd ☎ 094 2832 6575. Owned by the same family that runs *Linn Htet* restaurant (see p.243), this smart little eatery is most notable for its excellent English-language cooking classes (K15,000). Start at 9.30am and you can eat your own Shan-style creations for lunch; start at 3pm and you can do likewise for dinner.

SPAS AND MASSAGE

Aqua Lilies Museum Rd ☎ 094 2836 3584. The town's best spa option, offering all sorts in a charming location: foot rubs, body scrubs and wraps, facials and more. Massage is also available; figure on K8000 for 30min, or K11,000 for their traditional special. Lastly, if you feel like playing "good cop, bad cop" with your body, their rooftop space is a great sunset cocktail spot (see above). Daily 8am–9pm.

FROM TOP HILL-TRIBE WOMEN, NEAR INTHEIN (P.248); NAUNG TUNG LAKE, KENGTUNG (P.253) >

5

Khaung Daing Natural Hot Spring Nyaung Wun Village
📞 094 936 4876, 🌐 hotspringinle.com. Excellent hot spring
resort within cycling distance to the west of town (see p.248).

Win Nyunt Off Myawady Rd. Far cheaper than Aqua Lilies
(see p.244), this offers traditional massage from K7000/hr
in a ramshackle building just south of the museum.

Inle Lake

အင်းလေးကန်

A placid expanse with forested mountains rising to its east and west, majestic **INLE LAKE**
is one of Myanmar's undoubted must-sees. Its appeal extends beyond this considerable
natural beauty, for dotting the lake and its immediate periphery are numerous stilt
villages of the **Intha** – "sons of the lake", and descendants of Mon people from the far
southeast (though now categorized as a subgroup of the Shan). You are also likely to see
fishermen using traditional conical nets, propelling their boats using a distinctive
leg-rowing technique, and other Intha residents of the lake tending to fruit and
vegetables on floating gardens.

The lake is, sadly, suffering from ever-increasing **pollution** – it's hard to imagine that
just one generation ago, its waters were clean enough to drink. These days, a greater
proportion of the vessels that work the lake are motorized; locals are producing more
litter; and chemicals from the "floating" tomato farms (and locals washing their
clothes) are seriously impairing the quality of the water, and the size of the fish stock.

While the lake is very firmly on the
beaten path, its size is such that you
only really notice just how many other
foreigners are around when your boat
pulls up at one of the stops. Even now, its
markets are aimed more at villagers of the
various ethnic groups that live in the area –
among them Shan, Pa-O, Kayah and Danu
– than they are at tourists. Most visit these
as part of a **boat trip** (see box opposite),
while other sights hereabouts include the
beautiful **Phaung Daw Oo Paya** and **Ngaphe
Kyaung**, the former "jumping cat"
monastery, and the lovely **hot springs** near
Khaung Daing. Note that the sights have
been listed here in an order heading
vaguely clockwise around the lake; this is
the route that most boatmen take.

In common with the rest of Myanmar,
visitor numbers are highest from
December to February. One other
good time to be around is during the
Thadingyut Festival of Lights in October;
since locals like to decorate their houses
with lanterns and candles, taking a
night-time boat ride through the stilt
villages is particularly pleasing.

Maing Thauk

မိုင်းသောက်

On four days out of every five, the
charming village of **MAING THAUK** is

TAKING A BOAT TRIP ON INLE LAKE

It would be a pity – not to mention rather strange – to leave Inle Lake without having taken a **boat trip** on its placid waters. This is not only a beautiful and thoroughly enjoyable experience, but by far the best and easiest way in which to see the various sights around the lake, and take in its unique way of life.

Most trips follow a fairly standard route. Your boat will first spend some time chugging along the canal joining Nyaungshwe to the lake. As soon as you hit the lake proper, you'll see a bunch of fishermen, their boats surprisingly devoid of fish. They'll ask for money if you take pictures; you'll get plenty of chances to snap "real" fishermen later on. Then it's off south to **Nampan**; if it's market day at **Maing Thauk** (see box, p.230), you'll probably stop there too. At Nampan there are a couple of good options for early lunch (see p.250). After that, it's off to the **Phaung Daw Oo Paya** (see below), which features more lunch options (see p.250), and possibly a side-trip to **Inthein** (see p.248). Then, after a trip to see the long-necked **Padaung ladies** and have a stroll on the **floating gardens** (see p.248), it's off to **Ngaphe Kyaung** (see p.248), and finally off home; if it's before 4.30pm, you could ask your boatman to aim instead for the Khaung Daing **hot springs** (see p.248).

Lastly, on the way around, your boatman will inevitably call at various floating cottage industries: **lotus-fibre eavers**, **goldsmiths**, **cheroot-makers**, **boat-builders** and the like. These are all free to visit, and there's little pressure to buy souvenirs, but feel free to tell your boatman if you've tired of these soft-sell activities.

left off most boat-trip itineraries. The exceptions are, of course, the day that the five-day market lands here (see box, p.230); at such times the market is a pleasingly photogenic throng of commerce. The village itself is split into two halves: one for landlubbers, and a "floating" one accessible only by boat. You can walk towards the latter on a long pier, though you'll get stuck at the end.

Thit Tha Kyaung (Forest Monastery)
တောရဘုန်တော်ကြီးကျောင်း
Sitting pretty up a steep hill to the east of Maing Thauk is the gorgeous "**forest monastery**". From lake level you'll be able to make out the stupa at its front; the lake views from here are excellent, if somewhat sullied by electricity wires. The monastery itself provides some great picture-taking opportunities (such as monks eating or washing dishes against whitewashed walls), though do try not to be intrusive. It's a long, sweaty walk here from Maing Thauk, one that will take almost an hour; coming by bike, you'll have to drag the thing up the last few hundred metres, though coming back down is joyfully fast.

Nampan
နန်းပမ်
One of the lake's larger villages, **NAMPAN** is the first stop on most boat tours. Here you'll likely be directed towards weaving workshops, goldsmiths or cheroot factories, though if the particular location is suitable, do take the opportunity for a little walk around some beautiful stilt houses. There are a couple of good lunch spots hereabouts (see p.250), and those not yet temple-tired could ask to be dropped off at **Alodaw Pauk** (actually a shrine), one of the oldest religious structures in the area.

Phaung Daw Oo Paya
ဖောင်တော်ဦးဘုရား • Daily 24hr • Free; packets of gold leaf from K5000
Boats converge on the tiered lakeside **Phaung Daw Oo Paya**, west of Nampan and south of Ywama, to the extent that you'll probably need to climb over a logjam of them in order to reach the shore. The pagoda building is nothing special, but men crowd around

5

to add gold leaf to five Buddha figures that are already so coated that they are no longer recognizably human in shape. Females are not allowed to perform this activity, or approach the figures directly, though there's no problem entering the building.

Inthein

အင်းတိန်

The canal ride west from Ywama to the over-touristy village of **INTHEIN** (also romanized as Indein) starts among reed beds before continuing between more solid banks with jungle on both sides: a striking contrast to the wide-open space of the lake. Just behind the village, at the base of a hill, is **Nyaung Oak**, a set of picturesquely overgrown stupas with carvings of Buddhas, chinthe, devas, elephants and peacocks. Head uphill along a covered walkway to reach **Shwe Inthein Paya**, a collection of seventeenth- and eighteenth-century stupas which are being slowly and heavy-handedly restored. On the way down, look out for a path on the left which runs through a bamboo forest back to the riverside.

Floating gardens

ကျွန်းမျော

On your way around the lake, keep an eye out for boats piled high with twin piles of fertilizer (the gap is for the boatman to stand in while loading and unloading). This weedy bounty is culled from the shallow lakebed, and used for floating **tomato farms**, the crops tethered to the earth with tall bamboo poles. Walking around on these "floating gardens" is a surreal, and rather beautiful, experience – your boatman will likely try to persuade you to eat a couple of tomatoes for proof that the practice works.

Ngaphe Kyaung

ငါးဖယ်ကျောင်း• Near Ywama • Daily 24hr • Free

Previously referred to as the "jumping cat" monastery, **Ngaphe Kyaung** was formerly famed for its felines, which resident monks had once trained to jump through hoops in exchange for edible rewards. This is what most people still come for, though the current crop of cats have not been trained to do anything at all. Nevertheless, the monastery remains a highly attractive place filled with elaborate carvings; if you're in luck, the ceiling will be ashimmer with sunlight reflected from the lake. The monastery is backed by a small, touristy market that makes one of the lake's best souvenir-shopping spots.

Khaung Daing hot springs

ခေါင်တိုင်ရေပူစမ်း• Daily 8am–6pm • Old wing K5000, new wing K9500 • 40min by bicycle from Nyaungshwe, or K7000 return by boat

Located off the west side of the lake, and easily reachable under your own steam from Nyaungshwe, the fantastic **Khaung Daing hot springs** are a real treat to those who've been travelling hard. The place was recently made more tourist-friendly with the opening of a stylish new wing – more expensive though far prettier, and with a bar serving soft drinks and cocktails. The pools here are a joy to wallow in, while those in the old wing are more basic, and more of a local experience. The best time to be here is around sundown, when the shadow from the mountains to the east starts to inch, then race, across the surrounding fields. Mercifully, the horrendously bumpy road from Nyaungshwe – one that saw many cyclists come a cropper with punctured tyres – was in the process of being upgraded at the time of writing; it's also a lovely journey by boat.

Further south

5

If you're prepared to stump up more for a boat, and spend a bit more time on a noisy vessel, the south end of the lake is relatively untouristed. Most head that way to see the markets at **Thaung Tho** and **Kyauk Thaung**, which are far more authentic affairs than others around the lake; they're located on a wide canal which eventually leads to yet another lake. Once off limits, **Moebye Lake** is now drawing a few adventurous travellers; the main targets are **Sankar**, a beautiful village, and **Tharkong Pagoda**, a crumbling assortment of stupas. Note that these latter sights are around three hours from Nyaungshwe, each way – a long time to spend on a boat, so consider bringing a book. The mountains hereabouts would make for excellent hiking territory, but they conceal a substantial opium trade: an estimated five tonnes of the stuff per year, with the crops protected by local militia.

GETTING AROUND

INLE LAKE

By boat Most hotels, guesthouses and travel agencies in Nyaungshwe can arrange boat trips, though it's pretty easy – and often cheaper – to do things yourself. Walk around the main canal, and boatmen will find you; while walking around Nyaungshwe, touts will also regularly cycle upto you offering such services. The standard rate is K12,000–18,000 per boat; these fit a maximum of five people, though three or four is far more comfortable. If you're planning on heading to Inthein, it'll cost around K5000 extra; further south to Sankar, it'll cost more like K60,000, and take three hours longer each way. Ask if your vessel has life jackets and cushioning on the seats. You'll all be seated in series, and essentially unable to talk to each other over

the jagged rattle of the engine – consider bringing earplugs, as well as a sun hat (the boats have no cover), sunblock and water. Something with long sleeves can also come in handy during the occasionally chilly early morning. Tours can take most of the day, meaning that an early start is advisable: pre-sunrise departures are popular, though some prefer to start later on and return at dusk.

By bicycle It's possible to hit a few of the sights around the lake by bike (see box, p.240). These include the Khaung Daing hot springs (see opposite), Maing Thauk (see p.246) and the Forest Monastery (see p.247); for anything longer, ask the staff at Active & Authentic (see p.241), who also run good bike tours.

ACCOMMODATION

There are now more than a dozen resorts dotting the shores of the lake, and you'll see a fair few when taking a boat trip. Many are quality affairs staffed by local villagers, while the price usually includes pick-up in Nyaungshwe (or, sometimes, the airport); some are owned by government cronies, most notably Tay Za's *Aureum Palace Hotel*. Do note that you'll essentially be stranded at many of these places, and that wi-fi access should not be relied upon.

★**Golden Island Cottages** Nampan and Thale U ☎095 154 9019, ⓦgichotelgroup.com. One of the most affordable options around the lake – two, in fact, since they have locations in both Nampan and Thale U. Both are staffed by Pa-O people, and feature decent stilt-house rooms boasting gorgeous lake views; the Nampan location is set above the lake, while the one in Thale U is closer to shore. $70

★**Inle Princess Resort** North of Maing Thauk ☎081 209055, ⓦinleprincessresort.net. A dreamily beautiful, undeniably romantic place where rooms and common areas alike have been designed with rare attention. The furnishings and fabrics are all top-notch, the lily-filled ponds could tempt out the artist in you, and the on-site restaurant is fantastic. $180

Inle Resort Near Maing Thauk ☎095 154444, ⓦinleresort.com. Terrific option near to Maing Thauk, a gigantic complex set around a restaurant that feels more like that of an ocean liner. Their cottages are affordable, but you'll have to splash out far more for a deluxe room ($175)

or villa ($210) with lake view. Also note that the place is actually accessible by land as well as boat, meaning that you're not entirely trapped. $110

Ngwe Zin Yaw Near Phaung Daw Oo Paya ☎095 211996. Though primarily functioning as a restaurant (see p.250), this place lets out simple rooms too. It's one of the only lower-end options in the whole area. $35

Paramount Inle Resort Khaung Daing ☎094 936 0855, ⓦparamountinleresort.com. Near the village of Khaung Daing and its hot springs, this is the best option at this price level – and you can certainly enquire about discounts. While its rooms aren't exactly huge, they're pleasantly decorated, and all have appealing balconies with lake views. $105

Shwe Inn Tha Near Phaung Daw Oo Paya ☎095 192592, ⓦinlefloatingresort.com. High-end venue with luxuriantly appointed stilthouse rooms, impeccable service and an excellent bar and restaurant. There's an on-site spa, as well as that true Inle rarity, a swimming pool. $170

5

EATING

Boat trips can take up the whole day, so it's fortunate that there are plenty of places to eat on the lake, especially in and around Nampan village (see p.247), and in stilt houses abutting the Phaung Daw Oo Paya. If you want to dine anywhere specific, however, let your boatman know – otherwise, you may well be taken to a commission-friendly place of his choosing.

Golden Kite Nampan Village ✆ 081 209327. Like *Green Chilli*, this is a Nampan-based twin to a more established Nyaungshwe restaurant (see p.243). This time the food isn't quite as good, but the charming above-the-lake location means that it still makes a good stop for pizza or pasta. Daily 9am–7pm.

Green Chilli Nampan Village ✆ 095 214101. The most beautiful restaurant on the lake area, this elegant stilt house has more or less the same Thai-heavy menu as its sister venue in Nyaungshwe (see p.243). The fact that most dishes are available most of the time is rather astonishing, given the far-flung location. Daily 9am–7pm.

★**Inle Heart View** North of Myatheintan Village ✆ 094 2831 4979. A *Far Side* cartoon come to life, this quirky, solar-powered restaurant is located in almost comical solitude on a shallow hillside east of the lake, and east of the main road south to Maing Thauk, so keep an eagle eye out for the sign. They serve organic dishes, most of them using veggies grown in the surrounding fields. It's one of those places where the menu rarely bares much resemblance to what's actually on offer – just ask the affable chef (whom you may have to stir from slumber or hail from a field), and before long you could be devouring delectable steamed fish (K3000), potato soup with ginger (K1500), "dancing" pomelo and avocado in balsamic vinegar (K1500) and more besides. Fantastic, and they also do cooking lessons (see p.244). In theory, daily 24hr.

Ngwe Zin Yaw Near Phaung Daw Oo Paya ✆ 095 211996. A cheery-looking place with lime-green tablecloths and dangling parasols, this is the best option near the Phaung Daw Oo Paya, and also a cheap place to stay (see p.249). The menu itself holds few surprises, but simple mains are yours for around K2000, and fruit juices (K15000) and beer (K2000) are also available. It's located just over one of the several footbridges you'll see: just look for the sign. Daily 5am–10pm.

Taunggyi

တောင်ကြီး

You're unlikely to spend too much time in **TAUNGGYI**, the capital of Shan State – though agreeable in a bustling, dusty sort of way, there's precious little of interest here. One might expect it to function as a travel hub, but in reality the buses it fires west can be booked and boarded just as easily in Nyaungshwe or Kalaw (saving you an hour or two to boot), and the few it sends east remain off limits to foreign adventurers. Though the city has the regular Burmese dole of religious monuments (none particularly notable), there are two decent reasons to come to Taunggyi: one is when the city takes its comparatively tourist-free turn on Shan State's rotating five-day market schedule (see box, p.230), and the other is in the autumn, when it plays host to a fantastic **balloon festival** (see box below).

THE TAUNGGYI FIRE-BALLOON FESTIVAL

Mention Taunggyi to a Shan local, or perhaps even Burmese from other states, and they'll likely rhapsodize about the city's famed **balloon festival** – even if they've never been themselves. It takes place in October or November, but ask one of the Nyaungshwe or Inle Lake hotels for the actual date if you're in the area around this time. Most visit by taxi on a day-trip from Nyaungshwe (figure on at least K40,000 return, including waiting time), though traffic can get snarled up when heading back in the late evening, partly down to the fact that many of those on the road will be rather drunk. Rather like unmanned hot-air balloons, and decorated with all manner of images and text (often made up of small, cleverly arranged candles), the fire-balloons themselves aren't the safest of objects – fireworks are attached to many of them, so it may be prudent to keep your distance. Before or after the viewing, do take the chance to simply stroll around town while everyone's in party mode.

5

KAYAH STATE

Located south of the Inle Lake area, and populated by tribal groups including Padaung, Kayin and Karenni, tiny **Kayah State** is one of Myanmar's least-visited divisions. One reason for this is the fact that the area has only recently been opened to foreign travellers – in theory, independent travellers can visit the state capital, **Loikaw**, the only place in Kayah with accommodation licensed to accept foreigners, and take day-trips into the surrounding area. In practice, however, an abundance of red tape means that it's still very tough both to arrive here and to get around, and for now you're still advised to join a tour (see below).

Loikaw itself is a likeable enough place, though there's little to see bar the colourful **Thiri Mingalar** tribal market and the pretty view from the stupas on **Taung Kwe**, a craggy hillock overlooking the town. Those staying on could try tracking down **Christ the King Church**, the oldest Catholic place of worship in Kayah; it contains a small cultural museum featuring minority dress and the like, though nothing is signed in English.

Day-trip options from the city include **Chikae Village**, notable for traditional Kayah flagpoles known as *kay htoe poe*; **Dor Sor Bee**, home to a series of Kayah animist shrines; and "**Seven Steps Lake**", a series of pools surrounded by delightfully unspoiled countryside. Those on a tour can also try the easy (and mostly flat) half- or full-day trek to the Padaung village of **Panpet** – a far less touristy "giraffe lady" experience than that available on Inle Lake (see box, p.247).

Tours are best organized in Yangon (see p.83), although the majority actually start from Inle Lake; most begin with a boat ride from Nyaungshwe to Loikaw, and some finish with an overland journey to Kalaw. They don't come cheap – figure on at least $300 for a two-night trip. With the Kayah tourist scene still in its infancy, it's worth keeping your ear to the ground – at the time of writing, Exotissimo (see p.25) were in the process of piecing together an exciting cycling tour around parts of the state.

ARRIVAL AND DEPARTURE
TAUNGGYI

By plane Heho airport (see p.241) is the closest one to Taunggyi; it would be a minor miracle to find other foreigners headed to Taunggyi, rather than Inle Lake, but if you'd like to share a taxi (around K30,000) you may get some luck asking locals.

By bus Though the vast majority of buses heading west from Inle Lake and Kalaw start in Taunggyi, don't come here to board one – you'll add hours to your travel time, and may find it difficult to track down the correct bus stop. These are clustered west of the National Highway which forms the city's main north–south thoroughfare, between Kon The (Merchant) Rd and Na Ga Pwat Rd; ask at one of the many offices on the west side of the

highway for details. Juddering buses to Kalaw (3hr) leave from a stop next to the Na Ga Pwat Kyaung; these can also drop you at Shwenyaung, for Inle Lake, though less problematic are the direct pick-ups to Nyaungshwe (see p.238).

Destinations Bagan (3 daily; 9hr); Bago (daily; 12hr); Lashio (daily; 15hr); Mandalay (3 daily; 7–8hr); Meiktila (3–4 daily; 4hr); Thazi (3–4 daily; 3hr 30min).

By pick-up Crowded pick-ups (K1000) connect Nyaungshwe and Taunggyi with surprising regularity; they drop off just southeast of Na Ga Pwat monastery.

ACCOMMODATION

Note that accommodation becomes scarce during the balloon festival (see box opposite) – even hotels in Nyaungshwe are known to jack up their prices during this period.

KBZ FC Khwar Nyo Rd ☏ 081 22009. Named after the city's football team (whose players sometimes roost here), this is a reliable choice, located a short motorbike taxi ride northwest of the centre. Rooms are large enough, and come equipped with basic mod cons – including, on occasion, more than one TV. Breakfast not

included; no wi-fi. $\overline{\$30}$

Sun Min National Highway ☏ 081 22353. Located opposite the stadium that the aforementioned local football team play in, this is one of the few decent budget choices in town. Breakfast not included; no wi-fi. $\overline{\$15}$

5

Kengtung

ကျိုင်းတုံ

The third-largest settlement in Shan State after Taunggyi and Lashio, **KENGTUNG** (also known as Kyaingtong, and in either case pronounced "Chengtong") is a love-it-or-loathe-it sort of place. Adherents delight in its unhurried, untouristed vibe; its profusion of Buddhist places of worship; the charming lake at its centre; and the opportunities for **trekking** and **hill-tribe** visits on its periphery. Detractors find that the place simply isn't worth the occasionally considerable expense of getting here. Foreigners are still barred from taking overland transport to or from areas west (ie, almost all of Myanmar), meaning that you'll face a steep fee to fly in, out, or both. In addition, it's a dusty place that somehow contrives to feel windswept, even when there's no wind, while the accommodation is almost all vastly overpriced, and there are few good culinary options to speak of. On balance, it's probably only really worth heading here if you're combining a Myanmar trip with a visit to northern Thailand.

The **Thai border** is, indeed, a mere five-hour bus ride away (see box, p.256), and it's easy to spot several manifestations of this proximity. Thai products line the shelves of Kengtung's shops, while Leo and Singha beer are imbibed alongside Myanmar around the night-time barbecue stands; Thai tourists pop into town in ever-increasing numbers; while many local places of worship are known as "Wat", and some are distinctively Thai in style.

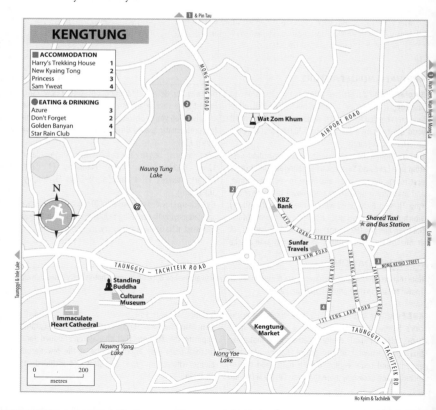

Kengtung Market

ကျိုင်းတုံ့ဈေး • Between Zeigyi Rd and Main Rd • Daily 6am–6pm • Free

Kengtung's **market** is as colourful a place as any of its Shan State contemporaries, with hill folk descending to sell their wares. Entering from the town side, you'll have to run a gauntlet of kitchenware, cheap clothing and other uninteresting fare, though before long you'll track down one of the smaller sections in which ethnic beads and fabrics are sold. There was once also a **water buffalo market** on the way out to Taunggyi; though this had ceased to trade at the time of writing (apparently due to a combination of tax increases and the villagers' increasing propensity to trade by mobile phone instead), it's certainly worth enquiring at your accommodation, just in case it has resurfaced.

Naung Tung Lake

နောင်တုံ့ကန် • Best accessed from Main Rd to south, or small road south of *New Kyaing Tong* hotel to the east • Daily 24hr • Free

Pretty much the only attractive place in a rather ugly city is the small **Nang Tung Lake** at its heart. The best views are from the east side, near the *Azure* bar and *Don't Forget* restaurant (see p.255); from here you'll be able to make out the standing Buddha statue (see below), and see the Shan mountains cascading into the distance – particularly beautiful during sunset. You'll be able to walk around the whole lake in half an hour; the road circling it is small and relatively traffic-free. Lastly, looking out over the lake from the east is the town's old **colonial quarter**, where several buildings still stand proud; best is the **Colony House** on Mine Yen Road.

Wat Zom Khum

On hill between Mong Yang Rd and Airport Rd • Daily 4am–8pm • Free

Peeking down on Kengtung from a lofty vantage point atop a small hill, **Wat Zom Khum** – also known as Wat Jong Kham – is by far the most appealing of the town's many, many religious sites. As with most of the others, the "Wat" in its name reflects Kengtung's proximity to Thailand. It's certainly worth the walk up, for there are delightful views both inside and out. The interior has stencilled gold markings on a burgundy background (making it somewhat Vietnamese in feel) and a panoply of golden statues, no two of which are identical. From the pavilion to the rear of the complex, you can see the lake, the standing Buddha statue (see below) and the mountains muscling away beyond.

West of the centre

There are a few sights located in a small huddle just west of the town centre. From the market or lake, track down the busy Main Road and make the steep plod west. Once over the ridge, you'll see the **Immaculate Heart Cathedral** on your right; this has been educating and otherwise assisting local orphans since the days of empire. Accessible from the rear gate of the complex, and visible from all over town, is a **Standing Buddha** statue some 18m in height. Finally, near its foot is the local **Cultural Museum**.

Cultural Museum

ယဉ်ကျေးမှုပြတိုက် • Off Main Rd, near foot of Buddha statue • In theory Tues–Sun 10am–6pm, though you may have to hunt down the keyholder • K2000

Kengtung's small **Cultural Museum** isn't really worth the modest entrance fee: it merely portrays, rather than explains, what goes on in the hills and mountains surrounding the town, and it's often locked in any case. If lucky enough to find the keyholder, you'll find costumes from all of the main minority peoples hereabouts, as well as an assortment of beads, necklaces and farming equipment.

5

VISITING THE VILLAGES AROUND KENGTUNG

For most, the main reason to visit Kengtung is to take advantage of the **trekking opportunities** in the hills around town. Clutches of Akha, Eng, Lahu, Loi, Padaung and Shan live hereabouts, amid some splendid scenery. Diverse though these peoples are, most travellers feel that a single day of village-visiting suffices; things can get samey rather quickly, and overnight stays are currently forbidden by the Shan State authorities.

The most common target is the **Pin Tau** area 16km north of town, in which it's possible to visit several villages on a loop trek. It's an easy walk, though the area's popularity with foreign visitors means that you may encounter begging or over-persistent vendors. Alternatively, the lofty **Ho Kyim** area is 16km south of town; the journey up is rather beautiful, and rewarded with some pleasant Loi and Akha villages. Further south and east, on a separate mountain range around 32km from Kengtung, is the equally high **Loi Mwe** area; despite its name, most villages here are Ahka and Lahu, rather than Loi. This has the most to get one's teeth into of all the village areas around town, and is also easiest to access for single travellers (see below); the steep, luxuriantly forested drive up is smooth yet quite spectacular (look for a miniature Golden Rock on the way, opposite the hydroelectric system used to power the villages), while near the top are a small, pretty lake, a decent little market (great for lunchtime noodles) and a clutch of colonial structures dating back to the area's time as a minor hill station. Farther afield, nestled into a small valley on the way out towards Mong La (see box opposite), are the Loi villages of **Wan Saen** and **Wan Nyek**; here, people still live in communal longhouses, which sometimes play host to more than ten families at a time. Also check out the gorgeous carved panels and doorways on Wan Nyek's beautiful Wat; it looks like they're awaiting donations to bring the cheap roof into line.

Most hit one or more of these areas as part of a day-long **tour**; most hotels will be able to organize these for you. This generally costs $25 for the guide (which you'll need to be able to find most villages) and $40 for the car or minibus, all split between the group. You'll be able to hit the Pin Tau and Ho Kyim areas in one day; if you want to head further out to the Wan Saen and Wan Nyek villages, figure on an extra $20–30 for the vehicle. These prices are too steep for many single travellers, who are instead advised to head to the shared taxi rank (see below) behind the *Golden Banyan* restaurant (see opposite). Here you should be able to meet a motorbike driver; $20 is a fair price for a trip out to Loi Mwe and back. This is the best place to head, since most of its villages and sights are accessible by road. Trips to Pin Tau or Ho Kyim involve more walking, and as such you'll likely be charged additional guide-service fees ($20); the going isn't too tricky on any of these trails, but it's prudent to bring along sensible footwear and a bottle of water.

ARRIVAL AND DEPARTURE   KENGTUNG

By plane If you're combining Kengtung with any Myanmar destination bar Tachileik, you're going to have to make use of its tiny airport, located 3km east of the centre – within walking distance, for sure, though since the route isn't terribly pleasant you may want to take a tuk-tuk (K2000) or bus (K500) to or from town. To fly to or from Yangon, you'll need to go via Heho or Mandalay; tickets are available from agencies dotted around the town centre, though given the fact that foreigners have no other option, flights are usually very expensive (figure on $135 to Heho, one-way).

Destinations Heho (1 daily; 55min); Mandalay (1 daily; 50min–1hr 30min); Tachileik (1 weekly; 25min).

By bus Foreigners are still prohibited from using overland transport between Taunggyi and Kengtung: you've no option but to fly, but though the situation doesn't look like changing in the foreseeable future, there's no harm in re-checking before you travel. The only route you're allowed to take is south to Tachileik on the Thai border, and even for this it's *essential* to get permission from the local immigration office (see box, p.256). This is free, and only takes a few minutes: you'll need to present your passport, as well as your bus ticket, and these will also need to be photocopied up to six times for presentation at road-blocks; though your bus company should take care of this before you board, it's safer to have it taken care of the day before. Several companies make the run to Tachileik (ask at your accommodation for the closest one), though strangely they all make the run in near-convoy at the same times (8am and noon; 5hr); the times are the same back from Tachileik.

By bus and shared taxi To Mong La, shared taxi is the only option (2hr; K5000); they depart from a yard-like area behind the *Golden Banyan* restaurant (see opposite). Your driver will likely pop by the immigration office on the way to get your trip stamped and signed off.

5

ACCOMMODATION

Kengtung has very few decent places to stay, and most find that a couple of nights here is more than enough. Note that though the following places claim to have wi-fi, it often goes down across the whole town (see p.256).

Harry's Trekking House Mong Yang Rd ☎ 084 21418. Though Harry is sadly no longer around, this guesthouse remains excellent value, and is the only real recommendation at this price level despite a far-flung location north of the lake. Rooms are set in three separate buildings and differ a fair bit, so look at a few before plumping for one. **$15**

New Kyaing Tong Mong Yang Rd ☎ 084 21620, ⓦ kyaingtongnewhotel.com. If you're looking for something resembling a real hotel, this is your only option, with smartish rooms and a swimming pool (out of service since incurring earthquake damage in 2011). Though it's apparently no longer government-owned, there are still questions about where the money is

going; in addition, the place can feel utterly empty at times. **$65**

Princess Zaydan Kalay Rd ☎ 084 21319, ⓔ kengtung @main4u.com.mm. Reliable mid-range choice, though you really won't get what you're paying for. Rooms have tellies, a/c and a fridge for stowing your booze, and the location near the market is a plus point. **$50**

Sam Yweat Kyaing Lan Rd ☎ 084 21235. Surprisingly pleasant place, at least once you're past the motorbikes in the open-air reception area. These are the only rooms in town which could be described as "cheery", with some painted decorations, though they're still rather basic. Breakfast is taken in the atmospheric old block. **$35**

EATING AND DRINKING

If you think that Kengtung's accommodation options are uninspiring, just wait until you try finding a decent place to eat. Some solace can be found in the many snack-shacks around the market, and those leading down to the lake from Mong Yang Rd. At night, you could try to track down one of the town's many barbecue-stick places for some cheap, tasty snacks (K100–200 each); there's one on the east shore of the lake, near the corner where the road comes down.

Azure East side of lake. Tiny place across the small road from the lakeshore, selling tasty draught beer (K1000 per glass, K4000 for a pitcher). You could always ask to plonk your plastic chair in the grassy area by the lake. Daily 10am–9pm.

Don't Forget East side of lake ☎ 094 4100 6438. An odd, cutesey little place popular with young couples or couples-to-be. Their food is OK (mains K1500–3000), though given the lakeside location it's also a nice place for a strawberry shake by day (K1000) or beer by night. Daily 10am–11pm.

Golden Banyan Zaydan Loang Rd ☎ 084 21421. Not great, though somehow still the most reliable place to eat in town. They've a wide range of Chinese dishes; try the hot

and sour fish soup (K4000), fried aubergine (K2500), fried noodles (K2000) or tofu dishes (K3000). As long as the weather agrees, it's most pleasant to eat outside under the banyan tree – not a garden, sadly, but a sort of concrete shelf. Daily 10am–9pm.

Star Rain Club Airport Rd. 2km east of the centre, this nightclub is a decidedly surprising find in a far-flung location such as Kengtung. Firstly, outside Yangon, Myanmar doesn't have many such venues; secondly, though not officially a gay venue, it's certainly gay-friendly, and when cavorting with its (usually very young, mostly male) crowd it can feel more like you're in Thailand than Myanmar. Daily 8–11pm.

MONG LA

Way out near the Chinese border, **Mong La** has a bit of a reputation. Essentially a part of China, and even running on Beijing time, it has long been popular with (almost exclusively male) Chinese tourists, who come across the border to throw down cash at the town's brothels and casinos. Pressure from the Chinese government forced many to close in 2005, though in the words of one chuckling local police officer, "we just moved them all back ten miles, and made them much larger". Unfortunately, the border crossing here is closed to third-party nationals, but the place does draw a few curious Westerners. Other than the odd Myanmar-meets-Vegas-meets-Bangkok atmosphere, the most interesting sight here is the town **market**, though it makes depressingly clear the continuing Chinese trade in endangered animals – live pangolins and monkeys, as well as tiger claws, elephant skin, bear paws and the like.

5

DIRECTORY

Banks The KBZ bank here does not yet have an ATM or provide foreign exchange services, though they can perform Western Union transfers in an emergency. In short, it's best to arrive in Kengtung with as much kyat as you'll need; you'll be able to change foreign currency (especially Thai baht) in Tachileik, if you're headed to or from Thailand.

Internet Kengtung has not yet caught up with the rest of Myanmar in the internet connectivity stakes, and service regularly goes down for days or weeks on end. If you're in luck, you should be able to get online at most hotels; failing that, try the large internet café on the west bank of the lake.

Tachileik

တာချီလိတ်

You'll find yourself passing through bustling **TACHILEIK** if making the trip between Kengtung and northern Thailand. There's a palpable frontier atmosphere here – it's almost as if a zest for foreign currency has physically yanked the place right up to the border, and Thai baht is indeed the main currency accepted everywhere, from hotels to the tiny stores dealing in black-market goods. That said, these days Chinese is quite possibly the second language here – a sign of the times.

Though there's no reason to visit the place on its own merit, Tachileik has long been a popular visa-run destination for expats living in Thailand, and travellers wanting to peek inside Myanmar without shelling out on a visa or benefiting the regime. At one point foreigners were allowed all the way to Kengtung on a free **temporary visa** (see box below), but now you're not permitted to use this to stray any further than the Tachileik city limits.

ARRIVAL AND DEPARTURE   TACHILEIK

By plane Tachileik's small airport is 10km northeast of the town centre, just east of the Kengtung road (100 baht by motorbike, or 300 baht by tuk-tuk). Note that while there's a daily flight to Kengtung, the machinations of local flight schedules mean that flights only arrive from there once a week. You can buy tickets from various agencies around the junction just up from the Thai border; if you're in Thailand and intending to fly from Tachileik to other parts of Myanmar than Kengtung, try to find out the schedule before crossing the border, or you could be in for a boring few days' wait.
Destinations Heho (3 weekly, sometimes via Lashio; 1hr); Kengtung (1 daily; 25min); Lashio (2–3 weekly; 1hr 5min); Mandalay (1–2 daily; 1hr 10min); Yangon (5 weekly; 1hr 35min).

By bus Numerous companies have two daily services to Kengtung (5hr), all departing at either 8am, then again at 11am. It's best to buy tickets at the town's hotels, even if you're not staying. You'll also need official permission for this journey; the guards on the Burmese side of the Thai border will tell you which particular office to head to, and you'll need to present your bus ticket and passport. The permission slips must be photocopied up to six times for presentation at local checkpoints – this can usually be done when buying the ticket, though it sometimes incurs an extra fee. The station itself is 2km from the centre on the Kengtung road, and easily accessible by tuk-tuk (10 baht) or motorbike (40 baht).

TACHILEIK–MAE SAI BORDER CROSSING

Using this border to cross into Thailand has been a far, far simpler affair since 2013, when fiddly restrictions were relaxed. You no longer need permission from Yangon to cross, or pre-booked transport to the border, merely government permission to take the bus from Kengtung (see p.254). Coming into Myanmar is a slightly different matter; **visas** are not issued at the border, so you'll need one arranged beforehand, unless you're opting for one of the free 14-day **temporary visas** (which allow you no further than the Tachileik city limits). The border **immigration offices** are open daily 6am–6pm.

The pleasant Thai town of **Mae Sai** hugs up against the border. Small red buses make the trip between the border and the bus station for 15 baht, while it's more like 40 baht by motorbike, or 80 baht by taxi. Mae Sai has regular connections to and from Chiang Rai (1hr 30min), slightly less frequent ones to Chiang Mai (4–5hr), and others to destinations across Thailand.

ACCOMMODATION AND EATING

In general, you'll get far more bang for your baht by staying over the Thai border in Mae Sai instead. Baht's the preferred currency in Kengtung's hotels, though they'll accept kyat and (usually) dollars too.

Erawan Mahabondola Rd ⊕012 892 863. Extremely good value for the price, with a range of clean, ample-sized rooms; you'll pay extra for those with a/c and/or wi-fi. To get here from the Thai border, turn right at the junction, then take the first proper road on the left (after the Ayeyarwady Bank). $10

Valentine Main Rd. A nice hi-hi or bye-bye to Burmese cuisine, just around the corner from the Thai border – turn right at the junction, and it's almost immediately on your right. They sell Thai and Chinese-style mains too (K1500–2500), as well as Burmese tea (K300). Daily 5am–9pm.

DIRECTORY

Banks There are money-changers all over town, though to avoid being ripped off, do get a handle on rough rates beforehand; at the time of writing, it was around K30 to the baht. There's also a KBZ Bank, with an ATM that usually works, just a short walk from the Thai border; with Thailand at your back, turn right at the junction, and you're almost there. If that one fails, there are more banks further up the same road.

Mandalay
and around

U BEIN BRIDGE, AMARAPURA

Mandalay and around

Myanmar's second city and de facto cultural capital, Mandalay is one of the country's "big four" destinations. Such popularity is well deserved, since the city and its surrounding area constitute the country's densest concentration of sights – many areas would be proud to boast of a former royal capital, but here you'll find a full four of them, all within cycling distance of each other. Mandalay is, of course, the main centre of affairs; initially unassuming despite the exotic-sounding name, it's a real grower that tempts many an independent traveller to stay longer than expected.

Though most travellers only stay for a night or two, there's enough in **Mandalay** to keep you busy for a week. The appeal here lies not just in the city's sights – ascend Mandalay Hill, visit the reconstructed palace, hunt down the Mahamuni Paya or any number of other Buddhist monuments – but also in the opportunities for eating, shopping and entertainment that are hard to find elsewhere in Myanmar. A single day could see you wolfing down a fried English breakfast, heading to the driving range to practise (or get started on) your golf swing, following up a nice swim with a Thai lunch and some durian ice cream, shopping for gold leaf, then catching a marionette show or the famed Moustache Brothers in action.

You'll need two days, at the very minimum, to exhaust the many sights lying further afield. Just south of Mandalay is **Amarapura**, a former capital boasting the world's longest teak footbridge – a truly splendid creation, and especially photogenic during the rising or setting of the sun. Further on is **Inwa**, capital on at least four occasions but now essentially rural in nature; after taking a short ferry ride to access the main area, most travel around this bucolic village by horse-drawn carriage. Crossing the Ayeyarwady bridges from Inwa will bring you to **Sagaing**, yet another former capital, and one possessed of a stupa-studded hill that rivals the famous one visible way to the north in Mandalay. Some way north of Mandalay, and usually accessed by ferry from the city, is little **Mingun**, a delightful village which would have been home to the world's largest stupa had certain things gone according to plan. The part that *did* get built is still a grand sight, and you can also content yourself with the world's largest functional bell.

Mandalay

မန္တလေး

Rudyard Kipling has a lot to answer for. Thanks to his evocative poem, the name of **MANDALAY**, Myanmar's second city, suggests – for many Western travellers, at least – images of a bygone Asia. Arriving in the city itself tends quickly to dispel such thoughts, however, as visitors find themselves confronted by an initially faceless grid of congested streets. These centre around the walls of the old palace compound – though

WOODCARVINGS, SHWE IN BIN KYAUNG

Highlights

❶ Shwe In Bin Kyaung Far less visited than the similar Shwenandaw Kyaung, this teak monastery is equally beautiful and free to enter. **See p.271**

❷ Shan food So what if you're not in Shan state? There are plenty of ethnic Shan in Mandalay, and their yummy food is available at many buffet-style eateries such as *Shan Mama*. **See p.277**

❸ Sunset over the Ayeyarwady Myanmar's most important waterway is at its most beautiful around sunset; take it in from the riverside road, or over cocktails on the roof of the *Ayarwaddy River View Hotel*. **See p.279**

❹ Mandalay shows Myanmar's capital of culture, Mandalay boasts a series of tempting traditional performances to enjoy. **See p.279**

❺ U Bein Bridge Just south of Mandalay, this iconic bridge – more than 1km in length – is one of Myanmar's most famous sights. See p.282

❻ Biking around Inwa Most make their way around this delightful rural village in a horse-drawn carriage, but with your own two wheels you'll be able to explore roads that see no other tourists. **See p.284**

❼ Boat trip to Mingun Slide up the Ayeyarwady River on a boat towards Mingun, a tiny village featuring the remains of what was intended to be the world's largest stupa. See p.289

HIGHLIGHTS ARE MARKED ON THE MAP ON P.262

even this potentially redeeming feature is largely taken up by a huge military base. There is, however, a great big "but". As with many other places of regal pedigree, Mandalay still exudes a relaxed, traditional feel quite at odds with, say, Yangon. Kipling never actually visited Mandalay, but those who *do* spend a bit of time here often end up loving the place.

Of the city's attractions, **Mandalay Hill** is probably the most popular – most choose to pant up its lengthy covered staircases in time to see the sun go down behind the Ayeyarwady. **Kuthodaw Pagoda** is the pick of the several temples nearby; you could, indeed, spend a whole day in the Mandalay Hill area alone. To the west, and at the dead centre of the city, is the old **palace** compound – now largely a military zone, though many of its former royal buildings have been reconstructed. Down in the southern part of the city you'll find the excellent **Mahamuni Paya**, and the teak **Shwe In Bin Kaung**.

The city's draws extend beyond mere tourist sights. It's one of Myanmar's most important cultural centres, which allows for some interesting **shopping** opportunities – much of the nation's gold leaf is walloped into submission here, while it's also the main

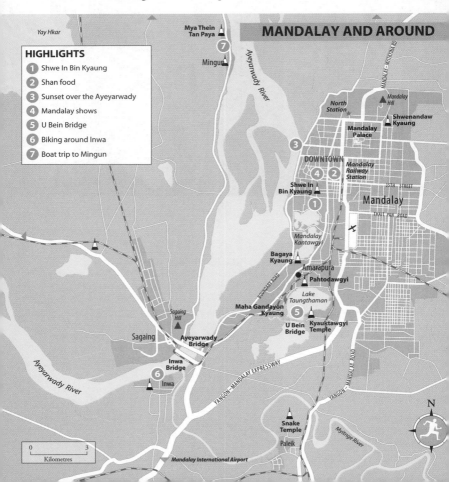

MANDALAY AND AROUND

HIGHLIGHTS

1. Shwe In Bin Kyaung
2. Shan food
3. Sunset over the Ayeyarwady
4. Mandalay shows
5. U Bein Bridge
6. Biking around Inwa
7. Boat trip to Mingun

A RIGHT ROYAL MERRY-GO-ROUND

From the mid-fourteenth century until the British arrived some half a millennium later, Mandalay and its surrounding area played host to a curious travelling circus as the national capital regularly shifted from one city to another. It all followed the unification of the Sagaing and Pinya kingdoms; Thihathu, the Pinya king, had made his base just a few kilometres east of the Ayeyarwady River, but in 1364 this was moved to **Inwa** (then known as Ava) by his great-grandson Thadominbaya, mastermind of the reunification. Things stayed this way until 1555, when the city was ceded to the **Taungoo dynasty** after repeated attacks. Based in Taungoo, then Bago, this dynasty soon started to crumble, and Inwa became capital again in 1599; it remained the seat of power until the death of King Mahadammayaza in 1752, when the French, then busying themselves in the area, encouraged a rebellion. The capital of the nascent **Konbaung dynasty** was moved out to Shwebo (see p.317), though this lasted only eight years before its second king decided that a riverside location would be more beneficial – step forward **Sagaing**. Again, it was only a few years before the capital moved across the river, back to Inwa; less than two decades later, in 1783, it was **Amarapura**'s turn, when King Bodawpaya chose to relocate the national centre of power. After fifty years functioning as a centre of Buddhist teachings, the capital was then shifted back to Inwa by Bodawpaya's grandson, King Bagyidaw – troubled by instability in the eastern Indian states, he viewed Inwa as a stronger base. Inwa was, however, devastated by a great earthquake in 1838, whereupon the capital was transferred back to Amarapura; this time it lasted only twenty years, before King Mindon received a vision showing him that the capital had to be moved north to **Mandalay**. This was to become Burma's final royal capital, since shortly after occupying the country the British banished the royals to India in 1885.

6

source of Jataka tapestries telling the life of the Buddha. The surprisingly good **entertainment** options include dance and puppet shows, and the famed Moustache Brothers (see box, p.279). The **culinary** scene is also pretty diverse, with Thai, Western and Korean cuisine to track down, as well as plenty of excellent Shan restaurants. Then, of course, there's the wonderful array of attractions within cycling distance of the city – plenty to do, in other words.

Brief history

Given its reputation as a place of historical importance, Mandalay is a surprisingly young city. Locals love to tell of how Buddha climbed Mandalay Hill and prophesied that 2400 years into the future, a grand city would be founded at its foot; it was duly founded in 1857 by **King Mindon**, said to be the reincarnation of San Da Mukhi, an ogress who impressed the Buddha by lopping off her breasts and presenting them to him. Legend aside, one other reason for Mandalay's establishment would have been to show the British, who were ruling Lower Burma from Rangoon, that Mindon's kingdom was still mighty. After being taken by the British in 1885, the city prospered until the Japanese occupation during World War II, which saw many of the old buildings levelled by Allied bombing. Today, Mandalay is the commercial hub of northern Myanmar, and particularly important for trade with China – as made evident by the large Chinese community. There are also plenty of ethnic Shan, mostly concentrated in low-lying areas west of 86th Street; Hindus, many of whom worship at a couple of colourful temples in the centre (see p.269); and pockets of Christians and Muslims. This ethnic patchwork exists in harmony most of the time, though trouble does occasionally flare up – 2014 saw night-time curfews imposed across the city after a spate of Buddhist–Muslim violence, ignited by the alleged rape of a local woman.

Mandalay Hill and the northeast

Visible from much of the city, **Mandalay Hill** lifts its multi-turreted head just northeast of the centre. This is up there with the city's most-visited attractions, particularly

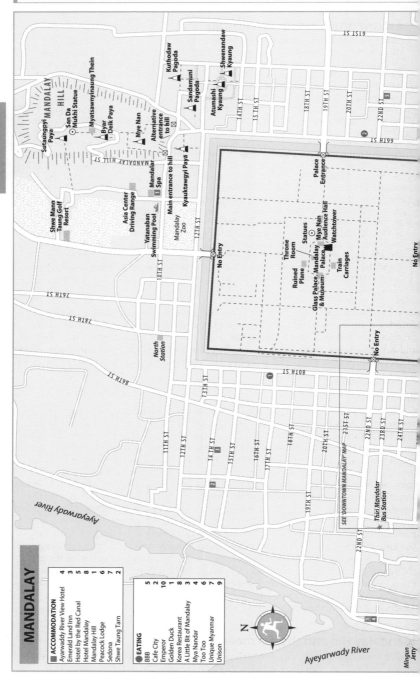

MANDALAY
ACCOMMODATION
Ayarwaddy River View Hotel 4
Emerald Land Inn 3
Hotel by the Red Canal 5
Hotel Mandalay 8
Mandalay Hill 1
Peacock Lodge 6
Sedona 7
Shwe Taung Tarn 2
EATING
BBB 5
Cafe City 2
Emperor 10
Golden Duck 1
Korea Restaurant 8
A Little Bit of Mandalay 3
Mya Nandar 4
Too Too 6
Unique Myanmar 7
Unison 9
MANDALAY HILL
Sutaungpyi Paya
San Da Mukhi Statue
Myatsawnyinaung Thein
Byar Deik Paya
Mye Nan
Alternative entrance to hill
Kuthodaw Pagoda
Sandamuni Pagoda
Atumashi Kyaung
Shwenandaw Kyaung
Kyauktawgyi Paya
Main entrance to hill
Mandalar Spa
MANDALAY HILL ST
Asia Center Driving Range
Shwe Mann Taung Golf Resort
Yatanaban Swimming Pool
Mandalay Zoo
No Entry
Palace Entrance
Throne Room
Statues
Mye Nan Audience Hall
Watchtower
Mandalay Palace
Ruined Plane
Glass Palace & Museum
Train Carriages
No Entry
No Entry
North Station
Thiri Mandalar Bus Station
SEE 'DOWNTOWN MANDALAY' MAP
Ayeyarwady River
Ayeyarwady River
Mingun Jetty
10TH ST
11TH ST
12TH ST
13TH ST
14TH ST
15TH ST
16TH ST
17TH ST
18TH ST
19TH ST
20TH ST
21ST ST
22ND ST
23RD ST
24TH ST
61ST ST
66TH ST
76TH ST
78TH ST
80TH ST
86TH ST
N

6

MANDALAY AND AROUND

Entrance ⊠
Escarpment ⁄⁄\

Pyi Gyi Myat Shin
Bus Station

61ST ST

62ND ST
63RD ST

41ST STREET

66TH ST

Chinese
Consulate

MAHA MYAING ST

THEIK PAN ST

Mandalay
University

ADIPADILI RD

Mandalay
Marionettes

Zone
Express

Mintha
Theater

MTT

Exotissimo

GGG
Massage

Smile
Massage

CB Bank

Diamond Plaza &
Mingalar Diamond Cineplex

Mandalay
Railway
Station

Myanmar Golden
River Group (MGRG)

Moustache
Brothers

Mahamuni Paya

Stone
Carvers' Workshops

Eindawya
Pagoda

Jade Market

Shwe In Bin Kyaung

Thingyo Yazar Channel

Gawein Jetty & IWT office

STRAND ROAD

▲ ❸

⚓ ❹

▶ Kwe Se Kan Bus Station, Airport & Yangon

▶ Stone Carvers' Workshops

▶ Amarapura, Sagaing & Inwa

26TH ST
27TH ST
28TH ST
29TH ST
30TH ST
31ST ST
32ND ST
33RD ST
34TH ST
35TH ST
36TH ST
37TH ST

21ST ST
22ND ST
23RD ST
74TH ST
75TH ST
76TH ST
77TH ST
78TH ST
79TH ST
80TH ST

63RD ST
64TH ST
65TH ST
66TH ST
68TH ST

27TH ST
28TH ST
29TH ST
30TH ST
31ST ST
32ND ST
33RD ST
34TH ST
35TH ST

81ST ST
82ND ST
83RD ST
84TH ST
85TH ST

86TH ST
87TH ST
88TH ST
89TH ST

90TH ST

78TH ST
38TH ST
39TH ST
40TH ST
41ST ST
42ND ST
43RD ST
44TH ST
45TH ST

106TH ST
168 ST

DRINKING
1 Ayar Sky Bar
2 Central Park
3 Win Win III

SHOPS
2 Diamond Plaza
5 Jade Market
3 King Galon
1 Rocky
4 Shwe Pathein

0   500
metres

6

FESTIVALS IN AND AROUND MANDALAY

Traditional **festivals**, known as *pwe*, take place throughout the year in Mandalay – ask staff at your hotel or guesthouse, or one of the city's many motorbike taxi drivers. These can be incredibly noisy affairs, and some go on well into the night – people have reported having to change hotels to get away from the din. However, *pwe* are hugely important to the city and its inhabitants, and experiencing one, however briefly, will give you an insight into how Mandalay functions. Note that since most are based on the lunar calendar, the dates on which they take place vary year by year – run a quick internet search if you're in town around any of the following times.

Mahamuni Paya Pwè This colourful event sees villagers from across the region arriving in their thousands at the fantastic Mahamuni Paya. The festival lasts two full weeks, and features umpteen evening shows – if you're in luck, you may see a traditional *anyeint* that *doesn't* feature the Moustache Brothers. Usually early Feb.

Irrawaddy Literary Festival ⓦ irrawaddylitfest.com. A relatively recent arrival on the local festival scene, this brings together players in Myanmar's literary scene. International authors also pop by to give talks and share opinions. Feb.

Thingyan Water Festival Major event taking place across the land (see p.41); just like anywhere else in the country, participants are likely to get totally drenched. Mid-April.

Sand Stupa Festival In three areas of Mandalay (check with your accommodation for the one closest to you), large sand stupas are erected over the course of a single night; each layer is supported with bamboo rods and mats. Usually May.

Shwe Kyun Pin Nat Pwè Taking place across the Ayeyarwady in the delightful village of Mingun (see p.287), this festival celebrates a brother and sister who drowned in the river and then became *nats*. Expect to see hundreds of farmers from across the area, who arrive on bullock carts wearing richly colourful costumes. Usually July.

Taungbyone Nat Pwè Held in the town of Taungbyone, around 18km north of Mandalay, this huge event is one of the most famous *nat pwè* (see box, p.49) in the land – don't miss out on it if you're in the area near this time. The *nat pwè* honours two brothers, Min Gyi and Min Lay (see box, p.217), who apparently assumed supernatural powers after eating the body of a dead *zawgyi* (alchemist); legend aside, the thousands attending are more interested in eating, dancing and making offerings. July/Aug.

Yadanagu Nat Pwè The week after Taungbyone's *pwe*, the circus moves south to Amarapura to honour Mai Wunna, the brothers' mother (see box, p.217). Usually Aug.

Thadingyut Festival Marking the end of Buddhist Lent, this festival takes place across the land, and constitutes the largest festival in central Mandalay. Buddhist monuments and city parks are illuminated with streams of lanterns, and festivities continue throughout the full week. Usually early Oct.

---

around sunset time. You can make a full half-day of the area by visiting the slew of attractions just south of the hill – these include several temples, a teak monastery and "the world's largest book".

Mandalay Hill

မန္တလေးတောင် · Accessible from 10th St · Daily 24hr · Free; K200 to store footwear at base, though you can take it with you for free · Motorbike taxis to top around K4000 including waiting time, pick-ups K1000; both are available on 10th St

For many people, the 45-minute walk up **Mandalay Hill** for sunset is one of the highlights of a visit to the city. The usual starting point is the staircase between a large pair of chinthe on 10th Street; there is another entrance a little further east. Whichever route you choose, the concrete steps run uphill beneath corrugated iron roofs lined with stalls selling drinks and souvenirs. The two routes meet just before **Byar Deik Paya**, from which a large standing Buddha points back the way you came; he's actually pointing at Mandalay rather than telling you to go back down.

There are numerous other shrines on the way up the hill, including **Ngon Minn**, a stupa where the names of donors are written on the white columns. Further up is the **Myatsawnyinaung Thein**, an almost preposterously ugly affair made of cracked concrete. Though such monstrosity inspires precious little devotion, the ordination hall is notable for being attached to a fort that dates back to imperial days; you can see part of the structure by peering out of the hall's eastern flank.

As you get higher, the crowds become thicker, particularly around sunset. After a fair few "Is *this* one the top?" false dawns, the actual summit is quite obvious; the wide terrace of **Sutaungpyi Paya** ("Wish-Granting Temple") accommodates a mixture of pilgrims, tourists and novice monks, with many of the latter there to practise their English. Note that even at these times, simply moving down a level or two will ensure you some breathing space. At the eastern side of the first major level on the way back down, don't miss the tiny statue of **San Da Mukhi**, merrily holding her severed breasts; it was this act which prompted Buddha to eventually have her reincarnated as King Mindon, creator of Mandalay (see p.263).

Mandalay Zoo

မန္တလေးတိရစ္ဆာန်ရုံ • 12th St • Mon–Fri 8am–5pm, Sat & Sun 8am–2pm • K2000

The city's awful **zoo** has been included here as a warning alone – even by the almost uniformly low standards of such facilities across Asia, this is a real shocker. Most of the animals here are kept in featureless, undersized concrete cages, some of which sport tree stumps or leafless branches – presumably to make the poor creatures feel at home. Unless you fancy seeing depressed hippos standing for hours on end with their heads to the floor, bears and big cats endlessly pacing the same side of their enclosure, or monkeys making all-too-obvious calls of distress, leave this place well alone.

Kyauktawgyi Paya

ကျောက်တော်ကြီးဘုရား • Off 10th St, south of the Mandalay Hill entrance • Daily 5am–7pm • Free

Worth popping into on your way down from the hill, the small **Kyauktawgyi Paya** is centred on a giant Buddha, hewn from a single slab of marble – no mean feat, since the statue is 12m tall. The sight is "enhanced" by the LED disco-Buddha lights so beloved by the Burmese; these provide a playground for local sparrows, as do other parts of the multi-mirrored complex, which is one of the more pleasant and relaxing such places in Mandalay. One major exception is October's Thadingyut festival (see box opposite), during which time this is one of the focal points of Mandalay proceedings.

Kuthodaw Pagoda

ကုသိုလ်တော်ဘုရား • Off 12th St • Daily 6am–9pm • Covered by Mandalay combination ticket (see box, p.268)

Huddled in two groups northeast of the palace moat is a series of engraved marble slabs which collectively are often referred to as "the world's biggest book". There are a whopping 729 of them, each housed in a small stupa and relaying the entire fifteen books of the Tripitaka, ringing the **Kuthodaw Pagoda**. King Mindon commissioned the construction of the complex in 1857, and it took more than a decade to complete and check for errors – the creation of the complex is, in fact, described on yet another slab, bringing the total here to 730. The complex was heavily damaged during British rule, with bricks from the stupas used for military roads, though rebuilding came quickly and was impressively conducted.

Sandamuni Pagoda

စန္ဒာမုနိဘုရား • Off 12th St • Daily 6am–9pm • Free

Amazingly, Kuthodaw is trumped by nearby **Sandamuni Pagoda**, which boasts another 1774 slabs engraved with commentaries on the Tripitaka scripture. Unlike the concentric formations of Kuthodaw, here they're arrayed in an almost military-like formation. However, it's still a strikingly beautiful compound in the heat of the day – the dazzlingly whitewashed stupas make great camera fodder if you can find the right sight lines.

6

THE MANDALAY COMBINATION TICKET

Many of Mandalay's sights, as well as some in the surrounding area, are covered by a **combination ticket** (K10,000), valid for five days – unfortunately, it's not possible to purchase individual tickets to the sights it covers. At each sight you visit the relevant section of the ticket will be stamped, which means it can't really be transferred between travellers. Tickets can be purchased from booths at most of the most sights that it covers, though do have a think before you buy, since some of them aren't that great, and there are free (and sometimes better) alternatives to others.

You'll most likely need a ticket to get into **Mandalay Palace** (see below), though many visitors don't find the place all that interesting; some travellers have reported being able to sneak in by merely asking a question at the ticket booth, then simply ambling past the guards who'll assume that you've purchased a ticket. You'll also need one for **Atumashi Kyaung** (see below), though this place is terribly dull and can be missed without causing you sleepless nights; note that you can't purchase tickets here either. You'll also need one for nearby **Shwenandaw Kyaung** (see below), though the Shwe In Bin monastery to the southwest (see p.271) is free, less touristed, and perhaps even more beautiful. Tickets are only checked at certain entrances at the **Kuthodaw Pagoda** (see p.267), though the nearby Sandamuni Pagoda (see p.267) is very similar, and free to visit.

The palace aside, the only things you'd miss by not purchasing a combination ticket are the main sights at **Inwa** (see p.284), way to the south. Then again, these are visible and easy to photograph from the outside, and for many the area's bucolic charm – particularly if you have your own transport – is the main draw anyway.

Atumashi Kyaung

အတုမရှိကျောင်း • Off 14th St • Daily 9am–5pm • Covered by Mandalay combination ticket (see box, p.268)

The **Atumashi Kyaung** was originally built in the 1850s to house a Buddha statue that went missing – complete with the diamond in its forehead – when the British took the city. The current building is a dull reconstruction dating back to the 1990s, its only noteworthy aspects being the preposterously tiny altar hiding away in its large main hall, and the unusually shaped formation of terraces leading up to it.

Shwenandaw Kyaung

ရွှေနန်းတော်ကျောင်း • Off 14th St • Daily 9am–5pm • Covered by Mandalay combination ticket (see box, p.268)

A glorious teak construction, the **Shwenandaw Kyaung** was originally built within the palace walls as a residence for King Mindon. The building was converted to a monastery and moved to its current site east of the palace after Mindon died in it, as it was considered bad luck by his son, Thibaw; this later saved it from burning alongside the palace's other buildings. Nowadays, it's most notable for the elegantly carved Jataka stories in its raised main hall, whose atmospheric interior glows a dim gold.

Mandalay Palace

မန္တလေးနန်းတော် • Entrance on 66th St • Daily 8am–5pm • Covered by Mandalay combination ticket (see box, p.268)

Mandalay is centred on the moated square of land that once hosted the large **royal palace**. The area has belonged to the military for decades, and the palace itself is long gone, though a huge replica has been erected. As part of his fulfilment of Buddhist prophecy, King Mindon had the palace constructed almost immediately after making the city his capital in 1857. It followed a traditional design informed by links with China – much like Beijing's famed Forbidden City, it consisted of a geometrically auspicious alignment of buildings set inside a heavily walled fort and surrounded by a moat. However, only Mindon and his successor, Thibaw, actually ruled from here before the British came to town; almost all remaining buildings were flattened by Allied bombs in World War II, and what you see today is a 1990s reconstruction. The whole area is still a functional part of town, though one controlled by the military and, as such, mostly off-limits to foreigners; you're free to visit the shops and teahouses just off the main road heading in from the east, but precious little else bar the reconstructed palace at the centre.

Foreigners may only enter the old palace area from the east gate. Nearby, a sign states "Tatmadaw and the people, co-operate and crush all those harming the union", and the army enhance their already stellar international reputation by insisting that foreign cyclists leave their vehicles at the gate; tour buses, of course, get to boom straight to the centre.

The palace grounds

The palace itself is more impressive as a whole than for any particular part. A spine of reconstructed main halls runs down the centre, with signs stating what each was used for – none of the details are terribly interesting, though they're occasionally rather bombastic (such as the cannons which "can crush all enemies"). Starting from the east is the **Mye Nan Audience Hall**, which contains then-and-now pictures which attest to the accuracy of the remodelling. Of the other main halls, the **throne room** is the most handsome; the throne itself is a richly decorated affair featuring lions and other carved imagery. Elsewhere, many of the minor structures are empty shells; it's better to head for the **watchtower** to the south of the complex, for after dragging your way up the spiral staircase you'll have a fantastic view. There's also a small **museum** at the western end, housed in what was known as the "Glass Palace"; this was named after a glass bed brought from France by King Thibaw. The bed is still here, and rather impressive, as is a series of traditional costumes which seemed designed to make pagodas of those who wore them.

The rest of the complex

The rest of the complex is out of bounds, which is a pity since those with eagle eyes will be able to spot plenty of interesting things on its periphery. Look out from the northern wall, towards the west of the complex, and you'll make out a ruined **plane**; do likewise from the south, and you'll see a few rusting **train** carriages. Just northeast of the main entrance, there's a circle of nine **statues** of kings and other historical figures: out of bounds, but you can usually visit. Lastly, you may care to buck the system slightly by stepping out of the museum to the west for a freshly pressed sugar-cane juice (take that, officialdom!).

The city centre

There are a few sights dotted around Mandalay **city centre**, whose contemporary reincarnation is located to the west of the palace. Poke around awhile and you'll find a few pretty Buddhist and Hindu monuments, but better than this is the chance to simply take the pulse of Myanmar's second city – the grid of streets teems with traffic, snack-stands and stray dogs, yet things somehow feel rather orderly. In addition, the area is home to many of the city's best places to eat and drink (see p.277).

The Hindu district

Sri Krishna 27th St, at 81st St; Sanatan Dharma 27th St, between 79th & 80th sts • Both usually daily 9am–5pm • Free

If you haven't spent time in Bali, Singapore or southern India, the two Hindu temples off 27th Street might hold some interest. With its steeply inclined mass of colourful detail, the **Sri Krishna** temple is the more architecturally beautiful, though there's not much to see inside. The interior of the red-coloured **Sanatan Dharma** down the road is larger and features several statues, though is more functional than beautiful. During the daytime you'll often find snack trolleys outside the temples, selling incredibly sugary Indian sweeties.

The fire lookout tower and fire station

If you're in the area, keep an eye out for the city's former **fire lookout tower** (29th St, at 81st St), from which lofty vantage point dangers were surveyed – essential in a large city whose buildings were mostly made of wood. It's no longer in use, but the city's

6

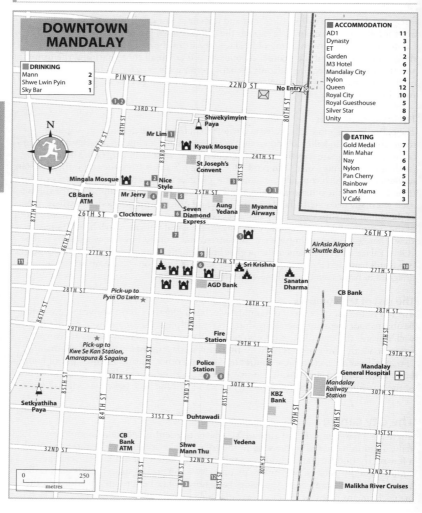

main **fire station** remains alongside on 29th Street; the firemen certainly don't mind visitors popping in to see their pair of vintage 1970s engines, which look at least two decades older and are still used on occasion.

Eindawya Pagoda

အိမ်တော်ရာဘုရား • Off 28th St • Daily 24hr • Free

The most striking temple in central Mandalay, the **Eindawya Pagoda** is centred on a glittering, gold-leaf-covered stupa – it's a delight to pad around it (barefoot, of course) in the early evening, when the play of light produces a rather magnificent effect. The temple was constructed in 1847 on the orders of King Pagan Min, who was living on this very site when he ascended to the throne. If you've a little time, head out of the western entrance and cross the road to a lovely, secluded area of monastic dwellings – arguably the calmest, most charming place in the whole city.

South of the centre

South of the centre, the city's atmosphere becomes more workaday; this is best exemplified by the gold-pounders on 36th Street (see p.280), and the stone-carvers near **Mahamuni Paya**. Said temple is probably the most attractive in the city, and well worth a look, as is the "forgotten" teak monastery of **Shwe In Bin**.

Mahamuni Paya

မဟာမုနိဘုရား• Off 82nd Rd, just east of Mandalay–Sagaing Rd • Daily 24hr; Buddha cleaning daily 4am • K1000

Host to one of Mandalay's biggest festivals (see box, p.266) and the most important Buddhist site in the city, the large **Mahamuni Paya** complex is a joy even for non-religious visiting travellers. At the heart of the pagoda is a **Buddha figure** some 3.8m in height, taken from Mrauk U in 1784 by the army of King Bodawpaya (see p.127) – this tale is portrayed in a series of paintings, lining a gallery-like wing to the northeast of the main hall.

Male devotees visit to apply **gold leaf** (from K1600) to the figure; women are not allowed within the inner area and instead hand their ultra-thin golden squares to a male assistant. The figure itself is said to weigh six tonnes, and the gold leaf covering it adds another two tonnes; pictures here show just how much bling has been accreted here since 1984, and the weight has really gone to Buddha's calves, to such a degree that he appears to have elephantiasis. In the early morning, a small crowd of early birds gathers while the face of the statue – pretty much the only part not covered in gold leaf – is tenderly washed.

Northwest of the main shrine is a cream concrete building containing Hindu figures taken originally from Angkor Wat by the Rakhine, before being appropriated by Bodawpaya at the same time as the large Buddha.

Stone carvers' workshops

Off 82nd St

Just outside the Mahamuni Paya complex, to the west, is a dusty, noisy and visually absorbing district of **stone-carving workshops**. Here you'll see Buddha statues in various sizes and stages of completion, with the most interesting the ones awaiting specific facial design instructions.

Shwe In Bin Kyaung

 ရွှေအင်းပင်ကျောင်း• 89th St, between 37th & 38th sts • Daily 24hr • Free

Raised on stilts and housing around thirty monks at any one time, the teak **Shwe In Bin Kyaung** is a real stunner – and one which is, rather surprisingly, left alone by most visitors. The monastery was built in the late nineteenth century by jade merchants from China (whose legacy is still evident in the nearby Jade Market; see p.280), and is most notable for the fantastically rich profusion of carvings in and around its upper level; you'll see them in every doorway, eave and balustrade, many of them covered in spiders' webs, and they extend way up to the heavily spiked roof.

ARRIVAL AND DEPARTURE
MANDALAY

BY PLANE

Mandalay International Airport Flights to Mandalay touch down at Mandalay International Airport (🖥mandalayairport.com), some 45km south from the city centre. At the airport you'll find a few ATMs, and a café.

MANDALAY ADDRESSES

Mandalay's roads are laid out along a numbered **grid system**, which makes it easy to find your way around the city. One common source of traveller confusion, however, is that streets up to 50th are east-to-west (ie the "wrong" way around), and numbers above 50 north-to-south. Our addresses give the street on which the place sits first (81st St, for example) and then the cross streets between which it lies (eg 29th & 30th streets).

6

Transport to/from town Getting into town is easy if you've arrived from Thailand with AirAsia – just hop on one of their free buses, which drop off by the railway station, then at their office on 79th St (between 26th & 27th sts). Back to the airport, these depart the office at 9am & 9.15am. If you've arrived with other airlines, hunt down the taxi booking desk, which charges a set K4000 per seat, or K12,000 for the full cab; heading back to the airport, get your accommodation to call a taxi, or enquire about booking a shared cab at an agency such as Nice Style (p.274). These are also the best places to go when buying tickets. Do note that, in common with the rest of Myanmar, you may drop by one or two other airports on the way to your destination.

Airlines AirAsia (26th St, between 78th and 79th sts; ☎02 61328); Air Bagan (78th St, between 27th and 28th sts; ☎02 61791); Air Mandalay (78th St, between 29th and 30th sts; ☎02 61513); Asian Wings (30th St, between 77th and 78th sts; ☎02 74791); Myanmar Airways International (78th St, at 27th St; ☎02 69551); Yangon Airways (78th St, between 29th and 30th sts; ☎02 34405).

Destinations (domestic) Bagan (at least 3 daily; 30min); Bhamo (9 weekly; 45min–1hr 55min); Heho (9 daily; 25min, sometimes via Bagan); Kengtung (4 weekly; 50min); Lashio (1 daily; 45min); Myitkyina (at least 1 daily; 45min–2hr); Naypyitaw (3 daily; 50min); Putao (3 weekly; 2hr 20min); Tachileik (4 weekly; 1hr 10min, sometimes via Kengtung); Yangon (19 daily; 50min–2hr 5min).

BY BUS

Bus stations Mandalay has three bus stations. The main terminus is teeming Kwe Se Kan (Main) Station, which serves destinations south and lies around 10km south of the centre. If your ticket doesn't come with a pick-up or drop-off service, make use of the motos (K3000) and taxis (K6000) that ply the route. Pyi Gyi Mat Shin Station is 3km east of the centre and serves destinations to the northeast. Finally, Thiri Mandalar Station is the most central of Mandalay's three stations, though only covers a few destinations.

Booking tickets You may have to jump through a few hoops before leaving Mandalay by bus. In general, for long-distance journeys it's best to book ahead – not least because the main station is quite a distance from the city centre. You're best advised to book at your hotel, or make use of the many travel agents dotted around town (see p.274); they'll charge commission (anything up to K2000), but this works out far cheaper and less time-consuming than taking a motorbike taxi or taxi out to the main station and back. In addition, many of these offers include transfers to the stations, at which it's usually hard enough to find your bus, let alone buy tickets too. There's a great glut of them in the area bordered by 80th, 83rd, 30th and 33rd sts. Most long-distance services also

include "ferry" shuttles to or from the stations, with pick-up either at your hotel or one of the booking offices; do double-check the times, though, as some pick up too early, or too late for comfort.

Destinations (Kwe Se Kan Station) To Bagan there's not much choice, though Shwe Mann Thu (32nd St, between 82nd and 83rd sts) have at least 6 daily a/c services (7hr) between 7.30am and 10pm. To Inle Lake (7–8hr) there are various services, all via Kalaw; some stop at the entrance to Nyaungshwe, others drop off in Shwenyaung on their way to Taunggyi, and most services come with pick-up. There must be a dozen operators heading to Yangon (frequent; 8–10hr), and again you'll have a choice between express services (featuring two-plus-one seating, small TVs on the seats and on-board toilets) and ordinary services; these are also your best option if heading to or from Bago (4 daily; 10–12hr). There are also services to Hpa-An (12 daily; 15hr); Magwe (1 daily; 8hr); Mawlamyine (2 daily; 12hr); Meiktila (7 daily; 3hr); Mrauk U (1–2 daily; 25hr); Naypyitaw (7 daily; 4hr); Pyay (2 daily; 13hr); Sittwe (1 daily; 30hr); and Taungoo (2 daily; 7hr).

Destinations (Pyi Gyi Mat Shin Station) Departures to Kyaukme (8 daily; 5hr), Hsipaw (6 daily; 6hr) and Lashio (3 daily; 9hr) tend to leave early in the morning, though there are a couple of afternoon departures too, and some night services. Yedena (81st St, between 31st & 32nd sts; ☎02 36196) have a service to all three destinations (you'll have to pay to Lashio) leaving at 6pm, and to Kyaukme alone at 1.30pm. Duhtawadi (31st St, between 81st & 82nd sts; ☎02 61938) have a/c services to Hsipaw at 5.30am and 2.30pm. None of these services includes pick-up.

Destinations (Thiri Mandalar Station) Hourly services run to Shwebo until 4pm (3hr); Monywa 'til noon (3hr 30min); and Pyin Oo Lwin (2hr); there are services to Bhamo too, but foreigners still can't use them. Buy your tickets from the windows on the south side of the station.

BY PICK-UP OR SHARED TAXI

Pick-ups Pick-ups to Pyin Oo Lwin (3hr; K2500) run between 5am and 5pm, departing when full from the corner of 28th St and 83rd St. They are most frequent early in the morning, and may not run after 3pm.

Shared taxis Duhtawadi bus company runs shared taxis to Hsipaw (5–6hr; K15,000) from its office in town (see above). Aung Yedana (25th St, between 81st and 82nd sts; ☎02 24850) has shared taxis to Kalaw and Nyaungshwe (from K35,000) and will pick you up from your hotel. Several operators have services to Pyin Oo Lwin (2hr; K6000–7000), collecting passengers from their hotels, plus there are morning departures from the corner of 27th & 83rd sts. Lastly, it's also quite possible to visit Monywa on a day-trip; figure on $60–70 for the return journey, plus waiting time.

BOAT TRIPS FROM MANDALAY

Considering the wealth of destinations both up and down the **Ayeyarwady River**, it's no surprise that a fair proportion of visitors to Mandalay rock up on a boat. Bar the government services, for which you can usually buy your ticket on the ferry itself just before it departs, you're advised to book ahead; again, travel agencies will help if your accommodation can't (and occasionally include transfers to the jetty), though some companies now allow you to book online. Unless otherwise stated, the following services arrive at and depart from the **Gawein jetty** area, 3km west of the centre at the end of 35th St; the exact point will depend upon the river level. Boat trips to **Mingun** are covered in the Mingun section (see p.289).

6

TO BAGAN

There are a number of services to Bagan; think about whether you'd like to go fast and expensive, or slow and cheap. Faster and more expensive first, with three private companies running services (10–12hr), departing at 7am but not running every day: **Shwe Keinnery** (upper floor of railway station, 30th St, between 78th and 79th sts; ☎ 096 813472, ⓦ nmaihka .com; $40), **Malikha River Cruises** (between 77th and 78th, and 32nd and 33rd sts; ☎ 02 72279, ⓦ malikha-rivercruises.com; $40); and **Myanmar Golden River Group** (MGRG; 38th St, between 79th and 80th sts; ☎ 011 202734, ⓦ mgrgexpress.com; $45). All include breakfast, and MGRG includes lunch too. The slower **government ferry** (two days; $10) leaves at 5.30am on Wednesday and Sunday; they are run by IWT (35th St; daily 9.30am–4.30pm; ☎ 02 36035; look for the faded yellow building by the main road).

TO THE NORTH

Katha Irra (☎ 09 650 1155) runs the main service to Katha (12–14hr; $25), stopping at Kyaukmyaung, Tagaung and Tigyiang (see box, p.311). Fancier, more expensive **Shwe Keinnery** services run to Katha ($80) and Bhamo (18–22hr; $100), but during high season they use the boat on the Bagan route instead. From a booth marked "Pan Lon Co Ltd", **Shwe Eyama** (Strand Rd; ☎ 094 309 9102) sell tickets for daily services to Katha ($35), leaving at 5am; you can change here for one to Bhamo, though you can buy a single through-ticket in Mandalay ($55). Lastly, an **IWT government** boat runs to Bhamo (at least 30hr; $12 on deck, $60 in a cabin) via Kyaukmyaung and Katha at 6am, theoretically on Monday, Thursday and Saturday.

LUXURY RIVER CRUISES

Several local and overseas operators run cruises on the Ayeyarwady between Bhamo and Mandalay, including these listed below. In addition, a few luxury cruises starting from Mandalay run on the Chindwin River (see box, p.222).

Amara ⓦ amaragroup.net. Four beautiful teak boats with 5–7 cabins for scheduled trips to Bhamo, which are also available to charter.

Belmond ⓦ voyagesinmyanmar.com. Formerly known as Orient Express, Belmond operates two boats,

the *Road to Mandalay* and *Orcaella*, and organizes cruises as far north as Bhamo.

Pandaw 1947 ⓦ pandaw1947.com. A luxurious sixteen-berth vessel built in 1947 on the same design as the original Irrawaddy Flotilla Company's steamers.

BY TRAIN

Mandalay Railway Station The simplest way to depart or arrive in Mandalay is by train, though standards on the national rail network are not particularly high. The main station is centrally located just off 30th St, between 78th and 79th sts; it's usually pretty easy to buy tickets here, though the queues get longer and the station far busier as departure times approach.

North Station Note that there's also a small station just off the palace's northwest corner, though the line heading north from here doesn't go anywhere of tourist interest;

services to Myitkyina and other places to the north actually still use the main station, and start their journey by heading south.

Destinations Bagan (1 daily; 8hr); Bago (3 daily; 14hr); Hopin (3 daily; 16hr); Hsipaw (1 daily; 12hr); Kyaukme (1 daily; 11hr); Lashio (1 daily; 16hr); Monywa (1 daily; 5hr); Myitkyina (3 daily; 19hr); Naba (for Katha; 3 daily; 12hr); Nawngpeng (for Gokteik Viaduct; 1 daily; 8hr); Naypyitaw (2 daily; 6–7hr); Pyin Oo Lwin (daily; 6hr); Shwebo (3 daily; 5hr); Taungoo (3 daily; 8–9hr); Thazi (3 daily; 3hr); Yangon (3 daily; 16hr).

6

GETTING AROUND

By bicycle Almost pancake-flat, Mandalay is a great city in which to cycle; the traffic can be bad, but most drivers are well mannered and respectful of bikes. Everywhere in this chapter can actually be reached by bike (though Mingun is a bit of a stretch), so you may wish to rent one out on your first day and keep it with you until leaving Mandalay. There are a few operators renting out bikes in the centre of town; try Mr Lim, just outside the *ET* hotel (see below) on 83rd St, between 23rd and 24th sts (daily 7.30am–7.30pm), or Mr Jerry, opposite *Mann* bar (see p.279) on 83rd St, between 25th and 26th sts (daily 7am–7pm). Both charge K2000/ day for a bike, and from K10,000/day for a motorbike. If you fancy a fun little trip, try crossing the small bridge which starts just beyond the western end of 14th St; a more delightful village would be hard to find.

By bus and pick-up Mandalay does actually have a bus network of sorts, though precious few foreigners will ever

end up using it – the numbers are all in Burmese, the routes change as often as the wind, vehicles are packed to the gills and it's simply so easy to find easier and only slightly more expensive alternatives. The only possible exceptions are pick-ups heading south to Amarapura (see p.282) and Sagaing (see p.286), which you can find rolling down 84th St, near the junction with 29th St; do note, however, that these will put you nowhere near the sights in those two towns, so you'll have to find onward transport in any case.

By taxi and motorbike taxi Mandalay's many taxi and motorbike taxi drivers will take you anywhere you need to go. A motorbike taxi to the Mingun ferry terminal will set you back K1500, to the Gawein jetty K2000 and to the bus terminal K3000; you can double these fees for taxis. Hiring one for the day is the most popular way for independent travellers to get themselves to the various sights around Mandalay (see p.282).

INFORMATION AND TOURS

Exotissimo 70th St, between 28th and 29th sts ☎ 02 38786, ⊛ exotissimo.com. Mandalay branch of one of the country's most reputable tour operators (see p.25).

MTT 68th St, between 26th and 27th sts ☎ 02 60356. The office of this government-run travel agency is actually a fairly decent – not to mention friendly – place to head for advice, and the booking of flight or ferry tickets.

★ Nice Style 25th St, between 82nd and 83rd sts ☎ 02 64103, ⊛ nicestyletravel.com. The amiable team at this small office are particularly good at organizing anything

from flight tickets to shared taxis to the airport.

Seven Diamond Express 25th St, between 82nd and 83rd sts ☎ 02 65865, ⊛ sevendiamondtravels.com. Another agency that has cultivated a good reputation with travellers, one founded on their fair, competent sales of flight and bus tickets. Can also organize shared taxis to the airport.

Zone Express 68th St, between 26th and 27th sts ☎ 02 74651, ✉ zone.mandalay@gmail.com. One of the better places in town for flight tickets.

ACCOMMODATION

First, the bad news – even more so than the rest of the country, accommodation in Mandalay is, almost as a rule, horrendously overpriced. Foreigners are excluded from the very cheapest places, meaning that you'll have to figure on at least $10 per head as a minimum; even some of the places charging $30 per double (which seems to be the default lower-end rate now) are atrocious. Moving a tiny bit up the price scale can result in a palpable increase in quality; for something resembling a real hotel room, you're talking $90 or so, while the city's luxury options (all located quite far from the centre) will see you fortunate to get change from $200. Most travellers stay in and around the city centre, in the quadrant bordered by 84th St to the west, 27th St to the south, 83rd St to the east and 23nd St to the north; there are some mid-range options further south, and a couple in the partly rural area way up north on 14th St. Lastly, many places now claim to have wi-fi, though don't rely upon it.

DOWNTOWN

AD1 Between 87th and 88th sts, and 27th and 28th sts ☎ 02 34505, ✉ ead.1hotel@gmail.com; map p.270. Simple, colourful and friendly, this is a popular place with those willing to brave a very slightly out-of-the-way location. Some beds are better than others, so give yours a quick bounce before choosing a room; upper rooms have views that could best be described as "featureful". No wi-fi. $20

Dynasty 81st St, between 24th and 25th sts ☎ 02 35801, ✉ hoteldynasty@myanmar.com.mm; map p.270. Overpriced but just about acceptable as a fallback,

this small hotel's corridors hint at a sort of Bauhaus minimalism, but the rooms make clear that the whole place is just cheaply designed. The saving grace here is a decent travel service in the lobby. Rates do not include breakfast, and there's no wi-fi. $30

ET 83rd St, between 23rd and 24th sts ☎ 02 65006, ✉ ethotel129a@gmail.com; map p.270. For one reason or another, this is just about the most popular place in town at this price level, its lobby area playing host to a steady hubbub of traveller chat and Facebook messaging each and every evening. Rooms are merely okay but the location's

6

good, and though staff are occasionally surly they're also helpful at doling out travel advice. $30

Garden 83rd St, between 24th and 25th sts ☏ 02 31884, ✉ gardenhotelmdy@gmail.com; map p.270. Budget choice competing with the *Nylon* around the corner. This one's appealing in a grubby sort of way, with decent beds, lots of channels on the telly, a/c and 24hr hot water (sometimes way too hot). Staff are professionally minded and adept at arranging onward tickets. No wi-fi. $22

★**M3 Hotel** 26th St, between 82nd and 83rd sts ☏ 02 67171, ⊛ mhotelmandalay.com; map p.270. This eight-floor venue was one of the newest options in town at the time of writing, and it's well worth splashing out on a room here if you can afford to. Stylishly attired staff bid every entrant a warm welcome, then lead the way along carpeted corridors to rooms that do a fair approximation of international standards; all feature attractive bathrooms (showers only at Standard level, tubs otherwise) and flatscreen TVs (still a rarity in Myanmar), while some also boast weighing scales. A fine place. $45

★**Mandalay City** 26th St, between 82nd and 83rd sts ☏ 02 61700, ⊛ mandalaycityhotel.com; map p.270. The most luxurious choice in the city centre, though wi-fi doesn't carry through to the wood-panelled rooms, which don't quite live up to the promise of the lovely lobby and entrance area. Service is professional, there's complimentary tea and water, and the hotel also features a small swimming pool out back, underneath the palm trees (and also open to non-guests; see p.281). $90

Nylon 83rd St, at 25th St ☏ 02 33460, ✉ nylonhotel25 @gmail.com; map p.270. Sharing its lobby with an electrical equipment store, this guesthouse is in near direct competition with the *Garden* around the corner; some prefer this, some prefer the other, so you're best advised to have a good look at both. This is a wee bit cheaper, especially for single travellers ($15); some rooms feature mirror panelling, and a few have surprisingly large bathrooms. No wi-fi. $20

Queen 81st St, between 32nd and 33rd sts ☏ 02 39805, ⊛ hotelqueenmandalay.com; map p.270. Presentable mid-range choice located in the low thirties, a sort of no-man's-land just south of the city centre. All rooms have bathtubs and wi-fi (in theory); their cheapest rooms are all doubles, while the best are the $55 choices at the front. $45

Royal City 27th St, between 76th and 77th sts ☏ 02 66559, ⊛ royalcityhotelmandalay.com; map p.270. In a quiet area just east of the centre and south of the palace moat, this hotel has made a decent stab at smartening itself up – all rooms are comfy enough, though the corner ones are particularly nice. Breakfast is taken on the rooftop, with lovely views. $35

★**Royal Guesthouse** 25th St, between 82nd and 83rd sts ☏ 02 31400; map p.270. Small and amiable, this is the best of the area's budget choices, and usually the cheapest too, though you'll pay $5 extra for an en-suite room. Common

areas have been decorated with rare care (perhaps using a Rubik's cube as a colour palette). Wi-fi doesn't run to all rooms, and not all have windows, so do look at a few if possible. The guesthouse's yellow sign is a little hard to spot; it's next door to Casper the Friendly Woodmachinery Trader. $17

Silver Star 27th St, at 83rd St ☏ 02 33394, ⊛ silverstarhotelmandalay.com; map p.270. One of the town's taller hotels, with eight full levels; rooms have wi-fi and all mod cons, while the service is pretty good too. It's worth paying an extra $10 for one of the corner rooms, which catch a lot of light. $45

Unity 27th St, at 82nd St ☏ 02 66583, ✉ unity @mandalay.net.mm; map p.270. It's hard to single out a Mandalay cheapie for praise; this hotel has rough edges to smooth out, for sure, but it's one of the more reliable choices. Plus-points include a lobby that feels like that of a "real" hotel, a functional lift, and a nice little coffee bar on the ground level. Also think about splashing out on one of their suites ($40), which are large and well appointed. $25

OUTSIDE THE CENTRE

Ayarwaddy River View Hotel Strand Rd, at 22nd St ☏ 02 64945, ⊛ ayarwaddyriverviewhotel.net; map pp.264–265. A perfectly acceptable hotel for the price, with some rooms sporting great views of the famed Ayeyarwady River. They've also some cheap singles ($55) way up on top, in quirky rooms with sloping ceilings; also worth mentioning are a swimming pool (open to non-guests; see p.281), and the fantastic rooftop *Ayar Sky Bar*, which often doles out free sunset cocktails (see p.279). $70

Emerald Land Inn 14th St, between 86th and 87th sts ☏ 02 26990; map pp.264–265. Good rooms in a large complex some distance north of the centre – the surrounding area is charmingly local, pleasing to the eye, and refreshingly tourist-free. Back on site, there's a good pool (though one used more by local pigeons than by guests) and a neat rooftop lookout point – good for birdspotting. $55

★**Hotel by the Red Canal** 63rd St, at 22nd St ☏ 02 61177, ⊛ hotelredcanal.com; map pp.264–265. Now this is a treat, a traditionally styled affair lurking away by a canal in the side roads east of the palace. After making your way past the kidney-shaped pool, you'll find a range of rooms divided into areas named after some of Myanmar's ethnic groups: the Rakhine section is cheapest, the Shan rooms have views, and the Kachin boast gorgeous outdoor showers. Free cocktails are available from the balcony in the evening. $288

Hotel Mandalay 78th St, between 37th and 38th sts ☏ 02 71582, ⊛ hotelmandalaymm.com; map pp.264–265. One of the few central options if you want a "real" hotel with foreign exchange, tour operators, international restaurants and the like. Rooms are a bit poky for the price, though things get a little better in the new wing at the rear. $90

Mandalay Hill 10th St, by Mandalay Hill ☎ 02 35638, ⓦ mandalayhillresorthotel.com; map pp.264–265. This luxury hotel boasts by far the most attractive pool in all Myanmar – with the hill as a backdrop, it's a wonderful place to swim, and even open to non-guests (see p.281). The rooms themselves are opulently decorated affairs, and those on the upper levels boast predictably good views; unfortunately for shower-lovers, most have bathrooms that are bathtub-only. A great on-site spa (see p.281) and rather pricey restaurant round out a pleasing picture. **$276**

Peacock Lodge 60th St, between 25th and 26th sts ☎ 02 61429, ⓦ peacocklodge.com; map pp.264–265. An interesting choice way out to the east of town, and a decent recommendation if you feel like basing yourself somewhere more remote in feel. Their nine rooms (reserve ahead) are modern, lovingly decorated affairs, and the main building backs onto a pleasant, mango tree-shaded garden area. It's a little hard to find; from 26th St, look for the sign heading north down a side road to "Hotel Treasure". **$35**

Sedona 26th St, at 66th St ☎ 02 36488, ⓦ sedonahotels .com.sg; map pp.264–265. The Mandalay branch of this Singaporean chain forms the de facto base for higher-end tour groups, and as such often finds itself fully booked despite the stratospheric price tag – one which often can be halved if booking through an online engine. The appearance of rooms and common areas alike approximates international luxury norms, though staff aren't always as on-the-ball as one would expect at this level. **$300**

Shwe Taung Tarn 14th St, between 88th and 89th sts ☎ 02 75405, ⓦ shwetaungtarnhotel.webs.com; map pp.264–265. Way up north in the high eighties, this hotel may tempt those who don't fancy a city feel – the scent from the neighbouring fields can be somewhat fresh. They're decently sized, though, and an evening dip in the swimming pool can feel joyously relaxing at the end of a long day. **$70**

EATING

In keeping with its status as the second-largest city in the land, Mandalay has a decent little selection of places to eat. The area of greatest interest is the quadrant bounded by 84th St to the west, 27th St to the south, the palace moat to the east and 22nd St to the north; you'll find plenty of cheap, local choice here, including a fair few buffet places operated by the city's substantial Shan community. Also of note are the chapati snack-shacks which spring up in the evening around the junction of 27th St and 82nd St, and a few carts selling super-sugary Indian sweets; you're usually most likely to find them outside the Hindu temples on 27th St. Poking around further afield increases the range of possibilities to upper-class local fare and Western-style grub, as well as other Asian tastes from Thai to Korean via Chinese crispy duck.

DOWNTOWN

Gold Medal 30th St, between 81st and 82nd sts ☎ 02 35025; map p.270. Decent little bakery selling tasty treats – ideal if you're heading off on a long bike journey. Best are the Portuguese-style egg tarts (K500) and mutton puffs (K500); you can eat on site, but it's perhaps more enjoyable to devour the goodies in the calm police residential compound just to the east. Daily 8am–9.30pm.

Min Mahar 23rd St, at 86th St ☎ 09 508 7882; map p.270. Large, centrally located teahouse whose extremely young staff run around bearing cups of tea (K250), bowls of tasty Shan noodles (K800), samosas (K350) and the like. Also notable are a unique strain of banana pancake (K500), and the oddly named "nutritious meal" – a curious mix of banana, boiled egg, strawberry cream and sweetened condensed milk. Daily 5am–5.30pm.

Nay 27th St, at 82nd St; map p.270. The pick of this area's many street-side chapati-shacks, as evidenced by the crowd that's gathered around every single evening. They even have a menu of sorts, though there are no prices on it – ask when ordering to avoid any unpleasant surprises. You'll usually pay K1000–2000 to fill up, perhaps a little more if you plump for the "mutton brain", which gets you a little sheep cerebellum sitting in a curry sauce – surprisingly tasty, though served lukewarm. No alcohol, though they're happy for you to bring your own. Daily 3pm–1am.

★ **Nylon** 25th St, at 83rd St ☎ 02 32318; map p.270. Across the road from the guesthouse of the same name (see opposite), this deceptively simple place is one of Mandalay's more enduringly popular spots with locals and travellers alike. They serve fantastic ice cream from just K600, as well as a range of drinks (avocado shake K1000). Do note that foreigners sitting street-side are likely to be hassled by beggars while eating their treat. For a look at how said treat is made, pop into the preparation room out back. For a puerile laugh, step outside and look at the sign atop the café – a splendidly inappropriate name for a brand of sweetened condensed milk. Daily 8am–9.30pm.

★ **Pan Cherry** 81st St, between 26th and 27th sts ☎ 02 39924; map p.270. The best of the several South Asian choices in this area, this cheery Indian restaurant serves refillable curry platters that are effectively all-you-can-eat. They're pretty tasty, too, not to mention pretty cheap at just K2500 for meat and K1500 for veggie – a small price to pay. Daily 10am–9pm.

Rainbow 23rd St, at 84th St ☎ 02 23266; map p.270. Reasonable choice for cheap, simple local food; figure on around K3500 per main, or a bit less for the fried noodles. The top level also constitutes one of this area's nicer places to drink. Daily 8am–9pm.

★ **Shan Mama** 81st St, between 29th and 30th sts ☎ 02 71858; map p.270. You'll find plenty of ropey Shan buffet restaurants around the *Nylon* hotel, but if you're prepared to head a teensy bit further south, this is an infinitely better bet. It's not all-you-can-eat, but you're almost guaranteed to leave full – the friendly, English-speaking owner and her all-female coterie of giggling staff will insist that you try free samples of every single dish before making your choice. It'll all work out at around K2500–4000. Daily 6am–9.30pm.

V Café 80th St, at 25th St ☎ 09 680 4928; map p.270. A respite from the realities of Mandalay for those who need it, this is a relaxed, Western-style venue parping National Geographic, Shania Twain and the like from their screens and speakers. The food's okay – try a pizza (K6500), sardine sandwich (K1600) or Thai-style spicy beef salad (K5000), then wash it down with a so-so espresso (K800). Note that the *Sky Bar* upstairs is also a grand drinking spot (see opposite). Daily 9am–10.30pm.

OUTSIDE THE CENTRE

★ **BBB** 76th St, between 26th and 27th sts ☎ 02 73525, ⓦ bbbrestaurant.com; map pp.264–265. Quiet, urbane and stylish, it's no surprise that each and every one of Mandalay's expats seems to make a weekly pilgrimage to this restaurant. Their dishes are certainly on the pricey side, though this surplus gets you a range of flavours simply unavailable elsewhere in town; try the sea perch (K8500), salmon steak (K9500) or fish kebab (K6300). Also of note are the excellent burger and chips (K2900), banana and peanut smoothies (K2200), and well-made cocktails (from K2500). Daily 10am–10.30pm.

Cafe City 25th St, at 66th St ☎ 09 522 4054; map pp.264–265. Precisely the same menu as you'll find at *BBB* (see above), though a bit further out (just east of the palace walls), and decorated more like an American bar. Daily 10am–10.30pm.

Emperor 85th St, by Kandawgyi Paya; map pp.264–265. Way down south by the lakeside, this is an extremely popular local sunset spot. They've cheap barbecued snacks, as well as a range of local, Chinese and Thai mains (most in the region of K3000). The atmosphere is most compelling after sundown, when lanterns are illuminated around the complex – and the lake's army of resident mosquitoes takes to the air for an evening meal. Daily 10am–10pm.

Golden Duck 80th St, at 16th St ☎ 02 36808, ⓦ goldenduck.com.mm; map pp.264–265. The most revered of Mandalay's many Chinese places to eat, and particularly popular with local middle-class sorts and their families. The food's quite authentic; most mains are in the K3000–5000 range, though their signature crispy duck is a fair bit more (K11,800, serves two). Lastly, a location just west of the palace walls makes the place a great sunset-time spot. Daily 10.30am–3pm & 5.30–10pm.

Korea Restaurant 76th St, between 28th and 29th sts ☎ 02 71822; map pp.264–265. Run by a Korean–Burmese

couple, the pleasingly authentic Korean flavours here can come as a nice change to tired tastebuds. Go for a *bibimbap* (veggies and egg on rice, served in a hot clay bowl; K2500) or squid on rice (K3000); most mains are served with a small armada of mainly veggie side dishes known as *banchan*, meaning that it's easy to fill up on the cheap. The only negative is a curious layout designed around the kimchi-hungry Korean tour groups that form the bulk of diners here; single travellers may find themselves shunted into a weird side room. Daily 8am–9.30pm.

★ **A Little Bit of Mandalay** 28th St, between 52nd and 53rd sts ☎ 02 61295; map pp.264–265. Way out east in a delightfully secluded location, this is one of the best places in which to sample Burmese food – not truly authentic but in a good way, since the oil, spice and salt parameters are all kept way below national norms. Veggie curries (K4000) and fried, honey-drizzled chicken (K5000) are the best picks from the menu, though there's plenty more besides, including Red Mountain wine from Inle Lake (see box, p.244). Daily 10am–10.30pm.

Mya Nandar Strand Rd ☎ 02 66110; map pp.264–265. Housed in an almost preposterously large venue by the Ayeyarwady, this is a popular choice with tour group operators – try to dine here outside the main lunch and dinnertime hours, especially if you want a riverside table. The menu is mainly Thai fare; rice and noodle mains go for K3000 and the cheapest meat-based staples for K4000, or you could try something more exotic like sea bass (K7000). Daily 9am–10pm.

★ **Too Too** 27th St, between 74th and 75th sts ☎ 02 66351; map pp.264–265. A favourite with international visitors, even since a hike in prices following expansion to the street-front. You'll be given a single choice – chicken, mutton, prawn or fish, with your selection (K2800–4000) served in curry with at least five side dishes. Service is super-friendly, and on the whole it's up there with the city's best places for local grub. Daily 10am–9pm.

Unique Myanmar 27th St, at 65th St ☎ 02 21237; map pp.264–265. Popular with tour groups, and near-deserted outside of mealtimes, this open-air venue is a good place to eat before or after catching a performance at the nearby Mandalay Marionettes or Mintha Theater (see p.280). Despite the name, much of the MSG-free menu is made up of Chinese-style dishes; large sets go for K9000, while mains go from K3000. Also try an organic coffee or pot of Shan tea (K1000). Daily 9am–10pm.

Unison 38th St, at 87th St; map pp.264–265. A good pit stop if you're on a bike tour of Mandalay, this round-the-clock operation is surely the largest teahouse in Mandalay, housed in an odd octagonal structure by the canal – views of said waterway are blocked, though given the water pollution this is not really a bad thing. You'll pay K500 for a very large, very milky cup of the local brew. Daily 24hr.

THE MOUSTACHE BROTHERS

It's not easy to criticize the regime in Myanmar, especially in public – however, the internationally famed **Moustache Brothers** have been doing just this for decades, playing on the edges of what's acceptable to the regime. This comic dissidence has, inevitably, landed them in trouble – in 1996 the three brothers performed at Aung San Suu Kyi's compound in Yangon, after which two of them (Par Par Lay and Lu Zaw) were sentenced to six years of hard labour. Undeterred, they resumed their show in 2002; barred from performing in any public area, they decided to do so at their Mandalay home instead, satirizing national politics under the watchful gaze of the authorities. Officialdom then decreed that they weren't allowed to perform there either; the brothers then decided to do the same act without costumes and make-up, since it then couldn't be called a "show". Somehow, this ruse worked, and they've been performing ever since. Sadly, Par Par Lay died in 2013, but the two remaining performers have carried on (see p.280). Despite his fame, and the fact that he meets curious foreigners every single day, Lu Maw (the only English-speaker) is actually very willing to chat to those who pop by during the day.

DRINKING

Don't expect nightclubs (or, indeed, anything with a dancefloor), but Mandalay does have its fair share of decent, low-key places to drink. As well as the following, most of the restaurants listed in the Eating section (see p.277) serve alcohol; you could also make use of any number of identikit "beer stations" dotted liberally around the city.

Ayar Sky Bar Strand Rd, at 22nd St ☎ 02 64945; map pp.264–265. Don't shout this too loudly, but every evening this open-air bar atop the *Ayarwaddy River View Hotel* (see p.276) gives out free cocktails to guests and non-guests alike. The only condition is that you have to be here during sunset hours, with gorgeous views out over the river... what a pity. Even if greedy freeloaders prompt the hotel to retract this generous offer, it's a good place with drinks that aren't too pricey at all, given the location (cocktails K6000, beer K3000, or K2000 for a can of pop). Daily 5.30–10pm.

★**Central Park** 27th St, between 68th and 69th sts ☎ 09 9101 3500; map pp.264–265. Occasionally outdoing *Mann* (see below) in the debauchery stakes, this fun, open-air venue serves super-cheap drinks – a glass of draught Tiger will be yours for K800, rum sours go for K1200 and most cocktails cost K2800, while even the incredibly potent Long Island Iced Tea will only set you back K5000. They serve pizza (K4500) and other bar snacks; happy hour runs 6.30–7.30pm. Daily 10am–10.30pm.

★**Mann** 83rd St, between 25th and 26th sts ☎ 02 66025; map p.270. Entirely devoid of tour groups and also popular with locals, this bar feels almost like Myanmar "back in the day", when almost every traveller to the country was a worldly, backpackery type. The place is full each and every night thanks to cheap booze (beers K1500, small

bottles of rum K700) and a raucous atmosphere; given the lack of table space most nights, you're almost guaranteed to get talking to locals or other travellers. It's a restaurant of sorts too, though the service is slow and the food terrible; the scent of rat poison out back on the way to the toilets – plus some curious clangs, bangs and squeaks from the kitchen area – should be enough to put you off. Drink here for sure; dine somewhere else. Daily 9am–10pm.

Shwe Lwin Pyin 82nd St, between 32nd and 33rd sts ☎ 02 66328; map p.270. Exuding a chilled vibe unique to Mandalay, the rear yard of this simple restaurant is a delightful place for draught Myanmar (K800) of an evening. The interior has been pleasingly decorated, and usually features paintings by local artists. Daily 10am–10pm.

Sky Bar 80th St, at 25th St ☎ 09 680 4928; map p.270. Sitting pretty above the *V Café* (see opposite), this open-air bar is essentially part of the same venue – you'll be picking from the same menu. It's often near deserted, and a beautiful place from which to watch the palace walls flaring up with the sun's last rays. Daily 9am–10.30pm.

Win Win III 39th St, between 80th and 81st sts; map pp.264–265. This beer station (draught beers K700) is nothing out of the ordinary, but it does function as a handy place to wait before catching the Moustache Brothers performance (see above). Daily 9am–11pm.

ENTERTAINMENT

There are a few great shows to catch in Mandalay, with all of the acts listed below having found fame – or actually performed – overseas. It's just a pity that they all take place at precisely the same time.

CINEMA
Mingalar Diamond Cineplex 5F Diamond Plaza,

between 33rd & 78th sts. The only cinema in town to show subtitled, rather than dubbed, foreign films – though not every day, or every film, so ask before buying your ticket (from K1200). Daily 6am–6pm.

SHOWS

Mandalay Marionettes 66th St, between 26th and 27th sts ☎02 34446, ⓦmandalaymarionettes.com. Controlled from behind the tiniest stage imaginable (though the one in Nyaungshwe is smaller still; see p.244), colourful puppets re-create scenes from the life of the Buddha – given the subject, the hour-long show is actually quite light-hearted, and even rather funny in places. Do, however, try to read the programme before the lights go down – you'll be a little lost otherwise. Curtain goes up at 8.30pm daily; tickets K8000.

Mintha Theater 27th St, between 65th and 66 sts ☎09 680 3607, ⓦminthatheater.com. A great opportunity to see traditional dance with extravagant costumes, accompanied by live music, with ten different performances packed into the show. Daily 8.30pm; tickets K8000.

Moustache Brothers 39th St, between 80th and 81st sts ☎09 4303 4220, ⓔbosoeoo@gmail.com. The only chance you're likely to get to experience *anyeint*, a traditional form of comedy combining political satire and broad slapstick, delivered in a mix of Burmese and English. Two of the performers, Par Par Lay and Lu Maw, served six years' hard labour after making jokes about the regime in 1996 (see box, p.279), and this context is reason enough to attend even if the jokes don't always hit the mark. Daily 8.30pm; K8000.

SHOPPING

Pretty much all of the **gold leaf** applied to Buddha images by devotees in Myanmar comes from a small area of Mandalay. There are about fifty gold-leaf workshops across the city, many of them based in homes in the blocks around 36th St, just east of the railway line. Mandalay is also famed for the production of wonderful **tapestries**, most of which depict the Jataka. Finally, if you can fit a giant Buddha statue into your backpack, go hunting in the fascinating area just west of the Mahamuni Paya (see p.271).

Diamond Plaza 33rd St, at 78th St; map pp.264–265. The newest mall-like space in town at the time of writing, consisting of five floors of brand-name (usually ones you won't have heard of) clothing and cosmetics. There's a cinema sitting here on the top floor (see p.279), next to a few cheap restaurants and cafés, and Myanmar Book Centre, the city's best bookstore, down below. Daily 6am–6pm.

Jade Market 38th St, at 87th St; map pp.264–265. You'll hear lots of Chinese being spoken at this extraordinarily busy market, which in theory charges foreign visitors a K1000 entry fee; you're more likely to be asked for it at the western entrance, and less likely at the northern one. If you're in the market for some jade, the first prices will, of course, be rip-offs; you should be able to haggle these down to more acceptable levels, particularly if using the nearby *Unison* teahouse (see p.278) as part of a "look, I'm *really* walking away" strategy. Also of note are the workhouses off the eastern side of the market, which are where the stones get cut and polished – quite an absorbing spectacle. Daily 8.30am–5.30pm.

★ **King Galon** 36th St, between 77th and 78th sts ☎09 4714 3078; map pp.264–265. By far the best of several gold-pounders' workshops on 36th St. The sound of various chaps bonking the gold into super-fine thickness

can be quite beautiful – and, in fact, almost musical. They also, on occasions, show how bamboo paper is made. The place is free to enter, and though they sell souvenirs there's very little pressure to buy; one thing you may wish to invest in is a stash of gold leaf (from K3000), for putting onto an appropriate Buddha image (see p.271). Daily 7am–6pm.

Rocky 27th St, between 62nd and 63rd sts ☎02 74106; map pp.264–265. A terrific little place selling all sorts of local crafts, including Mandalay's famed marionettes. They'll first point you towards the jade and other precious stones (which can be yours for as little as K5000), and there are also good necklaces and woodcarvings on sale (the latter on the upstairs level). However, the shop is perhaps most notable for its superb Jataka tapestries and other images. Daily 8.30am–8.30pm.

Shwe Pathein 36th St between 77th and 78th sts ☎09 504 3067; map pp.264–265. Not worth dragging yourself way across town for, but certainly worth popping into if you're visiting the King Galon gold pounders (see above), this tiny store sells gorgeous paper parasols, which come in a range of sizes – there are even some for kids, who often find the things delightful. The cheapest cost around K9000; it's just a pity that the staff are usually so grumpy. Daily 6am–6pm.

SPORTS AND ACTIVITIES

However long you stay in Mandalay, there's plenty to keep you occupied – whack golf balls towards Mandalay Hill from a cute driving range, swim off the day's exertions in a hotel pool, go for a massage or relax at a spa.

GOLF

Asia Center Driving Range 10th St, behind Mandalay Hill hotel. A nice alternative to paying fee after fee at the

Shwe Mann Taung course (see opposite) is this driving range, just north of the *Mandalay Hill* hotel (p.277), where you can whack balls in the direction of the hill without even

6

leaving the comfort of your flip-flops. It'll cost you K700–2000 for a tray of sixty balls (depending on quality), and an extra K1000 per club; all locals also splash out on a caddy (K2000 per tray), though this is not necessary. All in all, a fun way to spend an hour or so.

Shwe Mann Taung Golf Resort 73rd St, at Lan Thit Rd ☎ 02 75898, ✉ shwemanntaung.mdy@gmail.com. An eighteeen-hole golf course in Mandalay? You bet, and a fairly decent one at that – with nice views of Mandalay Hill to boot. Even stranger is the fact that the course attracts upwards of 200 golfers per day, the vast majority of them local. The green fee will cost you K30,000 whether you're playing eighteen or nine holes; otherwise, you can chop the buggy (K30,000), caddy (K12,000) and trolley fees (K1000) in half if you're playing over nine. They also rent out sets of clubs for K15,000–30,000, depending on quality.

MASSAGE

GGG 27th St, between 74th and 75th sts ☎ 09 4025 77711. A reliable place for a good rubdown; 1hr massage K6000. Daily 9am–7pm.

Smile 27th St, at 75th St ☎ 09 9100 9487. Massage from blind masseurs – a 1hr session costs just K6000. Daily 9am–11pm.

MEDITATION

Dhamma Mandala Yaytagun Hill ☎ 02 39694, ✇ mandala.dhamma.org. A large complex with room for 160 visitors, located on a rise around 16km from central Mandalay. Their ten-day introductory courses, which can also be conducted in English, are paid for by donations from those who've already benefited from the experience, meaning that there are no set fees.

Kyunpin Meditation Centre Kanphyu Village, Wetlet Township, Sagaing ☎ 099 102 6653, ✇ kyunpin.com. Located in Sagaing, around 20km southeast of Mandalay (see p.286), this centre receives good reports from foreign visitors. There are no set fees for food or accommodation, and in common with similar places around the land, those staying here should refrain from smoking, drinking alcohol or socializing; you'll be expected to meditate for 12–14hr/day.

SWIMMING

Having a swim can feel like the best thing in the world at the end of a hot Mandalay day, and there are a number of places to do it. Other than the public venue listed here, those fancying a swim can take a dip in the pools at the *Ayarwaddy River View*, *Mandalay City* or *Mandalay Hill* hotels, where it'll cost K5000 per person. You didn't read it here, but note that the one at the Mandalay Hill is the easiest to sneak into without paying, and by far the most attractive too.

Yatanaban Swimming Pool 10th St, west of Mandalay Hill hotel. Abutting the city's wretched zoo (see p.267), but using a separate entrance to the east of the compound, this is a fairly decent public facility – and cheap as chips at just K1000 for entry. There are a few diving boards and the like, though you'll see that using them comes with extra difficulties beyond the usual ones – they're kind of dangerous. Daily 6am–6pm.

SPA

Mandalar Spa 10th St, by Mandalay Hill ☎ 02 35638, ✇ mandalayhillresorthotel.com. Located at the rear of the *Mandalay Hill* hotel (see p.277), this is the best and most attractive spa in town. There are various options available, but they're a bit pricey – figure on K35,000 for a basic course, or K65,000 for a full-body treatment. Daily 8am–10.30pm.

DIRECTORY

Banks There are foreign exchange counters and ATMs in the arrivals section at the airport (see p.271). Centrally located banks with currency exchange include AGD, 82nd St, between 27th and 28th sts, and Small & Medium Industrial Development Bank (SMIDB), 83rd St, between 27th and 28th sts. CB Bank, 78th St, between 27th and 28th sts, also has an ATM. Diamond Plaza, to the east of the railway line, has a UAB bank plus several ATMs.

Hospital Mandalay General Hospital is on 30th St, between 74th and 77th sts (☎ 02 39001; call ☎ 192 in an emergency).

Police There are many police offices around town, with even the far-flung ones often featuring an English-language "How may I help you?" sign outside. The main office is on 81st St, between 29th and 30th sts (☎ 02 36869).

Post office The main post office is at 22nd St, between 80th and 81st sts. There's also a DHL office on 78th St, between 37th and 38th sts, outside the *Hotel Mandalay* (see p.276).

Around Mandalay

Beyond the city, it only takes a day – whether by bike or as part of a tour – to see **Amarapura** and its famed teak footbridge; take a horse-driven carriage through **Inwa**'s web of dusty lanes and make the sweaty trudge up **Sagaing**'s stupa-studded hill. All of these former capitals are tethered together by the mighty Ayeyarwady, a river which – as elsewhere in the country – functions as the lifeblood of the region, and also slides idly by the delightful village of **Sagaing**, which never functioned as a capital but boasts a building which (had it been completed) would have beaten any in the area for size.

<table>
<tr><td colspan="2">

GETTING AROUND

</td><td>

AROUND MANDALAY

</td></tr>
</table>

By pick-up Pick-ups leave Mandalay in the direction of Amarapura and Sagaing, though since they don't go anywhere near any of the sights in those cities, they're barely worth bothering with – you'd have to get a taxi in any case.

By taxi/motorbike taxi Most people choose to hire a motorbike driver or taxi for a day or half-day; a motorbike taxi will ask for K8000 to Amarapura, K12,000 to Sagaing, and around K15,000 for these two and Inwa too. By taxi it'll be more like K35,000 to visit all three, though you can split this between up to four people. To add Paleik onto these itineraries will cost an additional K10,000 or so, or K12,000 as a stand-alone trip.

By bike It's possible to visit all the sights around Mandalay by bike, though Mingun is an awfully long return trip if you're not taking the ferry there or back. Do note that you'll be sharing the main road from Mandalay to Sagaing with plenty of buses, lorries and the like – it's not terribly pleasant. However, having a bike certainly makes a visit to Inwa a lot more interesting; rather than sitting in a cart and following all the other carts around, you can plot your own course, and even take off into the area's rather arresting countryside.

By ferry Both private and government boats operate to Mingun (see p.289).

Amarapura

အမရပူရ

Just 11km south of central Mandalay is the small town of **AMARAPURA** (pronounced with the stress on the first "ra"). Though a decidedly scruffy place today, it has substantial historical pedigree, having twice served as Myanmar's royal capital (see box, p.263). Though there are some pleasing stupas and other Buddhist monuments dotted around the place, Amarapura is most famed for the **U Bein Bridge**, a lengthy teak construction that's up there with Myanmar's most photogenic – and most photographed – sights.

The bridge stretches across pretty **Lake Taungthaman**; ostensibly named after an ogre who came here in pursuit of the Buddha, it's a shallow expanse whose shore and surrounding area are by far the most pleasant part of town. Hunt around the maze of lanes inland from the bridge's western end (beyond the umpteen trinket stalls by the bridge itself) and you'll see plenty of villagers making longyi and other garments – despite the horde of tourists padding along the bridge nearby, this is up there with Myanmar's cheapest places in which to shop for **fabrics**.

Note that there's nowhere for foreigners to stay in Amarapura, and since there are no particularly exciting restaurants, you're also advised to eat elsewhere.

U Bein Bridge

ဦးပိန်တံတား• Daily 24hr • In theory part of the Mandalay combo-ticket (see box, p.268), but nobody usually checks; boat rental K8000–10,000 for 45min or so

An absolute must-see if you're in the Mandalay area, the spectacular **U Bein Bridge** stretches more than 1200m across Lake Taungthaman – it is, in fact, the world's longest teak footbridge. Most evenings it probably also hosts the world's longest unbroken line of tourists: no bad thing, and in fact quite a spectacle when the colours of everyone's shirts are flared up by the sun's last rays. Though most visit at this time, early birds can catch something similar with far fewer people at daybreak.

The bridge's existence stems from a salvage job that took place following one of Myanmar's many changes of regal power: after the palace was shifted north to Mandalay in 1859, Amarapura's mayor **U Bein** decided to create a bridge using the teak support columns left behind. There are, today, just over a thousand pillars along the course of the bridge, some of which have been replaced with concrete poles. If you're wondering why the thing was built so high above the lake, you're obviously visiting in the dry season – the water level rises considerably after the rains.

A visit to the bridge can complicate some day-trip itineraries – most visitors like to walk the length of the bridge, so unless you want to walk it twice, ask your driver to pick you up from the other end. It's also possible to rent **paddle boats** here; these are usually only available at the western end, where most of the tour buses drop off.

Maha Gandayon Kyaung

မဟာဂန္ဓာရုံကျောင်း • Daily 24hr • Free

Home to hundreds of monks, the huge, nationally renowned **Maha Gandayon Kyaung** sprawls across the area to the west of the U Bein Bridge. The monastery is a pleasant place to poke around, with some lovingly decorated halls, but try not to visit during the monks' lunchtime (around 11am) when tour buses disgorge droves of trigger-happy camera-toters, and the resultant crowd while the monks eat silently feels rather like panda feeding time at a zoo.

Pahtodawgyi

ပုထိုးတော်ကြီး • Entrance to south of complex • Daily 24hr • Free

If cycling south from Mandalay, **Pahtodawgyi** will be the first hint that you're nearing Amarapura – a giant, bell-shaped stupa protruding from the flatlands, completed in 1819 at the beginning of King Bagyidaw's reign. Both the stupa and its reflection are also clearly visible from the bridge, the spectacle creating lovely pictures for those with powerful camera lenses. If you're male (for women are not allowed), you'll also get a great view of the surrounding countryside by ascending to the stupa's upper level.

Bagaya Kyaung

ဘားကရာကျောင်း • Just east of Mandalay–Sagaing road • Daily 9am–5pm • Part of Mandalay combination ticket (see box, p.268)

Around 2km north of the lake, the **Bagaya Kyaung** is a recent reconstruction of a monastery built here during Amarapura's first stint as royal capital. It's surely the most curious component of the Mandalay combination ticket, for bar a moderately pretty wooden exterior featuring a couple of steeply tapering towers, there's almost nothing to get your teeth into – perhaps one to avoid.

ARRIVAL AND DEPARTURE   AMARAPURA

By pick-up It is possible to get to Amarapura by pick-up from Mandalay (see p.274), though these drop off nowhere near the sights, which are also rather distant from each other – far more trouble than it's worth.

By bike You can cycle to Amarapura from Mandalay in well under an hour; use the tall Pahtodawgyi stupa (see above)

as a reference point for when to turn off the main road.

Tours Most visit Amarapura as part of a motorbike or taxi tour (see opposite); your driver is certain to stop by the bridge, but let them know if you'd like to add other sights to your itinerary here.

Paleik

ပုလိပ်

The village of **PALEIK**, around 18km south of Mandalay, is famous for one thing and one thing only – the "**Snake Temple**" (Hmwe Paya) at its centre. An unassuming little place, it has earned fame thanks to a clutch of resident pythons – some made the temple their home in 1974, and despite efforts from the monks to keep them out, the serpents kept on coming back. The monks decided that the snakes were probably holy, and allowed them to roost here – if you're in luck, you'll see them wrapped around one of the various Buddha statues. Most people visit at 11am, when the snakes are lovingly washed in a bath filled with petals. If you're not on too tight a schedule, think about combining your visit with a short trip to some decaying **stupas**, just to the south of the temple.

By bike Paleik is a little far from Mandalay, but with an early start and a good breakfast it's quite possible to cycle here and back in a day.

Tours Most visit the temple as part of a motorbike or taxi tour (see p.282).

Inwa

အင်း:ဝ

6

One of the most enchantingly beautiful parts of the wider Mandalay area, the sleepy, semi-rural village of **INWA** was once a place of great importance. Originally known as **Ava**, it served as the capital of Myanmar on four separate occasions, totalling over three hundred years (see box, p.263) – almot impossible to imagine today while you're rumbling between fields along the dusty village lanes.

Scattered in and around the ancient **city walls**, sections of which remain visible (as do the ditches which once formed the surrounding moats), the various sights pertaining to Inwa's period in the regal sunshine are quite spread out and not all that easy to track down by yourself; the vast majority of visitors chalk them off as part of a **horse-drawn carriage** tour (see opposite). These follow a fairly set route, and the sights here have been listed in the same order that you're likely to follow. A pleasurable alternative is to make the rounds yourself on a **bicycle**, though you'll have to ride this down from Mandalay (see p.274). Cycling will give you the opportunity to strike off along roads left alone by the cart drivers, or even into stupa-studded fields surrounding the central clutch of sights.

If you're on a day-trip around the Mandalay area, Inwa makes by far the best place in which to take lunch – there are a couple of good **restaurants** just up from the jetty where the ferries drop off (see opposite).

Shwedagon Paya

ရွှေတိဂုံဘုရား • Daily 24hr • Free

You'll usually race straight past this gleaming golden stupa on your horse-drawn carriage, and your driver most likely won't want to stop to let you see it, but the hefty **Shwedagon Paya** is unmissable when making the trot west to Bagaya Kyaung (see opposite). It forms the southwestern corner of the ancient city wall, and is splendidly photogenic.

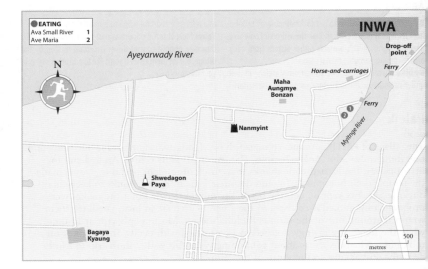

● EATING	
Ava Small River	1
Ave Maria	2

INWA

Ayeyarwady River

Drop-off point

Horse-and-carriages

Ferry

Maha Aungmye Bonzan

Ferry

Myitnge River

Nanmyint

Shwedagon Paya

Bagaya Kyaung

0   500
metres

N

Bagaya Kyaung

ဘားကရာကျောင်း • Daily 24hr • Covered by Mandalay combination ticket (see box right)

Cart drivers usually make a beeline straight to Inwa's most memorable sight – the **Bagaya Kyaung**, a truly captivating teak monastery built in 1834, during Inwa's final stint as royal capital. It's still a functioning place of worship, residence and study – for proof of the latter, check out the globes placed in the teaching hall to help young monks with their geography skills. The moodily dim main hall is more beautiful; keep an eye out for peacocks and lotus flowers painted onto the columns. The exterior, too, is a highly attractive affair featuring all sorts of carved detail. Independent travellers can take off into the surrounding fields, many of which are punctuated with small stupas. Finally, one brief word of warning here – the postcard peddlers can be rather persistent.

> A **Mandalay combination ticket** (see box, p.268) is needed for most sights in Inwa; you can get one from a booth near the Maha Aungmye Bonzan (see below).

Nanmyint

နန်းမြင့် • Daily 6am–7pm • Covered by Mandalay combination ticket (see box above), though you may not be asked for it

Referred to by almost all of the travellers who see it as the "Leaning Tower of Inwa", the wonky **Nanmyint** tower is the only surviving structure from King Bagyidaw's palace. The tilt came as a result of the 1838 earthquake which eventually resulted in Inwa finally losing its status as capital forever (unless the powers that be get sick of Naypyitaw and fancy moving to the countryside). It's possible to ascend the structure for superlative views of the Inwa area.

Maha Aungmye Bonzan

မဟာအောင်မြေဘုံစံ • Daily 6am–7pm • Covered by Mandalay combination ticket (see box above)

Cart drivers usually round up their tour with a visit to the **Maha Aungmye Bonzan**, a gorgeous structure located on a slight rise. The place looks like it's ready to fall apart, with the stucco slowly turning to powder and breaking from the brick walls. A harbinger of doom if ever there was one, a colony of bats has taken roost in the eaves – given Inwa's location, you're unlikely to be around in the evening when they flit off, en masse, for a bite to eat. If you fancy a walk, head towards the rear of the complex, which eventually backs onto the river; the many golden spires of Sagaing (see p.286) glisten beyond the opposite bank.

ARRIVAL AND DEPARTURE
INWA

You can visit Inwa as part of a **motorbike or taxi tour** (see box, p.282), on a **bicycle** (just over 1hr from central Mandalay) or by public transport: **pick-ups** from Mandalay (corner of 29th St and 84th St; 30min) can drop you at a junction from which it's a 10min walk southwest down a long, straight, tree-lined road to the jetty. Whichever way you arrive, you'll have to take a very short **ferry** ride (regular departures daily 6am–6pm; K800 return, K1000 with a bicycle, or K1500 with a motorbike) across a river; horse-and-carriage drivers lie in wait on the other side.

GETTING AROUND

By horse-drawn carriage The easiest way to get around Inwa's scattered sights is on a horse-and-cart tour – for some it's this experience that sticks in the memory, rather than any of the sights in particular. Drivers typically ask for K6000 for a 2hr tour (penny-pinchers could try the walking-on technique, which usually results in the driver following you along the road and willing to accept a little less). The horses probably need little commandeering, since they essentially trot the same course every time.

EATING

Ava Small River ☎ 09 9100 1921. A friendly little open-air place selling regular Chinese mains, with their veggie dishes particularly good; expect to pay around K4000 to fill up. Daily 8am–6pm.

Ave Maria ☎ 09 26328. Pleasant and more local in terms of its menu than the *Ava Small River*. Go for one of their surprisingly large curry sets (K2000); staff will often come by to refill the various components, meaning that you can eat a lot for very little. Daily 8.30am–6pm.

Sagaing

စစ်ကိုင်း

The low-key city of **SAGAING** sits just 25km south of Mandalay on the opposite side of the Ayeyarwady River, which slides lazily past its eastern flank. If the name seems familiar, you may have spent some time looking at a map of Myanmar – this unassuming place is actually the capital of **Sagaing Region**, which stretches way up north, almost all the way to Tibet. In common with Mandalay and many of its present-day satellite towns, it once functioned as the royal capital of Myanmar, though its stint was the shortest by far at just four years (see box, p.263); it was also the centre of a Shan kingdom during the fourteenth century. However, it wears its history better than other places hereabouts, and remains an important religious centre.

The main reason to come here is clearly visible from the Ayeyarwady bridges (one built by the British in 1934, the other a 2005 construction), and sometimes even from Mandalay itself – **Sagaing Hill**, a modest rise bristling with so many Buddhist spikes that it resembles some sort of Burmese Hellraiser. Few visit anything else in the town (there are plenty more of said spires to track down, if you so desire), though some enjoy the chance to take a walk in the delightful area north of Sagaing Hill, and others choose to stay the night – this is the only one of the Mandalay satellite towns with foreigner-licensed accommodation, and those staying on will get the chance to see another, more local, side of Burmese life. This is also true of those who choose Sagaing as their meditation base, since there's a great centre hereabouts (see p.281).

Sagaing Hill

စစ်ကိုင်းတောင် • Access from Thall Ta Pan St • Daily 24hr • Covered by Sagaing-Mingun combination ticket (see box below); K300 camera and K500 video fees, usually only collected from road entrance • Motorbike taxis cost around K2000

Around 250m high, splendid **Sagaing Hill** pokes its omni-spired head out just north of the city centre. The views from the top are predictably fantastic, though for some the ascent from Thall Ta Pan Street (around 25min) is the best part of the experience; the covered pathway gets steeper as you go, and if you can make it to the top without pausing for a breather you're officially in decent shape.

The 30m stupa of the **Sone Oo Pone Nya Shin Paya** lies in wait at the top, a handsome, pleasingly decorated reward for your endeavour, with fancily colourful tiling and rich turquoise-and-green tessellated glass behind the main statue. In addition, the views of the river are quite superb from here, and with decent enough weather you'll see Mandalay's grey sprawl way to the north. There are several other religious structures on the hill, the most interesting of which is **Umin Thounzeh**, a curved chamber containing 43 seated and two standing Buddha images, a twenty-minute walk from the Sone Oo Pone Nya Shin Paya.

Kaunghmudaw Paya

ကောင်းမှုတော်ဘုရား • 7km northwest of central Sagaing • Daily 24hr • Covered by Sagaing-Mingun combination ticket (see box below) • Motorbike taxis charge K6000

Some way to the northwest of Sagaing but easily visible from a distance, **Kaunghmudaw Paya** is the town's most interesting religious monument. Looking

---

THE SAGAING-MINGUN COMBINATION TICKET

In theory, to enter Sagaing or Mingun you'll need to buy or show a **combination ticket** (K3000), valid for both towns yet separate from the similar one used for Mandalay and Inwa (see box, p.268). Before the 2012 earthquake, this was collected from travellers before they boarded the ferry to Mingun; these days it's rarely collected at all. Sagaing is a different matter, since efforts to collect the fee have been ramped up in recent years; vehicles crossing the bridge are checked for foreigners, and those on board asked to show the ticket or cough up. Mysteriously, travellers on bicycles are occasionally waved through – perhaps as congratulations for completing the long journey from Mandalay.

somewhat like a whitewashed, 50m-tall mammary gland, it was completed in 1648, its decidedly non-Burmese design based on the Ruvanvalisaya stupa in Anuradhapura, Sri Lanka. Like its counterpart, it is said to house a number of relics of the Buddha, including a tooth – actually an ox-bone fake – and several strands of hair.

ARRIVAL AND DEPARTURE | SAGAING

By pick-up It's possible to get to Sagaing on one of the smoke-hooting pick-ups from Mandalay (see p.282), but these drop off near the market – nowhere near Sagaing Hill, but fine if you're planning to stay in or otherwise make use of the town itself. It's a 2km climb from the market to the hill – walkable, just about, though it's far easier to hop on a motorbike taxi.

Tours Most travellers arrive in Sagaing on a motorbike or taxi tour (see box, p.282). Some drivers will take you to the base of Sagaing Hill, and others to the top – ask about this when arranging your trip, since you might be asked extra for the latter, unless your driver is also planning to visit a commission-friendly silversmiths on the way down.

ACCOMMODATION AND EATING

Outside Mandalay, Sagaing is the only place in the area with foreigner-licensed accommodation – and there's one whole hotel to choose from. While a day-trip is enough for some, there's certainly some merit to staying the night – it's an appealing place which won't have any other foreigners after sundown.

Pyi San One road north of Aoe Tann Lay ☎ 072 34505. A passable place to eat, located one street parallel to the *Shwe Pyae Sone* hotel; as with any restaurant in Sagaing, you'll have curious locals gazing at you throughout your meal. The fare on offer includes hefty-sized Chinese staples (from K1500), and good draught Dagon beer. Daily 8am–9pm.

Shwe Pyae Sone 20 Aoe Tann Lay ☎ 072 22781,

☻ shwepyaesonehotel.sgg@gmail.com. If you feel like staying in the Mandalay area but not in Mandalay itself, here's your only option. It's actually a very nice little place, with courteous staff and surprisingly presentable rooms; the $35 ones are far nicer than the standards, but all have a/c, flatscreen TVs and a minibar. They also rent out bicycles (K3000/day) and motorbikes (K10,000/day). §30

Mingun
မင်းကွန်း

The small, village-like town of **MINGUN** is, for many visitors, the most appealing of the many attractions surrounding Mandalay. By making a trip here, you'll get historical attractions, a look at village life and a delightful ferry ride, all rolled up into one ball. The place would likely be ignored today were it not for King Bodawpaya, who in 1790 decided to build the gigantic **Mingun Pagoda** here. All that was completed by the time of his death, 29 years later, was the bottom portion – an imposing cube of bricks on top of a huge terrace, its bulk clearly visible from across the river in Mandalay. There are a few other modest sights around the unfinished pagoda, but perhaps more appealing is the chance to take the pulse of local life – you may well have no other option than to do so, since the schedule of the ferries linking Mingun to Mandalay more or less obliges you to while away a couple of hours here. Mercifully, there are a few little places to eat and drink (see p.289).

Mingun Pagoda
မင်းကွန်းဘုရား • Currently off limits • In theory, part of Sagaing-Mingun combination ticket (see box opposite)

Quite possibly the world's largest pile of bricks, it's hard to imagine how majestic a sight **Mingun Pagoda** would have been if finished – using thousands of prisoners of war and other slave labour, the project was originally intended to reach a final height of around 150m. Though only one-third was completed, it's still an astonishing sight – and one made more dramatic by the jagged, lightning-like fissures created when earthquakes hit in 1819 and 2012. The latter 'quake saw the pathway heading up to the pagoda closed to visitors; it's unlikely to reopen any time soon, though keep your fingers crossed.

6

KILLING TIME IN MINGUN

The ferries to Mingun usually afford you around three hours in the village – a little too much time for some, since the giant Mingun Pagoda can no longer be climbed, and it takes only a short time to circumnavigate. Although it looks tempting, you're advised to save the pagoda for last – you've plenty of time, and by hitting the other sights first you'll see them without being part of a large group of tourists. Just north of Hsinbyume Paya is the start of a small residential area; many travellers eventually gravitate here, to pad slowly along its pleasant, dusty roads, and perhaps drop into one of the several teahouses. If you really, really need something to do, there's also a snooker hall here, just on the right as you enter the village – Burmese often joke that the country has more snooker tables than school tables.

On your way up to the pagoda from the river, you'll pass a pair of **chinthe** – half lion and half dragon, these giant figures were built to guard the giant structure. Though they're almost entirely ruined, it's still possible to get a vague idea of their shape, especially from the roadside.

Settaya Paya

စက်တော်ရာဘုရား • Daily 24hr • Free

Just south of Mingun Pagoda, the smaller **Settaya Paya** is a decidedly ugly structure, though useful if you fancy leaving Buddha some shoes as an offering – inside the small hall you'll see what locals claim to be **Buddha's footprint**, a metre-long indentation with shells on the toes and a flower on the heel.

Pondaw Pagoda

ပုံတော်ဘုရား • Daily 24hr • Free

In common with other important Burmese super-structures, a smaller-scale replica of Mingun Pagoda sits nearby – it's located just south of Settaya Paya. **Pondaw Pagoda** is certainly worth a look, if only to better imagine how Bodawpaya's vision may have appeared when completed.

Mingun Bell

မင်းကွန်းခေါင်းလောင်း • Daily 5.30am–5.30pm • Free

As well as the globe's largest pile of bricks, Mingun also boasts one of the world's heaviest functioning **bells**, just north of Mingun Pagoda, on the west side of the road. Like its fellow record-breaker, this was commissioned by King Bodawpaya, to whom size clearly meant everything – it weighs 55,555 viss (corresponding to around ninety tonnes), and is around 5m wide at the base. The done thing here – quite probably down to human nature, for every single visitor seems genetically programmed to do precisely the same thing – is to duck inside, then get someone to clang the bell with their fist. Despite the size, it's not particularly sonorous – the graffiti daubed inside can't help.

Hsinbyume Paya

ဆင်ဖြူမယ်ဘုရား • Daily 24hr • In theory, part of Sagaing-Mingun combination ticket (see box, p.286)

The town's final sight, located just north of the Mingun Bell, is handsomely whitewashed **Hsinbyume Paya**. Its wavy design is said to represent Mount Sumeru, the mountain at the centre of the Buddhist cosmos, and the seas that surround it – there are seven such "layers", and if you walk up past all of them you'll be rewarded with a superlative view of the Mingun area, the countryside beyond, and the river on which you've most likely arrived.

ARRIVAL AND DEPARTURE

By ferry There are two ways of getting to Mingun by ferry. The government boats (1hr; K5000) leave from the pier on 26th St in Mandalay at 9am, and return at 1pm; if there aren't enough seats on the deck, simply pop downstairs to fetch your own. The alternative is to take one of the MGRG (see box, p.273) services, which depart at 9.30am and 2.30pm, and stay in Mingun for three hours (K8000 return) – a lot of time to kill (see box opposite), though quite pleasant if you approach things in the right mind; note that these run Jan–April only.

On a day-trip It's also possible to combine Mingun with Sagaing and other destinations on a motorbike or taxi day-trip, though this will add two hours of travel to the day, and a fair bit more to the price – though taking the boat is way more fun, on rented transport you may get to see the place without the passengers disgorged by the ferry.

EATING

The village has a few cute places to eat and drink. There are a couple of touristy ones just north of the Mingun Pagoda, but for a more authentically local experience, push on north into the small clutch of houses just beyond Hsinbyume Paya.

Kaungkin Tar North of Hsinbyume Paya. Pleasant teahouse near the sights just at the start of the main village, and quite a pretty place with its mint-green stools and tan-coloured tables. A cup of tea will cost you K200. Daily 4am–9pm.

Point Behind Settaya Paya. Good for a small meal, this lazy place has a river view, and can rustle up simple dishes such as omelette with chicken meat (K2500). They also sell beer (K700). Daily 8am–10pm.

Northern Myanmar

KACHIN FESTIVAL, MYITKYINA

Northern Myanmar

With its dripping jungles, ice-bound mountains, fiercely independent hill tribes and fabulous natural resources, northern Myanmar fuels the imagination like few other places. This fascinating land has been criss-crossed by armies and explorers for centuries, and yet it remains one of the least-known places in Asia. Overland travel is controlled in much of the region, but it is currently possible to travel on most of the major rail and river routes without permits.

7

The most accessible part of **northern Myanmar** lies in the hills east of Mandalay between balmy **Pyin Oo Lwin** and the modern town of **Lashio**. Once summer capital of British Burma, Pyin Oo Lwin is still redolent of the Raj, with colonial piles dotting its leafy suburbs. Further east, train enthusiasts and those with a head for heights will appreciate the creaky **Gokteik Viaduct**, constructed in 1901 and made famous by Paul Theroux in *The Great Railway Bazaar*. Further along the old **Burma Road** are **Kyaukme** and **Hsipaw**, both excellent bases from which to trek into tea-growing hills and explore the villages of northern Shan State.

In northern Myanmar, as elsewhere in the country, the **Ayeyarwady River** is a major transport artery. At the time of writing, it was possible for foreigners to travel upstream as far as **Bhamo**, a pleasant riverside town with a long history as a trading post. Downstream from Bhamo, there are interesting stops to be made in **Shwegu** with its ranks of overgrown, island-bound pagodas, and **Katha**, the inspiration for "Kyauktada" in George Orwell's must-read novel, *Burmese Days*. Further south again the river flows through Sagaing Region past the riverside potteries of **Kyaukmyaung**, not far from the remains of the ancient city of **Hanlin**, today the site of a major archeological dig, and the town of **Shwebo**, a one-time Burmese capital.

In the far north, the modern town of **Myitkyina** is a springboard into the wilds of northern **Kachin State**. The bumpy journey to **Indawgyi Lake** is a great permit-free way to experience the region's incredible natural environment and to see one of northern Myanmar's few important pagodas, **Shwe Myitzu**. However, for a true wilderness experience, you'll need to get as far as **Putao** and the national parks that line Myanmar's Himalayan border, for which you'll need to sign up to a tour.

Much of vast **Sagaing Region** is closed to foreign travellers without permits – particularly along the Indian border in the state's mountainous northwest. Further south, it's possible to cruise along the Chindwin River (see box, p.222) north to Kalewa, with occasional boats all the way up to Khamti, and the southeast of the state – between Sagaing and Shwebo – is completely open.

GOKTEIK VIADUCT

Highlights

1 Pyin Oo Lwin With horse-drawn carriages and strawberry fields, colonial hill station spirit lives on in British Burma's former summer capital. **See p.295**

2 Gokteik Viaduct A century after its construction, trains still cross this creaking bridge at a crawl on one of Myanmar's iconic rail journeys. **See p.300**

3 Shan State treks Hike across hillsides lined with tea plantations and stay in remote Palaung villages around Hsipaw and Kyaukme. **See boxes, p.301 & p.304**

4 Ayeyarwady River trips Float past logging camps and waterside pagodas on Myanmar's most important river. **See box, p.311**

5 Katha Hunt down locations from George Orwell's novel *Burmese Days* in this quaint riverside town. **See p.314**

6 Myitkyina Time your visit to Kachin State's capital to coincide with one of its colourful festivals, or console yourself with a Kachin feast if you miss them. **See p.320**

7 Indawgyi Lake Kayak to the beautiful Shwe Myitzu Pagoda, or hike in the forested hills that surround the placid waters of Myanmar's largest lake. **See p.325**

HIGHLIGHTS ARE MARKED ON THE MAP ON P.294

TRAVEL RESTRICTIONS

Travelling in northern Myanmar is made considerably slower and more complicated by a frustrating array of travel restrictions. A consequence of the north's numerous ethnic insurgencies, restricted areas (see map, p.28) may be completely closed (the jade rush town of **Hpakant**), or accessible only with a pricey permit (**Putao** and the surrounding area). Even in open areas, overland travel is frequently limited – **Myitkyina** can be accessed by rail but not by boat, while **Bhamo** could *only* by reached by boat – and flying is frequently the best option.

If you do want to visit a no-go zone in the region, you'll need to contact MTT (see p.52) or a tour operator well in advance of your trip – permit applications can take upwards of a month. For the latest on local restrictions, foreigner-orientated hotels and guesthouses are the best places for up-to-date information.

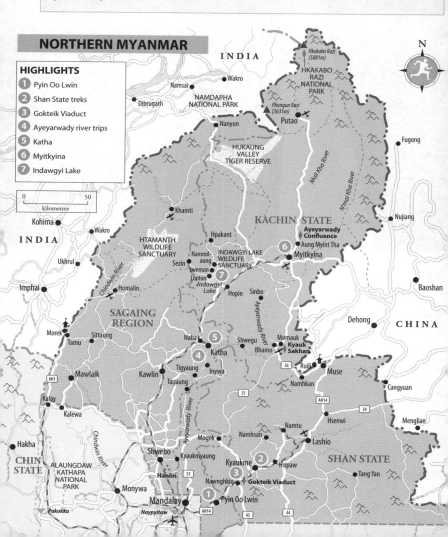

NORTHERN MYANMAR

HIGHLIGHTS

1. Pyin Oo Lwin
2. Shan State treks
3. Gokteik Viaduct
4. Ayeyarwady river trips
5. Katha
6. Myitkyina
7. Indawgyi Lake

Pyin Oo Lwin and around

ြ◌င့◌်ဦ◌းလ◌ွင◌်ြမ◌ို◌့

Situated on a lush plateau 65km east of Mandalay, the town of **PYIN OO LWIN** sits far above the dust of Central Myanmar. At an elevation of 1070m, the town is famed for its pleasant climate, with temperatures seldom creeping above 30°C, even in summer. It was established formally only in 1896, as a hill station providing refuge from the searing heat of Yangon and Mandalay, and originally named **Maymyo**, or "May Town" after a Colonel James May who was stationed on an early army base here. From the 1900s onwards the entire establishment of British Burma decamped here at the start of each summer, gradually covering the town's gently rolling hills with half-timbered government offices and graceful brick villas.

Pyin Oo Lwin's history is still in evidence today in other ways, making it a wonderful place to explore. Horse-drawn carriages clip-clop past colonial mansions, the **Purcell Tower's** bells – cast in London in 1935 for King George V's Silver Jubilee – chime every quarter hour, and strawberries nestle alongside tropical fruit in the **Shan Market**. Another British leftover is the recently revamped **National Kandawgyi Gardens**, a huge botanic garden where neat beds of tulips thrive alongside half-wild groves of teak trees. Further afield, it's possible to float away in the plunge pools of the **Anisakan Falls** and stroll through **Peik Chin Myaung Cave**'s humid cavern, making Pyin Oo Lwin an excellent place to linger.

7

The town centre

The 1936 **Purcell Tower** marks the centre of Pyin Oo Lwin's compact town centre. More down to earth than the posh suburbs, the centre is home to large ethnic Indian and Nepali communities, the descendants of soldiers and labourers from across the subcontinent who moved here under British rule. Today, many run shops selling the fruit wine, jam and woolly jumpers for which Pyin Oo Lwin is known, and mosques and Hindu temples abound.

As Maymyo, the town was an important **military cantonment** for the British Burmese government and, while the regime has changed, the military connections remain – the Burmese Army's Defense Services Academy (training the "Triumphant Elite of the Future") is just west of the centre.

Governor's House

ဘ◌ုရ◌င◌်ခ◌ံအ◌ိမ◌်တ◌ော◌် • 1km southwest of Purcell Tower, Mandalay–Lashio Rd • Daily 8am–6pm • $2 • ☏ 085 21901

Built in 1903, the British governor's summer residence, **Government House**, stood for just forty years before it was destroyed in World War II. Rebuilt in 2005 according to the original blueprints, today it is part of the *Governor's House Hotel* and run by the Htoo Group (see box, p.350), which has been subject to international sanctions. The mansion has been set up as a small **museum**, filled with greenish waxworks of colonial personalities and decorated with sepia photographs of the original – not terribly exciting, but it's one of the few colonial-style buildings open to visitors and a favourite with domestic film-makers. If you're feeling seriously plush, the five-bedroom house (complete with indoor pool) can be yours for $2175 a night.

Shan Market

ရ◌ှမ◌်းဈ◌ေး • 2km northeast of Purcell Tower, Mandalay–Lashio Rd • Daily 6am–4pm

Start the morning at the bustling **Shan Market** on the eastern side of town, at its best between 6.30am and 8am. Originally, Shan farmers gathered here to sell their produce because of the market's proximity to their villages east of Pyin Oo Lwin. While it's still a great place to visit, rents have risen and the majority of stallholders and customers are

PYIN OO LWIN

ACCOMMODATION

Bravo	1
Golden Dream Hotel	2
Grace Hotel I	3
Hotel Pyin Oo Lwin	6
Kandawgyi Hill Resort	7
Royal Green Hotel	4
Royal Parkview	5

EATING

Club Terrace	7
December	1/2/5
Feel	8
Golden Triangle	6
Krishna South Indian Restaurant	4
Ruby	3

now Yunnanese migrants – the Shan have moved to a muddy lane 1km further east along the Mandalay–Lashio Road.

Circular Road and the suburbs

မြို့ပတ်လမ်း

Circular Road (or Myo Part Lan in Burmese) started life as a forest ride for British officers. Today the leafy thoroughfare inscribes a semicircle around the eastern half of Pyin Oo Lwin, leading south from the Shan Market and the main Mandalay–Lashio Road into the wealthier suburbs and the richest seams of colonial buildings. Of particular note are the buttercup yellow **Seventh-day Adventist Church** on Cherry Street, and the half-timbered **No. 4 Basic Education High School** (formerly St Michael's), a missionary school for Anglo-Burmese students.

The British government departments were clustered on **Yone Paung Sone Street**. Several attractive colonial-era offices still occupy similar government functions today – the former Survey Office is now the Myanmar Survey Training Centre, and across the road the old Forestry Department is today's Myanmar Forest School.

It's also worth seeking out the old **Candacraig** and **Croxton** hotels, both formerly company guesthouses of the Bombay Burmah Trading Company that operated as state-run hotels until they were privatized in 2013. Both properties were closed for renovation at the time of research.

Chan Tak Temple

Forest Rd • Daily 6am–6pm • ☎ 09 204 5570

Despite its relative newness, **Chan Tak Temple** is a classically styled Chinese complex, its ornate halls and pagoda set among attractive gardens and replete with flying eaves and concrete dragons. The temple's dining hall serves a vegetarian buffet at lunchtime (10am–1pm), making it a pleasant spot for a break.

National Kandawgyi Gardens

အမျိုးသားကန်တော်ကြီးဥယျာဉ် • Nandar Rd, 4km southeast of Purcell Tower • Daily 8am–6pm (some attractions close at 5.30pm, and staff may be reluctant to let you in after 5pm) • K5000 • ☎ 085 22497 • Horse-drawn carriages cost K10,000 (see p.299)

Pyin Oo Lwin's major visitors' attraction, the **National Kandawgyi Gardens**, was established in 1915–17, when hundreds of Turkish prisoners of war were put to work excavating the central **Kandawgyi Lake** and landscaping its surroundings. After independence, the park gradually deteriorated, until the Htoo Group (see box, p.350) took it over in 2000 and redeveloped it as a scenic spot.

Today, the gardens can be divided into two areas: the highly manicured and picturesque area around the lakeside, filled with pansies and tulips and popular for photo opportunities, and the more interesting and unkempt areas beyond, with stands of bamboo, exotic orchards and a jungly swamp walkway. Overlooking both is the distinctive twelve-storey **Nan Myint Tower**, looking not unlike an ancient oriental helter-skelter. The 380-acre gardens take at least two hours to explore properly; with an aviary, a butterfly museum, a swimming pool and a surprisingly decent café all on-site, it's easy to spend half a day here. The garden hosts a flower festival each December.

Around Pyin Oo Lwin

The lush, rolling countryside around Pyin Oo Lwin is peppered with worthwhile sights, from cascading waterfalls to busy religious spots. Most are situated within a few kilometres of the Mandalay–Lashio road, making them straightforward to access, especially if you have your own transport.

Anisakan Falls

အနီးစခန်း ရေတံခွန် • Near Anisakan, 9km southwest of Pyin Oo Lwin • Free • Motorbike taxis (K5000 return) depart from the roundabout near the Green Luck Petrol Station, or take a Mandalay-bound pick-up (K300) to Anisakan and walk the remaining 2km • **Dat Taw Gyaint Waterfall Resort** ☎ 085 50262

Just outside the village of Anisakan, the plateau on which Pyin Oo Lwin is situated drops away dramatically into a forested canyon, carved out by a tributary of the Dokhtawady River as it plunges down the **Dat Taw Gyaik** waterfall to the valley floor. It takes 45 minutes to walk down from the road to the foot of the falls, and a sweaty hour to hike back to the car park, but the scenery and the chance to cool off in the jade-green plunge pools make it worthwhile.

Once at the trailhead, local children with a ready supply of cold drinks can accompany you down the trail – be sure to agree a price with them in advance, K1000–2000 being customary. There is an alternative route up the opposite side of the falls to the **Dat Taw Gyaint Waterfall Resort** from where it's a 2.5km walk back to the main road. The crony-owned resort is not open to overnight guests, but there's an elegant restaurant on-site, which you may have better luck with – call ahead to check it's open before you trek up there.

Maha An Htu Kan Tha Paya

မဟာအံ့ထူးကံသာဘုရား • 8km northeast of Pyin Oo Lwin • Daily 5am–7pm • Free • K3000 (return) by motorbike taxi

The main reason to visit the **Maha An Htu Kan Tha Paya** ("Reluctant Buddha Paya"), completed in 2000, is for its back story. In 1997, a temple in China's Yunnan Province commissioned three marble Buddha statues from Mandalay. When the statues came to be delivered, one fell off its truck just outside Pyin Oo Lwin; a large concrete Buddha's footprint at the side of the Mandalay–Lashio road marks the spot today.

After several attempts to reload the massive statue, the head of a nearby village claimed that the Buddha visited him in a dream to tell him that the statue wished to stay where it was. The story drew widespread attention inside Myanmar and the donations it attracted funded the construction of the cream and gold hilltop *paya*. A major **festival** takes place here around the Tazaung full moon in November each year, when locals gather on the hillside below the *paya* to release huge bamboo and paper hot-air balloons shaped like animals.

Pwe Kauk Waterfall

ပွဲကောက်ရေတံခွန် • Pwe Kauk, 8km northeast of Pyin Oo Lwin • Free • Turn north opposite the Maha An Htu Kan Tha Paya entrance

Pwe Kauk Waterfall was a favourite picnic spot for the British, who knew it as Hampshire Falls. A series of short, wide waterfalls in a woodland dell, it occupies a setting that's pretty rather than dramatic, with plenty of man-made attractions along the riverbank, including a water-powered merry-go-round.

Peik Chin Myaung Cave and around

ပိတ်ချင်းမြောင်ဂူ • Near Wet Wun village, 20km northeast of Pyin Oo Lwin • Daily 6.30am–5pm • Free, K300 camera fee • K5000 by motorbike taxi from central Pyin Oo Lwin

Peik Chin Myaung Cave snakes into a hillside some 3km east of the village of Wet Wun. Until recently the humid cavern was bare rock, but today donors have filled it with gold-coated Buddha statues and dioramas from Jataka stories, and an underground stream gushes alongside the concrete path. While you'll need to stoop in places, for the most part the cave is open and well lit. It takes around fifteen minutes to reach the end of the walkway and no socks or shoes are allowed.

WET WUN itself is also worth a brief stop – several ancient Banyan trees line the roadside, and the largely Shan villagers frequent the attractive roadside **Wet Wun Zeigaun** monastery with its steeply tiered roofs.

ARRIVAL AND DEPARTURE

By bus Buses and minibuses to Hsipaw leave from *San Pya* restaurant, 3km northeast of the Purcell Tower on the main road. Buses to most other destinations leave from the Thiri Mandalar Bus Station just southeast of *San Pya* – tickets can be purchased from offices along the Mandalay–Lashio road in the town centre.

Destinations Bago (daily; 10hr 30min); Hsipaw (6 daily; 4hr); Kyaukme (6 daily; 3hr); Lashio (3 daily; 6hr); Mandalay (hourly; 2hr); Monywa (3 daily; 7hr); Naypyitaw (2 daily; 8hr); Taungoo (daily; 10hr); Yangon (daily; 12hr).

By pick-up Pick-ups to Mandalay (3hr, K2500) leave when full from just north of the first roundabout southwest of the Purcell Tower. Services start around first light, petering out later in the afternoon.

By shared taxi The fastest way to get to Mandalay (2hr), Kyaukme (2hr 30min), Hsipaw (3hr 30min) and Lashio (5hr 30min) is by shared taxi. Book through your accommodation and the car will pick you up and drop you off at your destination. Mandalay-bound taxis (K7000) depart from the roundabout southwest of town on the Mandalay–Lashio Rd from 6am until they run out of passengers, leaving when full. Shared taxis to Kyaukme, Hsipaw and Lashio leave from the *San Pya* restaurant from 8am onwards – regardless of your destination, you'll need to pay the full fare to Lashio (K14,000).

By train Pyin Oo Lwin's small railway station is northwest of the town centre, 600m north of the Mandalay–Lashio road. Officially it's not possible to book seats in advance, but the station staff can make a note of your name and save you a seat.

Destinations Hsipaw (daily; 6hr 30min); Kyaukme (daily; 5hr); Lashio (daily; 11hr); Mandalay (daily; 6hr).

GETTING AROUND

By motorbike taxi A short journey around town ought to cost no more than K1000. English-speaking driver, Bathein (☏09 4315 2931), who works at the Gandamar Land handicraft store near the main market, can be both guide and driver for similar prices.

By bicycle Bikes are available to rent from most hotels and Crown Bicycle Rental (daily 7.30am–7pm) on the Mandalay–Lashio road near the Purcell Tower for K2000/

day or K2500/24hr.

By motorbike Motorbikes are available to rent from guesthouses and hotels around town for around K8000/day.

By horse-drawn carriage Pyin Oo Lwin's iconic horse-drawn carriages cost around K6000/hr, or K10,000 for a trip to the Kandawgyi Gardens including waiting time – the exact price will depend on your bargaining skills.

ACCOMMODATION

Bravo Mandalay–Lashio Rd ☎085 21223, ✉soemoe @mandalay.net.mm. Not far from the Purcell Tower, this is a good central option. Although some of the rooms are getting a little shabby around the edges, all are clean and neat, plus the staff are friendly and more than usually helpful. Singles from $20, wi-fi available. **$30**

Golden Dream Hotel 64 Mandalay–Lashio Rd ☎085 21302, ✉goldendreamhotel@gmail.com. The pastel-coloured rooms here may be dilapidated and the bathrooms may smell of damp, but *Golden Dream* is the cheapest foreigner-friendly hotel in central Pyin Oo Lwin. All rooms have wi-fi and en-suite bathrooms with hot water. The $20 rooms are in better shape than the cheapies, and single travellers pay half. Breakfast not included. **$14**

Grace Hotel I 114 Nan Myaing Rd ☎085 21230. The only budget option in Pyin Oo Lwin's leafy suburbs, *Grace I* has decent, spacious rooms with en-suite bathrooms in a new building, and scruffier versions of the same in the older block next door. There's plenty of outdoor space for lounging in the sun and the staff are clued in on how to deal with travellers. Wi-fi included, with singles from $15. **$25**

Hotel Pyin Oo Lwin 9 Nandar Rd ☎085 21226, ✇hotelpyinoolwin.com. Not far from the Kandawgyi Gardens, this luxury hotel opened in 2011. The 36 bungalows are beautiful, with dark wood panelling, plenty of space and private verandas, and the service is good – as you'd expect at these prices – but there are still a few

quirks; the large pool is unheated, the wi-fi slow and the huge TVs have no international channels. **$120**

Kandawgyi Hill Resort Nandar Rd ☎085 21839, ✇myanmartreasureresorts.com. Housed in a 1910 brick mansion with sweeping lawns close to the Kandawgyi Gardens, this Htoo Group-owned hotel doesn't really live up to its potential. The rooms are dusty, the bathrooms worn, and staff seem startled to have guests. However, at the time of writing it was one of the few genuine colonial-house hotels still in operation – if you do decide to stay, it's worth paying a little extra for a room in the main house. **$75**

★ **Royal Green Hotel** 17 Ziwaka St ☎085 28422. Impeccable standard rooms come with fresh new linen, satellite TV and wi-fi, free bottled water and hot drinks, making this hotel excellent value for money, especially given the high prices elsewhere in Pyin Oo Lwin. For $45 you get a balcony and bathtub, while the $55 corner rooms are beautiful and airy. **$35**

Royal Parkview 107 Lanthaya St ☎085 22641, ✉royalparkview107@gmail.com. In a quiet spot 2km southeast of the centre, rooms here are tastefully decorated with parquet floors. The standard rooms are arranged in ageing bungalows, while the more expensive options ($70–80) are in a small newly constructed block, some with their own gardens. There's wi-fi and all rooms have a/c. **$50**

EATING

Club Terrace 25 Club Rd ☎085 23311. Housed in an attractive red-brick building near the golf club, this classy restaurant offers a pretty patio and excellent service. The Thai and Chinese food (most dishes around K4500) is decent, and there are a few Burmese and Western options available, but the surroundings are the main attraction. Daily 10am–10pm.

★ **December** Mandalay–Lashio Rd ☎085 21053 & Zaygyi St. This small local chain started life as a rest stop on the Mandalay–Lashio road, 12km out of Pyin Oo Lwin towards Lashio, serving up fresh juice, noodles and ice cream to hungry travellers. While there are two branches in the centre of town, the original roadside store is the nicest, with a petting zoo and pavilions scattered around the strawberry fields. All branches daily 7am–9pm.

★ **Feel** Off Nandar Rd ☎085 22083. The kitchen here copes surprisingly well with the restaurant's ridiculously extensive menus (plural), which cover everything from sushi to hamburgers and hotpot. There's a pretty lakeside deck with views towards the Kandawgyi Gardens, and it's

popular with visitors and locals alike. California rolls cost K4000, fried rice from K3000, and there's a good range of cakes available too. Daily 9.30am–9.30pm.

Golden Triangle Mandalay–Lashio Rd ☎085 24288. With Western food, pastries, locally grown coffee and fast wi-fi, what foreign-owned *Golden Triangle* lacks in atmosphere it makes up for with familiar comforts. Coffee from K1800, breakfast dishes from K1500. Daily 8am–9pm.

Krishna South Indian Restaurant Gurkha Rd. Of the many Indian–Burmese restaurants in town that seem to have been set up in someone's front room, *Krishna* has among the best and the most Indian-influenced food. A meal with curry and chapatis will set you back K3000. Vegetarian options available. Daily 10am–9.30pm.

Ruby Mandalay–Lashio Rd ☎085 21395. Run by third-generation immigrants from Yunnan, *Ruby* serves up a range of reasonably priced halal Chinese dishes (K2000) along with a few international options, like kimchi fried rice. Daily 8am–9pm.

7

7

THE MANDALAY–LASHIO RAILWAY

The 280km railway between Mandalay and Lashio took eight years to complete, thanks to a series of major geographical challenges en route. First, between Mandalay and Pyin Oo Lwin, it relies on a series of zigzags and reverses to climb a steep escarpment onto the Shan Plateau. More dramatically, near Nawnghkio the single strand of track soars 102m above the Dokhtawady River on the famous **Gokteik Viaduct**.

Still Myanmar's highest bridge over a century after its construction, the Gokteik Viaduct was completed in 1901, built by a US contractor using parts cast by the Pennsylvania Steel Company, and shipped from the United States. The viaduct has been repeatedly renovated, but trains still cross the span at a crawl – leaving those unafraid of heights with plenty of time to lean out of the windows and enjoy the view.

Gokteik Station is on the Mandalay side of the viaduct. If you wish to cross the bridge and catch the train back to Mandalay in a single day, you'll need a ticket to Nawngpeng, fifty minutes beyond Gokteik Station, where it's possible to scurry onto the single daily train back to Mandalay.

DIRECTORY

Banks KBZ Bank, opposite the Purcell Tower, and the CB Bank, further down the Mandalay–Lashio road, both have ATMs and exchange facilities.

Golf Once the site of a colonial-era polo field, the eighteen-hole Pyin Oo Lwin Golf Club, Sanda Rd (daily 6am–6pm; ☏ 085 22382), is one of the country's more popular courses – perhaps because the ball flies 10 percent further at this altitude. Green fees $10, caddy $5,

club and shoe rental available.

Internet Net Star (daily 8.30am–10pm), just off the Mandalay–Lashio rd near the town centre, and Green Garden Internet Café (daily 7am–9pm) on Ziwaka St both offer internet access for K400/hr. The latter also has free wi-fi if you buy a drink or snack.

Post office Pyin Oo Lwin's post office is tucked away down a side street, just south of *Golden Triangle* café.

Kyaukme

ကျောက်မဲမြို့

A major tea- and gem-dealing town for many years, **KYAUKME** is a relatively wealthy little place. With a lively market, several hilltop **pagodas** and a fragrant tea-trading quarter, it's an engaging place to stay in its own right, but the main draw for visitors is the chance to get out of town. The surrounding countryside, where the tea itself is grown, sees far fewer foreigners than nearby Hsipaw, and offers plenty of brilliant opportunities to trek and motorbike to incredibly friendly and remote **Palaung villages**, where you can stay overnight in bamboo-built houses.

Kyaukme was an established tea-dealing centre well before the arrival of the British in the 1890s (see box, p.302). Today, the tea warehouses are concentrated in a few blocks immediately southwest of the railway station. The town beyond is dotted with characterful, peeling old buildings, including a 1933 **synagogue** on Paklu Street. The **main market** between Paklu Street and Aung San Road is the centre of town life, attracting a mix of Shan, Bamar and Palaung customers – the latter often in their traditional clothing.

Kyaukme is flanked to the east and west by pagoda-topped hills, both of which can be reached via covered staircases from the town. In the east, **Sunrise Pagoda**, also known as Le Kaun Pagoda, holds a few pretty shrines and a small monastery, while **Sunset Pagoda** on the west side of town has great open views.

ARRIVAL AND DEPARTURE

KYAUKME

By bus Buses to most destinations leave from the highway bus station on the north side of the railway line 600m west of the station. Hsipaw-bound buses leave from the southwest corner of the main market each morning at

7am, and a few buses to Lashio and Muse leave from here as well. *A Yone Oo* can help book tickets, as can the friendly Kyaw Swar – also known as Mr Ticket (☏ 09 4037 19692) – who works at the highway bus station.

Destinations Hsipaw (6 daily; 1hr); Kalaw (2 daily; 12hr); Lashio (3 daily; 3hr); Mandalay (daily; 5hr); Muse (daily; 8hr); Pyin Oo Lwin (6 daily; 3hr); Yangon (daily; 13hr).

By train Kyaukme's railway station is slightly northwest of the town centre, about a 10min walk from *A Yone Oo*. There's a decent teahouse in the station, making it a popular place to gulp down lunch when heading in either direction.

Destinations Hsipaw (daily; 1hr 30min); Lashio (daily; 7hr); Mandalay (daily; 11hr); Pyin Oo Lwin (daily; 5hr).

By motorbike taxi The trip to Hsipaw will set you back K10,000. A short trip around town costs the usual K500.

ACCOMMODATION AND EATING

At the time of writing there was a single **hotel** option for foreigners in Kyaukme, *A Yone Oo*, owned by a local councillor with a monopoly on the town's tourist facilities. Several other **guesthouse** owners were optimistic that they would be able to obtain the permits needed to receive foreign guests, but whether that optimism is well founded or not remains to be seen. The *Northern Rock Guesthouse* (☏082 40660), opposite *A Yone Oo*, was one of the contenders. As for food, during market hours the small noodle shops inside the **covered market** are one of the most interesting places to eat, serving up *moun-di* and *mi-shay* noodles to hungry shoppers.

A Yone Oo Shwe Pyi Oo Rd ☏082 40669. A range of rooms on a quiet street running parallel to the railway line between the station and the market. The cheapest fan-cooled rooms are noisy and faintly depressing and it's worth forking out a bit more for the good-value rooms in a 1940s building ($24), while for the most comfort go for those in the modern block ($56). Singles are available at half-rates. $12

Thiripyitsaya 4/54 Shwe Pyi Oo Rd ☏082 40340.

Opposite *A Yone Oo*, this bare little place has an English menu and serves simple snacks — things like omelettes (K1000) and Shan noodles (K500) feature heavily. Daily 7am–9pm.

Shwe Mae Song Aung San Rd. One block south of the main market along Aung San Rd, this busy Shan Chinese restaurant serves up tasty stir-fries (K1500) along with platefuls of fried rice that are particularly popular with locals. Daily 8am–9pm.

DIRECTORY

Bank KBZ Bank on the south side of the market offers currency exchange, but as yet Kyaukme has no ATMs.
Doctor English-speaking Dr Khin Mg Nyo runs a small clinic (daily when he's in town, 8–10.30am and 4–7.30pm; ☏09 527 5292) and lending library just opposite *A Yone Oo*.
Internet Internet Access, next to *A Yone Oo*, has wi-fi (K200/hr) and computers (K400/hr) available.

Hsipaw and around

သီပေါမြို့

Known in Burmese as Thibaw, **HSIPAW** is the former seat of an independent Shan state. Today the small town has an attractive air of tranquillity — venerable tamarind and rain trees line the main street, the **Dokhtawady** (or Namtu) River flows languidly to the east of town and the nearby hills conceal thatch-roofed Palaung and Lisu villages. Add to this a good range of accommodation and some excellent cafés, and it's unsurprising that Hsipaw is a popular base for trekking into the surrounding countryside (see box, p.304).

HIKING AROUND KYAUKME

A trip into the hills around Kyaukme often starts with a motorbike ride along rough country lanes to a village or trailhead, with this element of the trip raising the price compared to other destinations. Several excellent **trekking guides** work out of Kyaukme, starting at K25,000 per person per day for a group of two, dropping to around K10,000 per person for a group of six; prices vary little from one to the next.

Naing Naing (☏09 2564 22077, ✉naingninenine@gmail.com), an ethnic Palaung, is the most experienced and adventurous of the local guides, taking groups deep into the hills. **Kyaw Hlaing** (☏09 4037 06070, ⊛shanprinces.webs.com), a young Shan guy who goes by the English name Joy, leads motorbike excursions and speaks excellent English. Both have useful maps of the area and sheaves of good testimonials.

PLATE OF TEA, VICAR?

Northern Shan State is one of the original homes of **Camellia sinensis**, which originated somewhere in the hills that range between northeast India, northern Burma and southwest China. When the British first surveyed the Shan states in the nineteenth century, Palaung and Shan villagers had already been cultivating tea for several centuries. In 1855 Burmese officials told a visiting British delegation that they thought the very idea that the Chinese grew their own tea was "preposterous", so great was their neighbour's demand for Burmese exports of the crop.

Tawngpeng, a largely Palaung district that surrounds the (currently off limits) hill town of Namhsan, is Myanmar's main tea-growing region, with the best of their fragrant harvest being reserved for the production of **lahpet** (fermented tea leaves). The fresh leaves are lightly steamed and then packed into lengths of bamboo, buried and left to ferment for anything up to a year, before they're ready to be eaten as **lahpet thouq** (tea-leaf salad), served as an afternoon tea staple from Yangon's *Strand Hotel* to the hawkers on Myanmar's trains.

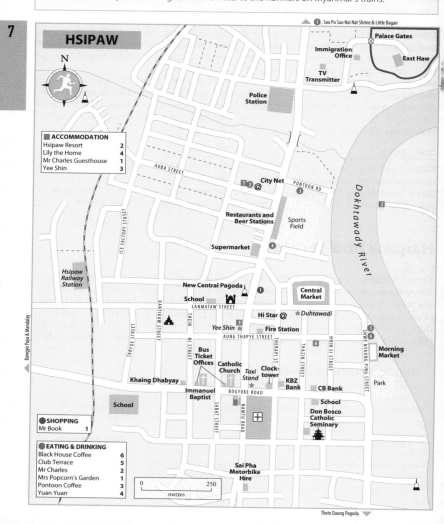

7

HSIPAW

ACCOMMODATION
Hsipaw Resort	2
Lily the Home	4
Mr Charles Guesthouse	1
Yee Shin	3

SHOPPING
Mr Book	1

EATING & DRINKING
Black House Coffee	6
Club Terrace	5
Mr Charles	2
Mrs Popcorn's Garden	1
Pontoon Coffee	3
Yuan Yuan	4

Sau Pu Sao Nai Nat Shrine & Little Bagan

Palace Gates
Immigration Office
East Haw
TV Transmitter
Police Station
City Net
PONTOON RD
AUBA STREET
Dokhtawady River
Restaurants and Beer Stations
Sports Field
Supermarket
Hsipaw Railway Station
ICE FACTORY STREET
New Central Pagoda
School
LANMATAW STREET
Central Market
Hi Star @
★ Duhtawadi
Yee Shin
Fire Station
AUNG THAPYE STREET
KANTIKAW STREET
TATPOE STREET
THEIN
NI STREET
THERAPI ST
THAZIN STREET
HNIN SI STREET
SHWE NYUNG PING STREET
Morning Market
Bus Ticket Offices
Catholic Church
Taxi Stand
Clock-tower
KBZ Bank
Park
CB Bank
Khaing Dhabyay
BOGYOKE ROAD
School
Immanuel Baptist
SABAI STREET
NAMTU ROAD
Don Bosco Catholic Seminary
School

Bawyo Paya & Mandalay

Sai Pha Motorbike Hire

0 — 250
metres

Thein Daung Pagoda

The town itself is an engaging place to explore, with a worthwhile **morning market** along the riverbank if you can get up early enough to see it, and many small workshops around town, where it's possible to watch tea being sorted and cheroots being rolled. The most interesting sights all lie on the outskirts of town, a short bike ride away.

Brief history

The Shan *saophas*, or "sky lords", of Hsipaw were among the most powerful leaders in the Shan states, thanks to Hsipaw's strategic location at the edge of the Shan Plateau, poised above the Bamar-dominated lowlands. In 1886, **Sao Hkun Hseng** was among the first Shan *saophas* to submit to British rule, and the first Shan chieftain to meet Queen Victoria. His colourful son, Sao Hke (later **Sir Sao Hke**), took forty wives and ruled from a jewel-encrusted throne in his magnificent court at Sakandar, which now lies in ruins just outside Hsipaw.

The most well known of Hsipaw's *saophas*, however, was **Sao Kya Seng**, who ruled Hsipaw with his Austrian *mahadevi*, Inge Sargent, from 1954. Hsipaw flourished under their rule, until in 1962 Sao Kya Seng disappeared on his way home from a political conference in the immediate aftermath of Ne Win's coup. Save for two letters that were smuggled to his wife from a military camp near Taunggyi, Hsipaw's last *saopha* was never heard from again, and the regime never acknowledged his death – a story told in Inge Sargent's book *Twilight over Burma,* written after she and the couple's two daughters had left Burma for the US. Sao and Inge's wedding portrait can be seen around Hsipaw today, a lasting testament to their popularity.

East Haw

သီပေါ်ဟော် • 1km northeast of the town centre • Daily 9am–noon & 3–6pm • Free

While Sakandar, the Neoclassical summer palace of the Hsipaw *saophas*, was destroyed in World War II, the 1924 **East Haw** still stands, and it was here that Sao Kya Seng and Inge Sargent lived in the 1950s (see above). The buildings and swimming pool are overgrown and sorely in need of maintenance, but the last *saopha*'s niece-in-law, Mrs Fern, opens the palace gates and receives visitors. While the state of the buildings is sad, it's a rare opportunity to hear first-hand stories of Hsipaw's colourful recent history.

Little Bagan

500m west of Namtu Rd, 1.5km north of Hsipaw • Free

The northwest corner of Hsipaw is dotted with a handful of crumbling and overgrown brick pagodas, earning it the jokingly overblown name of **Little Bagan**. It may be a fraction of its namesake's size, but it's still an appealing place to explore. At the eastern extremity is **Kotaun Kyaung**, which is marked by a dramatically cracked pagoda with a tree sprouting from its crown. As you make your way west you'll pass **Madhaya Shwe Kyaung** and **Maha Nanda Kantha Kyaung**, a pair of attractive 150-year-old teak monasteries that flank the road, the latter with a Buddha figure woven from bamboo and covered with gold leaf. A few further groups of pagodas lie northwest of here.

Sao Pu Sao Nai Nat Shrine

100m west of Namtu Rd, 1.5km north of Hsipaw • Daily dawn–dusk • Free

Between Namtu Road and Little Bagan is **Sao Pu Sao Nai Nat Shrine**, a vibrant temple filled with picturesque statues of animals, dedicated to Hsipaw's guardian *nat*, Tong Sunt Bo Bo Gyi, whose effigy stands in the offering-filled main hall. The compound is also home to several smaller pavilions furnished with miniature beds, and covered with pink satin sheets – the last word in *nat* hospitality. Towards the rear of the complex is a

7

HIKING AROUND HSIPAW

The most popular hike from Hsipaw is the four- to five-hour walk to **Pan Kam village**, where it's possible to stay overnight. The trail starts at the Muslim cemetery on the western edge of Hsipaw, and winds uphill through the villages of Nar Loy, Nar Moon and Man Pyit. The headman at Pan Kam, O Maung, works closely with *Mr Charles Guesthouse* and the village is beginning to feel a little touristy during high season. If you don't fancy staying in Pan Kam itself, it's possible to hike a further 75 minutes to **Htan Sant**. The standard way to get to Htan Sant is to take the left-hand path at a fork just after you leave Pan Kam, but the longer right-hand path has truly exceptional views of the valley. Accommodation at Htan Sant can be arranged through the headman, Khao San Aye, and the following day you can retrace your steps or press on to Sar Maw village and thence to **Bawgyo Paya** (see below), from where it's possible to hitch the 8km back to Hsipaw.

At the time of research, the Palaung village of **Namhsan** – the starting point for a great three-day hike to Hsipaw – had been off limits to foreigners since July 2013. There are various theories as to why the area was closed, ranging from a local flare-up in fighting between a Palaung militia and the army to a localized gold rush. Ask at any Hsipaw guesthouse for the latest information on this situation. Treks can be organized through all of Hsipaw's guesthouses and through Sai John (☎09 4037 03322), although it is also possible to strike out on your own. Expect to pay around K10,000 per person per day including food and accommodation.

green-canopied shrine that holds two swings; local people push the (empty) swings to please the female *nat* depicted behind them and gain her blessing.

Thein Daung Pagoda

2.5km south of Hsipaw • Daily dawn–dusk • Free

Also known as Sunset Pagoda, **Thein Daung Pagoda** offers great views out over Hsipaw and the hills that bracket the town and river. To get here, head south along the Mandalay–Lashio road and cross the Dokhtawady River. Just beyond the bridge there's a decorative gateway by the roadside – the pagoda is a thirty-minute walk uphill from here.

Bawgyo Paya

တော်ကြီးဘုရား • 9km west of Hsipaw • Daily dawn–dusk • Free

A twenty-minute drive west of Hsipaw is the strikingly tiered, Shan-style **Bawgyo Paya**. The central shrine contains four wooden Buddha statues believed to date from the thirteenth century, when they were carved from a piece of wood given to Bagan's King Narapatisithu by an immortal. The leftovers were buried in the temple complex, where they miraculously took root, growing into a tree that still thrives today. The Buddha images are shown publicly once a year, during a huge festival that takes place here around the Tabaung (February/March) full moon.

ARRIVAL AND DEPARTURE

HSIPAW AND AROUND

By bus There is no bus station in Hsipaw, with buses and minibuses departing from a motley collection of restaurants and guesthouses that double as ticket offices, including *Yee Shin* guesthouse, *Duhtawadi Café* on Lanmataw St and *Khaing Dhabyay* on Bogyoke Rd.
Destinations Kalaw (1–3 daily; 13hr); Kyaukme (6 daily; 1hr); Lashio (3 daily; 2hr); Mandalay (6 daily; 6hr); Monywa (daily; 11hr); Naypyitaw (3 daily; 12hr); Nyaungshwe (for Inle Lake, 3 daily; 15hr); Pyin Oo Lwin (6 daily; 4hr); Yangon (3 daily; 16hr).
By shared taxi Shared taxis east to Lashio (2hr; K6000/person), and west to Kyaukme (1hr), Pyin Oo Lwin (3hr

30min) and Mandalay (5hr 30min) depart Hsipaw around 6–7am. Book a seat through your accommodation or through *Khaing Dhabyay* on Bogyoke Rd. Westbound you will pay the same fare (K15,000) regardless of your destination.
By train Hsipaw's railway station is west of the town centre, 500m west of Namtu Rd. Tickets only go on sale 30min before each train arrives. If you are heading for Mandalay you can knock 3hr off the journey by getting off the train in Pyin Oo Lwin and taking a bus for the remaining distance.
Destinations Kyaukme (daily; 1hr 30min); Lashio (daily; 4hr 30min); Mandalay (daily; 13hr); Pyin Oo Lwin (daily; 6hr 30min).

GETTING AROUND

By tuk-tuk A short journey around town ought to cost no more than K500.

By bicycle Most of Hsipaw's sights are within easy cycling distance of the town centre. Bikes are available to rent from *Mr Charles*, *Yee Shin* and *Lily the Home* for K2000/day.

By motorbike It's possible to rent motorbikes from guesthouses around town, with prices around K8000–K10,000/day. Sai Pha at the southern end of Namtu Rd (daily 7am–7pm) rents out motorbikes for K8000/day.

ACCOMMODATION

Hsipaw Resort 29/30 Myohaung Village ☎ 082 80721, ⓦ hsipawresort.com. Owned by Amata Resorts, Hsipaw's most upmarket hotel offers twenty comfortable tartan-filled rooms in pretty riverside bungalows with wonderfully comfortable beds. On the opposite bank of the Dokhtawady River from the town, the hotel operates a free boat service and there's a good hotel restaurant. Wi-fi available. $85

★ **Lily the Home** 108 Aung Thapye St ☎ 082 80318, ⓦ lilythehome.com. Tucked away in the middle of a quiet block, this family-run hotel is an excellent choice. The cheapest fan-cooled rooms have shared bathrooms, but you don't need to pay much more to get an en-suite room with a/c ($20). The hotel was undergoing expansion at the time of writing, with a rooftop restaurant and 36 more rooms on the way – it remains to be seen if this will change the feel of the place. Wi-fi included. $14

Mr Charles Guesthouse 105 Auba St ☎ 082 80105, ⓦ mrcharleshotel.com. The most established guesthouse in town, *Mr Charles* has had rather a monopoly on Hsipaw's tourist business, offering a gamut of services including aggressively marketed hikes and day-trips. There's a range of rooms on offer, with those at the cheaper end of the spectrum providing better value than the overpriced mid-range ones. The cheapest singles go for $9, and there's decent wi-fi available. $20

Yee Shin Namtu Rd ☎ 082 80711, ⓔ shinthant291 @gmail.com. This small guesthouse has fourteen tiny rooms, most with little space beyond the beds. The rooms and (mainly shared) bathrooms are clean and neat, all with hot water and wi-fi. The cheapest rooms are rather cramped, but the $12 doubles with fans and shared bathrooms are undeniably good value, and single travellers pay half. $10

EATING AND DRINKING

While Hsipaw has plenty of appealing places to relax with a drink, the food options are less exciting. In addition to the establishments below, Namtu Road is lined with inexpensive teahouses and small restaurants, and there are a few cheap food stalls in the main market.

Black House Coffee Shwe Nyaung Pin St. Owned by a friendly Shan family, this low-key place on the riverside serves up hot drinks and cake – and opens early to offer sustenance to those who make it to the nearby morning market. Daily 6am–6pm.

★ **Club Terrace** 35 Shwe Nyaung Pin St ☎ 09 4027 52971. This outpost of the *Club Terrace* in Pyin Oo Lwin shares its sister restaurant's understated style, with a pretty wooden deck overlooking the river and a menu that covers the usual bases – Thai, Chinese and Burmese. It's pricier than most other restaurants in Hsipaw (K2500 for a bottle of Myanmar Beer, K3500 for meat and fish dishes), but the food, service and environment all make it worth visiting. Daily 10am–10pm.

Mr Charles 105 Auba St ☎ 082 80105. The comfortable dining room at *Mr Charles* serves a range of Asian dishes, along with a few Western favourites aimed squarely at homesick travellers, including perfectly adequate pizza and burgers starting from around K2500. Daily 7am–10pm.

★ **Mrs Popcorn's Garden** Near Little Bagan ☎ 09 4026 64925. In a lovely garden on the road that runs between Little Bagan and the *nat* shrine, the cheerful Mrs Popcorn and her daughter serve up locally grown tea and coffee, plus simple snacks (no popcorn, though – Mrs Popcorn's moniker dates from a previous business venture), making it a perfect place to spend the afternoon lazing in the sun. Cooked meals are available if you order in advance. Daily 9am–dusk.

Pontoon Coffee Pontoon Rd. Run by Maureen, an Australian expat who has lived in Hsipaw for many years, this café near where an old pontoon bridge used to span the river serves excellent coffee (from K1000) and a small range of snacks like pancakes, sandwiches and delicious guacamole. Daily 9am–9pm.

Yuan Yuan Namtu Rd ☎ 09 4037 31865. This little café on Hsipaw's main road serves a range of delicious fruit juices (K800) concocted by "Mr Shake", and the excellent chicken rice (K1500) cooked by his wife, Ayeyong. Daily 11.30am–10pm.

SHOPPING

Mr Book Namtu Rd. The kindly Ko Zaw Tin, aka Mr Book, runs a small bookshop from a dusty shack, with a small collection of English books on sale. He's also involved with several charitable projects and often donates school supplies and funds to village schools near Hsipaw – donations of any kind are gratefully received. Daily 6am–9pm.

DIRECTORY

Banks Hsipaw's banks are clustered around the clocktower on Bogyoke Rd, with branches of KBZ Bank and CB Bank offering currency exchange, although neither has an ATM. In a pinch most guesthouses will change US dollars too.

Internet Head to Hi-Star on Theraphi St (daily 9am–10.30pm; K400/hr) or City Net on Aura St (daily 8am–11pm; K500/hr).

Lashio

လားရှိုးမြို့

The last major town before the Chinese border, **LASHIO** sprawls over a series of hillsides 170km south of the Muse–Ruili border crossing (see box, p.308). The town itself has repeatedly risen from its own ashes like an ungainly phoenix, most recently after a devastating fire in 1988 ripped through many of its old wooden houses. Formerly the seat of a Shan *saopha*, Lashio has become an important regional hub – sitting between the **Burma Road** (see box opposite) leading east, and the Mandalay–Lashio railway heading west.

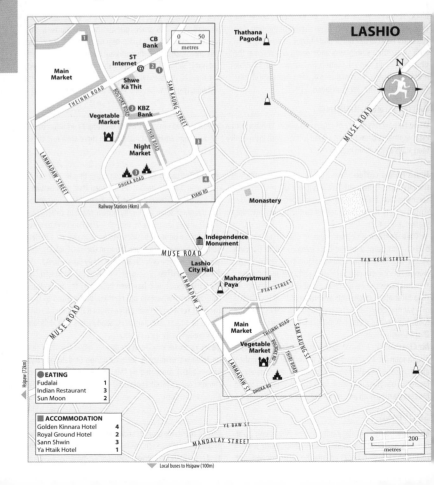

LASHIO

EATING
Fudalai	1
Indian Restaurant	3
Sun Moon	2

ACCOMMODATION
Golden Kinnara Hotel	4
Royal Ground Hotel	2
Sann Shwin	3
Ya Htaik Hotel	1

THE BURMA ROAD

In November 1937, when the Japanese Imperial Army took control of Shanghai after a savage three-month battle, China lost Nanjing, its largest port and the last obstacle between Japanese forces and the Chinese capital. The government scrambled to relocate to a provisional capital in Chongqing, deep in the interior as the ports along China's eastern seaboard toppled to the Japanese. Alternative supply routes were urgently needed, and work on the **Burma Road**, linking the Chinese city of Kunming to the Burmese railhead at Lashio, began.

A rough, cobbled track that crossed countless sodden, jungle-covered hills as well as the Mekong and Salween rivers, the Burma Road was built by an estimated 200,000 Burmese and Chinese labourers and 1150km long at its completion in 1939. This vital supply route functioned for just three years before the Japanese overran Burma in April 1942, occupying Lashio and closing the road. After months of airlifting supplies from Assam to Kunming – over the infamous "Hump" at the eastern end of the Himalayas – the Allies began construction on an arduous alternative route, the **Ledo Road** between Ledo in Assam and Kunming, which finished construction early in 1945, just months before the Japanese surrender.

Today, there's little reason to visit Lashio unless you are heading on to Hsipaw (Lashio's airport being the closest), or to China or overland to Bhamo via Namhkan if you have the right permits. However, there's a large Chinese community, a small collection of temples and several thronging markets to occupy you if you do find yourself here for a day.

The markets and around

The closest thing to a town centre in Lashio is the area around the covered market between Lanmadaw Street and Samkaung Street. A morning **vegetable market** spreads out along Bogyoke Road before dawn (sadly no longer lit picturesquely by candles – the traders prefer fluorescent lamps these days) before the action moves into the **main market** around 7am. To end the day, a lively **night market** sets up each evening along Bogyoke and Thiri roads. Just south of all the market action is Lashio's pretty **central mosque**, which was rebuilt after its predecessor was torched during anti-Muslim riots in May 2013.

Thathana Pagoda

သာသနာ ၂၅၀၀ ဘုရား • Thathana Pagoda Hill, off the Mandalay–Muse road, 2km north of the market

A gilded octagonal pagoda, **Thathana Pagoda** sits on a ridge north of town surrounded by wooded slopes offering excellent views over Lashio to the rounded hills beyond. The most interesting way to reach it is along a steep staircase that leads from the Muse road uphill to an unusual monument on stilts, before turning north to the pagoda.

ARRIVAL AND DEPARTURE — LASHIO

By plane Some 8km from the central market area, Lashio Airport is served by Asian Wings, Air KBZ, Myanma Airways and Yangon Airways. Most services to Yangon are "hopper" flights, stopping in Mandalay or Heho (or both). Tickets cost around \$90 to Mandalay and \$170 to Yangon. When arriving in Lashio Airport, note that the baggage reclaim shed is actually just outside the gates. Shwe Ka Thit, 34 Theinni Rd (T 082 25702), offers decent ticket prices and has helpful, English-speaking staff.

Destinations Heho (for Inle Lake, 2 weekly; 1hr); Mandalay (daily; 45min); Tachileik (2–3 weekly; 1hr); Yangon (daily; 1hr 45min–3hr).

By bus Lashio's main bus station is on the Muse road, 3km northeast of the market, just south of Mansu Pagoda. There's also a more central local bus station just south of the market on Mandalay St, which has a few services to Hsipaw. At the time of research, foreigners were not allowed on buses to Muse, and you may also have difficulty buying tickets to Taunggyi.

Destinations Hsipaw (3 daily; 2hr); Kalaw (3 daily; 15hr); Kyaukme (3 daily; 3hr); Mandalay (3 daily; 9hr); Meiktila (5 daily; 10–11hr); Muse (daily; 4hr); Naypyitaw (daily;

13hr); Pyin Oo Lwin (3 daily; 6hr); Taunggyi (daily; 15hr); Yangon (2 daily; 18hr).

By shared taxi Shared taxis to Muse (4hr; K10,000) and west to Hsipaw (2hr), Pyin Oo Lwin (5hr 30min) and Mandalay (7hr 30min; all three destinations K15,000) depart from around the main bus station each morning when full. Book a seat through your accommodation and

the car will pick you up from your hotel.

By train Lashio's railway station is 5km northwest of the market, K1500 by pick-up or motorbike taxi. The daily train to Mandalay (17hr), which stops at Hsipaw (4hr 30min), Kyaukme (6hr) and Pyin Oo Lwin (11hr) en route, departs at 5am, with tickets on sale from 4.30am.

GETTING AROUND

By motorbike taxi Motorbike taxi drivers gather around the railway station, bus station and the market, with a journey around town typically costing K1000–1500.

By tuk-tuk A chartered tuk-tuk around town will cost

around K1500 per journey. Some shared tuk-tuks run from the railway and bus stations to the market, with a trip on either costing K300/person.

ACCOMMODATION

Golden Kinnara Hotel Kyani Rd ☎082 30891, ✉goldenkinnarahotel@gmail.com. Opened in 2014 in a fairly central location, this is one of Lashio's more comfortable hotels. The rooms are bland but immaculate, with high ceilings and plenty of space, staff are kind and wi-fi is included. $50

Royal Ground Hotel 34 Theinni Rd ☎082 25516. Around 50m downhill from the market, this place is larger than it looks from the street, with a collection of decently priced rooms, all with a/c and private bathrooms – some with

extravagantly cracked bathtubs. Little English spoken. $20

Sann Shwin Dhuka Rd ☎082 25290. This friendly family-run place, just downhill from the night market, is one of Lashio's cheaper options, with a collection of white-tiled twin rooms with high ceilings and bathrooms. K18,000

Ya Htaik Hotel Bogyoke Rd ☎082 22655, ✉yahtaiklso@gmail.com. Yet another option close to the market, this echoing high-rise block has a few cheapish single rooms with shared bathrooms ($15) as well as plenty of very average doubles with private bathrooms. $35

EATING AND DRINKING

Food options in central Lashio are decidedly casual – the **market** area is a good place to try chewy Chinese *ersi* noodles, while the **night market** (daily 5–9pm) along Bogyoke Rd has several stalls selling Shan noodle soup and Burmese curries among the cheap Chinese clothes and cosmetics.

Fudalai Theinni Rd ☎082 22691. This Chinese–Burmese restaurant is one of the few proper restaurants in the market area, serving barbecued skewers, fried rice (K1500) and cold beer (K600). There's no English menu. Daily 8am–10pm.

Indian Restaurant Dhuka Rd. Sandwiched between Hindu and Sikh temples, just south of the night market – look for the "Indian Restaurant" sign – what this tiny

restaurant lacks in size, it makes up for with flavour. Rice, dhal and a curry will set you back K1500–2000, and all are served with their delicious tamarind pickle. Daily 9am–9pm.

Sun Moon Bogyoke Rd ☎082 30606. With several branches around town, this brightly lit bakery sells bread, cakes and hamburgers in boxes – perfect if you have a long train ride ahead of you. Daily 8am–9pm.

MUSE AND THE CHINESE BORDER

The small, scrappy town of **Muse** (pronounced Mu-say) sits just across the Shweli River from the high-rises of **Ruili** on the Chinese side of the border. While the border (daily 6.30am–10pm) is nominally open to foreigners, at the time of writing travellers still needed an official guide and permit as well as a valid Chinese or Myanmar visa to get across, although there were rumours that this would be relaxed in the near future.

Check with a Yangon- or Kunming-based tour operator before you commit to using this route as the **permits** take up to a month to process and the whole package (including guide and transport) usually costs $200–250 for the single day from Ruili to Lashio. There is a Myanmar consulate-general in Kunming (☎+86 871 6816 2804, ✇mcgkunming.org) where visas take three days to process. **Chinese visas** are available from the embassy in Yangon (see p.93) and the consulate-general in Mandalay (35th St, between 65th and 66th sts; ☎02 35937, ✇mandalay.china-consulate.org).

DIRECTORY

Banks The CB Bank on Theinni Rd and the KBZ Bank on Bogyoke Rd have ATMs and currency exchange.

Internet ST Internet (daily 8am–10pm), next to the *Royal Ground Hotel* on Theinni Rd, has internet for K500/hr.

Bhamo and around

ဗန်းမော်မြို့

For centuries, caravans carrying jade and other exotic Burmese products passed through **BHAMO** on their way to the markets of southwest China. While this small town on the eastern bank of the Ayeyarwady belies these romantic origins, today it's a pleasantly relaxed place, punctuated with aged rain trees, dark teak houses and busy markets. There are a couple of fun things to do nearby as well – cycle across a

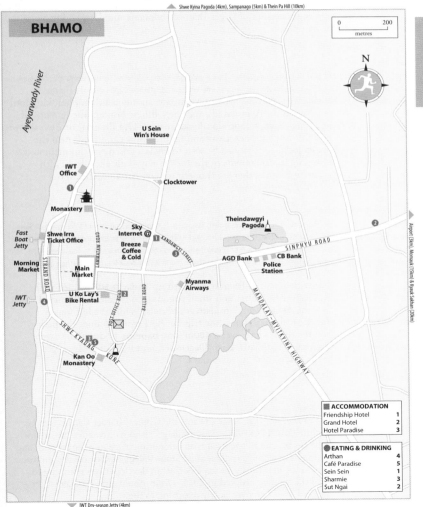

Shwe Kyina Pagoda (4km), Sampanago (5km) & Thein Pa Hill (10km)

BHAMO

7

0   200
metres

N

Ayeyarwady River

U Sein Win's House

IWT Office

❶

Clocktower

Monastery

Theindawgyi Pagoda

❷

Fast Boat Jetty

Shwe Irra Ticket Office

Sky Internet @

Breeze Coffee & Cold

Morning Market

Main Market

Myanma Airways

U Ko Lay's Bike Rental

AGD Bank

CB Bank

Police Station

SINPHYU ROAD

IWT Jetty ❹

Kan Oo Monastery

STRAND ROAD

POST-OFFICE ROAD

BALILI ROAD

KANDAWGYI STREET

THEINNI ROAD

SHWE KYAUNG KONE

MANDALAY–MYITKYINA HIGHWAY

Airport (3km), Momauk (15km) & Kyauk Saktan (20km)

❚ **ACCOMMODATION**
Friendship Hotel	1
Grand Hotel	2
Hotel Paradise	3

● **EATING & DRINKING**
Arthan	4
Café Paradise	5
Sein Sein	1
Sharmie	3
Sut Ngai	2

IWT Dry-season Jetty (4km)

wonderfully rickety bamboo bridge and along the river to **Thein Pa Hill** or rumble down the cobbled road towards China and quaint **Kyauk Sakhan**, the "Stone Village". For many, however, the main reason to visit Bhamo is in order to leave again on a boat down the Ayeyarwady (see box opposite) to Shwegu and beyond. There's also a rough-but-interesting overland route to Lashio via Namhkan that requires permits and an official guide.

Oddly, Bhamo doesn't make much of its waterfront. The town's Strand Road is dominated by shops selling tractors and seeds to the farmers who gather to sell their produce at the rather messy **vegetable market** that sets up here each morning (Mon–Sat 6.30–8am). The **main market**, hidden away one block east of the river, is worth a look as well, though more for the quaint covered market – surrounded by a small moat – than the goods on sale.

Bhamo's pagodas pepper the outskirts of town, the most important being the elongated **Theindawgyi Pagoda**, 500m east of the river on Sinphyu Road – keep an eye out for the photogenic procession of larger-than-life concrete monks queuing along the western side of the complex.

Sampanago

စမ္ပာနဂိုရ် • 5km north of Bhamo • Daily dawn–dusk • Free • From Bhamo, cycle north to the prison, turn left shortly after, and follow this road for 1.5km to Shwe Kyina Pagoda; Sampanago's remains are on the left-hand side of the road 200m southwest of the pagoda

The plains around Bhamo were once part of Manmaw, an independent Shan kingdom that ruled the area between the Ayeyarwady and the Chinese border. The remains of Manmaw's ancient capital, **Sampanago** (locally known as "Old Bhamo" or *Bhamo myo haung*), lie 5km north of town hidden away among the houses and fields near the modern **Shwe Kyina Pagoda**. All that can be seen today is a raised embankment and a ditch running alongside it – fragments of the former city walls and moat, with occasional rammed earth hillocks that are thought to have been watchtowers.

Thein Pa Hill

10km north of Bhamo • Daily dawn–dusk • Free • Cycle north towards Sampanago (see above) and turn left just before you reach Shwe Kyina Pagoda, which will bring you to the bamboo bridge (Dec–June only; K300/person). When the bridge is out of service, a long-tail boat (K300/person; K200/bike) ferries people across the river. Beyond the river go straight until you reach the second village, where there's a small turning that leads to the riverbank; Thein Pa is a few kilometres further north. It's also possible to take a boat here from Bhamo (see p.312)

A ninety-minute bike ride north of Bhamo, the path up **Thein Pa Hill** is lined with meditation halls, monastery buildings and small pagodas, and there are beautiful views from the hilltop over the Ayeyarwady's midstream islands. While the hill makes a tranquil picnic spot, the real attraction is the trip out here from Bhamo, the path winding along sandy riverbanks and over a **400m-long bamboo bridge** that's swept away by the monsoon rains each year. Each December, hundreds of villagers get together to rebuild the bridge over just two days.

Kyauk Sakhan

ကျောက်စခန်း • 20km east of Bhamo • Daily 9am–6pm • Free

Tucked up at the foot of the hills that range towards the Chinese border (here closed to foreigners), small Kachin **KYAUK SAKHAN** ("Stone Village") is so named after the boulders that erupt from nearby fields. The village itself is an interesting place to poke around, and there's a great swimming hole at the grandly named **Stone Village Resort**, twenty minutes further down a bumpy track that runs southeast. A Kachin developer was planning to open a hotel here until the fighting erupted in 2011 – four mouldering bungalows on the hillside above the cool, clear river are slowly returning to the wild.

AYEYARWADY RIVER TRIPS

The **Ayeyarwady River** north of Mandalay sees far fewer visitors than the stretch to Bagan (see box, p.273). Although the scenery is largely flat – save for the brief drama of the "second defile", where the hills close in and the river deepens and narrows (see p.312) – the journey between Bhamo and Mandalay offers more scope for interacting with local people, as well as the opportunity to jump ship at some interesting and little-visited spots en route.

The river **north of Bhamo** has been closed to foreigners since fighting between the government and the Kachin Independence Army flared up in 2011. Since you aren't allowed to get to Bhamo by road, the easiest way to do the whole available route is to fly into Bhamo then take the boat downriver; the cheapest is to take a train to Katha (via Naba), then travel upriver to Bhamo and back by boat.

Three types of boat ply this stretch of the river: government-run IWT ferries, privately operated fast boats (both of which run regularly year-round), and a handful of scheduled departures on luxury riverboats organized by upmarket tour operators (see box, p.273).

IWT FERRIES

The journey by **IWT ferry** from Bhamo to Mandalay ($12 on deck, $60 in a cabin) takes around thirty hours when water levels are high – during the dry season the boats moor each night to avoid hitting exposed sandbanks and the journey will take longer. Shwegu, Katha and Kyaukmyaung are the main stops of interest to visitors. Note that while in theory there are three departures each week in either direction, in practice the schedule is more erratic – but as long as you have plenty of time, these boats are a great way to experience the river.

FAST BOATS

Between Bhamo and Katha, **Shwe Irra** (☏09 470 10004) has daily departures that stop briefly at Shwegu en route. Between Katha and Mandalay, **Katha Irra** (☏09 650 1155) runs the main service, stopping at Tigyiang, Tagaung and Kyaukmyaung. Seating is usually on cramped, hard wooden benches under an awning, where you may be subjected to a Burmese pop music marathon. Food is available at most stops, and while the departures are daily and the service is far faster than the IWT boats, it's as well to be prepared for a few delays.

7

The interesting journey out here is an added incentive to visit. The road passes checkpoints and IDP (internally displaced person) camps – another legacy of the 2011 fighting – before the cobbled road to the village and the border forks right off the main road at Momauk, and runs towards the hills through fields of watermelons and emerald rice paddies.

ARRIVAL AND DEPARTURE

BHAMO

At the time of research foreigners were not allowed to travel in and out of Bhamo by bus. A railway linking Katha, Shwegu and Bhamo is currently under construction, but is not expected to be completed any time soon.

By plane Originally built as a Japanese Air Force base in World War II, Bhamo's airport is 3km east of town. Air Bagan, Asian Wings, Myanma Airways and Yangon Airways operate a handful of flights each week – purchase tickets through your hotel, or through the Myanma Airways office (☏074 50269) on Kandawgyi St.

Destinations Mandalay (9 weekly; 45min–2hr); Myitkyina (2 weekly; 30min); Yangon (6 weekly; 2hr 30min).

By boat As river travel upstream to Sinbo and Myitkyina is off limits, foreigners are only permitted out of Bhamo by boat downstream. Daily fast boats to Shwegu (4hr; K6000) and Katha (8hr; K12,000) leave at 8.30am from the riverside by the Shwe Irra ticket office on Strand Rd; if you're travelling on downstream to Mandalay you will need to spend the night in Katha before continuing your journey south. Slower IWT ferries depart Bhamo on Mon, Wed and Fri for Shwegu (5hr), Katha (9hr) and Mandalay (30hr) in theory, but the schedule is less reliable in practice. During the dry season the IWT boats need to leave from a jetty 4km south of Bhamo, but you can buy tickets from the IWT office (☏074 50117; daily 9am–5pm), housed in a colonial building set back from Strand Rd just north of the main waterfront.

GETTING AROUND

By tuk-tuk Chartering a tuk-tuk to the IWT dry-season jetty or airport costs K2000. The long trip out to Kyauk Sakhan or similar will cost around K20,000 including waiting time.

By bicycle Bikes (K2000/day) are available to rent from U Ko Lay's shop down the alley opposite the *Grand Hotel*.

Breeze Coffee and Cold, opposite the *Friendship Hotel*, offers bike rental too but is seldom open.

TOURS

U Sein Win ☎09 2563 50518. A fascinating septuagenarian polymath, U Sein Win speaks excellent English and can guide you around Bhamo's sights for K10,000/day. His house is just north of the clocktower and is signed in English. With a little notice he can arrange boat trips to an elephant camp (dry season only) or to Thein Pa Hill – there's a chance of seeing dolphins on the latter (Nov–Feb only).

ACCOMMODATION

★**Friendship Hotel** Balldi Rd ☎074 50095. The cheapest rooms may be getting a little shabby, but the *Friendship* still offers great service and one of northern Burma's finest breakfast buffets. The budget rooms have a/c and shared bathrooms, while the more expensive ones ($50–60) are in better repair with smarter linen and decoration. Light sleepers beware – there's a karaoke lounge downstairs. Achingly slow wi-fi is included, and the hotel produces a useful map of town. $20

Grand Hotel Post Office Rd ☎074 50317. Less luxurious than its name would have you believe, the *Grand* has decent doubles with a/c, wi-fi and slightly musty bathrooms – pay an extra $10 and you'll qualify for one of their large, over-furnished suites. Rooms are the same price for double and single occupancy. $25

★**Hotel Paradise** 36 Shwe Kyaung Kone ☎074 50136, ✉hotelparadisebanmaw@gmail.com. The newest hotel in town has a range of tidy new rooms in a block at the southern end of town, though they do smell of mothballs. The spacious $15 singles with a/c and en-suite bathrooms are a good-value option. $30

EATING AND DRINKING

After dark, Bhamo's centre of gravity shifts from the waterfront to the **beer stations** on Sinphyu Road, but across town most places close down by 9.30pm.

Arthan Strand Rd. This airy teahouse is the only place in Bhamo with views of the riverside over the main jetty. The kitchen serves up the usual teahouse menu; tasty noodles, fried things and endless cups of tea and coffee. Daily 6am–7pm.

Café Paradise Next to Hotel Paradise, Shwe Kyaung Kone ☎074 50136. With an English menu and a range of Western food – from French fries (K2000) to burgers, decent coffee (from K1500) and cocktails – this cheesily decorated, popular little place might hit the spot if you've been living off fried rice for a few weeks. Daily 7am–9.30pm.

Sein Sein Strand Rd ☎074 50031. With Myanmar Beer on tap (K600) and an extensive menu of stir-fried dishes (from K2500), this is considered one of the best Chinese restaurants in town, even if the chef shows a rather Burmese enthusiasm for cooking oil. Despite its promising location, there is no view of the river from the dining room. Daily 9am–9pm.

Sharmie Kandawgyi St ☎074 50108. This Indian canteen serves a selection of excellent halal curries Burmese-style with plain rice or biryani, soup and vegetables (K2000). The owners manage to keep the restaurant spotless despite it being home to an exotic range of pets. Daily lunch and dinner.

★**Sut Ngai** Sinphyu Rd. This Kachin restaurant and beer station just north of Theindawgyi Pagoda serves a range of traditional Kachin dishes including *sipa* (steamed vegetables with herbs) and chicken and pork steamed in banana leaves, as well as delicious barbecued skewers. Daily 9am–9pm.

DIRECTORY

Banks Bhamo's banks are all on Sinphyu Rd near the police station. Ignore the KBZ Bank, which has neither exchange facilities nor ATM. Head instead to AGD Bank or CB Bank, which have both; the latter has a slight edge on exchange rates.

Internet Sky Internet (daily 9am–9pm) opposite the *Friendship Hotel* has slow wi-fi and wired internet access for K500/hr.

Bhamo to Katha

The main spectacle along the Ayeyarwady between Bhamo and Katha is the 13.5km **second defile** where the river narrows dramatically from 2km wide to just 200m across, and flows through a tight s-bend. Towards the western end of the defile a **parrot's head** is painted on the rocky cliffs – when the water rises to touch the bird's beak, the river currents are judged to be too dangerous for certain craft, and larger boats stop and wait downstream. The Ayeyarwady defiles (there are three of them) are said to be extremely deep and the Burmese believe that *naga* – the local equivalent of Scotland's Loch Ness monster – lurk in the river's depths.

The most interesting place to stop along this stretch of the river is at **Shwegu** where there are a few simple guesthouses and an attractive island pagoda.

Shwegu
ရွှေကူမြို့

Spread-eagled along the Ayeyarwady River's southern bank, **SHWEGU** sees few foreign visitors. Those who do disembark here are either on their way to **Shwe Baw Kyun**, on the mid-river island of **Kyun Daw** where hundreds of pagodas in varying states of decay picturesquely cover the island's southeastern tip, or searching for pottery workshops in the town's dusty backstreets. Either way, it's a quirky place to break the journey between Bhamo and Katha. The main road runs a block inland of the river, and the main **pottery district** is further inland again, although you'll need to look hard to find much evidence of it.

Shwe Baw Kyun Pagoda
ရွှေပေါ်ကျွန်းဘုရား • Kyun Daw Island, 2.5km southwest of Shwegu jetty • Daily dawn–dusk • Free • Boat from near Shwe Andaw K500 one-way

Hidden away above the wide sandy shores of **Kyun Daw** ("Royal Island") in the middle of the Ayeyarwady is **Shwe Baw Kyun**. An estimated seven thousand pagodas forest the eastern end of the island, some gleaming with new gold leaf while others are barely recognizable piles of bricks. The site's origins are murky, but it was apparently already in need of renovation by the mid-eleventh century, when King Anawrahta (see p.331) perked it up and gave the central pagoda a new *hti*.

Today it makes an intriguing if somewhat uncomfortable (you'll need to carry your shoes) place to wander barefoot for an hour or two. Long whitewashed corridors radiate outwards from the main shrine surrounded by *tazaung* (tier-roofed chapels), birds sing from the undergrowth that curtains many of the older stupas, and fragments of stucco decoration cling to exposed brickwork.

If you've had enough pagodas, the island village next to Shwe Baw Kyun also makes an attractive place to explore, while on the riverbank opposite Kyun Daw is **Shwe Andaw**. This small pagoda is the site of a lively festival around the time of the Tabaung (February/March) full moon.

ARRIVAL AND DEPARTURE SHWEGU

By boat Catching a boat out of Shwegu requires a willingness to lurk around the jetty and wait. Fast boats to Katha (4hr) pass through at around 11.30am, while Bhamo-bound boats arrive around 1.30pm (5hr) – buy tickets for both services on board. The IWT ferries to Mandalay theoretically stop at Shwegu just after noon on Mon, Wed and Fri. Delays are frequent on all services.

GETTING AROUND

By boat Long-tail boats (K500 one-way) run out to Shwe Baw Kyun from a logging jetty 400m north of Shwe Andaw; 8am is the peak time to find one. It's also possible to charter a boat straight from the main jetty to the island, which ought to cost K10,000 for the return trip including waiting time.

By tuk-tuk and motorbike taxi Tuk-tuks and motorbike taxis are hard to find in Shwegu – you'll probably have more luck hitchhiking. The 15min drive from one end of Shwegu to the other costs around K2000.

ACCOMMODATION AND EATING

Shwegu's only accommodation options are around a 15min walk northwest of the jetty (turn right once you reach the road). The northwest end of Shwegu's main road is lined with Burmese restaurants, teahouses and beer stations, most of which serve decent and reasonably priced dishes, but none of which seem to have many customers – pick the busiest and prepare to point and order.

Mya Myint Moe Main Rd ☎074 52134. With a collection of basic rooms with a/c and shared bathrooms, this little guesthouse (Burmese sign only) is just off the main road next to a rambling red-brick mansion. Rather excitingly, the bathrooms have Western toilets. Breakfast not included. K10,000

SAG Guesthouse 3 Saigon Quarter ☎074 52647.

A 15min walk west of the jetty, the enthusiastic owners here have a collection of colourful fan-cooled rooms with grubby shared bathrooms, and more expensive ones with a/c and en suites (K16,000). It's tucked away one block south of the main road and the staff have a useful-ish map of town. Breakfast not included. K6000

Katha

ကသာပြို

For travellers, **KATHA** would be just another quaint riverside town of stained teak houses had not one Eric Blair (later better known as **George Orwell**; see box, p.316) spent his last posting as a colonial policeman here in 1926–27. Orwell used the town as the setting for his novel *Burmese Days*, and while it was renamed "Kyauktada" and the layout disguised – Orwell's publisher being concerned that the book was potentially libellous – several colonial buildings that played a part either in the novel or in Orwell's life here are identifiable today.

Katha is orientated north–south along the western bank of the Ayeyarwady. Its attractive **Strand Road** is lined with dark chocolate-coloured teak houses, most of the town's accommodation and several attractive pagodas – the largest of which stands at the southern end of the Strand, near the British-built **jail**, which is still in use. The small town's action is concentrated around the **market** (daily 6.30am–4pm), a few blocks inland from the riverside – if you have time to spare, it's also worth checking out the antiquated 1890 **railway station** hidden away a little further to the northwest.

The most interesting Orwell-era buildings are north of the town centre on **Club Street**, although they are neither signposted as such nor formally open to visitors – do bear this in mind before you invite yourself in for a look around. The easiest to find is the 1924 **tennis club** with its tiny mint-green clubhouse. Just behind the tennis court is the half-timbered former **British Club**, which is still much as Orwell himself described it – "a dumpy one-storey building with a tin roof" – now housing a government-run co-operative. It's usually locked but the caretaker may unlock the door and produce the visitors' book for you. One block north of the tennis club on the west side of Club Street is the 1928 **District Commissioners' House**, which stands empty and alone in a huge lot full of thistles. The **Police Commissioner's House** immediately to the north of the DC's is in much better repair, and off limits – it is still in use by the police today.

ARRIVAL AND DEPARTURE

KATHA

By train While trains do run directly to Katha, the single daily service between Katha and Naba (3hr) on the Mandalay–Myitkyina line is so slow that it barely counts – it's far quicker to get a pick-up (1hr; K1000) over the same distance from the roadside just north of Katha's market. Naba is served by three trains in each direction each day, with the last departure to Myitkyina (3 daily; 11hr 30min) leaving at 7.55am. Train times towards Mandalay (3 daily; 12hr) are slightly friendlier, departing between 4.55–11.35pm.

By boat Fast boats depart daily at 5.30am for Mandalay (12–14hr; $25) and 9am for Bhamo (8hr; K12,000), with tickets for either service available shortly before departure from Katha Irra ticket booth (☎09 4004 35212) on Strand Rd. Tickets for IWT ferries are available an hour before departure from the IWT office (☎074 25057) on Strand Rd, a little north of the fast ferry ticket office – look for the Myanmar flag outside. The IWT ferries themselves depart from a jetty 600m south of the IWT ticket office, just south of the large riverside pagoda.

ACCOMMODATION

Katha's accommodation is rudimentary – shared bathrooms and cold bucket showers are the norm across the board. Single travellers stay for half-price everywhere and none of the following options includes breakfast.

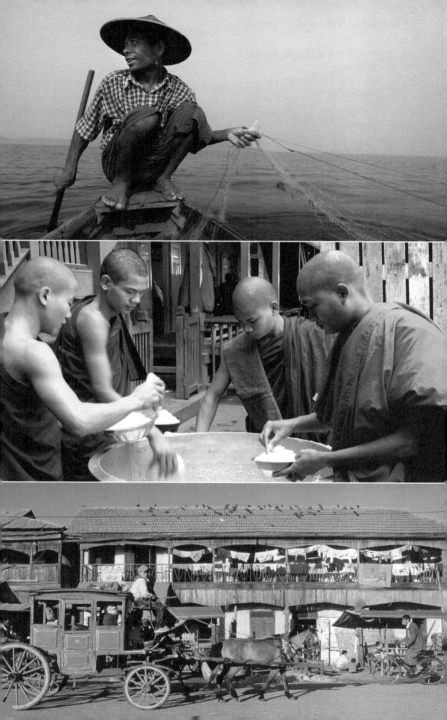

GEORGE ORWELL IN BURMA

Eric Blair (1903–50), who would later find fame under the pen name of **George Orwell**, arrived in Burma in November 1922 as a youthful member of the Indian Imperial Police. Sent first to Mandalay, he also spent time in the Ayeyarwady Delta and Moulmein (now Mawlamyine, where his mother grew up) before being posted to Katha.

Orwell's experiences in Burma convinced him of the wrongs of imperialism and he gained a reputation as an outsider more interested in spending time with the Burmese than in more "pukka" (appropriate) pursuits for a British officer. In this he resembled **Flory**, the protagonist of his first novel *Burmese Days* (1934), which was set in a thinly disguised Katha. Orwell also wrote about Burma in his essays *A Hanging* (1931) and *Shooting an Elephant* (1936).

There's a long-standing joke that Orwell actually wrote three books about Burma, including his denunciations of totalitarianism *Animal Farm* (1945) and *Nineteen Eighty-Four* (1949). Unlike the anti-imperialist *Burmese Days*, until recently both of the later works were banned by the regime.

7

Annawah Guesthouse Strand Rd ☎075 25146. More darkly chaotic than *Ayarwady* or *Kant Kaw*, *Annawah* has cheap, partitioned fan-cooled rooms that range from claustrophobia-inducing singles to a couple of more decent river-facing rooms upstairs. All have shared bathrooms. **K8000**

Ayarwady Guesthouse Strand Rd ☎075 25140. This old-school Burmese guesthouse has a collection of neat but small rooms, all of which have shared bucket showers. Try to get one of the rooms with a/c and river views at the front of the building (K14,000) – the rooms at the back also play host to cockroaches from time to time. The hotel offers guests a useful sketch map of town, although the representation of the town centre is misleading. **K12,000**

Kant Kaw Strand Rd ☎075 25144. The northernmost of Katha's Strand Rd guesthouses, this little place has friendly owners, hard beds, shared Burmese-style bathrooms and – the height of luxury in Katha – a Western loo. **K10,000**

EATING AND DRINKING

Katha has a particularly good **night market** (daily 5–9pm) with various options beyond the typical fried rice and skewers, including fresh fruit lassis and good curry-and-rice combos. The market is held on a street running away from the river, just south of the fast boat jetty and locally known as "Night Market Street".

Jet Sun Night Market St. This small teahouse is one of the few places open early in the morning, and therefore the best option for a breakfast of sweet tea and hot paratha before you get on the ferry to Mandalay. Daily 5am–6pm.

Shwe Sisa Strand Rd. Riverside restaurant offering grills and tasty stir-fries, draught beer, Premiership football and a balcony overlooking the river. Barbecued fish is their speciality. Daily 9am–10pm.

★Yangon Myin Myin Market Rd ☎075 25558. Near the entrance to the main market (Burmese only sign – look for the Golden Island Rum advert), this popular restaurant serves up excellent Burmese curries with fresh vegetables and a range of side dishes for K2500, with an unusual tamarind-spiked jaggery for dessert. Few vegetarian options. Daily 9am–9pm.

DIRECTORY

Bank If you're in need of cash and here during banking hours the CB Bank, two blocks back from the waterfront, can exchange US dollars, but there's no ATM in town – yet.

Internet Ozone Internet (24hr), hidden down an alley behind the waterfront, has a decent connection for K500/hr.

Katha to Mandalay

The broad ribbon of the Ayeyarwady flows almost straight due south between Katha and Mandalay, through low denuded hills that have been intensively logged for teak – elephants hauling tree trunks and barges loaded with logs can still be spotted along the river. Just before the town of **Inywa** river traffic negotiates its way around the **Shweli sandbar** where the Shweli River dumps its heavy load of silt at the river's confluence with the Ayeyarwady.

Fast and slow boats alike stop at Tigyaing and Tagaung, but the place most likely to be of interest to travellers is **Kyaukmyaung** where potters produce huge **Martaban jars**, using techniques that have remained unchanged since King Alaungpaya forcibly relocated thousands of Mon captives here from Mottama (formerly Martaban) near Mawlamyine in the eighteenth century. Alaungpaya also left his mark on his birthplace, **Shwebo**, which he made capital of his new dynasty between 1752 and 1760. Outside Shwebo, the ruins of a far more ancient city, **Hanlin**, are also worth visiting.

Kyaukmyaung

ကျောက်မြောင်း

Some 74km north of Mandalay, **KYAUKMYAUNG** is the last major stop on the way south. From the jetty the main pottery area of **Ngwe Ngein** is 1.5km south along the riverside road, just north of the Radana Thinga Bridge. Kyaukmyaung is a sleepy little place, and save for the potteries and a few pagodas that were badly cracked in a 2012 **earthquake**, there's little to occupy you – which is just as well, seeing as the nearest accommodation for foreign visitors is 17km west in Shwebo (see p.319).

While Kyaukmyaung's workshops produce a variety of earthenware jars, the most recognizable are the large Martaban jars that were used for centuries by Mon merchants in their Indian Ocean trade – also known as "Ali Baba jars" after their cameo in *Ali Baba and the Forty Thieves*. In shady huts set back from the riverside it's possible to see potters shaping the jars using wheels that they turn with their feet, later firing them in low brick kilns fuelled by rice husks.

7

ARRIVAL AND DEPARTURE
KYAUKMYAUNG

By bus Buses for Shwebo (1hr) and Mandalay (3hr) depart when full from in front of the market, with the last bus leaving mid-afternoon.

By motorbike taxi A motorbike taxi to Shwebo will set you back K3000–5000, depending on how late you arrive in Kyaukmyaung and how much luggage you have.

By tuk-tuk Tuk-tuks to Shwebo (1hr; K700) leave hourly until 3pm, and drivers usually wait around to meet each boat.

By boat Slow boats pull in at the Kyaukmyaung jetty (northbound on Mon, Thurs and Sat; southbound on Sat, Tues and Thurs), but departure times are unreliable – ask at the IWT office opposite the jetty for upcoming departures. Southbound fast boats pass through Kyaukmyaung at around 2–4pm, but don't always pull in – you may need to take a long-tail out to join the boat midstream. Northbound fast boats pass through at around 7–9am. On all services it's possible to buy tickets on board.

Shwebo and around

ရွှေဘိုမြို့

Once known as Moksobo or "Hunters' Village", **SHWEBO** was given its current name ("Golden Leader") when Alaungpaya, an ambitious native of the town, founded

---

IRRAWADDY DOLPHINS

Despite its name, the **Irrawaddy dolphin** can be found in estuaries, rivers and along coasts from the Bay of Bengal to the Great Barrier Reef. Although not a true river dolphin – they're closely related to killer whales – subpopulations do live in several Southeast Asian rivers, with one such group eking out an existence in the turbid waters of the upper Ayeyarwady River.

While there are many stories of the dolphins co-operating with fishermen, the use of gill- and drag-nets by those same fishermen has seen Myanmar's dolphin population drop alarmingly, and CITES lists the Ayeyarwady's dolphins as being critically endangered.

In 2005 the Burmese government established a protected area for the dolphins in a 68km stretch of the river between Kyaukmyaung and Mingun in which there has been a ban on certain types of fishing nets and the use of mercury in riverside gold mines. While Irrawaddy dolphin numbers initially showed a slight recovery, the mammals are now facing a new threat as the Ayeyarwady's fisheries decline due to overfishing, with just an estimated 63 individuals left in 2014.

Burma's last empire in 1752. Today only Shwebo's fine selection of royally bestowed names (of which there are five), and a concrete reproduction of Alaungpaya's throne hall at **Shwebon Yadana**, hint at its glorious past. Nowadays the town is better known for its fragrant *thanaka* sandalwood, said to be the best in the country.

Shwebo makes a good base for exploring the ruins of the ancient Pyu city of **Hanlin**, 20km to the southeast, and it's possible to do a day-trip to the potteries in Kyaukmyaung (see p.317) from here. The town is also a useful stop if you want to travel between Kyaukmyaung and Bagan without stopping in Mandalay, with transport on to Monywa and Pakokku. You may see signs of the 2012 **earthquake**, which registered 6.8 on the Richter scale, although Shwebo escaped without major damage.

Shwe Taza Paya

ရွှေတန်ဆာဘုရား· Shwe Taza Paya Rd · Daily 5am–7pm · Free

Just off the main road to Mandalay, an alluring array of golden spires punctuates the skyline – these belong to **Shwe Taza Paya**, Shwebo's most important religious complex. The main shrine can be reached along a dim covered corridor populated with *thanaka* vendors sawing at sandalwood logs and customers daubing samples on their cheeks.

Established in the eleventh century, the *paya*'s main treasure is a small golden **Buddha statue** in the main hall, which is said to emit rays of light from its head and is paraded around Shwebo to hasten the rains each year around the Waso (July) full moon. Keep an eye out for the *nat* shrine on the southern side of the *paya*, where you can see Shwebo's council of nine guardian *nats*, offerings piled in front of each one.

Shwebon Yadana

ရွှေဘုံတာနာ· Alaungpaya St · Daily 8am–5pm · K2000

After King Alaungpaya founded the Konbaung dynasty in 1752, he set about building a new palace in his humble home town. He ruled from **Shwebon Yadana** until his death in 1760, whereupon his successor moved the capital to Sagaing (see p.286).

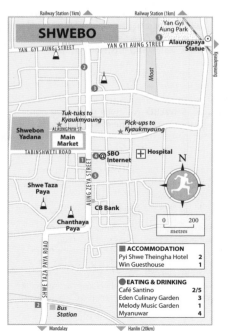

The original palace buildings were destroyed by the British after the annexation of Upper Burma, and the area was used as a **prison** until 1994 (the colonial-era courthouse still stands just inside the gates), when the military government decided to reconstruct two of the throne halls. Today the peeling halls are best viewed from a distance and there's no real reason to go inside.

Hanlin

ဟန်လင်း· 20km southeast of Shwebo · Site and museum Tues–Sun 9.30am–4.30pm; K5000 · Motorbike taxis charge K12,000 return; to get there under your own steam from Shwebo head south of town towards Mandalay, turning left at the Shwebo Canal, which you follow for 10km until a turning signposted "Han Lin Pyu City" (in English); Hanlin village is 9km down this road

Between the first and ninth centuries AD the walled city of **Hanlin** flourished in the bone-dry hills southeast of Shwebo, one of the largest and most important Pyu city-states. Archeologists have been systematically excavating the area enclosed by Hanlin's rectangular brick walls (3.2km long by 1.6km wide) since 1962, uncovering inscribed stones, coins and attractive jewellery made from gold and semi-precious stones, samples of which are on display in the surprisingly informative **museum** in Hanlin village. The dig has also exposed several of the city's curved gates as well as mass graves. The latter being covered by locked huts, it's best to visit the museum first and find someone who has the keys to accompany you as you tour the scattered sights.

At present there are 33 excavation sites scattered across the countryside north of Hanlin village. While these are signed in English, it's a good idea to have a local driver or guide to show you the way. Pits 26, 29 and 30 all contain human remains, with some of the skeletons in Pit 29 still wearing bracelets around their bony wrists. Further afield, site 22 is an interesting religious building with altars of polished stones arranged on three sides.

HANLIN village is an attractive place in its own right, with hot springs, salt wells and a host of crumbling stupas to occupy you.

ARRIVAL AND DEPARTURE   SHWEBO AND AROUND

By bus and tuk-tuk The bus station is just south of Shwe Taza Paya, with regular departures to Mandalay and Monywa until mid-afternoon, and a daily service to Pakokku at 7.30am. To Kyaukmyaung you'll need to take one of the regular tuk-tuks (K700), which leave from just north of the market, or a pick-up (K500) departing from a side street 100m further east.

Destinations Kyaukmyaung (regular; 1hr); Mandalay

(hourly; 3hr); Monywa (hourly; 3hr); Pakokku (daily; 6hr).
By train Shwebo's railway station is 2.5km north of the market, just inside the northern side of the city moat. The town is on the main line between Mandalay and Myitkyina, with three "up" and three "down" trains daily.
Destinations Mandalay (3 daily; 5hr); Myitkyina (3 daily; 19hr); Naba (3 daily; 7hr).

GETTING AROUND

Motorbike rental Motorbike rental (K10,000) is available from *Win Guesthouse*.

Tours Friendly English-speaking motorcycle taxi driver Kyaw Soe (✉ kyawsoe040@gmail.com) can organize tours

of Shwebo, Hanlin (K13000) and Kyaukmyaung (K10,000). He has no telephone number, but can often be found waiting on the street just south of *Win Guesthouse*.

ACCOMMODATION

★**Pyi Shwe Theingha Hotel** Shwe Taza Paya Rd ☎ 075 22949, ✉ pyishwetheingha@gmail.com. One of Myanmar's fancier bus station hotels with the only elevator in Shwebo, this brand-new block has a range of clean, spacious rooms all with private bathrooms, hot water and a/c. Single rooms start at a reasonable K15,000. **K20,000**
Win Guesthouse Aung Zeya St ☎ 075 22049. This

modern guesthouse soaks up most of Shwebo's foreign visitors thanks to both its location between Shwe Taza Paya and the market, and its decent rooms. The cheapest are plain but bright and clean with shared bathrooms, and there are a few nicer rooms upstairs with a/c and en suite. Single travellers pay half the regular rate, but you'll need to head outside for breakfast. **$20**

EATING AND DRINKING

★**Café Santino** Aung Zeya St ☎ 09 4004 25714. With two cavernous teashops on Aung Zeya St, *Café Santino* is popular with locals all day long – from their breakfast-time fried rice and *moun-di* to late-night football matches, with plenty of coffee and tea served up in between. Daily 6am–10pm.
Eden Culinary Garden Aung Zeya St ☎ 075 21651. With a dining room and some tables set around a little courtyard, *Eden* serves Burmese and Chinese standards, with the promise of a few Western dishes to boot. Check the prices before you order – while it's not an expensive place overall (a meal for two costing from

K4000), there are a few surprises, like a K7000 omelette. Daily 6am–9pm.
Melody Music Garden Yan Gyi Aung St ☎ 075 22011. One of the few places in town to take advantage of the city moat, with a veranda that's a great spot for sitting and enjoying the view with an icy glass of beer – just don't forget your mosquito repellent. Daily 10am–10pm.
Myanuwar Tabinshweti Rd ☎ 09 616 1123. Not far from the market, this little local diner serves up cheap curry and rice (K1000, or K1500 with side dish), as well as K200 fried rice for breakfast. Daily 9am–8pm.

7

Banks There are branches of the main banks on Aung Zeya St, none with ATMs as yet. *Win Guesthouse* and *Pyi Shwe Theingha* can also change US dollars at decent rates.

Internet SBO Internet (daily 9am–10pm) on Tabinshweti Rd has a good connection for K400/hr.

Myitkyina and the far north

Despite the exotic allure of its jungles and hill tribes, Myanmar's **far north** – where the country forms a wedge between China and India – sees few foreign visitors. In part this is down to the byzantine **travel restrictions** that govern much of the region, but the north's rusting infrastructure and damp, steamy climate both play their parts.

However, for those willing to stump up for permits or happy to brave long, uncomfortable journeys, Myanmar's northern tip has plenty to offer. The main town, **Myitkyina**, is the best place to get a taste of Kachin culture, while the peaceful **Indawgyi Lake Wildlife Sanctuary** is the most accessible of the region's nature reserves. Further north, the small town of **Putao** is a useful base for adventurous expeditions into the surrounding jungle-clad mountains.

Myitkyina and around

မြစ်ကြီးနားမြို့

Capital of Kachin State, **MYITKYINA** is a fascinating place. The town was largely destroyed in the three-month **Battle for Myitkyina** during World War II and few old buildings survive, but what it lacks in history it makes up for with variety. It's a major centre for the six hill tribes that comprise the **Kachin** (see p.353), as well as substantial communities from the Indian subcontinent – churches decorated with geometric Kachin patterns stand alongside mosques and Sikh gurdwara – with everyone speaking Burmese as the lingua franca.

While travel restrictions limit day-trips outside the town, one straightforward excursion is to head north along the Ayeyarwady to the site of the **Myitsone Dam** (see box, p.322) and the confluence of the Mali Kha and N'Mai Kha rivers that is considered the **source of the Ayeyarwady**.

Thanks to its proximity to the **jade mines** of Hpakant (see box, p.326), Myitkyina is a major jade trading centre. Along with a steady stream of Chinese buyers and ready money, the semi-precious stone has bought a slew of problems, ranging from inflated prices for everyday goods to an alarming increase in drug abuse – the town feels noticeably less safe after dark than elsewhere in Myanmar. A lesser problem is that Myitkyina's English road signs are rather inconsistent and a single road name may have several different spellings.

Brief history

Myitkyina was a small Kachin trading post when the British arrived here in the 1890s and established a military base. Roman Catholic and Baptist missionaries followed, one of whom was the Swedish–American **Ola Hanson** (1864–1927), who translated the Bible into Kachin. Originally animists, today most Kachin identify as **Christians**.

FESTIVALS IN MYITKYINA

On Kachin National Day (January 10) each year Myitkyina hosts the **Manau festival**, originally a *nat*-propitiating ceremony and now an important expression of Kachin unity. The town stops for days of feasting and dancing, with the focus on Manau Park north of the town centre, where the totem-like Manau poles are on display year-round. In early February, Myitkyina also plays host to the **Lisu New Year** celebrations, when Lisu people from Kachin State and neighbouring regions of China gather together for a three-day party.

During World War II the Kachin levies who fought alongside the Allies in this region were legendary for their jungle survival skills and fighting spirit. For much of the period since independence, that same fighting spirit has been directed at the Myanmar government, with the Kachin insurgency led by the **Kachin Independence Army** (KIA) being one of the country's fiercest and longest running. Although a ceasefire has nominally been in place since 1994, fighting periodically flares, and the ceasefire collapsed entirely in 2011. Today Myitkyina itself is peaceful, but you will see the KIA flag (crossed *machetes* on a red and green background) decorating T-shirts and motorbikes around town.

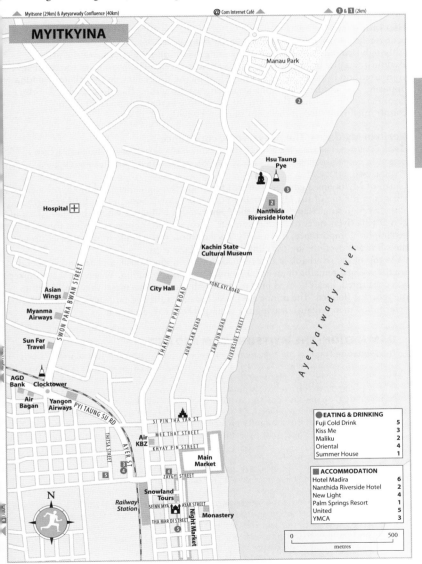

MYITKYINA

Myitsone (29km) & Ayeyarwady Confluence (40km)

Com Internet Café

1 & 1 (2km)

7

Manau Park

Hsu Taung Pye

Nanthida Riverside Hotel

Hospital

Kachin State Cultural Museum

City Hall

YONE GYI ROAD

A y e y a r w a d y   R i v e r

Asian Wings

SWON PARA BWAN STREET

Myanma Airways

THAKIN NET PHAY ROAD

AUNG SAN ROAD

ZAW TUN ROAD

RIVERSIDE STREET

Sun Far Travel

AGD Bank   Clocktower

Air Bagan

Yangon Airways

PYI TAUNG SU RD

SI PIN THA YAR ST

MEE THAT STREET

Air KBZ

KHYAY PIN STREET

THITSA STREET

AYER ST

Main Market

ZAYGYI STREET

Snowland Tours

Railway Station

SEINN MYA   AYAR STREET

THA MAR DI STREET

Monastery

Night Market

N

EATING & DRINKING
Fuji Cold Drink	5
Kiss Me	3
Maliku	2
Oriental	4
Summer House	1

ACCOMMODATION
Hotel Madira	6
Nanthida Riverside Hotel	2
New Light	4
Palm Springs Resort	1
United	5
YMCA	3

0   500
metres

7

Kachin State Cultural Museum

ကချင်ယဉ်ကျေးမှုပြတိုက် • 1km north of the market, on the corner of Thakin Net Phay Rd and Yone Gyi Rd • Mon–Sat 9.30am–4pm; closed on national holidays • K2000

The small **Kachin State Cultural Museum** is worth a visit to see its display of Kachin and Shan costumes and the Latin scripts that European missionaries adapted to express the complexities of Kachin pronunciation in the 1890s. The most interesting exhibits are upstairs, however, where a collection of Manau headdresses shaped like hornbills and a wide selection of everyday items made out of bamboo and rattan are held.

Hsu Taung Pye

ဆုတောင်းပြည့် • Northern end of Zaw Jun and Aung San roads • Daily dawn–dusk • Free

Although **Hsu Taung Pye** (its name meaning "wish fulfilling") is one of the main Buddhist temples in Myitkyina and has an attractive golden pagoda on the riverbank, your attention is more likely to be captured by the slinky 30m-long **reclining Buddha** opposite, and another interesting arrangement of standing Buddhas nearby. A former Japanese soldier donated the main Buddha statue in memory of 1280 of his countrymen who died in the 1944 Battle for Myitkyina.

North of Myitkyina: The Ayeyarwady confluence

မြစ်ဆုံ • 40km north of Myitkyina • Daily during daylight hours • Free; camera fee K1000, parking K300; boat trips K7000 (per boat) for a short trip around the confluence, K30,000 to the Myitsone Dam and back • Motorbike taxi from Myitkyina (90min each way) cost K15,000

North of Myitkyina a good road winds for 30km through a series of modern Kachin villages to the site of the **Myitsone Dam** (see box below). Some 11km further north, along a rough single-lane track, is the **Ayeyarwady confluence** where the Mali Kha and N'mai Kha rivers meet to form Myanmar's most important artery. Despite the site's geographical importance, it is a fairly low-key spot, with simple restaurants set up on the silt beach overlooking the confluence, and boat trips.

On top of the riverbank is a reproduction Kachin **longhouse**, and around the bend are the ravaged remains of an artisanal **gold-panning** operation. When the dam project was confirmed, locals flocked here to extract all the precious metal they could before the area was flooded. The minor gold rush has now subsided (although a few determined men remain), leaving the bank pocked with deep holes.

DAM NATION: THE MYITSONE DAM PROJECT

The **Myitsone Dam** on the Ayeyarwady, 8km south of its confluence, is one of Myanmar's most controversial engineering projects. The 140m-high dam is expected to flood 447sq km and force the relocation of 11,800 local people, as well as preventing fertile sediment from washing down the river to Myanmar's "rice bowl", the Ayeyarwady Delta. Critics also point out that the site sits upon the unstable Sagaing fault line, and that, as with many of Myanmar's mooted mega-projects, a foreign nation will reap the benefits while leaving Myanmar to deal with the substantial environmental and social costs – in return for financing the project, much of the electricity generated will be exported to China's Yunnan province.

Despite President Thein Sein's announcement in 2011 that the project would be suspended for the remainder of his term, locals say that the construction is continuing in secret using imported workers from China. Opposition to the dam has led to skirmishes between the KIA and government troops in the area.

The road from Myitkyina to the Ayeyarwady confluence passes **Aung Myint Tha**, a new village with eerie rows of suburban-style housing that was constructed for local people who will be displaced by the dam. The village has not been a notable success – today most inhabitants continue to work the fields near their old village, where the land is more fertile than Aung Myint Tha's heavy clay.

ARRIVAL AND INFORMATION

MYITKYINA AND AROUND

At the time of research, the only ways to get in and out of Myitkyina were by flying in or taking the phenomenally slow and frequently delayed train from Mandalay, 600km away.

By plane Air Bagan, Asian Wings, Myanma Airways and Air KBZ all have flights to Myitkyina's airport, 5km west of the town centre. On arrival, don't worry if you're herded out of the airport without your bags – the luggage reclaim is done in a shed outside the airport gates. Most airline offices are concentrated on and around Swon Para Bwan St, but opening hours at all the offices are unreliable – if you're out of luck and unable to book through your accommodation, try Sun Far Travel (daily 9am–5pm; T 074 23392 or T 09 240 1141), also on Swon Para Bwan St.

Destinations Bhamo (2 weekly; 30min); Mandalay (8 weekly; 45min–2hr); Putao (5 weekly; 50min); Yangon (7 weekly; 2hr 20min).

By train Myitkyina's railway station is right in the centre of town. The ticket office is open from 7am to 9.30pm, and it's possible to buy tickets one day in advance. While basic English is spoken at the station, the timetables are all in Burmese – the fastest services to Mandalay are the 34 and 38 down.

Destinations Hopin (3 daily; 5hr); Mandalay (4 daily; 16–22hr); Naba (3 daily; 9hr 30min); Shwebo (3 daily; 19hr).

Information The *YMCA* produces a photocopied map of Myitkyina and its outskirts.

7

GETTING AROUND

By motorbike taxi A motorbike taxi around town will cost K500–1000, while a trip up to the area around Manau Park is K2000 and the journey to the airport K3000. The drivers wait at designated spots on the streets, marked "Taxi".

By cyclo-rickshaw A cyclo-rickshaw around downtown Myitkyina will cost K500.

By bike and motorbike The *YMCA* rents out bicycles for K2000/day and motorbikes for a fairly steep K15,000/day.

Tours The staff at the YMCA can arrange day-trips by motorbike to the sights around Myitkyina with one of their English-speaking staff for around K20,000/day – pretty decent, considering the cost of renting a motorbike alone. Snowland Tours (T 074 23499, W snowlandmyanmar.com) on Aung San Rd can arrange tours further afield in Kachin State.

ACCOMMODATION

Central Myitkyina is stuffed with cheap accommodation, little of which is open to foreign travellers – nowhere with "guesthouse" in its name will allow you to stay.

Hotel Madira Yuzana Rd T 074 29455, E madira.hotel.mka@gmail.com. Although its location (2km northwest of the railway station towards the airport) is a little inconvenient, the clean, bright rooms here are a cut above its town-centre competition, with international TV channels and minibars. Variable wi-fi available. $65

Nanthida Riverside Hotel Zaw Jun Rd T 074 22362. Overlooking the river, this old-school, state-owned hotel is in a slightly awkward location at the northern end of Zaw Jun Rd, just south of Hsu Taung Pye. Avoid the dingy bungalows, and opt instead for one of the spacious rooms in the main building with high ceilings, bathtubs and river views. $45

New Light 70 Zaygyi St T 074 23576, E newlight_47@yangon.net.mm. The cheapest white-tiled rooms here are small and neat with shared bathrooms and cheerful Chinese-style decoration, while their pricier (K40,000) counterparts have slightly ragged en-suite bathrooms. Not to be confused with the *New Light Guesthouse* near the *YMCA*. K20,000

Palm Springs Resort 7/8 Sitarpu Quarter T 074 22938, W palmspringresort.com.mm. Around 4km north of town, this luxury hotel has wonderfully comfortable rooms set in bungalows around nicely landscaped gardens, a tiny infinity pool overlooking the river, as well as substantial government connections. $120

United 38 Thitsa St T 074 22085, E hotelunitedmyitkyina@gmail.com. Rooms here are clean and pleasant, and the slightly more expensive ones ($45) have balconies facing the street. Those on one side of the hotel look directly into the neighbouring building a few metres away, so do check before you pay up. All include a/c, wi-fi and bathrooms with hot water. $35

YMCA Ayer St T 074 23010, E shkawnmai2012@gmail.com. A favourite with the few backpackers that make it this far north, the *YMCA*'s (women welcome) ten rooms range from cheap twins with stained lino, old sheets, and worn-out shared bathrooms, to some slightly nicer options upstairs with en suite ($15). The saving grace here is the Kachin staff, who are friendly and knowledgeable about everything from local restaurants to national politics. No breakfast. $10

KACHIN CUISINE

Kachin cooking places a greater emphasis on fresh herbs and spices than Bamar cuisine, generally to delicious effect. Dishes to try include *chekachin* (chicken steamed with herbs in a banana leaf), *amedha thouq* (a spicy salad made with pounded dried beef) and pretty much anything on a skewer – Kachin barbecue dishes being a particular highlight.

EATING AND DRINKING

Each evening a brightly lit **night market** sets up on Aung San Rd south of Zaygyi St. Food options are concentrated at the lively southern end of the street, with the usual noodle dishes and kebabs dominating. At the northern end of town in the area around Manau Park, the backstreets are full of Kachin restaurants – usually indicated by the word *luseng* on their sign in Latin letters.

Fuji Cold Drink Aung San Rd. This street-side store whisks up delicious seasonal fruit juices and cold drinks without tooth-rotting amounts of sugar. Locals come here for *falooda* but their lassis are also among the best in town. Daily 9am–5pm.

★ **Kiss Me** Zaw Jun Rd. Hidden away between Hsu Taung Pye and the river, *Kiss Me* has a great terrace and extra-enthusiastic tea boys. The menu covers everything from Kachin to Malaysian dishes, with some delicious snacks as well – their "rolls" (paratha with various stuffings, K500) are particularly good. Daily 6am–9pm.

Maliku South of Manau Park. You'll need some help both finding this place and ordering once you get here (ask someone to write down a few dishes in advance), but it's rumoured to be the best Kachin restaurant in town. Daily, lunch and dinner.

Oriental Ayer Rd. Next to the *YMCA*, this friendly little restaurant has a fairly pan-Asian menu – the Kachin owner once lived in Japan – with good kimchi fried rice (K1800) and a range of other dishes at similar prices. Mon–Sat 7am–9pm, Sun noon–9pm.

★ **Summer House** Off Thakin Net Phay Rd, 1km north of Manau Park. *Summer House* has a collection of little huts scattered around a wooded section of riverbank north of Manau Park. While they specialize in Kachin dishes, their *mala-je* (a Chinese dish of vegetables doused in a spicy peanut sauce) and barbecued fish are also delicious. Daily, lunch and dinner.

DIRECTORY

Bank The bank situation is unusually poor in Myitkyina, with the AGD way out on Pyi Taung Su Rd the only place that will exchange dollars at official rates, and at the time of writing there were no ATMs in town.

Internet Com Internet Café, 100m north of the roundabout by the Manau Park, has a decent connection (K300/hr).

JUNGLE FEVER

Hundreds of rare and endemic species inhabit the mist-cloaked hills of northern Myanmar, where the humid jungles of the Indian subcontinent meet China's bamboo forests on the southern slopes of the Himalayas. As yet – thanks to obstacles both geographic and political – little work has been done to catalogue what's out there. But despite the challenges of exploring this region, Burma's northern rainforests have been catnip for Western scientists since the first British surveys in the late nineteenth century.

Plant collector **Frank Kingdon Ward** made ten epic journeys across northern Burma between 1914 and 1956, collecting seeds from new species as he went. On these expeditions Ward survived multiple bouts of malaria, "hordes of famished leeches", and impalement on a bamboo spike in his hunt for new species for Britain's herbaceous borders.

American zoologist **Alan Rabinowitz** travelled widely through Kachin State and Sagaing Division in the 1990s to establish a series of nature reserves, including the Hkakabo Razi National Park, the country's largest. While his main objective has been to preserve the habitat of Myanmar's vanishing tigers, critics hold that the government sees the four reserves established so far simply as another way of curtailing ethnic insurgencies in the region.

Most recently, **Joe Slowinski**, an American herpetologist, was leading a multidisciplinary expedition to northern Kachin State when he was bitten by a many-banded krait, Asia's deadliest land snake. On September 12, 2001, while the world was reeling from the terrorist attacks on the US – and after his colleagues had kept him alive by mouth-to-mouth resuscitation for more than 24 hours – Slowinski died when the monsoon rains and red tape delayed the arrival of a vital rescue helicopter.

Indawgyi Lake

အင်းတော်ကြီးကန်

Despite being Myanmar's largest lake, beautiful but remote **Indawgyi Lake** is well off Myanmar's tourist trail. The few travellers who do brave the rough journey to get here do so to enjoy the peaceful natural environment, spending days hiking in the hills, kayaking across or cycling around the lake, and exploring remote Shan villages that have just a few hours' electricity each evening. Note that the road to the lake from the railhead town of **HOPIN** is frequently impassable during the rainy season, and roads around the lake are bumpy at any time of year.

The lake is part of the **Indawgyi Lake Wildlife Sanctuary**, established in 1999 in an effort to protect the area's bird and animal species, which include several **endangered species** as well as gibbons, gaur, banteng and wild elephants. At certain times of year your fellow guesthouse residents are as likely to be birdwatchers and field biologists as backpackers (Dec–March is the main birdwatching season). The only accommodation and visitors' facilities are in the small village of **LONTON**, which sits at the southern end of the lake, making it handy for excursions to either the east or west lakeshore.

7

Shwe Myitzu Pagoda

ရွှေမြို့ဇူဘုရား • 10km north of Lonton • Daily during daylight hours • Free • Shwe Myitzu can be reached from the village of Namde, halfway up Indawgyi's western shore and 8km north of Lonton, from where the pagoda is 2km down an access road, with the turning signed in English

There is a plethora of local legends surrounding Indawgyi's origins, many of them related to the mid-lake **Shwe Myitzu Pagoda**, which was built in the mid-nineteenth century. The picturesque pagoda seems to float above the lake's surface for most of the year, except around the time of the annual **festival** (held a week before the Tabaung full moon, usually in March) when the waters recede to reveal two sandy causeways – one for humans and one for *nats*. Today a concrete path covers both natural causeways, but even this is inundated during rainy season, when it is replaced by a boat service.

Lwemon and Nammilaung

လွယ်မွန် / နမ့်မီးလောင်

The most interesting places to stop on the western side of Indawgyi Lake are the villages of **LWEMON** and **NAMMILAUNG**. Neither receives many visitors, but both are filled with attractive weathered teak houses and have basic snacks available. According to a local legend, Indawgyi was once the site of a thriving city that was flooded by two *nagas*. Only one person, a widow, escaped from the city alive and settled in Lwemon – there's a shrine telling the full story in the village, 11km north of Lonton; on full moon nights locals claim to be able to hear the sounds of the drowned city coming from below the water. Some 4km further north from Lwemon, Nammilaung is home to a cane Buddha image and a family of working **elephants**, with plenty of attractive sandy lanes to explore.

ARRIVAL AND DEPARTURE
INDAWGYI LAKE

To reach Indawgyi Lake, take a train as far as **Hopin** on the Mandalay–Myitkyina line (16hr from Mandalay, 5hr from Myitkyina). From Hopin you'll need to clamber on one of the phenomenally slow and uncomfortable pick-ups to **Lonton**, 40km away (3–5hr; K4000), or find a willing motorcycle taxi driver. The trucks leave when full from a yard just south of the station along the tracks. Pick-ups in the opposite direction leave from Lonton's main street between 7am and 2pm – book a spot through your accommodation and the truck will pick you up first.

ACTIVITIES

Inn Chit Thu Between In Daw Ma Ha and Indawa guesthouses, Lonton. Since 2013 Fauna & Flora International (ⓦ fauna-flora.org) have been working with this small local organization to develop community-based tourism in Indawgyi, with the profits being ploughed back into conservation projects. They offer kayak (K15,000/day), bicycle (K7000/day) and motorbike (K10,000/day) rental, have good maps of the lake and can provide guides for K10,000/day. Fishing and trekking trips can be arranged on request.

7

HPAKANT: MYANMAR'S WILD NORTHWEST

An incredible ninety percent of the world's **jadeite** is mined in and around **Hpakant** in Kachin state, 70km north of Indawgyi Lake. The area's mineral wealth is so great that local people used to find lumps of jadeite when they were digging wells and house foundations. This semi-precious stone has been exported to China since the nineteenth century, but after a 1994 ceasefire between the KIA and the Myanmar government (see p.321) paved the way for both sides to extract Hpakant's jade, mining practices have become increasingly destructive.

Today the countryside around Hpakant has been reduced to a hellish moonscape; once forested hills have been reduced to heaps of tailings, and in the town itself prostitution, drug abuse and even murder are all on the increase. It is impossible for foreigners to get beyond Nyaung Bin at the northern tip of Indawgyi Lake without tough-to-score permits, but the extent of the mines is visible even on Google Earth. In 2013 it was reported that 43,000 tonnes of jadeite worth $8 billion was exported from Myanmar in 2011/12, less than 0.05 percent of which went through official channels – it's clear that somebody somewhere is making a lot of money from Hpakant's misery.

ACCOMMODATION AND EATING

While Hopin has plenty of food options, the choice around Indawgyi Lake is much more limited – prepare for oodles of noodle-based meals in Lonton and the other lakeside villages. The only accommodation at the lake itself is in Lonton, with single travellers staying for half-price at both guesthouses.

HOPIN

Hopin Star Pyay Doung Su Rd ☎ 074 62261. The only foreigner-friendly accommodation in Hopin, this place is useful if your train arrives too late to make it out to Lonton. There's little English spoken, but the owners are friendly and the simple rooms with shared bathrooms aren't terrible. There are also a few rooms with en suite (K10,000). Breakfast is not included. <u>K8000</u>

LONTON

In Daw Ma Ha Guesthouse ☎ 09 3615 2269. This very basic guesthouse by the side of the lake has six simple rooms with mosquito nets, cold bucket showers and a few hours' electricity each evening. Breakfast isn't included but the kindly owner will ply you with all the coffee-mix you can drink. Trucks from Lonton will drop you outside. <u>K14,000</u>

Indawa Guesthouse This little family-run place is the closest thing in Lonton to an official guesthouse, and their three rooms are occasionally occupied by people attached to the small military camp next door – there's no telephone though, so you'll need to cross your fingers and turn up on spec. <u>$20</u>

The far north

Located at the point where the subtropical rainforests of Southeast Asia abut the Himalayas, Myanmar's thickly forested northern tip is a hotspot of biodiversity – a treasure-trove of endangered and endemic species. These mysterious hills are also home

---

THE TARON

With an average height of just 129cm, Asia's only pygmies – the **Taron** – live in the hills of Naung Mun Township outside Putao. When the community was first surveyed in the 1960s, Burmese researchers discovered just fifty pureblooded Taron left. Even then, mental and physical disabilities – the result of inbreeding – were rife. By 2005 the population had dwindled to just four individuals following the Taron's decision, en masse, simply to stop having children rather than risk future generations suffering ever more severe birth defects or diluting their tribe's genes by marrying outsiders. They thus effectively made themselves one of the planet's most endangered human populations.

This particular story, however, may yet have a happy ending. In 2009 genetic links were discovered between the Taron and the diminutive Dulong, who live in the area around China's Dulong River. The youngest pure Taron, a 111cm-tall man named Dawi, now in his early fifties, plans to travel to China in hope of finding a Dulong bride.

to Asia's shortest people (and the only true Mongoloid pygmies), the **Taron** (see box opposite), and Southeast Asia's tallest mountain, **Hkakabo Razi** (5881m), which was summited for the first time in 1996 by a Burmese–Japanese team.

The far north is home to a slew of Myanmar's wildlife sanctuaries and national parks, including the world's largest tiger reserve in the **Hukaung Valley**. Unfortunately, in the latter case, the sanctuary's creation doesn't seem to have stopped logging companies and gold-miners from destroying the once rich natural environment, leaving scant evidence of the big cats it was created to protect. Happily, ecosystems elsewhere are more intact, making this area still your best chance of spotting wild animals.

Putao

ပူတာအိုမြို့

The small town of **PUTAO** is the gateway into this region, but at the time of writing it was only possible to access it as a paid-up member of a tour (with permits taking three weeks to process; see box, p.26), or as a guest of the eye-wateringly expensive (and crony-owned) *Malikha Lodge*. Once a Shan stronghold, and subsequently known by the British as **Fort Hertz**, the town has a market, a sprinkling of pagodas and plenty of enticing views of distant mountains.

Excursions out of Putao range from two-day trips to nearby Kachin villages to multi-day whitewater rafting trips and the twelve-day round-trip hike to **Phongun Razi**, at 3635m the region's most accessible trekking peak. Once out of Putao, the only accommodation options are wild camping and the occasional village house.

ARRIVAL AND DEPARTURE PUTAO

By air Given uber-crony Tay Za's investments in Putao (see box, p.43), it's unsurprising that his Air Bagan airline is also your best bet for getting to the town, with several scheduled flights each week from Putao to Mandalay via Myitkyina. Air KBZ, Myanma Airways and Yangon Airways occasionally organize charter flights when there are enough bookings.

Destinations Mandalay (3 weekly; 2hr 20min); Myitkyina (5 weekly; 50min).

ACCOMMODATION

Malikha Lodge Mulashidi Village ☎09 860 0659, ⓦmalikhalodge.net. In an isolated setting a 12km drive from Putao, the rooms at this genuinely stunning Tay Za-owned property are housed in thatched cabins complete with log-burning stoves and an on-site spa. Service is excellent, and the food selection is limited but good – perhaps not as good as you'd expect at these prices, but given the location maybe that's understandable. Room rates (minimum two-night stay; prices quoted are per person for two nights) include hotel transfers, day-trips and all meals. Open Oct–April. $3000

★**Putao Trekking House** 424/425 Htwe San Lane ☎09 840 0138, ⓦputaotrekkinghouse.com. Pricewise this is the closest thing in Putao to a budget hotel. Accommodation is in tastefully decorated wooden bungalows with small verandas, private bathrooms and fires for warmth in both the dining room and on the outdoor deck. The largely Kachin staff also organize a good range of tours – full details on their useful website. Closed June–Oct. $120

BURMESE SCRIPT

Contexts

History

Myanmar's past reflects its unique geographical location at the cultural watershed between China, Southeast Asia and the Indian subcontinent, and the country has been buffeted throughout its history by the rival claims of competing kingdoms and cultures – not to mention the conflicting demands of its numerous ethnic groups and the traumatic effects of colonial occupation. Myanmar's tendency to disintegrate into competing kingdoms (often divided along ethnic lines) has been a repeated feature of its history, like a kind of tropical Yugoslavia, and the threat of imminent Balkanization continues to hang over the country right up to the present day.

Physically, Myanmar grew up around its great river valleys, particularly the mighty **Ayeyarwady** – a cradle of civilization every bit as impressive as the Ganges, Indus or Nile. Culturally, the unifying effect of **Theravada Buddhism** has played a major role in uniting Bamar, Mon and other Burmese peoples throughout their history, although significant Christian and Muslim minorities remain.

Written **records** of early Burmese history are slight – much of what is known about the Pyu – the first recorded settlers – for example, comes from Chinese annals (and the now extinct Pyu language itself wasn't deciphered until the early twentieth century) – while even some quite basic assumptions about Burmese history have been repeatedly questioned. Many details remain politically charged to this day (the exact role of the Mon in the development of the Bagan Empire, for example). Early **dates** can also be problematic – two different dating systems exist for the rulers of Bagan, for instance, meaning that sources don't always agree.

Prehistory

The first modern humans, **Homo erectus**, are thought to have arrived in Myanmar as early as 750,000 BC, settling around the Ayeyarwady River. **Homo sapiens** appears to have been present in Myanmar since at least 11,000 BC, judging by archeological finds from the Padah-Lin Caves near Taunggyi, including pieces of charcoal, stone tools, fragments of bone and simple cave paintings in red ochre.

By 1500 BC, the inhabitants of Myanmar had spread along the Ayeyarwady and Chindwin rivers and out into the areas that now form Shan and Kachin states. Inhabitants of the copper-rich Shan hills had begun to smelt **bronze**, while in the river valleys the art of growing rice had also been mastered – although perhaps the most notable achievement of the early Burmese is to have been among the first people in the world to have domesticated the chicken. By 500 BC villages in the vicinity of modern Mandalay were producing **iron**, while there is also evidence of trade both locally and as far afield as China – a precursor of the human migrations from southern China into Myanmar that were to prove so crucial in the country's early development.

750,000 BC	11,000 BC	1500 BC	c.200 BC
Arrival of *Homo erectus* in Myanmar	Evidence of prehistoric settlement at Padah-Lin Caves	Early human settlement of Ayeyarwady River valley	Development of early Pyu city-states along northern Ayeyarwady River

HISTORY AND POLITICS IN MODERN MYANMAR

The history of Myanmar is a multi-faceted, complex and frequently controversial subject. The official government-sponsored narrative emphasizes Myanmar's status as a country forged out of a patchwork of disparate peoples joined together in the glorious cause of national unity, sovereignty and the greater good, while travelling around the country you'll probably notice posters and displays promulgating the "Three Main National Causes" promoted by the military rulers: "Non-disintegration of the Union/Non-disintegration of national solidarity/Perpetuation of Sovereignty".

Not surprisingly, official history tends to focus on the primacy of the country's Bamar majority and their role in building the modern nation state of Myanmar, while huge statues of the country's three great Bamar unifiers and nation-builders – Anawrahta, Bayinnaung and Alaungpaya – tower symbolically over the new capital of Naypyitaw. Such history inevitably tends to be written at the expense of smaller ethnic groups – the Mon, Shan, Rakhine, Kayin and many others – who have found themselves at the margins of the majority Bamar world-view, and whose cultures, languages and identities have been progressively swamped and suppressed.

Pyu city-states

Myanmar's recorded history begins with the arrival of the **Pyu** in the second century BC. Migrating south from Yunnan in southern China, the Pyu gradually settled along the northern Ayeyarwady valley, establishing a string of mutually independent city-states along local trade routes between China and India. Tang-dynasty Chinese annals record eighteen Pyu statelets including eight walled cities (each with twelve gates – one for each sign of the zodiac). The largest early Pyu city was at **Hanlin** (see p.318), although as the Pyu migrated south down the Ayeyarwady this was eventually eclipsed, in around the seventh or eight century, by **Sri Ksetra** (aka Thayekhittaya; see p.184).

Pyu civilization lasted roughly a thousand years – the "Pyu Millennium", as it's sometimes described – laying the foundations for the great Bagan Empire that would eventually succeed it and, by extension, much of the basis of modern Burmese culture. Religious and cultural ideas travelling north from India played a profound role in Pyu society. By the fourth century most Pyu had converted to a local form of "Ari Buddhism" (see p.355), while they also developed an alphabet based on the Indian Brahmi script and adapted architectural ideas from the subcontinent – Myanmar's first stupas, later to become the country's defining architectural and religious symbol, made their first appearance at Sri Ksetra.

Mon kingdoms

Meanwhile, the second of Myanmar's two major early civilizations was taking root in the south of the country. The first **Mon** peoples began to migrate into Lower Burma from the kingdom of Dvaravati (roughly equivalent to present-day Thailand) from the sixth century onwards (although some studies, particularly by Mon historians, claim that they arrived much earlier). Like the Pyu, the Mon established a series of miniature kingdoms and city-states, the most notable being at **Thaton** and **Bago** (aka Pegu), both founded in the ninth century.

c.700 AD	c. 825	832 & 835	849
Sri Ksetra (Thayekhittaya) emerges as main Pyu city in Ayeyarwady valley	Foundation of the Mon cities of Thaton and Bago in southern Myanmar	Bamar raiders from Yunnan attack Pyu settlements in northern Ayeyarwady valley	Bamar settlers establish Bagan

As in the Pyu city-states, the Mon traded extensively with India, and were strongly influenced by Indian culture and ideas. They were among the first peoples to convert to **Theravada Buddhism** and followed (at least to begin with) a relatively pure form of the religion – unlike the heterogeneous Ari Buddhism practised further north by the Pyu.

Bagan and the Bamars

The beginning of the end of the Pyu Millennium came in 832 with the arrival of a new wave of invaders and settlers who would subsequently become the nation's dominant ethnic group: the **Bamar** (see p.351). Following migratory routes first taken by the Pyu a thousand years previously, Bamar raiders descended upon the Ayeyarwady valley from the Nanzhao Kingdom in Yunnan, sacking the major Pyu city of Hanlin in 832 before returning in 835, raiding and pillaging further Pyu towns. Some of the invading Bamar appear to have brought their families with them and to have settled in the region. The exact details are vague, although what is known is that sometime in the mid-ninth century – the traditional date given is 849 – the Bamar settled and fortified the small town of **Bagan** (aka Pagan), located in a strategic location close to the confluence of the Ayeyarwady and Chindwin rivers in the middle of the old Pyu heartlands.

After their initial raids, the migration of the Bamar appears to have been a relatively peaceful affair – not so much an apocalyptic clash of cultures as a gradual merging of two related ethnic groups, Pyu and Bamar, both originally hailing from southern China and speaking similar Sino-Tibetan languages. Further Bamar from Nanzhao continued to arrive in the region during the ninth and tenth centuries, assimilating many aspects of the already thousand-year-old Pyu civilization. Bagan, meanwhile, gradually extended its authority over the surrounding plains and by 1044 had expanded to become the centre of its own sizeable statelet, covering an area stretching across the central plains as far as modern Mandalay, Meiktila and Magwe.

King Anawrahta and the rise of Bagan

The history of the Bagan Empire began in 1044 with the accession of **King Anawrahta** (aka Aniruddha; ruled 1044–78), who transformed Bagan from one of several minor kingdoms in Upper Burma into the pre-eminent power in the land. In doing so, he united most of the territories now comprising modern Myanmar into a single state and laid the foundations of the modern nation, at the same time establishing the primacy of the Bamar people within it.

Anawrahta began by strengthening Bagan's economic base, launching ambitious irrigation schemes whereby large swathes of formerly arid land were opened to new settlers. Canals were constructed and villages created, establishing the Bagan area as the rice bowl and commercial powerhouse of Upper Burma. Having consolidated Bagan's wealth and influence, Anawrahta gradually expanded the territory under his control. Formerly independent Pyu towns were taken under Bagan's rule, while expeditions were also sent south into Mon territories. The ruler of **Bago** submitted to Bagan's authority, while in 1057 the kingdom of **Thaton** (which had resisted Anawrahta's demands for tribute) was conquered, and its king, Manuha, taken back to Bagan as a captive.

The conquest of Thaton is traditionally seen as pivotal in the history of Bagan. Anawrahta, it is said, returned to Bagan with over 30,000 Mon slaves, including many

1044–77	1057	1174–1211
Bagan emerges as a major power during rule of King Anawrahta; Theravada Buddhism is established as the state religion of expanding Bagan Empire	Thaton falls to Bagan forces under King Anawrahta	Bagan Empire reaches its apogee under King Narapatisithu

craftsmen and artists, who would subsequently play a key role in helping create the thousands of flamboyant temples which survive to this day. Anawrahta's conversion to Theravada Buddhism by the Thaton-born monk **Shin Arahan** (see p.355) also proved crucial in establishing this branch of Buddhism as the country's dominant faith, as it continues to this day. Anawrahta also safeguarded the religion elsewhere in Southeast Asia by stopping the advance of the (then) Hindu Khmer, and helped to restart Theravada ordinations in Sri Lanka, whose Buddhist monasteries had been destroyed by the Indian Cholas.

Age of empire

The following two centuries marked the golden age of Bagan, led by a succession of capable rulers who continued Anawrahta's grandiose building works at home and conquests abroad, establishing the Bagan dynasty as one of the two great Southeast Asian powers, rivalled only by the Khmer Empire of Angkor.

Anawrahta was succeeded by his eldest son, **Sawlu** (ruled 1078–84), whose brief reign ended when he was killed during a rebellion in the south. Sawlu was succeeded in turn by Anawrahta's second son, **Kyansittha** (ruled 1084–1112), and Kyansittha's grandson, **Alaungsithu** (aka Sithu I; ruled 1112–67), both of whom continued to push back the frontiers of the Bagan Empire while launching into ever more spectacular temple-building projects at home. Alaungsithu was murdered by his homicidal son, **Narathu** (ruled 1167–71; see box, p.200), who was himself assassinated shortly afterwards. Order was restored under **Narapatisithu** (ruled 1174–1211), under whom the empire reached its greatest geographical extent, stretching south to the Malay peninsula and east into present-day Thailand.

The period also saw the emergence of a new and distinctive **Bamar culture**. Bagan's temple architecture began to develop its own distinctive flavour, transcending earlier Mon and Pyu models, while Burmese script became the primary vehicle for the written language, displacing Mon and Pyu scripts. The region's ethnic Pyu increasingly merged with the Bamar majority, during which their language died out and their legends and histories were appropriated by the rulers of Bagan.

Decline and fall

A further four decades of peace and stability followed under Narapatisithu's successors, the devout but ineffectual **Htilominlo** (ruled 1211–35), the last of Bagan's great temple builders, and his successor **Kyazwa** (ruled 1235–50). The empire's former dynamism had been lost, however. Revenues remained static, while expenses continued to rise, as kings and nobles continued their attempts to accrue religious merit by endowing yet more temples and monastic foundations – by 1280, it's estimated, as much as two-thirds of Upper Burma's available agricultural land had been donated to the Buddhist clergy, effectively destroying the rulers' own revenues.

The agents of change came, once more, from the northeast. In 1271, and again in 1273, the **Mongol** armies of Kublai Khan demanded tribute of King **Narathihapate** (ruled 1256–87; see p.204) and, when this was refused, launched a series of attacks against the northern Bagan provinces in 1277, 1283 and 1287, moving progressively southwards on each occasion, eventually reaching Bhamo. Narathihapate fled south and was subsequently murdered, at which point many of the empire's tributary states,

1287	1300 onwards	1364	1369
Mongol invasion leads to the collapse of Bagan Empire	Emergence of independent Shan States in northeastern Myanmar, and the Hanthawaddy Kingdom in the south	Foundation of the Kingdom of Ava	The Hanthawaddy Kingdom establishes its new capital at Bago

including Arakan and the southern Mon territories, rebelled and declared independence. Almost overnight, the great empire of Bagan had ceased to exist.

A period of confusion ensued. The Mongols moved still further south into Tagaung, north of Mandalay (although it appears they possibly never reached Bagan itself), but showed no signs of wishing to permanently occupy the lands of the empire whose demise they had just precipitated. A new king, **Kyawswa** (ruled 1289–97), appeared in Bagan, although real power was held by three local brothers and former military commanders – Athinhkaya, Yazathingyan and Thihathu. Kyawswa submitted to Mongol authority and was recognized as governor of Bagan in 1297, only to be promptly overthrown by the three brothers, who proceeded to found the short-lived **Myinsaing Kingdom**. The Mongols despatched yet another force to reinstate Kyawswa, but this was beaten back, and Mongol forces finally left Myanmar for the final time in 1303, never to return.

Bagan, meanwhile, had been reduced from a once flourishing city of 200,000 people to an unimportant town. Further descendants of Anawrahta continued to rule as local governors owing allegiance to subsequent kingdoms until 1369, but the town itself would never regain its former political pre-eminence.

After Bagan: the successor kingdoms

The collapse of Bagan left a power vacuum in Myanmar during which a series of smaller successor kingdoms – **Ava**, the **Shan States**, the **Mon** territories and **Arakan** – jostled for pre-eminence over a period of almost three centuries before the rise of the next great Burmese dynasty, the kingdom of Taungoo.

Ava

The remains of Bagan itself mutated, via the Myinsaing Kingdom and other local fiefdoms (including the Pinya and Sagaing statelets, which had emerged following the collapse of Bagan), into the **Kingdom of Ava**, the dominant power in Upper Burma for almost two centuries. Based in the city of Ava (at Inwa, near Mandalay; see p.284), the dynasty was founded by King Thadominbya, an ethnic Shan, in 1364. Despite their non-Bamar origins, Thadominbya and his successors regarded themselves as descendants and rightful heirs to the kings of Bagan and fought a series of wars in an attempt to reconquer former Bagan territories, although with only partial success. Long battles against the Mon, in particular, exhausted and impoverished the kingdom. The **Forty Years' War** (1385–1424) against the southern kingdom of Hanthawaddy (see p.334) took a particular toll, as did attacks on Ava by the Shan States, which succeeded in conquering Ava itself in 1527. The enfeebled kingdom never recovered, and in 1555 was toppled once again by the armies of the emerging Taungoo dynasty.

The Shan States

Yet another people from Yunnan in southern China, the **Shan** had been moving down into northern Myanmar from at least the tenth century, establishing a series of minor kingdoms, at first under the authority of Bagan, and then, following the Mongol invasion of 1287, independently. Shan rulers gained increasing power during the two centuries after the fall of Bagan, establishing the Kingdom of Ava (see above) as well as a series of

1385–1424	**1430**	**1510**	**1527**
Repeated clashes between the Ava and Hanthawaddy kingdoms during the Forty Years' War	Mrauk U becomes capital of the Kingdom of Arakan	Foundation of the first Taungoo dynasty	Shan forces capture the city of Ava

other Shan states including Mohnyin (Mong Yang) and Mogaung (Mong Kawng) in present-day Kachin State, along with Thibaw (Hsipaw), Theinni (Hsenwi), Momeik (Mong Mit) and Kyaingtong (Kengtung) in what is now Myanmar's northern Shan State.

Hanthawaddy

Meanwhile in the south, the Mon territories had reasserted their independence immediately after the fall of Bagan, establishing the **Hanthawaddy Kingdom** (aka "Hanthawaddy Bago" or "Ramannadesa"), a loose confederation of three semi-independent statelets – **Bago** (Bago), **Mottama** (formerly known as Martaban), near present-day Mawlamyine, and the **Ayeyarwady Delta**. The kingdom's first capital was at Mottama, but it was moved to Bago in 1369. After repulsing Ava in the Forty Years' War, the Hanthawaddy enjoyed a miniature gold age, growing rich from trade with India and becoming a major centre of Mon language and literature, and also Theravada Buddhism – as witnessed by the numerous pagodas which still dot Bago to this day.

Arakan

In the far west of the Myanmar, the kingdom of **Arakan** (modern-day Rakhine State) had already been in existence for centuries (see box, p.115), squeezed between the Bagan Empire on one side and the Bengal Sultans on the other. Arakan suffered repeated attacks by the rulers of Ava following the collapse of Bagan, finally repulsing only during the reign of King Narameikhla (aka Min Saw Mon; ruled 1429–33), who founded the kingdom of **Mrauk U** in 1429 with military assistance from the Sultanate of Bengal. Indian influence was strong: in return for their help, Narameikhla recognized Bengali sovereignty over the kingdom and also ceded territory to the sultan. Close links with Bengal also led to the arrival of many Indian Muslims, perhaps the ancestors of the modern **Rohingya** (see box, p.116).

The first Taungoo empire

In the end, the second great pan-Burmese empire came from an unexpected direction. The kingdom of Ava was gradually crumbling in the face of repeated Shan attacks, and in 1510 the minor statelet of **Taungoo** (often spelt "Toungoo") in the far south of the Ava kingdom rebelled against its Ava rulers under the leadership of King Mingyinyo (ruled 1510–30), inaugurating the first Taungoo dynasty. Following the Shan conquest of Ava in 1527, many ethnic Bamar fled to Taungoo, now the only independent kingdom under Bamar rule, but menaced by much larger and more powerful states – Shan, Arakanese and Mon – on all sides.

Nothing daunted, Taungoo ruler **King Tabinshwehti** (ruled 1530–50) set out to expand his territories, taking on and eventually defeating his southern neighbours in the Taungoo–Hanthawaddy War (1535–41) and subsequently moving his capital to newly conquered Bago in 1539. By 1544 Taungoo forces had taken control of the country as far north as Bagan but failed in later campaigns against Arakan and the Thai city of Ayutthaya, leading to Tabinshwehti's assassination in 1550.

It was left to Tabinshwehti's former military commander and successor, the legendary **King Bayinnaung** (ruled 1550–81), to restore the fortunes of the struggling kingdom. Born (it's said) the son of a lowly toddy-tapper, Bayinnaung succeeded by force of

1531–54	1535–41	1550–81
The Kingdom of Mrauk U reaches its apogee under King Minbin	Taungoo forces overrun Mon territory during the Taungoo–Hanthawaddy War, moving their capital to Bago in 1539	The Taungoo Empire reaches its apogee during the reign of King Bayinnaung

character and military prowess in rising through the ranks. Following the assassination of the former king, he succeeded in beating off a series of rivals, laying siege to Taungoo and ultimately claiming the throne.

Having quelled dissension at home, Bayinnaung set out on a series of ambitious campaigns which brought a swathe of far-flung regions under the rule of Taungoo. Ava and the Shan States were conquered, along with further-flung territories including Ayutthaya, Manipur (in what is now northeastern India) and the Lao state of Lan Xang – establishing the largest and most powerful kingdom in Southeast Asia of its time.

Not surprisingly, the kingdom struggled to outlast the death of Bayinnaung, and by 1597 all the Taungoo dynasty's former possessions (including, ironically, their former home city of Taungoo itself) had rebelled, while in 1599 Arakanese soldiers sacked Bago.

Back in Arakan: the rise of Mrauk U

Meanwhile, back in the west, **Arakan** had remained subordinate to Bengal until 1531 and the arrival of Mrauk U's greatest king, **Minbin** (aka Min Pa Gyi; ruled 1531–54). After seizing the throne, Minbin took advantage of a weakened Bengal Sultanate, sending an army of 12,000 to claim large swathes of what is now Bangladesh and celebrating his victory with the construction of the landmark Shittaung Paya, the first of Mrauk U's great temples.

Even after recovering their independence, Arakanese Buddhist rulers continued to style themselves as "sultan", and court fashions were widely modelled on those at the Islamic Sultanate of Bengal. Mrauk U's uniquely multicultural kingdom was also the first part of Myanmar to experience the full impact of Western traders and invaders, suffering repeated attacks from Portuguese mercenaries as well as hosting a large community of Arab and European merchants.

Threats from the Portuguese and from the emerging Kingdom of Taungoo remained an ever-present danger during the reigns of Minbin's successors. Min Phalaung (ruled 1572–93) was obliged to fight off a major invasion by Taungoo in 1580–81, while his successor Min Razagyi (ruled 1593–1612) managed to defeat Taungoo forces in 1599 and even succeeded in sacking the Taungoo capital of Bago itself.

The empire strikes back

Reports of the demise of the Taungoo dynasty turned out to be somewhat premature. Following Arakan's sack of Bago in 1599, the empire revived dramatically under Bayinnaung's son, **Nyaungyan** (ruled 1599–1606), who by the end of his reign had regained control of much of northern Myanmar and the Shan States, ushering in the so-called **Restored Taungoo Dynasty** (aka the Nyaungyan dynasty). His son and successor, **Anaukpetlun** (ruled 1606–28), further reasserted Taungoo's control over large parts of Myanmar as well as defeating the army of Filipe de Brito e Nicote, the rogue Portuguese ruler of Thanlyin (see p.80), in 1613. The old city of Ava became the capital of the kingdom from 1599 to 1613, after which it was returned to Bago until 1635 before once again returning to Ava, where it remained.

Almost a century of relative peace and stability followed until the 1720s and 1730s, during which period growing external pressures led to the empire's slow disintegration.

1555	1599	1606–28
Taungoo dynasty forces conquer and destroy the Kingdom of Ava	King Min Razagyi of Mrauk U sacks the Taungoo Empire capital of Bago; the Taungoo dynasty establishes a new capital at Ava	Armies of the Restored Taungoo Dynasty under King Anaukpetlun reconquer large areas of the former Taungoo Empire

Raiders from Manipur began encroaching along the Upper Chindwin valley while Taungoo's Thai provinces in Lan Na (Chiang Mai) also rebelled, and Qing-dynasty forces from China seized parts of Shan and Kachin states. Then, in 1740, the Mon also cast off the Taungoo yoke, founding the **Restored Hanthawaddy Kingdom** (with the support of the French). Not content with reasserting their own independence, Mon forces invaded northern Myanmar in 1751, assisted by Portuguese and Dutch mercenaries and using weapons supplied by the French. In 1752 they captured Ava itself, ending two and a half centuries of Taungoo rule.

The Konbaung dynasty

Scarcely had the Taungoo dynasty been erased from the face of Myanmar when the last of Myanmar's three great pre-colonial empires appeared in the shape of the **Konbaung dynasty** – which would eventually go on to wield control of the second-largest empire in Burmese history. The dynasty was founded in Shwebo, northwest of Mandalay, in 1752 by one Aung Zeya, a village chief who refused to accept the authority of the new Restored Hanthawaddy rulers in Ava. His initial territory was small – just 46 villages – but Aung Zeya had himself crowned nonetheless, taking the name **King Alaungpaya** (ruled 1752–60). Three attempts by Hanthawaddy forces to capture Shwebo were repulsed and growing numbers of recruits arrived to fight for Alaungpaya's anti-Hanthawaddy cause. By early 1754 he had acquired sufficient forces to recapture Ava and to drive out all Hanthawaddy forces from northern Myanmar.

The conflict had by now acquired an increasingly ethnic dimension: a possibly decisive battle between the Mon south and the Bamar north. Hanthawaddy persecution of Bamar living in Mon lands played directly into Alaungpaya's hands, and in 1755 he struck south, taking control of the Ayeyarwady all the way down to the small town of Dagon, which he renamed **Yangon** – only to be brought to a halt by French forces defending the port city of Thanlyin. A fourteen-month siege ensued before the city finally capitulated, after which Konbaung forces marched to Bago, capturing and sacking the city in 1757, signalling the demise of the Hanthawaddy dynasty – and, indeed, the end of the very last independent Mon kingdom in Myanmar, a blow from which the Mon people, culture and language have yet to recover.

Following the capture of Bago, various territories including Chiang Mai and other Thai provinces that had once formed part of the Taungoo Empire sent tribute to Alaungpaya, as did the governor of Mottama in the south. Konbaung forces also recaptured former Taungoo territory in the northern Shan and eastern Kachin states taken by the Qing dynasty in the 1730s, while Manipur was overrun in 1756. Scarcely had Alaungpaya finished fighting in the north, however, when a Mon rebellion broke out in the south, with Thai backing. In 1759 Alaungpaya led an army of forty thousand men into southern Myanmar before heading east, eventually reaching and laying siege to the Thai capital at Ayutthaya in April 1760. Just a few days into the siege, however, Alaungpaya suddenly fell ill and died, and Konbaung forces retreated back into Myanmar.

Ayutthaya again

The brief reign of Alaungpaya's son and successor **Naungdawgyi** (ruled 1760–63) was plagued by further rebellions – in Ava, Taungoo, Mottama and Chiang Mai – and it

1635	**1740**	**1752**
The Dutch East India Company establishes a trading base at Mrauk U	The Mon rebel against their Taungoo rulers, founding the Restored Hanthawaddy Kingdom	Mon armies of the Hanthawaddy Kingdom capture Ava, signalling the end for the Taungoo dynasty; King Alaungpaya founds the Konbaung dynasty

was left to his younger brother, the formidable **Hsinbyushin** (ruled 1763–76), to complete Alaungpaya's expansionist work. Having moved the Konbaung capital to a newly rebuilt Ava in 1765, Hsinbyushin conquered the Lao kingdoms of Vientiane and Luang Prabang and then led his armies east, slowly fighting his way south to the Thai capital of **Ayutthaya** in 1766. A fourteen-month siege ensued before the city finally fell. Kongbaung forces proceeded to devastate what was then one of Asia's largest and most magnificent cities, taking thousands of captives back to Myanmar.

Thai forces succeeded in recapturing most of their lost territory over the next few years. Ayutthaya, however, never recovered, and the Thai capital was subsequently moved to a new location, later to become known as Bangkok.

The return of the Chinese

Meanwhile, just as Konbaung forces were marching towards Ayutthaya, the Chinese launched successive invasions of their own into northeastern Myanmar. The first two were repulsed, but in late 1767 a Chinese army of fifty thousand defeated Konbaung forces at the **Battle of Goteik Gorge** and marched south to within 50km of Ava. Stretched perilously thin, Hsinbyushin finally recalled his armies from Thailand, eventually beating off the Chinese at the **Battle of Maymyo** in 1768 and repulsing yet another invasion the following year.

Hsinbyushin's achievement in simultaneously taking Ayutthaya while holding off the Chinese is often considered one of the greatest strategic feats in Burmese history, although the increasingly militarized nature of the Konbaung state and the cost of endless wars had its inevitable effect. The now ever-present Chinese threat, a resurgent Thailand, endless rebellions in Manipur and (in 1773) another Mon rebellion all conspired to cast a major shadow over the king's achievements, as did the wanton destruction of Ayutthaya, the root of widespread anti-Burmese sentiments which persist in Thailand right up to the present day.

Bodawpaya and the fall of Mrauk U

Hsinbyushin's successor, **King Singu** (aka Singu Min; ruled 1776–82), largely put an end to his father's endless wars, ceding Chiang Mai province (which had by then been a Burmese possession for most of the past two centuries) to Thailand in 1776. He was succeeded by his uncle (and King Alaungpaya's fourth son), **Bodawpaya** (ruled 1782–1819), who moved the capital to Amarapura (see p.282) and also commissioned the lunatic Mingun Pagoda, which would have been the world's largest stupa had it ever been finished (see p.287). Bodawpaya launched two further (unsuccessful) attacks against Thailand, although it was in the west that his forces had their most notable success, particularly in 1784, when a Konbaung army captured the great city of **Mrauk U** – ending the golden age of Arakan, and also bringing Konbaung rulers, for the first time, into direct contact with the British in neighbouring India.

The arrival of the British

By the beginning of the nineteenth century, European adventurers and traders had already been sniffing around Myanmar for over two centuries. Portuguese mercenary Filipe de Brito e Nicote (see p.80) had carved out his own personal fiefdom back in

1754	1755	1757
Konbaung forces under Alaungpaya capture Ava and drive Mon armies out of northern Myanmar	Konbaung forces take the town of Dagon, which is renamed Yangon	Hanthawaddy, capital of Bago, falls to Konbaung armies, marking the end of Myanmar's last independent Mon kingdom

1603 in the port of Thanlyin while the **Dutch East India Company** had established a trading base in Mrauk U in 1635. Later, in the 1740s, the **French East India Company** established their own HQ in Thanlyin, supplying arms to the local Mon during their rebellion against the Taungoo Empire.

The first **British** presence in Myanmar was the small colony of **Cape Negrais**, at the far southwestern corner of the Ayeyarwady Delta, established in 1753 following the collapse of the Taungoo Empire – although it was destroyed by Konbaung soldiers in 1759, after which relations between the two nations remained strained.

The First Anglo-Burmese War

Bodawpaya's capture of Mrauk U in 1784, and his subsequent seizure of Assam in 1816, created a long and only vaguely defined border between Konbaung territories and British India. Clashes were inevitable, given the British desire to neutralize what was seen as growing French influence at the Konbaung court, and also to seize more of the border territories for themselves. After some preliminary skirmishes, war – the **First Anglo-Burmese War**, as it's now known – was officially declared in March 1824.

Led by **General Mahabandoola** (see p.61), Burmese forces enjoyed some spectacular early successes in Arakan thanks to their greater experience of jungle warfare. The British countered by sending a large naval division to attack Yangon, causing the local population to flee. Eventually, in November, the rival armies met outside Yangon. British forces resisted repeated attacks by the numerically superior but poorly armed Burmese, who were cut down in their thousands and then forced back into the small town of Danubyu. At the same time, a counteroffensive was launched against Konbaung troops still in Arakan. On March 29, 1825, British forces simultaneously attacked Danubyu, killing Mahabandoola, and captured the Arakan capital, Mrauk U. The war was effectively over. An armistice was subsequently declared, and although Konbaung troops attempted a daring counterattack against British troops in Pyay in November, they too were defeated and forced to sign the humiliating **Treaty of Yandabo** (1826). Under this, the Konbaung were obliged to cede Arakan, Manipur and Assam in the west and a large slice of territory in Tenasserim (modern Tanintharyi) in the far south, as well as paying a colossal indemnity of £1 million.

The Second Anglo-Burmese War

The effect of the conflict on both Konbaung finances and morale was devastating, with the empire left economically crippled and its leaders in disarray. **King Bagyidaw** (ruled 1819–37), relocated the capital to Ava in 1823 but became increasingly reclusive and ineffectual following the disastrous war. He was overthrown by **Tharrawaddy** (ruled 1837–46) who continued to plot fruitlessly against the British, and then by his son **Pagan Min** (1848–53).

The origins of the **Second Anglo-Burmese War** (1852) were little more than a minor diplomatic squabble after the captains of two British merchant ships were detained in Bago on charges of customs violations. The British, seeing a chance of making further inroads into Burmese territory, blew the incident up out of all reasonable proportion, demanding a staggering £100,000 in compensation, blockading Yangon harbour, shelling the city and provoking a conflict in which the odds were stacked very heavily in their favour.

1760	1766	1783	1784
Death of Alaungpaya during the siege of Ayutthaya	Siege and sack of Ayutthaya by Konbaung armies under King Hsinbyushin	King Bodawpaya establishes a new Konbaung capital at Amarapura	Konbaung forces sack the city of Mrauk U and take possession of Arakan

A very one-sided war ensued, with overwhelmingly superior British forces encountering only modest Burmese resistance. Mottama, Yangon and Pathein were all seized within less than a fortnight in April, with Bago following in June and Pyay in October. The British issued a "Proclamation of Annexation" stating that it was taking possession of Bago and the lower half of the country up to Pyay. Konbaung humiliation was complete.

King Mindon
The Second Anglo-Burmese War had at least one positive side effect for the Konbaung dynasty. Following the conclusion of hostilities, King Pagan Min was dethroned in favour of his half brother **Mindon** (ruled 1853–78). The most progressive of all Konbaung rulers, Mindon saw the urgent need to modernize what was left of his country, sending envoys to Europe and the US to learn about technological developments while enacting numerous reforms at home aimed at reducing corruption and modernizing the national army. He also founded a new royal capital at **Mandalay** in 1857, introduced Myanmar's first machine-made currency and encouraged trade with Britain by acquiring steamers after the opening of the Suez Canal.

The Third Anglo-Burmese War
Mindon died in 1878 and was succeeded by his son, **Thibaw** (ruled 1878–85). The British soon became concerned at Thibaw's attempts to ally himself with the French, while relations were further strained following the so-called "Great Shoe Question", when British officials who refused to remove their shoes before entering the royal palace were banished from Mandalay.

The tipping point arrived in 1885, when a dispute over logging rights was used as an excuse by the British to insist on further concessions from King Thibaw – demanding not only that they to all intents be given a free commercial hand throughout Myanmar, but also that Britain take control of all Burmese foreign policy decisions, effectively surrendering national sovereignty and making Burma a British colony. Faced with an impossible situation, King Thibaw granted all British demands bar the surrender of sovereignty.

Thibaw's many concessions notwithstanding, the British parliament decided that the moment for the annexation of the last remaining piece of independent Myanmar had finally arrived. The resultant **Third Anglo-Burmese War** was even shorter and more one-sided than the second. British troops advanced on Mandalay virtually unopposed, seized the palace and despatched Thibaw into exile in India (just as the last Mughal emperor of India had been sent by the British into exile in the opposite direction; see p.69).

Colonial Burma
Now in complete and undisputed control of the country, the British set about remodelling their new possession in their own image, with **Burma** (as it was now known) being administered – rather insultingly – as a province of British India. **Rangoon** (as Yangon, already the principal city of British southern Burma, had become known) became the new national capital, developing into one of the British Empire's

1824–25	1852	1853
First Anglo-Burmese War: the British seize Arakan, Manipur, Assam and much of southern Myanmar	Second Anglo-Burmese War: the whole of southern Myanmar falls to the British, who establish a new capital at Yangon (Rangoon)	King Mindon assumes power, initiating wide-reaching reforms in an attempt to modernize the country

great imperial showcases with its alien, European-style courthouses, clocktowers and doughty red-brick edifices.

The opening of the Suez Canal in 1869 had greatly increased the demand for Burmese rice and large new areas of countryside were reclaimed and opened up for cultivation, particularly in the formerly swampy, disease-ridden and mangrove-choked lowlands of the Ayeyarwady Delta. Relatively little of the country's burgeoning wealth found its way to the Burmese themselves, however. British firms controlled much of the nation's economy, while the plight of the country's native Burmese was further exacerbated by a massive influx of Indian merchants and labourers. Secular schools were established and Christian missionary activity encouraged. Improvements to the country's infrastructure also followed. Railways were built and the Irrawaddy Flotilla Company (see p.63) launched. Meanwhile, all signs of opposition to British rule were suppressed, with rebellious villages being razed to the ground and their leaders exiled, forcing many Burmese into banditry and other criminal activities.

The nationalist movement

By the turn of the twentieth century the first signs of organized nationalist resistance had already begun to emerge. As elsewhere in Asia, many leading anti-colonialists were young people educated in Europe who returned home demanding change through constitutional reform, rather than by taking up arms. In 1920, university students went on strike in protest at the new University Act (seen as privileging Myanmar's western-leaning, European-educated elite), while locally sponsored "National Schools" were created to counterbalance the colonial education system. The Buddhist clergy also played a leading role in anti-British protests – one of the first to speak out against colonial rule (particularly Christian missionary activity) was the remarkable Irish-born monk known as U Dhammaloka, while other prominent figures included U Ottama in Sittwe and U Wisara, who died in prison after a lengthy hunger strike.

The first major uprising was the **Saya San Rebellion** (1930–32), named after its leader, Saya San, who organized mass peasant protests, vowed to expel the British and had himself crowned king. The popular uprising was put down with considerable difficulty, after which Saya San and over a hundred other rebels were hanged.

The year 1930 also saw the creation of the **Thakin** movement (also known as the **Dobama Asiayone**, or "Our Burma", movement) – a nationalist group formed largely of students and operating mainly out of Rangoon University. The Thakins were instrumental in organizing a second university students' strike in 1936 to protest the expulsion from Rangoon University of a certain young **Aung San** and his colleague **U Nu**, both of whom would go on to play seminal roles in the history of the country.

Burma was uncoupled from India in 1937 and given a new constitution, including its own elected assembly and prime minister (although with limited actual powers). Despite these concessions, major protests erupted in 1938–39, leading to the so-called **1300 Revolution** (1300 being the Buddhist calendar equivalent to 1939). Strikes by employees of the Burmah Oil Company in the centre of the country developed into nationwide protests. The subsequent crackdown claimed 33 lives including thirteen unarmed protesters shot dead in Mandalay – a small but chilling foretaste of atrocities yet to come.

1885	**1920**	**1930**
Third Anglo-Burmese War: British forces seize the whole of Myanmar, which is now administered as a province of British India	University students strike in Rangoon in protest at colonial educational policies	Establishment of the nationalist Thakin movement by students at Rangoon University

World War II

Agitations for independence took a back seat, however, with the outbreak of **World War II**, during which Burma would become a pivotal region in the fight between Japanese, Allied and Chinese forces. Many nationalists saw the war as a chance to wring further concessions out of the British in return for Burmese help; others, including the Thakins, were resolutely opposed to any form of involvement in the fighting.

The rebellious young student **Aung San**, meanwhile, had given up his university studies in order to devote himself to the anti-colonial struggle and in 1940 was forced to flee Burma after the British issued a warrant for his arrest. He travelled to China, hoping to gain assistance from the Kuomintang government, but was intercepted by the Japanese authorities in Amoy, who offered their help instead. Aung San and 29 of his other fellow nationalists – the so-called "**Thirty Comrades**" (whose number also included future dictator Ne Win) – were subsequently taken by the Japanese to Hainan Island and given military training.

The Japanese occupation

Meanwhile, in Southeast Asia the war was advancing steadily closer to Burma. In November 1941 the Japanese forces invaded British-ruled Malaya and began moving into Thailand (which had signed a military alliance with Japan). Two months later, further Japanese forces (accompanied by the Thirty Comrades, including Aung San) moved through northern Thailand and into Tenasserim (Tanintharyi) in southern Burma, capturing Moulmein (Mawlamyine) after fierce fighting. Rangoon was evacuated in March 1942, there being insufficient troops available to defend the city, leaving the Japanese to enter unopposed. Allied troops retreated northwards and, after further fighting, were ordered to leave Burma for India. The Thai army, meanwhile, occupied Kayah and Shan States, as previously agreed in their treaty with the Japanese.

Many Burmese initially saw the Japanese – fellow Asians and Buddhists alike – as liberators come to help them shake off British rule, although it soon became obvious that the life under the Japanese was no better than it had been under the British – in fact quite possibly the opposite. The country was renamed the State of Burma and a puppet government installed, but real independence remained as distant as ever. Increasingly disgruntled, Aung San (who had served as war minister and head of the army in the Japanese-sponsored government) put himself and the Burmese National Army (of which he was now commander) at the service of the British.

The Allied counterattack

Allied attempts to retake Burma following the Japanese occupation were put on hold, the battles in Europe and the Middle East being considered of more pressing importance, while political disturbances and famine in Bengal were also tying up large numbers of troops. It was not until October 1943 that a combined force of British, Indian, African, American and Chinese soldiers began moving back into northern Burma. Progress through the jungles was slow and difficult, but by May 1944 the airfield at Myitkyina had been taken, establishing an air link with India and China. At the same time the Japanese launched a counterattack, attempting to drive through to Imphal, the capital of Manipur in British India, but their advance was halted at

1930–32	1939	1940
The Saya San Rebellion sees mass popular protests against colonial rule	Outbreak of World War II	Nationalist leader Aung San and the rest of the "Thirty Comrades" are given military training by the Japanese in preparation for overthrow of British rule

Kohima, and they were forced to retreat with heavy losses – most caused by disease, starvation and exhaustion.

The tide slowly turned. Japanese forces fell back from the Chindwin to the Ayeyarwady. Allied troops were sent into Rakhine while Chinese forces moved south to Bhamo, followed by a decisive push into central Burma, with the Allies now able to make the most of their superior numbers and air power in the flat central plains. **Meiktila** fell in March 1945 after a devastating battle during which most of the town was destroyed and almost every member of the Japanese garrison killed, while **Mandalay** was captured shortly afterwards, following further fierce fighting which left much of the historic old town in ruins. Simultaneously, the Burmese National Army led by Aung San rose up against the Japanese. Allied forces now proceeded with increasing speed towards **Rangoon**, following the rapidly repeating Japanese. Gurkha and Indian forces arriving in Rangoon on May 1 discovered that the Japanese had already abandoned the city and fled.

To independence

Four years of fighting had left the country in physical and economic tatters, with estimates of the number of civilians who died during the Japanese occupation ranging from 170,000 up to a quarter of a million. Following the Japanese surrender, the **Anti-Fascist Organisation (AFO)** – which Aung San had founded in 1944 along with others including future prime minister Ba Swe, socialist leader Thakin Soe, communist leader Than Tun and old student comrade U Nu – emerged as the leading mouthpiece for Burmese nationalist aspirations.

Two years of uncertainty followed, as the British attempted to stall demands for immediate independence and Burmese communists, socialists and conservatives manoeuvred for position. In January 1947 Aung San led an AFO team to London, signing an agreement with British prime minister Clement Attlee guaranteeing Burma independence within a year, while in February he convened the Panglong Conference, during which leaders of the Shan, Kachin and Chin (but not, notably, Kayin) agreed to form part of a future unified Burma. In general elections in April 1947, Aung San's **Anti-Fascist People's Freedom League** (AFPFL), as the AFO had now been renamed, won 176 out of 210 seats.

Aung San was by now firmly established as Burma's post-independence leader in waiting. Or would have been. On July 19, 1947, Aung San and the Executive Council of his provisional government were in a meeting at Rangoon's Secretariat when a group of gunmen stormed the rooms and **assassinated Aung San** along with six of his ministers. The attack was eventually traced to former colonial-era prime minister U Saw, who was subsequently hanged (although as with the assassination of another national political hero, American John F. Kennedy fifteen years later, conspiracy theories continue to abound; many suggest British involvement, while others point to the hand of future military ruler Ne Win).

The catastrophic effect of Aung San's death on Burma can hardly be overestimated, given his status as the one leader who might have been capable of uniting the country's widely divergent peoples, and it's often speculated how much more peaceful the country's subsequent history might have been, had he lived.

1941	1943	1947
Japanese forces invade and capture Myanmar	Allied forces reconquer Myanmar, aided by Aung San and other nationalist leaders disillusioned with Japanese rule	Aung San signs an agreement with British authorities guaranteeing Burmese independence within a year, but is assassinated shortly afterwards

Independence and after

It was left to socialist leader (and Aung San's old university friend) **U Nu** to oversee **independence** on January 4, 1948, becoming post-colonial Burma's first prime minister. The country was immediately wracked by a series of armed insurgencies featuring a wide-ranging cast of communists, army rebels, Arakanese Muslims and Kayin militia. Then, from 1949, fleeing Kuomintang forces, recently driven out of China by Mao Zedong's communists, took over remote areas of the north (covertly supported by the US). Physical and economic reconstruction of the ravaged country continued apace, even so. Regular elections were held, with U Nu continuing as prime minister except for a brief period in 1956–57 when he was replaced by his communist-leaning AFPFL colleague, Ba Swe.

In 1958, the ruling AFPFL split into two factions led by U Nu and Ba Swe respectively, during which U Nu narrowly survived a vote of no confidence brought by Ba Shwe. U Nu subsequently "invited" army chief of staff General **Ne Win** to take over the country (some say he was coerced) until fresh elections were held. Ne Win duly obliged, taking the opportunity to arrest over four hundred alleged communist sympathizers and close three daily newspapers – a very modest taste of things to come.

Fresh elections in 1960 returned U Nu's faction of the AFPFL with a large majority, although Shan separatists almost immediately commenced agitating for independence. Faced with bickering politicians, closet communists and endless separatist uprisings by Myanmar's ethnic minorities, the army appears to have come to the conclusion that only strong leadership could save the country from disintegration. On March 2, 1962 Ne Win, along with sixteen other senior army officers, staged a **coup**, arresting U Nu and others and proclaiming the establishment of a socialist state to be run by a military-led revolutionary council, initiating a period of army rule which persists (albeit in neutered form) to this day. Myanmar's age of the generals had begun.

Ne Win and military rule

The coup itself was almost completely bloodless, while protests following the announcement of military rule were allowed to run their course until July 1962, when soldiers fired into a student protest at Rangoon University, killing over a hundred people. In March 1964 all opposition political parties were banned, and hundreds of activists arrested. Meanwhile, there were ongoing insurgencies by the **Kachin Independence Organization** (from 1961), and in 1964 a rebellion by the Shan State Army.

In response, Ne Win commenced slamming all Myanmar's doors on the rest of the world firmly shut. Around 15,000 private firms were nationalized, causing the economy to stagnate; foreign aid agencies and the World Bank were expelled; the study of English was cut back in schools; and visitors limited to 24-hour visas. The few Burmese who were allowed to travel were sent mainly to the Soviet Union for training; mass press censorship was put in place and foreign-language publications and privately owned newspapers banned. Over 200,000 expat Chinese, Indians and Westerners quit the country, along with almost the whole of the country's remaining Jewish population (see p.66).

More than a decade of isolation and underachievement passed. Ne Win retired from the army in 1974 but continued to run the country through the **Burma Socialist Programme Party** (BSPP), the nation's one and only officially recognized political

1948	**1958**	**1960**
Myanmar gains independence; U Nu becomes the country's first post-colonial leader	Faced with growing disorder, U Nu "invites" military leader Ne Win to take charge of the country pending fresh elections	U Nu wins the general election, but is unable to bring stability to country

GENERAL MADNESS

The despotic excesses of modern Myanmar's two leading generals, Ne Win and Than Shwe, have been widely reported. What is less well known is their quaint shared beliefs in antique superstitions and old wives' tales – some of which appear to have played a major role in shaping huge national policy decisions and other affairs of state.

Rumours abound concerning **Ne Win**'s (1910–2002) penchant for numerology and *yadaya* (see p.358). Warned by his astrologer of potential assassination attempts, the great dictator is said to have stood in front of a mirror, stamping on a piece of meat and then shot himself in the mirror in order to deflect the anticipated bloodshed. In 1987 he was also responsible for disastrous currency reforms during which new K45 and K90 notes (both divisible by nine, and said to be numerologically auspicious) replaced former high-denomination notes, wiping out the lifetime savings of many Burmese at a stroke – a decision which played a major role in the 8888 Uprising which erupted the following year.

Ne Win's successor **Than Shwe** (b.1933) was no less superstitious. The grandiose new multi-billion capital of Naypyitaw was established, it's rumoured, largely at his astrologers' say-so, while he is also thought to have indulged a weakness for many other forms of almost cabalistic superstition. On one occasion following the Saffron Revolution in 2007 – an incident entertainingly related in Emma Larkin's *Everything is Broken* (see p.363) – his wife Kyaing Kyaing is reported to have walked a pig and a dog counterclockwise around the Shwedagon Pagoda in a *yadaya* ritual aimed either at breaking the power of Aung San Suu Kyi and/or protecting Than Shwe's own family from a cowardly people (with pig and dog symbolizing either Aung San Suu Kyi or the backsliding Burmese populace – or possibly both). Whatever its intentions, Kyaing Kyaing's attempt at Buddhist black magic had little influence on subsequent events – although at least no animals appear to have been harmed in the making of this particular military fable.

organization. Further strikes and demonstrations took place in 1974, during which a further hundred-odd students and workers were shot, while in 1978 the army drove a quarter of a million Rohingya Muslims (see box, p.116) into Bangladesh.

Ne Win's disastrous currency reforms (see box above) in 1987 caused further suffering and provoked a further round of protests and riots, while new government policy forcing farmers to sell produce below market values (following on from the UN's decision in late 1987 to downgrade Myanmar to "Least Developed Country" status) led to further violent rural protests. Public letters written by Ne Win's former second in command General Brigadier Aung Gyi described Burma as "almost a joke" compared to other Southeast Asian countries. Not surprisingly, he was arrested soon afterwards.

The 8888 Uprising

Popular discontent at military rule finally erupted during the **8888 Uprising** (named after the key events which occurred on August 8, 1988). The initial spark for the uprising occurred in March 1988 when a student was shot dead by police following a trivial after-dark altercation in Yangon. Protests rapidly spread across the city's universities and several more students were killed during a protest at Inya Lake. By June, demonstrations had spread nationwide, with widescale unrest and numerous deaths in cities across the country.

1962	1962 onwards	1974
Ne Win leads a military coup and seizes power, announcing a new policy dubbed the "Burmese Way to Socialism"	Myanmar becomes increasingly impoverished and isolated under Ne Win's leadership	The first widespread protests against the military regime are brutally suppressed

Then, at the height of the crisis, Ne Win unexpectedly announced his retirement, promising a multi-party democracy in the near future but also stating, ominously, that "If the army shoots, it has no tradition of shooting into the air. It shoots straight to kill." Further protests ensued, including a huge nationwide demonstration and general strike starting on August 8, 1988, a day of numerological auspiciousness. Entire neighbourhoods of Yangon were taken over by demonstrators, which now included people from all realms of Burmese society including doctors, monks, lawyers, army veterans and government workers, causing police and army to retreat in the face of the sheer scale of the protests.

On August 26, Aung San's daughter, **Aung San Suu Kyi**, made her first public speech, addressing half a million people at the Shwedagon Pagoda, urging the people and army to work together peacefully and becoming, almost overnight, the defining symbol of the nation's struggle for democracy in Myanmar. Events seemed to be moving definitively in the protesters' favour. Dr Maung Maung, a legal scholar and the only non-military member of the junta's political mouthpiece, the BSPP, was appointed as head of government, offering the promise of imminent elections.

Then, on September 18, 1988, the military suddenly and decisively struck back, imposing martial law and breaking up protests with new and unprecedented brutality in the name of the newly established **State Law and Order Restoration Council (SLORC)**. The military once again assumed total control of the country, under the leadership of Ne Win protégé **General Saw Maung**. Troops roamed through cities nationwide, shooting randomly at protesters: over 1500 were murdered in the first week of SLORC rule alone. Aung San Suu Kyi appealed for international help, but within a few days the protests had been effectively crushed. As many as ten thousand Burmese are thought to have died in the uprising, with many more missing or fled. The prospect of a democratic Myanmar – which had seemed so tantalizingly close for one heady month in August – was now as far away as ever.

The rule of SLORC

The new SLORC leadership was widely condemned by international leaders for its role in crushing the demonstrations – the military responded by more than doubling the size of the army (from 180,000 to 400,000). Aung San Suu Kyi, meanwhile, responded to the failure of the uprising by founding the **National League for Democracy (NLD)**, which would henceforth serve as the principal vehicle for all anti-government protests. Offers by SLORC to hold elections were rejected by Aung San Suu Kyi on the grounds that they could not be held freely and fairly so long as the generals remained in power.

One of SLORC's first major acts after crushing the 8888 Uprising was to officially change the name of the country from Burma to **Myanmar** (see box, p.8). It also, surprisingly, announced the first elections in the country since 1960, designed to elect a quasi-parliamentary body which would draft a new constitution and provide a semblance of democracy. The generals, having indulged in widespread electoral manipulation and media control and placed all major opposition leaders (including Aung San Suu Kyi) under arrest, were thus horribly surprised when the **elections of May 1990** provided a landslide victory for Aung San Suu Kyi's NLD, winning 392 of the 492 seats available and trouncing the SLORC-sponsored National Unity Party (the successor to the BSPP). SLORC refused to recognize the election result.

1987	**August 1988**
Ne Win's numerologically inspired currency reforms wipe out the life savings of many Burmese	The 8888 Uprising sees mass nationwide protests against military regime; Ne Win resigns and Aung San Suu Kyi emerges as the figurehead of the democracy movement

AUNG SAN SUU KYI

The world's most famous former prisoner of conscience, **Aung San Suu Kyi** has for many years served as the human face of the Burmese freedom struggle – as synonymous with her country's democratic aspirations as Nelson Mandela was with the anti-Apartheid movement in South Africa.

Much of Aung San Suu Kyi's standing undoubtedly derives from her status as the daughter of the revered **Aung San** (1915–47), father of modern Myanmar (see p.340), although despite her illustrious parentage there was little in her early life to suggest the path she would later follow. Born in Yangon in 1945, Aung San Suu Kyi was just two when her father was assassinated and subsequently spent many of her younger years abroad, first in Delhi (where her mother, **Khin Kyi**, served as Burmese ambassador to India and Nepal) before studying at Oxford University, where she met her future husband, the late distinguished Asian scholar **Dr Michael Aris**. She subsequently worked for the UN in New York before marrying Aris in 1971. They spent their first year of married life in Bhutan (where Aris was tutor to the royal family), after which they returned to England, living in Oxford where Aris had been made a university lecturer. Meanwhile, Aung San Suu Kyi continued her studies at London University's School of Oriental and African Studies and also became the mother of two sons.

THE STRUGGLE BEGINS

The spectacular rise to global prominence of the formerly bookish and retiring wife of an Oxford don followed a remarkably serendipitous chain of events. In 1988, Aung San Suu Kyi returned to Yangon to care for her sick mother, who had been admitted to the Rangoon General Hospital. Within weeks of her return, Aung San Suu Kyi found herself caught up in the greatest popular uprising in modern Burmese history (see p.344), with the hospital itself at the epicentre of events. Swept along in the sudden political upheavals, she determined to devote herself to the fight for democracy, espousing **political beliefs** rooted in non-violent resistance, dialogue, reconciliation and inclusivity, which owed much to the ideas of Mahatma Gandhi as well as her own Buddhist faith. Her first official **public speech**, at the Shwedagon Pagoda, was attended by thousands of Burmese whose imaginations had been fired by the unexpected return of Aung San's own daughter at the hour of their greatest need, while opposition activists began to see in Aung San Suu Kyi the perfect figurehead for their aspirations – the daughter of the country's greatest national hero, and someone entirely untainted by former political or military connections.

Than Shwe

In April 1992 SLORC leader General Saw Maung "resigned" on health reasons – although rumours suggest he was effectively deposed by rival generals worried by his apparent willingness to hand over power to the NLD – and was succeeded by the second of Myanmar's two infamous military despots, **Than Shwe**. Than Shwe proved an apt successor to Ne Win – similarly ruthless and repressive, and totally lacking in personal charisma. A reclusive leader, he rarely made public appearances or spoke to the press and was believed to take many major decisions based on the advice of his astrologers (see box, p.344). He also enjoyed the trappings of wealth – a leaked video of his daughter Thandar Shwe's wedding in 2006 caused widespread outrage due to its ostentatious extravagance, with Thandar Shwe herself wearing diamonds worth millions of dollars at a time when (as now) most Burmese were still living in abject poverty.

Than Shwe relaxed some state controls on the economy (although without any significant beneficial effect), cracked down on corruption and, in 1997, led Myanmar into ASEAN (the Association of Southeast Asian Nations). Ceasefires were also

September 1988	1989
Founding of the National League for Democracy; protests are violently suppressed, with thousands killed by the military, who re-establish control under the newly established State Law and Order Restoration Council (SLORC)	The country's colonial-era name, Burma, is changed by military government to Myanmar

HOUSE ARREST

The 8888 Uprising itself was soon brutally crushed. Undeterred, Aung San Suu Kyi established the **National League for Democracy** (NLD) in September 1988 with former eminent generals turned regime opponents Aung Gyi and Tin Oo. Her newly launched political career was brought to an abrupt halt in July 1989, however, when she was placed under **house arrest** – the first in a long sequence of home detentions which would last for fifteen of the next 21 years. Her international profile, meanwhile, rose ever higher, cemented by the award of the Nobel Peace Prize in 1991. This Mother Teresa-like status in the West largely insulated her from criticism – and continues to do so to this day – although some questioned both the usefulness of Gandhian passive resistance in the face of brutal military rule and the NLD's isolationist stance, with its self-declared **tourism boycott** and support of ineffectual Western sanctions which (it's argued) served to plunge the country into further atrophy.

Brief periods of release from house arrest and attempts to travel the country were met with repeated military intimidation, most notably in 2003 when at least seventy NLD supporters travelling with Aung San Suu Kyi were killed in the **Depayin Massacre** in Sagaing. Meanwhile Aung San Suu Kyi herself was repeatedly caricatured in government media as a "Western poster girl" and "foreigner" thanks to her years abroad and UK-based family.

2010 AND AFTER

Aung San Suu Kyi was finally freed from house arrest in **November 2010** and immediately threw herself straight back into her political work – subsequently announcing her intention of running for president in the elections of 2015. The military, meanwhile (once again playing on her expatriate past), have conveniently inserted a clause in the constitution barring anyone with a foreign spouse or children from serving as president – legislation specifically aimed at denying her the chance of achieving the political office she would doubtless otherwise attain.

Curiously, since her release in 2010 Aung San Suu Kyi has shown notable signs of entering into a murkier sort of *Realpolitik*, hobnobbing with generals and government cronies, as well as singularly failing to speak up in support of the horribly oppressed Rohingya (see box, p.116). To what extent her idealistic beliefs survive prolonged contact with Burmese political realities remains to be seen, although for the time being she continues to provide a beacon of hope as the country emerges, slowly, from decades of military rule.

---

negotiated with Kachin and Shan rebels (although fighting against the Kayin would continue until 2012). Despite these modest reforms, spending on the army continued to soar even while investment in health and education remained among the lowest in the world. The junta was also accused of increasingly widespread and serious **human rights abuses**: as many as a million Burmese were shipped off to rural labour camps and forced to work unpaid on government projects, while there are also reports of hundreds, possibly thousands, of summary executions.

In 2003, **Kyin Nyunt**, the (relatively) moderate prime minister of the regime – now renamed the **State Peace and Development Council (SPDC)** – announced a seven-step "roadmap to democracy". A subsequent power struggle with Than Shwe saw him arrested – possibly on account of his apparent willingness to reach an agreement with the NLD – and stripped of power. Most surprising was the sudden announcement, in November 2005, that the national capital was to be moved to **Naypyitaw** – a huge new project dreamt up by Than Shwe, costing billions of dollars and confirming, in the eyes of many observers, the true scale of the generals' out-of-control megalomania.

1990	**1991**	**1992**
The National League for Democracy wins a landslide victory in general elections; the military refuse to recognize the results and confine Aung San Suu Kyi to house arrest	Aung San Suu Kyi is awarded the Nobel Peace Prize	Hardline general Than Shwe assumes leadership of the military government

The Saffron Revolution

The next major upheaval in Burmese society – the **Saffron Revolution** (as it has been named in honour of the monks who played a leading part in it) – was in some ways a rerun of the previous protests of 1988. After a decade during which anti-government protests had been virtually unknown, simmering popular discontent with military rule once again abruptly boiled over in August 2007 following the junta's decision to suddenly remove fuel subsidies, causing petrol prices to rise by two-thirds overnight.

The first protests were held by monks in the town of **Pakokku**, from where public shows of dissent rapidly spread nationwide. By September, thousands of monks and other demonstrators were marching daily through Yangon and Mandalay (on September 24 as many as 100,000 are estimated to have taken to the streets in Yangon alone).

Then, just as in 1988, the military hit back with their customary brutality – Than Shwe was rumoured to have taken personal charge of the army after senior commanders had refused to use force against the demonstrations. Rumours circulated that the military had purchased large quantities of monastic robes and were busily shaving their heads in order to penetrate the ranks of the protesting monks; convicted criminals were also released, and being ordered to do the same. Starting in late September soldiers began attacking and tear-gassing protesters. Thousands were beaten and dozens shot, while reports of monks being abducted, beaten and possibly murdered were widely circulated. Protesters were arrested and sentenced, usually to many years of hard labour. Although the orgy of killing seen in 1988 was not repeated, the crackdown was sufficient to eventually quell the uprising.

Further international sanctions and trade restrictions ensued. Rumours of dissension within the ranks of the generals, however, and reports that many soldiers and army officers had refused orders to take violent action against demonstrators, particularly monks, suggested that the tide might finally be turning against the regime, who subsequently announced that nationwide elections would be held in 2010.

Cyclone Nargis

Then, just as it seemed there might finally be light at the end of the tunnel, Myanmar suffered the greatest natural disaster in its entire recorded history. On May 3, 2008, **Cyclone Nargis** swept in from the Bay of Bengal, hitting the Delta region with little warning and unprecedented force. Large swathes of the densely populated, low-lying region were erased from the map in a matter of hours, with an estimated 130,000 dead, and a million left homeless and without food or water.

The biblical scale of the cyclone's devastation was impossible to grasp. Even more shocking, however, was the response of the embattled junta, who over the following month systematically blocked all offers of international aid, while doing almost nothing themselves to assist the survivors of the tragedy. International aid supplies and disaster experts were kept waiting in Yangon while the generals dithered in far-off Naypyitaw, and European and US naval ships stood waiting off the coast of the Delta, primed to provide relief but denied access. Hundreds of thousands of cyclone survivors are thought to have perished due to starvation, dehydration and disease thanks to the regime's paranoia and incompetence – perhaps the most damning indictment of the entire period of military rule, and certainly the most disastrous.

1992 onwards	1997	2005
Than Shwe initiates modest economic reforms accompanied by widespread political repression and human rights abuses	Myanmar joins ASEAN	The military government establishes a multi-billion-dollar new capital at Naypyitaw

Towards democracy

The **elections** announced by the military in 2008 were held as promised in November 2010, although they were boycotted by the NLD since many of its most prominent members were banned from running. These included Aung San Suu Kyi herself, whose period under house arrest had been conveniently (from a military standpoint) extended after she had reluctantly given shelter to US citizen **John Yettaw**, who had swum across Inya Lake to her house in order to gain an audience. Given the non-participation of the NLD, widespread allegations of electoral intimidation and other irregularities, and the fact that a quarter of all seats were reserved for the military, the subsequent landslide victory for the government-backed **Union Solidarity and Development Party (USDP)** was therefore largely inevitable, though on a more positive note, a few days after the election Aung San Suu Kyi was finally released from house arrest, apparently this time for good.

The SPDC was officially dissolved on March 30, 2011 and replaced by the newly elected (or, at least, "elected") USDP government led by former general and junta prime minister **Thein Sein** – 77-year-old Than Shwe having decided to stand down from politics, although rumours suggest that he remains a powerful behind-the-scenes influence. The new leader was widely seen as a moderate and reformist – although he was also known for his key role in blocking relief efforts following Cyclone Nargis, as well as his anti-Rohingya policies (see box, p.116).

Despite its military background, the new government set about initiating a series of landmark **reforms**. Anti-corruption legislation was passed, hundreds of political prisoners released, strike laws eased and the formerly stifling press censorship (see p.39) significantly reduced – with images of Aung San Suu Kyi, banned just a few years previously, now seen everywhere from newspapers to T-shirts. Signs of economic reform could also be seen – a normalization of government-fixed currency exchange rates led to a virtual disappearance of the formerly ubiquitous black market, while foreign companies were allowed to do business in Myanmar for the first time in half a century, with Ford, Nissan, Suzuki and Coca-Cola among the first arrivals. Political progress also followed, with the NLD participating in 2012 **by-elections**, winning 43 out of the 44 seats they contested. Aung San Suu Kyi herself won the seat of Kawhmu township in Yangon and has continued to be allowed to travel freely around the country.

Towards the 2015 elections

After half a century of despotic rule, Myanmar appears to be finally headed for something approaching normality. To what extent the reforms represent genuine change or are simply window-dressing by the generals anxious to present a more acceptable face to the world remains to be seen, however. Serious restrictions on the freedom of speech persist, large sections of the economy remain in crony hands (see box, p.350), while a corrupt legal system and army abuses – particularly in ethnic-minority areas – continue to be reported. A clause in the new military-sponsored constitution of 2008 banning those with foreign next of kin from standing for president, specifically aimed at Aung San Suu Kyi, remains in place, casting a shadow over political reforms, while growing Buddhist–Muslim tensions (see boxes, p.116 & p.180) have been a conspicuous feature of the past few years. Even Aung San Suu Kyi herself has shown worrying signs of cosying up to the generals and their business cronies, while her failure to speak up for the persecuted Rohingya drew widespread condemnation in 2014.

2007	2008
The Saffron Revolution sees further nationwide protests, again brutally suppressed by the military	Cyclone Nargis devastates the Delta, killing around 130,000 people; the government leaves many survivors to die, while blocking all offers of international assistance

THE CRONIES: A BRIEF WHO'S WHO

Much of Myanmar's wealth and economy is controlled by a group of so-called **crony capitalists**, fewer than twenty businessmen and their families who grew fabulously wealthy during the years of Than Shwe's military regime in a mutually beneficial arrangement whereby the cronies would supply services to the regime (and jobs for their family members) in return for lucrative contracts and import licences. Many have been the target of US and EU sanctions, although given the proximity of huge and sanction-free markets in India and China these have had little effect. Some have also been implicated in human rights abuses, the trafficking of arms and drugs, money laundering, land theft, forced labour and assorted other crimes.

The cronies face an uncertain but possibly lucrative future following the return to partial democracy. Some are window-dressing their activities in an attempt to appear less odious, including establishing links with Aung San Suu Kyi and donating generously to NLD causes. Ironically, despite the West's attempt to restrict their wealth and influence, the formerly pariah cronies (or their immediate families) may soon prove essential partners to Western companies looking to break into the Myanmar market, while their vast reserves of capital and local nous may prove key to ensuring the country's future economic growth.

Tay Za (b.1964) is Myanmar's most high-profile tycoon, now allegedly devoting himself to charitable works through his Htoo Foundation following a near-fatal helicopter crash. His Htoo Group owns numerous hotels (see box, p.43), Air Bagan and Asian Wings airlines and the AGD (Asia Green Development) Bank. Another leading crony is **Zaw Zaw** (b.1967), chairman of sprawling Max Myanmar Group which has interests in logging, gems, jade mining, rubber plantations, construction and hotels, and holdings including the Ayeyarwady Bank and Max Hotels group.

More reclusive but no less influential is **Aung Ko Win**, a former schoolteacher closely connected with the old junta, particularly General Maung Aye, the junta's former second-in-command. His KBZ Group controls the KBZ Bank (Myanmar's largest private bank), two airlines (Air KBZ and Myanmar Airways International), plus lucrative jade- and gem-mining concessions. Shadier still is **Steven Law** (real name Tun Myint Naing; b.1958). The son of the late Lo Hsing Han ("one of the world's key heroin traffickers", according to the US Treasury), Law is himself alleged to have been involved in drugs trafficking. Now owner of the huge Asia World conglomerate, as an ethnic Chinese Law has served as a major conduit for Chinese investment and led Asia World into several large and controversial Chinese-funded joint ventures, including the Myitsone hydroelectric dam (see box, p.322).

Reforms notwithstanding, Myanmar's **economy** remains among the least developed in Asia, with a per capita GDP of just $1700 (giving it a global rank of 201 out of 228 countries worldwide), compared to a similar figure of $9900 in neighbouring Thailand. A third of all Burmese still live below the poverty line, a situation made worse by raging inflation and rampant population growth (over a quarter of the population are now aged under 14). A fifth of all Burmese in rural areas have no reliable source of drinking water, and spending on healthcare and education remains among the lowest in the world. At least, on a more positive note, the national adult literacy rate is a respectable 93 percent.

Politically, the local and international community continues to express cautious optimism over the reforms so far enacted, although perhaps the real litmus test of the country's fledgling democracy will come in the general elections scheduled for **2015**, in the army's true willingness to give up its still considerable power, and in the ability, despite continuing religious and ethnic clashes, of this profoundly diverse and multicultural country to survive intact in the coming years.

2010	2010 onwards	2012–13
First general elections in twenty years are won by military-backed USDP; Thein Sein becomes Myanmar's new leader; Aung San Suu Kyi is released from house arrest	USDP introduces wide-ranging economic and political reforms	Anti-Rohingya riots in Rakhine and anti-Muslim riots in Meiktila and elsewhere

Myanmar's ethnic groups

Myanmar is home to an extraordinary patchwork of peoples. No fewer than 135 different ethnic groups are officially recognized by the government, arranged into eight "major national ethnic races": Bamar, Chin, Kachin, Kayah, Kayin, Mon, Rakhine and Shan. There are also some major ethnic groups not officially recognized, including the Burmese Chinese (three percent of the population), Burmese Indians (two percent of the population) and the embattled Rohingya (see box, p.116), not to mention the mixed-race Anglo-Burmese. Most ethnic groups speak their own language, with Burmese as a second language – although some (such as the Rakhine) speak a dialect of Burmese as their first language.

Ethnically, Myanmar is dominated by the **Bamar**, who have occupied the fertile Ayeyarwady valley and central plains for the past thousand years. Other ethnic groups tend to inhabit the country's mountainous margins, battling inhospitable terrain and (in recent decades) widespread military repression and human-rights abuses – every single major ethnic group in the country has been at war with the central government at some point since independence, with most insurgencies dragging on into the 1990s or – in the case of the Kayin – even more recently.

Bamar

Far and away Myanmar's largest ethnic group are the **Bamar** (still occasionally referred to by their old colonial-era name, "Burmans", or, less accurately, as the "Burmese", although properly speaking this adjective refers to all citizens of Myanmar rather than the Bamar alone). The Bamar now make up over two-thirds of the national population – almost 34 million people – and have largely assimilated formerly distinct ethnic groups including the now vanished Pyu people (see p.330) as well as large numbers of formerly independent Mon and other minorities who have been steadily Burmanized over the past centuries.

Originally hailing from Yunnan in southern China, the Bamar's traditional heartlands were the fertile Ayeyarwady River valley and surrounding plains, where they first settled around 1000 AD, establishing the kingdom of Bagan. Bamar culture and language are now inextricably bound up with that of the nation as a whole – the Bamar language, Burmese, is now Myanmar's official mother tongue, and many other marks of Bamar identity (the wearing of longyi and *thanaka*, for example; see box, p.7) have become synonymous with the country as a whole.

Shan

Myanmar's second-largest ethnic group – roughly nine percent of the population (around 4.5 million people) – the **Shan** live mainly in eastern Myanmar (as well as across the border in northern Thailand), where they have given their name to the country's largest state. Culturally and linguistically the Shan are closely related to the Tai peoples of Thailand and Laos – indeed, the Shan refer to themselves as "Tai", the name "Shan" being a Burmese corruption of "Siam". Originating, like the Bamar, from Yunnan in southern China, the Shan have inhabited eastern Myanmar since at least the tenth century, playing a major role in the country's history. Most are Buddhist and speak the Shan language, closely related to Thai and Lao.

Though the Shan are the most populous group in the east, you may not actually see all too many of them – the main Shan heartlands lie east of Taunggyi, an area off limits to foreign travellers due to the civil conflict that has been rumbling on for decades between the **Shan State Army** and the national government. Guerrilla attacks are still common in the mountains near the Thai border, and military reprisals occasionally see whole villages burned down, with Shan often forced to flee into Thailand – a country that refuses to afford them refugee status. Recent years have seen a slight improvement in relations, though Shan (and, of course, other minority groups) are still excluded from prominent military and government positions, and calls by many Shan for the creation of an independent Shan nation persist.

There are myriad other different hill tribes in eastern Myanmar, nominally classified as subgroups of the Shan and including the **Intha** (see below), the **Palaung, Pa-O, Eng, Danu, Akha, Lahu** and **Loi**. Many of these tribes have villages in both Myanmar and Thailand, and some of them, such as the Akha and Lahu, are more easily visited on hill-tribe treks on the Thai side of the border.

Intha

One of the country's more visible minorities, the **Intha** ("sons of the lake") number approximately 70,000 people and live mainly around Inle Lake where they eke out a living cultivating small plots and floating gardens on and around the water. They are believed to have originally come from Dawei in southern Myanmar and still speak their own distinctive Burmese dialect. They're best known for their unusual style of leg-rowing, as featured in innumerable tourist literature.

Kayin (Karen)

The **Kayin** – aka **Karen** – are Myanmar's third-biggest ethnic group, with around 3.5 million, who live mainly in Kayin State in the south of the country (seven percent of the national population), while many more have fled to Thailand. The Kayin are the most heterogeneous of Myanmar's ethnic groups, comprising a disparate collection of hill tribes speaking various languages, most of them mutually unintelligible. They were first grouped together under the umbrella term "Kayin" in the 1800s by Baptist missionaries who had considerable success converting the region's Buddhist natives. Today, a quarter of all Kayin in Myanmar are Christian, with the rest professing Buddhism, sometimes with strong animist elements.

Strongly favoured under British rule thanks to their Christian leanings, the Kayin have suffered even more than most other Burmese ethnic minorities in the decades since independence. The separatist **Karen National Union (KNU)** was founded in 1947 to push the case for their own independence, although peaceable efforts to create a Kayin sovereign nation (provisionally named Kawthoolei) collapsed just two years later when government troops slaughtered eighty Kayin villagers in Palaw, Tanintharyi. The resultant conflict, fought between the KNU's military arm, the **Karen National Liberation Army**, and government troops, was the longest running of Myanmar's many ethnic insurgencies, displacing as many as 200,000 people before a formal ceasefire was signed in 2012. Save for the occasional KNU truck rumbling down the streets of Hpa-An, visitors to the Karen heartlands of Myanmar will see little sign of the conflict's impact, although an estimated 120,000 Kayin people still live in Thai refugee camps.

Rakhine

Living mainly in Rakhine State, in the west of the country, and in neighbouring Bangladesh, the **Rakhine** (also spelt "Rakhaing", and previously known as the Arakanese) share much in common with the Bamar but have also been significantly influenced by their proximity to the Indian subcontinent, claiming to have been among the first converts to Buddhism in Southeast Asia as the new religion spread east from India. Comprising around four percent of the national population (roughly two million people), the Rakhine speak a distinctive form of Burmese (considered a dialect by some, a separate language by others). A brief account of Rakhine history is given in chapter 2 (see box, p.115).

Mon

Formerly the largest and most powerful ethnic group in southern Myanmar, the **Mon** people have now been relegated to the status of an embattled minority. The last independent Mon kingdom was toppled in 1757 (see p.336), since when they have been largely assimilated into the Bamar mainstream – only around two percent of Burmese (roughly a million people) now class themselves as Mon, living mainly in the south of the country, particularly in Mon and Bago states and the Delta region. As with many other ethnic minorities, the Mon have periodically rebelled against the central government in an attempt to gain independence – a series of insurgencies ended only by a general ceasefire agreement of 1995.

Kachin

"Kachin" is an umbrella term used to describe some six ethnic groups living in far northern Kachin State, with a total of just under a million people; the **Jinpo** are the major subgroup. Core Burmese beliefs are less in evidence here – most Kachin are Christian, and animist beliefs remain strong too – while traditional styles of Kachin dress (although now rarely worn except on festive occasions; see box, p.320) are among the most flamboyant in the land. The **Kachin Independence Army** (KIA) has been involved in a long-running conflict with the government (see p.321), with hostilities recommencing in 2011 following the collapse of a previous ceasefire.

Kayah

Living in the remote hills of Kayah State are the **Kayah** people, also known as the Red Karen or the Karenni (and sometimes classified as a subgroup of the Karen) – the name "Red Karen" derives from their fondness for red clothing. Now numbering fewer than half a million (with more over the border in Thailand), the Kayah can be divided into

THE PADAUNG "GIRAFFE LADIES"

The long-necked ladies of the **Padaung** tribe are without doubt the most startling of all Myanmar's ethnic minorities (although "Padaung" is actually a Shan name and they're more accurately called the Kayan Lahwi). From the age of around five, Padaung girls are fitted with heavy brass **neck rings**, with more being added as their necks elongate, causing their collarbones to sink. No one knows exactly why the practice began. One theory claims that it started as a means of making local girls less appealing to raiders from neighbouring tribes; another legend suggests that the neck rings were designed to protect against biting tigers – although quite possibly it simply originated as a fashion statement and marker of cultural identity. The rings are only rarely removed and it's popularly believed that the ladies would not be able to support the weight of their own heads without them, although in fact a number of women have jettisoned their rings safely in recent years and reported nothing but passing discomfort.

These days, the practice is a moneymaker. A number of long-necked ladies have left their homes in remote Kayah State to set themselves up around touristy Inle Lake; their houses are free to visit, but they're basically all souvenir shops. Though undeniably photogenic, many visitors feel uncomfortable given that the ladies themselves are treated almost like zoo animals.

numerous subgroups including the famous **Padaung** (see box, p.353). As with other minorities, the Kayah have suffered repeated military persecution and human rights abuses, which led to clashes between the Burmese army and the **Karenni People's Liberation Front** until the agreement of a ceasefire of 1995.

Chin

Forming the majority of the half-million inhabitants of remote Chin State in Myanmar's far west, the **Chin** people share many ethnic links with the Zo (aka Mizo) people in the adjacent Indian state of Mizoram. Always remote from the Burmese mainstream, the majority of Chin converted to Christianity during the colonial period – and have suffered significantly for their beliefs since independence (see box, p.218). They are perhaps best known to outsiders for their curious practice of tattooing the faces of their women (see box, p.126).

Wa

Myanmar's million or so **Wa** people (descended, according to one legend, from two female tadpoles) live mainly in northern Shan and eastern Kachin states along the Chinese border and around Kengtung. Left largely alone by the British thanks to their wild reputation (including a fondness for animal sacrifice and headhunting), the Wa retained considerable autonomy following independence and were often in armed conflict with the government until the signing of a ceasefire in 1989. Their heartlands comprise one of the country's major drug-producing areas (originally opium, more recently heroin and methamphetamine), with the lucrative trade policed and protected by the **United Wa State Army**, formerly one of the world's largest drug militias, with as many as ten thousand men under arms.

Naga

Perhaps Myanmar's most truly remote people, the **Naga** tribes are spread across northwestern Myanmar and northeastern India, living mainly – on the Burmese side of the border – around the Chindwin River and in the hills of western Sagaing Region. A patchwork of tribes, all speaking different languages, the Naga had little contact with the outside world under the British colonial era. Headhunting was formerly a popular pastime, although the practice largely died out following widespread conversion by Christian missionaries (rumour has it, however, that the practice continued into modern times). The Naga people are now increasingly Burmanized, although some traditional settlements and customs remain. Naga men traditionally wear few clothes but many tattoos, while the Naga are also known for their exuberant dancing, drumming and singing, at its most flamboyant during the Naga New Year celebrations, when the men also don their extraordinary traditional headdresses.

Burmese Buddhism and traditional beliefs

Almost ninety percent of all Burmese people classify themselves as Buddhist. Buddhism permeates every aspect of Burmese life, with Myanmar often claimed to be the world's most devout Buddhist nation, both in terms of the amount of money dedicated to religious expenses and judged by the proportion of monks relative to the overall population – easy to believe when you've seen quite how many red-robed clergy there are in virtually every corner of the country.

There are also significant numbers of **Christians**, **Muslims** and other religious groups, although these are found mainly among ethnic minorities and exist very much at the margins of Burmese society – particularly given the prolonged discrimination against non-Buddhist individuals and groups, which has been a feature of the years since independence.

History of Burmese Buddhism

Buddhism arrived early in Myanmar, although exactly who converted to the religion and when remains conjectural. According to one tradition the religion was introduced by two monks despatched by the great Indian Buddhist emperor Ashoka (ruled 268–232 BC), although the arrival of the religion was most likely a piecemeal affair, as the new religion travelled east from India, mingling with existing beliefs and religious practices. The Rakhine, living close to the subcontinent, claim to have been among the first to convert, while the Mon were also early adherents. Further north, the Bamar adopted an eclectic version of the faith known as **Ari Buddhism** including *nat* worship (see p.356) alongside elements drawn from Hinduism and Mahayana and Tantric Buddhism, as well as other magical astrological and alchemical beliefs.

The establishment of a relatively orthodox form of **Theravada Buddhism** as the dominant religion came in the eleventh century during the reign of the great King Anawrahta of Bagan (see p.331). Much of the credit for Anawrahta's reforming zeal goes to the legendary Mon monk, **Shin Arahan**, who persuaded the king to abandon the heterogeneous Ari faith in favour of the more conservative Theravada form – although Anawrahta made the concession of installing images of the traditional *nats* on the stupa of his great Shwezigon Pagoda (see p.192), and *nat* worship remains very much alive to this day.

Myanmar subsequently became one of the main strongholds of the Theravada faith, surviving the resurgence of Hinduism in India (which virtually wiped out the religion in the country of its birth), as well as the arrival of Islam and the onslaught of colonial-era Christianity – although missionaries had considerable success among some of the country's ethnic minorities, and significant numbers of Kayin, Kachin, Chin and Naga still profess Christianity to this day.

Surprisingly, Buddhism has never been the official state religion of Myanmar except for a brief period in 1961–62. Nonetheless, the identification between state and Buddhism has always been strong. Early Burmese kings traditionally saw themselves as patrons and upholders of the faith, while in more recent years Myanmar's ruling generals have traditionally made much of their temple-building projects and other religious activities in an effort to distract attention from their murderous rule.

Theravada Buddhism

Myanmar follows the **Theravada** (the "Law of the Elders") school of Buddhism, the older and more conservative version of the religion which also predominates in Sri Lanka, Thailand, Cambodia and Laos (in contrast to the later and more eclectic Mahayana Buddhism followed in China, Japan, Korea, Vietnam and elsewhere). As the older of the two main schools, Theravada claims to embody the Buddha's teachings in their original form. These teachings emphasize that all individuals are responsible for their own spiritual welfare, and that any person who wishes to achieve enlightenment must pursue the same path trodden by the Buddha himself, giving up worldly concerns and developing spiritual attainments through meditation and self-sacrifice. This path of renunciation is, of course, impossible for most members of the Theravada community to follow, which explains the importance of **monks** in Myanmar (and in other Theravada countries), since only members of the Sangha (see opposite) are considered fully committed to the Theravada path.

Nats

Despite its adherence to the "pure" form of Buddhism, the religion in Myanmar still shows the influence of other eclectic beliefs pre-dating the arrival of the Theravada faith. Most notable is the countrywide practice of **nat** (spirit) worship, still particularly prevalent in rural areas (although educated urban Burmese often dismiss the tradition as folk superstition). Burmese *nats* come from a variety of sources including local animist nature spirits, folk deities (such as Mai Wunna, the flower-eating ogress of Mount Popa; see box, p.217), Burmanized versions of major Hindu gods and *nats* related to real-life historical figures (such as Min Situ, the *nat* spirit of Bagan's King Alaungsittu) – all of whom merge in a bewildering historical and mythological melange. Some have followers nationwide; others may be linked to a single area, or even a single village.

The survival of the *nats* as an essential element in modern Burmese Buddhism owes much to King Anawrahta, the great religious reformer of Bagan, who first established Theravada Buddhism as the national religion. Realizing the hold that the *nats* had over his people, Anawrahta chose to incorporate them into his new-look Buddhist faith in an attempt to encourage the Burmese to follow the new Theravada doctrines. Some of the most important of Myanmar's myriad *nats* were chosen to form a royally sanctioned pantheon known as the **37 Nats** (see box, p.194) under the leadership of Thagyamin (a Burmanized version of the Hindu god Indra, often portrayed, like Indra himself, seated on top of a three-headed elephant). Thaygamin excepted, every one of the 37 *nats* died a violent death, lending them something of the character of Christian martyrs. At the same time they're also an engagingly humanized bunch, in stark contrast to the exalted qualities of the Buddha himself. Popular *nats* include some decidedly raffish characters with very recognizable personal flaws and earthly failings such as Min Kyawzwa, the "Drunken Nat", whose image at Mount Popa is draped with offerings of whisky bottles and cigarettes in homage to his life spent boozing, cockfighting and hunting.

Nats have been thoroughly integrated into Burmese Buddhism, and *nat* shrines or images can be found in most temples in the country. All pagodas have a resident guardian *nat* spirit, or **Bo Bo Gyi**, typically shown as a man dressed in pink robes with a white turban. In addition, you'll also see many shrines dedicated to **Shin Upagot** (or Upagutta), a much venerated figure who is believed to protect worshippers against watery perils such as floods and storms. He's easily recognizable thanks to his distinctive pose, seated, with one hand dipping into an alms bowl on his lap, and his head tilted upwards, looking skywards as if in search of rain.

Myanmar's main centre of *nat* worship is Mount Popa, while there are also several important *nat* shrines around Mandalay. All of these places host raucous **nat pwè** festivals (see p.40) with celebrations led by spirit mediums know as **nat kadaw** (see box, p.49).

The Sangha

Myanmar's community of Buddhist monks, the **Sangha**, is one of the world's largest – the sight of monks (and also nuns) doing their daily morning rounds, bearing alms bowls and possibly a brightly coloured umbrella, is one of the country's most emblematic sights. Exact figures are hard to come by, although there are probably between 300,000 and half a million monks (plus at least fifty thousand nuns) in the country at any one time.

Burmese monks usually wear maroon-coloured robes rather than the orange robes worn in countries like Sri Lanka and Thailand. There are nine officially recognized **monastic orders** (*nikaya*); easily the largest is the Thudhamma Nikaya, followed by the more conservative Shwegyin Nikaya. All Burmese Buddhist men are expected to experience monastic life at least once. This often happens as a child – anytime after the age of seven. Young boys are entered into the monastery during an elaborate **shinbyu** ceremony, a major Burmese rite of passage during which their heads are shaved and normal clothes exchanged for robes; better-off parents may also arrange a *shinbyu* procession for their offspring, providing a symbolic re-enactment of the Buddha's own renunciation of royal life. Most boys enter a monastery for a short period only, perhaps as little as a week, although poorer children may become novices and be educated at the monastery. Full ordination (*upasampada*) for those who choose to enter the Sangha for life follows at the age of twenty or later.

Buddhism in daily life

Daily religious life for the Burmese laypeople is mainly concerned with observing the religion's Five Precepts (a kind of Buddhist five commandments) and accumulating spiritual **merit** through good deeds and alms-giving (*dana*) – all of which, it is hoped, will ensure a favourable rebirth in the next life. **Meditation**, particularly Vipassana meditation, is also popular among both monks and laity.

Many Burmese homes have their own small Buddhist shrine, but local **temples** remain very much at the heart of religious, and indeed social, life – larger places come equipped with their own shops, resident palmists and astrologers, food vendors, flower shops (and, nowadays, ATMs, wi-fi zones and lifts). There is no congregational worship in Buddhism, meaning that people come to pay their respects at all times of the day and night – early evening after work is particularly popular.

Worshippers often come bearing **offerings** of flowers, money and quaint paper umbrellas, while also popular is the practice of rubbing fine slivers of gold leaf on particularly revered Buddha images (the statue at the Mahamuni Paya in Mandalay, for example, whose nether regions have now largely been buried under an estimated two

---

BUDDHISM AND POLITICS

Myanmar's monks play an important role in Burmese life as spiritual leaders and have also assumed an important role in many of the last century's political struggles. **U Ottama** and **U Wisara** (both of whom starved themselves to death while in British prisons) were two leading figures in the anti-colonial movement. The Sangha also played a leading part during the **1988 and 2007 uprisings** (see p.348) – despite their revered status they suffered particularly badly from military brutality, with hundreds, perhaps thousands, of monks being murdered during the 1988 uprising (during which numerous government informers reportedly shaved their heads and donned robes in an attempt to infiltrate the monastic orders and identify protesters). Their decision during the 2007 uprising to "overturn the alms bowl" (*thabeik hmauk*) and refuse all offerings from the military – a kind of Buddhist version of excommunication – served as a powerful, if ultimately unsuccessful, symbolic statement against military rule.

Not all members of the Sangha are irreproachably peaceful, however, as proved by the influential **969 Movement**, led by controversial monk Ashin Wirathu, whose sermons have been accused of stoking Burmese Islamophobia, declaring (with reference to his Muslim fellow nationals) that "You can be full of kindness and love, but you cannot sleep next to a mad dog".

tonnes of additional gold applied by visiting devotees). Inside the temple the devout will offer prayers, perhaps ringing one of the gongs with which all temples are equipped in the hope that their prayer will be answered. Depending on which day of the week they were born on, they will visit the relevant planetary post (see box, p.71) and wash its Buddha image, dousing it in water once for every year of their age, plus once more for luck.

Burmese Buddhism and the occult

Running alongside the country's orthodox Buddhist beliefs is a string of arcane and outlandish beliefs. First and foremost is a strong belief in **astrology** many Burmese will consult an astrologer when planning, say, a new business or preparing to sit an exam. The day of the week on which one is born is considered especially important.

Numerology

Numerology is considered particularly significant. Ne Win's disastrous 1987 currency reforms (see box, p.344) can be blamed on numerology, while the ultra-auspicious date of August 8, 1988 was chosen for the date on which the main thrust of the 8888 Uprising (see p.344) was launched; another rebellion was later planned for September 9, 1999, but failed to materialize. More recently, the 969 Movement (see box, p.357) chose its name (whose three digits "symbolize the virtues of the Buddha, Buddhist practices and the Buddhist community") in overt numerological opposition to the popular Islamic cipher 786, corresponding to the opening phrase of the Qu'ran (the fact that $7 + 8 + 6 = 21$ being seen as proof by the 969 Movement that Muslims intend to take over Myanmar during the current century).

Yadaya

Linked to numerology and also popular among many Burmese – including past rulers Ne Win and Than Shwe – is **yadaya**, the practice of quasi-magical Burmese rituals, prescribed by astrologers in order to ward off possible misfortune. Most *yadaya* rituals simply involve a visit to the temple and making certain specific offerings and prayers outlined by an astrologer, although some rituals can be considerably stranger – as when Ne Win elected to shoot himself in a mirror in order to avert a possible assassination attempt (see box, p.344). *Yadaya* is also said to have influenced affairs of state both major and minor. The decision in 1970 to change the side of the road on which traffic drives from left to right, for example, is rumoured to have been taken to ward off political or military attack from right-wing groups – even though this means that virtually every vehicle in Myanmar has its steering wheel on the wrong side, right up to the present day. Likewise, in 2010 when the country's military leaders greeted the Thai prime minister at Yangon airport dressed in women's longyi, the influence of *yadaya* – in this case an attempt to harness the distaff power of Aung San Suu Kyi – was again suspected.

Weizza

Combining many of Myanmar's weirder and more wonderful occult traditions is the practice of **weizza**. A uniquely Burmese Buddhist cult, *weizza* (also spelt "*weikza*") attempts to evade the usual laws of karma through rituals including magic, meditation and alchemy. Powerful practitioners of *weizza*, it is said, can live for centuries and choose the exact moment of their next reincarnation, among other supernatural powers.

Weizza incorporates many traditional beliefs including a local fascination with *zawgyi* (wizards and alchemists, who feature heavily in popular Burmese folklore) as well as elements dating perhaps all the way back to Ari Buddhism. The modern form of the tradition emerged in the late seventeenth century when **Bo Bo Aung**, a monk in Sagaing, discovered manuscripts revealing the secrets of *weizza*. Bo Bo Aung's image, traditionally dressed in an all-white robe and turban, can still be found in many temples and homes, devotees believing he has the power to assist all those who pray to him with a pure heart.

Burmese architecture

Few other countries are as abundantly endowed with religious architecture as Myanmar, from the thousands of ancient brick temples blanketing the plains of Bagan through to the huge gilded pagodas rising up above the bustling modern streets of Yangon, Mandalay, Bago, Pyay, Mawlamyine and pretty much every other city in the country. By contrast, relatively little secular architecture survives from the past, excepting the magnificent European-style colonial streetscapes of Yangon (see box, p.62).

Temple names

Temple names in Myanmar can be confusing. Buddhist temples are generally named using either the English **pagoda** or its Burmese equivalent, **paya**, with the two words being used more or less interchangeably – the Shwedagon in Yangon, for example, is widely referred to as both the Shwedagon Pagoda and Shwedagon Paya. In Bagan the word **pahto** is also sometimes used, generally when referring to "hollow" temples such as the Ananda or Sulamani, rather than solid stupas. Bagan's hollow temples can also sometimes be identified by the fact that they have the word **gu** (meaning "cave") in their name – the Gubyaukgyi, Alotawpyi-gu-hpaya and Shwegugyi temples, for example. The Burmese word for stupa is **zedi**, as in Bagan's Mingalazedi and elsewhere.

Pagoda architecture

The sheer number and size of Buddhist pagodas in Myanmar owes much to the Burmese obsession with **merit-making** – doing good works in this life in order to secure a favourable rebirth in one's future reincarnations. The rulers and nobles of Bagan virtually bankrupted their own kingdom thanks to their obsession with temple-building, while modern rulers have also left a string of pagodas in their wake, including Than Shwe, who sought to atone for a lifetime of greed, repression and murder by raising the huge Uppatasanti Pagoda in Naypyitaw. Such edifices also serve as notable memorials to their creators, handily combining religious good works and self-glorification in a single architectural package.

The vast majority of Burmese pagodas remain very much living places of worship rather than historic monuments. Many date back hundreds of years, although most have been repeatedly refurbished, remodelled – and sometimes completely rebuilt – many times over the centuries, making it difficult to get a sense of the antiquity of the country's major shrines. (Even many of the seemingly ancient-looking temples at Bagan have actually been reconstructed over the past few decades according to local aesthetic whim rather than sound archeological principles, which is why UNESCO has so far refused to inscribe it on the list of global World Heritage Sites). The general sense of timelessness is also exacerbated by the fact that new pagodas being constructed today are essentially not that much different in style from those erected a thousand years ago, tradition rather than innovation being of the essence.

Parts of a pagoda

The typical Buddhist pagoda follows a basic plan which you'll see repeated all over the country. The vast majority are arranged around a central **stupa**; these are usually solid, although there are a few hollow modern pagodas with shrines inside (notable examples including the Botataung Pagoda in Yangon, the Uppatasanti Pagoda in Naypyitaw and the Lawkananda Pagoda in Sittwe). Surrounding the stupa there's usually a **terrace** ringed with subsidiary **shrines** containing assorted Buddha images, along with the occasional *nat* (see p.356). Pagodas are often built in raised positions, with **stairways** (often covered and lined with shops in larger pagodas) leading up from the streets below – grander temples typically have four entrances, one at each of the cardinal points. Larger temples often have a **monastery** (*kyaung*) attached.

Stupas

The soaring gilded **stupas** that dot Myanmar's towns and countryside are the country's most emblematic and memorable sight – vast masses of shimmering gold, dazzling by day, mysteriously glowing in the half-light of dusk, magnificently illuminated after dark. The classic Burmese-style stupa is perhaps the most beautiful in Asia: tall and slender, with a distinctive shape that seems to blend monumental size and presence with an elegantly simple outline, softened with organic, almost feminine, curves.

The country's first stupas, at Thayekhittaya (see p.184), are little more than massive but rather crude cylindrical towers. These gradually developed at Bagan into the classic design – typified by the stupas at pagodas such as the Shwezigon and Shwesandaw – with their bell-shaped bodies rising to a delicately tapering spire above.

THE ARCHITECTURE OF BAGAN

Much of the history of Burmese temple architecture can be seen at **Bagan**. The buildings of Bagan divide into two periods: early and late. Temples of the **early period** (roughly 850–1120), such as the Pahthothamya Paya, are heavily influenced by early Pyu and Mon architectural styles – typically low and heavy one-storey structures topped by a small and rather cursory stupa. Interiors are kept deliberately dark in order to create a sense of mystery: most early shrines have just a single door and small windows with tiny latticework openings. Inside, there's usually a central shrine plus antechamber, with perhaps an ambulatory around the central shrine. Stupas, like the Bupaya and that at the Lawkananda Pagoda, are modelled on earlier Pyu examples at, for example, Thayekhittaya: cyclindrical or slightly bulbous in outline, with little of the shapely finesse of later examples.

The city's **late period** architecture (roughly 1120–1300) shows the emergence of the unique Bagan style. Temples become taller, with the addition of a second shrine (often the main shrine) on the upper storey. Windows become much larger and interiors much lighter; many later temples also have four entrances ("four-faced" temples, as they're sometimes called) rather than the previous single entrance, also admitting more light. The rooftop stupa grows in size, ultimately developing into the soaring stupa-spires which top many temples, usually combining a rather Indian-looking tower with curved sides (known as a "shikhara") with a stupa on top. Tiers of gradually smaller terraces connect the three parts of the structure – the two shrines and the stupa-spire – their corners decorated with miniature stupas or Indian-style *kalasa* (nectar pots), while many also have educational carvings showing scenes from the Buddhist Jataka tales. The central shrine of earlier is now filled in to support the weight of the superstructure above, and an ambulatory (occasionally a double ambulatory) built around this solid central core, with a Buddha standing at each of its four sides.

Builders also achieved a remarkable mastery in the art of **brick vaulting**, at least a century in advance of anything else achieved in Asia at that time (the expertise proved by the fact that most temples survived the massive earthquake that hit Bagan in 1975). These skills were lost after the fall of Bagan, as demonstrated by the failed Mingun Pagoda project initiated by King Bodawpaya near Mandalay in 1790.

Late-period **stupas**, like the Mingalazedi and those at the Shwesandaw and Shwezigon pagodas, are also dramatically different from earlier models, typically much taller and more slender in outline, with a bell-shaped body set on an octagonal base and surmounted by a tall spire, with the whole structure set upon a huge square plinth. This design set the prototype for most subsequent stupas built across the country. There are also a couple of rare examples of stupas set upon **pentagonal** bases (the Dhammayazika is the best example) in order to accommodate a fifth shrine to the future Buddha Maitreya – a design feature unique in the Buddhist world.

The massive Shwedagon Pagoda in Yangon is perhaps the ultimate Burmese stupa, and typifies many standard design elements found across the country, albeit on an unusually grand scale. The entire stupa sits on a massive square **base**, surrounded by miniature stupas, and with shrines to the four Buddhas (see box, p.71) at each of the cardinal points. Above the base rises a series of octagonal **terraces** (*pyissaya*) – access to these is restricted to monks. Surmounting this is the main body of the stupa, shaped like an inverted **almsbowl** (*thabeik*), its top decorated with lotus petals. This provides a base for the stupa spire, culminating in the distinctive "**banana bud**" (*nga pyaw bu*). At the very top, the stupa is crowned by a latticework **umbrella** (*hti*), typically decorated with precious stones, hung with bells and topped with a gilded flag.

Shrines

Surrounding the central stupa you'll usually find a ring of **shrines** (*tazaung*), typically decorated in a riot of colour and ornamentation. Most shrines are topped by a gilded **pyatthat**, a kind of cross between a roof and a spire, with tiers of flamboyantly carved, superimposed flying eaves rising to a needle-thin finial – a symbolic representation of the Buddhist cosmos, with the different tiers standing for the various realms of human and celestial beings rising to the mythical Mount Meru, home of the gods, above. (*Pyatthat* were also a common feature of royal palace complexes – the higher one's status at court, the more tiers the *pyatthat* over one's residence were permitted.)

Inside, walls and pillars are often decorated in dazzlingly intricate **glass mosaics**, another Burmese speciality. Virtually every shrine will have a Buddha image inside, often several. Some will also house images of *nats*, while in bigger shrines you'll find additional objects of veneration such as symbolic **Buddha footprints**, decorated with arcane symbols, or **reliquaries** containing sacred objects – typically replicas of the Buddha's Tooth or other bodily remains.

Benign Buddhas

Burmese Buddhas are everywhere, from the supersized colossi in Yangon, Monywa, Bago and elsewhere through to the myriad smaller images which can be found in every temple. The array of styles is strikingly wide, ranging from manneristic, slightly extraterrestrial-looking Shan- and Thai-influenced figures through to more realistic images such as the square-faced and rather portly-looking images that were the speciality of the Rakhine (such as the revered Mahamuni Buddha, now in Mandalay). Most images show the Buddha clad in simple monk's robes, although in later images (particularly Mandalay-style statues) these are often replaced with sumptuous royal regalia, including lavish sculpted robes and extravagant crowns.

The **Mandalay-style Buddha**, which developed during the Konbaung era, is particularly popular, showing the Buddha with a round and realistic-looking face (unlike the rather alien-featured Shan- and Thai-style Buddhas), and a full head of closely cropped hair with a hair-bun looking slightly like a woollen cap. Most Mandalay-style seated images are shown in the *bhumisparsha mudra* (see box, p.362) with the robe tied over the left shoulder (the right shoulder is left bare).

Magical animals and mythical monsters

Mythical **beasts** are another essential feature of Burmese temple architecture, their fearsome features designed to offer supernatural protection to the building they guard. The entrances to many temples are protected by huge pairs of **chinthe**, lion-like figures (with a hint of dragon), while **sphinx**-like creatures (basically chinthe with human heads) are often placed at the corners of stupas. Grotesque **kirtimukha** (aka *kala*) – pop-eyed ogre heads swallowing chains of garlands or pearls – decorate the walls of many Bagan temples, referring to an old Hindu legend in which Shiva accidentally creates a ravenous monster and then orders it to eat his own body. Other mythological monsters commonly encountered include the bird-like **garuda** and the snake-like **naga**,

BUDDHIST MUDRAS AND THEIR MEANINGS

Buddha images are traditionally shown in one of various iconic poses, known as **mudras**, whether standing, sitting or reclining.

Abhaya mudra The "Have No Fear" pose shows the Buddha standing with his right hand raised, the palm facing the viewer.

Bhumisparsha mudra The "Earth-Witness" pose shows the seated Buddha touching the ground with the tips of the fingers of his left hand, commemorating the moment during his enlightenment when the demon Mara, attempting to break his concentration, caused the Earth to shake beneath him, and the Buddha stilled the ground by touching it.

Dana or **varada mudra** The "offering" pose, with the Buddha seated and his right hand placed palm upwards signifying the act of giving and compassion.

Dhyani or **samadhi mudra** Shows the Buddha in meditation, seated in the lotus or half-lotus position, with his hands placed together in his lap.

Namaskara mudra Shows the Buddha (or other devotee) with hands placed together in a gesture of prayer.

Parinirvana mudra Shows the Buddha in a reclining pose to represent the moment of his death and entrance into nirvana.

Vitarka mudra ("Gesture of Explanation") and **dharmachakra mudra** ("Gesture of the Turning of the Wheel of the Law"). In both positions the Buddha forms a circle with his thumb and one finger, representing the "wheel of dharma" (dharmachakra), which symbolizes the Buddhist route to nirvana. Used in both standing and sitting poses.

half-animal and half-human creatures with god-like powers. Another bird, the **hamsa** (translated either as "goose" or "swan"), is also commonly found as a decorative element and is strongly associated with the Hindu god Brahma, who also appears in some Buddhist temples as a protector of the faith.

Secular architecture

Temples apart, traditional Burmese buildings were constructed entirely of wood and have entirely vanished as a result of fire, earthquakes, World War II and the depredations of time – the now empty plains surrounding the temples of Bagan, for example, would once have been filled with wooden houses, palaces and monastic and administrative buildings. The reconstructed royal palace at Mandalay gives a slight (if not massively inspiring) sense of what old Myanmar looked like. More authentic are the few surviving wooden religious buildings such as the Yoke Sone Kyaung monastery in Salay (see p.219).

Books

Myanmar has a rich English-language literary heritage dating back to colonial times, when authors from quintessential Empire tub-thumper Rudyard Kipling through to anti-imperialist freethinker George Orwell penned various poems, essays, travelogues and novels about the country. Post-independence literature largely focuses on the desperate plight of the country under military rule – often sombre reading, but offering unparalleled insights into life under the generals. Sadly, there's virtually no Burmese literature available in translation, although Burmese authors writing in English have provided a handful of excellent memoirs, histories and other works. All the following titles are widely available overseas, although less easily obtainable in Myanmar itself. Particularly recommended titles are marked with a ★ symbol.

LITERATURE

★Amitav Ghosh *The Glass Palace.* Set in Burma, India and Malaya, this acclaimed historical novel follows the fortunes of four Indian and Burmese families (including that of the exiled King Thibaw) during the six tumultuous decades between the fall of Mandalay in 1885 and the end of World War II. Essential Burmese reading.

Rudyard Kipling *Barrack-Room Ballads; From Sea to Sea.* Rudyard Kipling's entire experience of Burma consisted of brief visits to Rangoon and Moulmein (Mawlamyine) during a sea journey from India to the US in 1889 – which didn't stop him from leaving a heavy literary mark on the land. Originally published in *Barrack-Room Ballads*, "Mandalay" (which he never visited) remains the most famous poem ever written about the country, though Burma appears in several other poems and short stories. An account of his 1889 visit can be found in *From Sea to Sea*, which is also the source of his endlessly repeated quote: "This is Burma, and it will be quite unlike any land you know".

Daniel Mason *The Piano Tuner.* Bestselling novel by American writer Daniel Mason, set in 1886 and telling the story of piano tuner Edgar Drake, despatched to the remote Shan States to repair the Érard grand of an eccentric army doctor – full of convincing historical detail, and a very enjoyable read.

George Orwell *Burmese Days.* Orwell's classic critique of British colonialism has its moments, although it's a turgid read at times, with heavy-handed satire and cast of profoundly unsympathetic and largely one-dimensional characters who are little more than mouthpieces for Orwell's anti-imperialistic screed. Burma also appears in two of Orwell's most celebrated essays, "A Hanging" and "Shooting an Elephant", both of which say more about the canker of empire in just a few pages than *Burmese Days* manages in its entire length.

Amy Tan *Saving Fish From Drowning.* Richly comic send-up of modern tourism when a group of bumbling American visitors go missing near Inle Lake, with memorable consequences.

TRAVELOGUE AND REPORTAGE

★Emma Larkin *Everything is Broken: Life Inside Burma.* Even better than Larkin's earlier Burmese book (see below), *Everything is Broken* provides a harrowing portrait of Myanmar in the aftermath of Cyclone Nargis and a damning indictment of the ruling junta's spectacular inaction in the face of the country's greatest ever natural disaster.

Emma Larkin *Finding George Orwell in Burma.* Enjoyable and insightful mix of travel writing and reportage: part travelogue, following in the footsteps of Orwell during his stint as a colonial police officer in Burma; part examination of the state of Myanmar under the generals – and its

uncanny resemblance to the Orwellian dystopias of *Animal Farm* and *Nineteen Eighty-Four*.

★Norman Lewis *Golden Earth: Travels in Burma.* Classic tome by one of the twentieth century's finest travel writers, describing a 1951 journey the length of the country from Myeik to Myitkyina during the turbulent early years after independence, all narrated with Lewis's characteristic insight and wit.

Rory Maclean *Under the Dragon: A Journey Through Burma.* Genre-bending book cross-cutting an account of Maclean's travels in the footsteps of Sir George Scott with a series of novel-like episodes portraying the lives of ordinary Burmese in the shadow of the 8888 Uprising. It's somewhat uneven, although a couple of the novelistic interpolations are very fine.

★ **Andrew Marshall** *The Trouser People*. Inspired by the diaries of colonial empire-builder Sir George Scott – who also appears in Rory Maclean's *Under the Dragon* (see p.363) – *The Trouser People* serves up a compelling mix of travelogue and reportage as Marshall ventures into some of Myanmar's remotest ethnic minority areas. Brave, black and savagely funny.

W. Somerset Maugham *The Gentleman in the Parlour*. Travel-diary-style jottings describing journeys up the Ayeyarwady to Mandalay and into the Shan hills (plus a voyage down the Mekong to Saigon), with plenty of quaint characters and exotic scenery on the way. A good record of 1930s travel in the grand style.

POLITICS AND CURRENT EVENTS

Maggie Lemere & Zoe West *Nowhere to Be Home: Narratives from Survivors of Burma's Military Regime*. Interviews with 22 persecuted Burmese including child conscripts, sex workers, refugee monks and representatives from ethnic minorities forced to labour for the regime – a simple but eloquent indictment of life under the generals.

David I. Steinberg *Burma/Myanmar: What Everyone Needs to Know*. A perceptive introduction to the history and politics of Myanmar, covering all the major issues affecting the country today in handy, bite-sized chapters.

Thant Myint-U *Where China Meets India: Burma and the New Crossroads of Asia*. Wide-ranging analysis of Myanmar's possible future role as the geographical and economic conduit between the two great Asian superpowers. Mixing history, travelogue and reportage, it has thought-provoking nuggets of information and insight on virtually every page.

AUNG SAN SUU KYI

Aung San Suu Kyi *Freedom from Fear and Other Writings*. This varied collection of essays, speeches and open letters serves as a useful introduction to Aung San Suu Kyi's political credo, and includes her Nobel Prize acceptance speech and her famous address at the Shwedagon Pagoda in 1988 (see p.345).

Aung San Suu Kyi *Letters from Burma*. Rather less interesting than *Freedom from Fear*, this second collection of essays on assorted aspects of Burmese politics and culture gives the distinct sensation of a barrel being rather thoroughly scraped.

Aung Zaw *The Face of Resistance: Aung San Suu Kyi and Burma's Fight for Freedom*. Interesting short book by former political prisoner Aung Zaw, founder and editor of the excellent *Irrawaddy* magazine (see p.40). It focuses not just on Aung San Suu Kyi herself but also on the rainbow tapestry of other organizations and individuals working towards a free Myanmar.

Bertil Lintner *Aung San Suu Kyi and Burma's Struggle for Democracy*. Concise, up to date (published in 2012) and balanced survey of Aung San Suu Kyi's life and politics – and refreshingly free of the sycophantic hagiography which colours most writing about The Lady.

Peter Popham *The Lady And The Peacock: The Life of Aung San Suu Kyi of Burma*. The blockbuster biography is more up to date (2012) than Wintle's book (see below) but not its equal in other respects, leaning towards biopic cliché in places and haphazardly organized in others – although worth a look if you want to read up on events of recent years.

Justin Wintle *Perfect Hostage: Aung San Suu Kyi, Burma and the Generals*. The first major study of Aung San Suu Kyi (originally published in 2007) and still the best of the English-language biographies currently available, combining heaps of detail with a well-structured and very readable narrative. Wintle's also not afraid to ask some hard questions about the effectiveness (or otherwise) of Gandhian-style non-violent protest against a brutal military regime.

HISTORY

Michael Aung-Thwin and Maitrii Aung-Thwin *A History of Myanmar Since Ancient Times*. The only complete scholarly history of Myanmar in English currently available – although it's far from your average academic tome. A strong polemic element runs through the entire book, with the authors launching a series of broadsides against a wide range of received historical and political opinions – everything from Mon influence at Bagan through to the military's renaming of the country and transfer of the capital to Naypyitaw. An often interesting read, although the final chapter is little more than government propaganda.

Michael W. Charney *A History of Modern Burma*. Covering the period from 1886 to 2008, this book provides a useful continuation to Thant Myint-U's history (see opposite). Full of interesting detail, and particularly good on the post-1962 period.

Thant Myint-U *The Making of Modern Burma*. Microscopic examination of the history of Myanmar between the latter days of the Konbaung dynasty and the establishment of nationwide British rule. Thant Myint-U's unravelling of the intricate social and economic structures of Myanmar under kings Mindon and Thibaw is an academic *tour de force*, while accounts of the Machiavellian intrigues, infighting and palace coups at the royal court add welcome spice.

★ **Thant Myint-U** *The River of Lost Footsteps: A Personal History of Burma*. Easily the best general introduction to the history of Myanmar, Thant Myint-U's superb "personal history" covers the country from ancient times to the present, combining exemplary scholarship, vivid prose and razor-sharp insights into a superbly readable and informative whole.

MEMOIRS

David V. Donnison *Last of the Guardians: A Story of Burma, Britain and a Family*. Enjoyable portrait of life in colonial Burma between 1923 and World War II, based on the memoirs of Donnison's parents.

James Mawdsley *The Heart Must Break: The Fight for Democracy and Truth in Burma*. Gripping account of British activist James Mawdsley's fight for democracy in Myanmar and his fourteen months spent in jail there in 1999–2000.

Pascal Khoo Thwe *From The Land of Green Ghosts: A Burmese Odyssey*. Lyrical memoir describing the author's boyhood in a remote Padaung village, his years as a rebel guerrilla fighter in the 1990s and, eventually, his escape to Europe and graduation from Cambridge University. An unrivalled portrait of life among Myanmar's repressed minorities.

Zoya Phan *Little Daughter: A Memoir of Survival in Burma and the West*. Simple but affecting memoir by Kayin refugee Zoya Phan describing her family's flight from their native village in 1994 and the following two years spent dodging Burmese armed forces, before her eventual escape to Thailand and the West.

MISCELLANEOUS

Naomi Duguid *Burma: River of Flavors*. This attractive cookbook provides a good introduction to Burmese cuisine, with solid coverage of basic ingredients and cooking techniques as well as recipes, plus lovely photos of the country to boot.

Myat Yin Saw *CultureShock! Myanmar: A Survival Guide to Customs and Etiquette*. Handy introduction to Burmese culture, customs and manners, plus plenty of general background on the country.

Robert Carmack & Morrison Polkinghorne *The Burma Cookbook: Recipes from the Land of a Million Pagodas*. Original and enjoyable cookery book featuring dozens of colonial-era recipes alongside good coverage of contemporary dishes and cooking techniques, all lavishly illustrated with a mix of modern photographs and colonial prints.

Language

Around a hundred different languages are spoken in Myanmar. Far and away the most widely used is Burmese, or "Myanmar Language" (*myanma bhasa*) as it's officially called, the native language of the country's Bamar majority as well as many other ethnic groups including the Mon. Burmese is spoken by around two-thirds of the population (32 million) as their first language and a further ten million as their second language. As well as Burmese proper, there are also several major regional dialects spoken in different parts of the country such as Intha, Danu, Yaw and Taungyo, not to mention Arakanese, spoken in Rakhine State, which is sometimes considered a dialect, and sometimes as a separate language. English is taught in schools and quite widely spoken in larger towns and cities, less so out in the countryside.

Part of the Tibeto-Burman group of tongues, Burmese is a tricky language for Westerners, although locals will appreciate any effort you make to speak it. The major difficulty derives from its **tonal** system (see opposite). Most words are monosyllabic, but word order and many other basic linguistic features of the language are also quite different to English.

There aren't many **study resources** available for learning Burmese. The best is *Burmese By Ear* by John Okell of the University of London's School of Oriental and African Studies, comprising a series of audio recordings plus accompanying book in PDF format, all of which can be downloaded for free at ⓦwww.soas.ac.uk/bbe. The audio files can be loaded onto a tablet or MP3 player and make for educational listening during long bus journeys and suchlike. Lonely Planet's pocket-sized *Burmese Phrasebook* is also a useful travelling companion.

Transliteration

There's no universally agreed way to show Burmese in Roman script – the same Burmese sound might be transliterated as *me*, *may*, *mei*, *mey* or *mae*, for example, while place names are similarly subject to random variation (the national capital, for example, is known variously as Naypyitaw, Naypyidaw, Nay Pyi Taw and Nay Pyi Daw). The difficulty of representing Burmese sounds in Roman script can lead to a degree of confusion, given how some Roman letters are commonly used to represent Burmese sounds with a notably different pronunciation. The only real way to grasp the language's pronunciation is to listen to Burmese-speakers themselves.

THE BURMESE ALPHABET

The Burmese alphabet's distinctively rounded appearance ("bubble writing", as some people describe it) derives from the fact that palm leaves inscribed with a stylus were historically used as the main material for writing upon, rather than paper and ink, with circular characters preferred given that numerous straight lines would have torn the leaves being used.

Like many other Southeast and South Asian languages, Burmese is written in a **consonant**-based script – **vowels** and **tones** are signified by adding additional accents and symbols to the basic consonant, rather than written separately, as in Western languages. There are 33 basic Burmese **consonants**, with distinctions made between unaspirated and aspirated consonants (see opposite). The script is written from left to right with no spaces between words, although modern written Burmese usually inserts spaces after each clause to enhance readability.

Pronunciation

There are five **tones** in Burmese – three main tones plus two additional modifiers:

Creaky high tone High, short pronunciation with tightened throat (akin to the pronunciation of the English word "squeak"). Transliterated using an acute accent, eg **á**.

Plain high tone Longer pronunciation, starting high and falling (like the English "fall" pronounced with a falling intonation). Transliterated using a grave accent, eg **à**.

Low tone Starts and stays low. Transliterated with no additional symbol.

Stopped syllable High sound cut short with a glottal stop at the end (like the first syllable of "bot-tle" spoken in a Cockney accent). Transliterated with a -q, eg **aq**.

Reduced (or "weak") syllable Usually applied to the first syllable of a two-syllable word where the first syllable is short and unstressed (as in the English "beneath", or for that matter, "reduced"). Transliterated with a breve accent, eg **ă**.

Burmese also distinguishes between **aspirated** and **unaspirated** consonants, the latter pronounced with a slight puff of air (put your hand in front of your mouth and say the English words "bin" and then "pin" to get a clear idea of the difference). Aspirated consonants are transliterated by placing an apostrophe after them (eg **k'**); those in the following section marked "whispered" begin with a sound similar to the start of the English "hmm".

ă as in "about"
a as in "car"
a in aq and an as in "cat"
ai in aiq and ain as in "site"
au in auq and aun "ou" as in "lounge"
aw as in "saw"
e as in French "café"
e in eh as in "sell"
e in eq as in "set"
ei in eiq and ein "a" as in "late"
i as in "ravine"
i in iq and in as in "sit"
o as in the French "eau"

ou in ouq and oun "o" as in "tone"
u as in "Susan"
u in uq and un "oo" as in "foot"
b as in "bore"
ch same as "ky" but aspirated
d as in "door"
dh "th" as in "this"
g as in "gore"
gy as in "judge"
h as in "hot"
hl same as "l" but whispered
hm same as "m" but whispered

hn same as "n" but whispered
hng same as "ng" but whispered
hny same as "ny" but aspirated
hw same as "w" but whispered
k as in French "corps"
k' as in "core" (aspirated)
ky "ch" as in "cello"
l as in "law"
m as in "more"
n as in "nor"
ng as in "long"
ny "gn" as in Italian "gnocchi"

p as in French "port"
p' as in "pore" (aspirated)
q glottal stop
r as in "raw"
s as in "soar"
s' same as "s" but aspirated
sh as in "shore"
t as in French "tour"
t' as in "tore" (aspirated)
th as in "thaw"
w as in "war"
y as in "your"
z as in "zone"

USEFUL WORDS AND PHRASES

GREETINGS AND BASIC PHRASES

Goodbye	thwà-meh-naw?
Excuse me (to get past)	nèh-nèh-lauq
Sorry	sàw-ri-naw
Please	kyè-zù pyú-bì
Thank you	kyè-zù tin-ba-deh
Thanks (less formal)	kyè-zù-bèh
Yes	houq-kéh
No	hín-ìn
Do you speak English?	ìn-găleiq sagà pyàw-daq-thălà?

What's that called in Burmese?	èh-da Băma-lo beh-lo k'aw-dhălèh?
Could you repeat that?	pyan-pyàw-ba-oùn?
I don't understand	nà măleh-ba-bù
Can you help me?	k'ăná-lauq louq-pè-ba
Good/bad	kaùn-deh/s'ò-deh
Hot/cold (weather)	pu-deh/è-deh
When (in the future)?	beh-dáw-lèh?
Who?	bădhu-lèh?
Where?	beh-hma-lèh?
Why?	ba-p'yiq-ló-lèh?

There is no word for a simple "**hello**" – rather, greetings are nonverbal or based on the situation (e.g. "Where have you been?"). Locals greet foreigners with the very formal *min-găla-ba* (see p.45)

COMMON SIGNS

Open	ဖွင့်သည်
Closed	ပိတ်ထားသည်
Entrance	အဝင်
Exit	အထွက်
No entry	ဝင်ခွင့်မရှိ
Men	ကျား
Ladies	မ
Toilets	အိမ်သာ / ရေအိမ်
No smoking	ဆေးလိပ်မသောက်ရ

Open/closed	pwín-deh/peiq-t'à-deh
Bank	ban
Post office	sa-daiq

MEETING PEOPLE

When answering where you come from, for most nationalities simply say the name of your country in English – one of the very few exceptions is France, which is Pyin-thiq.

My name is ….	cănáw/cămá nameh …. (m/f)
Where do you come from?	beh-gá la-dhălèh?
I come from …	…-gá la-ba-deh
I'm here for … weeks	cănaw/cămá di-hma (m/f) … paq ne-meh
Husband/wife	ămyò-thà/ămyò-thămì
Child/children	k'álè/k'álè-myà
It's very hot, isn't it?	theiq pu-deh-naw?
Can I take a photograph?	di-hma daq-poun yaiq-c'ìn-ba-deh
No problem	yá-ba-deh

EMERGENCIES

Help!	keh-ba!
Fire!	mee!
Go away!	thwà-zàn!
Stop!	yaq!
I'm lost	làn pyauq-thwà-bi
I've been robbed	ăk'ò-k'an-yá-deh
Police station	yèh-t'a-ná
I'm ill	ne-măkàun-bù
Call a doctor!	s'ăya-wun-go k'aw-pè-ba!
Hospital	s'è-youn
Pharmacy	s'è-zain
Where is the…?	…beh-hma-lèh?
…toilet?	ein dha…

DIRECTIONS

Where is the…?	…beh-hma-lèh?
How far is it?	beh-lauq wè-dăhlèh?
Left/right	beh-beq/nya-beq
Straight ahead	téh-déh

Near/far	nì-deh/wè-deh
This way	di-beq
Over there	ho-beq-hma

TRANSPORT

Ticket	leq-hmaq
Airport	le-zeiq
Boat (ferry)	thìn-bàw
Bus	baq-săkà
Bus station	kà-geiq
Train station	bu-da
Taxi	teq-si
Car	kà
Bicycle	seq-bein
When will the … leave?	… beh-ăc'ein t'weq-mălèh?
bus	baq-săkà
plane	le-yin-byan
train	mì-yăt'à

ACCOMMODATION

Hotel	ho-teh
Guesthouse	tèh-k'o-gàn
Can I reserve a room?	ăl'àn ăk'àn co-yu jin-ba-deh
Do you have any rooms?	ăk'àn à-là?
Double room	hnăyauq-k'àn
Single room	tăyauq-k'àn
Bathroom	ye-c'ò-gàn
How much for …	…beh-lauq-lèh?
…one night?	tăyeq…
…two nights?	hnăyeq…
How much is it?	beh-lauq kyá-dhălèh?
Cheap/expensive	zè cho-deh/zè kyì-deh
Passport	paq-săpó
Air-conditioning	èh-kun
Fan (electric)	pan-ka

SHOPPING

How much is it?	beh-lauq kyá-dhălèh?
Do you have any…?	…shi-là?
lacquerware	yún-deh
silk	pò-deh
silver	ngwe
jade	cauq-sein
Yes, I have	shí-ba-deh bya
No, I haven't	măshí-ba-bù
Cheap/expensive	zè cho-deh/zè kyì-deh
Can you give me a cheaper price?	zè-sháw-ba
That one	èh-da
I like that one	èh-da caiq-pa-deh
I'll take it	yu-meh
I'm just looking	cí-youn-ba-bèh

BURMESE NUMBERS

0	၀	thoun-nyá	13	၁၃	s'éh-thoùn
1	၁	tiq	20	၂၀	hnǎs'eh
2	၂	hniq	21	၂၁	hnǎs'eh-tiq
3	၃	thoùn	30	၃၀	thoùn-zeh
4	၄	lè	40	၄၀	lè-zeh
5	၅	ngà	100	၁၀၀	tǎya
6	၆	chauq	200	၂၀၀	hnǎya
7	၇	k'un(-hniq)	300	၃၀၀	thoùn-ya
8	၈	shiq	1000	၁၀၀၀	tǎt'aun
9	၉	kò	2000	၂၀၀၀	hnǎt'aun
10	၁၀	tǎs'eh	10,000	၁၀၀၀၀	tǎthaùn
11	၁၁	s'éh-tiq	100,000	၁၀၀၀၀၀	tǎthèin
12	၁၂	s'éh-hniq			

TIMES AND DAYS

Today	di-né	**Monday**	tǎnin-la-né
Tomorrow	mǎneq-p'an	**Tuesday**	in-ga-né
Morning	mǎneq	**Wednesday**	bouq-dǎhù-né
Midday	né-leh	**Thursday**	ca-dhǎbǎdè-né
Afternoon	nyá-ne	**Friday**	thauq-ca-né
Night/evening	nyá	**Saturday**	sǎne-né
		Sunday	tǎnin-gǎnwe-né

FOOD AND DRINK

GENERAL TERMS

Restaurant	sà-thauq-s'ain
Café/teahouse	lǎp'eq-ye-s'ain
Breakfast	mǎneq-sa
Lunch	né-leh-za
Dinner	nyá-za
Knife	dà
Fork	k'ǎyìn
Spoon	zùn
Chopsticks	tu
Plate	bǎgan-byà
Glass	p'an-gweq
Vegetarian (food)	theq-thaq-luq
I don't eat meat or fish	thà-gyì ngà-gyì … shaun-deh
Hot (spicy)	saq-teh
Sweet/sour	c'o-deh/c'in-deh
Cheers!	Chì-yà!
Delicious	kaùn-laiq-ta
What does it come to?	beh-lauq kyá-dhǎlèh? (ie the bill)

MEAT, FISH AND BASICS

ǎmèh-dhà	beef
bǎzun	prawns
bèh-dhà	duck
kyeq-thà	chicken
ngà	fish
s'eiq-thà	mutton
weq-thà	pork
chís	cheese
hìn	curry
t'ǎmin hin	curry and rice
ngǎpí	fish paste
ngǎyouq thì	chilli
paun-moún	bread
pèh-byà	tofu
ǎthouq	salad
s'à	salt
s'i	oil
t'ǎw-baq	butter
thǎgyà	sugar

VEGETABLES AND SALAD

hìn-dhì-hìn-yweq	vegetables
ǎthouq	salad
a-lù	potato
bù-dhì	gourd
c'ìn-baun	roselle leaf
céq-thun-byu	garlic
céq-thun-ni	onion

RICE AND NOODLES

kya-zan	rice vermicelli
k'auq-s'wèh	noodles
nàn-gyì	thick noodles
t'ǎmìn	rice
t'ǎmìn-gyaw	fried rice

OLD NAMES OF MYANMAR

Some of Myanmar's old colonial-era names are still in occasional circulation. The main ones you're likely to come across are:

NEW NAME	OLD NAME	NEW NAME	OLD NAME
Ayeyarwady	Irrawaddy	Pyay	Prome
Bagan	Pagan	Pyin Oo Lwin	Maymyo
Bago	Pegu	Rakhine	Arakan
Dawei	Tavoy	Sittwe	Akyab
Mawlamyine	Moulmein	Tanintharyi	Tenasserim
Mottama	Martaban	Thandwe	Sandoway
Myeik	Mergui	Thanlyin	Syriam
Pathein	Bassein	Yangon	Rangoon

hmo	mushroom	peìn-nèh-dhì	jackfruit
k'ãyàn-jin-djì	tomato	thãyeq-thì	mango
moun-la-ú-wa	carrot	thìn-bãw-dhì	papaya
p'ãyoun	pumpkin		
s'ãlaq-yweq	lettuce	**DRINKS**	
thãk'wà-dhi	cucumber	thauq-ye	drinking water
		ye-thán	purified water
FRUIT		ye-thán-bù	bottle of purified water
thiq-thì	fruit	ãè	soft drink
ceq-mauq-thì	rambutan	bi-ya	beer
dù-yìn-dhì	durian	kaw-p'ï	coffee (with milk sugar)
lein-maw-dhì	tangerine	kaw-p'ï nwà-nó-néh	coffee with milk
ma-lãka-dhì	guava	lãp'eq-ye	black tea
mìn-guq-thì	mangosteen	lahpet-ye-gyàn/ye-nwè-gyàn	green tea
na-naq-thì	pineapple	p'yaw-ye	fruit juice
ngãpyàw-dhì	banana	t'àn-ye	toddy
oùn-dhì	coconut	nó mãt'éh-néh	don't put milk in
p'ãyèh-dhi	watermelon	thãgyà mãt'éh-néh	don't put sugar in
pàn-dhì	apple	ye-gèh mãt'éh-néh	don't put ice in

Glossary

abhaya mudra "Have no fear" Buddhist mudra

amalaka lotus-shaped feature found in some stupa designs between the *anda* and spire

anda the main, bell-shaped section of the stupa, symbolizing the Buddha's upturned alms bowl (*thabeik*)

andaw Tooth relic

anyeint traditional Burmese entertainment combining music, dancing and comedy

Ari Buddhism early, eclectic form of Burmese Buddhism

ASEAN Association of Southeast Asian Nations

Avalokitesvara the Boddhisattva of universal compassion

banana bud the slightly bulbous decorative feature immediately below the topmost section of a stupa spire

betel popular snack mixing betel nut with other ingredients (see box, p.10)

bodhi tree type of fig tree (*Ficus religiosa*) beneath which the Buddha is said to have gained enlightenment; also known as the bo or peepal tree

Bodhisattva a future Buddha who, rather than passing into *nibbana*, has chosen to stay in the world to improve the spiritual welfare of other, unenlightened, being

BSPP Burma Socialist Programme Party

Burman colonial-era name for Bamar

chaung/gyaung stream or small river

chinlone popular Burmese "keepy-uppy" game using a rattan ball

chinthe mythical lion-like creature

dana mudra traditional Buddhist "offering" mudra; also known as the *varada* mudra

daw "Mrs" or "aunty"

deva divine being or god

Dhamma the Buddha's collected teachings

dharmachakra mudra Buddhist mudra symbolizing the "Gesture of the Turning of the Wheel of the Law"

dhyani (samadhi) mudra traditional mudra showing the Buddha seated in meditation

Ganesh the elephant-headed Hindu god of prosperity

garuda mythical bird-like creatures, sacred to both Buddhism and Hinduism

hamsa sacred geese (or sometimes swan), and the mount of the Hindu god Brahma. Also known as the *hintha*

harmika relic chamber found at the base of the spire in some stupas

hintha see "hamsa"

hti the umbrella-like feature placed at the very top of a stupa spire

in lake

Indra Hindu king of the gods

IWT Inland Water Transport Authority

Jataka collection of popular folk tales describing the 547 previous lives of the Buddha

kala alternative name for *kirthimukha* (see below)

kalasa decorative "nectar pots", derived from Indian architecture and sometimes found adorning the corners of stupa terraces

kalpa the current world cycle in Buddhist cosmology

karaweik mythical bird; also known as the *karavika*

kirthimukha mythical ogre-like creature

KNLA Karen National Liberation Army

Konagamana the second of the five Buddhas of the present world cycle

kyaik Mon temple

kyaung monastery

kyi/gyi suffix, meaning "big"

kyun island

Lokanat Burmese name for Avalokitesvara (see above)

longyi sarong-like garment worn by the majority of Burmese

Mahayana the later and more eclectic of the two main schools of Buddhism, centred on the cult of the Boddhisattva

Maitreya the future Buddha Maitreya is predicted to be the fifth and last of the five Buddhas of the current world cycle

mi-gyaung/kyam traditional crocodile-shaped, three-string Burmese zither

mudras a series of canonical poses used in most visual representations of the Buddha (see box, p.362)

myo town

naga mythical serpent-like creature with divine powers (although can also refer to the Naga people living in northwest Myanmar)

namaskara mudra traditional Buddhist mudra showing the Buddha or other figure in the act of praying

nat Burmese spirits

nat kadaw *nat* spirit medium

nat pwè *nat* festival

ngwe silver

nibbana nirvana

nikaya monastic order

NLD National League for Democracy

paccaya terrace at base of stupa

pagoda temple

pahto temple (used mainly in Bagan in reference to "hollow" temples)

Pali extinct Indian language in which most of Buddhism's oldest scriptures were first recorded – the Buddhist equivalent to Hebrew in Christianity or Sanskrit in Hinduism

palm leaf used as an alternative to paper thanks to its greater durability in the tropics, with dried leaves bound together into long, narrow books

parinirvana mudra traditional mudra showing the reclining Buddha at the moment of entering nirvana

paya temple (literally, the Burmese word for "pagoda")

pwe festival

pyatthat Southeast Asian-style multi-tiered roof

pyigyimun royal barge

pyissaya stupa terraces

Ramayana famous Hindu epic describing the life of Rama, an incarnation of the god Vishnu

samadhi mudra see *dhyani* mudra

Sangha the worldwide community of Buddhist monks

saopha a "sky lord" – the hereditary rulers of the Shan peoples

sariputra one of Buddha's disciples

sayadaw abbot

shikhara Indian-style temple tower

shinbyu ceremony marking induction of young boys into the Sangha

shwe golden

SLORC State Law and Order Restoration Council

SPDC State Peace and Development Council

stupa Buddhist monument found in most Burmese temples

sutra Buddhist (or Hindu) religious text

taik library

Tatmadaw the Burmese Armed Forces, comprising army, navy, air force and police

taung mountain

taw/daw suffix (as in, for instance, Naypyitaw), signifying somewhere sacred or royal

tazaung pavilion-style shrine

Temptation of Mara popular subject of Buddhist art, showing hordes of monsters unleashed by the demon Mara attempting to distract Buddha at the moment of his enlightenment

thabeik alms bowl

thanaka general-purpose Burmese powder/paste used as all-in-one make-up, sunscreen and insect repellent

thein ordination hall

Theravada the older of the two main schools of Buddhism and the dominant form of the religion in Myanmar

Thingyan water festival celebrating the Buddhist New Year

Tripitaka the main collection of Buddhist scriptures

trishaw cycle rickshaw (although sometimes used to describe motorized vehicles as well)

U "Mr" or "uncle"

USDP Union Solidarity and Development Party

varada mudra see *dana* mudra

viss Burmese unit of weight (equivalent to 1.6kg)

Vitarka mudra "Gesture of Explanation" – one of the traditional Buddhist mudras

weizza (weikza) Burmese Buddhist cult dedicated to magical practices and beliefs

yadaya quasi-magical rituals prescribed by astrologers to ward off misfortune (see box, p.358)

Yama Zatdaw Burmese version of the Ramayana

yoma mountain range

zaungdan stairway

zawgyi alchemist/magician

zedi stupa

zei market

Small print and index

A ROUGH GUIDE TO ROUGH GUIDES

Published in 1982, the first Rough Guide – to Greece – was a student scheme that became a publishing phenomenon. Mark Ellingham, a recent graduate in English from Bristol University, had been travelling in Greece the previous summer and couldn't find the right guidebook. With a small group of friends he wrote his own guide, combining a highly contemporary, journalistic style with a thoroughly practical approach to travellers' needs.

The immediate success of the book spawned a series that rapidly covered dozens of destinations. And, in addition to impecunious backpackers, Rough Guides soon acquired a much broader readership that relished the guides' wit and inquisitiveness as much as their enthusiastic, critical approach and value-for-money ethos.

These days, Rough Guides include recommendations from budget to luxury and cover more than 120 destinations around the globe, as well as producing an ever-growing range of ebooks.

Visit **roughguides.com** to find all our latest books, read articles, get inspired and share travel tips with the Rough Guides community.

Rough Guide credits

Editors: Edward Aves, Eleanor Aldridge, Emma Gibbs
Layout: Jessica Subramanian
Cartography: Deshpal Dabas, Ashutosh Bharti
Picture editor: Marta Bescos
Proofreader: Jan McCann
Burmese proofreader: John Okell
Managing editor: Keith Drew
Assistant editor: Prema Dutta
Production: Emma Sparks

Cover design: Nicole Newman, Marta Bescos, Jessica Subramanian
Photographer: James Tye
Editorial assistant: Rebecca Hallett
Senior pre-press designer: Dan May
Programme manager: Helen Blount
Publisher: Joanna Kirby
Publishing director: Georgina Dee

Publishing information

This first edition published February 2015 by
Rough Guides Ltd,
80 Strand, London WC2R 0RL
11, Community Centre, Panchsheel Park,
New Delhi 110017, India
Distributed by Penguin Random House
Penguin Books Ltd,
80 Strand, London WC2R 0RL
Penguin Group (USA)
345 Hudson Street, NY 10014, USA
Penguin Group (Australia)
250 Camberwell Road, Camberwell,
Victoria 3124, Australia
Penguin Group (NZ)
67 Apollo Drive, Mairangi Bay, Auckland 1310,
New Zealand
Penguin Group (South Africa)
Block D, Rosebank Office Park, 181 Jan Smuts Avenue,
Parktown North, Gauteng, South Africa 2193
Rough Guides is represented in Canada by Tourmaline
Editions Inc. 662 King Street West, Suite 304, Toronto,
Ontario M5V 1M7
Printed in Singapore by Toppan Security Printing Pte. Ltd.

© Rough Guides, 2015
Maps © Rough Guides
No part of this book may be reproduced in any form
without permission from the publisher except for the
quotation of brief passages in reviews.
384pp includes index
A catalogue record for this book is available from the
British Library
ISBN: 978-1-40935-661-5
The publishers and authors have done their best to
ensure the accuracy and currency of all the information in
The Rough Guide to Myanmar, however, they can accept
no responsibility for any loss, injury, or inconvenience
sustained by any traveller as a result of information or
advice contained in the guide.
1 3 5 7 9 8 6 4 2

MIX
Paper from responsible sources
FSC™ C018179
www.fsc.org

Help us update

We've gone to a lot of effort to ensure that the first edition of **The Rough Guide to Myanmar** is accurate and up-to-date. However, things change – places get "discovered", opening hours are notoriously fickle, restaurants and rooms raise prices or lower standards. If you feel we've got it wrong or left something out, we'd like to know, and if you can remember the address, the price, the hours, the phone number, so much the better.

Please send your comments with the subject line **"Rough Guide Myanmar Update"** to ✉ mail @uk.roughguides.com. We'll credit all contributions and send a copy of the next edition (or any other Rough Guide if you prefer) for the very best emails.

Find more travel information, connect with fellow travellers and plan your trip on ⓦ roughguides.com.

ABOUT THE AUTHORS

Joanna James started her career as a commodity broker in London, before affecting a daring escape to Beijing, where she studied at Peking University. She now lives in Hong Kong and works as a freelance writer and photographer. *The Rough Guide to Myanmar* is the first book Jo has co-authored.

Gavin Thomas (ⓦgavinthomas.net, @gavinthomastrav) is a freelance travel journalist specializing in Asia and Arabia. He has worked for Rough Guides for over fifteen years, writing and contributing to numerous books including the Rough Guides to Sri Lanka, India, Rajasthan, Dubai, Oman and Cambodia.

Martin Zatko has written or contributed to more than twenty Rough Guides, including those to Korea, China, Japan, Vietnam, Turkey and Europe. He first visited Myanmar in 2008, and often leans on the country as an answer to the tricky question of his favourite place to travel.

Acknowledgements

Joanna James A heartfelt thank you to everyone who helped me, whether knowingly or unknowingly. In particular, I would like to thank: U Win Naing, U La Shu, Ma Myat, U Tin Naing, Daw Zin Mar, Mr Myo, James Lable and his son, Tang Bau Jacob and Hawng Lum, U Sein Win and his daughter, Kyaw Soe Ko Ko, U Bathein, Stephen, Verena, Dave and Jenna, Andrea, Myo and Dani and everyone who helped get my passport from Shwebo to Pyin Oo Lwin on its first (and hopefully only) solo journey. *Ce zu tin ba deh!* Outside of Myanmar, my thanks go to Ed and, finally, to Jerry, with love wherever I am.

Gavin Thomas In Myanmar thanks to all the many people who assisted me on my travels particularly Ye Lin Kyaw in Bagan, Shwe Nue in Mrauk U, Min Naing in Pathein, Oscar in Meiktila, Nah Myo in Chaung Tha, Ko Toe and Tom Tom in Ngwe Saung, and everyone at the *Chan Myaye Guest House* in Yangon. In the UK and elsewhere, big thanks to: David Abram, John Oates, John Okell, Ma Saw, Keith Drew, Eleanor Aldridge and Emma Gibbs; to my fellow authors Martin Zatko and Jo James; to our great editorial leader Ed Aves for running the entire project with his customary élan and expertise; and of course to Jamie, Laura and Allison, who kept the home fires burning, as always.

Martin Zatko would like to thank James Mundy and the team at InsideBurma, Richard Ludwig at Exotissimo, and the kindly staff at the many hotels, restaurants, bars and tearooms he slept, ate and drank at.

Photo credits

All photos © Rough Guides except the following:
(Key: t-top; c-centre; b-bottom; l-left; r-right)

p.1 Flickr RF/Getty Images

p.2 Mick Shippen/4Corners

p.4 Jon Hicks/Corbis (tl); Jeremy Woodhouse/Blend Images/ Corbis (tr)

p.7 Gallo Images/Getty Images

p.9 Felix Hug/Getty Images (t); Peter Stuckings/Getty Images (c); Christophe Boisvieux/Corbis (b)

p.10 Nigel Pavitt/AWL Images

p.11 Stuart Black/Robert Harding Picture Library

p.12 Jochen Schlenker/Corbis

p.13 Christian Kober/John Warburton-Lee Photography Ltd/AWL Images (t); Karl Johaentges/Glowimages (c); Suronin/Dreamstime.com (b)

p.14 Michael Sheldon (t); Tuul/Robert Harding World Imagery/Corbis (b)

p.15 Thierry Falise/LightRocket/Getty Images (t); Pep Roig/ Alamy (b)

p.16 LOOK Die Bildagentur der Fotografen GmbH/Alamy (t); Simon Reddy/Alamy (c); blickwinkel/Alamy (b)

p.17 Richard Taylor/4Corners (tl); Tom Bourdon/4Corners (tr); Günter Gräfenhain/4Corners (b)

p.18 Michael Sheldon (t); Lee Frost/Robert Harding Picture Library (b)

p.19 Marc Dozier/Corbis (t); Luca Tettoni/Robert Harding Picture Library (b)

p.20 Travel Pix Collection/AWL Images (tl); Joao Almeida/ Robert Harding Picture Library (tr)

p.22 Martin Puddy/Corbis

pp.54–55 Stefano Brozzi/4Corners

p.57 Peter Sumner/Alamy

p.75 Tibor Bognár/Corbis (t); Katie Garrod/AWL Images (b)

pp.94–95 Frank Waldecker/Robert Harding Picture Library

p.97 Arco Images GmbH/Alamy

p.113 Michael Sheldon (t); Hemis/Alamy (b)

pp.130–131 Tuul/Robert Harding Picture Library

p.133 Günter Gräfenhain/4Corners

p.147 Amar Grover/John Warburton-Lee Photography Ltd/ AWL Images (t); Günter Gräfenhain/4Corners (b)

pp.168–169 Stefano Politi Markovina/Getty Images

p.187 Hemis/Alamy (t); SuperStock/Alamy (b)

p.205 Flickr Open/Getty Images (t); Peter Adams/AWL Images (bl)

p.227 Stuart Black/Corbis

p.245 Michael Sheldon (t); Stuart Black/Robert Harding World Imagery/Corbis (b)

pp.258–259 Dinhhang/Dreamstime.com

p.275 Stefano Politi/Corbis (t); Jeremy Horner/Corbis (b)

pp.290–291 Maurice Joseph/Alamy

p.293 blickwinkel/Alamy

p.315 National Geographic Image Collection/Alamy (t); Still Pictures/Robert Harding Picture Library (c); Tibor Bognar/Alamy (b)

p.328 Gavin Hellier/AWL Images

Front cover and spine A dug-out canoe on the Ayeyarwady River © Mint Image/Getty Images

Back cover U Bein Bridge, Amarapura © Hemis/Alamy (t); Buddhist monk at Shwedagon Pagoda, Yangon © Lee Frost/ Robert Harding Picture Library (bl); Bagan © Christian Kober/ AWL Images (br)

Index

Maps are marked in grey

Map symbols

The symbols below are used on maps throughout the book

Main road	⊠ Gate/entrance	Paya/pagoda	P Parking
Minor road	⊙ Statue	Buddha statue	Boat/ferry
Highway	Point of interest	Tower	Vineyard
Pedestrianized road	@ Internet access	Monument	Hot spring
Steps	Garden	Cave	Swimming pool
Unpaved road	Golf course	Escarpment/ridge	Church/cathedral
Railway	Bridge	Mountain peak	Building
Path	Ruin	Mountain range	Market
Wall	Border crossing	Viewpoint	Stadium
Post office	Chinese temple	Petrol station	Park/forest
(i) MTT office	Synagogue	International airport	Beach
Hospital	Mosque	Domestic airport	Cemetery
E Embassy	Hindu temple/gurudwara	Bus/taxi/pick-up	Swamp/Marsh

Listings key

- Accommodation
- Eating
- Drinking/nightlife
- Shopping

INSIDE
Burma

Small Group Tours

Fully Tailored Journeys

Experiences & Inspiration

Get beneath the Surface
with the Burma
travel experts

Tel: 0117 244 3381
www.insideburmatours.com
info@insideburmatours.com

Get beneath the surface

Part of **InsideAsia Tours Ltd,** an award-winning travel company
offering group tours, tailored travel and cultural experiences
across Japan, Vietnam, Cambodia, Laos and Burma.